NEGOTIABLE INSTRUMENTS

And Related Commercial Paper

(second edition)

NEGOTIABLE INSTRUMENTS
And Related Commercial Paper
(second edition)

STEVE H. NICKLES

ROGER F. NOREEN PROFESSOR OF LAW
UNIVERSITY OF MINNESOTA

BLACK LETTER SERIES

WEST GROUP
EAGAN, MINN.
1993

COPYRIGHT © 1993 By WEST PUBLISHING CO.
610 Opperman Drive
P.O. Box 64526
St. Paul, MN 55164–0526

Library of Congress Cataloging-in-Publication Data

Nickles, Steve H., 1949–
   Negotiable instruments / by Steve H. Nickles. — 2nd ed.
     p.   cm. — (Black letter series)
   Rev. ed. of: Commercial paper. 1988.
   ISBN 0–314–01979–0
   1. Negotiable instruments—United States—Outlines, syllabi, etc.
I. Nickles, Steve H., 1949–   Commercial paper. II. Title.
III. Series.
KF957.Z9N53 1993
346.73'096—dc20

[347.30696]   92–47440
                                 CIP

ISBN 0–314–01979–0

Nickles—Comm. Paper BLS
1st Reprint–1999

PUBLISHER'S PREFACE

This "Black Letter" is designed to help a law student recognize and understand the basic principles and issues of law covered in a law school course. It can be used both as a study aid when preparing for classes and as a review of the subject matter when studying for an examination.

Each "Black Letter" is written by experienced law school teachers who are recognized national authorities in the subject covered.

The law is succinctly stated by the author of this "Black Letter." In addition, the exceptions to the rules are stated in the text. The rules and exceptions have purposely been condensed to facilitate quick review and easy recollection. For an in-depth study of a point of law, citations to major student texts are given. In addition, a **Text Correlation Chart** provides a convenient means of relating material contained in the "Black Letter" to appropriate sections of the casebook the student is using in his or her law school course.

If the subject covered by this text is a code or code-related course, the code section or rule is set forth and discussed wherever applicable.

FORMAT

The format of this "Black Letter" is specially designed for review. (1) **Text.** First, it is recommended that the entire text be studied, and, if deemed necessary, supplemented by the student texts cited. (2) **Capsule Summary.** The Capsule Summary is an abbreviated review of the subject matter which can be used both before and after studying the main body of the text. The headings in the Capsule Summary follow the main text of the "Black Letter." (3) **Table of Contents.** The Table of Contents is in outline form to help you organize the details of the subject and the Summary of Contents gives you a final overview of the materials. (4) **Practice Examination.** The Practice Examination in Appendix B gives you the opportunity of testing yourself with the type of question asked on an exam, and comparing your answer with a model answer.

In addition, a number of other features are included to help you understand the subject matter and prepare for examinations:

Short Questions and Answers: This feature is designed to help you spot and recognize issues in the examination. We feel that issue recognition is a major ingredient in successfully writing an examination.

Perspective: In this feature, the authors discuss their approach to the topic, the approach used in preparing the materials, and any tips on studying for and writing examinations.

Analysis: This feature, at the beginning of each section, is designed to give a quick summary of a particular section to help you recall the subject matter and to help you determine which areas need the most extensive review.

Examples: This feature is designed to illustrate, through fact situations, the law just stated. This, we believe, should help you analytically approach a question on the examination.

Glossary: This feature is designed to refamiliarize you with the meaning of a particular legal term. We believe that the recognition of words of art used in an examination helps you to better analyze the question. In addition, when writing an examination you should know the precise definition of a word of art you intend to use.

We believe that the materials in this "Black Letter" will facilitate your study of a law school course and assure success in writing examinations not only for the course but for the bar examination. We wish you success.

THE PUBLISHER

SUMMARY OF CONTENTS

APPENDICES

TABLE OF CONTENTS

APPENDICES

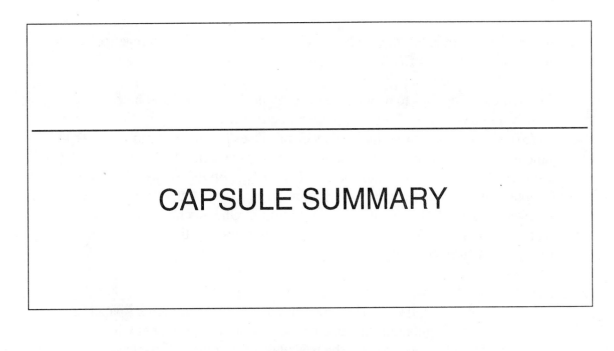

CAPSULE SUMMARY

PART ONE --
ARTICLE 3 NEGOTIABLE INSTRUMENTS

I. INTRODUCTION TO INSTRUMENTS AND NEGOTIABILITY

A. HISTORY AND SOURCES OF LAW

1. Early Law Of Commercial Paper

By the end of the 18th Century the English courts had developed, through common law, the basic principles of negotiable instruments, mainly drafts and notes.

2. Uniform Negotiable Instruments Law

In the United States in 1896, the National Conference of Commissioners on Uniform State Laws (NCCUSL) collected these principles in the Uniform Negotiable Instruments Act, which is often referred to as the Negotiable Instruments Law or the N.I.L.

3. Uniform Commercial Code

The N.I.L. was replaced by a comprehensive statute dealing comprehensively with the various areas of the law governing commerce -- the Uniform Commercial Code which is referred to as the U.C.C. or the Code. In 1986, work began to update the Code's law of commercial paper. The ultimate results were that a new Article 4A on funds (wire) transfers was added to the Code in 1989; and, **in 1990, the basic law of negotiable instruments, Article 3, was completely redrafted.** At the same time, **Article 4 on bank deposits and check collection was significantly changed** and conforming amendments were made elsewhere in the Code. **All references to the Code are to the 1990 Official Text except where otherwise indicated.**

U.C.C. Article 3 "applies to negotiable instruments," 3-102(a), and nothing else. Generally and basically, a "*negotiable instrument*" (or its synonym, "*instrument*," 3-104(b)) is "a signed writing that orders or promises payment of money," 3-104 comment 1, and that satisfies the other requirements described by section 3-104(a). These requirements are known as the *requisites of negotiability*, which are the subject of Chapter 2 infra. Wherever Article 3 refers to an instrument, it means a writing that satisfies all of the 3-104 requisites of negotiability. Only such an instrument triggers the application of Article 3, and only a writing that satisfies the requisites of negotiability is an instrument.

4. Supplemental Role Of Federal Law
The Uniform Commercial Code is the principal source of commercial paper law, but federal statutes and regulations are an increasingly large supplement which naturally preempts the U.C.C. Nevertheless, the basic law of commercial paper is state U.C.C. law, even with respect to check collection and even when checks are collected (as they often are) through the Federal Reserve System.

5. International Law
The international law of negotiable instruments is the Convention on International Bills of Exchange and International Promissory Notes.

B.   INTRODUCTION TO INSTRUMENTS: FORMS, PARTIES, AND USES
There are only two basic kinds of instruments -- *notes* (including *certificates of deposit*) and *drafts* (including *checks*), and only four capacities or roles in which a person can sign an instrument -- *maker*, *drawer*, *acceptor*, and *indorser*.

1. Notes
a. General Distinguishing Characteristics
The most elementary form of commercial paper is the *note*. It is an instrument that is a written promise to pay money signed by the person making the promise, 3-104(e), who is called the *maker*. 3-103(a)(5). The maker's *explicit* promise to pay is the distinguishing feature of notes and explains why they are commonly called *promissory* notes.

b. Transfer
In transferring a note, the payee usually signs the instrument and in doing so she becomes an *indorser*.

c. Some Uses of Notes
- ◆ Borrowing money
- ◆ Buying on credit
- ◆ Evidencing preexisting debt

2. Certificates Of Deposit

A *certificate of deposit*, often referred to as a "*CD*," is a form of note that a bank issues. It is "an instrument containing an acknowledgment by a bank that a sum of money has been received by the bank and a promise by the bank to repay the sum of money." 3-104(j).

3. Drafts

a. General Distinguishing Characteristics

A *draft* is an instrument that, on its face, is an order to pay money rather than a promise. 3-104(e). (The ancient name for a draft is *bill of exchange,* but neither the U.C.C. nor common practice uses this old term.) The person who issues the order is the *drawer*, 3-103(a)(3), and the person ordered to pay is the *drawee*. 3-103(a)(2). The principal distinguishing feature of a draft is that, in form, it orders payment instead of promising it. 3-104(e). This order commands the drawee, who ordinarily is a debtor of the drawer, to pay the payee of the instrument, either on demand or on a stated date, part or all of the sum that the drawee owes the drawer. The drawer of a draft does not expressly promise to pay it. Indeed, the normal expectation is that she will not have to pay the draft because the drawee, who is ordered to pay, will do so. If, however, the drawee does not pay (or preliminarily, in a proper case, refuses to accept), the drawer is obligated to pay the instrument herself. 3-414(b). So, while a taker of a note expects the maker to pay the instrument, a taker of a draft looks initially to the drawee for payment rather than the drawer.

b. Drawee Becoming Acceptor of Draft

The drawee is not obligated to pay a draft unless she accepts it. 3-408. Acceptance is the drawee's signed agreement to pay the draft. 3-409(a). The drawee's mere signature on the draft is sufficient as acceptance. 3-409 comment 2.

c. Transferring Drafts

In transferring a draft, the payee, like the payee of a note, usually signs the instrument and in so doing assumes the role and liability of an *indorser*.

d. Using Drafts to Finance Movement of Goods

Most generally, drafts are a means whereby a person can satisfy her own obligations by having debts she is owed paid to her creditors. Specific business applications are extremely wide and varied. Perhaps the most common specific use of ordinary or non-checks drafts, in a variety of forms, is to finance the movement of goods.

4. Checks

By far the most common form of draft, and the most widely used form of commercial paper, is the *check*. A check is a draft that is drawn on a bank, as drawee, and that is payable on demand. 3-104(f).

C. SIGNIFICANCE AND ADVANTAGES OF INSTRUMENTS

1. Convenience Of Form

2. Less Risk To Assignee Of Payment To Another

3. Procedural Advantages

4. Negotiability

Negotiability means that under limited circumstances defined by law, a transferee of property can acquire rights therein that are better or greater than the rights of the transferor.

D. NEGOTIABILITY: AN EXCEPTIONAL DOCTRINE

1. General Rule Of Derivative Title

A very basic general rule pervading the whole of English and American law is that title is derivative. A transferor of property can ordinarily convey nothing more or better than her own rights in the property. Even the most innocent bona fide purchasers for value acquire nothing more. This rule is codified throughout the U.C.C. **Derivative title is also a general rule of Article 3**: "Transfer of an instrument * * * vests in the transferee any right of the transferor * * *." 3-203(b).

2. Negotiability As Exception To Derivative Title

Competing policy goals sometimes override the desire to protect property rights so that, notwithstanding the rule of derivative title, a transferee of property can acquire rights therein that are better or greater than the rights of her transferor. In these circumstances, the property is treated as negotiable, which describes property in situations where an exception to the rule of derivative title applies.

A very important instance of negotiability concerns **rights to the payment of money that are Article 3 instruments.** The derivative title principle generally applies transfers of rights to payment, including such rights that have been reified in Article 3 instruments. Yet, the very heart of Article 3 is an important exception to the rule of derivative title known as the *holder-in-due-course doctrine.* "Holder in due course" is the name Article 3 gives a holder of a negotiable instrument who takes the instrument for value, in good faith, and without knowledge of any claim or defense to it. Such a person acquires the instrument free from all adverse claims and free from virtually all defenses to its enforcement, including claims and defenses that could have been asserted against the holder's transferor. See 3-305(b) & 3-306.

II. THE MEANING OF INSTRUMENT: ARTICLE 3's REQUISITES OF NEGOTIABILITY

A. MEANING AND SIGNIFICANCE OF REQUISITES OF NEGOTIABILITY

1. Article 3 Defined In Terms Of Instruments

Article 3 applies to writings that are instruments, which means negotiable instruments. 3-104(b). The statute governs nothing else.

2. Instruments Defined In Terms Of Requisites Of Negotiability

The requirements for negotiability under Article 3 are known as the *requisites of negotiability* which are spelled out in section 3-104(a). It provides:

> "[N]egotiable instrument" means an unconditional [written] promise or order to pay a fixed amount of money, with or without interest or other charges described in the promise or order, if it:
> (1) is payable to bearer or to order at the time it is issued or first comes into possession of a holder;
> (2) is payable on demand or at a definite time; and
> (3) does not state any other undertaking or instruction by the person promising or ordering payment to do any act in addition to the payment of money, but the promise or order may contain (i) an undertaking or power to give, maintain, or protect collateral to secure payment, (ii) an authorization or power to the holder to confess judgment or realize on or dispose of collateral, or (iii) a waiver of the benefit of any law intended for the advantage or protection of an obligor.

3. Negotiability Turns On Form

The negotiability of a writing is determined by the contents of the writing itself and nothing more. The language that appears there must satisfy the requisites of negotiability. The provisions that 3-104(a) requires must be there, and the provisions that it prohibits must not be there.

B. WRITING

The core requirement of a negotiable instrument is a promise or order to pay money, 3-104(a); and a promise or order, by its own definition, must be written. 3-103(a)(6) & (9). *"Written"* or *"writing"* includes any "intentional reduction to tangible form." 1-201(46).

C. SIGNED BY MAKER OR DRAWER

The order or promise that negotiability requires means a written instruction or undertaking that is *signed* by the person who instructs or undertakes to pay. The meaning of "signed" is very broad, including "any symbol executed or adopted by a party with present intention to authenticate a writing." 1-201(39).

D. PROMISE OR ORDER

Fundamentally, an instrument is a signed writing that, on its face, orders or promises the payment of money. 3-104 comment 1. At the core is the requirement of a promise or order. Either promising or ordering payment will satisfy negotiability, but the choice determines the nature of the instrument. An instrument that promises payment is a *note*. An instrument that orders payment is a *draft*.

1. Promise

The promise that satisfies negotiability "means a written *undertaking* to pay money signed by the person undertaking to pay." 3-103(a)(9) (emphasis added).

2. Order

An order that marks a draft is "a written *instruction* to pay money signed by the person giving the instruction." 3-103(a)(6) (emphasis added).

E. UNCONDITIONAL

Negotiability requires a promise or order that is *unconditional*. It must be expressed in absolute terms which are not subject to contingencies, provisos, qualifications, or reservations that undermine or impair the obligation to pay.

1. General Rule

Generally, a promise or order *is unconditional* unless the writing states:
- an express condition to payment,
- that the promise or order is subject to or governed by another writing, or
- that rights or obligations with respect to the promise or order are stated in another writing.

In other words, if the writing contains none of these provisions, the order or promise is unconditional. The writing is negotiable if it satisfies the other 3-104(a) requisites of negotiability. On the other hand, if the writing contains even one of the three kinds of provisions that 3-106(a) describes, the promise or order is conditional, negotiability is impossible, and the writing is not an Article 3 instrument.

2. Terms Of Instrument Determine Presence Of Condition

For the purpose of determining negotiability, the promise or order it contains is unconditional unless something *in the instrument itself* is to the contrary.

3. Effect Of Another Agreement

In terms of Article 3, "the obligation of a party to an instrument to pay the instrument may be modified, supplemented, or nullified by a separate agreement of the obligor and a person entitled to enforce the instrument, if the instrument is issued * * * as part of the same transaction giving rise to the agreement." 3-117. On the other hand, the separate agreement -- whether oral or written -- does not affect negotiability. Regardless of the provisions that any outside writing may provide, it does not destroy the negotiability of an instrument which otherwise meets the requisites of negotiability.

4. Referring To Another Agreement

The *existence* of another agreement does not affect negotiability. 3-117. The instrument *making express reference* to an outside agreement or other writing can affect negotiability depending on the nature of the reference. A statement is inoffensive that simply mentions the outside writing or reports that the instrument arises out of or in connection with the writing. Negotiability is denied, however, if the statement ties the instrument to the writing by providing either that the instrument is subject to or governed by the outside writing, or that the latter defines rights or obligations with respect to the former. 3-106(a)(ii-iii).

5. Implied Conditions Not Recognized, Only Express

A reference in an instrument to an underlying executory contract between the parties does not implicitly condition the instrument on due performance of the contract and thereby deny negotiability to the instrument. The rule is that an order or promise is conditional only if it states "an *express* condition to payment * * *," 3-106(a)(i) (emphasis added), which is not true of a statement in an instrument simply reporting that the instrument is given for an executory promise.

6. Express Conditions That Are Permitted

There are a couple of very narrow exceptions to the general rule against express conditions, such as:

- The countersignature in a traveler's check
- A statement in a note preserving claims and defenses

7. Reference To Account Or Fund

"A promise or order is not made conditional * * * because payment is limited to resort to a particular fund or source." 3-106(b).

F. MONEY

The unconditional promise or order that negotiability requires is a promise or order to pay *money.* An instrument is payable in money if it is stated as payable in "a medium of exchange authorized or adopted by a domestic or foreign government and includes a monetary unit of account established by an intergovernmental organization or by agreement between two or more nations." 1-201(24).

G. FIXED AMOUNT

The money payable must be a *fixed amount,* which means a total which the holder can determine from the instrument by any necessary computation at the time the instrument is payable, without reference to any outside source. This requirement applies, however, only to the principal. It does not apply to interest or to other charges. Therefore, "[t]he amount or rate of interest may be stated or described in the instrument in any manner" and, most significantly, "*may require reference to information not contained in the instrument.*" 3-112(b) (emphasis added).

H. PAYABLE ON DEMAND OR AT A DEFINITE TIME

Negotiability requires that an instrument "is payable *either* on demand *or* at a definite time." 3-104(a)(2) (emphasis added).

1. On Demand

An instrument is "payable on demand" if it:
- states that it is payable on demand or at sight,
- otherwise indicates that it is payable at the will of the holder, or
- does not state any time of payment. 3-108(a).

2. At A Definite Time

An instrument is payable at a definite time if it is payable:
- at a fixed date or dates,
- on elapse of a definite period of time after sight or acceptance, or
- at a time or times readily ascertainable at the time the instrument is issued,
even if it is subject to prepayment, acceleration, or certain extensions. 3-108(b).

3. At A Definite Time *And* On Demand

It is possible that an instrument may be payable *both* at a definite time *and also* on demand. Negotiability is not offended. The instrument is deemed payable "on demand until the fixed date and, if demand for payment is not made before that date, becomes payable at a definite time on the fixed date." 3-108(c).

I. PAYABLE TO ORDER OR TO BEARER (*WORDS OF NEGOTIABILITY*)

Negotiability requires that the instrument is "payable *to bearer* or *to order* at the time it [the instrument] is issued or first comes into possession of a holder." 3-104(a)(1). Words that satisfy this requirement are called *words of negotiability*. "To order" or "to bearer" are alternative forms of the words of negotiability. In determining if a writing is a negotiable instrument, it makes no difference whether it is payable to order or to bearer so long as it is payable one way or the other.

1. Payable To Order

Typically, an instrument is payable to order, which means it (1) is not payable to bearer and (2) is payable:

- to the order of an identified person, or
- to an identified person or order. 3-109(b).

a. Wording Important
The word "order" (or, perhaps, a very close equivalent) is essential.

b. Payable to Payee Without Order Language (Mercantile Specialty)
1) General Rule
   An instrument is not payable to order that provides only, "Pay Jane Doe" because the magic "order" word is missing. Neither is it payable to bearer. The writing therefore lacks words of negotiability, is not a negotiable instrument.

2) Exception -- 3-104(c) Check
   The single exception is the 3-104(c) check. It is an order to pay that satisfies all of the requisites of negotiability, and that otherwise falls within the definition of "check," except that it lacks words of negotiability. Section 3-104(c) deems that such a check, despite its missing words, is a negotiable instrument and a check. Therefore, a check payable "Pay Jane Doe" is fully negotiable.

c. To Whom Instrument *Can Be* Payable
An instrument may be made payable to the order of anyone, whether a natural person or legal or commercial entity, including the maker, drawer, or drawee.

d. To Whom Instrument *Is* Payable
A person to whom an instrument is payable may be identified in any way, including by name, identifying number, office, or account number. 3-110(c). The test to determine who the instrument identifies is the intent of the person signing as, or in the name or behalf of, the issuer, whether or not the person

signing is authorized to do so. 3-110(a). In case the signer is not human, as with a computer or checkwriting machine, the relevant intent is that of the person who supplied the payee's name, even if this person acts without authority and wrongfully. 3-110(b).

2. Payable To Bearer

"Payable to bearer" means that a promise or order:
- states that it is payable to bearer or to the order of bearer or otherwise indicates that the person in possession of the promise or order is entitled to payment;
- does not state a payee; or
- states that it is payable to or to the order of cash or otherwise indicates that it is not payable to an identified person.

3-109(a). If the instrument is payable to bearer and also to an identified person, the instrument is payable to bearer whether or not it is also payable to the person's order. An instrument that does not state a payee is also payable to bearer, 3-109(a)(2), as in "Pay to ____ " or "Pay to the order of ___."

3. When The Instrument Must Be So Payable

Basically, the instrument must contain the words of negotiability when the maker or drawer gives it to the payee. It is not an instrument if it lacks these words and the payee adds them.

J. NO OTHER UNDERTAKING OR INSTRUCTION

The final requirement of negotiability is that beyond the maker's order or promise to pay money, the instrument itself must not contain "any other undertaking or instruction" by the maker or drawer "to do any act in addition to the payment of money," 3-104(a)(3), with a few exceptions that Article 3 describes. For example, negotiability is not affected if the writing also contains:
- an undertaking or power to give, maintain, or protect collateral to secure payment,
- an authorization or power to the holder to confess judgment or realize on or dispose of collateral, or
- a waiver for the benefit of any law intended for the advantage or protection of an obligor. 3-104(a)(3)(i-iii).

K. NEGOTIABILITY (OR NOT) BY DECLARATION

1. Effect Of Declaration That Writing Is Negotiable

"[A] writing cannot be made a negotiable instrument within Article 3 by contract or conduct of its parties * * *." 3-104 comment 2.

2. Effect Of Declaration That Instrument Is Nonnegotiable

"A promise or order *other than a check* is not an instrument if, at the time it is issued or first comes into possession of a holder, it contains a *conspicuous* statement, however expressed, to the effect that the promise or order is not negotiable or is not an instrument governed by this Article." 3-104(d) (emphasis added). A declaration on a check that it is not negotiable is ineffective.

L.   INCOMPLETE INSTRUMENTS

An "incomplete instrument" is "a signed writing, whether or not issued by the signer, the contents of which show at the time of signing that it is incomplete but that the signer intended it to be completed by the addition of words or numbers." 3-115(a). It includes a true instrument that, though incomplete, satisfies the requisites of negotiability (e.g., a note for which the parties intended a due date but failed to state it), and also a writing that fails these requisites but is intended to satisfy them and be an instrument when complete. An "incomplete instrument" that is not truly an instrument will nevertheless become an instrument, and be treated as such in every respect under Article 3, if the requirements of negotiability are met when it is completed. 3-115(b).

M. DATES AND PLACES
1.   Date Of Instrument
a.   Date Normally Not Required
Negotiability normally does not require dating the instrument to show when it was created, signed, or issued by the maker or drawer.

b.   Except When Tied to Time of Payment
On the other hand, if a date is essential to fix maturity, as in an instrument payable "thirty days after date," the date is required for negotiability.

c.   Antedating or Postdating Instrument
Negotiability is not affected by antedating or postdating an instrument.

2.   Place Of Payment
Negotiability does not require that an instrument state the place where it is payable, and negotiability is unaffected if such a place is stated.

III. CONTRACT LIABILITY ON INSTRUMENTS

A. FUNDAMENTAL REQUISITES OF LIABILITY
1. Signature
The most basic rule governing liability on negotiable instruments is that "a person is not liable on an instrument unless (i) the person signed the instrument, or (ii) the person is represented by an agent or representative who signed the instrument and the signature is binding on the represented person under Section 3-402." 3-401(a).

a. Mechanics of Signature

"A signature may be made (i) manually or by means of a device or machine, and (ii) by the use of any name, including a trade or assumed name, or by a word mark, or symbol executed or adopted by a person with present intention to authenticate a writing." 3-401(b).

b. Signature by Agent

1) Liability of Principal

When a representative signs an instrument for someone else, the other person, i.e., the represented person, is bound on the instrument -- even if her name is not used - if she would be bound by extra-Code law that determines when agents can bind principals on simple contracts.

2) Liability of Agent

By the standard rule, the representative herself is also *prima facie* liable unless:

- the form of the signature shows unambiguously that the agent made the signature behalf of the represented person, and
- the instrument identifies the represented person.

3-402(b)(1). To rebut this liability the representative must prove that the original parties did not intend that the representative would be personally liable on the instrument. 3-402(b)(2).

c. Liabilities When Person's Name Is Signed by Unauthorized Agent (Including Forger)

When a person's name is placed on an instrument by someone acting without authority to do so, the person whose name is signed is not liable on the instrument because she has not signed it. 3-401(a) & 3-403(a). The signature operates, however, "as the signature of the unauthorized signer in favor of a person who in good faith pays the instrument or takes it for value." 3-403(a).

d. Liability Without Signature

Sometimes, exceptional rules apply to bind the person whose name is signed even though she did not authorize the signature and the signature was a complete forgery. For example, a person's unauthorized or forged signature binds her if she ratifies the signature. 3-403(a). More important, a person is bound even by her forged signature if she is responsible or culpable or at fault with respect to the making of the signature. This liability is based on rules such as:

- Estoppel
- Negligence -- 3-406
- Special Rules for Indorsements -- 3-404 and 3-405

e. **Signature Without Capacity or Liability**
A person whose signature appears on an instrument is not liable in any capacity if she signed for a benign purpose.

2. **Delivery (Issuance)**
Lack of delivery, i.e., nonissuance, is a defense to liability on an instrument.

B. NATURE OF LIABILITY

1. Significance Of Capacity

The nature of a person's liability on an instrument -- her *"contract of liability"* -- varies with the capacity in which the person signed the instrument. *Capacity* refers to the role the signer plays with respect to the instrument itself:

- maker,
- drawer,
- acceptor, or
- indorser.

2. Primary Versus Secondary Liability

In general, the liability of makers and acceptors is described as *primary*, while the liability of drawers and indorsers is *secondary*. For this purpose, *secondary liability* means that enforcing the drawer's or indorser's liability is conditioned on someone else not paying or accepting the instrument who (party or not) was expected to do so. This refusal is called *dishonor*, which is a condition on the liability of a drawer of a draft and the indorser of any instrument. *Primary liability* means that the maker or acceptor is obligated to pay without initial resort to anyone else.

C. CAPACITIES

1. Maker

"'Maker' means a person who signs or is identified in a note as a person undertaking to pay." 3-103(a)(5). Basically, the maker of a note "is obliged to pay the instrument * * * according to its terms at the time it was issued" or, if the maker signed an incomplete note, "according to its terms when completed * * *." 3-412.

2. Drawer

"'Drawer' means a person who signs or is identified in a draft as a person ordering payment." 3-103(a)(3). The drawer is obligated to pay the draft only if the instrument is dishonored, 3-414(b)&(d), which basically means that the drawee fails to pay or accept the draft upon due and proper presentment for payment or acceptance. See 3-502.

Dishonor that is a condition to the drawer's liability normally requires presentment of the draft, so that presentment too is normally a condition to her liability -- a derivative condition.   A drawer's liability is *not* conditioned on notice of dishonor, except in the case of a draft accepted by a non-bank. In this case, the acceptance effectively converts the drawer's liability to that of an indorser, whose liability is usually conditioned on notice of dishonor.   See 3-414(d); 3-415(a); & 3-503(a).

As a general rule, a drawer may avoid contract liability on an *ordinary draft* by adding words to her drawer's signature that disclaim liability to pay the draft. The most commonly-used disclaimer are the words "without recourse." 3-414(e). The drawer of a *check*, however, is not permitted to disclaim her liability. "There is no legitimate purpose served by issuing a check on which nobody is liable." 3-414 comment 5.

3. Acceptor

An acceptor is the drawee of a draft who has accepted the instrument by signing it for the purpose of agreeing to pay it as presented to her. 3-103(a)(1) & 3-409(a). The acceptor's liability on the draft, like a maker's liability on a note, is primary. If the instrument is complete when she accepts it, the acceptor becomes obligated to pay the draft according to its terms as of the time of acceptance. 3-413(a). A drawee accepts by signing anywhere on the instrument. Nothing more is required.

4. Indorser

An indorser is someone who is not a maker, drawer, or acceptor and who signs an instrument (whether a note or draft) in order to negotiate it, restrict payment, or just to incur liability on the instrument. 3-204(a). Her signature is called an *indorsement*. Id.   An instrument is most commonly indorsed for the purpose of negotiating an order instrument so that the transferee becomes a holder. An indorser's liability is secondary. Her obligation, like a drawer's, is to pay only if the instrument is dishonored. 3-415(a). **An indorser's liability is conditioned on dishonor regardless of the nature of the instrument, even when the instrument is a note.** Presentment usually is a necessary part of dishonor. Therefore, presentment usually is a derivative condition on the indorser's liability. Also, "[t]he obligation of an indorser * * * may not be enforced unless (i) the indorser * * * is given notice of dishonor of the instrument complying with this section or (ii) notice of dishonor is excused * * *." 3-503(a). Unexcused delay in notifying an indorser -- either on a note or a draft -- discharges her liability. 3-415(c) & 3-503(c). An indorser can disclaim her contract of liability on the instrument by *qualifying* her indorsement, which means adding to her signature words such as "without recourse" or the like. 3-415(b).

5. In Case Of Doubt About Person's Capacity

"The general rule is that a signature is an indorsement if the instrument does not indicate an unambiguous intent of the signer not to sign as an indorser." 3-204 comment 1.

D. DISHONOR AND OTHER CONDITIONS TO SECONDARY LIABILITY

The contract liability of drawers and indorsers is conditioned on *dishonor* of the instrument, which usually involves *presentment* of it. An indorser's liability is further conditioned on *notice of dishonor*, and so too the liability of a drawer when the draft is accepted by a person other than a bank. These three events -- presentment, dishonor, and notice of dishonor -- are the conditions of secondary liability. **If any of these conditions that is required for liability is not satisfied or excused, the liability is not enforceable. Absent excuse of the condition, enforcement must await satisfaction of the condition**. In concept, the conditions of secondary liability are easy to understand. Presentment involves requesting payment or acceptance of the expected payor; dishonor is this person's refusal of the request; and notice is alerting the secondary party whose own liability on the instrument is now triggered. Analytically, however, there are lots of details about the effects of not satisfying the conditions; the mechanics of meeting them; and the circumstances under which the law excuses the conditions altogether or excuses delay in presentment or notice of dishonor.

1. Dishonor

Dishonor is essential to the liability of a drawer of a draft and the indorser of any instrument. The meaning of dishonor -- what prompts it and how it occurs -- depends on the kind of instrument that is involved. There are many rules, and they are not safely summarized beyond the summary in the text of Chapter 3 infra.

2. Presentment

Secondary liability fundamentally requires dishonor of the instrument. Dishonor usually requires, as a necessary prerequisite, due and proper presentment which satisfies the procedural and other requirements of Article 3. Officially, "presentment" means:

> a demand made by or on behalf of a person entitled to enforce an instrument (i) to *pay* the instrument made to the drawee or a party obliged to pay the instrument or, in the case of a note or accepted draft payable at a bank, to the bank, or (ii) to *accept* a draft made to the drawee.

3-501(a) (emphasis added). Generally speaking, dishonor occurs if the demand is refused, so long as two conditions are met, one of substance and the other of procedure.

a. The Substance Or Nature Of The Presentment Must Be Appropriate

The kind of presentment made, either for payment or acceptance, must have been a kind that, if refused, triggers dishonor in the circumstances of the particular case. The kind of presentment that is appropriate in the circumstances -- the nature or substance of it -- is determined by the rules of dishonor which are described in Chapter III infra. It generally turns on the nature of the instrument, when it is payable, and when the presentment is made.

b. The Appropriate Procedures Must Be Followed

Second, if the kind or substance of the presentment is appropriate, the presentment must be procedurally correct. Presentment must be made by or on behalf of a person entitled to enforce an instrument; must be made to an appropriate person, who is designated by the rules of dishonor; and must be in line with Article 3's rules regarding where, how and when presentment is made.

3. Notice Of Dishonor

Notice of dishonor is always a condition to the liability of an indorser, and is a condition to a drawer's liability if a nonbank accepts the draft because, in this event, the drawer's liability is transformed into the liability of an indorser. 3-503(a), 3-414(d), 3-415(c). Notice of dishonor "may be given in any commercially reasonable manner, including an oral, written, or electronic communication." 3-503(b). No special words must be used to give notice of dishonor. Notice of dishonor may be given by *any* person or her agent, 3-503(b), whether or not the person is a party to the instrument and even though she lacks any connection to it. Generally, "notice of dishonor must be given within 30 days following the day on which dishonor occurs,." 3-503(c), but exceptional rules apply with respect to checks and other instruments that a collecting bank takes for collection.

4. Consequence Of Delay In Presentment Or Notice

When a party's liability is conditioned on dishonor, as is true of drawers and indorsers, the liability cannot be enforced until dishonor occurs, unless it is excused by law or agreement. The same is true of presentment and notice of dishonor when they are conditions of liability. A further issue with respect to presentment and notice is the consequence of delay with respect to either of them in cases where a time limit on presentment or notice of dishonor applies. A time limit applies to presentment only with respect to checks. Unexcused delay affects indorsers and drawers differently. Notice of dishonor is required for indorsers only, except that a drawer is also entitled to notice if the acceptor is not a bank. Unexcused delay in notice to an indorser or such a drawer discharges her liability. 3-415(c) & 3-503(c).

5. Excusing Conditions Altogether Or Delay

In some cases the law relaxes the conditions of secondary liability -- excuses the conditions or delay in meeting them. An excuse may extend to one or more conditions and may affect the liability of one or more parties. Regardless of which conditions and whose liabilities are affected, the legal effect of excusing a condition or delay is that the law regards the condition as having been properly met within the time normally allowed.

E. LIABILITIES ON SPECIALIZED "CHECKS"

1. Certified Check

A *certified check* is a check that has been accepted by the bank on which the instrument is drawn. Upon acceptance the bank is liable on the check as acceptor, but the drawer's liability is discharged and the liability of any indorser is also discharged.

2. Cashier's Check

A *cashier's check* is a draft and check "with respect to which the drawer and drawee are the same bank or branches of the same bank." 3-104(g). The person who procures the check must pay the bank for it and is known as the *remitter,* 3-103(a)(11), but is not liable on the check herself unless she signs it.

3. Money Order

A money order is a demand draft that the drawee creates and that a purchaser buys for use in paying a third person. The drawee can be a bank or a non-bank (that may be affiliated with a bank). Anybody can create a money order, which is only a check or ordinary draft that is distinguished by its use rather than its form.

4. Teller's Check

A *teller's check* is a check that a bank (broadly defined) draws on, at or through another bank.

5. Traveler's Checks

A *traveler's check* is "an instrument that (i) is payable on demand, (ii) is drawn on or payable at or through a bank, (iii) is designated by the term 'traveler's check' or by a substantially similar term, and (iv) requires, as a condition to payment, a countersignature by a person whose specimen signature appears on the instrument." 3-104(i). Like a money order, a traveler's check is always a draft but is not a check unless it is drawn on a bank.

F. LIABILITY OF JOINT OBLIGORS

1. Liability To Others

"Except as otherwise provided in the instrument, two or more persons who have the same liability on an instrument as makers, drawers, acceptors, indorsers who indorse as joint payees, or anomalous indorsers are jointly and severally liable in the capacity in which they sign." 3-116(a).

2. Liability Between Themselves

When two or more persons sign an instrument jointly in the same capacity, neither is liable to the other on the instrument, unless one of them is a surety for the other. Yet, if either of them is required to pay the instrument, she is entitled by the common law to contribution from her co-obligor.

G. DISCHARGE OF LIABILITY ON INSTRUMENTS

1. Meaning And Modes Of Discharge

"Discharge" means that an obligor is released from liability on the instrument for reasons of Article 3 or contract law.

2. Payment Of The Instrument

A person who signs an instrument becomes liable to pay it. It is natural, therefore, that her payment of the instrument should end her liability on it. The law confirms and reaches this outcome by way of discharge, by providing that "[t]o the extent of the payment, the obligation of the party obliged to pay the instrument is discharged * * *." 3-602(a). Also, by separate rule, payment of the instrument usually discharges the underlying obligation. 3-310(b-c).

3. Tender Of Payment

If the obligor on a negotiable instrument makes a proper tender of full payment to the holder at or after maturity, but the holder improperly refuses to accept the payment, the obligation of the party making the tender continues; but the holder's refusal of a proper tender completely discharges any indorser or accommodation party having a right of recourse with respect to the obligation to which the tender relates. 3-603(b). Furthermore, the party making the tender is discharged to the extent of her subsequent obligation to pay interest after the due date on the amount tendered. 3-603(c).

4. Fraudulent Alteration

An alteration of an instrument that is "fraudulently made discharges a party whose obligation is affected by the alteration unless that party assents or is precluded from asserting the alteration." 3-407(b). A non-fraudulent alteration is benign, but the instrument is enforceable only to the extent of its original, unaltered terms. Id.

5. Cancellation Or Renunciation

The holder of an instrument may discharge any party's obligation on an instrument by *cancellation* or *renunciation*. 3-604(a). The former is "an intentional voluntary act, such as surrender of the instrument to the party, destruction, mutilation, or cancellation of the instrument, cancellation or striking out of the party's signature, or the addition of words to the instrument indicating discharge * * *." Id. Renunciation occurs differently, "by agreeing not to sue or otherwise renouncing rights against the party by a signed writing." Id.

6. Discharge By Agreement Or Other Act

An agreement to discharge liability on an instrument is enforceable under Article 3 to the extent that contract law would enforce it, even in the absence of renunciation, cancellation, payment, or any other discharge provided by Article 3 itself.

7. Article 3 Discharge As A Defense Against Holder In Due Course

Normally, notice of a defense to an instrument prevents a person from becoming a holder in due course of it. 3-302(a)(2)(vi). Notice of an Article 3 discharge of liability on an instrument does not have this effect; but any party's "[d]ischarge is effective against a holder in due course * * * if the holder had notice of the discharge when holder in due course status was acquired." 3-601 comment.

H. RELATIONSHIP BETWEEN LIABILITY ON AN INSTRUMENT AND LIABILITY ON THE UNDERLYING OBLIGATION

1. Taking Instrument Usually Suspends Underlying Obligation

The usual effect of taking an instrument is to *suspend* the underlying obligation pro tanto, i.e., "to the same extent the obligation would be discharged if an amount of money equal to the amount of the instrument were taken * * *." 3-310(b). In the case of an ordinary note or uncertified check, the suspension continues until the instrument is paid or dishonored. 3-310(b)(1-2). Payment of the instrument serves a double purpose. It discharges the maker or drawer's liability on the instrument itself, 3-602(a), and also on the underlying obligation. 3-310(b)(1-2). If the instrument is dishonored, the underlying obligation is revived. Then, the payee-obligee "may enforce *either* the instrument or the obligation." 3-310(b)(3) (emphasis added).

2. When Taking An Instrument Discharges The Obligation

In two exceptional situations, taking an instrument for an underlying obligation discharges the obligation instead of only suspending it. Taking an instrument discharges the underlying debt when the parties to the deal agree to this effect regardless of the kind of instrument involved, or when the instrument is a certified check, cashier's check, or teller's check even though the parties have not agreed to a discharge of the underlying debt.

3. Accord And Satisfaction

Sometimes, in an attempt to settle a disputed claim, the person against whom the claim is asserted issues a check to the claimant for an amount less than the full amount the claimant demands. The check is commonly known as a *"full-payment check"* which, when successfully used, results in discharging the claim upon payment of the check. In contract terms, it is known as an "accord and satisfaction." Success would depend on the common law, but Article 3 provides its own rules of accord and satisfaction when instruments are used. These rules are collected in 3-311 and, for the most part, follow the common law.

IV. INSTRUMENTS AS PROPERTY: ENFORCEMENT, TRANSFER, AND NEGOTIATION

A. INTRODUCTION: MAIN PROPERTY ASPECTS OF INSTRUMENTS

Instruments are, first, contracts. They embody enforceable promises to pay money. Instruments are also property. Their ownership is assignable, and enforceability is transferable. The most fundamental property right with respect to an instrument is the right to enforce it.

B. THE RELATIONSHIP OF TITLE AND THE RIGHT TO ENFORCE AN INSTRUMENT: OVERVIEW OF TRANSFER, NEGOTIATION, AND HOLDER STATUS

1. Article 3 Determines Right To Enforce, Not Ownership

Who owns an instrument -- who has title -- is determined by principles of property law apart from Article 3. 3-203 comment 1. Who can use and enjoy an instrument -- who can enforce it and exercise its other rights -- is determined by Article 3.

2. Holder Can Enforce

Generally, any "holder" of an instrument can enforce it, and enforcement is normally restricted to a holder or someone with a holder's rights. 3-301. Holder does not mean owner, although typically the holder of an instrument owns it. Holder generally means someone in possession of an instrument that is payable to bearer or to her, meaning that she is identified by the instrument as the person to whom it is payable. 1-201(20).

3. Issue

The first holder of an instrument usually gets possession because the instrument is *issued* to her. "'*Issue*' means the first delivery of an instrument by the maker or drawer, whether to a holder or nonholder, for the purpose of giving rights on the instrument to any person." 3-105 (a). "Delivery" means "voluntary transfer of possession." 1-201(14). Thus, when Buyer gives Seller a check or note payable to Seller's order, Buyer issues the instrument and Seller is a holder.

4. Transfer

As holder, Seller is a person entitled to enforce the instrument. She can convey this right of enforcement by *transferring the instrument*. On the other hand, a transfer does not give the transferee a self-evident right of enforcement, only a derivative right that must be proved. Only when the plaintiff is herself a holder is she entitled to enforce an instrument on the basis of her status alone.

5. Negotiation

A person becomes a holder of an instrument, post-issuance, only by the process of *negotiation*. 3-201(a). A voluntary transfer is normally part of negotiation, 3-201 comment 1, but is not always necessary for negotiation. Basically, an instrument is *negotiated* to a person when (1) she gets possession of an instrument (2) payable to bearer or to her that has been indorsed by everyone to whom previously it has been payable.

6. Connection Between Ownership And Right To Enforce

Article 3's rules of transfer, negotiation, and enforcement are a means of protecting non-Code property principles of ownership.

C. ENFORCEMENT

1. Persons Entitled To Enforce

The contract liabilities of maker, drawer, indorser, and acceptor are alike in that each of them is obligated to:

+ "a *person entitled to enforce the instrument * * **," or
+ an *indorser* who pays the instrument, except that indorsers themselves are liable inter se only to subsequent indorsers.

3-412, 3-413(a), 3-414(b), 3-415(a). *"Person entitled to enforce"* means

+ the holder of the instrument,
+ a nonholder in possession of the instrument who has the rights of a holder, or
+ a person not in possession of the instrument who is entitled to enforce the instrument pursuant to Section 3-309 or 3-418(d), which concern instruments that are lost, were stolen, or paid by mistake.

3-301. Any person who fits any of these categories is entitled to enforce the instrument "even though the person is not the owner of the instrument or is in wrongful possession of the instrument." Id.

2. Procedures Of Enforcement

A person's liability on an instrument is based on her having signed it. Therefore, to make a prima facie case in court to enforce an instrument, the plaintiff need only produce the instrument and prove that she, the plaintiff, is a person entitled to enforce it under 3-301. Without more, the plaintiff "is entitled to payment * * *." 3-308(b), but this abbreviated procedure may lengthen at both ends and in the middle.

3. Using Extrinsic Evidence To Vary Liability From The Terms Of An Instrument

   a. Interpretation: The Rule That Reads Writings Together
   It is a general principle of law that writings executed as part of the same transaction must be read together as a single agreement -- at least as between the immediate parties. This principle applies to instruments by force of U.C.C. 3-117.

   b. Scope: The Parol Evidence Rule
   The parol evidence rule applies, in its common-law form, to negotiable instruments in much the same way that it applies, in various forms, to other written contracts. The rule trumps section 3-117 which would otherwise require giving effect to other writings executed before the instrument but as part of the same transaction. Accordingly, neither the issuing party nor the party to whom the instrument is issued is permitted to introduce any evidence, written or oral, of what occurred prior to signing or any oral evidence of what was agreed at the time of signing for the purpose of changing, adding to, or deleting, any terms of the instrument.

4. Liability Over
"In an action for breach of an obligation for which a third person is answerable over pursuant to this Article or Article 4, the defendant may give the third person written notice of the litigation, and the person notified may then give similar notice to any other person who is answerable over. If the notice states (i) that the person notified may come in and defend and (ii) that failure to do so bind the person notified in an action later brought by the person giving the notice as to any determination of fact common to the two litigations, the person notified is so bound unless after seasonable receipt of the notice the person notified does come in and defend." 3-119.

5. Statutes Of Limitations
Article 3 includes six statutes of limitations for suits on instruments. See 3-118. Which statute applies depends on the nature of the instrument and when it is payable.

D. NEGOTIATION -- BECOMING A HOLDER OTHER THAN BY ISSUANCE

1. Introduction And Basic Rules: Possession Always And Indorsement Sometimes
Basically, only a holder can enforce an instrument or someone who claims through a holder. 3-301. A holder is anyone in possession of an instrument payable to her or payable to bearer. 1-201(20). There are two ways to become a holder:

A person can become a holder of an instrument when the instrument is *issued* to that person, or the status of holder can arise as a result of an event that

occurs [apart from and usually] after issuance. *"Negotiation"* is the term used in Article 3 to describe this post-issuance event."

3-201 comment 1. Negotiation is both a noun and a verb, an end and the means for accomplishing it. The process itself -- the conduct necessary for this result -- is the verb form of negotiation and depends on how the instrument is payable:

- ◆ If an instrument is *payable to an identified person*, negotiation requires --
  - √ transfer of possession of the instrument, *and*
  - √ its *indorsement* by the holder.
- ◆ If an instrument is *payable to bearer*, it may be negotiated by transfer of possession alone. 3-201(b).

2. The Constant, Common Requirement For Negotiation: *"Transfer Of Possession"*

Whether the instrument is payable to bearer or an identified person, a *"transfer of possession"* is necessary. "Negotiation always requires a change of possession of the instrument because nobody can be a holder without possessing the instrument, either directly or through an agent." 3-201 comment 1.

3. Indorsement Required When Payable To Identified Person

Indorsement is necessary to negotiate an instrument if the instrument is payable to an identified person. An instrument originally drawn or made payable to order is -- by definition -- payable to an identified person. 3-109(b). Negotiation of the instrument requires the payee's indorsement, which means her signature on the instrument. Whether an instrument originally was payable to order or to bearer, it is payable to an identified person if it is specially indorsed. A "special indorsement" is "an indorsement * * * made by the holder of an instrument, whether payable to an identified person or payable to bearer," that "identifies a person to whom it makes the instrument payable * * *." 3-205(a). It usually consists of a simple instruction to pay an identified person, such as "Pay Jane Smith" or "Pay Named Bank," that is followed by the holder's signature. In the end, the whole process of negotiation can be encapsulated and summarized in two grand rules:

- ◆ **An instrument cannot be negotiated that is missing the indorsement of any former or present holder to whom, as an identified person, the instrument was or is payable. Except for her, nobody is or can become a holder until she indorses.**
- ◆ **An instrument is negotiated whenever any person gets possession of an instrument that is indorsed by every former holder to whom, as identified persons, the instrument was payable. Anybody in possession is a holder.**

4. Incomplete Negotiation: The Effect Of A Missing Indorsement When The Transferee Is Entitled To The Indorsement

Occasionally, an instrument payable to order or to a special indorsee is delivered for value by the payee or the indorsee without her indorsement. When this occurs, the transferee is not a holder and acquires only the rights of the transferor against prior parties.

5. Negotiation By Multiple Payees

An instrument payable to order may name several payees either in the alternative, as "A, B, or C," or together as "A, B and C." A special indorsement may do the same. Negotiability is unaffected, but there are special rules about how to negotiate such an instrument. See 3-110(d).

6. Negotiation When Name Is Misspelled Or Misstated

Occasionally, an instrument is made payable to a payee or indorsee under a misspelled name or name other than her own. In this case, the Code provides that any person paying or giving value for the instrument may require the indorser to sign both names. 3-204(d).

7. Effect Of Attempt To Negotiate Less Than Balance Due

If an instrument has been paid in part, it may be negotiated as to the balance due. To be effective as a negotiation, however, an indorsement must transfer the entire instrument or the entire unpaid balance. If the indorsement purports to transfer less, it operates only as a partial assignment, 3-203(d), and the partial assignee does not become a holder or acquire her advantages. "[N]egotiation of the instrument does not occur." Id.

8. Effect Of Negotiation That May Be Rescinded

A negotiation is effective even if it may be rescinded on the grounds of incapacity, fraud, duress, mistake, illegality, or for other reasons. The transferee is a holder with full power to negotiate it further as long as she retains possession; and the transferor loses her rights with respect to the instrument until, by other law, she rescinds the negotiation and recovers the instrument by replevin or otherwise.

E. RESTRICTIVE INDORSEMENTS

In addition to the qualities of qualified or unqualified and blank or special, every indorsement is also either restrictive or unrestrictive. A restrictive indorsement is an indorsement that would limit the purpose to which the proceeds of an instrument are applied, so that a person is accountable who pays the instrument for any other use. A restrictive indorsement generally does not prevent further transfer or negotiation or affect an indorsee's right to enforce the instrument. Moreover, neither the indorsement nor knowledge of it prevents or affects a person's becoming a holder in due course. The consequence of a restrictive indorsement occurs when the terms of an effective restriction are violated by someone who is bound by the indorsement. The violation can prevent the person becoming a holder of due course or result in her personal liability.

V. WARRANTY AND RESTITUTION: INSURING ENFORCEABILITY

A person incurs contract liability on an instrument because she signs it. A person incurs warranty liability with respect to an instrument because she transfers the instrument and also because the instrument is presented for payment or acceptance. Warranty liability is a property concept. It is not dependent on promise and contract. Therefore, warranty liability attaches whether or not the warrantor indorsed the instrument. In case she indorsed, her contract liability is in addition to the warranty liability.

A. SOURCE OF LAW FOR WARRANTIES

Article 3 is the general source of warranty law for all instruments. Section 3-416 creates transfer warranties and 3-417 presentment warranties.

B. TRANSFER WARRANTIES

1. Who Makes Them

The transfer warranties are made by any person, including a holder in due course, who (1) transfers an instrument *and* (2) receives consideration. 3-416(a).

2. Who Gets Them

Transfer warranties always run in favor of the immediate transferee, whether or not the transferor has signed the instrument. If, however, the transferor indorses the instrument, the transfer warranties she makes run in favor of "*any subsequent transferee.*" 3-416(a) (emphasis added).

3. What Are They

A person who makes transfer warranties, though she may in fact be unaware of them, warrants that:

- **she is a person entitled to enforce the instrument;**
- **all signatures on the instrument are authentic and authorized;**
- **the instrument has not been altered." 3-416(a)(3);**
- **the instrument is not subject to a defense or claim in recoupment of any party which can be asserted against the warrantor; and**
- **she "has no knowledge of any insolvency proceeding commenced with respect to the maker or acceptor or, in the case of an unaccepted draft, the drawer. 3-416(a).**

C. PRESENTMENT WARRANTIES

A person who pays or accepts an instrument may worry that she is doing so rightly, for the right person, and in the right amount. *Presentment warranties* provide some insurance against these risks. They are described in 3-417, which provides different warranty coverage for different payors. *Drawees of unaccepted drafts* are covered by 3-417(a). *All other payors* are covered by 3-417(d).

1. Presentment Warranties In The Case Of A Drawee Of An Unaccepted Draft

The presentment warranties of 3-417(a) are made by any person who presents an *unaccepted draft* for payment *or* acceptance and also by any prior transferor. The warranties run only to the drawee who pays or accepts the draft in good faith, not to the drawer or anyone else. he warranties are:

* **the warrantor is, or was, at the time the warrantor transferred the draft, a person entitled to enforce the draft or authorized to obtain payment or acceptance of the draft on behalf of a person entitled to enforce the draft, 3-417(a)(1);**
* **the draft has not been altered, 3-417(a)(2); and**
* **the warrantor has *no knowledge* that the signature of the *drawer* of the draft is unauthorized, 3-417(a)(3).**

2. Presentment Warranties In All Other Cases

Except in the case of a drawee of an unaccepted draft**, the only presentment warranty is that "the warrantor is, or was, at the time the warrantor transferred the instrument, a person entitled to enforce the instrument or authorized to obtain payment on behalf of a person entitled to enforce the instrument." 3-417(d)(1).** The warrantor effectively promises that, at the time of her transfer or presentment, there were no missing or unauthorized indorsements that were necessary for negotiation. The same warranty -- that the warrantor is entitled to enforce the instrument -- is part of the transfer warranties of 3-416, and is also a presentment warranty in the special case of a drawee of an unaccepted draft. 3-417(a)(1). The only significant difference under 3-417(d) is that this warranty is the only warranty that the payor gets.

D. SUPPLEMENTING PRESENTMENT WARRANTIES WITH RESTITUTIONARY RECOVERY

Only through mistake is a maker, drawer or acceptor likely to pay an instrument that has been materially altered, or an instrument that bears an unauthorized maker's or drawer's signature. The mistake cannot ordinarily be corrected by way of a warranty action because the presentment warranties covering these kinds of fraud are very limited. Yet, whenever mistake is involved, there is the possibility of recovering the mistaken payment on the different, extra-Code theory of restitution. After all, common-law and equitable principles supplement the Code unless they are displaced by it. U.C.C. 1-103. Thus, in many cases in which presentment warranties do not cover payors' losses, they assert restitution claims, instead of warranty actions, against persons who have received payment on altered instruments or instruments bearing a forged drawer's or maker's signature. Almost always, however, the plaintiff-payors lose because the common law of restitution provides a defense to their claims that is codified in Article 3 itself: "The remedies [of restitution] provided by [3-418(a)] or [3-418(b)] may not be asserted against a person who took the instrument in good faith and for value or who in good faith changed position in reliance on the payment or acceptance." 3-418(c). This defense effectively eliminates restitution except in rare cases because, almost always, the person who obtains payment or acceptance took the instrument in good faith from her transferor and paid value for it. In sum, therefore, mistaken payment or acceptance is rarely undone on the basis of restitution law.

E. REMEDYING BREACH OF WARRANTY

Many of the rules for remedying a breach of warranty are basically the same for both transfer and presentment warranties. The most basic rule is the measure of damages, which is the same but is stated differently for the two kinds of warranties. In the case of transfer warranties, the basic measure of damages is the amount of the loss suffered as a result of the breach not to exceed the amount of the instrument. 3-416(b). For presentment warranties in the case of a payor, the measure is the amount she paid, which naturally is her loss. 3-417(b) & (d). An acceptor who pays can recover the same damages; but breach of warranty is a defense to payment in the first place, 3-417(b), except as against a holder in due course. Id.

F. ELECTRONIC BANKING: ENCODING AND RETENTION WARRANTIES

Special Article 4 warranties are made by the keeper of checks that are truncated any by any person who encodes information with respect to the checks.

VI. CLAIMS AND DEFENSES TO INSTRUMENTS

A. REAL DEFENSES

A holder in due course is subject to *real defenses*. They always survive and, without exception, are good against everybody. Any person suing to enforce an instrument is subject to them. There are only a few of them. They are narrow and mostly depend on outside law. Article 3 collects them in 3-305(a)(1):

- infancy of the obligor to the extent that infancy is a defense to a simple contract;
- duress, lack of legal capacity, or illegality of the transaction which, under other law, nullifies the obligation of the obligor;
- fraud that induced the obligor to sign the instrument with neither knowledge nor reasonable opportunity to learn of its character or its essential terms, known as *fraud in the factum*; and

* discharge of the obligor in insolvency proceedings.

B. ORDINARY OR PERSONAL DEFENSES

Ordinary or *personal defenses* are reasons of the law for reducing or eliminating an obligor's liability on an instrument except as against a holder in due course. The rule is: "Except as stated in subsection (b) * * *, the right to enforce the obligation of a party to pay an instrument is subject to * * * a defense of the obligor stated in another section of this article or a defense of the obligor that would be available if the person entitled to enforce the instrument were enforcing a right to payment under a simple contract * * *." 3-305(a)(2).

1. Article 3 Defenses

The ordinary defenses created by Article 3 itself are spread throughout the statute, but they are conveniently listed in a comment to 3-305:
* nonissuance of the instrument, conditional issuance, and issuance for a special purpose (Section 3-105(b));
* failure to countersign a traveler's check (Section 3-106(c));
* modification of the obligation by a separate agreement (Section 3-117);
* payment that violates a restrictive indorsement (Section 3-206(f));
* instruments issued without consideration or for which promised performance has not been given (Section 3- 303(b)),
* and breach of warranty when a draft is accepted (Section 3-417(b)). 3-305 comment 2.

2. Discharge -- The Not-A-Defense Defense

The most important Article 3 defense is not on the list of defenses in Article 3. It is "discharge," which is discussed under the heading of contract liability on instruments.

3. Defenses Of Contract Law

In addition to the Article 3 defenses specifically stated in Article 3, the personal defenses to an instrument also include defenses "of the obligor that would be available if the person entitled to enforce the instrument were enforcing a right to payment under a simple contract." 3-305(a)(2). These defenses derive from the underlying obligation and are based on the contract law that governs it. *This law includes the common law and any applicable statutory law*, such as U.C.C. Article 2 when a sale of goods is involved.

C. RECOUPMENT (DEFENSIVE COUNTERCLAIMS)

Basically, recoupment is a cause of action that is related to the plaintiff's claim and is asserted defensively, so far as is possible and necessary, to reduce the amount of liability -- only to wipe out or cut down the plaintiff's demand. In sum, recoupment is essentially a counterclaim that is asserted defensively only. When a person lacks the rights of a holder in due course, her right to enforce the instrument is subject to "a claim in recoupment of the obligor against the original payee of the instrument if the claim arose from the transaction that gave rise to the instrument * * *." 3-305(a)(3).

D. CLAIMS (PROPERTY INTERESTS)
1. General Rule
A person can own a property interest in an instrument even though somebody else holds the instrument and is the person entitled to enforce it. On the other hand, everybody except a holder in due course takes an instrument "subject to a claim of a property or possessory right in the instrument or its proceeds, including a claim to rescind a negotiation and to recover the instrument or its proceeds * * * ." 3-306.

2. Obligor's Options When Third Party Asserts Ownership Claim
An obligor safely can pay the holder of an instrument and be discharged from liability even though the obligor knows of a third person's claim to the instrument and even though the claim is valid. 3-602(a). The claimant's remedy is to sue to recover the instrument and prevent payment.

VII. ACCOMMODATION PARTIES

The term *surety* is probably familiar to you. Article 3 has a special name for a surety who joins the principal debtor in signing an instrument. The name is *accommodation party,* which generally means anyone who signs an instrument with another person for the purpose of benefiting the other person and without being a direct beneficiary of the value given for the instrument. 3-419(a) & comment 1. The other person -- the principal debtor -- is known as the *accommodated party* on the instrument. The relevance of accommodation status, and the different treatment that results from it, is principally in the accommodation party's rights (on and dehors the instrument) against the principal debtor, and in the accommodation party's defenses to payment of the instrument against the payee and other holders and transferees. In these regards an accommodation party is better protected, more privileged than signers of instruments who do not enjoy accommodation status.

A. DECIDING WHO IS AN ACCOMMODATION PARTY
1. Defining *Accommodation Party* And *Accommodated Party*
In short, "[a]n accommodation party is a person who signs an instrument to benefit the accommodated party either by signing at the time value is obtained by the accommodated party or later, and who is not a direct beneficiary of the value obtained." 3-419 comment 1.

2. Proving Accommodation Status

A person is an accommodation party if she signed the instrument to benefit another party to the instrument, i.e., "for the purpose of incurring liability on the instrument without being a direct beneficiary of the value given for the instrument." 3-419(a). Ordinarily, a person proves that she signed for this purpose by presenting evidence that she received no *direct* benefit from the proceeds of the instrument.

B. LIABILITY ON THE INSTRUMENT

The rule is that an accommodation party's obligation on the instrument is determined by the capacity in which she signed it. 3-419(b). Capacity means maker, drawer, indorser or acceptor. Accommodation status, in itself, does not alter the person's liability on an instrument as defined by the usual rules governing the liability of people who sign instruments.

C. RIGHTS AGAINST PRINCIPAL DEBTOR

1. Exoneration

Ordinarily, a holder is not required to pursue the principal debtor before demanding payment of an accommodation party. Yet, the accommodation party enjoys the right, by suit in equity, to compel the principal debtor to pay if the principal debtor is capable of satisfying the obligation. This right is known as *exoneration.*

2. Reimbursement And Recourse

Under the common law, a surety who pays the debt enjoys the right to recoup the payment from the principal debtor. This right is known as the *right of reimbursement.* An accommodation party enjoys this common-law right. She also enjoys a right of recovery on the instrument itself. By the terms of Article 3, "[a]n accommodation party who pays the instrument is entitled to reimbursement from the accommodated party and is entitled to enforce the instrument against the accommodated party." 3-419(e). An accommodation party can avail herself of these rights, including the right of recourse on the instrument, without regard to the capacity in which she signed and even though the principal debtor would not be liable to her on the instrument in the absence of the suretyship relation between them.

3. Subrogation

An accommodation party who pays the instrument is subrogated to the holder's rights on the instrument against the accommodated party, i.e., the principal debtor, and also to the creditor's rights in collateral that secures the debt. So, when an accommodation party pays the holder, she can enforce her rights of reimbursement and recourse out of any collateral that secures the instrument.

D. DEFENSES TO PAYMENT

1. Defenses Based On The Instrument

First and foremost, an accommodation party is a signer of an instrument. For this reason she is liable thereon in the capacity in which she signed the instrument. Correspondingly, notwithstanding her accommodation status, she is freed from liability whenever, under the rules of Article 3 generally, a person who signed in her capacity would be discharged on the instrument. Her accommodation status does not deprive her of rights, including defenses, she would otherwise have as a signer of an instrument.

2. Failure Of Consideration Between Creditor And Principal Debtor And Other Derivative Defenses

Failure of consideration between principal and creditor is a defense available to the surety, including an accommodation party. Further, the reasoning that allows a surety to assert such failure of consideration applies equally as well to any defense of the principal debtor against the creditor, whether the defense is want of consideration, impossibility, illegality, fraud, duress or the like. A few defenses of the principal debtor are characterized as personal to her and for this reason are unavailable to the surety. The most important examples are the principal's lack of capacity, such as infancy, and the discharge of the principal in bankruptcy. 3-305(d).

3. Lack Of Consideration

a. Between Principal Debtor and Creditor

If no consideration supports the principal debtor's obligation to the creditor so that the former, for this reason, would have a defense against the latter, this lack of consideration is also a derivative defense for the surety that is effective against the creditor.

b. For the Surety's Undertaking

The obligation of an accommodation party may be enforced notwithstanding any statute of frauds and whether or not the accommodation party receives consideration for the accommodation. 3-419(b).

4. Suretyship Defenses -- U.C.C. 3-605

An accommodation party's most important defenses are a collection of reasons for discharging her from liability that are based on her status as a surety, thus the name *suretyship defenses*. Speaking very generally, these defenses, or reasons for discharge, are tied to conduct of the creditor that
- alters the principal's obligation or
- impairs collateral for the obligation.

Article 3's collection of suretyship defenses is in 3-605. Significantly, **the 3-605 suretyship defenses are also extended to *ordinary indorsers* -- anybody who** indorses an instrument whether or not for accommodation. It also includes a drawer of a draft that is accepted by a nonbank because the law treats her, upon the acceptance, as an indorser. 3-414(d), 3-605(a).

F. FTC RULE ON NOTICE TO CONSUMER SURETIES

A rule of the Federal Trade Commission requires creditors in consumer transactions to warn a surety of her responsibilities before the surety becomes obligated on the debt. Some states, by their local law, require the same or a similar warning to consumer sureties.

VIII. HOLDER IN DUE COURSE

A. REQUIREMENTS OF DUE-COURSE STATUS

1. For Value

A holder can become a holder in due course only if and to the extent that she gives *value* for the instrument. For this purpose an instrument is issued or transferred for "value" if:

- the instrument is issued or transferred for a promise of performance, to the extent the promise has been performed;
- the transferee acquires a security interest or other lien in the instrument other than a lien obtained by judicial proceeding;
- the instrument is issued or transferred as payment of, or as security for, an antecedent claim against any person, whether or not the claim is due;
- the instrument is issued or transferred in exchange for a negotiable instrument; or
- the instrument is issued or transferred in exchange for the incurring of an irrevocable obligation to a third party by the person taking the instrument.

3-303(a). So defined, **value is both broader and more narrow than consideration: broader because it includes preexisting debt and more narrow because it excludes an executory promise.**

2. Without Notice

A further requirement of holder in due course is taking the instrument "without notice" --

- that the instrument is overdue or has been dishonored or that there is an uncured default with respect to payment of another instrument issued as part of the same series,
- that the instrument contains an unauthorized signature or has been altered,
- of any claim to the instrument, or
- that any party has a defense or claim in recoupment described in 3-305.

3-302(a)(2). **If a holder takes with notice of any of these circumstances, she is not a holder in due course for any purpose as against any person and is subject to all** claims to the instrument, and also to the defenses of every party to the instrument, even though there is no connection between the information she knew, or is charged with, and the claims and defenses that are asserted against her.

3. Authenticity Of The Instrument

Former law provided that a person has notice of a defense or claim if "the instrument is so incomplete, bears such visible evidence of forgery or alteration, or is otherwise so irregular as to call into question its validity, terms or ownership or to create an ambiguity as to the party to pay." 3-304(1)(a) (1989 Official Text). *The 1990 Article 3 makes the condition of the instrument a wholly separate requirement of holder in due course*, requiring that "the instrument when issued or negotiated to the holder does not bear such apparent evidence of forgery or alteration or is not otherwise so irregular or incomplete as to call into question its authenticity." 3-302(a)(1). The word "'authenticity' is used to make clear that the irregularity or incompleteness must indicate that the instrument may not be what it purports to be." 3-302 comment 1. It makes no difference, at least not under the new law, that the obligor's claim or defense is unrelated to the irregularity or incompleteness of the instrument. It also makes no difference, technically, that the taker is without notice of the irregularity or incompleteness; but the problem must be "apparent" and in this event the taker ordinarily would have reason to know of the problem and thus would have notice of it.

4. Good Faith

Even though a holder acquires an apparently perfect instrument for value and without prohibited notice, she does not qualify as a holder in due course unless she also takes the instrument in "*good faith*." The test of good faith is both subjective and objective. It means "honesty in fact *and the observance of reasonable commercial standards of fair dealing*," 3-103(a)(4) (emphasis added), which is "concerned with the fairness of conduct rather than the care with which an act is performed." 3-103 comment 4. History explains that when this objective test is added to the subjective, "a business man engaging in a commercial transaction is not entitled to claim the peculiar advantages which the law accords to the * * * holder in due course * * * on a bar showing of 'honesty in fact' when his actions fail to meet the generally accepted standards current in his business, trade, or profession. 3-302 comment 1 (1952 Official Text).

5. Apart From Certain Unusual Circumstances

Even though she satisfies the usual requirements previously described, a person does not acquire the rights of a holder in due course of an instrument taken:
- by legal process or by purchase in an execution, bankruptcy, or creditor's sale or similar proceeding,

 ◆   by purchase as part of a bulk transaction not in the ordinary course of business of
      the transferor, or
 ◆   as the successor in interest to an estate or other organization.
3-302(c).

B. PAYEE AS HOLDER IN DUE COURSE

The payee of an instrument, like any other holder, can be a holder in due course so
long as she meets the usual requirements, "but use of the holder-in-due-course
doctrine by the payee of an instrument is not the normal situation." 3-302 comment
4. The doctrine assumes that in the typical case, the holder in due course is not the
payee but is an immediate or remote transferee of the payee. When the issuer and the
payee are the only parties, "the holder-in-due-course doctrine is irrelevant in
determining rights between Obligor and Obligee with respect to the instrument." Id.
About the only case in which it makes any difference that a payee is a holder in due
course is that in which she does not deal directly with the maker or drawer but
instead obtains the instrument from a remitter who obtained it from the maker or
drawer. In this case, if the payee qualifies as a holder in due course, she takes the
instrument free of any defense or claim based on the remitter's wrongdoing;
otherwise not. See 3-302 comment 4.

C. EQUIVALENT RIGHTS TO HOLDER IN DUE COURSE
1. Taking Through A Holder In Due Course -- The Shelter Principle

The "[t]ransfer of an instrument, whether or not the transfer is a negotiation, vests in
the transferee any right of the transferor to enforce the instrument, including any right
as a holder in due course * * *." 3-203(b). By virtue of this broad *shelter principle*
(which applies to most other forms of property as well), even though a person in her
own right does not satisfy the requirements for being a holder in due course, she is
entitled to enjoy the benefits of that status that were enjoyed by any holder in due
course prior to her in the chain of transfer of the instrument. The primary
significance of the shelter principle, and the basis for its name, is the fact that it
enables one who is not a holder in due course to share the shelter from claims and
defenses to the extent enjoyed by a holder in due course through or from whom she
acquired the instrument.

2. Estoppel

Although a transferee of an instrument is not a holder in due course and does not
claim through such a holder, and even though the obligation assigned to her is not in
the form of a negotiable instrument, an obligor of a promise might be precluded from
asserting a defense against the transferee because of equitable estoppel.

3. Contractual Waiver Of Claims And Defenses

An assignee of even a simple contract can take free of prior claims and defenses, and thereby enjoy rights equivalent to those of a holder in due course, if the contract contains a waiver-of-defenses clause. Such a clause is a provision in the contract through which the obligor agrees not to assert against any assignee any claim or defense she may have against her seller, the assignor.

4. Direct Financing

A lender who finances a person's acquisition of property or services by loaning her the purchase money directly, rather than by funneling it through the seller as happens when a lender buys the seller's instruments or sales contracts, is generally not subject to the person's claims and defenses against the seller. The lender is immune from these claims and defenses simply because the debtor's promise to repay the lender the loan is, in contemplation of the law, totally independent of the seller's obligations to the debtor. The lender's rights against the debtor are not derived from the seller's rights against her. The loan and the sale are two legally separate transactions, and the lender in the loan transaction is not accountable for the sins of the seller in the sale transaction.

5. Federal Immunity

Federal law can give immunity from adverse claims and defenses to holders of contracts that are not instruments; and it can give the same immunity to transferees of instruments who are not holders in due course.

D. RESTRICTIONS ON DUE-COURSE STATUS AND EQUIVALENT RIGHTS

1. Federal Law

a. Federal Trade Commission Rule Concerning Preservation of Consumers' Claims and Defenses

When the holder-in-due-course doctrine, a contractual waiver of defenses, or direct financing is used in financing sales of property or services, the effect is to separate the buyer's duty to pay from the seller's obligations under the parties' contract. The holder in due course, the assignee of a contract containing a waiver-of-defenses clause, or the lender who loaned the buyer the purchase price can recover the price of the property or services even though the buyer has claims or defenses against the seller for breach of the sales transaction. More than a decade ago the Federal Trade Commission promulgated a trade regulation rule designed to prevent this separation of duties in consumer credit transactions. The rule is entitled the Federal Trade Commission Trade Regulation Rule on the Preservation of Consumers' Claims and Defenses, which generally intends to preserve an obligor's claims and defenses against persons who directly or indirectly take or receive consumer credit transactions.

b. **Bank Credit Cards**
Federal statutory law provides that a credit card issuer *is* subject to all claims (other than tort claims) and defenses arising out of any transaction in which the credit card is used as a method of payment or extension of credit, subject to certain limitations.

2. **State Statutory Law**
   a. **Restricting Contractual Waivers of Claims and Defenses**
   Statutes in a large number of states outlaw contractual waivers of claims and defenses in consumer credit contracts involving sales of goods and services. Not only are such waivers prohibited, the statutes also declare unenforceable a waiver that is included in a consumer contract in violation of the statutory prohibition.

   b. **Due-Course Status**
   Some states have attempted to neuter the Article 3 holder-in-due-course doctrine in consumer credit sales by prohibiting sellers of goods or services from taking a negotiable instrument (except a check for the purchase price) from buyers who are consumers.

   c. **Direct Financing (Purchase Money Loans)**
   The Uniform Consumer Credit Code provides that a consumer who borrows money to purchase or lease goods or services can assert against the lender claims and defenses the consumer has against the seller in certain circumstances.

3. **Decisional Law**
   a. **Close-Connection Doctrine**
   The courts have developed their own restrictions that exist as a matter of decisional law, the most important of which is the *close-connection doctrine*. Basically, the close-connection doctrine holds that an assignee of a right to money cannot take free of the obligor's claims and defenses against the assignor if the assignee was so closely connected (functionally or otherwise) to the assignor (generally or with respect to the particular transaction) that the assignee should be accountable for assignor's misdealings with the obligor.

   b. **Public Policy**
   A few courts have held that in consumer transactions, contractual waivers of claims and defenses are unconscionable, violative of public policy, or for similar reasons are not enforceable as a matter of decisional law.

PART TWO --
BANK DEPOSITS AND COLLECTIONS

IX. CHECK COLLECTION PROCESS

A. DESCRIBING (VERY GENERALLY) THE PROCESS AND ITS ARTICLE 3 EFFECTS

There are many ways in which checks are collected. Four very basic models are these:

1. Personal Presentment By Owners Of Checks

The payee or subsequent holder of the check personally presents the item to the payor bank for payment. Presentment will be for cash or through deposit.

a. Presentment for Cash

The holder hands the check to a teller of the drawer's bank (the payor bank) and asks for money. This process is presentment for immediate payment over the counter for cash. Final payment occurs when the money is given to the holder, i.e., paid in cash. Final payment to a holder discharges the drawer on the check, and also on the underlying transaction. The payor bank recoups by charging the item against the drawer's account.

b. Presentment Through Deposit

If the holder maintains her own account at the payor bank, she may deposit the check instead of presenting it for payment over the counter. In this event, the payor bank is also the depositary bank. Ordinarily, the holder's account is credited with the amount of the check before the check is charged against the drawer's account, but this credit to the holder's account is usually provisional. The credit can be revoked -- the item can be charged back against the account -- until the check is finally paid. Final payment will not occur until the bank's midnight deadline expires.

2. Direct Presentment Between Banks

If the holder's account is with another bank (not the payor bank) where she deposits the check or cashes it, her bank is the depositary bank. (The drawer's bank, as always, is still the payor bank.) In this case the holder's bank will act as the holder's agent in getting payment from the payor bank. In this role the depositary bank is also known as the collecting bank. If the two banks are located close together, or in the case of a very large item or other special circumstances, the depositary bank may present the item directly to the payor bank, and in this event the depositary-collecting bank also becomes the presenting bank. The payor bank will immediately give the depositary bank a credit for the item. Until the check is finally paid, the payor bank can dishonor the check by returning it to the depositary bank, which will compensate the payor bank for the returned item. If this happens, the depositary bank can recoup any credit it gave the holder, whether this credit was cash given for the item or an entry in the holder's account. Upon the payor bank's final payment of the check, the credit given the depositary bank becomes final (i.e., cannot be revoked), as does the credit the depositary-collecting bank gave the holder.

3. Collection Through Clearinghouses

Commonly, banks grouped in a city or larger region will agree among themselves to a multilateral collection process, known as a *clearing house,* for the principal purpose of collecting checks they receive that are drawn on one another. In simple terms, a clearinghouse operates by the member banks presenting checks to a central point where the items are physically exchanged among the members, and collection is made by crediting the amounts presented by each bank against one another.

4. Long-Distance Collection Through Federal Reserve Banks

When the depositary and payor banks are located far apart, the check will typically be collected through the Federal Reserve whose banks, bank branches and regional service centers spread throughout the country operate collectively as a kind of a national clearinghouse. Each Federal Reserve Bank serves as the "switch" in collecting checks among banks within the Bank's district; and, when more than one Reserve Bank is involved in the collection process, the Interdistrict Settlement Fund is the switching mechanism.

B. FORWARD COLLECTION PROCESS

1. Depositary Bank Giving Customer Credit

A person who wants to "collect" a check will take it to her bank and ask for cash or credit to her account. The depositary bank is not legally obliged to give cash for the item immediately and typically will give the customer only a provisional credit that can be revoked in case of dishonor. Federal law dictates how soon funds must be made available for a check that a customer deposits for credit with her bank.

2. Collecting Banks' Indorsements

Every bank (other than the paying bank) that handles a check during forward collection must add a standardized, legible indorsement, including the depositary bank and intermediary banks.

3. Responsibilities Of Collecting Banks

Any bank handling a check or other item for collection, except the payor bank, is a *collecting bank.* 4-105(5). The role of a collecting bank is to assist the owner of the check in getting payment from the payor bank by forwarding the item for presentment for payment and, if the item is dishonored, to assist in returning it to the owner if the item is returned through the collecting bank. In this role collecting banks ordinarily serve as agents of the owner and are responsible to her for their collection conduct.

In general, they owe the owner a duty of good faith, and they must also act reasonably, according to a standard of ordinary care, in carrying out tasks with respect to both forward-collection and return of items.

4. Settlements

As a check is deposited and moves from bank to bank in the collection process, everybody usually gets an almost immediate credit or settlement for the item. Article 4 provides that these settlements in the forward collection process generally are provisional and can be revoked if the check is dishonored. Overriding federal law declares that settlements between banks for the forward collection of a check are final when made; but the same federal law provides for returning a dishonored check and requires a bank to which a return is made to compensate the returning bank for the item.

5. Presentment

Federal law lists the locations at which a paying bank must accept presentment of checks, and both federal and state law endorse electronic presentment of items as part of truncation agreements.

C. MAIN DUTIES OF THE PAYOR BANK IN THE RETURN PROCESS

1. Article 4 Return -- Mainly, The *Midnight Deadline* Rule(s)

A payor bank cannot indefinitely retain a check that has been presented for payment. The check usually belongs to the depositor who expects payment, and federal law will require the depositary bank to make funds available for the check in fairly short order unless the check is sooner dishonored. 12 USCA 4001-4010. By rule of Article 4 -- 4-302 -- the payor bank becomes accountable for the item -- liable for it -- unless it returns the check by the **midnight deadline** with respect to the item -- **midnight of the next banking day following the banking day on which the item is received**, 4-301(a)(1); and a payor bank that is not the depositary bank can retain the item this long only if the bank settles for the item -- gives credit for it -- by midnight of the banking day of receipt. Id. If the item is presented through a Federal Reserve Bank, accountability results at the end of the banking day unless the payor bank settles by then. 12 CFR 210.9(a). In practice, a payor bank almost always settles for an item on the day the item is received and often immediately, even when the payor bank is also the depositary bank. Accountability under 4-302 is thus avoided. Settlement is an accounting. Until the midnight deadline, however, this settlement can be recovered by a return that is timely under 4-301 and in compliance with other provisions of state law and federal Regulation CC. Failure to make such a timely return results in the settlement becoming final -- final payment occurs. The settlement cannot be recovered lawfully. Unlawfully recovering the settlement result in liability for converting the funds.

2. Large-Dollar Notice

Even when a payor bank makes a timely and otherwise proper return under 4-301, the bank is also bound to give quick, special notice if the item is for $2,500 or more. This special notice is required by a rule of Regulation CC commonly called the large-dollar notice requirement.

3. Expeditious Return

Banks returning checks must also abide by Regulation CC's requirement of *expeditious return.* This requirement is imposed not only on the payor bank that returns an item, but also on intermediary banks involved in the return process (known as returning banks). As applied to payor banks, the expeditious return rule is separate from and in addition to the large-dollar notice requirement and is also in addition to the midnight deadline rules of Article 4. A check must be timely returned under Article 4 and must also be expeditiously returned under Regulation CC. The midnight deadline and expeditious return rules are closely related but different. It is possible to meet one rule and not the other, and the consequences of violating the rules are different. A way to view the relationship between the two requirements is that a return must begin by the midnight deadline of state law and must be accomplished expeditiously under federal law. There are two alternative tests for expeditious return:

- Two-Day/Four-Day Test. A check is considered expeditiously returned if the check is returned such that it would normally be received by the depositary bank by 4:00 p.m. (local time of the depositary bank) two business days after the banking day of presentment in the case of a local check, or by 4:00 p.m. four business days after presentment in the case of a nonlocal check. 12 CFR 229.30(a)(1).
- Forward Collection Test. A check is nonetheless considered returned expeditiously if the paying bank uses transportation methods and routes for return comparable to those used for forward collection checks, even if the check is not received by the depositary bank within the two-day or four-day period. 12 CFR 229.30(a)(2).

D. RETURNING BANKS IN THE RETURN PROCESS

A returning bank is a bank (other than a paying or depositary bank) handling a returned check or notice in lieu of return. A paying bank is authorized to return a dishonored check through a returning bank rather than directly to the depositary bank, so long as doing so is expeditious and the returning bank has itself agreed to handle the returned check expeditiously. A returning bank is required to return a returned check expeditiously, that is, according to standards that are similar to the tests of expeditious return established for paying banks. Regulation CC imposes this duty and prescribes the returning bank's liability for breaching it. Article 4 echoes CC by separately requiring a collecting bank to act reasonably in returning a check.

E. DEPOSITARY BANKS' RIGHTS AND DUTIES UPON RETURN OF CHECKS

1. Paying For Returns

A depositary bank must pay the returning or paying bank returning the check to it for the amount of the check prior to the close of business on the banking day on which it received the check.

2. Main Rights Against Customer And Others When Returned Check Has Been Dishonored

a. Charging Back Against Customer's Account

A depositary bank can recover the amount of credit it gave its customer for a check if the check is dishonored, which requires the payor bank timely to return the item pursuant to Article 4. It is self-help recovery. The bank simply debits the customer's account for the amount of the check even though the specific credit attributable to the check has been withdrawn or applied. If the account is insufficient to cover the charge back, the bank can sue to obtain refund from its customer. The customer is personally liable for the refund. A depositary bank that is also the payor bank enjoys the same rights of charge back and refund against its customer; but, when the depositary bank is the payor bank, charging back equates with returning and dishonoring the item, so that the limits of the 4-301 midnight deadline rule and sooner final payment apply. Most significantly, if the bank credits the depositor's accounts and fails to return the check by its midnight deadline, final payment has occurred and the rights of charge back and refund are lost. Also, if the bank cashes the item, the effect is final payment of the item then and there. There is no right to return, charge back or seek refund even if the bank bounces the check, notifies the customer, or takes other action prior to the midnight deadline.

b. Suing On The Check

The payor bank's dishonor of the check triggers the secondary liability of the drawer and any indorser. Thus, the depositary bank can sue them on the check.

3. Rights When Returned Check Was Not Dishonored And Was Unlawfully Returned In Violation Of Midnight Deadline

When the payor bank finally pays an item, a depositary bank loses the rights of charge back and refund and thus cannot recover the credit the bank gave its customer for the item. The liability of the drawer or any indorser of the check is conditioned on dishonor of the instrument. Thus, if the payor bank violates 4-301 and thereby finally pays an item, the depositary bank cannot sue anybody on the check. In the end, therefore, the depositary bank is left with a returned check for which it paid and for which it cannot lawfully recover. The answer is to look for recovery in the other direction -- back up the collection stream toward the payor bank which wrongfully returned the item despite final payment. The best theory is federal warranty law.

F. FINAL PAYMENT
1. Why Final Payment Is Important
Final payment is the point beyond which payor banks cannot dishonor checks that have been presented for payment and cannot lawfully return the checks and take payment for them from the depositary bank or a returning bank. In short, a payor bank that finally pays a check is usually stuck with it as against persons upstream in the collection process, even if the drawer's account is empty or the check cannot properly be charged against the account. Final payment under Article 4 also has consequences under Article 3 because it gives meaning to the term "payment" as used in important provisions 3-602 (discharge through payment to a holder) and 3-418 (payment is final in favor of certain classes).

2. Who Makes Final Payment
Only a payor bank, i.e., the drawee of a check, makes final payment!

3. How Final Payment Is Made
Article 4 describes three different, alternative means of finally paying an item. Final payment occurs as soon as the payor bank has first done any of them.
* Paid the item in cash;
* Settled for the item without having a right to revoke the settlement under statute, clearinghouse rule, or agreement; or
* made a provisional settlement for the item and failed to revoke the settlement in the time and manner permitted by statute, clearing-house rule, or agreement.

4. Liabilities That Are Excepted From Final Payment (And 4-302 Accountability)
A payor bank can sometimes, in effect, avoid (by end run) the finality of final payment. Even though a settlement has become final under the rules of Article 4, the bank can recover damages on collateral theories and thereby effectively recoup the payment made, even when the payment was made in cash. With respect to an item that has been finally paid, the principal bases of recoupment are:
* breach of warranty of presentment,
* restitution for mistaken payment, and
* subrogation to rights of the drawer.

X. THE RELATIONSHIP BETWEEN A PAYOR BANK AND ITS CHECKING ACCOUNT CUSTOMERS

A. WRONGFUL DISHONOR

"A payor bank is liable to its customer for damages proximately caused by the wrongful dishonor of an item." 4-402(b).

1. What Is "Wrongful Dishonor"

Simply put, *wrongful dishonor* is dishonoring a check that is properly payable and thus should have been paid.

2. What Damages Are Recoverable

The customer can recover "damages proximately caused." This recovery includes consequential damages of all sorts, including damages for an arrest or prosecution of the customer (as when the customer is charged with writing bad or hot checks), for loss of credit, and for other mental suffering.

3. Who Can Complain Of Wrongful Dishonor

A payor bank is liable to "its customer" for wrongful dishonor.

4. Which Funds Are Counted In Determining The Sufficiency Of The Account -- The Problem And Law Of *Funds Availability*

The most common reason for dishonoring a check is insufficient funds in the drawer's account. Dishonor for this reason is wrongful, however, if the payor bank errs in deciding that the account is insufficient to cover the check. Whether or not an account is sufficient depends partly on how soon the bank must account for funds that the customer deposits in the account. This timing issue concerns the law of *funds availability*, which determines when the customer has the right to withdraw or apply credit to her account that results from deposits of cash, checks or other items. This law is mainly federal. If a check is dishonored because funds are not counted that should have been available to the customer, the dishonor is wrongful under any applicable federal law that is violated and is also wrongful under state law 4-402. The federal law is the Expedited Funds Availability Act and Regulation CC which implements the Act.

5. Other Problems In Determining If Dishonor Is Rightful Or Wrongful

Special rules govern the narrow problems of
- Unaccounted new credits,
- Priority between checks, and
- When legal events against the account trump checks drawn on the account.

B. OVERDRAFT LIABILITY
1.   Overdrafts Chargeable To The Drawer's Account
An *overdraft* is a check drawn on an account that contains insufficient funds to cover the item. Ordinarily, of course, the payor bank can and will dishonor an overdraft, but the bank can pay the overdraft and charge the amount to the customer's account even in the absence of an agreement with the customer authorizing the payment of overdrafts.

2.   Overdraft Liability Of Joint Account Holders
If there is more than one customer who can draw on an account, the non-signing customer is not liable for an overdraft unless that person benefits from the proceeds of the item.

3.   Contrary Agreements Regarding Overdrafts
a.   Bank Agreeing To Pay Overdrafts
A bank is obligated to pay an overdraft if it has made an enforceable agreement to do so.

b.   Joint Account Customer Assuming Liability For Another Customer's Overdrafts
A customer on an account who neither signed an overdraft nor benefited from it is nevertheless liable for the overdraft, despite 4-401(b), if she agreed (before or after) to pay overdrafts drawn by another customer on the account, ratified the overdraft, or is estopped to deny liability for it.

C. STOPPING PAYMENT
Stopping payment refers to the drawer of a check or other authorized person ordering the payor bank, usually after the check has already been issued, to dishonor the item upon presentment for payment even though the item is otherwise properly payable. The intent of an order to close an account is the same with respect to outstanding items.

1.   The Right To Stop Payment (Or Close An Account)
"A customer or any person authorized to draw on the account if there is more than one person may stop payment of any item drawn on the customer's account or close the account by an order to the bank describing the item or account with reasonably certainty * * *." 4-403(a).

2.   Payor Bank's Liability For Payment Over A Valid Stop-Payment Order
A valid stop order renders the affected check not properly payable. Therefore, a "payment in violation of an *effective* direction to stop payment is an improper payment, even though it is made by mistake or inadvertence." 4-403 comment 7

(emphasis added). On the other hand, "[t]he burden of establishing the fact and amount of loss resulting from the payment of an item contrary to a[n] [effective] stop-payment order or order to close an account is on the customer." 4-403(c).

3. Requisites Of An Effective Stop-Payment Order

Payment in violation of a stop order is improper only if the stop order was effective with respect to the item. To be effective a stop order "must be received at a *time* and in a *manner* that affords the bank a reasonable opportunity to act on it before any action by the bank with respect to the item described in Section 4-303." 4-403(a).

4. Stopping Payment Against A Holder In Due Course

Technically speaking, payment can be stopped against a holder in due course. On the other hand, "the drawer remains liable on the instrument * * * and the drawee, if it pays, becomes subrogated to the rights of the holder in due course against the drawer." 4-403 comment 7. The practical result is that the drawer cannot complain against the bank for violating the drawer's stop order if the drawer had no defense that was good against the holder in due course. At a minimum, the bank's recovery as subrogee is offset against its liability for wrongful dishonor.

5. Cashiers' Checks

In a very large number of recent cases the courts have considered if payment can be stopped on a cashier's check, which is a draft drawn by a bank on itself. 3-104(g). This broad concern involves two entirely separate issues. The easier issue is whether the bank that issues the cashier's check becomes liable to the person who procured it, i.e., the remitter, by refusing to dishonor the instrument upon the remitter's request. The answer is no. The second and harder issue is whether an issuing bank that refuses payment of its cashier's check, either on its own or at the request of the remitter, can escape liability to the payee or other holder of the instrument. The answer, usually, is no. When a bank refuses payment of a cashier's, certified, or teller's check on which it is liable and for which it has no good defense, the damages against the bank naturally include the amount of the item; but the damages are not limited to this amount. The damages also can include "compensation for expenses and loss of interest resulting from the nonpayment and may [include] * * * consequential damages if the obligated bank refuses to pay after receiving notice of particular circumstances giving rise to the damages." 3-411(b).

D. UNTIMELY CHECKS

1. Stale Checks

A *stale check* is an uncertified check of a customer which is presented more than six months after the check's date. Although not bound to pay a stale check, the payor bank has the right to do so *in good faith.*

2. Postdated Checks

A postdated check is a check issued before the stated date of the instrument. "A bank may charge against the account of a customer a check that is otherwise properly payable from the account, even though payment was made before the date of the check, unless the customer has given notice to the bank of the postdating describing the check with reasonable certainty." 4-401(c).

3. Mitigating Liability For Paying Untimely Checks

As in the case where a stop order is violated, a payor bank that wrongfully pays a stale or postdated check should not be liable if the drawer suffered no actual loss as a result of the wrongful payment. Moreover, 4-407 subrogates the bank to the rights of various parties to the instrument.

E. EFFECT OF A CUSTOMER'S INCOMPETENCE OR DEATH

A check drawn by a customer who was then incompetent, or who later dies or becomes incompetent, is properly payable so long as the bank is unaware of the death or an adjudication of incompetency. The check becomes not properly payable, however, a reasonable time after the bank knows of the death or adjudication. "Even with knowledge a bank may for 10 days after the date of death pay or certify checks drawn on or before that date unless ordered to stop payment by a person claiming an interest in the account." 4-405(b).

F. CHECK FRAUD

Check fraud mainly refers to wrongfully altering checks or making signatures on them that are unauthorized or otherwise ineffective. Who bears the loss in case of check fraud as between the payor bank and the customer whose account is charged with the tainted item? The usual answer is that the loss falls on the payor bank, unless the bank can establish a defense provided by Article 3 or 4 or extra-Code law.

1. Basis Of Payor Bank's Liability To Its Checking-Account Customer

In every instance of check fraud the fundamental basis of a payor bank's accountability to its customer, where the item has been charged to the customer's account, is the rule that only properly payable items can be charged against a customer's account. See 4-401(a). Checks that have been materially altered, or that carry an ineffective indorsement or drawer's signature, are not properly payable.

2. Payor Bank's Defenses

The U.C.C. and other law provide an array of defenses for a payor bank or another defendant in a check fraud case as against a customer or other person who complains of a loss. The most important of these defenses are:
  ◆ Authority

- ◆ Ratification
- ◆ Preclusion by estoppel
- ◆ Negligence (3-406)
- ◆ Breach of conditional duty to discover and report check fraud (4-406(c-d))
- ◆ One-year outside limit on customer's complaints about customer's unauthorized signature or alteration (4-406(f));
- ◆ Special rules for unauthorized indorsements in certain circumstances (3-404 & 3-405), namely when there is
  - √ An impostor;
  - √ A nominal or fictitious payee; or
  - √ Fraud by an employee with responsibility with respect to the check.

XI. SHIFTING CHECK FRAUD LOSSES

A. PAYOR BANK VERSUS PEOPLE UPSTREAM IN THE COLLECTION CHAIN -- PRIMARILY, PRESENTMENT WARRANTIES

A check that has been altered, or that carries an unauthorized signature of the drawer or an indorser, is not properly payable and cannot rightfully be charged to the account against which it was drawn. Thus, if the payor bank pays the check, the payment cannot be recouped from the account. So, as against its checking account customer, the bank must bear the check fraud loss. Usually, the only way the payor bank can shift the loss to someone else is by a claim for breach of warranty based on 4-208. It establishes implied warranties that benefit payor banks which pay or accept items:

> If an unaccepted draft is presented to the drawee for payment or acceptance and the drawee pays or accepts the draft, (i) the person obtaining payment or acceptance, at the time of presentment, and (ii) a previous transferor of the draft, at the time of transfer, warrant to the drawee that pays or accepts the draft in good faith that:
>> (1) the warrantor is, or was, at the time the warrantor transferred the draft, a person entitled to enforce the draft or authorized to obtain payment or acceptance of the draft on behalf of a person entitled to enforce the draft;
>> (2) the draft has not been altered; and
>> (3) the warrantor has no knowledge that the signature of the purported drawer of the draft is unauthorized.

4-208(a). As is apparent, these presentment warranties do not cover every kind of check fraud. Thus, the payor bank cannot unload every kind of check fraud loss.

A person who is liable to a payor bank for breaching a 4-208 presentment warranty can often pass the loss to someone else further upstream in the collection process on the basis of the transfer warranties implied by 4-207, which provides:

> A customer or collecting bank that transfers an item and receives a settlement or other consideration warrants to the transferee and to any subsequent collecting bank that:
>   (1) the warrantor is a person entitled to enforce the item;
>   (2) all signatures on the item are authentic and authorized;
>   (3) the item has not been altered;
>   (4) the item is not subject to a defense or claim in recoupment (Section 3-305(a)) of any party that can be asserted against the warrantor; and
>   (5) the warrantor has no knowledge of any insolvency proceeding commenced with respect to the maker or acceptor or, in the case of an unaccepted draft, the drawer.

4-207(a). In addition, each customer and collecting bank that transfers an item and receives a settlement or other consideration is obligated to pay the item if the item is dishonored. 4-207(b). As you can see, the 4-207 transfer warranties cover the same kinds of fraud and more that are covered by the presentment warranties of 4-208. So, in any case where a presentment warranty is breached, there is a corresponding transfer warranty. The transfer warranties thus ordinarily insure that any check fraud loss unloaded by a payor bank can be passed upstream to the very beginning of the collection chain, thereby protecting every collecting bank through which the check passed.

B. PAYEE VERSUS DEPOSITARY-COLLECTING BANK

The holder of a check is the owner of it and the only rightful recipient of its proceeds unless she, or someone acting by her authority, directs otherwise. Therefore, when a check is stolen from a payee, her indorsement forged and the proceeds of the instrument are misappropriated, the thief is guilty of converting the payee's property and is liable to the payee for common-law conversion; and so is every transferee involved in the misappropriation even though the transferee acted innocently and without knowledge of the payee's superior rights. As a result, the bank at which the thief cashes the stolen check, or deposits it, is liable for conversion to the payee. Article 3 recognizes and codifies this conversion liability by providing:

> An instrument is * * * converted if it is taken by transfer, other than a negotiation, from a person not entitled to enforce the instrument or a bank makes or obtains payment with respect to the instrument for a person not entitled to enforce the instrument or receive payment.

3-420(a). "This covers cases in which a depositary or payor bank takes an instrument bearing a forged indorsement." 3-420 comment 1. It is no defense for a depositary bank that it acted reasonably and in good faith in dealing with converted items.

C. OTHER DIRECT ACTION SUITS

1. Payee Versus Payor Bank

In the typical check fraud case involving a payee's unauthorized indorsement, there is no doubt that the payee can recover directly from the payor bank for conversion if the check is paid. Paying a check over a forged indorsement amounts to conversion. Because the payee is the owner of the check and is entitled to its proceeds, she is a proper party to complain of the wrong by the payor bank.

2. Drawer Versus Depositary-Collecting Bank

The traditional view is that in the typical unauthorized indorsement case, the drawer of the check cannot directly recover from the depositary-collecting bank for conversion, money had and received, or otherwise. Article 3 expressly adopts this view, at least with respect to conversion. It provides that "[a]n action for conversion of an instrument may not be brought by * * * the issuer or acceptor of the instrument * * *." 3-420(a).

PART THREE --
ORDINARY DRAFTS USED WITH OTHER COMMERCIAL PAPER

XII. ORDINARY DRAFTS AND DOCUMENTS OF TITLE IN SALES FINANCING

A. DOCUMENTS OF TITLE

Negotiable instruments embody rights to the payment of money. Documents of title represent title to goods. The principal source of state law on documents of title is U.C.C. Article 7, which is the basis of what is said here about documents. Under Article 7, a *document of title* (or its short-form synonym, *document,* 7-102(1)(e)) is a writing "which in the regular course of business or financing is treated as adequately evidencing that the person in possession of it is entitled to receive, hold and dispose of the document and the goods it covers." 1-201(15). The most common examples are the bill of lading and the warehouse receipt. How a document serves these functions, and its effectiveness in doing so, are largely determined by whether the document is negotiable or non-negotiable.

1. Distinguishing Negotiable Documents

a. The Test for Negotiability

Except in overseas trade, the test of negotiability is whether "by its [the document's] terms the goods are to be delivered to bearer or to the order of a named person." 7-104(1). That's it! "Any other document is non-negotiable." 7-104(2).

b. Article 7's Coverage of Non-Negotiable Documents

Article 7 generally applies to both negotiable and non-negotiable documents. Making the distinction is important only in applying particular rules within Article 7, not in deciding whether the statute, as a whole, is the general source of governing law.

2. How Documents Control Access To The Goods

The bailee of goods who has issued a document of title, whether a bill of lading or a warehouse receipt, is generally obligated to "deliver the goods to a *person entitled under the document* * * *." 7-403(1) (emphasis added). The meaning of "person entitled under the document," which is the key to deciding who is entitled to the goods, depends on whether the document is negotiable or not.

a. When the Document Is Non-Negotiable

The person entitled to the goods under a non-negotiable document is "the person to whom delivery is to be made by the terms of or pursuant to written instructions * * *." 7-403(4). Such written instructions, directed to a bailee who has issued either a warehouse receipt or a bill of lading, are referred to as a *delivery order,* 7-102(1)(d), which is itself a document of title. 1-201(15).

b. When the Document Is Negotiable

The person to whom the bailee is obligated to deliver goods covered by a negotiable document is the *holder* of the document. 7-403(1) & (4). The term "holder" has the same basic meaning here that it has for purposes of Article 3, except that documents are held instead of instruments: "'Holder' with respect to a document of title means the person in possession [of the document of title] if the goods are deliverable to bearer or to the order of the person in possession." 1-201(20).

c. Bailee's Accountability for Non- or Misdelivery

A bailee is obligated to surrender goods to a person entitled to their delivery under a document covering the goods. A bailee who refuses to deliver the goods to such a person or is unable to do so because the goods have been lost or destroyed (nondelivery), or who cannot deliver them because she has given the goods to someone else (misdelivery), is liable, usually for conversion, to the person entitled to delivery.

d. Excuses for Non- or Misdelivery
Article 7 provides a list of seven excuses for nondelivery and misdelivery. See 7-403(1)-(3). Only the most important excuses are discussed here.

1) Major Excuses for Nondelivery
- Damage to or delay, loss or destruction of the goods for which the bailee is not liable, 7-403(1)(b);
- Bailee's lien is unsatisfied, 7-403(2);
- Negotiable document covering the goods has not been surrendered. 7-403(3).

2) Major Excuse for Misdelivery: Claimant With a Better Right
A bailee is not liable for having delivered the goods to someone other than the person entitled under the document if the bailee made "delivery of the goods to a person whose receipt was rightful as against the claimant." 7-403(1)(a). According to the commentary, the principal case covered by this excuse "is delivery to a person whose title is paramount to the rights represented by the document." 7-403 comment 2.

3. How (And The Extent To Which) Documents Control Title To The Goods

a. The Security of Documented Title (Protection Against Subsequent Claims)
Even though a document represents title to the covered goods, a person who buys the goods and is a transferee of the document risks having her rights therein defeated in certain cases by subsequent claimants of the property.

1) Resale by Transferor
In the case of a sale of goods covered by a non-negotiable document, title to the goods, i.e., the seller's rights, passes to the buyer when she gets the document. 7-504(1). Yet, her title can be defeated by certain creditors of, and buyers from, her transferor until such time as the bailee receives notification of the sale to the buyer. See 7-504(2)(a) & (b), which applies only in the case of a non-negotiable document. Most threatening to the buyer is the rule of 7-504(2)(b) that if the seller resells the goods in the ordinary course of business to a third person, this person will defeat the original buyer's rights if the bailee has delivered the goods to the third person, or received notice of the third person's rights, before learning of the original buyer's claim to the goods. 7-504(2)(b). Cf. 2-403(2).

2) Sale By Bailee

A buyer's title to goods covered by a document might be threatened by the bailee's sale of the property. As a general rule, however, a transferee of the bailee cannot defeat the buyer's title whether the title is represented by a negotiable or non-negotiable document. The transferee acquires only the rights of her transferor, 2-403(1), and in this case the transferor, i.e., the bailee, had nothing but a limited right of possession. There is an important exception, however: "A buyer in the ordinary course of business of fungible goods sold and delivered by a warehouseman who is also in the business of buying and selling such goods takes free of any claim under a warehouse receipt even though it has been duly negotiated." 7-205. Cf. 2-403(1) & 9-307(1).

b. The Credibility of Documented Title (Protection Against Prior Claims)

1) Post-Documentation Claims

Generally, a transferee of a document, whether negotiable or non-negotiable, takes the goods subject to legal and equitable claims against the goods existing at the time of the transfer to her. There is, however, a most important exception to this general rule: Just as a holder in due course of an instrument takes free of all claims to the instrument, "a holder to whom a negotiable document of title has been duly negotiated acquires thereby * * * title to the document [and] title to the goods," 7-502(1)(a) & (b), which essentially means that a holder of a document by due negotiation takes free of all claims to the document and the goods. There are three keys to this freedom under Article 7. The transferee must be a *holder,* and she must be holding a *negotiable document.* The third key is *due negotiation,* which requires the holder to purchase the document:

- in good faith,
- without notice of any defense against or claim to it on the part of any person,
- for value other than receiving the document in settlement or payment of a money obligation, and
- in the regular course of business or finance.

7-501(4).

2) Pre-Documentation Claims

Even a holder of a negotiable document who acquires it through due negotiation is generally not protected from claims to the goods that existed before the document was issued, except when the true owner:

- delivered or entrusted them or any document of title covering them to the bailor or his nominee with actual or apparent authority to ship, store or sell or with power to obtain delivery under this Article (7-403) or with power of disposition under this Act (2-403 & 9-307) or other statute or rule of law; or, ·

* acquiesced in the procurement by the bailor or his nominee of any document of title.

7-503(a) & (b).

B. PAYMENT AGAINST DOCUMENTS

This payment scheme permits a simultaneous exchange of goods for cash or other payment, even when the buyer and seller are located far apart, by addressing payment to documents covering the goods rather than to the goods themselves.

1. How The Payment Scheme Works

Upon shipping the goods to the buyer, the seller has the carrier issue a negotiable bill of lading to the seller's order. The seller will attach the bill of lading to an Article 3 draft, in the amount of the price of the goods, drawn against the buyer. The seller is both the drawer and payee of the draft, which is payable at sight or on demand. The draft with the accompanying bill of lading is referred to as a *documentary draft*. The seller will ask her bank to send the draft through banking channels for the purpose of collecting it from the buyer.

The seller will indorse both the draft and document that comprise her documentary draft and transfer them to her bank. The seller's bank, which in Article 4 terms is the depositary-collecting bank, must present or send the draft and accompanying documents for presentment. 4-501. The bank, however, does not send the documentary draft to the buyer. Rather, it is sent, through banking channels, to a bank, i.e., the *presenting bank,* where the buyer is located for the purpose of having the latter bank present the item to the buyer for payment.

The presenting bank is obligated to present the documentary draft to the buyer-drawee for payment. Upon receiving payment, the presenting bank is obligated to deliver the documents to the drawee. 4-503(1). Here is the exact point at which the simultaneous exchange of goods for cash takes place. The buyer tenders actual payment, which is cash or a cash equivalent in the form of a bank obligation and not just the buyer's own commitment. This payment is sent back down the collection chain to the seller's bank which will credit it to the seller's account. In return, the buyer gets the bill of lading covering the goods. Remember that the bill was indorsed in blank by the seller to whose order the bill was issued. Thus, the buyer, by taking possession of the bill, becomes the holder of the document, and thus the holder of the key to the goods, because the carrier-bailee's obligation to deliver the goods now runs to the buyer qua holder of the negotiable bill of lading. 7-403(1) & (4).

2. Buyer's Protections

a. Exclusive Access to the Goods

By taking possession of the negotiable bill of lading which the seller has indorsed in blank, the buyer becomes the holder of the document, 1-201(20) & 7-501(1), and is the only person to whom the carrier can rightfully deliver the goods. 7-403(1) & (4).

b. Title to the Goods

Transfer of the document to the buyer will pass the seller's title, that is, the buyer will thereby acquire the title and rights the seller had or had actual authority to convey. 7-504(1).

c. Rights Acquired Through Due Negotiation

In the typical case, the buyer will be a holder of the document through "due negotiation." 7-501(4). As a result, she will take title to the document and also title to the goods free of claims to them that arose after the document was issued. 7-502.

d. Warranties

1) Upon Issuance of the Document

The issuer of the document warrants that the issuer has the goods described in the document and that the goods are as described there. 7-203 & 7-301(1).

2) Upon Negotiation of the Document

In negotiating the bill of lading to the buyer, the seller warrants, in addition to any warranty made in selling the goods, that

* the document is genuine; and
* he has no knowledge of any fact which would impair its validity or worth; and
* his negotiation or transfer is rightful and fully effective with respect to the title to the document and the goods it represents.

7-507.

3) Upon Sale of the Goods

The seller also makes warranties with respect to the goods themselves. 2-313 (express warranties), 2-314 (merchantability) & 2-315 (fitness for a particular purpose).

e. Contract Remedies

In the event the goods, or the seller's performance, fail to conform to the sales contract, the buyer may pursue against the seller the remedies that Article 2 provides for breach of contract, including breach of warranty. See 2-711 & 2-714.

3. Seller's Protections Upon Breakdowns In The Scheme
a. Buyer Dishonors
The buyer's dishonor of the documentary draft is a breach of contract which trigger's the seller's Article 2 remedies. See 2-703. In most instances the seller will react by reselling the goods and suing the buyer for the difference between the contract price and the resale price. See 2-706.

b. Bailee Misdelivers Goods
The carrier, which issued the document covering the goods, is obligated to deliver only to a person entitled under the document, which is the seller in the case of a negotiable document still in possession of the seller or her agent. If the carrier violates this obligation, as by delivering the goods to the buyer before the buyer gets the document, the carrier is liable to the seller for misdelivery.

c. Presenting Bank Misdelivers Documents
If the presenting bank surrenders the document without getting payment of the draft, the bank is liable to the seller for breaching a duty of ordinary care which the bank, as a collecting bank, owes to the seller as the owner of the documentary draft. See 4-202 & 4-103(e).

d. Depositary Bank Is Negligent
The seller's bank, which is the depositary bank, owes the seller a duty of ordinary care in handling the documentary draft for collection. If the bank violates this duty, as by delaying in sending the draft for collection or by acting unreasonably in giving the seller notice of dishonor or in forwarding instructions to the presenting bank, the depositary bank is liable for damages.

4. Variations In The Scheme
a. Discounting Documentary Drafts
Typically, when a depositary bank takes a documentary draft for collection, the amount of the draft is not credited against the seller-customer's account until the draft is actually paid by the buyer-drawee and payment is remitted through banking channels to the depositary bank. The seller, however, may convince her bank to purchase the draft from her rather than simply take it for collection. This arrangement is referred to as *discounting the draft.*

b. Shipping Under a Non-Negotiable Document
Payment against documents can be structured so that the goods are shipped under a non-negotiable bill of lading instead of, as is usual, a negotiable document. When a non-negotiable bill is used, the seller retains control of the

goods by consigning them to herself or her agent so that the carrier is obligated to deliver the goods according to the seller's instructions. 7-403(1) & (4). The seller or her agent will instruct the carrier to surrender the goods to the buyer upon the buyer's payment of the draft. This variation involves more risks to the buyer.

C. CREDIT AGAINST DOCUMENTS: TRADE ACCEPTANCES
1. Description Of The Scheme
Payment against documents requires the buyer to pay the documentary draft upon presentment to her. The seller may agree, however, that the buyer can acquire the documents accompanying the draft by accepting the instrument upon presentment instead of paying it. Acceptance is the drawee's signed engagement to honor the draft as presented, and is accomplished by the drawee signing the draft. 3-409(a). The buyer qua acceptor engages that he will "pay the draft according to its terms at the time it was accepted." 3-413(a). A draft accepted by a buyer in a sale of goods arrangement such as that described here is referred to as a *trade acceptance*.

2. Advantages To Seller Compared To Sale On Account
A trade acceptance captures the buyer's promise to pay in a negotiable form, which is easier to enforce (even for the seller-payee) than a mere contractual promise, see 3-308, and for which there may be a wider market should the seller-payee decide to discount her rights against the buyer.

3. Advantage To Buyer Compared To Signing Instrument Up Front
From the buyer's perspective, credit against documents is preferable to signing a note at the time the sales contract is made because, in accepting a documentary draft, her engagement on an instrument is concurrent with acquiring control of the goods.

D. BANKER'S ACCEPTANCES
Another means for financing the buyer's purchase of goods is the *bankers' acceptance*. By this means the buyer usually can get funds more easily and more cheaply because the buyer's draft is accepted by a bank and thereby is backed by the credit of the acceptor-bank as well as the buyer's own credit.

XIII. LETTERS OF CREDIT

An Article 5 *letter of credit* is "an engagement by a bank or other person made at the request of a customer * * * that the issuer will honor drafts or other demands for payment upon compliance with the conditions specified in the credit." 5-103(1)(a).

A. DEFINING BASIC TERMS AND RELATIONSHIPS

1. Commercial Credits

a. The Main Players

The traditional use of a letter of credit is to facilitate sales of goods (especially in international transactions) by insuring payment of the price to the beneficiary of the credit, i.e., the seller, upon her performance. A letter of credit so used is referred to as a *commercial credit.* In the commercial letter of credit, the *issuer,* 5-103(1)(c), usually a commercial bank, issues the *credit,* which is shorthand for *letter of credit,* 5-103(1)(a), in favor of the seller of goods. The issuer does so in response to a request or application of the buyer, i.e., the *customer.* 5-103(1)(g). The seller is known as the *beneficiary* of the credit. 5-103(1)(d).

The *credit* is a writing in which the issuer engages that it pay or accept drafts or other demands for payment that comply with the terms of the credit. See 5-102(1); 5-103(1)(a) & 5-104. Typically, the terms require the seller to present documents, which usually consist of the seller's invoice; a shipping document (e.g., bill of lading, airway bill); an insurance certificate; various additional certificates (e.g., of inspection or origin); and consular documents, if necessary. The terms of credit also typically require presenting the documents together with a draft, or other form of a demand, ordering the issuer to pay or accept.

b. The Relationship Between Issuer and Beneficiary: Duty to Honor

Once a credit is established, the issuer is burdened with a statutory *duty to honor* owed directly to the beneficiary. This duty is stated in 5-114(1), which is the heart and soul of Article 5 and the statute's most important provision: "An issuer must honor a draft or demand for payment which complies with the terms of the relevant credit *regardless* of whether the goods or documents conform to the underlying contract for sale or other contract between the customer and the beneficiary." (Emphasis added.) An issuer that violates the duty to honor is guilty of *wrongful dishonor* and is liable to the beneficiary.

c. The Relationship Between Issuer and Customer: The Right of Reimbursement

Upon duly honoring a draft or demand for payment under a credit, the issuer acquires a *right of reimbursement* against the customer. 5-114(3). This right entitles the issuer to recoup "any payment made under the credit and to be put in effectively available funds not later than the day before maturity of any acceptance made under the credit." Id.

2. Standby Credits

The main players, and the basic rights and duties of the issuer, are the same in both commercial and standby letters of credits. Yet, a standby credit differs fundamentally from a commercial credit. While the traditional commercial credit insures payment to the beneficiary upon the shipment of goods or other performance by her in the customer's favor, the standby credit protects the beneficiary in the event of the customer's default.

B. DETERMINING COMPLIANCE WITH THE CREDIT

An issuer's fundamental and principal duty under Article 5 is to "honor a draft or demand for payment which *complies* with the terms of the relevant credit," 5-114(1) (emphasis added), whether the credit is commercial or standby.

1. What Determines Compliance

The most important point to remember about credit law is that the issuer deals only in the documents (and other papers), not in actual performance of the underlying transaction between customer and beneficiary. This means that the issuer's duty to honor depends exclusively on whether the beneficiary has presented the kinds of documents and other papers called for in the credit, not on whether the beneficiary has otherwise satisfied the underlying contract with the customer. In deciding if the papers satisfy the credit, the issuer is obligated only "to examine documents with care so as to ascertain that *on their face* they appear to comply with the terms of the credit * * *." 5-109(2) (emphasis added).

2. Degree Of Compliance

a. General Rule Applicable in Deciding Whether There Has Been Wrongful Dishonor

The courts generally follow the rule that a beneficiary is not entitled to honor of a credit unless the documents she presents comply literally, precisely and strictly with the terms of the credit.

b. Caveats to the General Rule

1) Distinguish the Issue of Interpretation

In interpreting the language of a credit for the purpose of deciding the meaning of the terms with which a beneficiary must strictly comply, the courts almost always resolve ambiguities and doubts against the issuer and in favor of the beneficiary.

2) Different Standard in Deciding the Issue of Reimbursement

On the issue whether the issuer has rightfully honored a credit so as to earn the right of reimbursement, the test is whether the documents presented by the beneficiary *substantially complied* with the terms of the credit.

3. Timing Of Compliance

A typical credit specifies an expiration date, also known as expiry date, upon which the issuer's duty to honor terminates. This date is part of the terms of the credit, and any draft or demand for payment that violates the date is not in compliance with the credit even though the documents are in perfect form and otherwise satisfy the terms of the credit.

4. Procedural Concerns

a. Presentment

Generally speaking, the mechanics of the beneficiary's presentment to an issuer are governed by Article 3, especially the many technical rules in Part 5 of Article 3.

b. Examination

1) General Obligation

"An issuer must examine documents with care so as to ascertain that on their face they appear to comply with the terms of the credit * * *." 5-109(2).

2) Time Allowed for Honor or Rejection

An issuer is allowed three banking days to determine whether to honor or reject a documentary draft or demand for payment that is presented under a credit. 5-112(1)(a). Failure to honor the draft within this time constitutes dishonor of it and the credit. 5-112(1).

c. Dishonor

1) Returning the Documentary Draft

Ordinarily, a payor bank that dishonors a documentary draft must physically return the instrument to accomplish dishonor. See 4-302(a)(2).

2) Providing Reasons For Dishonor

The courts generally require an issuer to state the reasons for the dishonor or rejection of a draft or demand for payment.

C. RIGHTFUL DISHONOR DESPITE FACIAL COMPLIANCE

1. Overview

As a general rule, an issuer is guilty of wrongful dishonor, and is accordingly liable to the beneficiary, by refusing to pay a demand that facially complies with the credit. There are, however, a few exceptions where hidden or latent defects justify dishonor.

2. Hidden Defects That Justify Dishonor

- Breach of warranty with respect to documents or other papers necessary for proper presentment

- ◆ Document forged or fraudulent
- ◆ Fraud in the transaction

3. Issuer's Dilemma And Privilege Upon Notification Of Hidden Defects

"[In all] cases as against its customer, an issuer *acting in good faith* may honor the draft or demand for payment despite notification from the customer of the fraud, forgery or other defect not apparent on the face of the document [including fraud in the transaction] * * *." 5-114(2)(b) (emphasis added).

4. Enjoining Payment Because Of Hidden Defects

Even when an issuer has decided to ignore the customer's allegations of hidden defects, such as fraud in the transaction, "a court of appropriate jurisdiction may enjoin such honor." 5-114(2)(b).

5. Absolute Duty To Pay Certain Innocent Third Parties

In no event can an issuer dishonor a credit, or a court enjoin such honor, even if there is in fact a hidden defect such as forgery or fraud in the transaction,

> if the honor is demanded by a negotiating bank or other holder of the draft or demand which has taken the draft or demand under the credit and under such circumstances which would make it a holder in due course and in an appropriate case would make it a person to whom a document of title has been duly negotiated or a bona fide purchaser of a certificated security.

5-114(2)(a).

D. ALIENABILITY OF CREDITS

1. Transferring The Right To Draw

The beneficiary cannot transfer her right to draw under a credit, i.e., she cannot delegate performance of the conditions under the credit, unless "the credit is expressly designated as transferable or assignable." 5-116(1).

2. Negotiating Drafts

The issuer is not obligated to honor the beneficiary's drafts negotiated or assigned to third parties unless the credit itself includes a commitment to such persons. A credit that contains no commitment of this type is known as a *straight credit*. Where the commitment is provided for, the credit is known as a *negotiation credit*.

3. Assigning Right To Proceeds

Even though a credit is straight and nontransferable, the beneficiary may assign her right to proceeds of the credit, and she may do so even before performance of the conditions of the credit. 5-116(2). In assigning proceeds, the beneficiary is transferring her Article 5 right to the money that the issuer is obligated to pay upon compliance with the terms of the letter of credit. This right to assign proceeds is not conditioned on the credit allowing such an assignment. Indeed, the right is not abridged by a provision in the credit purporting to prohibit assignment of proceeds. See 5-116 comment 3 & 9-318(4).

   a. **How Is the Assignment Effected?**
       "[T]he assignment is ineffective until the letter of credit * * * is delivered to the assignee * * *." 5-116(2)(a).

   b. **What Is Necessary to Make the Issuer Accountable to the Assignee?**
       In order to bind the issuer so that the issuer must respect the assignment, the issuer must receive "a notification of the assignment signed by the beneficiary which reasonably identifies the credit involved in the assignment and contains a request to pay the assignee." 5-116(2)(b). Until the issuer receives such a notification, the issuer may honor drafts or demands for payment drawn under the credit without any accountability to the assignee, id., notwithstanding that the assignment was fully effective between the assignee and beneficiary.

   c. **How Does the Assignee Protect Her Right to Proceeds Against Subsequent Transferees**
       An assignee protects her right to the proceeds of a credit against subsequent transferees and other claimants by perfecting her interest, which is accomplished by delivery of the credit to the assignee.

4. **Back-To-Back Credits**
    Back-to-back credits describes a financing and security arrangement in which a bank issues a letter of credit on the strength of an assignment of the right to proceeds of a separate credit.

E. INVOLVEMENT OF OTHER BANKS
1. Advising Bank
An *advising bank* is "a bank which gives notification of the issuance of a credit by another bank." 5-103(1)(e). An advising bank is only a messenger, and assumes no obligation to honor drafts drawn or demands for payment made under the credit, 5-107(1), not even when the advising bank has issued a written advice of credit. Its principal duty is simply to transmit accurately information about the credit that has been issued. See 5-107(1).

2. Confirming Bank
A *confirming bank* is "a bank which engages either that it will itself honor a credit already issued by another bank or that such a credit will be honored by the issuer or a third bank." 5-103(1)(f). Unlike a bank that only advises a credit, a confirming bank

is itself "directly obligated on the credit to the extent of its confirmation as though it were its issuer." 5-107(2). Therefore, to the extent of the confirmation, Article 5 saddles a confirming bank with the same fundamental duty of the issuer under 5-114(1): to honor a draft or demand for payment which complies with the terms of the relevant credit. In so honoring, the confirming bank acquires a right of reimbursement from the issuer which procured the confirmation.

3. Negotiating Bank

A *negotiating bank* is a bank that purchases drafts drawn by the beneficiary of a negotiation credit.

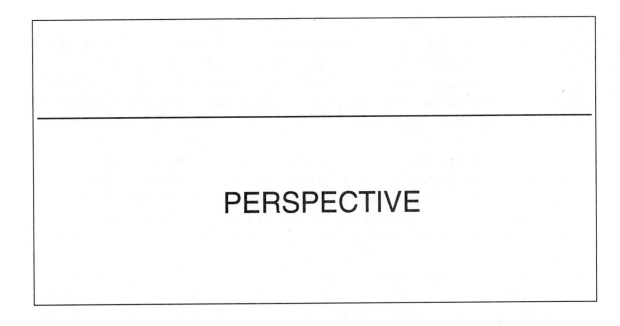

PERSPECTIVE

Defined most broadly, commercial paper refers to any writing embodying rights that are customarily conveyed by transferring the writing. A large subset of commercial paper consists of such writings that are negotiable, which means that the law enables a transferee to acquire the embodied rights free of claims and defenses good against the transferor. A wide variety of rights can be embodied in negotiable writings, including money, rights to the payment of money, and rights to other property. The most common examples of the last group are documents of title (such as bills of lading and warehouse receipts) and certificated securities (such as stocks and bonds). The most common and important examples of the second group -- rights to money -- are notes and drafts (which include checks). They are promises or orders to pay money that are principally governed by the Uniform Commercial Code (U.C.C.) Article 3 and are referred to, collectively, as *negotiable instruments* (or simply as *instruments*). They are the primary subject of this book, and the largest part of the outline -- **Part One** -- is wholly devoted to explaining them in terms of Article 3.

Described most simply, *an Article 3 instrument is a contract* that, because of its form, is governed by the special rules of liability codified in the U.C.C., principally Article 3. *An instrument is also a form of property*, the transfer of which is likewise governed by special rules of the U.C.C.

Contract implies an enforceable promissory obligation, that is, a promise for the breach of which the law gives a remedy. Every Article 3 instrument embodies either an explicit or implicit promise to pay money according to the terms expressed in the instrument itself and the terms implied by statute. Anyone who signs an instrument thereby makes this promise, and the promise is enforceable solely by force of, and to the extent provided by, Article 3. A common-law basis of validation, such as consideration or reliance, is unnecessary to prima facie liability. In sum, anybody who signs an Article 3 instrument thereby makes, and becomes liable on, a contract to pay the instrument simply because the writing that was signed is in the form of an Article 3 instrument.

The term *contract liability* is commonly used in referring to the liability that Article 3 imposes on a person for having signed an Article 3 instrument. The nature of this liability varies depending on the kind of instrument a person signs and the capacity in which she signs it. Article 3 explains this liability and codifies a host of rules that describe, limit, condition, extinguish and otherwise regulate it.

The promise or contract made by a person who signs an instrument is *reified* or embodied in the instrument itself. Buried there too, of course, along with the promisor's obligation to pay money, is a corresponding right of someone to receive the money. This right usually belongs, originally, to a promisee named in the instrument -- the payee. The right is valuable property which is freely assignable. The payee or other person entitled to enforce the right to payment can assign it and so can her immediate assignee and any subsequent assignee.

An assignment of a right to the payment on money locked in an instrument is ordinarily accomplished by *transferring* the instrument itself. Usually, the transferor will sign the instrument and in doing so will incur contract liability on the instrument. Yet, through the transfer process itself, the transferor, whether this person is the original promisee or an assignee, makes certain warranties with respect to the right to payment and the instrument itself. Article 3 implies these warranties just as Article 2 implies warranties in the sale of goods. This warranty liability is in addition to the contract liability on an instrument that a person incurs by signing it. Warranty liability, however, is not dependent on the transferor having signed the instrument, although the scope of her warranties is affected somewhat by whether or not she signed.

According to the general principle of derivative title, which usually governs the transfer of any kind of property, a transferee acquires only her transferor's rights. Under this principle any assignee of an instrument would step into the shoes of the assignor, that is, the assignee could not enforce the right to any greater extent than the assignor. Therefore, any third-party claims to the right to the payment of money locked in the instrument, and any defenses of the promisor to payment, that could be asserted against the assignor can also be asserted against the assignee.

The central doctrine of Article 3, the *holder-in-due-course doctrine*, is an exception to the general principle of derivative title. The doctrine applies to rights embodied in Article 3 instruments and provides that certain transferees of instruments acquire the reified rights free of all claims and most defenses that could have been asserted against the assignor. As a result, Article 3 instruments can be less risky and thus more desirable forms of rights to the payment of money than ordinary contract rights. The transferees who benefit from the holder-in-due-course doctrine are, in general terms, good faith purchasers for value who take the instruments through a special form of transfer called *negotiation.* By taking instruments in this manner, the transferees are *holders,* and they are said to take *in due course* by giving value in good faith and innocently, that is, without notice of claims or defenses to the instruments.

All of these and the many other special rules of Article 3 apply only to *instruments.* Therefore, following a brief introduction, Part One jumps immediately to the form of Article 3 instruments -- the requirements that a writing must satisfy to qualify as an instrument. These requirements are referred to as the *requisites of negotiability.* The next step is to consider contract liability on instruments and thereafter to examine their property aspects, which are collected in two chapters dealing separately with the transfer of instruments and the holder-in-due-course doctrine.

Part Two focuses on checks, considering an assortment of special concerns that are peculiar to them and the check collection process. A check is a kind of Article 3 negotiable instrument. The person who writes (i.e., issues) a check, known as the *drawer,* thereby orders a bank, known as the *drawee* or *payor,* to pay money to the *payee* of the check. Ordinarily, the drawer has an account at the drawee-payor bank, and this account is the intended source of funds to pay the check. Check collection is the process whereby the payee (or a person claiming through her) gets payment of the check from the drawee-payor bank where the drawer maintains the account against which the check is drawn. The payee may deal with this bank directly, or she may have her own bank act for her. The payee's bank may deal directly with the drawee-payor bank, or an intermediary such as a Federal Reserve bank may act for the payee's bank. In this capacity the Federal Reserve System plays a very important role in the check collection process.

The check collection process is largely governed by Article 4, although federal law sometimes controls because of the involvement of the Federal Reserve. To a great extent, however, federal law on check collection is consistent with Article 4 and supplements more than it displaces Article 4. The main concerns of state and federal check collection law are encouraging the speedy payment of instruments and allocating risks of loss due to fraud that attend the movement of money credits in and out of deposit accounts and through the check collection system.

The focus on checks begins with a chapter describing the check collection process and relating the rules of Article 4 to the principles of Article 3. Thereafter follow chapters focusing on the rights and duties that exist between a drawee-payor bank and its customers, and on the distribution of check fraud losses among participants in the check collection process.

Part Three consists of two chapters on documents of title and letters of credits. Documents and credits are commercial paper but are not Article 3 negotiable instruments and are governed principally by Articles 7 and 5, respectively. This book covers documents and credits principally because they often are used in conjunction with Article 3 instruments (primarily, ordinary drafts) and also because, for whatever reasons, they are commonly covered in commercial paper courses.

Some commercial paper courses go beyond the edge of traditional commercial paper law and include materials on credit cards and electronic fund transfers (EFT). These most modern payment devices usually operate without negotiable paper and can be entirely paperless. They are linked to traditional commercial paper, especially negotiable instruments, because of similarity in use, problems, and analysis. Eventually, these modern devices will in every sense overtake cash and checks as means of paying for property and services. Already, in terms of dollar amounts, more money credits are passed electronically each business day through wholesale wire transfers than by any other means.

Nevertheless, despite the growing importance of modern payment systems, most ordinary business transactions still use ordinary negotiable instruments -- drafts, checks, and promissory notes. The common, widespread importance of Article 3 instruments explains why they remain the principal topic of the typical commercial paper course and the main subject of this book. Expanded coverage of instruments leaves no room for credit cards and EFT.

PART ONE

ARTICLE 3 NEGOTIABLE INSTRUMENTS

Chapters

I

INTRODUCTION TO INSTRUMENTS AND NEGOTIABILITY

Analysis

A. HISTORY AND SOURCES OF LAW

1. Early Law Of Commercial Paper

"By the close of the 1700's * * * the basic principles of the law of negotiable instruments had been laid down in the decisions of the English courts." W. Britton, BILLS AND NOTES 9 (2d ed. 1961). From then until codification of the law of commercial paper in the late 19th Century, the courts amplified and applied these principles in response to the demands of a growing and complex economy.

a. Drafts

Before 1702, the common-law development favored the *draft* or *"bill of exchange"* over the promissory note. Domestic and foreign merchants in England used the "bill" as early as 1300 to exchange foreign currency, transfer domestic funds and finance the sale of goods. The mercantile courts prior to 1600 and the common-law courts thereafter developed various principles of liability and remedy and the concept that a bill was freely transferable. By the end of the 17th Century, the courts applied these principles to all parties on a bill of exchange, whether merchants or not. By the end of the 18th Century, the common law, aided by Lord Mansfield, had begun to explore the rights of good-faith purchasers and the relationship between the bill and the underlying obligation.

b. Notes

It was another story for *promissory notes*. Notes, then called *"bills obligatory,"* were used before 1600, but the law then did not accept their free transferability. English courts, along with continental and Roman law, did not recognize the concept that the owner of an intangible promise could transfer it to a third person without the delivery of some tangible token. Delivery of a simple writing was not enough. Fictions were developed to circumvent this limitation, but it was not until the Statute of Anne in 1702 that the law made notes "assignable or indorseable over" in the same manner as bills of exchange. Once the law recognized the concept of free transferability for the note, the courts developed its key function as a facilitator of credit transactions.

2. Uniform Negotiable Instruments Law

In 1896, the National Conference of Commissioners on Uniform State Laws (NCCUSL) promulgated the Uniform Negotiable Instruments Act, which is often referred to as the Negotiable Instruments Law or the N.I.L. Like the British Bills of Exchange Act (1882), after which it was in most respects modeled, the N.I.L. was largely declaratory of the common law. By 1924 all states had adopted it with only minor variations.

3. Uniform Commercial Code

Eventually, the N.I.L. failed. It could not accommodate changing commercial practices. Also, differences in interpretation among the courts tended to destroy the uniformity which it was intended to provide. Similar weaknesses appeared in other areas of commercial law. Some legal authorities believed that these difficulties should be overcome by piecemeal amendments of existing statutes; others thought that a comprehensive statute was needed to deal with the various areas of the law governing commerce. The efforts of the latter group during several decades resulted in the Uniform Commercial Code -- usually referred to as the U.C.C. or the Code.

The Code was primarily the joint work of the National Conference of Commissioners on Uniform State Laws (NCCUSL) and the American Law Institute (ALI). In preparing the Code, these organizations used the knowledge, experience, and talents of literally hundreds of judges, lawyers, professors, bankers, merchants, and other professionals from throughout the country. However, the first version of the Code, the 1952 Official Text, was adopted in only one state, Pennsylvania. The other states rejected it primarily because of New York's reaction. The legislature of New York, a key state in commercial matters, referred the Code to its Law Revision Commission. This Commission studied the Code for several years and reported in 1956 that "the Code is not yet ready for enactment." Legislative Document 1956 No. 65(A) 5. The Commission made a large number of detailed criticisms and suggestions for the Code which were reflected in 1957 Official Text. Many of these amendments affected the provisions on commercial paper. The 1957 provisions on commercial paper changed very little through subsequent revisions of the Official Text over the next 30 years.

In 1986, however, a drafting committee of the NCCUSL began to update the Code's law of commercial paper. The ultimate results were that a new Article 4A on funds (wire) transfers was added to the Code in 1989; and, **in 1990, the basic law of negotiable instruments, Article 3, was completely redrafted.** At the same time, **Article 4 on bank deposits and check collection was significantly changed** and conforming amendments were made elsewhere in the Code.

The Code is now the law in every state, as well as in the District of Columbia and certain territories of the United States; but the Code is not everywhere exactly the same. Changes in the Official Text are not universally adopted or not in their recommended forms, and every state's legislature adds its own local amendments. Also, each state's courts add peculiar interpretations to the local version of the Code. Nevertheless, the essentials are more or less the same in every jurisdiction and, in this sense, the Code and commercial law are uniform throughout the nation.

The Code deals not only with negotiable instruments and wire transfers in Articles 3, 4 and 4A, but also with sales of goods (Article 2), leases of goods (Article 2A), letters of credit (Article 5), bulk transfers (Article 6), documents of title (Article 7), investment securities (Article 8), and secured transactions (Article 9). Article 1 contains general provisions which apply throughout the whole Code, including definitions and rules and principles of construction and interpretation. Article 10 provides the effective date of the Code and also repeals the N.I.L. and a number of other state laws. Article 11 is a transition provision dealing with 1972 changes in Article 9.

Because this book focuses on negotiable instruments, it is based primarily on U.C.C. Article 3; but other parts of the Code get attention that relate to negotiable instruments and that govern related kinds of commercial paper, especially Articles 4, 5, and 7. **All references to the Code are to the 1990 Official Text except where otherwise indicated.** Any reference to the 1989 Official Text means the uniform version of the U.C.C. at the time of the 1990 changes.

a. The Scope Of U.C.C. Article 3 -- Negotiable Instruments
>   1) Direct Application
>   U.C.C. Article 3 "applies to negotiable instruments," 3-102(a), and nothing else. Generally and basically, a "*negotiable instrument*" (or its synonym, "*instrument*," 3-104(b)) is "a signed writing that orders or promises payment of money," 3-104 comment 1, and that satisfies the other requirements described by section 3-401(a). These requirements are known as the *requisites of negotiability*, which are the subject of Chapter 2 infra. Wherever Article 3 refers to an instrument, it means a writing that satisfies all of the 3-104 requisites of negotiability. Only such an instrument triggers the application of Article 3, and only a writing that satisfies the requisites of negotiability is an instrument.
>
>   Instruments, however, are not all alike. The requisites of negotiability permit differences. The principal difference is between drafts and notes, which are the two general categories of instruments. A *draft* is an instrument that is an order to pay money, and a *note* is an instrument that is a promise to pay. 3-104(e) & comment 4. They can be different and both qualify as instruments because order and promise are alternative requirements of negotiability. Either an order or a promise will do. This small difference in notes and drafts leads to very large differences in how the instruments are used, and leads Article 3 to treat them differently in some very important respects. Still, notes and drafts that are negotiable under 3-104 are equally instruments; and the principal source of law that governs them, while distinguishing between them, is equally U.C.C. Article 3.

2) Application by Analogy

An order or promise that is not within the scope of Article 3 because it fails the requirements of 3-104(a) may nevertheless be similar to a negotiable instrument in many respects and may deserve the same or similar treatment as a negotiable instrument. Directly applying Article 3 is not possible, but the same result can sometimes be reached because of other legal rules, from the terms of the parties' agreement, or by applying the principles of Article 3 by analogy. See 3-104 comment 2.

b. Exclusions from Article 3

Article 3 "does not apply," in any event, "to money, to payment orders governed by Article 4A , or to securities governed by Article 8." 3-102(a). This exclusion applies even to a writing that satisfies the requisites of negotiability and is otherwise an instrument within Article 3. For example, "[o]ccasionally a particular writing may fit the definition of both a negotiable instrument under Article 3 and of an investment security under Article 8. In such cases, the instrument is subject exclusively to the requirements of Article 8." 3-102 comment 2. In other words, Articles 3 and 8 are mutually exclusive, and so are Articles 3 and 4A which governs wholesale wire transfers.

c. Shared Jurisdiction

Other articles of the Code can share jurisdiction of instruments. An instrument may be collateral for a debt and be governed, in this role, by Article 9. The collection of a check through banking channels is governed in large part by Article 4. In both cases, Article 3 continues to apply. If there a conflict, Articles 4 and 9 govern over Article 3. 3-102(b).

4. Supplemental Role Of Federal Law

The Uniform Commercial Code is the principal source of commercial paper law, but federal statutes and regulations are an increasingly large supplement which naturally preempts the U.C.C. Federal law is growing fastest in the areas of bank deposits and check collection, which the Code covers in Article 4. Indeed, many of the 1990 changes in Article 4 were made to conform state law with new federal law, principally the Expedited Funds Availability Act. 12 U.S.C.A. §§ 4001-4010. Nevertheless, the basic law of commercial paper is state U.C.C. law, even with respect to check collection and even when checks are collected (as they often are) through the Federal Reserve System.

United States agencies often hold commercial paper. In this case, federal law controls rights and obligations with respect to the paper, but there is no separate body of federal commercial paper law. It is federal common law that usually controls, and the courts generally define this law by reference to otherwise applicable state law, which is ordinarily the U.C.C. Thus, even with respect to paper the United States holds, the U.C.C. is the basic law.

This book covers, in context, the most significant slivers of supplemental federal law. Throughout, however, the main concern is state law -- mainly U.C.C. Article 3.

5. International Law

There is an international law of negotiable instruments, the Convention on International Bills of Exchange and International Promissory Notes. ("*Bill of exchange*" is an ancient synonym for draft. The older term "bill of exchange" is commonly used in Europe but not in the United States.) "If the United States becomes a party to this Convention, the Convention will preempt state law with respect to international bills and notes governed by the Convention." 3-102 comment 5.

B. INTRODUCTION TO INSTRUMENTS: FORMS, PARTIES, AND USES

All Article 3 instruments share the same essential characteristics that are called the *requisites of negotiability.* U.C.C. 3-104(a) lists these requisites, and Chapter 2 of this book discusses them in detail. For now it is enough to know that, basically, every instrument -- irrespective of particular form and use -- is a signed writing that orders or promises payment of money. 3-104 comment 1. Any writing that satisfies the 3-104 requisites is called a *negotiable instrument* or, more simply, an *instrument.* The two terms are synonymous. 3-104(b).

Despite this sameness, instruments can differ in form, use, and in the parties to them. The main purpose of this chapter is to outline these differences, beginning with different forms and parties. It is only an introduction. Everything said here is repeated elsewhere (usually several times) with increasingly more context and detail.

Start with the conceptual and organizing theme that there are only two basic kinds of instruments -- *notes* (including *certificates of deposit*) and *drafts* (including *checks*), and only four capacities or roles in which a person can sign an instrument -- *maker, drawer, acceptor,* and *indorser.* A person's liability on an instrument depends on the capacity in which she signed it, and this capacity partly depends on the kind of instrument involved -- note or draft.

- A *note* is an instrument that contains an explicit promise to pay. 3-104(e). The note is issued and the promise is made by the *maker.* 3-103(a)(5). A *certificate of deposit*

(CD) is essentially a specialized note issued by a bank as a receipt for a deposit of money coupled with a promise to repay it. See 3-104(j).

◆ A *draft* is an instrument that orders someone else to pay. The draft is issued and the order is given by the *drawer*, 3-103(a)(3). The person ordered to pay is the *drawee*. 3-103(a)(2). The drawee is not liable unless she signs the draft. In this event, she becomes the *acceptor* and is liable in this role. See 3-103(a)(1), 3-409 & 3-413. A *check* is a draft on which the drawee is a bank that is ordered to pay on demand. See 3-104(f).

Makers belong to notes. *Drawers* and *acceptors* belong to drafts. *Indorsers* belong to both kinds of instruments. An indorser usually signs an instrument in the process of transfer, and usually her liability is secondary -- someone else is expected to pay rather than her. See 3-204, 3-415. The same is true of a drawer's liability. Much more is said later about the nature of signers' liability.

1. Notes
a. General Distinguishing Characteristics

The most elementary form of commercial paper is the *note*. It is an instrument that is a written promise to pay money signed by the person making the promise, 3-104(e), who is called the *maker*. 3-103(a)(5). The maker's *explicit* promise to pay is the distinguishing feature of notes and explains why they are commonly called *promissory* notes. (This adjective is, however, redundant and indifferential. Every note is promissory.) Like other forms of instruments, a note may be made payable to a named person or her order, or to bearer. If a note or any other form of instrument when first issued is made payable to a named person or to her order, she is called the *payee* and is the person entitled to enforce the instrument.

A note may take any of a number of different forms, depending on its purpose, the understanding of the parties, and other factors. A note may be payable at a definite time or be payable on demand. It is common to refer to a note that is payable at a definite time as a *time* or *term note* or instrument and to refer to one that is payable on demand as a *demand note* or instrument. If an instrument is payable on demand, the holder normally is entitled to payment at any time on or after the date of the instrument. Usually, the date is the day of issue, and the note is thus due as soon as the maker issues it. It is due from its inception. If a demand instrument is postdated, however, the holder must wait until the date shown on the instrument. 3-113(a).

Usually, a note is prepared on a printed form which, before completion, contains blank spaces for the date of issue, the amount, the name of the payee, and the signature of the maker. If the payee is a bank or other financial institution, the name of the payee will likely be preprinted on the form. Typically, the form also contains words "value received" and "with interest at the rate of" and leaves blanks for the interest rate, the due date, the place of payment, the number of the note, a memorandum of the transaction, the address of the maker and for other details. A note might also contain provisions relating to security, payment in installments, acceleration, renewals, other notes in the same series, and many other matters. Very little of what might be included is necessary for a negotiable, enforceable note.

A note is most often used as the means of capturing a seller's or lender's right against a debtor when credit is extended. By executing and delivering a note to her creditor, the debtor is said to have *issued* the instrument and is its *maker*. The debtor-maker is liable on the instrument itself, 3-412, and this liability is distinct from her accountability to the creditor under contract or sales law to repay the money borrowed or to pay the price of property or services purchased on credit.

b. Transfer

The promise in a note that is payable to a named payee runs to this person. She is entitled to enforce the instrument. The payee's name is placed on the note by the maker. Unlike the maker, the payee qua payee does not sign the instrument, and thus is not liable thereon. No one is liable on any instrument unless she signs it. 3-401(a). Yet, in transferring the note, the payee usually signs the instrument and in doing so she becomes an *indorser*. By her indorsement, the payee becomes liable on the note, which means that the instrument now embodies two rights, i.e., a right against the maker, 3-412, and a right against the indorser. 3-415(a).

An indorser of a note or draft is obligated to pay the instrument if the maker or other payor refuses to do so. An indorsee of a note or other instrument can herself transfer the instrument and she, too, becomes liable as an indorser if she signs the instrument. There is no limit on the number of times a note or other instrument can be transferred, or the number of indorsers who can add their liability to the instrument.

c. Some Uses of Notes

A note may be used for many different purposes, but generally these purposes fall into one of three important categories: (1) a means of borrowing money, (2) a means of buying on credit, and (3) a method of evidencing a preexisting debt.

1) Means of Borrowing Money

This use of a note is probably the most obvious. For example, assume that a business borrows $50,000 from a bank to help finance the purchase of raw materials. As evidence of the loan, an agent for the business is required to sign and deliver to the bank a negotiable note in which the business promises to pay to the bank's order, six months after date, the sum of $50,000. The bank may disburse the full $50,000 to the maker, who must repay this sum plus interest when the note matures. Alternatively, the bank may compute the amount of interest on $50,000 for six months at the agreed rate, deduct (or discount) this amount from the $50,000 and place the balance as a credit in the maker's checking account.

a) Rediscount

The bank may hold this note until it is paid, or rediscount it at another bank which charges a lower rate of interest, thus obtaining cash or credit and netting a profit for the difference between the two rates of discount. In order to induce a second bank to rediscount the note, the payee will indorse (or endorse) it, so as to assume secondary liability. (The indorser's secondary liability is discussed in Chapter III infra.) Normally, a person indorses an instrument by signing her name on the back of it. By indorsing, the payee bank becomes an indorser which is liable if the maker of the note does not pay it. 3-415(a). While the payee bank is in possession of the note as payee, it is the holder. After the payee bank duly indorses and delivers the instrument, the transferee bank becomes the new holder. (The precise meaning of "holder" is discussed in Chapter IV infra.)

b) People As Collateral -- Accommodation Parties

Very often the lender insists, before making a loan, that a note be signed by someone other than the maker. When the debtor is a business entity, this someone is usually an insider, such as a related entity or a natural person who is a principal in the business. Sometimes this person signs along with the borrower as a co-maker. Other times, she is required to sign on the back or in the margin as an indorser. In either case, this cosigner is called an *accommodation party* if she did not receive the consideration for the instrument. She signs to lend her name, i.e., her credit, to the borrower who received the money and who is the accommodated party. 3-419(a). (Accommodation parties are discussed in Chapter VII infra.) When a small or newly formed corporation wishes to borrow money, the lender usually insists that one or more of the maker's principal stockholders or officers sign as accommodation makers or accommodation indorsers.

c) Property As Collateral

An accommodation party is a form of security, somebody else to pay the note. Property can be security too, something to sell in satisfaction of the note if a default occurs. Instead of or in addition to adding an accommodation party to the note, the parties may agree on property as collateral for the note. They describe this property in the note or in a writing apart from it such as a real estate mortgage or formal Article 9 security agreement. A security interest or other lien is thereby created, and the lender perfects the lien against third persons by recording or otherwise giving notice of it. The lien gives the lender the right, if the maker defaults, to sell the property and use the proceeds to pay the note. Article 9 usually governs the process of creating and enforcing liens whenever the collateral is personal property. Real estate finance law governs when the collateral is real property.

d) Other Lenders

Banks are not the only lenders of money. There are other financial institutions that lend and other businesses and individuals who lend by themselves and collectively. Any lender can evidence its loans by notes and require security for them or not, and any holder of a note can rediscount or otherwise sell it to whomever will buy it.

Further, any borrower can use notes in other ways to borrow money. Businesses, especially big and credible businesses, can borrow from the public by issuing short-term, unsecured notes that are payable to bearer at a definite time, usually from 90 days to nine months after issue. Securities firms or other brokers sell these notes which are treated as investments by players in the financial markets. Investors usually refer to such notes so used as commercial paper, which we know is a very, very narrow use of the term. This commercial paper is a "security" under the Glass-Steagall Act, which means that commercial banks cannot underwrite it. *Securities Industry Ass'n v. Board of Governors of the Federal Reserve System*, 468 U.S. 137, 104 S.Ct. 2979, 82 L.Ed.2d 107 (1984). It may also be a security for purposes of U.C.C. Article 8, which applies to investment securities. In this event, Article 8 governs the commercial paper in place of Article 3. "[A] particular writing may fit the definition of both a negotiable instrument under Article 3 and of an investment security under Article 8. In such cases, the instrument is subject exclusively to the requirements of Article 8." 3-102 comment 2.

2) Means of Buying on Credit

In a common transaction, a merchant sells goods and receives as "payment" the buyer's note naming the seller as payee. The note is definite evidence of the debt. Also, the seller may indorse the note to some other firm in payment for goods she has purchased, or she can use the note to raise money at the bank by selling the note or using it as collateral for loans. When the seller indorses, she normally binds herself to pay if the buyer does not. Sometimes a note passes through a number of hands before maturity, gaining credit by virtue of the secondary liability assumed by each indorser. A vast amount of credit is extended to consumers of goods and services on the basis of notes, particularly installment notes which are secured by liens on the goods purchased.

3) Means of Evidencing Preexisting Debt

Very often a debtor who is short of funds can obtain temporary relief from the pressures to pay the debt by giving the creditor a promissory note payable at a later time. From the creditor's point of view this forbearance is more satisfactory than bringing suit to collect because the creditor can maintain the good will of the debtor, who is often a customer, and secure indisputable evidence of the debt in a new form with a fresh statute of limitations. The creditor may use the note, in turn, to pay her own debts, to sell, or to use as security to bolster her credit with her bank or other lender.

2. Certificates Of Deposit

A *certificate of deposit*, often referred to as a "*CD*," is a form of note that a bank issues. It is "an instrument containing an acknowledgment by a bank that a sum of money has been received by the bank and a promise by the bank to repay the sum of money." 3-104(j). In practice, a CD represents a special form of deposit account. The depositor cannot reach the funds in the account by check and usually can recover the funds only after a specified period of time rather than upon demand. The CD is the bank's receipt for the deposit and also the bank's promise to the depositor to pay the amount of the CD at the time fixed in the instrument. Banks use time certificates of deposit (CD's), with maturities varying from a few months to several years, mainly as a device for encouraging individuals to deposit funds. In return for the depositor giving up her right to withdraw the funds on short notice, the bank is willing to pay a higher rate of interest than it pays on its ordinary savings and demand accounts.

In real life, negotiable certificates of deposit -- CDs that are Article 3 instruments -- are very rare. Increasingly, CDs are maintained as electronic, book-entry accounts that are uncertificated. Even when a certificate is issued, its terms commonly declare that the writing is "NON-NEGOTIABLE." This declaration precludes negotiability under Article 3, 3-104(d), so that the certificate or other writing is not an Article 3 instrument even if it carries the legend "Certificate of Deposit."

3. Drafts
a. General Distinguishing Characteristics

A *draft* is an instrument that, on its face, is an order to pay money rather than a promise. 3-104(e). (The ancient name for a draft is *bill of exchange,* but neither the U.C.C. nor common practice uses this old term.) The person who issues the order is the *drawer*, 3-103(a)(3), and the person ordered to pay is the *drawee*. 3-103(a)(2). Typically, the drawee is named in the lower left-hand corner of the instrument, and the drawer signs in the lower right-hand corner. A draft is basically like a note. They share the same essential characteristics of form, 3-104(a) (requisites of negotiability), and each of them carries a right against the person who issued it. Also, like a note, a draft may be payable to bearer or to some specific person or her order. Sometimes the drawer names herself as payee, but normally names a third party. Like a note, a draft may be payable on demand or at a definite time. Like a note, a draft is usually prepared in a printed form with blanks that the drawer completes. A draft can be filled with terms and information, but most drafts are simple and even bare.

The principal distinguishing feature of a draft is that, in form, it orders payment instead of promising it. 3-104(e). In virtually all drafts the order to pay is implied by use of the word "pay." See 3-103(a)(6) ("'[o]rder'" means a written instruction to pay money"). This order commands the drawee, who ordinarily is a debtor of the drawer, to pay the payee of the instrument, either on demand or on a stated date, part or all of the sum that the drawee owes the drawer.

When a draft orders payment on a future date, it effectively also orders the drawee to accept if the draft is presented for acceptance before the date of payment. Acceptance is the drawee's signature that binds her to pay the draft when the instrument becomes due. The drawee is not liable without acceptance. Sometimes, the draft is drawn to tie the time of payment to acceptance, as when the draft orders payment 30 days after sight or acceptance.

The drawer of a draft does not expressly promise to pay it. Indeed, the normal expectation is that she will not have to pay the draft because the drawee, who is ordered to pay, will do so. If, however, the drawee does not pay (or preliminarily, in a proper case, refuses to accept), the drawer is obligated to pay the instrument herself. 3-414(b). Implicitly, therefore, the drawer of a draft promises to pay the sum herself, personally, if the drawee fails to pay or, in an appropriate case, fails to accept the draft.

So, while a taker of a note expects the maker to pay the instrument, a taker of a draft looks initially to the drawee for payment rather than the drawer. A drawee who fails to pay or accept is not herself liable *on the instrument* because a drawee is not obligated on a draft unless she accepts it, 3-408, which requires the drawee to sign the instrument. 3-409(a). No person is liable on an instrument unless she signs it. 3-401(a). Being named on an instrument as drawee, payee, or in any other capacity is not enough for liability on it. In refusing to pay, however, the drawee may incur liability apart from the instrument to the drawer, the payee, or a transferee. On the other hand, when a drawee fails to pay, the drawer's implicit liability is triggered.

b. Drawee Becoming Acceptor of Draft
  1) Meaning of Acceptance
     The drawee is not obligated to pay a draft unless she accepts it. 3-408. Acceptance is the drawee's signed agreement to pay the draft. 3-409(a). The drawee's mere signature on the draft is sufficient as acceptance. 3-409 comment 2. Customarily, a drawee accepts by signing vertically across the face of the instrument, but a drawee's signature anywhere on the instrument -- even on the back of it -- is sufficient as an acceptance. Having accepted the draft, the drawee becomes an acceptor and in this new role is liable on the instrument according to its terms at the time it was accepted, 3-413(a); but a drawee is never liable *on the instrument* merely as drawee.

  2) Why Drawee Accepts
     Before acceptance there is no right on the draft against the drawee because she has not signed the instrument. Nothing in Article 3 imposes a duty on a drawee to accept a draft drawn against her. Usually, a drawee accepts because she is committed to do so by an agreement between her and the drawer to whom the drawee owes some debt.

  3) When Drawee Will Accept
     A drawee can accept any draft, including a draft payable at sight or upon demand, i.e., payable whenever the instrument is presented to the drawee. Of course, a person who takes a demand draft normally expects immediate payment by the drawee, not acceptance which is a promise to pay later. Acceptance ordinarily involves a draft payable, by its terms, on a stated date, or following a fixed period after sight. The draft may, or may not, require acceptance before payment. In any event, the taker of such a draft presents it before the instrument is due seeking assurance of payment at maturity. The drawee gives the desired assurance by accepting the draft. When presentment for acceptance is duly and properly made, the drawee's refusal

to accept is as much a dishonor of the draft as is her refusal to pay a draft that is due.

c. Transferring Drafts

A draft, like a note or any other instrument, is transferable. (Indeed, transferability is the essential attribute of all instruments!) The payee of a draft (or a note) thus can use the instrument as a means of satisfying or securing a debt of her own by transferring the instrument to her creditor. In transferring a draft, the payee, like the payee of a note, usually signs the instrument and in so doing assumes the role and liability of an *indorser*. The transferee acquires the right against the drawer which is embodied in the draft, 3-414, and also becomes the beneficiary of the drawer's order that the drawee pay the instrument. Moreover, the transferee acquires a right on the instrument against the payee qua indorser. 3-415. This entire bundle of rights in turn can be transferred again and again by successive transferees. Each of them will acquire an ever lengthening chain of obligors, any one of whom can be forced as an indorser to make good on the instrument should the drawee or acceptor refuse to pay. The drawer herself, of course, ordinarily remains an obligor on the instrument without regard to the number of transfers and indorsements.

It is more likely that the drawee will pay the draft, or accept and thereafter pay, to a person properly entitled to payment. In this event, there is no dishonor which is necessary to charge the drawer and any indorser. In effect, the instrument expires. Moreover, payment of the instrument discharges, pro tanto, the correlative liability on the underlying obligation for which the instrument was taken. 3-310.

d. Using Drafts to Finance Movement of Goods

Most generally, drafts are a means whereby a person can satisfy her own obligations by having debts she is owed paid to her creditors. Specific business applications are extremely wide and varied. Perhaps the most common specific use of ordinary or non-checks drafts, in a variety of forms, is to finance the movement of goods. Assume that a merchant in Wilmington is selling goods to a merchant in Cleveland. The shipment is large and the seller is not entirely satisfied with the buyer's credit rating; or perhaps the seller must keep her funds liquid by quick collections. She therefore contracts for a means of payment that requires the buyer to honor a demand draft for the price, plus charges, upon delivery of a bill of lading for the goods. Accordingly, when the seller ships the goods, she obtains from the railroad or other carrier a negotiable bill of lading representing the goods. She then draws a sight or demand draft for the total cost naming the buyer as drawee. The seller delivers the draft (with the bill of lading attached) to her own bank, which is named as payee in the draft. This bank forwards the draft and attached bill of lading to a correspondent bank in Cleveland for presentment to the buyer-drawee. (Technically, a draft with attached papers such as a bill of lading is called a *documentary draft*. 4-104(a)(6). A draft without such papers is called a *clean draft*.)

When the Cleveland bank receives the draft and bill of lading, it notifies the buyer. If the buyer wishes to obtain the goods, she needs the bill of lading. To get the bill of lading the buyer pays the draft to the correspondent bank and this bank surrenders the bill to her. The bill of lading entitles the buyer to require the carrier to deliver the goods to her. Meanwhile, the Cleveland bank remits the proceeds of the draft, less its charges, to the forwarding bank in Wilmington which credits the seller's account at the bank.

1) Trade Acceptance

Essentially the same procedure can be used if the seller agrees to credit instead of requiring immediate payment. The only difference is that instead of paying the draft, the buyer accepts it and thereby creates a *trade acceptance*. The acceptance is the buyer's agreement to pay for goods at a future time by accepting a time draft drawn on her by the seller. When the trade acceptance is returned to the seller, she may hold it until maturity or indorse it and discount the acceptance at her bank, thereby obtaining ready cash for the sale. Such paper is highly regarded by banks because it is backed by the credit of the acceptor and the drawer.

2) Bankers' Acceptance

Still another form of draft used to finance the shipment of goods is the *bankers' acceptance*, which is simply a draft that a bank has accepted. For example, a buyer in Austin, Texas, wishes to buy goods from a merchant in Baltimore, Maryland. The buyer's credit may not be sufficient to enable her to buy goods on credit outside of Austin, but her credit is good at First Bank of Austin which agrees to finance her. The seller is willing to sell upon the well-known credit of First Bank. Accordingly, she ships the goods and draws a time draft for the price on First Bank as drawee. After attaching the bill of lading to the draft, the seller forwards them to First Bank, which writes its acceptance across the face and returns the draft to the seller. This banker's acceptance is readily salable because of the high credit standing of First Bank, the acceptor. By discounting or collecting the draft, the seller gets the price of the goods. The buyer also is satisfied because First Bank has given her the bill of lading entitling the buyer to delivery of the goods. Alternatively, First Bank may accept a draft drawn against it by the buyer. The buyer then transfers the acceptance to the seller; or, as is more likely, the buyer herself discounts the draft (maybe with First Bank itself) and uses the proceeds to pay the price of the goods to the seller. In any event, the buyer has agreed to provide First Bank with funds to pay the draft when it falls due. In some cases First Bank will insist on receiving some form of security from the buyer, perhaps including the goods financed by the Bank.

3) Letter of Credit

A means whereby the seller can get the bank's obligation far in advance is the *letter of credit*. The buyer gets First Bank to issue such a letter to seller. U.C.C. Article 5 then commits the bank to pay or accept the seller's draft (whichever the letter of credit requires) upon presentment of certain papers described in the letter itself, including especially the bill of lading. 5-114(1). If the bank duly complies with Article 5, it is entitled to immediate reimbursement from the buyer. 5-114(3). If the bank breaches its Article 5 obligation to the seller, the seller is entitled to damages. 5-115.

4. Checks

a. General Distinguishing Characteristics

By far the most common form of draft, and the most widely used form of commercial paper, is the *check*. A check is a draft that is drawn on a bank, as drawee, and that is payable on demand. 3-104(f). All other drafts and all forms of notes may be payable either on demand (for example, a demand note) or at some definite future time (for example, a 60-day note), but not a check. A draft is a check only if it is payable on demand and also is drawn on a bank. On the other hand, a check is always a draft. In practice, however, a check is rarely called a draft, and talk of drafts often intends to exclude checks. Sometimes, to avoid confusion, drafts that are not checks are called "*ordinary drafts*" or "*non-check drafts*." Nevertheless, when the law uses "draft" without qualification, the term includes checks unless the context indicates otherwise.

b. Drafts Drawn "Through" or "At" Rather Than "On" A Bank

A check is a draft that is drawn "on" a bank. Therefore, generally speaking, a draft drawn "through" a bank is not check. The bank is only an agent for collection of the item rather than the drawee. 4-106(a). "An item identifying a 'payable through' bank can be presented for payment to the drawee only by the 'payable though' bank." 4-106 comment 1. The Code is not uniform on how to treat a draft payable "at" a bank. The states are asked to chose between treating it as the equivalent of a check or as a "payable through" draft. 4-106(b) (Alternatives A & B).

c. Relationship Between Drawer-Depositor and Drawee-Bank

Normally, the issuance of a check is preceded by a contract between the bank and the drawer. The drawer, as customer, agrees to open an account; and the bank agrees to maintain the account and honor the drawer's orders for paying checks drawn on the account, always up to the amount of deposits and maybe in excess of them under a credit agreement. (Some special problems that arise from the relationship between the bank and its checking account depositors are discussed in Chapter X infra.) It is this checking account contract that obligates the bank to pay checks drawn on it as the drawee, but the obligation is not on the instrument and runs to the drawer rather than the payee or transferees. Thus, a person who takes an ordinary check in exchange for property or services is not getting the liability of the drawee-bank, only the liability of the drawer and any indorser. It is essentially a credit transaction unless and until the check is paid.

The drawer's checking or other deposit account establishes a debtor-creditor relationship with the bank. The bank owes the drawer the balance in the deposit account. When the drawer drafts against her account, she is ordering the drawee-bank to pay to the payee, or whomever the payee instructs, part or all of what the bank owes the depositor-drawer. If the bank complies with the order, the bank reduces its debt to the depositor-drawer accordingly.

If the bank refuses to follow the order, the bank is not liable on the instrument, but the check is enforceable against the drawer. The bank may be liable to the drawer but not on the instrument. The drawer's account is governed by a deposit agreement with the bank. This agreement and U.C.C. Article 4 obligate the bank to pay the drawer's checks that are properly payable. The bank is liable to the depositor if this agreement is breached by the bank's refusal to pay a check drawn against the account. This liability is based on common-law contracts and Article 4.

d. Bank Accepting A Check

The law does not obligate the drawee-bank on a check to accept the instrument, 3-409(d), and in the usual course there is no contractual agreement with the drawer to accept it. As a drawee of a draft that has not been accepted, a bank that fails for whatever reason to pay the instrument has no liability *on the instrument* to anyone. The bank may incur liability apart from the instrument, however, for having violated a duty to the drawer or another person that is imposed by contract or by the law governing the collection of checks, principally U.C.C. Article 4. Yet, a check, like any draft payable on demand, can be accepted. The process of a bank accepting a check is referred to as *certification*. By certifying a check, the bank-drawee incurs liability on the instrument as an acceptor. See 3-409(d). BE AWARE! Certification is rare. Banks prefer to issue their own instruments, such as cashier's checks, rather than certify depositors' checks. Moreover, certification never occurs as part of the normal check collection process.

e. Special Checks

Checks primarily serve as means of payment and as vehicles for the transfer of money. They make possible an enormous amount of business activity with a minimum amount of currency.   A check also furnishes a receipt; aids in keeping records; serves as evidence; reduces the risk of loss, destruction, and theft of currency; and in other ways serves a great commercial convenience. Occasionally, a postdated check is used as a short-term credit device. **Every check, however, is a credit risk.**   Ultimately, its worth depends on the ability and willingness of the drawer to pay it.

When the creditworthiness of the debtor is too risky, the seller or other creditor may be unwilling to take the debtor's check. The creditor is entitled to insist on payment in legal tender, 2-511, but she may be willing to take instead a check that someone else backs. Her willingness to do so increases with the solvency of the third person.

- One possibility is for the debtor's own check to be *certified* by the drawee-bank. The bank thereby becomes liable as acceptor and, incidentally, the drawer's liability is discharged. As already mentioned, however, certification is rare because the transactional problems and costs are high.
- There are checks drawn by or against third persons that a debtor can buy to satisfy her own obligations. The most familiar is the *cashier's check*. 3-104(g). It is the bank's own check that is drawn against itself. The debtor is the remitter, 3-103(a)(11), and she supplies the name of the payee. Banks would rather sell a customer a cashier's check than certify the customer's own check.
- Virtually every bank is itself also a depositor at another bank. Also, other kinds of financial institutions where a debtor can own accounts -- nontraditional "banks" -- may keep their money elsewhere, often in a traditional commercial bank. In this event, the debtor would buy from her "bank" a check that the debtor's bank draws directly against its own bank as drawee. The draft is called a *teller's check*. 3-104(h).
- *Money orders* (3-104 comment 4) and *traveler's checks* (3-104(i)), which may be issued and sold by banks and non-banks alike, are other variant drafts that put someone else's account or liability behind the instrument.

Liabilities on these special instruments are discussed in greater detail in Chapter III infra.

C. SIGNIFICANCE AND ADVANTAGES OF INSTRUMENTS

Deciding that a writing is an instrument means that the writing is a right to the payment of money in a distinctive form prescribed by U.C.C. Article 3. 3-104(a). By putting the right to payment in this form the process of *reification* occurs, which means that the right becomes embodied in the writing. By transferring the writing, the creditor or obligee thereby transfers her right to receive payment from the obligor. 3-203(b). Yet, transfer of a right to the payment of money does not require reification of the right in an instrument. Intangible property that is evidenced by an ordinary writing, or that exists only in the air, is transferable nonetheless through assignment. On the other hand, there are certain advantages of capturing a right to payment in an Article 3 instrument, including the following.

1. Convenience Of Form

Negotiable instruments are familiar and recognizable. They are reliable and efficient icons for the peculiar rights, duties, and risks that are established by Article 3 and related commercial paper law.

2. Less Risk To Assignee Of Payment To Another

When a right to the payment of money is reified in an instrument, an assignee is better protected against the risk that the obligor will pay the assignor instead of her, or that the assignor will make a successive assignment of the right to someone else who may collect the right from the obligor. A person who is obligated on a right embodied in an instrument cannot, with certainty, satisfy her obligation on the instrument without dealing with the person who holds the instrument.

3. Procedural Advantages

Reification of a right to payment in an instrument is also attractive because it simplifies collection of the debt. For example, when a credit seller of goods is forced to sue on an intangible right to payment, the creditor must plead and prove all the elements of the debtor's liability under U.C.C. Article 2 and the common law of contracts. The procedure is much easier if the debtor has signed and delivered an instrument to the creditor because, in so doing, the debtor has become liable on the instrument itself as the embodiment of the creditor's right against her. Thus, instead of suing to enforce the debtor's contractual obligation to pay the price, the creditor or the creditor's assignee can enforce the debtor's liability on the instrument, which is established prima facie simply by producing the instrument in court. 3-308(b).

4. Negotiability

The principal significance and advantages of an instrument spring from its negotiability, which is an exceptional concept of great importance throughout our law. In the law of commercial paper, negotiability -- broadly defined -- refers to "a concept designating a group of legal characteristics of certain commercial instruments, such as assignability, which confers on the assignee the power to sue upon the instrument in his own name, the immunity of certain holders of such instruments from claims of ownership, the immunity of certain holders from equities of defense of prior parties on their contractual liability, and a presumption of consideration." Waterman, *The Promissory Note as a Substitute for Money,* 14 MINN. L. REV. 313, 318 (1930). In general, however, negotiability means that under limited circumstances defined by law, a transferee of property can acquire rights therein that are better or greater than the rights of the transferor.

D. NEGOTIABILITY: AN EXCEPTIONAL DOCTRINE

1. General Rule Of Derivative Title

Property is not generally negotiable in the sense that a transferee's rights exceed those of the transferor. Suppose, for instance, that T steals equipment from O and sells it to B. B buys the property for value, in good faith, and without notice that it really belongs to O. Nevertheless, when O sues B to replevy the property, or for damages for having converted it, O will prevail. The basic authority for this result is U.C.C. section 2-403(1), which provides in pertinent part that "[a] purchaser of goods acquires all title which his transferor had or had power to transfer * * *." Because T had no rights whatsoever with respect to the equipment, B acquired none. Title remained in O.

U.C.C. 2-403(1) expresses a very basic general rule pervading the whole of English and American law: Title is derivative. A transferor of property can ordinarily convey nothing more or better than her own rights in the property. Even the most innocent bona fide purchasers for value acquire nothing more. The U.C.C. codifies this rule not only in Article 2, but also in Article 7 on documents of title (7-504(1)), Article 8 governing investment securities (8-301(1)), and Article 9 governing secured transactions (9-201, 9-306(2) & 9-318(1)).

Derivative title is also a general rule of Article 3: "Transfer of an instrument * * * vests in the transferee any right of the transferor * * *." 3-203(b).

2. Negotiability As Exception To Derivative Title

The rule of derivative title is an essential attribute of an economic-legal-social system such as ours which recognizes, protects and even sanctifies private ownership of property. Yet, our society is mercantilistic, as well as capitalistic; and a rule which fails to protect innocent purchasers does not promote society's interests in fostering trade and commerce. Imagine the effects on business if, in order to guarantee good title, buyers of goods and other personal property from merchants were required to investigate the chain of ownership as they do when purchasing real estate; and imagine a marketplace where merchants cannot assume that they receive good title to money paid by buyers of their products. Competing policy goals thus sometimes override the desire to protect property rights so that, notwithstanding the rule of derivative title, a transferee of property can acquire rights therein that are better or greater than the rights of her transferor. In these circumstances, the property is treated as negotiable, which describes property in situations where an exception to the rule of derivative title applies. Here are several important instances of negotiability:

a. Goods Delivered to Merchants

There is no general rule of law holding that a person buying goods from a merchant takes title free and clear of all adverse claims. Yet, in certain important instances in which a person gives or allows a merchant to hold goods in which the person has an interest, this interest can be snuffed out by a bona fide purchaser from the merchant.

Example: O owned equipment in need of repair. She took the property to T who was in the business of selling and servicing similar property. T agreed to fix O's equipment. T did fix it, but then sold the property to B. O sued B to recover the property. B wins. 2-403(2).

Example: Bank makes business loans to C Co., a retailer of tractors and other farm implements. To secure these loans, Bank has a fully perfected, Article 9 security interest in all of C's inventory. In other words, C's inventory is collateral for the loans from Bank. If C defaults by breaching its agreement with Bank, the Bank can grab the collateral, sell it, and apply the money to C's debts. Bank has given C permission to sell the collateral only if the proceeds are remitted to Bank. C defaults by selling a tractor to B, a regular customer, without remitting the sale proceeds to Bank. Bank sues B to replevy its collateral. B wins in this case even if she knew of Bank's interest. 9-307(1).

b. Money

In the classic case, *Miller v. Race*, 97 Eng. Rep. 398 (K.B. 1758), a thief robbed a mail coach that was carrying an English bank note, in bearer form, belonging to Finney. At this time in England, such a note was the practical equivalent of paper money. The robber or her transferee exchanged the note for value given by an innkeeper. The basic question in the case was whether the innkeeper got good title to the money, free and clear of Finney's claim. The court, through Lord Mansfield, held for the innkeeper. The law announced in the case is as true today in this country as it was then and now in England: "[I]n case of money stolen, the true owner can not recover it, after it has been paid away fairly and honestly upon a valuable and bona fide consideration." Id. at 401. This common-law rule applies whether or not the transferee of the money is a merchant so long as she innocently acquires it for value.

c. Rights to Payment of Money
1) Ordinary Contract Rights
   The principle of derivative title generally applies not only to transfers of tangible property, but also to assignments of intangibles of all types. When applied to an ordinary contract right to the payment of money, the principle is commonly restated as this familiar maxim: An assignee steps into the shoes of the assignor. For this reason an assignee of a right to the payment of money is ordinarily subject to whatever claims and defenses to payment the obligor has against the assignor. 9-318(1); Restatement (Second) of Contracts § 336 (1981).

   Example: B, a farmer, buys a tractor from S on credit and signs a sales contract which obligates B to pay the price of the tractor to S in one year. S sells to a local bank her right to receive payment from B. When B's obligation to pay the price matures, the bank demands payment. B refuses to pay because the tractor was not as warranted by S, and B thus justifiably revoked her acceptance of the tractor. Under U.C.C. Article 2, B would not be liable for the price to S because of the breach of warranty by S. This breach of warranty defense is also good against the bank as assignee of S's right to payment. 9-318(1)(a).

2) Article 3 Instruments
   The derivative title principle generally applies as well to transfers of rights to payment that have been reified in Article 3 instruments. U.C.C 3-203(b) declares that a transferee of an instrument gets her transferor's rights. U.C.C. 3-305(a) and 3-306 confirm that, in most respects, a mere transferee of an instrument stands in the shoes of the transferor.

   Yet, the very heart of Article 3 is an important exception to the rule of derivative title known as the *holder-in-due-course doctrine.* "Holder in due course" is the name Article 3 gives a holder of a negotiable instrument who takes the instrument for value, in good faith, and without knowledge of any claim or defense to it. See 3-302. Such a person acquires the instrument free from all adverse claims and free from virtually all defenses to its enforcement, including claims and defenses that could have been asserted against the holder's transferor. See 3-305(b) & 3-306.

Example: Shortly before leaving on a long journey, L remembers that she forgot to get cash to carry on her trip. O agrees to cash a check for her. L draws a $500 check payable to cash and hands it to O. (A check drawn payable to cash is a bearer instrument, as was the bank note in the *Miller v. Race* case, which means that a person obligated to pay the instrument is generally free to pay anyone in possession of it.) O gives L five $100 bills and puts the check in his wallet. A thief picks O's pocket, gets O's wallet, and finds the check. The thief then exchanges the check for a 1984 Ford sedan (with some rust) sold to her by a used car dealer. The dealer takes the check to L's bank which refuses to pay the item. The bank had been notified of the theft of the check. The car dealer sues L to enforce the check, and O intervenes. The car dealer has a better claim to the check and thus its proceeds.

Example: B, a farmer, buys a tractor from S on credit and signs a sales contract which obligates B to pay the price of the tractor to S in one year. B also signs a promissory note, that is an Article 3 negotiable instrument, in which B promises to pay S in one year an amount equaling the price of the tractor. S sells the note to a local bank. One year later, the bank demands payment of the note. B refuses to pay because the tractor was not as warranted by S, and B thus justifiably revoked her acceptance of the tractor. Under U.C.C. Article 2, B would not be liable for the price to S because of the breach of warranty by S. Under Article 3, S could not enforce the note against B. Yet, the bank, as a holder in due course of the note, can enforce it against B.

REVIEW QUESTIONS

1.   U.C.C. Article 3 governs _ _ g _ _ _ _ _ _ _   _ _ _ t _ _ _ _ _ _ s.

2.   When were the most recent significant amendments made to this statute?

3.   Identify the two basic kinds of instruments.

4.   T or F   A certificate of deposit is a type of note.

5.   T or F   A check is a type of draft.

6.   All Article 3 instruments share the same essential characteristics. What are they called?

7.   In terms of form, how are all Article 3 instruments alike?

8.   Distinguish the different kinds of instruments in terms of form.

9.   What is the principal significance of embodying a right to the payment of money in an instrument?

10.   Is derivative title an exception to negotiability, or is it the other way around?

11.   T or F   Any innocent, bona fide purchaser of property, whether tangible or intangible, generally takes free of all claims to the property and, if the property is a right to the payment of money, also takes free of the obligor's defenses to payment arising from the underlying transaction that gave rise to the right.

12.   T or F   *Miller v. Race* is the fundamental case for the proposition that money is negotiable, and it was decided by Judge Posner when he was a young trial judge in England.

II

THE MEANING OF INSTRUMENT: ARTICLE 3's REQUISITES OF NEGOTIABILITY

Analysis

A. *Meaning and Significance of Requisites of Negotiability*
  1. *Article 3 Defined In Terms Of Instruments*
  2. *Instruments Defined In Terms Of Requisites Of Negotiability*
  3. *Negotiability Turns On Form*
B. *Writing*
  1. *Meaning Of "Writing"*
  2. *Outer Limits*
C. *Signed By Maker Or Drawer*
  1. *Meaning Of "Signed"*
  2. *Any Symbol So Long As Purpose Is Authentication*
  3. *Signing Someone Else's Name*
d. *Promise Or Order*
  1. *Promise*
  2. *Order*
E. *Unconditional*
  1. *General Rule*
  2. *Terms Of Instrument Determine Presence Of Condition*
  3. *Effect Of Another Agreement*
  4. *Referring To Another Agreement*
  5. *Implied Conditions Not Recognized, Only Express*
  6. *Express Conditions That Are Permitted*
  7. *Reference To Account Or Fund*
F. *Money*

A. MEANING AND SIGNIFICANCE OF REQUISITES OF NEGOTIABILITY

1. Article 3 Defined In Terms Of Instruments

Article 3 applies to writings that are instruments, which means negotiable instruments. 3-104(b). The statute governs nothing else. 3-102(a). Therefore, nothing in Article 3 applies to any writing unless the writing is negotiable within the meaning of Article 3 itself. The inapplicability of Article 3 would not mean that the writing is unenforceable. It would mean that the legal consequences of the writing are determined by other law. Most significantly, therefore, no transferee could acquire the extraordinary rights that Article 3 gives a holder in due course.

2. Instruments Defined In Terms Of Requisites Of Negotiability

The requirements for negotiability under Article 3 are known as the *requisites of negotiability*. They define instrument. Without them, a writing is not negotiable, is not an instrument, and is not within the scope of Article 3. The requisites of negotiability are spelled out in section 3-104(a). It provides:

> **"[N]egotiable instrument" means an unconditional promise or order to pay a fixed amount of money, with or without interest or other charges described in the promise or order, if it:**
>> **(1) is payable to bearer or to order at the time it is issued or first comes into possession of a holder;**
>> **(2) is payable on demand or at a definite time; and**
>> **(3) does not state any other undertaking or instruction by the person promising or ordering payment to do any act in addition to the payment of money, but the promise or order may contain (i) an undertaking or power to give, maintain, or protect collateral to secure payment, (ii) an authorization or power to the holder to confess judgment or realize on or dispose of collateral, or (iii) a waiver of the benefit of any law intended for the advantage or protection of an obligor.**

3-104(a). A further, built-in requirement is that **the promise or order is in writing**. Promise and order are defined as a *written* instruction or undertaking. 3-103(a)(6) & (9).

3. Negotiability Turns On Form

The negotiability of a writing is determined by the contents of the writing itself and nothing more. The language that appears there must satisfy the requisites of negotiability. The provisions that 3-104(a) requires must be there, and the provisions that it prohibits must not be there. On the other hand, if a writing is negotiable on its face, the presence of a separate agreement (oral or written) does not affect negotiability, not even when the terms of the agreement would prevent negotiability if they were part of the writing itself. See 3-117 (by implication). Thus, it is usually possible to determine very quickly if a writing is negotiable simply by having the writing in hand and 3-104(a) in mind, except that 3-104(a) is amplified and supplemented by the balance of the provisions in Part 1 of Article 3. In effect, these provisions define the 3-104(a) requisites of negotiability, and these definitions are often more generous, tolerant and lenient than the plain language of 3-104(a) itself. Any decision about negotiability, especially that a writing is not negotiable, is not complete without checking these supplemental provisions. They mainly inform the following discussion which focuses, in turn, on each of the nine separate (but related) requirements that 3-104(a) describes.

Remember: A writing is not a draft, check, note, or certificate of deposit within the meaning and scope of Article 3 -- i.e., the writing is not governed by Article 3 -- unless the writing satisfies the requisites of negotiability. These requisites "go to matters of form exclusively," U.C.C. 3-103 comment 2 (1989 Official Text), not to the manner in which the instrument is used.

B. WRITING

1. Meaning Of "Writing"

The core requirement of a negotiable instrument is a promise or order to pay money, 3-104(a); and a promise or order, by its own definition, must be written. 3-103(a)(6) & (9). Commercial paper is usually executed on printed, paper forms, but this kind of writing is not necessary for negotiability. *"Written"* or *"writing"* includes any "intentional reduction to tangible form." 1-201(46). Therefore, the requirement of a writing can be met by engraving, stamping, lithographing, photographing, typing, or longhand writing in pencil or ink on anything tangible, or by any similar process or any combination of them. There are stories of instruments painted on cows and coconuts.

2. Outer Limits

There are also limits. Some authorities hold that an audio tape recording is not a writing under the Code. By this law, a verbal order or promise to pay money that is recorded, whether on audio or video tape, cannot qualify as a negotiable instrument. We would expect the same conclusion, perhaps for different reasons, if the order or promise was typed on a computer screen or saved to disk. The order or promise would be written, however, if printed with a laser or transcribed with a quill on 20-lb. bond paper or a 1000-lb. heifer.

C. SIGNED BY MAKER OR DRAWER

1. Meaning Of "Signed"

The order or promise that negotiability requires means a written instruction or undertaking that is *signed* by the person who instructs or undertakes to pay. The meaning of "signed" is very broad, including "any symbol executed or adopted by a party with present intention to authenticate a writing." 1-201(39). Normally, this requirement is met by a person using a pen to write her name in longhand. It may also be met by the person using a symbol that she affixes to the instrument by hand, machine or in any other manner. A smiley face drawn or stamped on a writing can be a signature as well as a rubber stamped signature or a name or number that a computer prints on paper.

> Authentication may be printed, stamped or written; it may be by initials or by thumbprint. It may be on any part of the document and in appropriate cases may be found in a billhead or letterhead.

1-201 comment 39. It may be a symbol the party adds to the writing or a symbol that is already there. Thus, a computer-produced check with a facsimile signature is a signed instrument; and a person can be found to have signed a writing because she wrote on paper preprinted with her name.

2. Any Symbol So Long As Purpose Is Authentication

In short, the decisive issue is never the kind or nature of graphic mark or how it got on the writing. Any symbol however done will do. The decisive issue "always is whether the symbol was executed or adopted by the party with present intention to authenticate the writing." Id. To *authenticate* means "to prove the genuineness or truth of." The New Lexicon Webster's Dictionary of the English Language 64 (1989). No symbol is a signature that lacks the purpose of authentication. Not even a person's name on a writing is, by itself, a signature. This explains why name and signature are not synonymous terms. A name is not a signature unless it is executed or adopted with the present intention to authenticate a writing.

3. Signing Someone Else's Name

A person's signing a writing using someone's else name is a signature so long as the signer does so with the requisite intent to authenticate. This is true even if the other person has not authorized using her name and doing so is a forgery. It nevertheless can operate as the signature of the signer. The other person's name is as good a symbol as a smiley face or a thumbprint. It is a further, different issue whether or not a person who signs an instrument, or whose name is signed, is liable on it. This issue is considered in Chapter III infra.

D. PROMISE OR ORDER

Fundamentally, an instrument is a signed writing that, on its face, orders or promises the payment of money. 3-104 comment 1. At the core is the requirement of a promise or order. Either promising or ordering payment will satisfy negotiability, but the choice determines the nature of the instrument. An instrument that promises payment is a *note*. An instrument that orders payment is a *draft*. By force of law, a draft obligates the drawer to pay if the drawee refuses to do so, but this obligation -- which is often described as an implied promise -- is irrelevant in determining the nature of the instrument. A note requires language of promise that is missing from a draft which, on its face, orders payment instead of promising it. For the purpose of characterizing the instrument, the law ignores the drawer's implied promise to pay if the drawee fails to satisfy the draft's order.

1. Promise

The promise that satisfies negotiability "means a written *undertaking* to pay money signed by the person undertaking to pay." 3-103(a)(9) (emphasis added). Typically, a note contains the very word "promise," providing "I or we promise to pay to the order of * * * ." It is not necessary, however, to use the word "promise." Other, equivalent language that expresses a promise will suffice. Mere acknowledgment of a debt, however, is not a promise for purposes of Article 3 negotiability. 3-103(a)(9) (second sentence). Therefore, "an I.O.U. or other written acknowledgment of indebtedness is not a note unless there is also an undertaking to pay the obligation." 3-103 comment 3. Accordingly, such statements as "I.O.U. $100" and "Borrowed $100" by themselves, are not promises; but courts have held that the requirement of a promise is met by adding such words as "to be paid on demand" or "due on demand." That such cases reach the courts is good reason for avoiding doubtful language.

2. Order

An order that marks a draft is "a written *instruction* to pay money signed by the person giving the instruction." 3-103(a)(6) (emphasis added).

a. Imperative Language

It is not sufficient that a person named in the writing is authorized to pay. The writing must also instruct her to pay. Id. The usual way of expressing the order is to use the imperative form of the verb "Pay." "Pay to the order of Steve" is clearly an order. The reason is not the use of the word "order," which satisfies the altogether different requirement that the writing is payable to order or bearer. The order to pay is inferred from the instruction that the drawee "Pay." Thus, the requirement of an order is met if the writing provides "Pay Bearer."

An instruction may be an order even though it is couched in courteous form such as "please pay" or "kindly pay." On the other hand, there must be more than an authorization or request to pay. Such uncertain language as "I wish you would pay" is not an order.

b. Name the Drawee

Moreover, an order must identify with reasonable certainty the person who is ordered to pay, i.e., the drawee. This requirement was explicit in earlier law and is necessarily implied by the current Article 3. In an ordinary draft, the requirement is usually satisfied by inserting the drawee's name immediately following the word "To" on the printed form in the lower left-hand corner of the instrument. A check usually meets the requirement because the drawee bank's name is printed and encoded on the face of the instrument.

1) Drawer Named as Drawee

Sometimes, the drawer orders itself to pay: the drawer and drawee are the same person. The most common example is a cashier's check, described in Chapter I supra, by which a bank draws a check on itself. Another common example is an insurance company issuing drafts drawn on itself and payable through a bank. Former law treated such an instrument as a note, but Article 3 is now somewhat truer to form. The definition of 'order' explicitly includes an instruction to pay that is addressed to the person giving the instruction. 3-103(a)(6). Because a cashier's check orders payment, Article 3 classifies and refers to it as a draft and a check rather than a note. Similarly, in line with form, Article 3 classifies insurance drafts as ordinary drafts. Nevertheless, Article 3 recognizes that, in substance, insurance drafts, cashier's checks, and other drafts drawn on their drawers are more like notes, and defines the liability of these drawers the same as the liability of a maker of a note. 3-412 comment 1. There are other differences from typical checks and ordinary drafts, especially with respect to cashier's checks.

2) Multiple Drawees

An order may be addressed to multiple drawees either jointly (To A *and* B) or in the alternative (To A *or* B). 3-103(a)(6). In either case the holder is required to present the draft only once. If the instrument is not paid or accepted when presented to any one of the drawees named, it is dishonored and the holder may proceed immediately against the drawer without presenting it to the remaining drawees. 3-103 comment 2, 3-501(b)(1) & 3-414(b). This authorization of multiple drawees "recognizes the practice of drawers, such as corporations issuing dividend checks, who for commercial convenience name a number of drawees, usually in different parts of the country." 3-103 comment 2. This practice is a convenience to the stockholder who can present the check to any drawee; and if that drawee dishonors it, she can proceed immediately against the drawer.

Naming drawees in succession (To A, and if A fails to pay, to B) is not an order and prevents negotiability. 3-103(a)(6) (order does not include instruction addressed in succession). This language would delay the holder's right to proceed against the drawer until the draft had been dishonored by all drawees, and is not permitted. The reason is that "the holder should not be required to make more than one presentment." 3-103 comment 2.

c. Implied Promise

Note again that, although the drawer does not expressly promise to pay the instrument, the law obligates her to pay the draft upon certain conditions. 3-414(b). In short, the drawer of a draft that the drawee dishonors may be liable on the instrument even though the draft itself contains no express promise to pay. This liability is discussed in Chapter III infra.

E. UNCONDITIONAL

Two major functions of commercial paper are to serve as a substitute for money and as a reliable basis for credit. If commercial paper is to perform either function effectively, business people must be assured that there are no strings attached to payment. Therefore, negotiability requires a promise or order that is *unconditional*. It must be expressed in absolute terms which are not subject to contingencies, provisos, qualifications, or reservations that undermine or impair the obligation to pay. It must be a "courier without luggage." *Overton v. Tyler*, 3 Pa. 346, 347 (1846).

1. General Rule

Generally, a promise or order *is unconditional* unless the writing states:

- an express condition to payment,
- that the promise or order is subject to or governed by another writing, or
- that rights or obligations with respect to the promise or order are stated in another writing.

3-106(a). In other words, if the writing contains none of these provisions, the order or promise is unconditional. The writing is negotiable if it satisfies the other 3-104(a) requisites of negotiability. On the other hand, if the writing contains even one of the three kinds of provisions that 3-106(a) describes, the promise or order is conditional, negotiability is impossible, and the writing is not an Article 3 instrument.

Example: "[A] promise states, 'I promise to pay $100,000 to the order of John Doe if he conveys title to Blackacre to me.' The promise is not an instrument because there is an express condition to payment." 3-106 comment 1.

Example: A note is not an instrument if it states, "'This note is subject to a contract of sale dated April 1, 1990 between the payee and maker of this note.'" Id.

Example: A note is not an instrument if it states, "Rights and obligations of the parties with respect to this note are stated in an agreement dated April 1, 1990 between the payee and maker of this note." Id.

2.   Terms Of Instrument Determine Presence Of Condition

As far as negotiability is concerned, determining if a promise or order is conditional requires an examination of the writing itself -- the putative instrument -- and nothing else. Its provisions are the only statements that matter in applying the tests of 3-106(a). What anyone has said about the instrument is irrelevant. For the purpose of determining negotiability, the promise or order it contains is unconditional unless something *in the instrument itself* is to the contrary. "Negotiability is determined from the face , the four corners, of the instrument without reference to extrinsic facts. The conditional or unconditional character of the promise or order is to be determined by what is expressed in the instrument itself." *Western Bank v. RaDec Const. Co., Inc.*, 382 N.W. 406, 409 (S.D. 1986).

Example: Assume that M hands P a note that provides, "I promise to pay $1000 to the order of P on demand. (Signed) M." In doing so M says, "This money will not be paid unless a bond is delivered to me." The note is negotiable because the promise contained in the note itself is unconditional and all other requirements for negotiability are satisfied.

The same is true if the condition is stated in a separate writing prepared before, after, or contemporaneously with the note. See 3-117. Other agreements, oral or written, are themselves irrelevant in deciding negotiability. In contrast, if the note itself provides that payment is to be made only if the bond is delivered, the note is not negotiable.

3.   Effect Of Another Agreement
a.   Separate Agreement Affects Obligation

Negotiable instruments are rarely issued in isolation. Usually, they are issued pursuant to or as part of some underlying transaction and agreement between the parties. For example, a check may be delivered to pay for property sold pursuant to a sales contract, or a note may be issued to evidence a loan agreement that is probably secured by collateral. The security aspect of the loan transaction will itself involve typically elaborate agreements about the lender's rights. When determining the respective rights and duties of the original parties to transactions of this kind, the Code follows the common-law rule that writings executed as part of the same transaction are to be read and enforced together as a single, integrated agreement. In terms of Article 3, "the obligation of a party to an instrument to pay the instrument may be modified, supplemented, or nullified by a separate agreement of the obligor and a person entitled to enforce the instrument, if the instrument is issued * * * as part of the same transaction giving rise to the agreement." 3-117. The supplemental agreement is a defense to payment of the instrument. Id. Here is the official example:

Example: "Suppose X requested credit from Creditor who is willing to give the credit only if an acceptable accommodation party will sign the note of X as co-maker. Y agrees to sign as co-maker on the condition that Creditor also obtain the signature of Z as co-maker. Creditor agrees and Y signs as co-maker with X. Creditor fails to obtain the signature of Z on the note. * * * Y is obliged to pay the note, but Section 117 applies. In this case, the agreement modifies the terms of the note by stating a condition to the obligation of Y to pay the note. * * * Section 3-117, in treating the agreement as a defense, allows Y to assert the agreement against Creditor * * * ." 3-117 comment 1.

Example: The only problem for Y in relying on 3-117 is that its rule that honors separate agreements is subject to applicable non-Code "law regarding exclusion of proof of contemporaneous or previous agreements." 3-117. Principally important is the parol evidence rule. If it applies, Y is barred from proving the separate agreement despite 3-117. The parol evidence rule overrides 3-117.

b. Negotiability Unaffected

On the other hand, the separate agreement -- whether oral or written -- does not affect negotiability. Regardless of the provisions that any outside writing may provide, it does not destroy the negotiability of an instrument which otherwise meets the requisites of negotiability. Thus, if the note in the example meets the requisites of negotiability, it is an instrument despite the agreement between Creditor and Y; and the rights and liabilities on the note are governed by Article 3, including 3-117.

4. Referring To Another Agreement

The *existence* of another agreement does not affect negotiability. 3-117. The instrument *making express reference* to an outside agreement or other writing can affect negotiability depending on the nature of the reference.

a. Rule -- Not Subject To Or Governed By

A statement is inoffensive that simply mentions the outside writing or reports that the instrument arises out of or in connection with the writing. Negotiability is denied, however, if the statement ties the instrument to the writing by providing either that the instrument is subject to or governed by the outside writing, or that the latter defines rights or obligations with respect to the former. 3-106(a)(ii-iii). The fact that the terms of payment cannot be determined by looking at the instrument itself, that it is necessary to look to an outside agreement, is contrary to the concept of negotiability. This is so even though the outside agreement, which governs or defines rights in the instrument, contains no conditions or other provisions that are contrary to the requirements of negotiability. "It is not relevant whether any condition to payment is or is not stated in the writing to which reference is made." 3-106 comment 1.

Example: A note is not negotiable that states it is subject to terms and conditions of the commitment letter in which the payee undertakes to lend the money that the maker promises to repay. *Sovran Bank v. Franklin*, 13 UCC Rep. Serv.2d 174 (Vir. Cir. Ct. 1990).

Example: A note is not negotiable that provides "payable as set forth in that certain agreement dated March 15, 1976." *Salomonsky v. Kelly*, 349 S.E.2d 358 (Vir. 1986).

Example: A note providing that it is subject to the terms of a partnership debt assumption agreement is not negotiable. *Growth Equities Corp. v. Freed*, 13 UCC Rep. Serv. 1134 (Cal. App. 1991).

Example: A refinancing agreement was not negotiable because its language "went beyond mere reference to the underlying agreement; it required reference to the contracts to determine terms of the agreement and spelled out the refinancing agreement's subservience to the contracts if the terms were not addressed in the refinancing agreement." *Massey Ferguson Credit Corp. v. Bice*, 450 N.W.2d 435, 442-43 (S.D. 1990). The agreement warned that it in no way affected the rights and obligations of the contracts. Also, there were other undertakings and instructions that 3-104 does not allow, including obligations with respect to the purchase of property damage insurance, the purchase of credit life insurance, provision for late payment fees, a provision for rebate of unearned finance charge, and an agreement to pay all taxes levied against the property.

b. Exception -- Security Agreements

There is a very important exception. Notes that are secured by collateral often refer to the mortgage or other security agreement for rights with respect to collateral, prepayment, or acceleration. This kind of reference is expressly excepted from the rule of 3-106 that would otherwise deny negotiability. 3-106(b)(i).

Example: "[A] note would not be made conditional by the following statement: 'This note is secured by a security interest in collateral described in a security agreement dated April 1, 1990 between the payee and maker of this note. Rights and obligations with respect to the collateral are [stated in] [governed by] the security agreement.'" 3-106 comment 1.

The reason for this exception is mostly business convenience and practice. Also, the obligation of an instrument is not diluted and can only be enhanced by rights with respect to collateral, prepayment or acceleration. Thus, a reference to such rights existing beyond the instrument should not impede its transfer or, therefore, its negotiability.

5. Implied Conditions Not Recognized, Only Express

Because the breach of a separate agreement can be a defense to an instrument, 3-117, it might be argued that a mere reference to an underlying executory contract between the parties, or even the existence of it, implicitly conditions the instrument on due performance of the contract and thereby denies negotiability to the instrument. This argument fails. Commercial paper often refers to contractual arrangements still to be performed. Usually such recitals are intended as statements of consideration without implications of any kind. If the maker or drawer intends to condition her liability, the Code requires him to do more than leave it to inference. The rule is that an order or promise is conditional only if it states "an *express* condition to payment * * * ," 3-106(a)(i) (emphasis added), which is not true when the statement simply reports that the instrument is given for an executory promise.

Example: "[S]uppose a promise states, 'In consideration of John Doe's promise to convey title to Blackacre I promise to pay $100,000 to the order of John Doe.' That promise can be an instrument if Section 3-104 is otherwise satisfied. Although the recital of the executory promise of Doe to convey

Blackacre might be read as an implied condition that the promise be performed, the condition is not an express condition as required by Section 3-106(a)(i)." 3-106 comment 1. See, e.g., *Carador v. Sana Travel Service, Ltd.*, 700 F. Supp. 787 (S.D. N.Y. 1988), aff'd, 876 F.2d 890 (2d Cir. 1989) (for security deposit for future performance of another contract); *Strickland v. Kafko Manufacturing, Inc.*, 512 So.2d 714 (Ala. 1987) ("for pool to be delivered").

Similarly, if an instrument otherwise negotiable provides that it is given in accordance with or "as per" some collateral contract, the possible inference that payment is conditioned on performance of the other contract does not destroy negotiability. Rather it is treated merely as a recital of the origin of the instrument or as an informational reference to another contract. In like vein, a statement in a draft that it is drawn under a letter of credit does not state a condition but merely identifies the occasion for the issuance of the instrument.

6. Express Conditions That Are Permitted

There are a couple of very narrow exceptions to the general rule against express conditions.

a. Countersignature In Traveler's Check

First, the requirement of a countersignature in a traveler's check does not affect negotiability. 3-106(c). Although this requirement "is a condition to the obligation to pay, traveler's checks are treated in the commercial world as money substitutes and therefore should be governed by Article 3." 3-106 comment 2.

b. Statement Preserving Claims And Defenses

Second, an instrument can contain a statement, that is required by other law, preserving the issuer's claims and defenses against the payee. 3-106(d). For example, federal law requires including the following notice in a consumer credit contract for the sale of goods or services, including a contract in the form of an instrument:

> ANY HOLDER OF THIS CONSUMER CREDIT CONTRACT IS SUBJECT TO ALL CLAIMS AND DEFENSES WHICH THE DEBTOR COULD ASSERT AGAINST THE SELLER OF GOODS OF SERVICES OBTAINED PURSUANT HERETO OR WITH THE PROCEEDS HEREOF.

16 C.F.R. 433.2(a). This notice does not prevent negotiability, even though the effect is to subject the note to the underlying transaction. This kind of notice nevertheless accomplishes its purpose because there cannot be a holder in due

course of the instrument. 3-106(d). Thus, any transferee takes subject to the claims and defenses that the issuer could assert against the original payee. Thus, if a consumer buys goods and signs a note for the price and the seller-payee fails to perform, the buyer can assert the breach as a defense or counterclaim against any third party who took the note and sues the buyer on it.

7. Reference To Account Or Fund
a. For Accounting Only
The fact that an instrument indicates a particular account to be debited or any fund or source from which reimbursement is expected does not render a promise or order conditional.

> *Example:* The drawer of a bill may direct the drawee to pay the money to the order of the payee and "charge the same to the amount of the drawer" or to the "merchandise account" or the like. Such directions are for accounting purposes, and the drawer's obligation is in no way contingent upon a credit balance in the account. Negotiability is unaffected.

b. To Limit Payment
The result would be different under former law if the instrument states that payment is to be made only from a particular fund or source. In this case, former law denied negotiability because the obligation to pay is necessarily contingent on the sufficiency of the fund. It was thought that to be unconditional, an order or promise must carry the general credit of the maker or drawer. The law changed its mind on this issue when Article 3 was amended in 1990. The rule now is that "[a] promise or order is not made conditional * * * because payment is limited to resort to a particular fund or source." 3-106(b). The explanation is this:

> There is no cogent reason why the general credit of a legal entity must be pledged to have a negotiable instrument. Market forces determine the marketability of instruments of this kind. If potential buyers don't want promises or orders that are payable only from a particular source or fund, they won't take them, but Article 3 should apply.

3-106 comment 1. This reasoning would justify eliminating every requirement of negotiability. A truer explanation, probably, is further relaxation and compromise in negotiability that reflect changes in business customs, practices, or expectations.

c. Nonrecourse Note

Under former law, a nonrecourse note is not negotiable because payment is tied to a particular fund. *United Nat'l Bank v. Airport Plaza Ltd. Partnership*, 6 UCC Rep. Serv. 1161, 7 UCC Rep. Serv. 488 (Fla. Ct. App. 1987, 1988). This reasoning on longer applies but the negotiability of a nonrecourse note remains doubtful. Arguably, such a note fails the separate requirement that the instrument promises or orders payment of a *"fixed amount* of money." 3-104(a) (emphasis added). Cf. *Dann v. Team Bank*, 788 S.W.2d 182 (Tex. Ct. App. 1990) (guaranty not negotiable because the ceiling on guarantor's liability failed the "sum certain" requirement).

F. MONEY

The unconditional promise or order that negotiability requires is a promise or order to pay *money*. An instrument is payable in money if it is stated as payable in "a medium of exchange authorized or adopted by a domestic or foreign government and includes a monetary unit of account established by an intergovernmental organization or by agreement between two or more nations." 1-201(24). Money, therefore, is not limited to United States dollars. If the instrument is payable in foreign money, the amount "may be paid in the foreign money or in an equivalent amount in dollars calculated by using the current bank-offered spot rate at the place of payment for the purchase of dollars on the day on which the instrument is paid." 3-107.

Example: X sold her cabinet shop to Y. Y agreed in writing to pay the price in cabinets that Y would make and X would resell to third persons. Y's obligation to X was reduced by an agreed value of the cabinets that Y made for X. This writing was not a negotiable instrument. The cabinets were not money. *Means v. Clardy*, 735 S.W.2d 6 (Mo. Ct. App. 1987).

G. FIXED AMOUNT

The money payable must be a *fixed amount*. The law formerly expressed this requirement as a "sum certain." The meaning is fundamentally the same -- a total which the holder can determine from the instrument by any necessary computation at the time the instrument is payable, without reference to any outside source. The requirement of a fixed amount applies only to the principal. 3-112 comment 1. It does not apply to interest or to other charges that are less commonly included in an instrument -- such as collection costs and attorneys fees which are notoriously uncertain in amount.

1. Interest

a. Unstated

An instrument is not payable with interest unless it so provides. 3-112(a). Negotiability is unaffected whether or not the instrument provides for interest, and is also unaffected by providing for interest without describing the rate. In the latter event, "interest is payable at the judgment rate in effect at the place of payment of the instrument and at the time interest first accrues." 3-112(b). Therefore, "if an instrument calls for interest, the amount of interest will always be determinable." 3-112 comment 1.

b. Variable

The typical note provides for interest and describes an amount or contract rate. Article 3 is very tolerant with respect to these provisions. "Interest may be stated * * * as a fixed or variable amount of money or it may be expressed as a fixed or variable rate or rates." 3-112(b). Also, [t]he amount or rate of interest may be stated or described in the instrument in any manner" and, most significantly, "*may require reference to information not contained in the instrument.*" Id. (emphasis added). The emphasized language specifically addresses a dispute among the courts under prior law. They disagreed on whether or not negotiability is denied when an instrument calculated interest by reference to an extrinsic formula or index, such as a bank's prime rate or an economic indicator published by government or a market. The law is now clear, because of the specific language of 3-112(b), that negotiability is unaffected. This result would seem to flow from the general principle that the requirement of "fixed amount" applies only to principal, not to interest or other charges.

2. Variable Principal

Presumably, however, negotiability is denied if the principal itself is tied to an extrinsic index. The reason is not that the amount is subject to change after issue. The reason is that the total principal cannot be calculated, at the time payable, from the face of the instrument. An exception is implied for a conversion rate in the event that an instrument stated in foreign money is paid in dollars. 3-107. It is also implied that fluctuations in such a rate do not render the amount unfixed.

As long as the principal can be determined when payable from information within the instrument, it is not always necessary for the instrument to state an indelible total. Mathematical calculation using the information is permitted, so that the amount is fixed if the instrument promises or orders 12 payments of $1,000 each. It is uncertain whether or not Article 3 continues the former law of tolerating a fixed discount or increase if the instrument is paid before or after a stated time for payment. The argument for tolerance is that the minimum amount is calculable. The possibility that an extra sum might be paid (icing on the cake) will not affect marketability or retard circulation and could even enhance it.

H. PAYABLE ON DEMAND OR AT A DEFINITE TIME

Negotiability requires that an instrument "is payable *[either]* on demand *or* at a definite time." 3-104(a)(2) (emphasis added).

1. On Demand
An instrument is "payable on demand" if it:

- states that it is payable on demand or at sight,
- otherwise indicates that it is payable at the will of the holder, or
- does not state any time of payment.

3-108(a). Most instruments that are payable on demand, including virtually all checks, are so payable for the last reason: they make no express provision for time of payment.

2. At A Definite Time
An instrument is payable at a definite time if it is payable:

- at a fixed date or dates,
- on elapse of a definite period of time after sight or acceptance, or
- at a time or times readily ascertainable at the time the instrument is issued,

even if it is subject to prepayment, acceleration, or certain extensions. 3-108(b).

Example: An instrument would be payable at a definite time if it were payable "on July 1, 1992," "thirty days after date" (assuming, of course, that the instrument is dated), or "on or before March 1, 1992." Although "on or before" may suggest indefiniteness, there is no reason to deny such instruments negotiability because there is no more uncertainty involved than in an instrument payable on demand. Similarly, when an instrument is payable at a fixed period after sight, the holder controls the matter and may determine maturity promptly by presenting the instrument for acceptance.

a. Acceleration Clauses
If the time for payment is otherwise definite, the fact that the instrument provides for accelerating payment does not render the time indefinite.

3-108(b)(ii). This is so whether the acceleration is automatic upon the occurrence of some event (certain to occur or not) or is at the option of one of the parties. For example, it is permissible that a term note accelerates the time for payment if the maker sells collateral securing the note, or permits the holder to demand earlier payment if she is insecure about the maker's financial condition. See 1-208. The instrument can also permit the maker to accelerate by allowing prepayment, 3-108(b)(i), but she may pay a penalty for doing so or remain liable for the unaccrued interest.

b. Extension Clauses
The requirement of payable at a definite time is not violated by making the time for payment subject to:

- an extension at the option of the holder,
- an extension to a further definite time at the option of the maker or acceptor, or
- an extension to a further definite time automatically upon or after a specified act or event.

A provision for extension by the holder need not specify a time limit for the extension. It can be open-ended because, even without the clause, the holder is naturally free to forebear for as long as she wishes. The holder cannot use this right to create additional interest charges over the obligor's objection. The obligor can tender payment on the due date and thereby escape liability for additional interest that she has not agreed to pay. 3-603(c) ("If tender of payment of an amount due on an instrument is made to a person entitled to enforce the instrument, the obligation of the obligor to pay interest after the due date on the amount tendered is discharged.").

A provision allowing the maker or acceptor to extend the time for payment, or automatically extending the time if an act or event occurs, must specify a definite time limit on the period of extension. So done, negotiability is unaffected by the provision because "the effect upon certainty of time of payment is the same as if the instrument were made payable at the ultimate date with a term providing for acceleration." 3-108 comment. Not done, negotiability is lacking because the unlimited right to extend negates the definite time for payment. No limit is ever implied by law, as sometimes happened under former law, that cures this violation of negotiability.

c. Tying Paying To An Event
Section 3-108(b) differs from former law by broadening definite time to include payable "at a time or times readily ascertainable at the time the promise or order

is issued." 3-108(b). This language presumably allows, for example, tying payment to a scheduled event certain to happen, such as "payable on the 150th anniversary of Northwestern University Law School" or "the day of Super Bowl XXXVI."   It would not allow tying payment to an event uncertain to occur. *Calfo v. D. C. Stewart Co.*, 717 P.2d 697 (Utah 1986) (A note is not negotiable if it provides for payment upon final closing of a deal between seller and buyers which shall be on or before May 1, 1980). Nor would it allow tying payment to an event certain to occur but at an uncertain time, such as the death of a particular person. It is nevertheless possible to accomplish the usual purpose of such a provision without offending negotiability by specifying a far distant definite time for payment subject to acceleration by the event.

3. At A Definite Time *And* On Demand

It is possible that an instrument may be payable *both* at a definite time *and also* on demand. Negotiability is not offended. The instrument is deemed payable "on demand until the fixed date and, if demand for payment is not made before that date, becomes payable at a definite time on the fixed date." 3-108(c). It is not certain, however, that a demand installment note is negotiable. It is a note for which the first installment payment is due on demand and the remaining installments are due at stated intervals thereafter. In one case the district court held that such notes were not negotiable; and the federal appeals court certified the issue to the Connecticut Supreme Court, commenting that the arguments were good on both sides of the issue. *In re Boardwalk Marketplace Securities Litigation*, 668 F. Supp. 115 (D. Conn. 1987), 849 F.2d 89 (2d Cir. 1988). The state court never reported a response.

I. PAYABLE TO ORDER OR TO BEARER (*WORDS OF NEGOTIABILITY*)

Negotiability requires that the instrument is "payable *to bearer* or *to order* at the time it [the instrument] is issued or first comes into possession of a holder." 3-104(a)(1). Words that satisfy this requirement are called *words of negotiability*. These words are the most common earmarks of negotiability. They most clearly indicate the intention of the maker or drawer to issue an instrument that is negotiable and subject to all the incidents attaching to this form of contract and property. They alert the prospective purchaser, more certainly than anything else, of the possibility that if the instrument is negotiated to a holder in due course, the effect is to cut off any claims and defenses of the maker or drawer against the payee. Also, requiring these words of negotiability provides a simple device to clearly exclude a writing that does not fit the pattern of typical negotiable instruments and which is not intended to be a negotiable instrument.

If a writing could be an instrument despite the absence of "to order" or "to bearer" language and a dispute arises with respect to the writing, it might be argued that the writing is a negotiable instrument because the other requirements of [3-104(a)] are somehow met. Even if the argument is eventually found to be without merit it can be used as a litigation ploy. * * * [By requiring words of negotiability for an instrument] [a]bsence of the words precludes any argument that such contracts [without the words] might be negotiable instruments.

3-104 comment 2; see, e.g., *Stone v. Mehlberg*, 728 F. Supp. 1341 (W.D. Mich. 1989) (mortgage nonnegotiable for lack of words of negotiability); *Mox v. Jordan*, 463 N.W.2d 114 (Mich. Ct. App. 1990) (mortgage); *Ramirez v. Bureau of State Lottery*, 463 N.W.2d 245 (Mich. Ct. App. 1990) (lottery ticket not negotiable); *First Nat'l Bank v. Fulk*, 13 UCC Rep. Serv.2d 1134 (Ohio Ct. App. 1989) (credit card sales slip not negotiable); *Dann v. Team Bank*, 788 S.W.2d 182 (Tex. Ct. App. 1990) (guaranty not negotiable because lacked words of negotiability); *Mauricio v. Mendez*, 723 S.W.2d 296 (Tex. Ct. App. 1987) (agreement for sale of a bar and restaurant business).

"To order" or "to bearer" are alternative forms of the words of negotiability. In determining if a writing is a negotiable instrument, it makes no difference whether it is payable to order or to bearer so long as it is payable one way or the other. The difference is important in deciding how the instrument is negotiated so that the transferee becomes a holder and is entitled to the rights of that status, which can include the rights of a holder in due course. An instrument that is payable to order (a/k/a *order paper*) is negotiated by transfer of possession *and* indorsement; *bearer paper* is negotiated by transfer of possession alone. 3-201(b).

1. Payable To Order

Typically, an instrument is payable to order, which means it (1) is not payable to bearer and (2) is payable:

- to the order of an identified person, or
- to an identified person or order.

3-109(b). This meaning covers the most common form of the words of negotiability: "Pay to the order of Jane Doe." It also covers the typical variation, "Pay Jane Doe or order." Significantly, an instrument that uses this form is payable to order even if Ms. Doe is fictitious. 3-109 comment 2.

a. Wording Important

The word "order" (or, perhaps, a very close equivalent) is essential. It makes clear that the maker or drawer intends payment to transferees as well as the identified person. It empowers this person, through the process of negotiation, to redirect the obligation that runs to her, as payee, to someone else she designates or to anyone who holds the instrument. Former law expressly tolerated using the word "assigns" as a synonym for "order" or designating the instrument as "exchange" or the like. These substitutes equally signal transferability by the named payee.

b. Payable to Payee Without Order Language (Mercantile Specialty)
1) General Rule
An instrument is not payable to order that provides only, "Pay Jane Doe" because the magic "order" word is missing. Neither is it payable to bearer. The writing therefore lacks words of negotiability, is not a negotiable instrument, and -- contrary to former law -- is entirely beyond Article 3. It is sometimes called a "*mercantile specialty*."

2) Exception -- 3-104(c) Check
The single exception is the 3-104(c) check. It is an order to pay that satisfies all of the requisites of negotiability, and that otherwise falls within the definition of "check," except that it lacks words of negotiability. Section 3-104(c) deems that such a check, despite its missing words, is a negotiable instrument and a check. Therefore, a check payable "Pay Jane Doe" is fully negotiable, is covered by Article 3, and a transferee of the check can become a holder in due course, even though the check lacks words of negotiability.

This exception for the 3-104(c) check is very narrow. Any other draft that is payable only to an identified person, and not also her order, is not negotiable. The order language is not supplied by the "order to pay" that distinguishes the draft from a note and that is implied by the direction "Pay." The "order to pay" in a draft satisfies a requirement of negotiability that is different from the requirement of words of negotiability. The former identifies the nature and purpose of the instrument and the issuer's undertaking. The latter signals transferability. A negotiable draft requires both an order to pay that, additionally, is payable to order or bearer, except for the 3-104(c) check.

c. To Whom Instrument *Can Be* Payable
An instrument may be made payable to the order of anyone, whether a natural person or legal or commercial entity, including the maker, drawer, or drawee. It may be made payable to the order of two or more persons together as "A, B and C," or in the alternative as "A, B or C." 3-110(d). Do not confuse multiple payees with multiple drawees. For discussion of the latter, see the earlier discussion in this chapter. For discussion of the former, see Chapter IV infra.

d. To Whom Instrument *Is* Payable

A person to whom an instrument is payable may be identified in any way, including by name, identifying number, office, or account number. 3-110(c). The test to determine who the instrument identifies is the intent of the person signing as, or in the name or behalf of, the issuer, whether or not the person signing is authorized to do so. 3-110(a).

Example: "If X signs a check as drawer of a check on X's account, the intent of X controls. If X, as President of Corporation, signs a check as President in behalf of Corporation as drawer, the intent of X controls. If X forges Y's signature as drawer of a check, the intent of X also controls." 3-110 comment 1.

Example: "In the case of a check payable to 'John Smith,' since there are many people in the world named 'John Smith' it is not possible to identify the payee of the check unless there is some further identification or the intention of the drawer is determined. * * * [T]he intention of the drawer determines which John Smith is the person to whom the check is payable." Id.

Example: "The same issue is presented in cases of misdescriptions of the payee. The drawer intends to pay a person known to the drawer as John Smith. In fact that person's name is James Smith or John Jones or some other entirely different name. If the check identifies the payee as John Smith, it is nevertheless payable to the person intended by the drawer." Id.

In case the signer is not human, as with a computer or checkwriting machine, the relevant intent is that of the person who supplied the payee's name, even if this person acts without authority and wrongfully. 3-110(b). The issue of whom the instrument names as payee usually translates into the issue of who can properly indorse the instrument. It concerns the process of negotiation, which is discussed in Chapter IV infra.

2. Payable To Bearer

An instrument that is not payable to order is not, automatically, payable to bearer. The two forms of the words of negotiability -- order and bearer -- are alternatives of the same requirement and either of them can be used in creating a negotiable instrument, but each of them has its own peculiar meaning. Failing one does not satisfy the other by default; and if the instrument does not use one form of the other, as Article 3 defines them, the instrument lacks the words of negotiability that 3-104(a) requires.

"Payable to bearer" means that a promise or order:

*   states that it is payable to bearer or to the order of bearer or otherwise indicates that the person in possession of the promise or order is entitled to payment;
*   does not state a payee; or
*   states that it is payable to or to the order of cash or otherwise indicates that it is not payable to an identified person.

3-109(a). The unofficial essence of payable to bearer is that anyone who possesses or holds the instrument can enforce it, which negatively implies that payment is not limited to a particular person or people. The issuer intends payment to anybody with the instrument. Thus, an instrument that expresses this intent in so many words is, officially, payable to bearer. 3-109(a)(1). The most common expressions of this intent, which meet the test of "payable to bearer," are:

*   "Pay to Bearer,"
*   "Pay to the order of Bearer"
*   "Pay to Cash," or
*   "Pay to Cash, or Order,"

as long as "Bearer" or "Cash" is not used to identify a person.

a.   Payable to Fictitious Payee

Naming a fictitious person who cannot be paid is different and does not qualify as "payable to bearer." In such a case the instrument indicates that is payable to an identified person whether or not, in fact, the person exists. If the fictitious person's name is coupled with order language, the instrument is payable to order; otherwise, it is not negotiable. See 3-109 comment 2.

b.   Payable to Bearer *And* Named Payee

If the instrument is payable to bearer and also to an identified person, the instrument is payable to bearer whether or not it is also payable to the person's order. Thus an instrument is payable to bearer that reads "Pay to Jane Doe or bearer" or "Pay to the order of Jane Doe or bearer." In the former case, the bearer language supplies words of negotiability that otherwise would be entirely lacking because "Pay to Jane Doe" is not payable to order. In the latter case, the order language itself constitutes words of negotiability, but the additional bearer language overrides. In the first case the bearer language is necessary for negotiability; in the second case the bearer language is not needed for negotiability and does not deny negotiability, but puts the instrument in bearer form and determines how, initially, it can be negotiated.

c. Payable to _____ (Blank)

An instrument that does not state a payee is also payable to bearer, 3-109(a)(2), as in "Pay to _____ " or "Pay to the order of ___." By leaving the space blank, the issuer might have intended that the instrument was payable to anybody. More likely, she intended to fill in someone's name and forgot, or she planned that someone else would fill in a name. In any event, the instrument is "payable to bearer" even if it is also an incomplete instrument. 3-109 comment 2.

3. When The Instrument Must Be So Payable

Negotiability requires that the instrument is payable to bearer or to order at *the time it is issued or first comes into possession of a holder.* The term "*issue*" means "the first delivery of an instrument by the maker or drawer, whether to a holder or nonholder, for the purpose of giving rights on the instrument to any person." 3-105(a). Basically, therefore, the instrument must contain the words of negotiability when the maker or drawer gives it to the payee. It is not an instrument if it lacks these words and the payee adds them. Thus, a note in which M promises to "Pay P" is not an instrument and does not become an instrument, as to M, by P later adding order language. Consider two variations:

- ◆ Suppose, however, that P nevertheless transferred the nonnegotiable note. It would be governed by law other than Article 3. Yet, in making the transfer, P followed the conventions of Article 3 despite the statute's inapplicability. Thus, P indorsed the note to T, "Pay to the order of T." These are words of negotiability. It could be argued that at this point, from P forward, the note becomes a negotiable instrument if it then satisfies the other requirements of negotiability. With a tug of the bootstraps, T would be a holder; and the note contained words of negotiability when it first came into her possession.
- ◆ A different case is a fully negotiable note payable to P's order that P indorses, "Pay T." The note remains negotiable because, at the time of issue, it contained words of negotiability.

The opposite case is the payee striking the words of negotiability in an instrument that is fully negotiable. The court held in *Key Bank v. Strober Bros., Inc.*, 423 N.Y.S.2d 855 (A.D. N.Y. 1988), that negotiability is destroyed.

J. NO OTHER UNDERTAKING OR INSTRUCTION

The final requirement of negotiability is that beyond the maker's order or promise to pay money, the instrument itself must not contain "any other undertaking or instruction" by the maker or drawer "to do any act in addition to the payment of money," 3-104(a)(3), with a few exceptions that Article 3 describes. For example:

- An instrument is not negotiable that also contains a promise or order to render services or to sell or lease property.
- An Article 9 security agreement or some other subsidiary understanding can live within a contract for the sale of goods or lease of real estate, but a negotiable instrument cannot reside there.
- Similarly, a combination note and real mortgage is not negotiable. *P & K Marble, Inc. v. La Paglia*, 537 N.Y.S.2d 682 (A.D. 1989).
- Also, a partnership subscription in the form of a note is nonnegotiable *Woodworth v. Richmond Indiana Venture*, 13 UCC Rep. Serv. 1149 (Ohio Ct. Com. Pl. 1990) (The note authorized the partnership to terminate the maker's partnership interest upon a default in paying the note.).

A negotiable instrument can freely exist along with a separate sales contract or other undertaking or instruction that supplements or even modifies the instrument, 3-117; but the latter must not be included within the former if the combination violates 3-104(a). It is their integration that precludes negotiability. On the other hand, if the whole passes the test of 3-104(a), it is a negotiable instrument even if it is also something else. See, e.g., *Accounts Management Corp. v. Lyman Ranch*, 748 P.2d 919 (Mont. 1987) ("check-note" divided in two halves with top being an inventory of the debt).

1. Some Additions Article 3 Allows

There are exceptions to the rule against additional undertakings or instructions. The principal exceptions are incorporated into 3-104(a) itself. Negotiability is not affected if the writing also contains:

- an undertaking or power to give, maintain, or protect collateral to secure payment,
- an authorization or power to the holder to confess judgment or realize on or dispose of collateral, or
- a waiver for the benefit of any law intended for the advantage or protection of an obligor.

3-104(a)(3)(i-iii). It is therefore possible to put an Article 9 security agreement in a note; and it is common for notes to include language whereby indorsers, sureties, and other parties waive requirements of notice and also waive other rights under Article 3 and rights to collateral and other protections under Article 9. Each of these exceptions strengthens the promise or order to pay money and has no independent value of its own.

There are other terms that can be included in an instrument (and often are) without affecting negotiability. Good examples are the place where the instrument is issued or payable, see 3-111 (place of payment), and the date of issue. See 3-113(b) (date of instrument). These and other terms are benign and permissible so long as they are not additional instructions or undertakings that negotiability forbids, and so long as the terms do not compromise any other provision of the instrument that is essential in satisfying another requirement of negotiability.

2. Common Extra Stuff Not Necessary
Relatedly, negotiability is unaffected by not including terms that are commonly included in instruments, except for terms that are essential for negotiability. Negotiability is exclusively defined by the requirements of 3-104(a). An instrument is created by any writing that meets them. Really, these requirements are very few and slim, so that very short and skimpy instruments are possible, not uncommon, and even encouraged by the narrowness and usual intolerance of 3-104(a) for anything beyond its plain letter.

K. NEGOTIABILITY (OR NOT) BY DECLARATION

1. Effect Of Declaration That Writing Is Negotiable
After tediously examining the requirements for negotiability, one might ask whether the parties can shortcut the matter by simply declaring on the writing that it is "intended to be negotiable" or by stamping it "NEGOTIABLE." Does such a declaration by the maker or drawer, by itself, establish a writing as a negotiable instrument under Article 3? No. "[A] writing cannot be made a negotiable instrument within Article 3 by contract or conduct of its parties * * *." 3-104 comment 2. The only way that a writing becomes an Article 3 instrument is to satisfy the 3-104 requisites of negotiability. Thus, for example, if a writing were payable in other than money or contained a conditional promise, a statement that "This Note is Negotiable" would not be effective to qualify the writing as an instrument.

On the other hand, if an otherwise negotiable note lacks the exact, magic words "payable to order" but declares on its face that it is "NEGOTIABLE," the declaration might itself satisfy the requirement of words of negotiability. It is intended as a substitute for the magic words, is a close equivalent, and does not undercut the commercial justifications for the concept of negotiability. The new Article 3, however, is less clear than former law that equivalent language is sufficient.

2. Effect Of Declaration That Instrument Is Nonnegotiable
a. General Rule
The opposite issue is whether or not the parties can use a form that is a negotiable instrument and avoid negotiability by declaring, on the instrument, that it is *not* negotiable. The answer is yes, except for a check.

A promise or order *other than a check* is not an instrument if, at the time it is issued or first comes into possession of a holder, it contains a *conspicuous* statement, however expressed, to the effect that the promise or order is not negotiable or is not an instrument governed by this Article.

3-104(d) (emphasis added). The effect is the same as eliminating the words of negotiability.

Example: "[A] promissory note can be stamped with the legend NOT NEGOTIABLE. The effect * * * is not only to negate the possibility of a holder in due course, but to prevent the writing from being a negotiable instrument for any purpose." 3-104 comment 3; see, e.g., *Isaacson v. Isaacson*, 508 So.2d 1131 (Miss. 1987) (CDs).

b. Exception for Checks

A declaration on a check that it is not negotiable is ineffective. The explanation is probably the same reason that a check without words of negotiability is fully negotiable. See 3-104(c). Such a declaration, like the absence of order or bearer language, is uncommon in checks and unexpected, and so could "easily be overlooked and should not affect the rights of holders who may pay money or give credit for a check without being aware that it is not in the conventional form." 3-104 comment 2.

L. INCOMPLETE INSTRUMENTS

"Incomplete instrument" is a term of art with a special, limited meaning and special rules, mainly about the effect of completion by someone other than the issuer. It is considered here because the term can include a writing that is not truly an instrument for the reason that the requirements of negotiability are not fully satisfied. Be careful! This is not to say that an incomplete instrument is any order or promise that for any reason fails any of the requisites of negotiability. It does not include, for example, a draft ordering "Pay to B." An "incomplete instrument" is "a signed writing, whether or not issued by the signer, the contents of which show at the time of signing that it is incomplete but that the signer intended it to be completed by the addition of words or numbers." 3-115(a). It includes a true instrument that, though incomplete, satisfies the requisites of negotiability (e.g., a note for which the parties intended a due date but failed to state it), and also a writing that fails these requisites but is intended to satisfy them and be an instrument when complete. In both cases the test is "whether the contents show that it is incomplete and that the signer intended that additional words or numbers be added." 3-115 comment 1.

An "incomplete instrument" that is not truly an instrument will nevertheless become an instrument, and be treated as such in every respect under Article 3, if the requirements of negotiability are met when it is completed. 3-115(b).

Example: An example is a check with the amount not filled in. The check cannot be enforced until the amount is filled in. If the payee fills in an amount authorized by the drawer the check meets the requirements of 3-104 and is enforceable as completed. If the payee fills in an unauthorized amount there is an alteration of the check and Section 3-407 applies. 3-115 comment 3.

In contrast, a note that the maker deliberately issues "Pay P" does not become an instrument by P adding words of negotiability. The rules of 3-115 would not apply as in the example of the check lacking an amount. In this case, the note was not an incomplete instrument. The maker intended the "Pay P" form. She did not intend that anybody would add order language.

M. DATES AND PLACES

1. Date Of Instrument
a. Date Normally Not Required
Negotiability requires that an instrument is payable on demand or at a definite time, but normally does not require dating the instrument to show when it was created, signed, or issued by the maker or drawer. For example, if an instrument is payable "on July 1, 1992," a date for the instrument is unnecessary. The same is true if the instrument is payable "on demand."

b. Except When Tied to Time of Payment
On the other hand, if a date is essential to fix maturity, as in an instrument payable "thirty days after date," the date is required for negotiability. Its absence prevents the order or promise from being payable at a definite time and, in this form, it is not payable on demand. It is thus not negotiable. If, however, the order or promise is an "incomplete instrument," it becomes negotiable by adding a date if the other requirements for negotiability are satisfied. 3-115(b).

c. Antedating or Postdating Instrument
1) Effect on Negotiability
Negotiability is not affected by antedating or postdating an instrument. 3-113(a). The time when it is payable is determined by the stated date if the instrument is payable at a fixed period after the date. Id.

Example: Suppose that a note was issued on June 1 but was dated July 1, and was payable one month after date. The time of payment is August 1. Also, a note dated April 20 and stated to be payable one week after date would be due upon issue if it were not issued until May 1.

Similarly, "an instrument payable on demand is not payable before the date of the instrument." Id.

Example: A demand note issued on May 1 but dated May 5 would not be due until May 5.

2) Effects of Postdating

The usual reason for issuing a postdated check is to obtain an extension of credit. By issuing such a check, a drawer promises in effect to have funds on deposit when the check falls due.

a) Criminal Liability Of Drawer

Absent an intent to defraud when the check is issued, there is no crime or civil wrong in issuing a postdated check knowing that there are not then sufficient funds on deposit to cover it, even though the check is dishonored for lack of funds on the date stated.

b) Civil Liability of Drawee

A different question is whether the drawee bank wrongs the drawer by paying the check earlier than the stated date. The answer is generally no, unless the bank had been alerted beforehand that the postdated check was issued and should not be earlier paid. 4-401(c).

2. Place Of Payment

Negotiability does not require that an instrument state the place where it is payable. Rather, the law implies that the place of payment is the place of business of the drawee or maker or her residence if she has no place of business. 3-111. The instrument can specify a different place. Negotiability is unaffected and the instrument is payable there. Id.

REVIEW QUESTIONS

1. What is an "instrument" within the meaning of U.C.C. Article 3?

2. List Article 3's requisites of negotiability.

3.   Name the two basic kinds of instruments, and distinguish them.

4.   Ms. Jones borrowed $100,000 from First Bank and signed the following writing:

NOTE

Thirty days after date, I (We) promise to pay to First Bank the sum of one hundred thousand dollars ($100,000) plus interest at the rate of ten percent (10%).

Explain why this writing is *not* an Article 3 instrument.

5.   Would the writing be an instrument if it were in the form of a check, ordering the drawer's own bank to pay First Bank?

6.   What is the significance of the nonnegotiability of the "Note" in Question 4.

7.   Suppose Ms. Jones signed and dated this writing:

NOTE

I (We) promise to pay to First Bank, or its order, at its principal office in Kansas City, Missouri, the sum of one hundred thousand dollars ($100,000) plus interest at the rate of ten percent (10%), secured by collateral described in a separate agreement executed herewith. Signatories waive presentment, dishonor, notice of dishonor, and all rights with respect to collateral.

Is this writing an instrument?

8.   Decide if the writing in Question 7, which Ms. Jones signed and dated, would be an instrument if its terms were changed so that:

     a.   the interest rate is "five points in excess of the Federal Reserve discount rate on the day of demand."

     b.   the reference to the collateral also provides that the agreement creating collateral controls over the terms of the Note.

     c.   the time for payment is "upon a five percent decline in gross sales of Maker's business."

     d.   payment is due "90 days after date."

e.   the Note provides for payment "90 days after date," and also provides for a 30-day extension if "Maker's gross sales increase by more than five percent during the initial term of this Note."

f.   the Note provides for payment "90 days after date," but also states that "signatories agree to such extensions as Bank in its discretion may allow."

g.   the Note provides for payment "90 days after date," but allows First Bank to accelerate payment "according to the provisions for acceleration specified in the agreement for collateral executed even date herewith."

h.   the Note restricts payment to available funds in a particular account.

9.   A written and signed promise states, "I promise to pay $100,000 to the order of Joe Doe if he conveys title to Blackacre to me." Is this promise an instrument?

10.   A signed note states, "This note is subject to a contract of sale dated April 1, 1990 between the payee and maker of this note." Is it negotiable?

11.   A signed note states, "Rights and obligations of the parties with respect to this note are stated in an agreement dated April 1, 1990 between the payee and maker of this note." Is this note netgotiable?

12.   Assume that M hands P a note that provides, "I promise to pay $1000 to the order of P on demand. (Signed) M." In doing so M says, "This money will not be paid unless a bond is delivered to me." Is the note negotiable?

13.   Suppose that a note contains the following statement: "This note is secured by a security interest in collateral described in a security agreement dated April 1, 1990 between the payee and maker of this note. Rights and obligations with respect to the collateral are [stated in] [governed by] the security agreement." Is it negotiable?

14.   Suppose a signed, written promise states, "In consideration of John Doe's promise to convey title to Blackacre I promise to pay $100,000 to the order of John Doe." Is this promise an instrument?

15.   Is the negotiability of a note destroyed if it is payable at a definite time and on demand?

III

CONTRACT LIABILITY
ON INSTRUMENTS

Analysis

A. *fundamental Requisites of Liability*
  1. *Signature*
  2. *Delivery (Issuance)*
B. *Nature Of Liability*
  1. *Significance Of Capacity*
  2. *Primary Versus Secondary Liability*
c. *Capacities*
  1. *Maker*
  2. *Drawer*
  3. *Acceptor*
  4. *Indorser*
  5. *In Case Of Doubt About Person's Capacity*
D. *dishonor and other Conditions To Secondary Liability*
  1. *Dishonor*
  2. *Presentment*
  3. *Notice Of Dishonor*
  4. *Consequence Of Delay In Presentment Or Notice*
  5. *Excusing Conditions Altogether Or Delay*
E. *Liabilities on Specialized "Checks"*
  1. *Certified Check*
  2. *Cashier's Check*
  3. *Money Order*
  4. *Teller's Check*
  5. *Traveler's Checks*

Fundamentally, an Article 3 instrument is a kind of contract -- a promissory obligation for the breach of which the law gives a remedy. This contract is distinctive, however. It is governed by Article 3 which explains such matters as how a person becomes liable on an instrument, the nature and extent of her liability, the procedures for enforcing the liability, the defenses to enforcement, and virtually every other aspect of the obligations borne by persons who are liable on instruments.

This liability on an instrument is separate from the obligor's liability on the underlying transaction that gave rise to the instrument. For example, when a purchaser of goods pays by check, or buys on credit and issues a note for the price, she is liable for the price of the goods under Article 2 which governs the sale transaction. She is also liable on the check or note under Article 3. Ordinarily, liability on an instrument is in addition to, rather than in place of, liability on the underlying transaction. The two bases of liability are naturally and legally related, but they are also different. The point is that liability on an instrument is a distinct obligation. Indeed, a person can be liable on an instrument even though there is no sale or other underlying transaction.

This chapter primarily addresses the incidents of liability on Article 3 instruments and incidentally deals with the relationship between liability on an instrument and the underlying transaction (if there is one) that produced the instrument.

A. FUNDAMENTAL REQUISITES OF LIABILITY

It is commonly said that a person's liability on an instrument depends on two conditions -- her signature on the instrument and delivery. A signature is certainly a condition to liability. Article 3 flatly declares that no person is liable on an instrument unless she or her representative signs it. 3-401(a). Technically, however, delivery is not a condition to liability. Rather, lack of delivery is a defense to liability, except as against a holder in due course. In any event, both signature and delivery are discussed here.

1. Signature

The most basic rule governing liability on negotiable instruments is that "[a] person is not liable on an instrument unless (i) the person signed the instrument, or (ii) the person is represented by an agent or representative who signed the instrument and the signature is binding on the represented person under Section 3-402." 3-401(a).

a. Mechanics of Signature

"A signature may be made (i) manually or by means of a device or machine, and (ii) by the use of any name, including a trade or assumed name, or by a word, mark, or symbol executed or adopted by a person with present intention to authenticate a writing." 3-401(b).

Example: B issued a check in payment of goods purchased from S. Instead of signing the check by hand, B impressed her name on the instrument using an inked, rubber stamp that bears her facsimile signature. B's signature appears on the check.

Example: The University's payroll carries thousands of people. Some of them are paid by direct deposit to their bank accounts. The majority, however, get checks that the University prints by computer, complete with the facsimile signature of the University president. These checks are signed.

b. Signature by Agent
1) Liability of Principal

A person may sign an instrument by a representative. The represented person is bound on the instrument -- even if her name is not used - if she would be bound by extra-Code law that determines when agents can bind principals on simple contracts. Under agency law, and thus under Article 3, "[t]he power to sign for another may be an express authority, or it may be implied in law or in fact, or it may rest merely upon apparent authority." 3-403 comment 1 (1989 Official Text). "If the represented person is bound [under the law of agency], the signature of the representative is the 'authorized signature of the represented person' and the represented person is liable on the instrument, whether or not identified in the instrument," 3-402(a).

2) Liability of Agent
a) Standard Rule

Even when an authorized representative is acting for someone else, her signature on the instrument may appear to be solely for her own benefit and can mislead third parties who know nothing different. Therefore, when an authorized representative signs her name to an instrument, even while acting for the principal and with the principal's specific authority, *the representative is herself prima facie liable* unless:

- ◆ the form of the signature shows unambiguously that the agent made the signature on behalf of the represented person, and
- ◆ the instrument identifies the represented person.

3-402(b)(1). By this rule the representative is freely and entirely safe only if both conditions are met, as by signing "P, by A, Treasurer." 3-402 comment 2. In this case she avoids liability as a matter of law. If the form of the representative's signature fails *either* of these conditions or both of them, she is liable on the instrument unless she "proves that the original parties did not intend the representative to be liable on the instrument." 3-402(b)(2). In effect, it is a defense to liability that the representative acted for someone else and that her signature was not intended to be personally binding. She can assert this defense against anyone, except a holder in due course who "took the instrument without notice that the representative was not intended to be liable on the instrument." Id. It makes no difference to the availability or applicability of the defense that the instrument shows nothing but the representative's signature in her own name and is entirely silent as to both the principal's identity and the representative's capacity. Even in this case, except as against the innocent holder in due course, the representative is free to prove the defense that the original parties did not intend to bind her on the instrument.

Example: John Doe is the authorized agent of Richard Roe. Doe signs a note for Roe. They and the payee intend that Roe will be liable on the instrument but not Doe. Doe signs for Roe in the following way:

- ◆ "Doe signs 'John Doe' without indicating in the note that Doe is signing as agent. The note does not identify Richard Roe as the represented person;
- ◆ "Doe signs 'John Doe, Agent' but the note does not identify Richard Roe as the represented person; or
- ◆ "The name 'Richard Roe' is written on the note and immediately below that name Doe signs 'John Doe' without indicating that Doe signed as agent."

3-402 comment 2. The payee sells the note. "In each case Doe is liable on the instrument to a holder in due course without notice that Doe was not intended to be liable. In none of the cases does Doe's signature unambiguously show that Doe was signing as agent for an identified principal. * * * But the situation is different if a holder in due course is not involved. * * * [In this event] Doe is prima facie liable * * *. But Doe can escape liability by proving that the original parties did not intend that he be liable on the note." Id.

b) Exceptional Rule for Checks

An exceptional rule that better protects the agent applies to checks. By law, the authorized agent is not liable to anyone on a check that she draws on the principal's account, *even if the agent neglects to indicate her agency status*, so long as the check identifies the principal. 3-402(c). The reason is that such a check effectively identifies somebody else as the owner of the account and thus the true obligor. Therefore, "nobody is deceived into thinking that the person signing the check is meant to be liable." 3-402 comment 3.

Example: John Doe is the authorized agent of Richard Roe. Doe signs a check for Roe. The check is drawn on Roe's account and names Roe as the owner of the account. Doe signs "John Doe" without indicating in the note that he is signing as agent. Nothing more identifies Richard Roe as the represented person. Doe is not liable, not even prima facie. There is no reason for him to prove anything about the original parties' intent.

c. **Liabilities When Person's Name Is Signed by Unauthorized Agent (Including Forger)**

When a person's name is placed on an instrument by someone acting without authority to do so, the person whose name is signed is not liable on the instrument because she has not signed it. 3-401(a) & 3-403(a). The signature operates, however, "as the signature of the unauthorized signer in favor of a person who in good faith pays the instrument or takes it for value." 3-403(a).

Example: T stole D's checkbook and forged D's name on a check she completed in the amount of $1000. T then used the check in paying for a snowmobile purchased from S. The check bounced, that is, D's bank dishonored it and promptly returned the check to S because D had notified the bank of the theft of her checkbook. S is looking for people to sue. D is not liable on the instrument, nor is D's bank. Neither of them signed the check, even though both their names appeared on the instrument. T is liable on the instrument, as well as on the underlying sales transaction.

d. **Liability Without Signature**

The general rule is that an unauthorized signature is ineffective to bind the person whose name is signed. 3-403(a). Therefore, an agent's unauthorized signature of a principal does not bind the principal. Similarly, an outright forgery by a thief who steals a checkbook does not create liability for the owner of the checking account even though the forger uses the owner's name and the owner's personal checks. In both cases, the only person liable on the instrument is the unauthorized signer. Id. In two situations, however, exceptional rules apply to bind the person whose name is signed even though she did not authorize the signature and the signature was a complete forgery.

1) Ratification

A person's unauthorized or forged signature binds her if she ratifies the signature. 3-403(a).

> Ratification is a retroactive adoption of the unauthorized signature by the person whose name is signed and may be found from conduct as well as from express statements. For example, it may be found from the retention of benefits received in the transaction with knowledge of the unauthorized signature. Although the forger is not an agent, ratification is governed by the rules and principles applicable to ratification of unauthorized acts of an agent.

3-403 comment 3.

2) Culpability or Fault

More important, a person is bound even by her forged signature if she is responsible or culpable or at fault with respect to the making of the signature. This statement of principle is a broad generalization that is not itself law but summarizes particular expressions of the principle that are law.

a) Estoppel

For example, there is the possibility of common-law estoppel against the person who name is signed, "as where he expressly or tacitly represents to an innocent purchaser that the signature is genuine * * * ." 3-404 comment 4 (1989 Official Text).

b) Negligence -- 3-406

A much wider example is the rule that a person cannot complain of her forged signature that results from her own negligence. It is codified in section 3-406, which provides:

> A person whose failure to exercise ordinary care substantially contributes to an alteration of an instrument or to the making of a forged signature on an instrument is precluded from asserting the alteration or the forgery against a person who, in good faith, pays the instrument or takes it for value or for collection.

3-406(a). For example, a person who is in the habit of using a signature stamp or an automatic signing device might substantially contribute to a forgery by negligently allowing outsiders to have access to it. Absent the negligence and 3-406, the person would escape liability because her signature would be missing from the instrument. Because of the negligence and 3-406, she is precluded or stopped or prevented from using the forgery as a defense. She is liable.

Section 3-406 does not protect or work in favor of everybody. It is, in effect, a defense that is only available to a person who, in good faith, pays the instrument or takes it for value or for collection. Moreover, under former law, even a person whom 3-406 was designed to protect would lose her protection if she herself had acted unreasonably in dealing with the instrument -- failed to follow the usual commercial standards and practices of her business. Now, under the 1990 Article 3, this negligence is considered only comparatively and is not a contributory, absolute bar. The rule is *comparative* negligence:

> Under [3-406(a)], if the person asserting the preclusion fails to exercise ordinary care in paying or taking the instrument and that failure substantially contributes to loss, the loss is allocated between the person precluded and the person asserting the preclusion according to the extent to which the failure of each to exercise ordinary care contributed to the loss.

3-406(b).

c) Special Rules for Indorsements -- 3-404 and 3-405
Wider culpability than negligence is behind two other rules that give effect to unauthorized signatures, 3-404 and 3-405, but they deal only with indorsements. They give effect to unauthorized indorsements when the maker or drawer is fooled by an impostor, does not intend the payee to have any interest in the instrument, or issues the instrument to a fictitious payee, and also when the indorser is an employee whom the employer entrusted with responsibility with respect to the instrument. Because indorsements typically are most important as part of the process of negotiating order instruments, 3-404 and 3-405 are discussed later in the context of negotiation. See Chapter IV infra.

e. **Signature Without Capacity or Liability**
Sometimes a person whose signature appears on an instrument is not liable in any capacity because it is clear that she signed for a benign purpose. For

example, a person normally would not be liable on the instrument if she placed "witness" after her name. Nor would she be liable if she signed below the words "payment received" because these words show a purpose to give a receipt. In each case the signature is benign -- no capacity, no liability -- because it unambiguously shows that the purpose of signing is something other than becoming a party to the instrument. See 3-204 comment 1.

> *Example:* The payee of a check cashes it at a collecting bank. The bank asks her to sign the back of the check as a receipt for the money. The payee signs her name with the accompanying words indicating that the signature was meant only as a receipt. The payee is not liable on the instrument.

> *Example:* The owner of a traveler's check countersigns the check when she uses it to pay for a Twins T-shirt.

2. Delivery (Issuance)

a. The Significance of Delivery (or Nondelivery)

Practically speaking, a maker of a note, or a drawer of a check, will not be liable on an instrument that she signs and immediately hides in a desk drawer. She must "*issue*" it, which means "the first *delivery* of an instrument by the maker or drawer, whether to a holder or nonholder, for the purpose of giving rights on the instrument to any person." 3-105(a) (emphasis added). "The general rule is that a promissory note [or other instrument] has no effect unless it is delivered." *Matter of Estate of Balkus*, 128 Wis. 2d 246, 253, 381 N.W.2d 593, 597 (App. 1985). In truth, however, a person can be liable on an undelivered instrument. The rule is that "[a]n unissued instrument * * * is binding on the maker or drawer * * *." 3-105(b). Nonissuance is only a defense, id., that is not an effective defense against a holder in due course. 3-305(a)(2)&(b); 3-305 comment 2. In any event, whether nonissuance is seen as preventing liability in the first instance, or as providing a defense to liability, the meaning of its core concept -- delivery -- is important because, under either view, lack of delivery and nonissuance can preclude liability on an instrument.

b. The Meaning of Delivery

The U.C.C. defines delivery as "voluntary transfer of possession," 1-201(14), and the first delivery of an instrument is referred to as "issue." 3-105(a). The common law gives content to these definitions because delivery is a long established and fully developed concept in the law of property. The issue of delivery most often arises in cases involving alleged gifts of instruments. In this context delivery means "the transfer of possession from one party to another * * * [requiring] the exercise of the will to transfer on the part of the transferor

* * * [and the actual passing] from the possession, that is, from the dominion and control, of the donor into that of the donee." R. Brown, THE LAW OF PERSONAL PROPERTY § 7.3 (3d ed. W. Raushenbush 1975). Although a constructive delivery may be sufficient, such "delivery occurs only when the maker indicates an intention to make the instrument an enforceable obligation against him or her by surrendering control over it and intentionally placing it under the power of the payee or a third person." *Matter of Estate of Balkus*, 128 Wis. 2d 246, 253, 381 N.W.2d 593, 597 (App. 1985).

Example: Upon Ms. Jones's death, her personal representative found among Ms. Jones's papers a demand note for $5000 made payable to a nephew. A notation on the instrument indicated that it was intended as a gift for the nephew. The nephew asserted a claim against the estate based on the note. The claim is invalid because there was no delivery sufficient to establish a gift, and there had been no delivery for purposes of Article 3 so that Ms. Jones never became liable on the note or had a defense to liability.

B. NATURE OF LIABILITY

1. Significance Of Capacity

A person's signature on an instrument subjects her to prima facie liability on the instrument, but the nature of this liability is not the same for every signer. It varies with the capacity in which the person signed the instrument. *Capacity* refers to the role the signer plays with respect to the instrument itself:

- maker,
- drawer,
- acceptor, or
- indorser.

The signature creates liability. The person's capacity defines and limits this liability by describing the statutory contours of liability, including when liability is triggered and discharged. So defined, a person's liability on an instrument that results from her signature is known as her "*contract of liability*."

2. Primary Versus Secondary Liability

In general, the liability of makers and acceptors is described as *primary*, while the liability of drawers and indorsers is *secondary*. For this purpose, *secondary liability* does not mean that somebody else is more or earlier *liable* on the instrument. It means that enforcing the drawer's or indorser's liability is conditioned on someone else not paying or accepting the instrument who (party or not) was expected to do so. This refusal is called *dishonor*, which is a condition on the liability of a drawer of a draft and the indorser of any instrument.

> *Example:* Consider, for example, an ordinary draft or check that has not been accepted. The only person *liable* on the instrument is the drawer. A drawee is named but is not *liable* on the draft because she has not signed it. On the other hand, the draft itself directs the holder to seek payment from the drawee, and everyone expects the drawee to pay. They also expect that the drawer will not be required to pay unless the drawee dishonors. It is in this sense that liability is secondary.

Primary liability means that the maker or acceptor is obligated to pay without initial resort to anyone else. Her liability is up front, not backup.

In detail, however, the liabilities of makers and acceptors are not exactly alike; and the differences in the liabilities of drawers and indorsers are even greater in some respects, especially under the new Article 3. Most noticeably, an indorser's liability requires giving her notice of dishonor that former law also required for a drawer. Under the new law, this notice is not generally a condition on a drawer's liability. This change in the terms of a drawer's liability is reported to mean that a drawer's liability is now primary rather than secondary. See 3-414 comment 2. This overstates the effect of the change because now, as before, a drawer is generally not liable unless the drawee dishonors. In this sense, a drawer's liability -- now as before -- is secondary. In truth, however, whether a drawer's liability is properly described as primary or secondary is mostly academic. Article 3 itself does not use the terms *primary* and *secondary* to describe liability or parties. The two terms are not themselves part of the law. Mainly, they are organizing concepts that aid in explaining the law. Article 3 itself separately and independently describes the terms and conditions of each capacity.

C. CAPACITIES

1. Maker
a. Definition
"'Maker' means a person who signs or is identified in a note as a person undertaking to pay." 3-103(a)(5). A maker normally signs in the lower right-hand corner of the note.

b. Primary Liability
Basically, the maker of a note "is obliged to pay the instrument * * * according to its terms at the time it was issued" or, if the maker signed an incomplete note, "according to its terms when completed * * *." 3-412. This obligation runs "to a person entitled to enforce the instrument or to an indorser who paid the instrument * * *." Id. It is primary liability. The maker must pay the note at maturity absent discharge or some other defense that is effective against the person who wants payment. Nobody else must first fail to pay the note; and normally, nobody else is liable to the maker on the instrument after she pays it. The instrument is then finished or expended, so long as the maker reacquires it and does not reissue it.

2. Drawer
a. Definition
"'Drawer' means a person who signs or is identified in a draft as a person ordering payment." 3-103(a)(3). A drawer normally signs in the lower right-hand corner of the draft and names the drawee in the lower left-hand corner.

b. Liability is Secondary -- Conditioned on Dishonor
The drawer is obligated to pay the draft only if the instrument is dishonored, 3-414(b)&(d), which basically means that the drawee fails to pay or accept the draft upon due and proper presentment for payment or acceptance. See 3-502. (What constitutes *dishonor* that fixes or triggers the drawer's liability in the ordinary case is discussed in more detail later in this chapter under conditions to secondary liability.) Unlike the maker of a note, the drawer of a draft does not expressly promise to pay the instrument. She does not even expect to pay it personally. Instead, the drawer orders someone else, the drawee, to pay the draft. It is only if the drawee fails to pay the instrument that the drawer expects to do so herself. Consider the ordinary check. The drawer in effect says to the bank, "Pay the amount of this check to the holder when she presents it and charge my account." In effect, she says to the payee, "Take this check to the bank and ask for payment and if it does not pay, come back to me and I will." This conditional promise is not stated in the draft she signs, which contains no promise but only an order expressed by the word "Pay" addressed to the drawee. Rather, the drawer's promise is implied in the draft.

1) Presentment Required
Dishonor that is a condition to the drawer's liability normally requires presentment of the draft, so that presentment too is normally a condition to her liability -- a derivative condition. In a rare case, delay in presentment

may discharge a drawer's liability on a check. 3-414(f). Presentment is discussed later in this chapter under conditions of secondary liability.

2) Notice of Dishonor NOT Required

A drawer's liability is *not* conditioned on notice of dishonor, except in the case of a draft accepted by a non-bank. In this case, the acceptance effectively converts the drawer's liability to that of an indorser, whose liability is usually conditioned on notice of dishonor. See 3-414(d); 3-415(a); & 3-503(a).

c. Qualifications/Exceptions

1) Primary Liability When Drawer Is Also Drawee

The drawee of a draft is usually someone other than the drawer. For some purposes, however, it is convenient for a drawer to draft against itself. The most common example is a cashier's check, but ordinary drafts are sometimes drawn this way. The negotiability of such an instrument is tested by the usual requisites of negotiability and, in typical form, passes the test. That the drawer and drawee are the same person does not defeat negotiability. On the other hand, the drawer's liability is different on a draft that she draws on herself. When the drawee is someone else, the drawer's liability is secondary. She promises to pay only if the drawee fails to pay. When the drawer is also the drawee, her liability is the very same as the maker of a note. It is primary liability. 3-414(a), 3-412. This liability is not denied or conditioned by the usual rule that a drawee lacks liability absent acceptance (3-408). Even without acceptance, the drawer-drawee is liable as a drawer with the primary liability which 3-412 equally applies to the maker of a note and the drawer of a draft who is also the drawee.

2) Liability Upon Acceptance

a) Liability Changes If Acceptor Is Not a Bank

If someone other than a bank accepts a draft, the drawer's liability changes slightly. It remains secondary -- conditioned on dishonored -- but, technically, is converted to an indorser's liability. 3-414(d). Here is the explanation:

> The drawer of an unaccepted draft is the only party liable on the instrument. * * * The drawee has no liability on the draft. Section 3-408. When the draft is accepted, the obligations change. The drawee, as acceptor, becomes primarily liable and the drawer's liability is that of a person secondarily liable as a guarantor of payment. The drawer's liability is identical to that of an indorser * * *.

3-414 comment 4. The largest effects are that, with the liability of an indorser, the drawer is entitled to notice of dishonor and has a right of recourse against the acceptor.

b) **Liability Is Discharged If Bank Accepts**
"If a draft is accepted by a bank, the drawer is discharged, regardless of when or by whom acceptance was obtained." 3-414(c). The explanation is that "[h]olders that have a bank obligation do not normally rely on the drawer to guarantee the bank's solvency." 3-414 comment 3.

d. Disclaiming Liability
1) Ordinary Drafts
As a general rule, a drawer may avoid contract liability on an *ordinary draft* by adding words to her drawer's signature that disclaim liability to pay the draft. The most commonly-used disclaimer are the words "without recourse." 3-414(e).

Example: Suppose, in a documentary sale, Seller draws a draft on Buyer for the price of goods shipped to Buyer. The draft is payable upon delivery to the drawee of an order bill of lading covering the goods. Seller delivers the draft with the bill of lading to Finance Company that is named as payee of the draft. If Seller draws without recourse Finance Company takes the risk that Buyer will dishonor. If Buyer dishonors, Finance Company has no recourse against Seller but it can obtain reimbursement by selling the goods which it controls through the bill of lading. 3-414 comment 5.

2) Checks
A drawer of a *check*, however, is not permitted to disclaim her liability. "There is no legitimate purpose served by issuing a check on which nobody is liable." 3-414 comment 5.

3. Acceptor
a. Definition
An acceptor is the drawee of a draft who has accepted the instrument by signing it for the purpose of agreeing to pay it as presented to her. 3-103(a)(1) & 3-409(a).

b. Liability Is Primary

The acceptor's liability on the draft, like a maker's liability on a note, is primary. If the instrument is complete when she accepts it, the acceptor becomes obligated to pay the draft according to its terms as of the time of acceptance. 3-413(a).

1) Liability for Changes In Instrument Before Acceptance

Note that the acceptor does not necessarily agree to pay the instrument according to the drawer's terms but rather according to the terms at the time of the acceptance. If between issue and acceptance the instrument has been altered in any respect, the acceptor is liable on and for the amount of the altered instrument, even if the draft states payable "as originally drawn." Id. She may have recourse against the presenter and one or more prior parties, however, as will be explained when liability based on warranties is discussed. See Chapter V infra.

2) Liability for Changes In Instrument After Acceptance

A different problem is an alteration *after* acceptance that raises the amount of the draft. To insure against liability for such a subsequently inflated sum, the acceptor should include in her acceptance the amount that is certified or otherwise accepted.   Otherwise, if the instrument is raised and thereafter acquired by a holder in due course, "the obligation of the acceptor is the amount of the instrument at the time it was taken by the holder in due course," 3-413(b), rather than the amount at the time of acceptance.

3) Liability When Draft Incomplete

If the acceptor signs a draft that is incomplete, as when the amount is blank, she is liable for any authorized amount that is later filled in. Someone filling in an unauthorized amount is treated as an alteration of the instrument. The acceptor is discharged if this alteration is fraudulent. Otherwise, she is liable on the instrument but only to the extent of the authorized amount, except that she is liable for the unauthorized, completed amount to a person who takes the instrument for value, in good faith, and without notice of the alteration.

c. How Accept

A drawee accepts by signing anywhere on the instrument. Nothing more is required. A bank's acceptance of a check is called *certification* and the instrument is then referred to as a *certified check*. 3-409(d). The acceptance "may consist of the drawee's signature alone." 3-409(a). It is customary for an acceptor to sign vertically across the face of the draft, but a drawee's signature anywhere on the draft normally is sufficient because usually the only possible reason for signing it is to accept. 3-409 comment 2. The acceptor may, and usually does, insert the word "accepted" above her signature. She may add the date, which is important information if the draft is payable a stated period "after sight." If the acceptor fails to insert the date of her acceptance, the holder may supply the date in good faith and the inserted date will bind the acceptor. 3-409(c). Also, the acceptor may indicate the place where the draft is payable. 3-410(b). None of this extra information is necessary, but none of it affects negotiability or undermines the acceptance, which is the signature alone.

Under the N.I.L. it was possible to accept by signing the instrument *or* a separate paper such as a telegram or a letter. Because these *extrinsic acceptances* caused a degree of uncertainty inconsistent with the free transferability of commercial paper, the Code provides that the acceptance "must be written on the draft" itself. 3-409(a).

d. When Accept Rather Than Pay
Acceptance occurs upon presentment for acceptance by the payee or other person entitled to enforce the instrument. Practically speaking, any draft can be accepted rather than paid, but acceptance is expected -- and refusing acceptance will amount to dishonor -- only in certain situations, most commonly:

- The draft is payable on a date stated in the draft and presentment for acceptance is duly made before the day the draft becomes payable; or
- The draft is payable on elapse of a period of time after sight or acceptance.

3-502(b)(3-4). In all other situations, payment is expected, and dishonor occurs if the drawee does not pay the draft upon due presentment for payment.

e. Why Accept
Nothing in Article 3 or in other commercial paper law obligates a drawee to accept a draft or a bank to certify a check. 3-409(d). Acceptance results because the drawer and drawee have so arranged under other law and have done so because of business needs and reasons of convenience.

f. Acceptance Affecting Other Parties' Liability
   1) Drawer's Liability
      An acceptance not only creates a contract of liability for the acceptor, it also diluted or discharges the liability of other parties. Always, the effect of acceptance is to convert the drawer's liability to that of an indorser. 3-414(d). The transactional reality is that, in the beginning, the drawer is the principal debtor on the draft because no one else is liable on it. Upon acceptance, the acceptor is typically considered the principal debtor and is

primarily liable, like the maker of a note. The drawer remains liable but is considered more like a surety. The law harmonizes with this custom and practice by transforming the drawer's liability to that of an indorser when the drawee accepts.

2) Drawer's and Indorser's Liability When Bank Accepts
The effect is even greater when the acceptor is a bank. In this case, because of the usually assured solvency of the bank, the reality is that holders rely only on the bank's obligation and not on the liability of other parties to the instrument. For this reason, acceptance of a draft by a bank, including certification of a check, discharges the liability of the drawer and any indorser. 3-414(c), 3-415(d). It makes no difference when acceptance was obtained or who procured it. 3-414 comment 3. Former law is changed that provided for discharge only if the holder obtained acceptance.

g. **Acceptance Varying Draft**
A drawee unwilling to accept a draft as presented to her may tender an acceptance that is different from or varies the draft's terms. She may vary the amount payable, the time of payment, or any other term. In a sense, this variance is an alteration to the instrument but, alone, does not discharge any party. When a drawee proffers an acceptance varying the terms of the draft, two courses are open to the holder. She may refuse the acceptance and treat the draft as dishonored. If she does so, she gives up whatever rights she had against the drawee as acceptor because the drawee may then cancel the acceptance. 3-410(a). On the other hand, the holder may assent and thereby acquire the obligation of the drawee-acceptor to the extent of the varied acceptance. 3-413(a). If the holder follows the latter course, each drawer and indorser who does not expressly, affirmatively assent to the variance is discharged. 3-410(c). The underlying reason for discharging a drawer or indorser who does not affirmatively assent is that she has agreed to be liable on a certain contract and should not be held liable on a different contract unless she agrees to it. The fact that the new contract may even be beneficial to the drawer or indorser is immaterial.

h. **Drawee Who Does Not Accept**
1) No Liability On Instrument
A drawee is the person who is ordered to pay a draft. 3-103(a)(2). A drawee who is not also the drawer is not liable on a draft until she *accepts* it, 3-408, which means signing the draft for the purpose of agreeing to pay it as presented. See 3-409(a). Therefore, so long as the drawee refrains from signing the draft, she incurs no liability to the holder *on the instrument* as the

result of refusing to pay or accept it. If the drawee accepts the draft, she becomes liable but in the role of acceptor rather than drawee.

2) Liability Dehors The Instrument -- Especially Bank as Drawee of Check
    Although a drawee who does not accept is not liable on the instrument, Article 3 does not prevent liability in contract, tort, or under other statutory law because of an obligation or representation that is not an acceptance. Banks as drawees of checks are especially vulnerable.

    A bank as the drawee of a check has no liability on the instrument. It incurs liability on the check only through acceptance. The act of a bank accepting a check is called *certification*.   Article 3, however, does not obligate a bank to certify a check for anyone. Moreover, neither certification nor acceptance otherwise occurs as part of the normal check collection process. So, when a check is dishonored, the person who presented it for payment cannot, in the ordinary course, successfully sue the drawee bank on the instrument. In certain cases, however, the drawee of a check may be liable apart from the instrument on common-law theories or under Article 4, most commonly:

    a) Assignment Theory.
        A bank account creates a debtor-creditor relationship between the bank and the depositor. The bank is indebted to the depositor to the extent of the account balance. A bank account, therefore, is simply a chose in action and is ordinarily assignable. Under Article 3, however, neither a check nor other draft operates of itself as an assignment of any funds in the hands of the drawee available for its payment. There is a soft spot in this rule: Although a check of itself is not an assignment of any funds held by the drawee, an "assignment may * * * appear from other facts, and particularly from other agreements, express or implied; and when the intent to assign is clear the check may be the means by which the assignment is effected." 3-409 comment 1 (1989 Official Text).

        Example: D and L make an express agreement whereby D assigned her checking account to L. L immediately notified D's bank of the assignment. In violation of the assignment to L, D cleans out the account by withdrawing half of the funds and ordering the bank (by check) to pay the rest to Z. Later, L makes a demand on the bank for the funds in D's account. The demand is made by L presenting a check issued to her by D. The check is dishonored because the account is empty. L sues the bank. U.C.C. 3-408 (no liability without acceptance) is no defense for the bank. L is not suing the drawee on the instrument, but rather on the theory that the account has been assigned to her and that, by notifying the bank of the assignment, the bank as obligor with respect to the account was bound to pay the funds only to L. Moreover, L is not basing the assignment on a check. The assignment is based on an express agreement between L and D. The ordinary rules of the common law of assignments would seem to impose liability on the bank. The bank might be protected, however, by statutory laws governing adverse claims to bank deposits. These laws generally immunize banks from accountability to adverse claimants to deposit accounts until such time as a claimant gets judicial recognition of her claim, or the claimant posts a bond indemnifying the bank for liability the bank might suffer in recognizing the claim.

b) **Common-Law Contract -- De Facto Acceptance**
A drawee of a check becomes liable on an instrument upon certifying it. Certification is a form of acceptance. Yet, acceptance, and thus certification, occurs only when the bank signs the instrument. An oral acceptance, or an acceptance written on paper other than the instrument itself, is not possible. Yet, nothing affects any liability in contract, tort or otherwise arising from any obligation or representation which is not an acceptance.

Example: B buys goods from S and tenders a check in payment. Before S accepts the check she telephones the drawee to see whether the check is good. The drawee reports that the account is full of funds and also guarantees that, in any event, the check will be paid. With this assurance S takes B's check. The instrument is ultimately dishonored. S sues the drawee bank. The theory is not that the bank is liable on the instrument as an acceptor or in any other capacity; the theory rather is that the bank made a promise to pay the instrument which is enforceable under common-law principles of contract and reliance. There is authority holding that S should prevail.

c) **Accountability Under Article 4**
In regulating the check collection process U.C.C. Article 4 imposes certain duties on drawee banks, which are referred to there as payor

banks. Especially important are a payor bank's duties in dealing with a check presented for payment. For example, a payor is obligated to act quickly in deciding whether to dishonor a check, usually by its midnight deadline, that is, by midnight of the next banking day following the banking day on which it received the instrument. If this deadline is violated, the drawee-payor bank is *accountable for the item.* See 4-215(a), 4-301 & 4-302. It is as though the payor has paid the item, and the proceeds, i.e., the amount of the item, must be passed to the person who presented it even if the drawer's account is empty. There are other ways in which a payor can be held accountable for a check even before expiration of the bank's midnight deadline. This Article 4 accountability is explored in detail in Chapter VII infra. For present purposes it is enough to know that Article 4 harbors theories on which a drawee can be liable *for* an instrument even though the bank is not liable *on* the instrument.

d) Conversion

Similarly, in the case of an ordinary draft, a drawee may become liable for conversion if, having had a draft presented to her for acceptance or for payment, she not only refuses to pay or accept but also refuses to return the instrument despite a demand for its return. 3-420(a). Although such a refusal does not constitute an acceptance, the result is possibly the same because damages for conversion can equal the face amount of the draft. 3-420(b).

4. Indorser
a. Definition

An indorser is someone who is not a maker, drawer, or acceptor and who signs an instrument (whether a note or draft) in order to negotiate it, restrict payment, or just to incur liability on the instrument. 3-204(a). Her signature is called an *indorsement.* Id. An instrument is most commonly indorsed for the purpose of negotiating an order instrument so that the transferee becomes a holder. See Chapter IV infra. An indorsement is usually in the margin or on the reverse side of the instrument but can appear anywhere. It is the purpose of the signature, not its placement, that determines indorsement. Yet, as is true of every signature, its placement on the instrument helps to define the purpose.

b. Liability Is Secondary -- Conditioned on Dishonor

An indorser's liability is secondary. Her obligation, like a drawer's, is to pay only if the instrument is dishonored. 3-415(a). **An indorser's liability is conditioned on dishonor regardless of the nature of the instrument, even when the instrument is a note.**

1) Presentment

Presentment usually is a necessary part of dishonor. Therefore, presentment usually is a derivative condition on the indorser's liability. In order to trigger an indorser's liability on a note, the instrument must be presented to the maker for payment. It is the maker's dishonor that triggers the indorser's liability on the note. In the case of a draft, the drawee's or acceptor's dishonor is the trigger. In the case of a check, delay in presentment discharges an indorser. 3-415(e).

2) Notice of Dishonor

"The obligation of an indorser * * * may not be enforced unless (i) the indorser * * * is given notice of dishonor of the instrument complying with this section or (ii) notice of dishonor is excused * * *." 3-503(a). Unexcused delay in notifying an indorser -- either on a note or a draft -- discharges her liability. 3-415(c) & 3-503(c)

c. **Exceptional Rule With Respect to Liability on Draft -- Effect of Bank's Acceptance**

"If a draft is accepted by a bank after an indorsement is made, the liability of the indorser * * * is discharged." 3-415(d). The drawer's liability is also discharged. 3-414(c).

d. **Multiple Indorsers**

Several people may indorse the same instrument. Upon dishonor and with proper notice, the person entitled to enforce the instrument may immediately proceed against any one of the indorsers without proceeding against the others. It can therefore become important to determine if the indorser who is required to pay has any rights against the other indorsers or anyone else. Generally, indorsers are liable to one another in the order in which they indorse, that is, each indorser is liable to every subsequent indorser. Thus, an indorser who pays can recover from people who indorsed before her, and any indorser can recover directly from the maker or drawer.

e. **Disclaiming Liability (Qualified Indorsement)**

An indorser can disclaim her contract of liability on the instrument by *qualifying* her indorsement, which means adding to her signature words such as "without recourse" or the like. 3-415(b). These words usually precede, but may follow, the signature. Although a *qualified indorser* incurs no contract liability on the instrument, she incurs liability on warranties as do unqualified indorsers and persons who transfer an instrument without any indorsement. See Chapter V infra. An indorsement that is not qualified is unqualified. Every indorsement is either qualified or unqualified. Typically, it is unqualified. Someone who gives value for an instrument is entitled to the transferor's unqualified indorsement. 3-203(c).

5. In Case Of Doubt About Person's Capacity

A person occasionally signs an instrument in some unusual place that creates doubt about her capacity, but capacity becomes apparent when the instrument is considered as a whole. For example, John Smith's signature in the lower left hand corner is obviously that of the maker of an instrument which states, "I, John Smith, promise to pay." When the capacity of the person signing is ambiguous, the law generally deems that her signature is an indorsement. Indorser is the catchall capacity by force of this rule:

> regardless of the intent of the signer, a signature and its accompanying words is an indorsement unless the accompanying words, terms of the instrument, place of the signature, or other circumstances unambiguously indicate that the signature was made for a purpose other than indorsement.

3-204(a). In other words, "[t]he general rule is that a signature is an indorsement if the instrument does not indicate an unambiguous intent of the signer not to sign as an indorser." 3-204 comment 1.

D. DISHONOR AND OTHER CONDITIONS TO SECONDARY LIABILITY

The contract liability of drawers and indorsers is conditioned on *dishonor* of the instrument, which usually involves *presentment* of it. An indorser's liability is further conditioned on *notice of dishonor*, and so too the liability of a drawer when the draft is accepted by a person other than a bank. These three events -- presentment, dishonor, and notice of dishonor -- are the conditions of secondary liability. **If any of these conditions that is required for liability is not satisfied or excused, the liability is not enforceable. Absent excuse of the condition, enforcement must await satisfaction of the condition**. The explanation is that secondary parties -- drawers and indorsers -- normally are not expected to pay unless someone else (the maker or drawee or acceptor) fails to do so. The conditions of secondary liability -- presentment, dishonor, notice of dishonor -- are the tools for asking the expected payor to pay. Thus, until the conditions have been met, the payor has not been properly asked to pay and secondary parties cannot be required to do so.

Postponement of secondary liability is not always the only consequence of not meeting these conditions. Delay in presentment or notice of dishonor can entirely discharge the liability of an indorser or, in a rarer case, the liability of a drawer.

In concept, the conditions of secondary liability are easy to understand. Presentment involves requesting payment or acceptance of the expected payor; dishonor is this person's refusal of the request; and notice is alerting the secondary party whose own liability on the instrument is now triggered. Analytically, however, there are lots of details about the effects of not satisfying the conditions; the mechanics of meeting them; and the circumstances under which the law excuses the conditions altogether or excuses delay in presentment or notice of dishonor. The major details are outlined here.

1. Dishonor

Dishonor is essential to the liability of a drawer of a draft and the indorser of any instrument. The meaning of dishonor -- what prompts it and how it occurs -- depends on the kind of instrument that is involved.

a. Note

Dishonor of a note is governed by the following rules that turn on when the note is payable:

- If the note is payable on demand, the note is dishonored if presentment is duly made to the maker and the note is not paid on the day of presentment;
- If the note is not payable on demand and is payable at or through a bank or the terms of the note require presentment, the note is dishonored if presentment is duly made and the note is not paid on the day it becomes payable or the day of presentment, whichever is later; and
- If the note is not payable on demand and the foregoing paragraph [3-502(a)(2)] does not apply, the note is dishonored if it is not paid on the day it becomes payable.

3-502(a)(1-3).

b. Ordinary Draft

A draft can order the drawee to pay or to accept and pay later. In either case, the time for payment can be on demand or at a definite time. How dishonor of a draft occurs depends on the particular combination of these variables.

1) Unaccepted

Dishonor of an unaccepted draft other than a documentary draft is governed by the following rules:

- If a draft is payable on demand and [is not a check to which 3-502(b)(1) applies] * * *, the draft is dishonored if presentment for payment is duly made to the drawee and the draft is not paid on the day of presentment;
- If a draft is payable on a date stated in the draft, the draft is dishonored if (i) presentment for payment is duly made to the drawee and payment is not made on the day the draft becomes payable or the day of presentment, whichever is later, or (ii) presentment for acceptance is duly made before the day the draft becomes payable and the draft is not accepted on the day of presentment; and
- If a draft is payable on elapse of a period of time after sight or acceptance, the draft is dishonored if presentment for acceptance is duly made and the draft is not accepted on the day of presentment. 3-502(b)(2-4).

2) Accepted

Dishonor of an accepted draft is governed by the following rules:

- If the draft is payable on demand, the draft is dishonored if presentment for payment is duly made to the acceptor and the draft is not paid on the day of presentment; and
- If the draft is not payable on demand, the draft is dishonored if presentment for payment is duly made to the acceptor and payment is not made on the day it becomes payable or the day of presentment, whichever is later.

3-502(d)(1-2).

c. Check
1) When Presented For Immediate Payment Over the Counter

Presenting a check for immediate payment over the counter essentially means presenting the instrument to a teller for cash right then and there. In this situation, dishonor is governed by rules that apply to ordinary drafts. By these rules, as they apply to a demand draft, dishonor of a check occurs "if presentment for payment is duly made to the drawee and the draft is not paid on the day of presentment." 3-502(b)(2). In truth, however, presenting checks for immediate payment over the counter is unusual. Checks usually are presented by their holders and owners -- directly or indirectly -- for credit.

2) All Other Cases -- Connection to U.C.C. Article 4

When a check is not presented for immediate payment over the counter, dishonor is governed by a very different, entirely peculiar meaning of dishonor that never applies to ordinary drafts. Here is the rule:

> If a check is duly presented for payment to the payor bank otherwise than for immediate payment over the counter, the check is dishonored if the payor bank makes timely return of the check or sends timely notice of dishonor or nonpayment under Section 4-301 or 4-302, or becomes accountable for the amount of the check under Section 4-302.

3-502(b)(1). That's right! It's pure gobbledygook which uses terms and refers to rules that are completely foreign. Indeed, it effectively incorporates major concepts of Article 4 and involves, indirectly, other Article 4 rules on which 4-301 and 4-302 depend. Thus, the complication in determining dishonor with respect to ordinary checks is that understanding and applying Article 4 is necessary, mainly its rules of check collection which are themselves affected by federal law. Check collection is sufficiently important to deserve its own chapter, and the applicable rules of Article 4 and federal law are discussed there in some detail. See Chapter IX infra. Here are the bare basics.

To begin, "payor bank" is Article 4's synonym for drawee-bank. 4-105(3). Checks are commonly presented to the payor bank by impersonal deposits for credit rather than over the counter for cash. Even more often, a check is presented by another bank acting for the check's owner as agent or subagent for purposes of collection, i.e., getting the payor bank to pay the check with hard funds. The reason for different banks is geography rather than law. The drawer and payee live in different places and use different banks. The payee deposits the check in her bank, known as the depositary-collecting bank, and this bank directly, or through an intermediary bank (such as a Federal Reserve Bank), presents the check for payment to the payor bank.

In any event, the payor bank then follows its own internal procedures to decide if the check is properly payable, i.e., if the check is an item for which the bank can rightly charge the drawer's account (another Article 4 issue), and also to determine if there are sufficient funds in the account to cover the check (a mixed issue of Article 4, federal law on funds availability, and arithmetic). In doing so, the payor bank cannot freely take whatever time it wants or is actually necessary for its internal processes. As a general rule, in the most typical case where another bank is the depositary bank, the payor bank must decide what to do -- to pay or dishonor -- by midnight of the banking day on which the check was received. If the bank keeps the check beyond this deadline, the bank itself is accountable for the amount of the check. 4-302(a)(1). The bank itself becomes liable and must pay the check with its own funds even if the check is not properly payable or the drawer's account is empty.

This accountability is not liability on the check because the bank has not accepted the instrument. It is liability that Article 4 imposes for violating its rules.

Section 4-302 provides two ways for the payor bank to avoid this liability.

- First, return the item on the banking day of receipt. Doing so is timely return under 4-302 and therefore amounts to dishonor for purposes of Article 3, namely 3-502(b)(1). Significantly, if there is no return by the deadline, there is dishonor whether or not the check is returned. By missing the deadline, the bank becomes accountable under 4-302 and this accountability, in itself, is dishonor under 3-502(b)(1). In this event, the holder can recover either from a secondary party whose liability was triggered by the dishonor, or from the payor bank who is accountable under Article 4.
- The other way for the payor bank to avoid 4-302 accountability is to settle for the check on the banking day of receipt. Settlement typically involves giving a provisional or soft credit to the person who presented the check. The collecting bank that presents the check gets a credit to an account maintained for this purpose with the payor bank, or to the collecting bank's account at a Federal Reserve Bank, or to some other account.

By settling on the day of receipt (which practically always happens), the payor bank buys more time but not much more. The bank gets an extra banking day. Now, the bank must return the item -- pursuant to 4-301 -- before midnight of the *next banking day* following the banking day of receipt. This extended next-day deadline, but not the shorter same-day deadline that applies absent settlement, is known as the bank's *midnight deadline*. By returning the check by this midnight deadline and in line with the procedures of 4-301, the payor bank can recoup the settlement it made even though it retained the check beyond the banking day of receipt. Also, and more important for present purposes, the check is thereby dishonored within the meaning of 3-502(b)(1). On the other hand, failure to meet the extended deadline and 4-301 in returning the check and recouping the settlement means that the check is finally paid under 4-215. The settlement hardens and cannot lawfully be reclaimed. 4-302. The final payment discharges the drawer's liability on the check, 3-602(a), and on the underlying obligation. 3-310(b)(1).

In the other common case in which the owner deposits the check in her own account at the payor bank, so that the payor is also the depositary bank, the longer midnight deadline always applies even though the payor bank does not settle with its customer. There is almost always a settlement, however, by a credit to the customer's account. As before, this settlement hardens unless the check is returned in line with 4-301 before the midnight deadline. Such a return is Article 3 dishonor.

There is much more to say on this subject, and some of it contradicts what is said here. The details of Article 4 provide exceptions, and federal law selectively overrides both the general and exceptional rules of the state law. For a more complete and more accurate explanation of the law of check collection, and for more about this law's ties to dishonor and other issues of Article 3, see Chapter IX infra

2. Presentment

Secondary liability fundamentally requires dishonor of the instrument. Dishonor usually requires, as a necessary prerequisite, due and proper presentment which satisfies the procedural and other requirements of Article 3. When presentment is required, there is no dishonor without it, not even if the facts prove an actual refusal to pay or accept the instrument; and, in terms of Article 3, there is no presentment absent compliance with Article 3's rules of presentment. Officially, "presentment" means:

> a demand made by or on behalf of a person entitled to enforce an instrument (i) to *pay* the instrument made to the drawee or a party obliged to pay the instrument or, in the case of a note or accepted draft payable at a bank, to the bank, or (ii) to *accept* a draft made to the drawee.

3-501(a) (emphasis added). Generally speaking, dishonor occurs if the demand is refused, so long as two conditions are met, one of substance and the other of procedure.

a. The Substance Or Nature Of The Presentment Must Be Appropriate

The kind of presentment made, either for payment or acceptance, must have been a kind that, if refused, triggers dishonor in the circumstances of the particular case. The maker of a note refusing presentment for acceptance is never dishonor. The kind of presentment that is appropriate in the circumstances -- the nature or substance of it -- is determined by the rules of dishonor, which are described above. They define dishonor in terms of the kind of presentment that must be refused for dishonor to occur. It generally turns on the nature of the instrument, when it is payable, and when the presentment is made. Thus, to judge if dishonor has occurred, the right approach is to decide first, under the rules of dishonor, if the person's refusal to pay or accept, whichever happened, is a defining event of dishonor.

b. The Appropriate Procedures Must Be Followed
Second, if the kind or substance of the presentment is appropriate, the presentment must be procedurally correct.

1) By Whom
Presentment is made "by or on behalf of a person entitled to enforce an instrument." 3-501(a). Thus, for example, a demand for payment by a thief of an unindorsed order instrument is never presentment. It is not necessary that the person making demand is herself a holder or other person entitled to enforce *if* she is acting on behalf of such a person, as by authority of that person. Who is a holder or other person entitled to enforce an instrument is discussed later. See Chapter IV infra.

2) To Whom
To whom presentment is made is really determined by the rules of dishonor. In general:

* Presentment for *acceptance* applies only to a draft and is always made to the drawee.
* Presentment for *payment of an unaccepted draft* is made, also, to the drawee.
* Presentment for *payment of a note or accepted draft* is made to the primary party, which is the maker of a note or the acceptor of a draft.

    √ An exception applies when the note or accepted draft is *domiciled*, which means the instrument is payable at a bank. In this event, presentment for payment is made to the bank, even though the bank is not the maker. The reason is that a domiciled instrument is the functional equivalent of a draft drawn on the bank or, minimally, designates the bank as an agent for collection. 4-106.

If there are multiple payors, presentment "is effective if made to any one of two or more makers, acceptors, drawees, or other payors." 3-501(b)(1).

3) How

a) Standard Requirements

Basically, presentment for acceptance is a *demand* for acceptance and presentment for payment is a *demand* for payment. To be effective as a presentment, however, the demand may have to satisfy certain requirements. What these requirements are depends in large part on what, if anything, is requested at the time of presentment by the person upon whom the demand is made. If the person upon whom the demand is made asks for nothing that the law permits her to request, any demand upon the party to pay, no matter where or how made, is generally an effective presentment. It "may be made by any commercially reasonable means, including an oral, written, or electronic communication * * *." 3-501(b)(1). Electronic presentment is an innovation that allows, most significantly, *truncation* of checks. The depositary bank of a check, or an immediately collecting bank, keeps and stores the actual instrument and presents directly to the payor bank, or through someone else, an electronic image or electronically transmitted information about the check. However made, presentment is effective when the demand "is received by the person to whom presentment is made * * *." 3-501(b)(1).

b) Custom Requirements

In any particular case, however, the meaning and requirements of proper presentment can be further defined and enlarged by the person to whom presentment is made. Section 3-501 gives this person the means to reduce the uncertainty of the barest presentment by giving her the right to request and require:

- exhibition of the instrument;
- reasonable identification of the person making presentment;
- evidence of authority if presentment is made for another;
- a signed receipt on the instrument for any payment made or its surrender upon full payment.

3-501(b)(2). If the party on whom presentment is made requests any of these things, the presentment is ineffective unless the presenting party complies. Also, without dishonoring the instrument, the party to whom presentment is made can return the instrument for lack of a necessary indorsement and, also without dishonor, can "refuse payment or acceptance for failure of the presentment to comply with the terms of the instrument, an agreement of the parties, or other applicable law or rule." 3-501(b)(3).

4) **Where**
Normally, presentment is made at the place of business or residence of the party who is expected to pay or accept, but no particular place of presentment is required. Even when the instrument specifies a place of payment, presentment there is not required unless the specified place is a bank in the United States. 3-501(b)(1). Otherwise, the Code allows the holder to make an effective presentment wherever he can find the payor or someone authorized to act for her.

5) **Time of Presentment**
There are two different issues with respect to time of presentment.

   a) **How Soon**
The first issue is when presentment can be made so that a refusal is dishonor. For example, a payor does not dishonor by refusing a presentment for payment made before the date for payment. It is really the question of how soon presentment can be made. When presentment is appropriate, in this sense, is defined in terms of dishonor and its rules which are explained earlier in this chapter.

   b) **How Late**
The other issue is when presentment must be made in the sense that delay dilutes the holder's rights by reducing or releasing a secondary party's liability. It is really the question of how late presentment can be made. The answer is found in the contract of liability that a person incurs when she signs as drawer or indorser. Generally, there is no time limit in this sense, except as may result from a statute of limitations or be required by good faith.

Checks are different. Presentment can be *too* late for checks.

- An indorser on a check is discharged unless the check is presented for payment or given to a depositary bank for collection within 30 days after the day the indorsement was made. 3-415(e).
- In a rare case, the drawer of a check may be discharged if the same action is not taken within 30 days after the date of the instrument: "If (i) a check is not presented for payment or given to a depositary bank for collection within 30 days after its date, (ii) the drawee suspends payments after expiration of the 30-day period without paying the check, and (iii) because of the suspension of payments, the drawer is deprived of funds maintained with the drawee to cover payment of the check, the drawer to the extent deprived of funds may discharge its

obligation to pay the check by assigning to the person entitled to enforce the check the rights of the drawer against the drawee with respect to the funds." 3-414(f).

3. Notice Of Dishonor

a. To Whom

Notice of dishonor is always a condition to the liability of an indorser, and is a condition to a drawer's liability if a nonbank accepts the draft because, in this event, the drawer's liability is transformed into the liability of an indorser. 3-503(a), 3-414(d), 3-415(c).

b. Method of Giving Notice

Notice of dishonor "may be given by any commercially reasonable means, including an oral, written, or electronic communication." 3-503(b). For example, it may be given in conversation face-to-face or over the telephone, by mail, by telegraph, through a clearing house, or by computer. The person giving notice should remember, however, when choosing a means of communication that she may be required to prove in court that she has given notice. Need for proof is one reason why notice of dishonor usually is given in writing and why, when given orally, it usually is confirmed in writing. It is noteworthy that notice of dishonor is effective when dispatched even though it is not received by the addressee. 1-201(26) (defining when a person "notifies" or "gives" a notice). Accordingly, notice sent by ordinary mail is given as soon as a properly addressed letter bearing sufficient postage and containing the notice is deposited in a mail box, chute, or other receptacle maintained by the Post Office for mailing letters.

c. Content of Notice

No special words must be used to give notice of dishonor. It "is sufficient if it reasonably identifies the instrument and indicates that the instrument has been dishonored or has not been paid or accepted." 3-503(b). Sending the dishonored instrument with a stamp, ticket, or writing, stating that acceptance or payment has been refused is sufficient. Indeed, even the "[r]eturn of an instrument given to a bank for collection is sufficient notice of dishonor." Id. The notice is intended to convey the idea that the party giving notice is asserting her rights against the party given notice. An assertion of these rights, however, need not be expressly stated. It is sufficiently implied by the notice alone.

d. Persons Giving Notice

Notice of dishonor may be given by *any* person or her agent, 3-503(b), whether or not the person is a party to the instrument and even though she lacks any connection to it. Even a stranger can give notice of dishonor.

e. Sequence in Which Notice May Be Given

An instrument that is well traveled may have multiple indorsements. Each of the indorsers is immediately liable to the ultimate holder without the holder having to resort first to any of the others. Each indorser, however, is entitled to her own notice of dishonor. Notice to one is not notice to another. On the other hand, to charge any particular indorser, it is not necessary to notify any of the others.

A holder may give notice of dishonor only to the indorser who is her immediate transferor, because this indorser is the person with whom the holder dealt and the person from whom the holder expects payment. This indorser will then look to and notify the indorser immediately before her. Notice and collection will thereby move back down the chain of indorsements to the drawer or primary party. The problem, both for the holder and each successive indorser, is that her immediate indorser may be unwilling or unable to pay. She can look further down the chain of liability, but a remote indorser may not have been given notice of dishonor. The problem is that the time for notice is limited. Except in the case of a check, notice of dishonor usually must be given within 30 days after dishonor. 3-503(c). Untimely notice discharges an indorser.

The better approach for the holder is immediately to notify all of the indorsers. Then, if she cannot collect from the first indorser she asks, rights against the others will have been preserved. Any one of them who pays need not give notice again to the indorser from whom recoupment is sought. Notice of dishonor that is duly given operates for the benefit of all parties who have rights on the instrument against the person notified. This rule is no longer explicit as under former law, but is equally true under the new Article 3. The key is that an indorser is timely notified of dishonor. It is unimportant who notifies her. Even a stranger can do it. Once an indorser is given timely notice of dishonor from someone and anyone, this condition of the indorser's liability is met for everyone who may sue her.

f. Time Allowed For Giving Notice

1) Usual Rule

Generally, "notice of dishonor must be given within 30 days following the day on which dishonor occurs." 3-503(c).

2) Exceptional Rules for Checks

Exceptional rules apply with respect to checks and other instruments that a collecting bank takes for collection:

- ◆ The bank itself must give notice before midnight of the next banking day following the banking day on which the bank received notice of dishonor.

♦ Anybody else must give notice within 30 days following the day on which she herself received notice.

Id.

Example: Suppose, for example, that the payor bank dishonors a check by returning it to the depositary-collecting bank that had presented the check for payment. This bank now wishes to sue an indorser on the check. It must have notified the indorser by the midnight deadline. Suppose that the bank had done so and the indorser paid the bank. This indorser now wishes to recover over, in turn, from a prior indorser who must be given notice of dishonor. The subsequent indorser gets 30 days to do so from the time she herself received notice.

3) **Effect of Unexcused Delay**
The effect of unexcused delay in giving notice of dishonor is to discharge the liability of the indorser or drawer entitled to the notice.

Example: Suppose the bank, in the first instance, delays giving notice of dishonor to the subsequent indorser. The effect is clearly to discharge her liability. It is less explicit under the new Article 3 that, technically, the prior indorser is concomitantly discharged, but she need not worry. The bank cannot sue the prior indorser because the bank will have equally missed its midnight deadline for notice of dishonor as to her. The subsequent indorser, because she was discharged by the bank's delay in notice to her, will have no reason to recover over against the prior party.

4. Consequence Of Delay In Presentment Or Notice

When a party's liability is conditioned on dishonor, as is true of drawers and indorsers, the liability cannot be enforced until dishonor occurs, unless it is excused by law or agreement. The same is true of presentment and notice of dishonor when they are conditions of liability. A further issue with respect to presentment and notice is the consequence of delay with respect to either of them in cases where a time limit on presentment or notice of dishonor applies.

a. Presentment
A time limit applies to presentment only with respect to checks. Unexcused delay affects indorsers and drawers differently:

1) Indorser

"If * * * the check is not presented for payment, or given to a depositary bank for collection, within 30 days after the day the indorsement was made, the liability of the indorser * * * is discharged." 3-415(e).

2) Drawer

"If (i) a check is not presented for payment or given to a depositary bank for collection within 30 days after its date, (ii) the drawee suspends payments after expiration of the 30-day period without paying the check, and (iii) because of the suspension of payments, the drawer is deprived of funds maintained with the drawee to cover payment of the check, the drawer to the extent deprived of funds may discharge its obligation to pay the check by assigning to the person entitled to enforce the check the rights of the drawer against the drawee with respect to the funds." 3-414(f).

b. Notice of Dishonor

Notice of dishonor is required for indorsers only, except that a drawer is also entitled to notice if the acceptor is not a bank. Unexcused delay in notice to an indorser or such a drawer discharges her liability. 3-415(c) & 3-503(c).

5. Excusing Conditions Altogether Or Delay

In some cases, presentment or notice of dishonor would be an empty formality contributing nothing to the persons intended to benefit by them. In other cases, whatever advantage might accrue from complying with these requirements is more than outweighed by the disadvantage to the person of whom compliance normally is required. Consequently, the law makes allowance in appropriate circumstances, relaxing the conditions of secondary liability. An excuse may extend to one or more conditions and may affect the liability of one or more parties. Regardless of which conditions and whose liabilities are affected, the legal effect of excusing a condition or delay is that the law regards the condition as having been properly met within the time normally allowed.

a. Presentment

Presentment for payment or acceptance is entirely excused if:

- the person entitled to present the instrument cannot with reasonable diligence make presentment,
- the maker or acceptor has repudiated an obligation to pay the instrument or is dead or in insolvency proceedings,
- by the terms of the instrument presentment is not necessary to enforce the obligation of indorsers or the drawer,

- the drawer or indorser whose obligation is being enforced has waived presentment or otherwise has no reason to expect or right to require that the instrument be paid or accepted, or
- the drawer instructed the drawee not to pay or accept the draft or the drawee was not obligated to the drawer to pay the draft.

3-504(a).

Example: D made a note to P who indorsed and delivered it to T. The note was not paid at maturity. Both D and P are in bankruptcy. P's bankruptcy does not excuse presentment to D which is a condition' on P's liability as indorser of the note. D's bankruptcy does not stay presenting the instrument to her. Nevertheless, because of 3-504(a), D's bankruptcy excuses presentment, so that presenting the note to D is not a necessary condition to P's liability.

Example: Same facts except that nobody is in bankruptcy. Presentment to D to charge P nevertheless will be excused if the terms of the note provide (as they usually do) that any indorser waives presentment.

b. Dishonor

Where dishonor is predicated on presentment that is excused for any of these reasons, the dishonor is deemed to occur "without presentment if the instrument is not duly accepted or paid." 3-502(e). There is no comparable express provision that deems notice of dishonor to be given if the instrument is not thereafter duly accepted or paid. It would therefore appear that any necessary notice is still required despite the fictional dishonor, unless notice is otherwise excused.

c. Notice of Dishonor

Notice is expressly excused, entirely, in only two situations:

- by the terms of the instrument notice of dishonor is not necessary to enforce the obligation of a party to pay the instrument, or
- the party whose obligation is being enforced waived notice of dishonor or presentment.

3-504(b). "Delay in giving notice of dishonor is excused if the delay was caused by circumstances beyond the control of the person giving the notice and the person giving the notice exercised reasonable diligence after the cause of the delay ceased to operate." 3-504(c).

E. LIABILITIES ON SPECIALIZED "CHECKS"

1. Certified Check

The bank on which a check is drawn, like the drawee of an ordinary draft, is not liable on the instrument unless the bank-drawee accepts. A bank accepts a check by certifying it, and the instrument becomes a *certified check* on which the bank is liable as acceptor. 3-409(d), 3-413(b). When the bank accepts, the drawer's liability is discharged regardless of when or by whom acceptance was obtained. 3-414(c). Any person who has already indorsed is also discharged. 3-415(d). Certification is rare.

2. Cashier's Check

When the transaction calls for a check that obligates a bank, the form that is almost always used is a *cashier's check*. It is a draft and check "with respect to which the drawer and drawee are the same bank or branches of the same bank." 3-104(g). The person who procures the check must pay the bank for it. She is known as the *remitter,* 3-103(a)(11), and is not liable on the check herself unless she signs it, which is rarely done.

Example: Suppose Seller of goods insists upon payment by cashier's check. Buyer will purchase such a check from a bank, usually the bank where she maintains her account. Bank will draw a check against itself to Seller's order. Put another way, an officer of the Bank will sign the check as Drawer ordering the Bank itself to pay the Seller or whomever the Seller orders. Buyer typically does not sign the instrument in any capacity. She is named on the check as *remitter* (3-103(a)(11)), but is not liable on it. The legal relationship on the check is between Seller (Payee) and Bank (both Drawer and Drawee). Buyer's account, however, has been debited by Bank for the amount of the check plus a fee, or the Buyer has otherwise paid or secured the Bank for the instrument.

3. Money Order

A money order is a demand draft that the drawee creates and that a purchaser buys for use in paying a third person. The drawee can be a bank or a non-bank (that may be affiliated with a bank). Anybody can create a money order, which is only a check or ordinary draft that is distinguished by its use rather than its form. The problem with money orders, as with any other financial service, is selling them. They must be marketed and credible, which means that the person who creates them must be financially credible and reliable. The market for Nickles' Money Orders would not be large.

The best example of a non-bank that creates and markets money orders is the United States Postal Service, but postal money orders are governed by federal law and are not directly governed by the rules discussed here.   Another good example is American Express. This company sells money orders in addition to its famous traveler's checks and credit cards.   American Express money orders are marketed through many retail businesses that sell them as just another product they offer their customers, such as at Tom Thumb and other neighborhood convenience stores.

When the drawee is a non-bank, the order technically is not a check unless it is payable at a bank, which is rare. Commonly, non-bank money orders are rather payable *through* a bank.   A *payable-through bank* functions only as a collecting bank to help collect the money orders from the drawee and has no responsibility to anyone to pay them.

Banks sometimes sell non-bank money orders and money orders of other banks. A common source of money orders that many community banks sell is a Minnesota vendor, Traveler's Express Co., Inc., which clears through a large regional bank in Minneapolis.

Probably the more common practice, however, is for banks -- especially larger banks -- to sell their own money orders. These money orders are checks on which the bank is itself the drawee but which may be payable through another, usually affiliated bank. Such a money order looks and functions like a cashier's check with a huge, fundamental difference. The bank does not sign this money order and thus has no liability on the instrument. The bank is merely the drawee. The purchaser who buys the money order is suppose to sign it as drawer, and in doing so she becomes liable on the instrument in this role. In effect, a money order is more like a check the purchaser would draw against her check accounting. It is like a one-shot, one-check checking account. The difference is that a money order will not be dishonored for insufficient funds because it is paid for in advance. A money order might be dishonored for other reasons, however, and is much less credible than a cashier's check for this reason and also because the bank is not liable on it.

4. Teller's Check

Commercial banks sometimes draw checks against other banks, not always against themselves. Other kinds of financial institutions often draw against commercial banks. Good examples are savings and loan associations (S&L's) and credit unions. They keep their customers' money and their own money in accounts maintained in their own names at commercial banks. A check that a bank (broadly defined) draws on, at or through another bank is called a *teller's check*. 3-104(h). In practice, "*bank draft*" is sometimes used as a synonym for teller's check. Bank drafts also may be used in the process of collecting checks deposited by bank customers. In this role, they are commonly referred to as *remittance drafts*. In the definition of teller's check and for other purposes under Articles 3 and 4, the term "*bank*" includes a savings bank, savings and loan association, credit union and trust company. 3-103(c); 4-105(1). Thus, a credit union or S&L may fund a loan to a customer by giving the customer a teller's check drawn on a commercial bank.

Commonly, a customer of an S&L or credit union can get to her account there by drafting the account. The drafts that she draws on the credit union or S&L are drawn through a commercial bank where the credit union or S&L keeps its deposits. They have common, unofficial names such as "*share drafts;*" but, technically and officially, they qualify as checks. The drawee S&L or credit union on which the instrument is drawn is not a commercial bank, but is nevertheless a bank for purposes of Articles 3 and 4. Therefore, these drafts are checks if they are payable on demand because they are drawn on a bank.

A draft drawn by a bank against a nonbank is a teller's check if the draft is payable through or at another bank. Such an instrument is relatively uncommon, however, and is forced into the definition of check because of function and practice rather than form.

5. Traveler's Checks

A *traveler's check* is "an instrument that (i) is payable on demand, (ii) is drawn on or payable at or through a bank, (iii) is designated by the term 'traveler's check' or by a substantially similar term, and (iv) requires, as a condition to payment, a countersignature by a person whose specimen signature appears on the instrument." 3-104(i). Like a money order, a traveler's check is always a draft but is not a check unless it is drawn on a bank. Many banks sell traveler's checks, but almost never are the checks drawn on the banks that sell them. Anybody, whether bank or non-bank, can issue traveler's checks and sell them through vendors including local banks and travel agents and anybody else whose customers are likely purchasers. The issuers who are successful in this business are banks and non-banks that are nationally and internationally known and reputable as reliable and finally sound. Without this reputation behind them, traveler's checks have no currency (meaning, sellers of property and services will not take them) and thus nobody will buy them. The same considerations limit the opportunities for marketing money orders and other instruments.

F. LIABILITY OF JOINT OBLIGORS

1. Liability To Others

"Except as otherwise provided in the instrument, two or more persons who have the same liability on an instrument as makers, drawers, acceptors, indorsers who indorse as joint payees, or anomalous indorsers are jointly and severally liable in the capacity in which they sign." 3-116(a).

Example: A and B borrow money from a bank and sign a note as co-makers. The note matures and is not paid. The bank sues B for the full amount of the loan. B is liable for the entire sum.

2. Liability Between Themselves

When two or more persons sign an instrument jointly in the same capacity, neither is liable to the other on the instrument, unless one of them is a surety for the other. Yet, if either of them is required to pay the instrument, she is entitled by the common law to contribution from her co-obligor. Article 3 codifies this common-law right of recovery:

> Except as provided in Section 3-419(e) or by agreement of the affected parties, a party having joint and several liability who pays the instrument is entitled to receive from any party having the same joint and several liability contribution in accordance with applicable law.

3-116(b). Section 3-419(e) deals with the different rights between accommodation parties (sureties). These rights are discussed later. See Chapter VII infra.

Example: A and B borrow money from a bank for their business and sign a note as co-makers. The note matures and is not paid. The bank sues B for the full amount of the loan. B is liable for the entire sum, but she is entitled to contribution from A. The general rule of apportionment in contribution is that all co-obligors must contribute equally in discharging their common obligation.

Example: Same facts except that B signed as surety for A. B can recover the whole amount from A.

Example: Same facts except that A paid the bank. A can recover from B a contributive share, unless B was a surety. In this event, A can recover nothing from B.

G. DISCHARGE OF LIABILITY ON INSTRUMENTS

1. Meaning And Modes Of Discharge

"Discharge" means that an obligor is released from liability on the instrument for reasons of Article 3 or contract law. Discharge is not thought of, technically, as a defense to liability on an instrument. See 3-302 comment 3. Nevertheless, "[d]ischarge is effective against anybody except a person having rights of a holder in due course who took the instrument without notice of the discharge." Id.; see also 3-601(b). It is, functionally, a defense. To be clear about the effect of discharge, keep in mind a few basic, fundamental propositions about it.

- First, the "instrument," itself, is not discharged. Rather, the liability of one or more parties on the instrument is discharged. The common expression, which far overstates the result, is that the parties themselves are discharged.
- Second, the liability of different parties may be discharged at different times.
- Third, a party may be discharged with respect to one person while remaining liable to someone else.
- Fourth, discharge of liability on an instrument is not always final. Liability that has been discharged can sometimes be revived. See, e.g., 3-418(d).
- Fifth, the discharge of any party is not effective against a subsequent holder in due course unless she has notice of the discharge when she takes the instrument. Such notice does not stop her from becoming a holder in due course but does subject her to the party's discharge defense.
- Finally, discharge can occur in several different, alternative ways:
  - √ payment, 3-602;
  - √ tender of payment, 3-603;
  - √ cancellation or renunciation, 3-604;
  - √ modification of the principal obligor's liability that causes loss to a surety, 3-605 (See Chapter V infra.);
  - √ impairment of collateral, 3-605 (See Chapter V infra.);
  - √ alteration, 3-407;
  - √ acceptance varying draft, 3-410 (See Chapter III supra.);
  - √ unexcused delay in presentment or notice of dishonor with respect to a check, 3-414(f), 3-415(e) (See Chapter III supra.);
  - √ an act or agreement with the obligor that would discharge an obligation to pay money under a simple contract, 3-601(a).

Some of these reasons for discharge are discussed elsewhere in the appropriate context. They are not repeated here. This discussion looks at the others, beginning with the most common and important reason for discharge -- discharge by payment.

2. Payment Of The Instrument
a. Requirements of the Discharge

A person who signs an instrument becomes liable to pay it. It is natural, therefore, that her payment of the instrument should end her liability on it. The law confirms and reaches this outcome by way of discharge, by providing that "[t]o the extent of the payment, the obligation of the party obliged to pay the instrument is discharged * * *." 3-602(a). Also, by separate rule, payment of the instrument usually discharges the underlying obligation. 3-310(b-c).

Three very important limits are built into the rule that payment of an instrument discharges liability on it.

1) Pro Tanto

First, the discharge is pro tanto only, "to the extent" of payment.

2) Payment Must Match Statute

Second, the actual payment must match the statutory definition of "payment" that applies here, which requires that payment is made:

- by or on behalf of a party obliged to pay the instrument, and
- to a person entitled to enforce the instrument.

3-602(a)(i-ii). Whenever someone other than a party gives value for the instrument, it is a purchase rather than "payment" and there is no discharge by this rule unless she acts for a party to the instrument. There is also no payment and no discharge if a right person pays the wrong person. The rule requires payment to a person entitled to enforce, who is usually the holder of the instrument. See 3-301.

Interestingly, the mechanics of "payment" are not described. The medium obviously is money; but other aspects are less clear, including the means of payment and the point at which payment is accomplished. These matters are important because they affect how and when the risks shift with respect to the funds.

3) Discharge Affects Only Person Who Pays

The third and final limit of 3-602(a) is that the discharge only affects the liability of the party who pays the instrument. For this reason, payment alone does not extinguish the whole instrument or discharge any other party's liability on it. For example, a maker remains liable on a note that an indorser pays. Former law agreed but also applied a supplemental rule that discharged everybody on the instrument when any party was discharged who herself had no right of recourse on the instrument. 3-601(3)(b) (1989 Official Text). Thus, if the maker of a note paid it, an indorser was discharged. The 1990 Article 3 lacks this rule, but the result is the same. An indorser's liability is conditioned on dishonor. 3-415(a). Because of the maker's payment, the indorser's liability never will mature.

b. Third-Party Claims

Significantly, while 3-602(a) conditions discharge on payment to a holder or other person entitled to enforce the instrument, the rule does not require this person to be the exclusive owner. The rule does not require her to have any interest whatsoever beyond having a right to enforce under the rules of Article 3. "The right to enforce an instrument and ownership of the instrument are two different concepts." 3-203 comment 1.

For this reason, a situation may arise in which the instrument is in the hands of a holder who wants payment but a third person objects, claiming that she owns the instrument or part of it or that she owns a better interest or superior possessory right than the holder. Paying the claimant is risky even if her claim is true. A holder in due course would take free of the claim and not be subject to the obligor's defense of having honored it. On the other hand, because of 3-602, the obligor would be safe in paying the holder. The obligor's knowledge of the third person's claim, in itself, does not jeopardize the discharge that 3-602(a) would give her if she paid the holder. The discharge applies "even though payment is made with knowledge of a claim to the instrument * * * by another person." 3-602(a). The third person's remedy is a court order blocking payment and giving her possession of the instrument.

Discharge is denied if payment is made in the face of certain other circumstances that are beyond bare knowledge of a third person's claim. Specifically, the discharge is denied if:

- a claim to the instrument under Section 3-306 is enforceable against the party receiving payment and
    - ✓ (i) payment is made with knowledge by the payor that payment is prohibited by injunction or similar process of a court of competent jurisdiction, or
    - ✓ (ii) in the case of an instrument other than a cashier's check, teller's check, or certified check, the party making payment accepted, from the person having a claim to the instrument, indemnity against loss resulting from refusal to pay the person entitled to enforce the instrument; or
- the person making payment knows that the instrument is a stolen instrument and pays a person it knows is in wrongful possession of the instrument.

3-602(b)(1-2). The knowledge that (b)(2) covers is much more than merely knowing of a third person's claim; in truth, it is knowing that the third person has no claim, which is true of any thief or anyone who holds through a thief. The exclusion in (b)(1)(ii) for bank checks is part of a scheme to encourage payment of these instruments, or to discourage dishonor of them. See also 3-411. The bank's payment to a holder effects a discharge even though the claimant has provided indemnification, but the bank is liable to the claimant for breaching any agreement not to pay the instrument. With respect to both (b)(1)(i) and (ii), they apply to deny the discharge only if the third person's claim is good against the person who is paid, which will not be true if this person is a holder in due course who took free of the claim. 3-602(b)(1). The obligor who pays in this case nevertheless faces liability apart from the instrument if the injunction ran personally against her, or if her payment to the holder violated an indemnity agreement with the claimant.

c. **Distinguishing Payment of the Underlying Obligation**

It is important to understand that the discharge of 3-602 is based on payment of the instrument, not payment of the underlying obligation. They are not the same. Paying the instrument also results, by separate rule, in discharge of the underlying obligation. See 3-310. The converse is not true. *Paying the underlying obligation, technically, does not discharge liability on the instrument.* By most accounts, this lack or absence of discharge is important.

> *Example:* Suppose, for example, that S takes B's note for the price of goods and immediately negotiates the instrument to T. B pays S. T sues B on the note. B does not have the 3-602(a) defense of discharge by payment. B paid S, but S was not then a person entitled to enforce the instrument. This right already had passed to T. The common understanding is that B must pay T even if T lacks the rights of a holder in due course. The reasoning is that when a negotiable instrument is assigned, the risk of paying the right person is on the obligor. The risk is on her even though she has not been notified of the assignment, which is different from the common-law and Article 9 rule that applies in the case of an ordinary contract right. See 9-318(3). The reasoning is that in the case of an instrument, "the right [to payment] is regarded as intimately connected with the writing, and performance rendered to a party that does not produce the writing is rendered at the obligor's peril, regardless of the lack of notification." E. Farnsworth, CONTRACTS § 11.7 at 806 (2d ed. 1990).

Possibly, however, this analysis is technically flawed and B should win. It is true that B's payment did not discharge her on the instrument. The payment nevertheless satisfied her underlying obligation to S. Satisfying this debt would have been a defense for her if S sued on the sales contract. T's rights on the instrument, if she is not a holder in due course, are subject to "a defense of the obligor * * * that would be available if the person entitled to enforce the

instrument were enforcing a right to payment under a simple contract."
3-305(a)(2). On this basis, B could argue that her payment of the sales contract
is a defense good against T, and that her lack of discharge on the instrument is
unimportant. This argument appears sound, but opposes commonly accepted
doctrine. In any event, the argument rightly fails and B flatly loses if T is a
holder in due course.

3. Tender Of Payment

If the obligor on a negotiable instrument makes a proper tender of full payment to the
holder at or after maturity, but the holder improperly refuses to accept the payment,
the obligation of the party making the tender is *not* discharged. Her obligation
continues, but the holder's refusal of a proper tender completely discharges any
indorser or accommodation party having a right of recourse with respect to the
obligation to which the tender relates. 3-603(b). Furthermore, the party making the
tender is discharged to the extent of her subsequent obligation to pay interest after the
due date on the amount tendered. 3-603(c).

The underlying reason for discharging a person who has a right of recourse against
the person whose tender is refused is that if the tender had been accepted, the party
having the right of recourse would have been completely discharged from liability. It
would be unjust to continue her liability and her risks solely because the holder
chooses to refuse payment.

An instrument sometimes is made or accepted to be payable at a particular place --
typically the place of business of the maker or acceptor or a bank. Unless the
instrument is payable on demand, tender is deemed to have been made on the due
date if the maker or acceptor is then able and ready to pay at every place of payment
stated in the instrument. Id.

4. Fraudulent Alteration
a. Meaning of Alteration

"'Alteration' means (i) an unauthorized change in an instrument that purports to
modify in any respect the obligation of a party, or (ii) an unauthorized addition
of words or numbers or other change to an incomplete instrument relating to the
obligation of a party." 3-407(a).

b. Rule of Discharge

An alteration of an instrument that is "fraudulently made discharges a party
whose obligation is affected by the alteration unless that party assents or is
precluded from asserting the alteration." 3-407(b). A non-fraudulent alteration
is benign, but the instrument is enforceable only to the extent of its original,
unaltered terms. Id.

c. Effect on Holder in Due Course

A discharge because of fraudulent alteration is not effective against a holder in due course who takes the instrument without notice of the discharge. Nevertheless, with one exception, such a holder can enforce the instrument only to the extent of its original, unaltered terms. 3-407(c). The exception is that in the case of an incomplete instrument altered by unauthorized completion, the holder in due course can enforce the instrument as completed. Id.

5. Cancellation Or Renunciation

The holder of an instrument may discharge any party's obligation on an instrument by *cancellation* or *renunciation*. 3-604(a). The former is "an intentional voluntary act, such as surrender of the instrument to the party, destruction, mutilation, or cancellation of the instrument, cancellation or striking out of the party's signature, or the addition of words to the instrument indicating discharge * * *." Id. Renunciation occurs differently, "by agreeing not to sue or otherwise renouncing rights against the party by a signed writing." Id. Neither cancellation nor renunciation requires consideration, id., but they must be (1) by a person entitled to enforce the instrument and (2) intentional. This means, for example, that surrender or mutilation of an instrument by mistake or because of fraud is not an effective cancellation. No discharge results.

Although canceling an indorsement discharges the indorser's liability on the instrument, it does not "affect the status and rights of a party derived from the indorsement." 3-604(b). The cancellation does not negate a negotiation of the instrument that depended on the indorsement. It does not create a missing necessary indorsement that, *nunc pro tunc*, undermines holder's status.

6. Discharge By Agreement Or Other Act

The reasons for discharge that Article 3 describes are geared to the character of a negotiable instrument as a special form of contract. Fundamentally, however, an instrument is and remains a contract; and the common-law rules of discharge that govern simple contracts apply equally to instruments. 3-601(a). Thus, an agreement to discharge liability on an instrument is enforceable under Article 3 to the extent that contract law would enforce it, even in the absence of renunciation, cancellation, payment, or any other discharge provided by Article 3 itself.

7. Article 3 Discharge As A Defense Against Holder In Due Course

Normally, notice of a defense to an instrument prevents a person from becoming a holder in due course of it. 3-302(a)(2)(vi). Notice of an Article 3 discharge of liability on an instrument does not have this effect; but any party's "[d]ischarge is effective against a holder in due course * * * if the holder had notice of the discharge when holder in due course status was acquired." 3-601 comment. Subject to this person's defense, the holder in due course can enforce the instrument against any other party and in doing so is immune to personal defenses, including any party's discharge of which the holder was unaware. "Discharge of the obligation of a party is not effective against a person acquiring rights of a holder in due course of the instrument without notice of the discharge." 3-601(b).

H. RELATIONSHIP BETWEEN LIABILITY ON AN INSTRUMENTAND LIABILITY ON THE UNDERLYING OBLIGATION

1. Taking Instrument Usually Suspends Underlying Obligation
a. Typical Case
1) Context And Issue
In the typical case, the maker or drawer issues an instrument because of an underlying transaction, specifically to evidence or effect payment of an obligation that the transaction creates. An obligee, however, is not ordinarily required, by law, to take an instrument that is issued for an underlying obligation; but the parties commonly agree on the use of an instrument and, for this reason, the payee takes the instrument that is issued to her. The overall effect between the parties, especially on the underlying obligation, is important to understand.

To begin, by getting possession of the instrument, the payee to whom the instrument is issued becomes a "holder," 1-201(20). She thereby acquires rights with respect to the instrument, most significantly including the right to enforce it against the issuer, 3-301, but normally does not lose rights against the issuer on their underlying deal. The issuer's liability on the instrument does not ordinarily replace her underlying obligation. This obligation usually continues; but the holder-payee-obligee gets no windfall, no possibility of double recovery.

2) Pro Tanto Suspension
The explanation is that the usual effect of taking the instrument is to *suspend* the underlying obligation pro tanto, i.e., "to the same extent the obligation would be discharged if an amount of money equal to the amount of the instrument were taken * * *." 3-310(b). In the case of an ordinary note or uncertified check, the suspension continues until the instrument is paid or dishonored. 3-310(b)(1-2).

3) Effects of Paying Instrument

Payment of the instrument serves a double purpose. It discharges the maker or drawer's liability on the instrument itself, 3-602(a), and also on the underlying obligation. 3-310(b)(1-2).

4) Effects of Dishonor

If the instrument is dishonored, the underlying obligation is revived. Then, the payee-obligee "may enforce *either* the instrument or the obligation." 3-310(b)(3) (emphasis added).

5) Choosing to Sue On Instrument

Upon dishonor, the payee-obligee is likely to choose enforcing the instrument because doing so is procedurally easier than suing on the underlying obligation. See 3-308. Principally, she makes her case on the instrument by producing it. The prima facie case requires nothing more.

a) If Instrument Lost

If the obligee loses the instrument, or it is stolen or destroyed, she is not free to pursue the underlying obligation. Rather, "the obligation may not be enforced to the extent of the amount payable on the instrument, and to that extent the obligee's rights against the obligor are limited to enforcement of the instrument." 3-310(b)(4) (second sentence). Special rules govern the enforcement of a lost, destroyed, or stolen instrument that aim to protect the obligor against a claim to the instrument that may appear at some later time. See 3-309.

b) Any Advantage In Suit on Instrument

Enforcing an instrument obligates the holder to observe Article 3's statute of limitations, 3-118, and to meet any applicable requirements of presentment, dishonor, and notice that Part 5 of Article 3 imposes. Also, enforcement of the instrument is generally subject to defenses and counterclaims that are produced by the underlying transaction. 3-305(a)(2). Enforcement is even subject to a claim in recoupment of the obligor against the original obligee that arose from the same transaction as the instrument. 3-305(a)(3). In short, the payee-obligee is generally in the same position as if she had sued on the underlying obligation. In sum, as between the immediate parties, there is not much substantive advantage in suing on the instrument. Of course, defenses and the like of the underlying transaction are rooted in the terms of the parties' underlying contract. If the instrument controls as the exclusive source of rights and duties, there is a fundamental advantage in suing on the instrument, which is to suppress the terms of the wider contract that could provide a defense. In truth, however, the instrument blends with other writings of the parties' transaction that are not barred by the parol evidence rule. The instrument is construed with the other writings, not apart from them, in determining the rights, duties, and defenses to the underlying contract and the instrument itself. The explanation comes later in this chapter in separate discussions about the interpretation and scope of the parties' agreement.

b. When Person Entitled to Enforce the Instrument Is Not the Original Obligee

Suppose that M makes a note to P that P indorses over to T. In both cases the instrument is taken for an underlying obligation. The effects on the relationship between M and P are already known, and the effects between P and T are essentially identical.

* The underlying obligation of P to T is suspended until paid or dishonored by M. 3-310(b)(2).
* In the latter case, T can sue P as indorser or on the underlying obligation P owes T, which will have been revived by the dishonor. 3-310(b)(3).
* T could also sue M as maker, but not on M's underlying debt to P. T is neither a party to this debt nor an assignee of it. She thus has no rights with respect to the debt.

M's payment of the note would discharge her liability on the instrument and, pro tanto, her underlying obligation to P. The payment by M would have the same functional effects for P, but the statute does not so neatly provide for them. M's payment precludes dishonor so that this condition to P's liability on the instrument is never met. The technical effect is only to bar enforcement of liability rather than discharge the liability that is created by P's signature on the instrument.

* Because there is no discharge of liability on the instrument, nothing triggers the rule that such a discharge also discharges the underlying obligation.
* Nevertheless, because dishonor is necessary to trigger liability on the instrument and to resurrect liability on the underlying obligation, payment preventing dishonor is as good as discharging these liabilities.

It is a different and easier case to explain if, instead of M paying the note to T, M dishonored the note. Suppose, then, that T notified P of the dishonor. P satisfied her indorser liability to T, "paying" and then reacquiring the instrument from T.

- ◆ The effects of P's payment would be to discharge P on the instrument, 3-602(a), and also discharge P, pro tanto, on her underlying debt to T. 3-310(b)(3) (second sentence).
- ◆ P could then recoup by suing M as maker of the note, or by suing M on M's underlying debt to P. Id. (first sentence).

2. When Taking An Instrument Discharges The Obligation

In two exceptional situations, taking an instrument for an underlying obligation discharges the obligation instead of only suspending it.

a. Agreement

Taking an instrument discharges the underlying debt when the parties to the deal agree to this effect. 3-310(b) ("Unless otherwise agreed * * *"). Such an agreement, which is very rare, is effective to discharge the underlying obligation regardless of the nature or kind of instrument that is taken, even if it is an ordinary note or check of the person who is the issuer of the instrument and the underlying obligor.

b. Bank Instruments

The other situation in which taking an instrument discharges the underlying debt is much more common. It is when the instrument is a certified check, cashier's check, or teller's check, or any other instrument on which a bank is liable as maker or acceptor. 3-310(a). This rule follows the common business understanding that such an instrument is the equivalent of cash. The obligor who remits the instrument thus satisfies the underlying debt and is freed of liability for it. Also, she ordinarily lacks any liability on the instrument itself. Thus, in the unlikely event the bank does not pay the instrument, the obligee cannot look to the obligor on any basis or theory.

There are exceptions to this exception:

- ◆ Even though a bank instrument is used, the parties can keep alive the underlying debt by agreeing to do so. Id. ("Unless otherwise agreed * * *").
- ◆ Also, even if they make no such agreement so that the debt is discharged, the obligor may indorse the instrument and thereby become secondarily liable on it behind the primary liability of the bank as "drawer-maker" (3-412) or acceptor.

3. Accord And Satisfaction

Sometimes, in an attempt to settle a disputed claim, the person against whom the claim is asserted issues a check to the claimant for an amount less than the full amount the claimant demands. The check is commonly known as a "*full-payment check*" which, when successfully used, results in discharging the claim upon payment of the check. In contract terms, it is known as an "accord and satisfaction." Success would depend on the common law, but Article 3 provides its own rules of accord and satisfaction when instruments are used. These rules are collected in 3-311 and, for the most part, follow the common law.

a. General Rule -- 3-311

The general rule is that the full-payment check fully discharges the claim for which it is given if these requirements are met:

- the check was tendered in good faith to the claimant as full satisfaction of the claim,
- the instrument or an accompanying written communication contained a conspicuous statement warning that the instrument was tendered in full satisfaction,
- the amount of the claim was unliquidated or subject to a bona fide dispute, and
- the claimant obtained payment of the check.

3-311(a-b). The discharge results even if the claimant expresses orally or in writing, on the instrument or elsewhere, that she rejects the settlement or that she still demands the balance of her claim.

b. Exceptions

There are two small exceptions.

1) If Claimant Is Organization

First, if the claimant is an organization, no discharge results unless the check is sent to the organization's office that handles disputed debts, so long as the person against whom the claim is asserted had prior warning to send full-payment checks there. 3-311(c)(1).

2) Claimant Repaying Full-Payment Check

Second, whether or not the claimant is an organization, a discharge can be undone by the claimant tendering repayment of the full-payment check within 90 days after the check was paid. 3-311(c)(2). This exception is designed for claimants who were unaware that the check was for full payment, not for claimants who have second thoughts about settling.

c. Limitation on Exceptions

Both exceptions are subject to a limitation. Neither exception applies, and the discharge stands, if the claimant actually knew within a reasonable time before trying to collect the check that it was tendered in full satisfaction of the claim. 3-311(d).

d. Warning About Scope of 3-311

Warning! There is no 3-311 discharge in the first instance unless the statute applies, which assumes that the instrument was negotiable so that Article 3 is applicable and that the four requirements for 3-311 discharge were met. When 3-311 is inapplicable for any reason, other law applies to determine if there was a valid accord and satisfaction. The other applicable law will almost certainly be common law, which is very unlikely to provide a discharge on facts that would fail the requirements of 3-311.

REVIEW QUESTIONS

1. What is the most basic rule governing liability on negotiable instruments?

2. Are you liable on a check on which a thief forges your signature? Is the thief liable on the check?

3. How should an agent sign an instrument when she acts for a principal? Why?

4. Explain the difference between primary and secondary liability on instruments.

5. T or F   Dishonor and notice of dishonor ordinarily are required to trigger the liability of a drawer of a draft and the indorser of a note or a draft.

6. What is the effect of unexcused delay in notifying an indorser of dishonor?

7. How does dishonor ordinarily occur with respect to a check in the check collection process governed by Article 4?

8. Give two reasons why a drawee is not liable on the instrument in the role of drawee.

9. Are there any circumstances under which the drawee bank on a check can be liable with respect to the instrument? If so, explain.

10. T or F   A party to an instrument is discharged from liability thereon by paying the instrument to anyone in possession of it.

11.   T or F   An unauthorized alteration of an instrument discharges the liability of a party whose obligation is thereby changed.

12.   Ordinarily, taking of an instrument for an underlying obligation affects the obligation by _____ [discharging] [suspending] it.

13.   Describe two circumstances in which taking an instrument discharges the underlying obligation.

14.   What are the requirements for a full-payment check to discharge the claim for which it is given?

15.   **T or F**   In any event, a claimant who takes a full-payment check can avoid the discharge by tendering repayment within 90 days.

Analysis

A. INTRODUCTION: MAIN PROPERTY ASPECTS OF INSTRUMENTS

Instruments are, first, contracts. They embody enforceable promises to pay money. Accordingly, the first chapters of this book focus on the contract liability of parties to instruments. Instruments are also property. Their ownership is assignable, and enforceability is transferable. Significantly, ownership and the right to enforce an instrument are not the same or inseparable. They often coincide, but they can split so that someone other than the owner of an instrument can enforce it, sometimes even when the instrument was stolen from the owner.

Typically, the right to enforce an instrument is deliberately transferred rather than stolen. *Transferring an instrument* vests in the transferee, derivatively, any right of the transferor to enforce the instrument. Normally, the transfer is part of a larger process of *negotiating* the instrument, which gives the transferee a fresh and independent right of enforcement. She enforces in her own name rather than through the transferor.

A transfer also involves duties because the law normally implies *warranties* that bind transferors of instruments. *Warranty liability* is different from contract liability on an instrument. Warranty liability usually is in addition to contract liability, but the former is not dependent on the latter and can exist without contract liability. Even a person who has not signed an instrument may incur warranty liability if she transfers the instrument or presents it for payment. In effect, transferors guarantee certain qualities about the instruments they convey and back this guarantee with their personal liability. So do the people who present instruments for payment. The transfer warranties differ somewhat from the presentment warranties, but both sets are alike in assuring a right to enforce the instrument.

A right to enforce, however, is not payment. Between the two are the risks that the obligor will be insolvent or can assert defenses that reduce or eliminate her obligation to pay the instrument. There is also the risk that a third party will intervene and assert an overriding claim of ownership. The transferee of an instrument -- even if she is a holder -- is generally subject to a fundamental principle of property law, *derivative title*. As applied to contract rights, it is normally expressed as the familiar rule that an assignee stands in the shoes of the assignor. It means that an assignee of a contract right or a transferee of an instrument is subject to the same claims and defenses that would prevent collection by the assignor or transferor.

Article 3 creates a very important exception that protects a *holder in due course* of an instrument. She takes free of most defenses to liability on the instrument that arose from an occurrence with a third party, and also takes free from a third party's claim to the instrument. Article 3 gives other favors to a holder in due course, but none so important as this immunity from claims and defenses. It is Article 3's most important property principle. A later chapter is dedicated to holders in due course. Before it are chapters devoted to warranty liability and claims and defenses to contract liability. This chapter begins the whole discussion of instruments as property by focusing on the most fundamental property right with respect to an instrument, the right to enforce it.

B. THE RELATIONSHIP OF TITLE AND THE RIGHT TO ENFORCE AN INSTRUMENT: OVERVIEW OF TRANSFER, NEGOTIATION, AND HOLDER STATUS

An instrument is property. It is a reified a right to the payment of money. 3-203 comment 1. Someone always owns the instrument in the sense of having title to it. Yet, an instrument is like other property that sometimes can be used or enjoyed by another person without the owner's permission, and that in exceptional circumstances can even be conveyed by the other person free of the owner's claim.   Always, it is a matter of balancing the importance of protecting the owner's claim against the need to insure the property's currency to the rest of the world.

1.   Article 3 Determines Right To Enforce, Not Ownership
Who owns an instrument -- who has title -- is determined by principles of property law apart from Article 3. 3-203 comment 1. Who can use and enjoy an instrument -- who can enforce it and exercise its other rights -- is determined by Article 3.

2.   Holder Can Enforce
Generally, any "holder" of an instrument can enforce it, and enforcement is normally restricted to a holder or someone with a holder's rights. 3-301. Holder does not mean owner, although typically the holder of an instrument owns it. Holder generally means someone in possession of an instrument that is payable to bearer or to her, meaning that she is identified by the instrument as the person to whom it is payable. 1-201(20). Why is such a person entitled to enforce an instrument?

> It is inherent in the character of negotiable instruments that any person in possession of an instrument which by its terms is payable to that person or to bearer * * * may be dealt with by anyone as a holder [that is, as someone entitled to enforce the instrument].

3-202 comment 2. It is inherent because of tradition and common understanding and also because the order or promise -- by its very terms -- extends to such a person.

3. Issue

a. Issue Usually Establishes First Holder

The first holder of an instrument usually gets possession because the instrument is *issued* to her. "'*Issue*' means the first delivery of an instrument by the maker or drawer, whether to a holder or nonholder, for the purpose of giving rights on the instrument to any person." 3-105 (a). "Delivery" means "voluntary transfer of possession." 1-201(14).

> *Example:* Buyer gives Seller a check or note payable to Seller's order. Buyer thereby issues the instrument. Seller takes it, gets possession, and is thereby a holder.

b. Issue to Nonholder

The possibility of issuance to a nonholder covers the issuance of an order instrument to a remitter who then delivers it to the payee -- a person purchases an instrument issued by someone else that is payable to a third party.

> *Example:* A cashier's check is payable to Seller but is issued by the Bank to the Buyer, who is the remitter only and not a holder. Buyer delivers the check to Seller who then becomes a holder because she is in possession of an instrument payable to her. Bank issues the check to Buyer, who is not a holder. Buyer delivers the check to Seller, who becomes a holder. Buyer's delivery is not issue. It is negotiation, which is another means of transferring an instrument so that the transferee becomes a holder. Negotiation is discussed later.

4. Transfer

As holder, Seller is a person entitled to enforce the instrument. She can convey this right of enforcement by *transferring the instrument*. This transfer is more than merely transferring possession of the instrument. Transferring the instrument means delivery of the instrument "by a person other than its issuer for the purpose of giving to the person receiving delivery the right to enforce the instrument." 3-203(a).

> *Example:* Seller, the payee of Buyer's note or check, sells the instrument to Bank or uses it as collateral or deposits it for collection. Seller thereby transfers it to Bank.

Transfer gives the transferee any right of the transferor to enforce the instrument. 3-203(b). Because Seller was a holder, Seller had the right to enforce the instrument. 3-301. Because of the transfer by Seller, Bank gets Seller's right of enforcement. On the other hand, a transfer does not give the Bank or any transferee a self-evident right of enforcement, only a derivative right that must be proved. Only when the plaintiff is herself a holder is she entitled to enforce an instrument on the basis of her status alone. A nonholder is entitled to enforce only by establishing that she claims through a holder. 3-301(ii). She must prove that the instrument was transferred to her by a holder or by someone who had the rights of a holder or that she acquired these rights by subrogation or succession. 3-308 comment 2.

5. Negotiation

A person becomes a holder of an instrument, post-issuance, only by the process of *negotiation.* 3-201(a). A voluntary transfer is normally part of negotiation, 3-201 comment 1, but is not always necessary for negotiation. Basically, an instrument is *negotiated* to a person when (1) she gets possession of an instrument (2) payable to bearer or to her that has been indorsed by everyone to whom previously it has been payable. No indorsements are necessary in the case of a bearer instrument that has never been payable to any identified person. Always, however, even in the case of a bearer instrument, holder status is never decided by possession alone. The nature or state of the instrument is an equal concern. A person in possession of a bearer instrument is not a holder solely because she is in possession of an instrument. She is a holder because of her possession of an instrument payable to bearer.

In the hypothetical case, Bank would become the holder of Buyer's note or check to Seller by taking possession of the instrument that Seller had indorsed. How Bank acquired possession of the instrument would not matter so long as the instrument carried Seller's indorsement. Typically, virtually always, possession changes by *delivery*, which is a voluntary transfer of possession. 3-203(a), 1-201(14). Seller intentionally and deliberately passes the instrument to Bank. Yet, the possession requirement of holder status would be met if Bank stole the instrument from Seller. All that matters to the Bank's holder status is possession, however obtained, of the instrument indorsed by Seller. Stealing the instrument would be wrong in every sense, and Bank would not own the instrument. Seller could retrieve it from the Bank, and could stop an action by the Bank to enforce the instrument. 3-305(c). On the other hand, so long as the Bank kept possession of the instrument and thereby its holder status, Buyer could discharge her liability on the instrument by voluntarily paying the Bank, even if Buyer knew of Seller's claim to the instrument, 3-602(a); also, a subsequent holder who took in due course from the Bank (or from a mediate transferee) could even enforce the instrument in a court action that the Seller could not stop despite her status as true owner. The holder in due course would take free of -- cut off -- Seller's claim. 3-305(b).

The Seller or any payee can avoid these consequences by not indorsing the instrument until the time she intends to transfer it. No one can become holder of an instrument, post-issuance, without the indorsement of a named payee; and the unindorsed instrument cannot be rightfully collected or enforced (in or out of court) by any person (immediate or remote), and cannot be freely paid, without proof that the payee voluntarily transferred her right to enforce.

6. Connection Between Ownership And Right To Enforce

Here, in the end, is the connection between property principles of ownership and Article 3 rules of transfer, negotiation, and enforcement. While title to an instrument and the right to enforce it are so far legally separate and distinct that neither establishes the other, the rules that determine the latter are a means of protecting the former. To insure this protection, owners respect Article 3's rules of transfer and negotiation so that, in practice, title and the right to enforce an instrument normally coincide throughout the instrument's life.

C. ENFORCEMENT

1. Persons Entitled To Enforce

The contract liabilities of maker, drawer, indorser, and acceptor are alike in a most important respect: each of them is obligated to:

- "a *person entitled to enforce the instrument * * **," or
- an *indorser* who pays the instrument, except that indorsers themselves are liable inter se only to subsequent indorsers.

3-412, 3-413(a), 3-414(b), 3-415(a). "*Person entitled to enforce*" means

- the holder of the instrument,
- a nonholder in possession of the instrument who has the rights of a holder, or
- a person not in possession of the instrument who is entitled to enforce the instrument pursuant to Section 3-309 or 3-418(d), which concern instruments that are lost, were stolen, or paid by mistake.

3-301. Any person who fits any of these categories is entitled to enforce the instrument "even though the person is not the owner of the instrument or is in wrongful possession of the instrument." Id.

a. Holder

A holder is a "person in possession" of an instrument that is "payable to bearer or, in the case of an instrument payable to an identified person, if the identified person is in possession." 1-201(20). A person becomes a holder either by issuance or negotiation, which are discussed elsewhere. For discussions of issue, see Chapter III supra and the first section of this chapter; for the details of negotiation, see the next section of this chapter.

b. Nonholder in Possession with Holder's Rights

A nonholder is entitled to enforce an instrument in her possession if she "has the rights of a holder." 3-301(ii). A nonholder having a holder's rights occasionally happens by subrogation or succession, and most commonly when a holder *transfers the instrument* to a person who does not herself become (i.e., qualify as or meet the requirements of) a holder.

> *Example:* Payee sells the instrument to Bank or pledges it as collateral for a loan and fails to indorse. A transfer occurred but not negotiation. Payee was a holder. Bank is not a holder. Nevertheless, as a result of the *transfer*, 3-203(a), the transferee acquires the right of the transferor, as a holder, to enforce the instrument. 3-203(b). The transferee therefore becomes a person entitled to enforce it within the meaning of 3-301, even though she is a nonholder. In sum, because a holder enjoys the right to enforce an instrument, so does her transferee even if the transferee is not herself a holder.

The same holds true for a remote transferee of a holder if the mediate conveyances between them were all transfers of the instrument, i.e., deliveries of the instrument intended to give each transferee the right to enforce the instrument. The right to enforce an instrument, which originates with any holder, will slide undiluted through an infinite number of transfers and can be asserted by the ultimate transferee as if she had taken the instrument directly from the holder. The transferee's only problem is proving that she claims through a holder and inherits the holder's right to enforce.

This derivative right of enforcement flows from the up side of a very basic principle of property law that title is derivative. The familiar down side is that a transferee gets only the interest in the property that belonged to her transferor and nothing more. All of the limits that applied to the transferor apply equally to the transferee. (A large exception is the holder-in-due-course doctrine which is not relevant at this point but terribly important later. See Chapters VI through VIII infra.)

The up side of derivative title, which applies here, is the rule that whatever interest the transferor could and did convey, it fully passes to the transferee with any accompanying benefits. This up side is known as the "*shelter principle*." It means that whatever rights a transferor could have enjoyed, these rights belong to her transferee who can freely assert them even though she does not personally and directly qualify for the rights.

c. Nonholder Without Possession In Exceptional Cases

Ordinarily, to enforce an instrument, a nonholder must not only have the rights of a holder, she must have possession of the instrument itself. 3-301(ii). The same is true for a holder because her very status requires possession. It is an element of the definition of "holder." 1-201(20). In sum, possession is essential for almost every person's right to enforce an instrument. Only in two very narrow, exceptional cases is a person entitled to enforce an instrument not in her possession.

1) Lost, Destroyed or Stolen Instruments

The easier exception to understand is the case in which the person would be entitled to enforce the instrument if she had possession of it, but the instrument was *lost, destroyed, or stolen*. Enforcement is possible in this case but only if these conditions are met:

* the person was in possession of the instrument and entitled to enforce it when loss of possession occurred,
* the loss of possession was not the result of a transfer by the person or a lawful seizure,
* the person cannot reasonably obtain possession of the instrument because the instrument was destroyed, its whereabouts cannot be determined, or it is in the wrongful possession of an unknown person or a person that cannot be found or is not amenable to service of process, and
* the person seeking enforcement proves the terms of the instrument and the person's right to enforce the instrument.

3-309(a-b). There is room here for harmful mischief or costly mistake. The instrument could be found or set free and end up in the hands of a holder in due course. This person would be entitled to payment even though the instrument had already been enforced through 3-309. For this reason, 3-309, provides for insurance:

> The court may not enter judgment in favor of the person seeking enforcement unless it finds that the person required to pay the instrument is adequately protected against loss that might occur by reason of a claim by another person to enforce the instrument. Adequate protection may be provided by any reasonable means.

3-309(b).

2) Different Rule for Bank Checks That Are Lost

Many states also deal specifically with the problem of enforcing cashier's, teller's and certified checks when such a check is lost, destroyed or stolen. In the typical situation, a person claims the right to receive the proceeds of a check that she has lost. The risk to the bank which honors the claim is that the check will end up in the hands of a holder in due course who can force the bank to pay the check. The bank will have paid twice. Perhaps the bank can recoup from the original claimant but the bank risks this person's solvency. The bank can protect itself by requiring the original claimant to provide security for any payment to her, but this imposes a large burden on this person.

Many states have enacted a statute that attempts to accommodate the interests of the bank and original claimant. See Minn. Stat. 336.3-312. The statute allows the claimant to make a claim for payment by providing the bank with a declaration of loss. The claim is enforceable at the later of the time the claim is made or the 90th day following the date or certification of the check. If the claim becomes enforceable before thc check is presented for payment, the bank is obliged to pay the claim and is discharged of all liability with respect to the check. The claim is legally ineffective prior to the time the claim become enforceable, and the bank must pay the check if the check is presented prior to the time of the claim's enforceability. The reasoning seems to be that if 90 days pass without presentment of the check, the claim of loss is probably legitimate and the possibility is small that someone will appear as a holder in due course of the instrument. In the unlikely event that such a person appears after the bank has honored an enforceable claim, the claimant is accountable for the check.

3) Instruments Paid by Mistake

In the other case in which a person can enforce an instrument not in her possession, a payor has paid the instrument by mistake and recovered the money. The person from whom payment is recovered should be free to collect from the right person; but the person who mistakenly paid the instrument probably got possession at that time and may be unable to return it in actionable form. In this case, the person from whom payment is recovered "has rights as a person entitled to enforce the * * * instrument." 3-418(d). Significantly, any discharge that resulted from the mistaken payment is effectively expunged because, upon recovery of the payment, the instrument is deemed dishonored. 3-418(d).

Example: Suppose, for example, that Buyer gives Seller a check as prepayment for goods that Seller promised to deliver. The Bank pays the check, but payment is a mistake because Buyer's account is empty. The Bank gets restitution from Seller. Seller can sue Buyer on the check, even if Bank inadvertently had returned the check to Buyer. Also, Buyer cannot defend on the basis of discharge by payment. When the Bank recovered the payment, the check was deemed dishonored .

d. Indorsers

The contract liability of parties to instruments runs not only to a "person entitled to enforce" the instrument, whom 3-301 defines. It also runs to an indorser who pays the instrument and to a drawer-turned-indoser in the case of an acceptor's liability. The reason is that an indorser is really a surety to any other party, except subsequent indorsers; and, as between a surety and the principal obligor, the latter should ultimately bear the responsibility of payment. Technically, however, an indorser is empowered to sue on an instrument only when and because she fits 3-301, not because a party's contract of liability is owed to her. Yet, in describing the persons entitled to enforce an instrument, 3-301 does not expressly include an indorser who paid the instrument and to whom, therefore, the maker, drawer, or acceptor is obligated. The paradox is avoided because the indorser, by other names, will usually fit 3-301.

1) Indorser Becoming Holder Against Upon Reacquisition

When an indorser pays an instrument, her liability is discharged but not the liability of persons liable to her. The instrument remains viable, and the indorser gets possession of it because, when she pays in full, the instrument is "surrendered" to her. 3-501(b)(2)(ii). In this case, her again getting possession of the instrument is called *reacquisition*. She can cancel or strike out her indorsement and any subsequent indorsement, including the indorsement that made the instrument payable to the person whom she paid. 3-207. By striking these indorsements, the instrument becomes payable to her or to bearer. By her own hand, she magically becomes a holder. Yes, it's legal! Id.

2) The Problem of the Anomalous Indorser

It is possible and not uncommon that an indorser who pays the instrument is not a former holder. It happens when the instrument was never negotiated to her; rather, she signed *only* as a surety, probably to lend her name and credit to the maker or drawer when the instrument was issued. In this case, her indorsement is out of the chain of transfer and is referred to as an *"anomalous indorsement*," 3-205(d), that is signed for *accommodation*. 3-419(a). She is an *accommodation party*, which is Aricle 3's name for a surety on a negotiable instrument. The magic of reacquisition, which allows striking indorsements, is not certainly available to her because, in terms of 3-207, she is not a "former holder." Prior law spoke in terms of reacquisition by a prior "party," 3-208 (1989 Official Text), N.I.L. 50, 121, and it was possible that reacquisition alone entitled an accommodation indorser to sue parties before her on the instrument. W. Britton, BILLS AND NOTES § 297 (2d ed. 1961). In a different way, the 1990 Article 3 provides in a limited way for the accommodation indorser. Because she is an accommodation party, and whether or not she is a holder, the indorser in this case who pays the instrument is, by special provision, a person "entitled to enforce the instrument against the *accommodated party*." 3-419(e) (emphasis added). More is said later about sureties and accommodation parties. See Chapter VII infra.

2. Procedures Of Enforcement

a. Plaintiff's Prima Facie Case

A person's liability on an instrument is based on her having signed it. Therefore, to make a prima facie case in court to enforce an instrument, the plaintiff need only produce the instrument and prove that she, the plaintiff, is a person entitled to enforce it under 3-301. Without more, the plaintiff "is entitled to payment * * *." 3-308(b), but this abbreviated procedure may lengthen at both ends and in the middle.

b. Establishing That Signature Binds Defendant

1) Presumed Effective Unless Denied

Because liability is based on the defendant's signature, the plaintiff's entitlement to payment assumes that the signature on the instrument binds the defendant, which would *not* be true if:

- the defendant did not make the signature, and it was not made by a representative whose signature bound the defendant; or,
- the defendant made the signature but she was acting with authority for someone else for the purpose of binding the other person rather than herself.

Generally, however, proving that the signature binds the defendant is not part of the plaintiff's case. *The law rebuttably presumes that the signature is effective unless the defendant pointedly challenges it.* Here is the rule:

> In an action with respect to an instrument, the authenticity of, and authority to make, each signature on the instrument is admitted unless specifically denied in the pleadings. 3-308(a).

2) Burdens If Effectivess Denied
    a) On Plaintiff To Persuade
        If the defendant properly denies the signature, "the burden of
        establishing validity is on the person claiming validity." Id. This means
        that the burden of persuasion, by a preponderance of the evidence, rests
        with the plaintiff to prove that the signature is authentic and authorized.
        1-201(8) ("persuading the triers of fact that the existence of the fact is
        more probable than its non-existence"). The plaintiff must carry this
        burden regardless of the reason the defendant denies the signature, even
        when the action is against an undisclosed principal. The plaintiff must
        prove that the instrument was signed for the defendant by an authorized
        representative whose signature bound the defendant.

    b) On Defendant To Go Forward First
        On the other hand, generally *the signature is presumed to be authentic
        and authorized,"* 3-308(a) (emphasis added). The effect is to put the
        burden of going forward with the evidence on the defendant. See
        1-201(31) (meaning of "presumed"). "[U]ntil some evidence is
        introduced which would support a finding that the signature is forged or
        unauthorized, the plaintiff is not required to prove that it is valid." 3-308
        comment 1. If the defendant produces this evidence, the plaintiff is put
        to her proof that the signature is authentic and authorized.

c. Proving Plaintiff's Entitlement to Enforce
Even if the defendant's signature is admitted or proved, the plaintiff suing on an
instrument cannot recover unless she "proves entitlement to enforce the
instrument under Section 3-301." 3-308(b). This proof is always part of the
prima facie case and is made from the instrument itself if the plaintiff is a
holder. 3-301(i); 3-308 comment 2 ("mere production * * * proves
entitlement"). Any other person in possession must prove by any admissible
evidence that she claims through a holder by transfer, subrogation, succession or
the like and thereby inherited the holder's right to enforce the instrument.
3-301(ii); 3-308 comment 2. In the rare case of a nonholder without possession,
she must prove that at the time of losing possession, she had holder status or the
rights of a holder. This requirement is explicit in the case of a lost, destroyed, or
stolen instrument, 3-309(a); it is necessarily implied in a 3-418(d) case to
enforce an instrument that was mistakenly paid.

d. Producing the Instrument
The plaintiff must produce the instrument to make her case. Production is
essential to judge authenticity and also to enable the defendant, in appropriate
circumstances, to acquire possession of the instrument upon paying it.

Otherwise, the defendant risks double payment of the instrument to a holder in due course. Production of the instrument is excused in only two very narrow cases, when the instrument was lost, stolen, or destroyed or the instrument was paid by mistake. See 3-301(iii), 3-309, 3-418(d). In these cases, which are discussed earlier in this chapter, the plaintiff is a person entitled to enforce even without possession of the instrument. 3-301(iii).

e. Defenses

The plaintiff is not home free even if she makes her prima facie case. Her right to payment is diluted or lost to the extent that "the defendant proves a defense or claim in recoupment * * *." 3-308(b). In this case, plaintiff nevertheless counters and finally wins "to the extent the plaintiff proves that the plaintiff has rights of a holder in due course which are not subject to the defense or claim." Id. On these very large issues, see Chapters VI and VIII infra, which are entirely devoted to them.

3. Using Extrinsic Evidence To Vary Liability From The Terms Of An Instrument

a. Interpretation: The Rule That Reads Writings Together

It is a general principle of law that writings executed as part of the same transaction must be read together as a single agreement -- at least as between the immediate parties. This principle applies to instruments by force of section 3-117, which provides:

> Subject to applicable law regarding exclusion of proof of contemporaneous or previous agreements, the obligation of a party to an instrument to pay the instrument may be modified, supplemented, or nullified by a separate agreement of the obligor and a person entitled to enforce the instrument, if the instrument is issued or the obligation is incurred in reliance on the agreement or as part of the same transaction giving rise to the agreement. To the extent an obligation is modified, supplemented, or nullified by an agreement under this section, the agreement is a defense to the obligation.

By this rule, therefore, the rights and duties of the immediate parties to an instrument, after issue, are determined by the instrument and also any other documents or writings that were executed as part of the same transaction. Everything is read together even though the different writings do not refer to each other.

The separate writings do not affect the negotiability of an instrument that accompanies them, but a holder in due course will probably take free of any limitations on enforcing the instrument contained in a separate writing unknown to her. An immediate party and anyone else, however, is subject to limitations and other terms of the separate writings. Disputes over the meaning of terms which are part of the total agreement should be resolved under the basic principles of contract interpretation, see Restatement Second of Contracts §§ 200-204, except where displaced by statutory rules of construction and substance.

b. Scope: The Parol Evidence Rule

Problems of a different kind are posed when one of the immediate parties tries to show that the rights and duties arising from the instrument are somehow altered by an oral statement made at the time of issue or by a written or oral agreement made before it was issued. The legal effect of these statements and agreements depends largely upon the *parol evidence rule* which may exclude them and thus narrow the scope of the parties' total effective agreement. The parol evidence rule applies, in its common-law form, to negotiable instruments in much the same way that it applies, in various forms, to other written contracts. The rule trumps section 3-117 which would otherwise require giving effect to other writings executed before the instrument but as part of the same transaction. Accordingly, with only minor exceptions which will be explained, neither the issuing party nor the party to whom the instrument is issued is permitted to introduce any evidence, written or oral, of what occurred prior to signing or any oral evidence of what was agreed at the time of signing for the purpose of changing, adding to, or deleting, any terms of the instrument. For example, such evidence would not be admitted for the purpose of changing the promise or order, the time or place of payment, the amount to be paid, or the words of negotiability.

1) Conditional Delivery and the Rule: Conditions Precedent and Conditions Subsequent

In applying the parol evidence rule to agreements made with or before a negotiable instrument, the courts make a vital distinction between *conditions precedent* and *conditions subsequent.* A condition precedent is intended to prevent an instrument from taking effect until the occurrence of the condition. A condition subsequent is intended to terminate the liability of a party on an instrument after it has taken effect. Courts have consistently held that the parol evidence rule does not exclude parol evidence that an instrument was delivered on a condition precedent, but a large majority of the courts have held that it does exclude evidence of delivery on a condition subsequent. Article 3 expressly agrees that, as against parties not holders in due course, extraneous evidence is admissible to show that an instrument was delivered on a condition precedent or for a special purpose only. It does so by providing that

[a]n instrument that is conditionally issued or is issued for a special purpose is binding on the maker or drawer, but failure of the condition or special purpose to be fulfilled is a defense.

3-105(b).

Example: Typical cases in which a person who signs and delivers a negotiable instrument is permitted to prove by parol evidence the existence of a condition precedent that will shield her from liability are those in which a party signs a note as maker and delivers it with the understanding that she is not to become liable on it until some other named person signs as comaker; where a maker signs and delivers a renewal note with the understanding that it is not to take effect until the original note is returned; or where a buyer signs and delivers her check as part payment of the price with the understanding that it will not bind her unless and until she is able to obtain a loan for the balance from a third person. In these cases the evidence of the condition is introduced to show that the instrument never took effect as a contract, and not to contradict the writing, and so it is admissible. See, e. g., *Weirton S. & L. Co. v. Cortez*, 157 W.Va. 691, 203 S.E.2d 468 (1974).

Example: Typical cases in which a person who signs and delivers a negotiable instrument is barred from introducing parol evidence of a condition subsequent are those in which the maker of a note offers to prove that, at the time of delivery, it was orally agreed that the maker would be discharged from liability by rendering some performance other than the payment of money or that, at the time of delivery, it was orally agreed that the maker would be liable only until some other specified person signed the note at which time the maker would be discharged. In cases such as these, the instrument is assumed to be an integrated writing that represents the true contract of the parties and the parol evidence is inadmissible because it is offered to change that contract.

2) Understanding Signer Is Not To Be Bound

Occasionally, a person sued on a negotiable instrument tries to avoid liability altogether by proving that, when she signed, it was agreed that she would not be liable under any circumstances. Various reasons have been given for such understandings. For example, it has been claimed that the instrument was signed as a mere formality, or was intended to conceal the identity of the true party or that it played a role in bookkeeping procedures. Sometimes it has appeared that there was a plan to deceive a third party such as a bank examiner. Obviously, to allow such a defense too readily would go far to undermine the stability of commercial paper. However, parol evidence offered to prove an agreement of complete immunity to liability on the instrument is akin to parol evidence of a condition precedent, which is clearly admissible. Nonetheless, in a large majority of the cases, parol evidence of such an agreement against liability has been excluded on the ground that it contradicts the writing and violates the parol evidence rule.

4. Liability Over

Often a party who loses an action on a negotiable instrument has a right of recourse against some prior party, who in turn may have recourse against a party prior to her, and so on. When a right of recourse exists, it is possible to have the matter settled in several lawsuits. Usually, however, it is more efficient to settle the various issues and determine the various liabilities in a single lawsuit. For the purpose of supplementing existing state and federal statutes relating to procedures for interpleader and joinder of parties, and also to help provide for more efficient disposal of multi-party litigation, Article 3 gives this rule:

> In an action for breach of an obligation for which a third person is answerable over pursuant to this Article or Article 4, the defendant may give the third person written notice of the litigation, and the person notified may then give similar notice to any other person who is answerable over. If the notice states (i) that the person notified may come in and defend and (ii) that failure to do so bind the person notified in an action later brought by the person giving the notice as to any determination of fact common to the two litigations, the person notified is so bound unless after seasonable receipt of the notice the person notified does come in and defend.

3-119.

5. Statutes Of Limitations

Article 3 was missing a statute of limitations until 1990 when 3-118 was added "to define the time within which an action to enforce an obligation, duty, or right arising under Article 3 must be commenced." 3-118 comment 1. Before then, other local law defined the limitations period. Actually, 3-118 includes six statutes of limitations for suits on instruments. Which statute applies depends on the nature of the instrument and when it is payable.

a. Common Instruments
Consider the most common instruments.

1) Ordinary Check

In the case of an *ordinary check*, or other unaccepted draft, "an action to enforce the obligation of a party * * * to pay the draft must be commenced within three years after dishonor of the draft or 10 years after the date of the draft, whichever period expires first." 3-118(c).

2) Note Payable At Definite Time

For a note payable at a definite time, it is "six years after the due date or dates stated in the note or, if a due date is accelerated, within six years after the accelerated due date." 3-118(a).

3) Demand Note

The rule for a *demand note* depends on whether or not payment has been demanded:

> [I]f demand for payment is made to the maker of a note payable on demand, an action to enforce the obligation of a party to pay the note must be commenced within six years after the demand. If no demand for payment is made to the maker, an action to enforce the note is barred if neither principal nor interest on the note has been paid for a continuous period of 10 years.

3-118(b). This design is intended "to require reasonably prompt action [six years] to enforce notes on which there is default" and "to bar notes that no longer represent a claim to payment [that someone intends to enforce]," 3-118 comment 2, which is likely of a note that has been dormant for ten years. The effect of a payment of principal or interest within ten years is to start a new ten-year period.

b. **Any Party's Liability Affected**

It is very important to understand that the applicable statute applies the same to any party's obligation on the instrument. Thus, for example, "indorsers who may become liable on an instrument after issue are subject to a period of limitations running from the same date as that of the maker or drawer." 3-118 comment 2.

c. **Applies to More Than Contract Liability**

Section 3-118 covers more than suits on instruments. Its subsection (g) "covers warranty and conversion cases and other actions to enforce obligations or rights arising under Article 3" that are extrinsic to instruments themselves. 3-118 comment 6.

d. Supplemental Law

It does not answer all questions that arise with respect to statutes of limitations. Most significant, "the circumstances under which the running of a limitations period may be tolled is left to other law pursuant to Section 1-103." 3-118 comment 1.

D. NEGOTIATION -- BECOMING A HOLDER OTHER THAN BY ISSUANCE

1. Introduction And Basic Rules: Possession Always And Indorsement Sometimes

Basically, only a holder can enforce an instrument or someone who claims through a holder. 3-301. A holder is anyone in possession of an instrument payable to her or payable to bearer. 1-201(20). There are two ways to become a holder:

A person can become holder of an instrument when the instrument is *issued* to that person, or the status of holder can arise as a result of an event that occurs [apart from and usually] after issuance. "*Negotiation*" is the term used in Article 3 to describe this post-issuance event."

3-201 comment 1 (emphasis added).

a. Review of Holder Status By Issuance

1) First Holder Usually Takes By Issuance

Almost always, the first holder of an instrument is the person to whom it is issued. "*Issue*" means "the first delivery of an instrument by the maker or drawer, whether to a holder or nonholder, for the purpose of giving rights on the instrument to any person." 3-105(a). The maker or drawer writes the instrument payable to the person's order, or payable to bearer, and delivers it to her.

2) First Holder Taking Other Than By Issuance

It is possible, but relatively rare, that the first holder acquires the instrument other than by issuance. It happens in two exceptional cases.

- The more common case is the issuance of an order instrument to a remitter who then delivers it to the payee.
- The other case is the original payee of an order instrument getting possession from the maker or drawer other than by delivery of it to her; or anyone getting possession of a bearer instrument from its maker or drawer without delivery.

In both exceptional cases, the person becomes a holder but not by issuance. It happens by negotiation in both cases, except when the payee of an order instrument takes it from the maker or drawer without delivery. In this very rare case, the payee fits the definition of holder but her possession results from neither issue nor negotiation.

b. Meaning of Negotiation

"'*Negotiation*' means a transfer of possession, whether voluntary or involuntary, of an instrument by a person other than the issuer to a person who thereby becomes its holder." 3-201(a). It most commonly explains how a person -- any person -- becomes a subsequent holder, either immediately or remotely, after the first holder who normally will have acquired the instrument by issue to her. Only by negotiation can "the status of holder * * * arise * * * after issuance." 3-201 comment 1.

c. Process of Negotiation: Depends on Whether Instrument Is Payable to Bearer or Identified Person

Negotiation is both a noun and a verb, an end and the means for accomplishing it. The purpose of 3-201(a) is only to label the process and explain the result of negotiation, which is that the transferee becomes a holder. The process itself -- the conduct necessary for this result -- is the verb form of negotiation and is explained in 3-201(b). It depends on how the instrument is payable:

* If an instrument is *payable to an identified person*, negotiation requires --
    √   transfer of possession of the instrument, *and*
    √   its *indorsement* by the holder.
* If an instrument is *payable to bearer*, it may be negotiated by transfer of possession alone.

3-201(b). To engage in this conduct is to negotiate the instrument. Doing so is a negotiation of the instrument, and the result of this negotiation is that the transferee of possession becomes a holder. Her situation thereupon matches the Article 1 definition of "holder." See 1-201(20).

2. The Constant, Common Requirement For Negotiation: *"Transfer Of Possession"*

Whether the instrument is payable to bearer or an identified person, a "*transfer of possession*" is necessary. "Negotiation always requires a change of possession in the instrument because nobody can be a holder without possessing the instrument, either directly or through an agent." 3-201 comment 1. *It is very important to understand that "transfer of possession" for purposes of 3-201 is not the same as the transfer of an instrument [when "[a]n instrument is transferred"] for purposes of 3-203.* The latter requires and is limited to a voluntary transfer. The former includes an involuntary transfer and any other change of possession. Indeed, how possession is acquired is unimportant, both as to means and motive. It is a transfer of possession when a thief steals an instrument. In sum, the clearer and more accurate meaning of negotiation is becoming a holder by *getting or taking possession in any manner*, even without a voluntary or involuntary transfer by the person who thereby loses possession.

3. Indorsement Required When Payable To Identified Person
   Whether or not an indorsement is necessary to negotiate an instrument depends on how the instrument is payable. Indorsement is necessary only if the instrument is payable to an identified person. If it is payable to bearer, getting possession of the instrument is alone sufficient for the process of negotiation, 3-201(b); and whoever gets possession is a holder because of the negotiation. 3-201(a). *There is more here than meets the eye because how an instrument is presently payable can turn on how it was formerly payable.*

   a. How An Instrument Becomes Payable to an Identified Person or Bearer and How It is Negotiated
      1) Original Negotiation -- Drawn or Made Payable To Order or To Bearer
         As originally drawn or made, an instrument is payable either to order or to bearer. See 3-104(a)(1).

         a) Drawn to Bearer Is Payable to Bearer
            If the instrument is payable to bearer, as defined in 3-109(a), it is equally payable to bearer for purposes of 3-201(b) and negotiation. The instrument "may be negotiated by transfer of possession alone." 3-201(b). For this purpose, "transfer of possession" means any change of possession. Negotiation occurs when anybody gets possession in any way. Anybody in possession is a holder.

            Example: Suppose Buyer issued a check or note payable to cash or otherwise to bearer. Thief stole the instrument before Seller indorsed. Thief is a holder. Seller's indorsement was unnecessary for negotiation.

         b) Drawn to Order Is Payable to Identified Person
            An instrument originally drawn or made payable to order is -- by definition -- payable to an identified person. 3-109(b). Negotiation of the instrument requires the payee's indorsement, which means her signature on the instrument. She or her authorized representative must

sign it. Nobody else's signature is her signature; therefore, nobody else's signature is her indorsement; thus, nobody can become a holder without her signature.

Example: Suppose Buyer's instrument was payable to Seller's order. Thief stole the instrument before Seller indorsed. Thief indorsed the instrument using Seller's name. Thief is not a holder. The result is the same if an unauthorized representative of Seller indorsed rather than Thief.

2) Negotiation Thereafter -- Depends on Nature of Indorsement
a) Special Indorsement

Whether an instrument originally was payable to order or to bearer, it is payable to an identified person if it is *specially indorsed.* A "*special indorsement*" is "an indorsement * * * made by the holder of an instrument, whether payable to an identified person or payable to bearer," that "identifies a person to whom it makes the instrument payable * * *." 3-205(a). It usually consists of a simple instruction to pay an identified person, such as "Pay Jane Smith" or "Pay Named Bank," that is followed by the holder's signature. It need not contain "order" language of 3-109(b), and can identify the person to pay in any manner that is permitted by 3-110, which contains rules for identifying the original payee.

A special indorsement changes an instrument from payable to bearer to payable to an identified person (the person whom the indorser named). The special indorsement would not be required for negotiation of a bearer instrument but would insure against enforcement by anyone except the identified person (or someone with her rights). Any further negotiation would require this person's indorsement. No one else could become a holder without it.

Example: Suppose Buyer issued a bearer instrument to Seller. Negotiation would occur by anyone getting possession of the instrument. Anyone who got possession would become a holder entitled to enforce even without Seller's consent. To guard against this happening, Seller could specially indorse to herself or another identified person whom Seller intends to become a holder. Negotiation would require the indorsement of whomever she named. No one could become a holder without the person's consent.

b) Blank Indorsement
An indorsement by a holder that is not special is a *"blank indorsement,"* which means that the holder indorses without identifying a person to whom the instrument is payable. A blank indorsement changes an instrument that is payable to the holder, as an identified person, to an instrument that is payable to bearer. 3-205(b). Thereafter, it "may be negotiated by transfer of possession alone until specially indorsed," id., just as if it had been issued originally as a bearer instrument. This was recognized by Lord Mansfield in 1781 in deciding *Peacock v. Rhodes*, 2 Doug. 633, 97 Eng. Rep. 871, wherein he said, "I see no difference between a note indorsed blank and one payable to bearer. They both go by delivery and possession proves property in both cases."

Example: Suppose Buyer's instrument is payable to Seller's order, which is typical. Therefore, Seller's indorsement is required to negotiate the instrument to Bank. How the instrument is thereafter negotiated is determined by how Seller indorses when she transfers the instrument to Bank. If Seller specially indorses to Bank, the Bank's indorsement is required for negotiation. If Seller indorses in blank, negotiation occurs whenever anybody gets possession. Anyone in possession is a holder. To prevent this happening, Bank could specially indorse, or it could convert the blank indorsement to special merely by inserting "Pay" followed by its name directly above the blank indorsement.

c) Special or Blank AND Qualified or Unqualified
Every indorsement is either special or blank, in addition to being either qualified or unqualified. See Chapter III supra. They describe different, entirely separate qualities of the indorsement. The typical indorsement is blank and unqualified.

3) The Grand Importance Of No Missing Indorsements
In the end, the whole process of negotiation can be encapsulated and summarized in two grand rules:

*   **An instrument cannot be negotiated that is missing the indorsement of any former or present holder to whom, as an identified person, the instrument was or is payable. Except for her, nobody is or can become a holder until she indorses.**
*   **An instrument is negotiated whenever any person gets possession of an instrument that is indorsed by every former holder to whom, as**

identified persons, the instrument was payable. Anybody in possession is a holder.

Everything else about negotiation really serves to explain and support these rules, but they cannot be understood or even stated without knowing everything else.

b.   Identifying Person To Whom Payable -- 3-110
A person to whom an instrument is payable may be identified in any way, including by name, identifying number, office, or account number. 3-110(c). The test to determine who the instrument identifies is the intent of the person signing as, or in the name or behalf of, the issuer, whether or not the person signing is authorized to do so. 3-110(a).

Example: If X signs a check as drawer of a check on X's account, the intent of X controls. If X, as President of Corporation, signs a check as President in behalf of Corporation as drawer, the intent of X controls. If X forges Y's signature as drawer of a check, the intent of X also controls. * * * In the case of a check payable to "John Smith," since there are many peope in the world named "John Smith" it is not possible to identify the payee of the check unless there is some further identification or the intention of the drawer is determined. * * * [T]he intention of the drawer determines which John Smith is the person to whom the check is payable. * * * The same issue is presented in cases of misdescriptions of the payee. The drawer intends to pay a person known to the drawer as John Smith. In fact that person's name is James Smith or John Jones or some other entirely different name. If the check identifies the payee as John Smith, it is nevertheless payable to the person intended by the drawer. 3-110 comment 1.

In case the signer is not human, as with a computer or check-writing machine, the relevant intent is that of the person who supplied the payee's name, even if this person acts without authority and wrongfully. 3-110(b). The issue of whom the instrument names as payee usually translates, of course, into the issue of who can properly indorse the instrument.

c.   Place of Indorsement on the Instrument
An indorsement must be written on the instrument. Normally, it appears on the reverse side of the instrument, but it may appear elsewhere. It can even be written on a paper affixed to the instrument even though there is room for the indorsement on the instrument, 3-204 comment 1. The paper is called an

allonge, 3-204 comment 1, and is considered part of the instrument. 3-204(a). To cover cases where the capacity in which a person signed is uncertain, "[t]he general rule is that a signature is an indorsement if the instrument does not indicate an unambiguous intent of the signer not to sign as an indorser." 3-204 comment 1, 3-204(a).

d. Exceptional Cases In Which Missing Indorsement Is Excused

1) Reacquisition

"Reacquisition" refers to the transfer of an instrument to a former holder. 3-207. If the instrument is payable to someone else because of indorsements that were added after she first became a holder, the former holder can cancel these indorsements so that the instrument once more is payable to her or to bearer. Id. She again becomes a holder and may negotiate the instrument even without the indorsement of the person to whom the instrument was payable when the former holder reacquired it.

2) Checks Deposited For Collection

Occasionally, through oversight or otherwise, a payee deposits a check or other item in a bank for collection without indorsing it. If ordinary principles applied, the bank could not become a holder without getting the depositor's indorsement. For the bank to return the item for indorsement in this situation, however, delays collection with little advantage to the drawer and none to the depositor or bank. This explains why Article 4 provides:

> If a customer delivers an item to a depositary bank for collection * * * the depositary bank becomes a holder of the item at the time it receives the item for collection if the customer at the time of delivery was a holder of the item, whether or not the customer indorses the item, and, if the bank satisfies the other requirements * * * is a holder in due course * * *."

4-205(1). Under this section a depositary bank that receives an item for collection without the depositor's indorsement is automatically a holder if the depositor was a holder. The depositor's indorsement is not necessary to the bank's holder status even if the instrument identifies the depositor as the person to whom the instrument is payable. Further, if the bank otherwise qualifies, it becomes a holder in due course. Also, if a drawee bank pays such an item, it is entitled to charge the drawer's account. The check is properly payable and chargeable to the drawer's account despite the missing indorsement of the depositor.

3) Risk Allocation

An indorsement is not effective unless it is the signature of the person whose indorsement is required, by her personally or an authorized representative. Because of special rules, however, a person's indorsement by a thief or other unauthorized person will be effective in certain situations. These rules cover situations of wrongdoing that the law believes are most easily prevented by the holder. She should police against them and should not be able to shift any losses that result from the wrongdoing to anyone else other than the wrongdoer. The technical means for effecting this policy is to deem that in these situiations, an indorsement by anybody in the name of the person to whom the instrument is payable is effective. These special rules are mentioned here because they apply to all instruments, but in practice they are most often applied to checks and thus are discussed more throughly in a later chapter that deals with check fraud.

a) Impostor

"If an impostor, by use of the mails or otherwise, induces the issuer of an instrument to issue the instrument to the impostor, or to a person acting in concert with the impostor, by impersonating the payee of the instrument or a person authorized to act for the payee, an indorsement of the instrument by any person in the name of the payee is effective as the indorsement of the payee in favor of a person who, in good faith, pays the instrument or takes it for value or for collection." 3-404(a).

b) Nominal or Fictitious Payee

"If (i) a person whose intent determines to whom an instrument is payable * * * does not intend the person identified as payee to have any interest in the instrument, or (ii) the person identified as payee of an instrument is a fictitious person, the following rules apply until the instrument is negotiated by special indorsement: (1) Any person in possession of the instrument is its holder. (2) An indorsement by any person in the name of the payee stated in the instrument is effective as the indorsement of the payee in favor of a person who, in good faith, pays the instrument or takes it for value or for collection." 3-404(b)

c) Employee Fraud

"[I]f an employer entrusted an employee with responsibility with respect to the instrument and the employee or a person acting in concert with the employee makes a fraudulent indorsement of the instrument, the indorsement is effective as the indorsement of the person to whom the instrument is payable if it is made in the name of that person." 3-405(b).

4. Incomplete Negotiation: The Effect Of A Missing Indorsement When The Transferee Is Entitled To The Indorsement

Occasionally, an instrument payable to order or to a special indorsee is delivered for value by the payee or the indorsee without her indorsement. When this occurs, the transferee's status may be summarized as follows: (1) The transferee is not a holder. (2) The transferee acquires only the rights of the transferor against prior parties. (3) Unless the transferor and transferee have agreed otherwise, "the transferee has a specifically enforceable right to the unqualified indorsement of the transferor." 3-203(c). It means that the transferee may obtain a decree of specific performance ordering the transferor, under pain of punishment for contempt of court, to indorse. Because this order is issued by a court of equity, the transferee is sometimes said to have equitable title prior to obtaining the indorsement. Actually, if her transferor owned the instrument, the transferee is the true owner even though she is not yet the holder. (4) When the transferor completes the negotiation by indorsing, only then does the transferee become the holder. "[N]egotiation of the instrument does not occur until the indorsement is made." Id.

5. Negotiation By Multiple Payees

An instrument payable to order may name several payees either in the alternative, as "A, B, or C," or together as "A, B and C." A special indorsement may do the same. Negotiability is unaffected, but there are special rules about how to negotiate such an instrument.

- If the instrument is payable to two or more payees in the alternative, it is payable to any one of them and it may be negotiated, discharged or enforced by any one of them who has possession of it. To negotiate such an instrument, the indorsement of only one of them is required.
- If the instrument is payable to several payees together, it may be negotiated, discharged, or enforced only by all of them acting together. To negotiate an instrument that names several payees together, it must be indorsed by all of them.
- If an instrument payable to two or more people is ambiguous as to whether it is payable to the persons alternatively, the instrument is payable to the persons alternatively.

3-110(d).

6. Negotiation When Name Is Misspelled Or Misstated

Occasionally, an instrument is made payable to a payee or indorsee under a misspelled name or name other than her own. In this case, an indorsement in the name that appears on the instrument is legally sufficient for an effective negotiation, but this alone is commercially unsatisfactory because of the difficulty a later holder might have in proving the identity of the indorser. An indorsement in her true name alone also is legally sufficient for a negotiation, but this is unsatisfactory because a later transferee may be uncertain about the state of title. To avoid this difficulty, the Code provides that any person paying or giving value for the instrument may require the indorser to sign both names. 3-204(d).

7. Effect Of Attempt To Negotiate Less Than Balance Due

If an instrument has been paid in part, it may be negotiated as to the balance due. To be effective as a negotiation, however, an indorsement must transfer the entire instrument or the entire unpaid balance. If the indorsement purports to transfer less, it operates only as a partial assignment, 3-203(d), and the partial assignee does not become a holder or acquire her advantages. "[N]egotiation of the instrument does not occur." Id. Other local law determines whether or not the partial assignee can sue to enforce her rights and the conditions under which she may do so. 3-203 comment 5. This rule against partial negotiation does not apply to an indorsement that transfers only a security interest in the instrument. Quite the opposite is true. The indorsement is fully effective as an unqualified indorsement of the instrument. 3-204(c).

8. Effect Of Negotiation That May Be Rescinded

A negotiation is effective even if it may be rescinded on the grounds of incapacity, fraud, duress, mistake, illegality, or because it was made in breach of duty, 3-202(a), and even if it is made by a thief, a finder, or someone else acting without authority. In fact, although the transaction in which it occurs is held to be entirely void because of illegality, an adjudication of incompetency, or on any other ground, a transfer meeting the requirements of negotiation is fully an effective negotiation. Consequently, the transferee of an instrument in any of these transactions is a holder with full power to negotiate it further as long as she retains possession; and the transferor loses her rights with respect to the instrument until, by other law, she rescinds the negotiation and recovers the instrument by replevin or otherwise. The ability to do so can be lost, however, because generally "those remedies may not be asserted against a subsequent holder in due course or a person paying the instrument in good faith and without knowledge of facts that are a basis for rescission or other remedy." 3-202(b). This immunity presumably applies even when the rescission is based on defects and infirmities akin to real defenses to payment that a holder in due course cannot avoid. Compare 3-305(a)(1) and 3-306. (For a discussion of claims and defenses to instruments, see Chapter VI infra.)

E. RESTRICTIVE INDORSEMENTS

In addition to the qualities of qualified or unqualified and blank or special, every indorsement is also either restrictive or unrestrictive. A restrictive indorsement is an indorsement that would limit the purpose to which the proceeds of an instrument are applied, so that a person is accountable who pays the instrument for any other use. The most familiar restrictive indorsements, which may also be the only legally effective ones, are collection and trust indorsements, such as "For Deposit Only" or "Pay to T in trust for B." Between them, collection indorsements are more common. Typically, however, indorsements are blank, unqualified, and silently unrestrictive, containing no restriction of any kind on the use or purpose of the instrument or its proceeds or how they should be applied. A restrictive indorsement generally does not prevent further transfer or negotiation or affect an indorsee's right to enforce the instrument. Moreover, neither the indorsement nor knowledge of it prevents or affects a person's becoming a holder in due course. The consequence of a restrictive indorsement occurs when the terms of an effective restriction are violated by someone who is bound by the indorsement. The violation can prevent the person becoming a holder in due course or result in her personal liability.

1. Collection Indorsements

a. Meaning of Collection Indorsement

Suppose that X intends to deposit her pay check in her account at DB Bank, a depositary bank. She wants to insure, as far as she can, that her account is actually credited and that the instrument is not misdirected or misused. Therefore, she will typically indorse in blank, write her account number, and add words such as "'for deposit,' 'for collection,' or other words indicating a purpose of having the instrument collected by a bank for the indorser or for a particular account * * *." 3-206(c). These added words constitute a restrictive indorsement, commonly known as a *collection indorsement*.

b. Who Is Effected

The indorsement binds:

- any nonbank,
- a depositary bank that purchases the instrument or takes it for collection, and
- a payor bank that is also the depositary bank or that takes the instrument for immediate payment over the counter from a person other than a collecting bank.

3-206(c)(1-3). Put another way, a collection indorsement generally binds every person except an intermediary bank (4-105(4)) or non-depositary payor bank (payor bank that is not also the depositary bank).

1) Conversion Liability

To be bound means that the person is liable for conversion unless the amount paid for the instrument is received by the indorser or applied consistently with the indorsement. Here is the drafter's example:

> ***Example:*** [S]uppose a check is payable to X, who indorses in blank but writes above the signature the words "For deposit only." The check is stolen and is cashed at a grocery store by the thief. The grocery store indorses the check and deposits it in Depositary Bank. The account of the grocery store is credited and the check is forwarded to Payor Bank which pays the check. * * * [T]he grocery store and Depositary Bank are converters of the check because X did not receive the amount paid for the check. Payor Bank and any intermediary bank in the collection process are not liable to X.

3-206 comment 3.

2) Violation Prevents Holder in Due Course

A "*purchaser*" of an instrument who is a converter is also *not* a holder in due course. 3-206(e). Here, the term "purchaser" probably includes any person who is a converter under 3-206(c), even though (c) appears to use the term more narrowly. The usual meaning of "purchaser" is very broad. See 1-201(32-33). Moreover, in the case of a collecting bank taking an instrument for collection, the usual approach of the law is to apply the same rules whether the bank purchases the item or is handling it only as agent for a customer. See 4-201(a) & comment 1. In any event, apart from 3-206(e), it would seem impossible for any converter to satisfy the requirements of innocence and good faith that every holder must satisfy to achieve due-course status. 3-302(a)(2). These requirements for becoming a holder in due course would not be avoided because of the inapplicability of 3-206(e), and its inapplicability would not mean that a person's conversion should be overlooked in deciding if she met the requirements.

> ***Example:*** Suppose that the Payor Bank, in the example above, dishonored the check for some reason, perhaps because the drawer stopped payment. The check would bounce back to the Depositary Bank and probably keep bouncing to the grocery store. In any event, whichever of them sued X or the drawer, neither of them would be a holder in due course because each of them violated the restrictive indorsement.

Example: For another example, if P, the payee, indorses a check, "for deposit," and delivers it to A, her agent, the depositary bank is charged with knowing that the proceeds must be credited to P's account. If the bank takes the check from A and pays A the amount of the check, or credits A's account or applies it toward satisfaction of A's indebtedness to the bank, the bank is liable to P for conversion because the value it gives is not applied consistently with P's restrictive indorsement. For the same reason, the bank could not qualify as a holder in due course and, if it sued the drawer, would be subject to any defense that the drawer might have. In contrast, if the bank credits the amount of the check to P's account and allows P to withdraw the proceeds, it could qualify as a holder in due course because in this case the value it gives is applied consistently with P's restrictive indorsement.

c. Instruments Affected

The rules of restrictive indorsements are not limited to the check collection process or to checks. They are equally applicable to collection indorsements on notes.

Example: Suppose that P, the payee of a note, indorses it "for collection," and delivers it to A, her agent, with instructions to obtain payment from M, the maker. Typically, A will present the note to the maker at maturity, obtain payment, and remit the proceeds to P. In this case A becomes a holder, but not a holder for value because she gives no value. Since she is not a holder for value, A is not a holder in due course; thus, if M has any defense against P, she can assert it against A. If A had paid P the amount of the note when she received it, or by mutual agreement they had cancelled some debt owed by P to A, A would have given value, and if she met the other requirements, A would have been a holder in due course. Consequently, A would not have been subject to the defense which M might have had against P, unless A had learned of it prior to giving the value.

Example: Suppose that A, instead of taking the note to M, transfers it to T; can T become a holder in due course? She can if the value she pays for the instrument is applied consistently with P's restrictive indorsement. If she actually pays A the amount of the note, she becomes a holder in due course despite the restrictive indorsement because such payment is contemplated by the indorsement itself.

The result is different if the value is not applied consistently with P's restrictive indorsement, as by crediting A personally with the amount of the note.

2. Trust Indorsements

Sometimes the purpose of a restrictive indorsement is to benefit the indorser or someone else in some way other than by providing for collection or deposit. For example, P, the holder of a note, wishing to benefit herself, may indorse it, "Pay T in trust for P," or, wishing to benefit C, may indorse it, "Pay T for the benefit of C." This restrictive indorsement is commonly known as a *trust indorsement*, "an indorsement using words to the effect that payment is to be made to the indorsee as agent, trustee, or other fiduciary for the benefit of the indorser or another person * * *." 3-206(d). The person who takes from the indorsee is not affected by the trust restriction, even if the indorsee violates a fiduciary duty to the indorser, unless "there is *notice* of breach of fiduciary duty as provided in Section 3-307." 3-206(d)(1) (emphasis added). Section 3-307 defines notice of breach of fiduciary duty that will prevent a holder from becoming a holder in due course. Subsequent transferees or the person who pays is affected only if she *"knows* that the fiduciary dealt with the instrument or its proceeds in breach of fiduciary duty." 3-206(d)(2) (emphasis added).

3. Indorsements With Ineffective Restrictions
a. Indorsements Purporting To Prohibit Further Transfer

"An indorsement limiting payment to a particular person or otherwise prohibiting further transfer or negotiation of the instrument *is not effective* to prevent further transfer or negotiation of the instrument." 3-206(a) (emphasis added). Even an indorsement which expressly prohibits further transfer cannot bar further transfer or negotiation under the Code. There are few practical reasons for a transferor to bar further transfer, and so such indorsements are rare. Under the Code, when they do occur they are given the same effect as unrestrictive indorsements. Thus, the indorsement, "Pay N. Dorsey only," is treated as if it were, "Pay N. Dorsey," or, "Pay to the order of N. Dorsey." This policy is consistent with the rule invalidating contract terms that prohibit the assignment of contract rights. See 9-318(4), 2-210(2).

b. Conditional Indorsements

A conditional indorsement purports to impose a condition on the right of the indorsee or any later holder to collect. Usually, the purpose of a conditional indorsement is to assure the indorser that some duty owed to her will be performed. For example, P, the payee of a note, may indorse it, "Pay X when she delivers 100 shares of Gold Stock to me. (Signed) P," and deliver it to X in return for X's promise to deliver the stock. A conditional indorsement should not be confused with a conditional promise by a maker or a conditional order by a drawer. A condition to a promise or order, if contained in the instrument, prevents the instrument from being negotiable. A conditional indorsement does not have this effect and does not prevent further transfer or negotiation of the instrument. Indeed, except as between the indorser and indorsee, a conditional indorsement is completely ineffective.

> An indorsement stating a condition to the right of the indorsee to receive payment *does not affect* the right of the indorsee to enforce the instrument. A person paying the instrument or taking it for value or collection may disregard the condition, and the rights and liabilities of that person are not affected by whether the condition has been fulfilled.

3-206(b) (emphasis added). It is wrong to think of conditional indorsements, or indorsements limiting transfer, as restrictive indorsements within the meaning of Article 3. Because their restrictions are not effective under Article 3, "they are no longer described as restrictive indorsements." 3-206 comment 2. They are indorsements with ineffective restrictions and thus, in legal effect, are unrestrictive indorsements.

REVIEW QUESTIONS

1. **T or F**   Article 3 determines who owns an instrument.

2. What is the difference between transfer and negotiation?

3. **T or F**   Negotiation of an instrument requires the transferor to sign the instrument as indorser.

4. **T or F**   There can never be a holder of an instrument following transfer of the instrument by a thief.

5. Name the three characteristics of an indorsement.

6. **T or F**   After an instrument originally payable to P's order is indorsed "P, Pay to A," the writing is no longer negotiable because the indorsement lacks words of negotiability.

7. Describe the indorsement in the preceding question, and decide if the indorsement is effective to prevent further negotiation by A.

8.   Law teacher poses this problem: "The payee of a check, P, indorsed the
        instrument by signing her name and adding the words, 'For Deposit Only.' A thief
        stole the check and transferred it to T, an innocent merchant of goods who paid
        value for it. The drawee dishonored the check, and T sued the drawer. The
        drawer's defense is that the check was stolen. T claims freedom from this defense
        because she is a holder in due course. Who wins?" Law student responds as
        follows: "Inasmuch as P indorsed the check in blank, T is a holder. T wins if she
        satisfies the requirements for holder-in-due-course status." How could you
        improve the response?

V

WARRANTY AND RESTITUTION: INSURING ENFORCEABILITY

Analysis

A person incurs contract liability on an instrument because she signs it. A person incurs warranty liability with respect to an instrument because she transfers the instrument and also because the instrument is presented for payment or acceptance. Warranty liability is a property concept. It is not dependent on promise and contract. Therefore, warranty liability attaches whether or not the warrantor indorsed the instrument. In case she indorsed, her contract liability is in addition to the warranty liability.

Warranty liability is personal liability that the law imposes on a person because of a breach of the warranties that Articles 3 and 4 separately impose with respect to the transfer and presentment of instruments. The purpose of transfer warranties, like warranties in the sale of goods or other property, is to insure the instrument's "title" and basic "quality." They assure or guarantee a right to enforce the instrument and against the existence of certain defenses and claims to the instrument that would dilute the instrument's value. The main purpose of presentment warranties is to assure the payor or acceptor that the person presenting the instrument for payment or acceptance is entitled to it.

Presentment warranties are not insurance that payment or acceptance was proper by the terms of the contract or other relationship that provides the underlying reason for the payment or acceptance. There is no warranty against payment or acceptance beyond these terms, by mistake. Avoiding mistake is within the personal control of the payor or acceptor and, for reasons of finality, the law is slow to provide any remedy for mistake. On the other hand, the common law of restitution permits recovering mistaken payments in limited circumstances. This law has always supplemented Articles 3 and 4, and the 1990 Article 3 codifies a restitution recovery for some mistakes. Restitution from any source is always very limited, however, because the remedy generally cannot reach innocent persons who gave value or who detrimentally relied on the mistaken payment or acceptance.

In largest effect, warranties and restitution serve the same purpose. They are the law's principal means for distributing risks (and thereby losses) in dealing with commercial paper; and the distribution is complete because the risks that are not covered by warranties or restitution are necessarily assigned and left to the transferee, payor, or acceptor who suffers the loss. What is not covered is therefore equally important to what is covered.

A. SOURCE OF LAW FOR WARRANTIES

Article 3 is the general source of warranty law for all instruments. Section 3-416 creates the transfer warranties and 3-417 the presentment warranties. Article 4 provides its own warranties, 4-207 for transfer and 4-208 for presentment. Also, 4-209 adds encoding and retention warranties that are peculiar to electronic check collection and truncation. Article 4's warranty provisions override Article 3 whenever Article 4 is applicable. It applies to the collection and payment of checks and other "items" by banks. An "item" is "an instrument or a promise or order to pay money handled by a bank for collection or payment * * *." 4-104(a)(9). Because the scope of "item" and Article 4 reach beyond negotiable instruments, the Article 4 warranties are applied more widely than Article 3's. More significant, the Article 4 warranties will apply to checks and other Article 3 negotiable instruments that are transferred and presented as part of the bank collection process. This is not a big deal, however, because the warranty provisions of the two articles are basically the same, and the warranties themselves are substantively identical.

In turn, Article 4's warranties are preempted to the extent that federal law provides different and additional warranties for items in the bank collection process. Regulation J describes warranties that are made to and by a Federal Reserve Bank. 12 CFR 210.5(a), 210.6(b). They are fewer than the Code's warranties but not very different and, in any event, apply only to a Reserve Bank. Regulation CC applies more broadly to all banks in the collection process; but, with an important exception, it mostly describes warranties that accompany the return of checks upon dishonor rather than forward-collection transfer and presentment warranties. 12 CFR 229.34. The exception is a warranty-like rule by which any bank that handles a check for forward collection or return is liable to any subsequent bank that does not receive payment for the check for any reason. Id. 229.35(b). Article 4 includes essentially the same rule. 4-207(b).

In sum, the federal preemption of Article 4 warranties is small, and these warranties are mostly the same as the warranties of Article 3. Thus, nothing significantly reduces Article 3's role as the general source of warranty law for instruments, which explains why this chapter mainly speaks in terms of Article 3 warranties.

B. TRANSFER WARRANTIES

1. Who Makes Them

The transfer warranties are made by any person, including a holder in due course, who (1) transfers an instrument *and* (2) receives consideration. 3-416(a). Be careful here! Throughout the Code, including provisions in Article 3, the term "value" appears. Value and consideration are not entirely the same. See 1-201(44); 3-303(a). Transfer warranties are triggered only by the transferor's receipt of *consideration,* which means "any [common-law] consideration sufficient to support a simple contract." 3-303(b).

2. Who Gets Them

Transfer warranties always run in favor of the immediate transferee, whether or not the transferor has signed the instrument. If, however, the transferor indorses the instrument, the transfer warranties she makes run in favor of "*any subsequent transferee.*" 3-416(a) (emphasis added). In other words, "[i]f there is an indorsement the warranty runs with the instrument and the [or any] remote holder may sue the indorser-warrantor directly and thus avoid a multiplicity of suits." 3-416 comment 1.

3. What Are They

A person who makes transfer warranties, *though she may in fact be unaware of them,* warrants that:

a. Warranty of Entitlement to Enforce

The very least a transferee of an instrument expects is that, by acquiring the instrument, she becomes a person a payor can safely pay, and who can sue on the instrument if it is dishonored. In sum, the transferee expects that she can enforce the instrument, which is true only if her transferor could do so. Thus, to assure the transferee in this regard, **the transferor warrants that she "is a person entitled to enforce the instrument." 3-416(a)(1).** Because this status basically is limited to a holder or a person who claims through a holder, 3-301, the warranty is "in effect a warranty that there are no unauthorized or missing indorsements * * *." 3-416 comment 2. If the signature of the payee or a prior special indorsee is forged or otherwise ineffective, the transferor is not a person entitled to enforce -- a holder or a person with a holder's rights -- and neither is her transferee. The warranty is obviously broken. Also, there can be no later holder unless the person whose indorsement is missing reacquires the instrument. Normally, therefore, if there is a forgery in the chain of transfer, the warranty is broken not only by the forger but also by any later transferor.

> *Example:* M issues a note to P's order. Acting without authority from P, Q indorses the note in P's name and transfers it for consideration to R. R transfers the note to S in exchange for property. M refuses to pay the instrument to S. Because P's indorsement was ineffective, R was not entitled to enforce the instrument. So S can sue R for breach of warranty whether or not R signed the instrument. Q breached the warranty, too. Thus, R can sue Q, and so can S inasmuch as Q indorsed the note. Q's signing P's name operated as Q's signature in favor of takers for value, including R and S. 3-403(a).

b. Warranty of Authentic Signatures

The second warranty a transferor gives is that "**all signatures on the instrument are authentic and authorized.**" **3-416(a)(2).** It covers indorsements necessary for negotiation, as does (a)(1); but only this warranty covers the signature of a maker, drawer, drawee, acceptor, or anomalous indorsee. The most obvious purpose is to protect the transferee against the risk that a person who appears to be liable on the instrument is really not liable because her signature is forged or unauthorized. The warranty is *not* tied to the transferor's knowledge. She is strictly liable for a breach whether or not she knew that the signature was forged or otherwise ineffective. Compare 3-417(a)(3) (presentment warranty of no knowledge that drawer's signature is unauthorized).

> *Example:* S sold diamonds on credit to B, whom S thought was acting for IMB, Inc. B executed a note for the price of the diamonds, signing "B, Executive Vice President, IMB, Inc." S indorsed the note in blank to her diamond wholesaler, W, in satisfaction of a preexisting debt. W sold the note to Big City Bank, which knew that IMB was very creditworthy. IMB refused to pay the note when it matured. B was not IMB's agent, and she acted without its authority. Moreover, IMB never even saw the diamonds purchased by B, who has disappeared with the loot. W is liable for breach of the 3-416(a)(2) warranty, whether or not W signed the note. S signed the note, but she has no warranty liability to anyone because she made no warranties. She transferred the note but did not receive consideration for it. Nevertheless, S is liable as indorser.

c. Warranty Against Material Alteration

A transferee usually assumes that she is entitled to enforce the instrument according to its terms at the time she acquired it. If the instrument has been altered, however, the liability of the parties who signed before the alteration usually is limited to the original terms of the instrument, and sometimes their liability is completely discharged. 3-407(b). Primarily to protect transferees against losses that result in this way, each transferor who receives consideration warrants that "**the instrument has not been altered.**" **3-416(a)(3).**

> *Example:* M issued a note to P's order. P materially and fraudulently raised the amount of the instrument from $5000 to $15,000. P thereafter negotiated the note to Q, who became a holder in due course. Q transferred the note for consideration to R. Upon the note's maturity, M agreed to pay only $5000, which was the original amount of the instrument. R has a breach of warranty claim against

Q, whether or not Q signed the note, even though Q was a holder in due course of the note and was ignorant of the alteration.

d. Warranty Against Defenses

A "transferee does not undertake to buy an instrument that is not enforceable in whole or in part, unless there is a contrary agreement." 3-416 comment 3. This assumption explains the warranty that **"the instrument is not subject to a defense or claim in recoupment of any party which can be asserted against the warrantor." 3-416(a)(4).** A "claim in recoupment" generally refers to a counterclaim arising from the transaction that gave rise to the instrument. Such a claim is an offset that reduces liability, as opposed to a defense that avoids liability in the first place. The warranty does not cover a third-party setoff, which is a debt or other claim unrelated to the instrument that the obligor has against the original payee of the instrument. The coverage is unnecessary because such a setoff cannot be asserted against a transferee, not even when the transferee lacks the status or rights of a holder in due course. 3-305 comment 3.

To breach the warranty, it is not necessary that the transferor is responsible for the defense, only that there is a defense that can be asserted against her. Also, it is not necessary for a breach that the defense is successfully asserted against the transferee. Even if the transferee is a holder in due course who takes free of the defense, "the warranty gives the transferee the option of proceeding against the transferor rather than litigating with the obligor on the instrument the issue of the holder-in-due-course status of the transferee." 3-416 comment 3.

e. Warranty Against Knowledge of Insolvency Proceedings

A transferor does not warrant that the party expected to pay or accept is a good credit risk or is financially solvent. The transferee is expected to determine these matters for herself before buying the instrument. In large part, it is a matter of opinion and judgment. On the other hand, the existence of insolvency proceedings against the payor is a fact that the transferor should disclose. Nondisclosure "amounts to a fraud upon the transferee," 3-416 comment 4, and accordingly **a transferor warrants that she "has no knowledge of any insolvency proceeding commenced with respect to the maker or acceptor or, in the case of an unaccepted draft, the drawer." 3-416(a)(5).** This warranty prevents a person who is aware that such proceedings have been commenced from passing her almost certain loss to a transferee. "Insolvency proceedings" means more than a federal bankruptcy case. It includes "any assignment for the benefit of creditors or other proceedings intended to liquidate or rehabilitate the estate of the person involved," 1-201(22), whether under federal or state law. It is not an absolute warranty that no insolvency proceedings are ongoing, only that the transferor has no "knowledge" of such proceedings. She must actually know of them. Notice is not enough for a breach.

f. Article 4's Additional Warranty of Absolute Liability
Article 4 provides an additional transfer warranty that, when applicable, swallows the other transfer warranties and goes well beyond them. Essentially, it warrants against dishonor *for any reason or no reason*. It is absolute, providing that:

> If an item is dishonored, a customer or collecting bank transferring the item and receiving settlement or other consideration is obliged to pay the amount due on the item (i) according to the terms of the item at the time it was transferred, or (ii) if the transfer was of an incomplete item, according to its terms when completed * * *.

4-207(b). The inspiration is federal regulatory law that implies basically the same warranty between banks involved in the collection and return of checks. 12 CFR 229.35(b). The other transfer warranties are swallowed, however, only to the extent that Article 4 or the federal rule applies, and both of them generally are limited to checks and other items within the banking industry's check collection system. Negotiable instruments outside of this system, including checks, are subject to the transfer warranties of Article 3, which do not include this absolute warranty against dishonor for any reason.

C. PRESENTMENT WARRANTIES

A person who pays or accepts an instrument may worry that she is doing so rightly, for the right person, and in the right amount. *Presentment warranties* provide some insurance against these risks. They are described in 3-417, which provides different warranty coverage for different payors. *Drawees of unaccepted drafts* are covered by 3-417(a). *All other payors* are covered by 3-417(d).

1. Presentment Warranties In The Case Of A Drawee Of An Unaccepted Draft
a. Who Makes Them
The presentment warranties of 3-417(a) are made by any person who presents an *unaccepted draft* for payment *or* acceptance and also by any prior transferor.

b. Who Gets Them
The warranties run only to the drawee who pays or accepts the draft in good faith, not to the drawer or anyone else.

c. **What Are They**
The warranties are:

- **the warrantor is, or was, at the time the warrantor transferred the draft, a person entitled to enforce the draft or authorized to obtain payment or acceptance of the draft on behalf of a person entitled to enforce the draft, 3-417(a)(1);**
- **the draft has not been altered, 3-417(a)(2); and the warrantor has *no knowledge* that the signature of the *drawer* of the draft is unauthorized, 3-417(a)(3).**

The warranty of right to enforce and the warranty against alteration are familiar. They are also included in the transfer warranties that are discussed earlier in this chapter.

Example: A was indebted to B. B drew a draft against A and issued it to her creditor, C. The draft ordered A to pay "30 days after acceptance." T stole the draft from C, forged C's indorsement, and sold the draft to Z. Z got A to accept. When Z presented for payment, A defended on the basis of breach of warranty. A wins.

Unlike a transferee, the drawee assumes -- in large part -- the risk that the drawer's signature is unauthorized. The only exception is when the warrantor has "*knowledge*" that the drawer's signature is forged or otherwise ineffective. In this case, the drawee is relieved of the risk because it is a fraud for a person to transfer or present an instrument that she knows is not genuine. Nevertheless, this warranty of no knowledge is very narrow because a breach requires *actual knowledge* that the signature is bogus.

Example: A was indebted to B. T forged B's name as drawer of a draft against A. The draft was drawn payable to P who was unaware of the forgery. The drawee paid the draft and later sought to recover the payment on the ground that the drawer's signature had been forged. There is no breach of warranty to support the drawee's action..

2. Presentment Warranties In All Other Cases
a. Who Makes Them
The warranties of 3-417(d) are made by the person obtaining payment and any prior transferor of the instrument.

b. Who Gets Them

The person making payment in good faith gets the warranties, including the drawer or an indorser of a dishonored draft that is presented to her for payment and a party obliged to pay any other instrument.

c. What Is The Warranty

Except in the case of a drawee of an unaccepted draft, **the only presentment warranty is that "the warrantor is, or was, at the time the warrantor transferred the instrument, a person entitled to enforce the instrument or authorized to obtain payment on behalf of a person entitled to enforce the instrument." 3-417(d)(1).** It is insurance against bogus indorsements that is given *by* the person who receives payment and prior transferors and is given *to* any person who pays if she was obliged to pay and did so in good faith. The warranty covers every case of payment by anyone, including:

* presentment of notes and accepted drafts to any party obliged to pay the instrument, including an indorser, and
* presentment of dishonored drafts if made to the drawer or an indorser.

3-417 comment 4. The warrantor effectively promises that, at the time of her transfer or presentment, there were no missing or unauthorized indorsements that were necessary for negotiation. The same warranty -- that the warrantor is entitled to enforce the instrument -- is part of the transfer warranties of 3-416, and is also a presentment warranty in the special case of a drawee of an unaccepted draft. 3-417(a)(1). The only significant difference under 3-417(d) is that this warranty is the only warranty that the payor gets.

> *Example:* M issues a note to P's order for an underlying obligation. Acting without authority from P, Q indorses the note in P's name and transfers it for consideration to R. R transfers the note to S in exchange for property. M pays the instrument to S. The loss starts with P, who can recover from M on the stolen instrument or the underlying obligation. M can recover from S who breached the presentment warranty of right to enforce. 3-417(a)(1). S can shift the loss using the transfer warranties. See 3-416(a).

> *Example:* S sold diamonds on credit to B, whom S thought was acting for IMB, Inc. B executed a note for the price of the diamonds, signing "B, Executive Vice President, IMB, Inc." Actually, B was not authorized to act for IMB in any respect, and the company had not approved of the deal and got nothing from it. S indorsed the note in blank to her diamond wholesaler, W, in satisfaction of a preexisting

debt. W sold the note to Big City Bank, which knew that IMB was very creditworthy. IMB paid the note when it matured and then discovered the wrongdoing. There is no breach of warranty that will allow IMB to recover the payment from Big City.

D. SUPPLEMENTING PRESENTMENT WARRANTIES WITH RESTITUTIONARY RECOVERY

Only through mistake is a maker, drawer or acceptor likely to pay an instrument that has been materially altered, or an instrument that bears an unauthorized maker's or drawer's signature. The mistake cannot ordinarily be corrected by way of a warranty action because the presentment warranties covering these kinds of fraud are very limited. Yet, whenever mistake is involved, there is the possibility of recovering the mistaken payment on the different, extra-Code theory of restitution. After all, common-law and equitable principles supplement the Code unless they are displaced by it. 1-103. Thus, in many cases in which presentment warranties do not cover payors' losses, they assert restitution claims, instead of warranty actions, against persons who have received payment on altered instruments or instruments bearing a forged drawer's or maker's signature. Almost always, however, the plaintiff-payors lose because the common law of restitution provides a defense to their claims that is codified in Article 3 itself.

1. Right Of Recovery
a. Deference to Common Law
The general rule of the common law is that "[a] person, who because of a mistake, has paid money to another in the payment or purchase of a bill of exchange [draft] or promissory note is entitled to restitution * * *." Restatement of Restitution § 29 (1937). Article 3 expressly endorses restitutionary recovery under the common law. The statute provides, as a general principle, that:

> [I]f an instrument has been paid or accepted by mistake * * * the person paying or accepting may, to the extent permitted by the law governing mistake and restitution, (i) recover the payment from the person to whom or for whose benefit payment was made or (ii) in the case of acceptance, may revoke the acceptance.

3-418(b).

b. Special Statutory Restitution
Also, restitutionary recovery is codified for a drawee who mistakenly pays or accepts a draft on which the drawer's signature is unauthorized, or who

mistakenly pays a draft for which the drawer has issued a stop order countermanding payment.

> Except as provided in subsection (c), if the drawee of a draft pays or accepts the draft and the drawee acted on the mistaken belief that (i) payment of the draft had not been stopped pursuant to Section 4-403 or (ii) the signature of the drawer of the draft was authorized, the drawee may recover the amount of the draft from the person to whom or for whose benefit payment was made or, in the case of acceptance, may revoke the acceptance. Rights of the drawee under this subsection are not affected by failure of the drawee to exercise ordinary care in paying or accepting the draft.

3-418(a).

c. Finality of Payment No Bar To Recovery

Neither common-law nor statutory restitution is barred by the rules of Article 4 or other law that determine when an instrument is paid provisionally or finally. 3-418 comment 4. Restitution is an exception to finality of payment, so much so that

> [I]f an instrument is paid or accepted by mistake and the payor or acceptor recovers payment or revokes acceptance under [restitution law], the instrument is deemed not to have been paid or accepted and is treated as dishonored, and the person from whom payment is recovered has rights as a person entitled to enforce the dishonored instrument.

3-418(d).

2. Defense To Recovery

Nevertheless, both the common-law recovery that Article 3 recognizes and the codified remedy it creates are limited by the usual immunity from restitution that the law affords good faith purchasers for value.

a. Common-Law Defense

The common-law of restitution recognizes a large defense to restitutionary recovery of money mistakenly paid:

> The holder of a check or other bill of exchange who, having paid value in good faith therefor, receives payment from the drawee without reason to know that the drawee is mistaken, is under no duty of restitution to him although the drawee pays because of a mistaken belief that * * * he is * * * under a duty to pay.

Restatement of Restitution § 33 (1937). This rule tracks as far back as the leading case, *Price v. Neal*, 3 Burr. 1354, 97 Eng. Rep. 871, which Lord Mansfield decided in 1762. The case involved two drafts drawn on Price and payable to Ruding. The first draft was indorsed to Neal who paid valuable consideration for it. Price paid the draft to Neal. The second draft was similarly drawn and indorsed to Neal, but Price accepted the draft before Neal purchased it. The end result was the same: Price paid the second draft to Neal. It turned out that both drafts were forged by Lee. He forged the drawer's signature on both instruments. Lee was hanged for the forgery. The hanging did not satisfy Price. He sued to recover the payments made to Neal, claiming that the payments were "paid by him by mistake only, on supposition 'that these were true genuine bills [of exchange].' " Price lost. He and Neal were both innocent parties, but Lord Mansfield decided that the drawee-acceptor could not recover either payment. In reaching this conclusion he said: "The plaintiff cannot recover the money unless it be against conscience in the defendant to retain it. * * * But it can never be thought unconscientious in the defendant to retain this money, when he has once received it upon a bill of exchange indorsed to him for a fair and valuable consideration, which he had bona fide paid, without the least privity or suspicion of any forgery." In Mansfield's view, the loss "was rather owing to the negligence of the plaintiff * * *. It was incumbent upon the plaintiff to be satisfied 'that the bill drawn upon him was the drawer's hand,' before he accepted or paid it: but it was not incumbent upon the defendant to inquire into it."

b. Statutory Defense
The following rule of Article 3 effectively codifies the defense of *Price v. Neal*:

> The remedies [of restitution] provided by [3-418(a)] or [3-418(b)] may not be asserted against a person who took the instrument in good faith and for value or who in good faith changed position in reliance on the payment or acceptance.

3-418(c). This defense effectively eliminates restitution except in rare cases because, almost always, the person who obtains payment or acceptance took the instrument in good faith from her transferor and paid value for it. In sum, therefore, mistaken payment or acceptance is rarely undone on the basis of restitution law.

Example: D drew a draft for $5000 on T. T paid the draft when P, the payee, presented the instrument for payment because T believed she owed D the amount of the draft. In fact, T owed D only $500. T cannot recover the overpayment from P. P breached no presentment warranty, and 3-418 gives P a good defense to a restitution or similar action.

Risks that the payor cannot easily detect, such as forged indorsements, are not forced on her by 3-418 because the provision does not bar breach of warranty actions, and the presentment warranties made to a payor include a warranty of good title, i.e., a warranty against forged indorsements.

E. REMEDYING BREACH OF WARRANTY

Many of the rules for remedying a breach of warranty are basically the same for both transfer and presentment warranties. The most basic rule is the measure of damages, which is the same but is stated differently for the two kinds of warranties.

1. Measure Of Compensatory Damages
a. General Rule for All Cases
In the case of transfer warranties, the basic measure of damages is the amount of the loss suffered as a result of the breach not to exceed the amount of the instrument. 3-416(b). For presentment warranties in the case of a payor, the measure is the amount she paid, which naturally is her loss. 3-417(b) & (d). An acceptor who pays can recover the same damages; but breach of warranty is a defense to payment in the first place, 3-417(b), except as against a holder in due course.

b. Special Rules in the Case of a Drawee Who Pays an Unaccepted Draft
The drawee of an unaccepted draft who has paid the instrument is entitled to the same damages any other payor gets, the amount paid. There are stated differences for the drawee, however, because of the triangular relationship among her, the drawer, and the payee or other person who obtains payment.

- First, the drawee's recovery is reduced by the "amount the drawee received or is entitled to receive from the drawer because of the payment." 3-417(b). To this extent, the drawee suffers no loss. This reduction envisages the case in which, despite the drawee's mistaken payment, she is entitled to recoup from or otherwise charge the drawer because of the terms of the contract or other relationship between the two of them.
- Second, the drawee's recovery may be precluded altogether if the breach of warranty is based on an unauthorized indorsement or alteration that, despite the wrongdoing, is chargeable to the drawer under 3-404, 3-405, 3-406 or 4-406. Warrantors can use these sections as defenses to warranty liability.

Nickles Comm. Paper 2nd—9

3-417(c). In general terms, each section forces the drawer to absorb the loss because of her own overriding fault or other responsibility. For this reason, the drawee can charge the drawer for the instrument and herself suffers no loss that she can shift to the warrantor. Two of the sections, 3-406 and 4-406, also stop a drawer from complaining about an ineffective drawer's signature, but 3-417(c) does not permit using them to block a warranty action based on such a signature. The reason is that an ineffective drawer's signature breaches no presentment warranty and supports no warranty claim, except when the warrantor knows of the forgery. In this event, the warrantor's own culpability is so great that the law is blinded to any fault or responsibility of the drawer that could otherwise bind her under 3-406 or 4-406.

The draw*ee*'s negligence is never considered. The statute is clear:

> The right of the drawee to recover damages [for breach of presentment warranties] is not affected by any failure of the drawee to exercise ordinary care in making payment.

3-417(b). On the other hand, lack of good faith denies a drawee a right to recover because the presentment warranties run only to a drawee who pays or accepts in good faith. 3-417(a). Ordinary negligence alone does not deny good faith, which concerns honesty and fairness "rather than the care with which an act is performed." 3-103 comment 4.

2. Incidental Damages

In every case of breach of warranty, whether transfer or presentment, the damages are not limited to direct compensatory loss. They also include expenses and loss of interest resulting from the breach. 3-416(b), 3-417(b) & (d). There is no express provision for attorney's fees, but they "are not meant to be necessarily excluded." 3-416 comment 6, 3-417 comment 5. It is not clear, however, if the provision for expenses is itself authority to award attorney's fees. In one place the comments report. "The intention is to leave to other state law the issue as to when attorney's fees are recoverable." 3-416 comment 6. Elsewhere, the report is that attorney's fees "could be granted because they fit within the language 'expenses * * * resulting from the breach.'" 3-417 comment 5.

3. Some Procedural Concerns

The statute of limitations for any breach of warranty action is three years after the claim accrues, 3-118(g), which is when the claimant has reason to know of the breach. 3-416(d), 3-417(f). A further, much shorter time limit also applies, both to presentment and transfer warranties, that requires giving the warrantor very early notice of breach:

> Unless notice of a claim for breach of warranty is given to the warrantor within 30 days after the claimant has reason to know of the breach and the identity of the warrantor, the liability of the warrantor * * * is discharged to the extent of any loss caused by the delay in giving notice of the claim. 3-416(c), 3-417(e).

4. Disclaiming Warranty Liability

Transfer and presentment warranties can be disclaimed except with respect to checks. 3-416(c) & 3-417(e).

a. Transfer Warranties

"Between the immediate parties disclaimer may be made by agreement. In the case of an indorser, disclaimer * * * must appear in the indorsement with words such as 'without warranties' or some other specific reference to warranties." 3-416 comment 5. Qualifying an indorsement with words such as "without recourse" does not disclaim warranty liability, only contract liability. Disclaimer is outlawed with respect to checks because the banking system relies on warranties and its automated processing systems cannot detect disclaimers.

b. Presentment Warranties

Nobody is liable for presentment warranties that she disclaims in the same way that transfer warranties are disclaimed. A general disclaimer that is not limited to either transfer or presentment warranties would seem to disclaim all of them, at least in favor of the person who makes the disclaimer. As is true with transfer warranties, however, presentment warranties cannot be disclaimed, either generally or specifically, with respect to checks. The warranties are too important to the banking industry's check-collection system.

F. ELECTRONIC BANKING: ENCODING AND RETENTION WARRANTIES

The trend in check collection is truncation. The payee, the depositary bank, or another bank -- known as the "keeper" -- retains the checks themselves and electronically forwards only the information or images of the checks. The payor is presented with electronic notices instead of paper items. The drawers receive reports of items charged to their account but do not receive the items themselves unless a special request is made. Even then the customer may receive only a copy of an image of the check. For many years a similar system has worked well for credit cards. Truncation is governed less by law than by contract, principally including agreements governing retention and other aspects of electronic presentment. Two warranties apply when truncation occurs.

- First, the keeper warrants to subsequent collecting banks and payors that its retention and presentment of the checks comply with the keeper's truncation agreements. 4-209(b).
- Second, any person who encodes information with respect to the checks "warrants to any subsequent collecting bank and to the payor bank or other payor that the information is correctly encoded." 4-209(a).

The encoding warranty applies, too, even in the absence of truncation. In the traditional collection process which moves the checks themselves, the depositary bank usually will encode on every check the amount of the item. This encoding enables electronic processing. Sometimes, encoding and retention, too, are done by customers who are payees of a large volume of checks. Whoever encodes information on a check, whether the depositary bank or its customer, warrants the accuracy of the encoding. Id.

The remedy is the same for a breach of either the encoding or retention warranty.

> A person to whom warranties are made under this section and who took the item in good faith may recover from the warrantor as damages for breach of warranty an amount equal to the loss suffered as a result of the breach, plus expenses and loss of interest as a result of the breach.

4-209(c).

REVIEW QUESTIONS

1. M makes a note to P. T steals the note, forges P's signature, and sells the note to U. U transfers the note to V. M pays V. Who has warranty claims against whom? Why does M care whether she has a warranty claim against anyone?

2. M issued a note to P's order. P materially and fraudulently raised the amount of the instrument from $5000 to $15,000. P thereafter negotiated the note to Q, who became a holder in due course. Q transferred the note for consideration to R. Upon the note's maturity, M agreed to pay only $5000, which was the original amount of the instrument. Does R have a good claim against Q?

3. Acting without authority from M, T signs M's name to a note. The payee, P, indorses the note for consideration to Q. If M refuses to pay the note, what actions, if any, does Q have against P? If M mistakenly pays the note, can she successfully recoup in actions against P or Q?

4. What is the measure of compensatory damages for breach of warranty?

5.   Computer, Inc. is a very large wholesaler of computer hardware and software. Before depositing checks that it receives from customers, Computer encodes certain information on each check, including the amount of the item. Suppose that a mistake was made in encoding a check received from ABC Retailer -- $50,000 was encoded as the amount of a $5,000 check. Because the depositary and payor banks' computers read and post information to amounts based on such encoding, Computer was credited with $50,000 and ABC was debited in the same amount. How does the law straighten out this mistake?

VI

CLAIMS AND DEFENSES
TO INSTRUMENTS

Analysis

Ultimately, the value of an instrument is determined by whether or not the obligor must pay the instrument and, if so, whether or not she is financially able to do so. The latter issue is beyond this book and mostly beyond the law. The former issue is discussed here and in the next chapter. It largely depends on whether or not a claim to the instrument or a defense to payment is proved and, if so, whether or not the plaintiff is subject or immune to the claim or defense. Usually, immunity depends on the plaintiff having the rights of a holder in due course, which means she takes free of most claims and defenses that arose before the instrument was negotiated to her. This chapter focuses on the full range of claims and defenses to an instrument that generally limit the right to enforce it.

◆ The outline begins with the so-called "*real defenses*" collected in 3-305(a)(1). They are the relatively few, mostly narrow defenses that are good against any person entitled to enforce the instrument, including a holder in due course. The issue of holder in due course is mooted to the extent that the defendant proves a real defense.

◆ Next discussed are the so-called "*ordinary*" or "*personal defenses*" and then *recoupment,* which generally refers to a related counterclaim for damages that is asserted defensively only. The personal defenses and recoupment are good against every person entitled to enforce an instrument, except a person having the rights of a holder in due course.

◆ Different from any class of defenses to payment of an instrument are "*claims*" to an instrument, which are discussed last in this chapter after all of the defenses. These claims are property interests and possessory rights in instruments that follow them everywhere and into the hands of every person, except holders in due course. Just as holders in due course take free of personal defenses, they also take free of all prior claims to instruments. 3-306. A claim in recoupment does not fit here. It is a cause of action that acts as a defense to payment of the instrument and is not a property interest or right to the instrument.

◆ Article 3 provides special personal defenses for parties who are *sureties* on an instrument, either actually or functionally. These parties include "*accommodation parties*" who are actual sureties. They signed the instrument for the deliberate purpose of backing or securing the obligation of another party to the instrument. Also included are *ordinary indorsers*. They functionally secure payment by a drawee or another party to the instrument whom everybody intends is the ultimate payor. Sureties are treated gingerly throughout the whole law with rules that guard against increasing their risks beyond what they agreed to undertake. The common law is the primary source of these rules, but Article 3 codified some of them in order to refine their application to sureties on instruments. Technically, the Article 3 rules usually are enforced by discharging a surety's liability rather than by giving her a defense. Practically, however, a discharge is a personal defense. Therefore, it is appropriate to treat the surety's special protections as a subclass of the personal defenses, which are commonly known as the "*suretyship defenses*." The subject is sufficiently large, important, and unique that accommodation status and suretyship defenses get a separate chapter of their own, Chapter VII infra.

If an ordinary defense is proved in a suit to enforce an instrument, or if the plaintiff is suing to replevy the instrument from the defendant because of a prior claim, the case reaches the issue of holder in due course and turns on this issue. Who wins usually is decided by whether or not the plaintiff has the rights of such a holder. How a person acquires these rights is the subject of Chapter VIII infra.

A. REAL DEFENSES

The principal advantage of being a holder in due course is that the person takes free of -- cuts off -- most of the defenses to payment that arose before the instrument was negotiated to her. These defenses are called *personal defenses*. They are good against everybody entitled to enforce an instrument, except a person with the rights of a holder in due course. She is immune to them. A holder in due course is not immune to *real defenses*. They always survive and, without exception, are good against everybody. Any person suing to enforce an instrument is subject to them. The *real defenses* are discussed here. There are only a few of them. They are narrow and mostly depend on outside law. Article 3 collects them in 3-305(a)(1):

* infancy of the obligor to the extent that infancy is a defense to a simple contract;
* duress, lack of legal capacity, or illegality of the transaction which, under other law, nullifies the obligation of the obligor;
* fraud that induced the obligor to sign the instrument with neither knowledge nor reasonable opportunity to learn of its character or its essential terms; and
* discharge of the obligor in insolvency proceedings.

1. Infancy

Infancy is a defense against a holder in due course to the same extent that it is a defense to an action on a simple contract under the non-Code state law governing the transaction. 3-305(a)(1)(i). Generally, with some exceptions usually provided by special statute, the contracts of an infant are voidable entitling the infant to disaffirm or rescind her contract even though she has received and enjoyed the benefits. In most states, the same applies to contracts for necessaries, but an infant who rescinds a contract for necessaries and does not return them may be bound to pay their fair value on the theory of quasi contract. The bottom line, therefore, is that an infant who incurs liability on a negotiable instrument usually may avoid this liability in whole or in part even against a holder in due course. See *Trenton Trust Co. v. Western Sur. Co.*, 599 S.W.2d 481 (Mo. 1980).

2. Duress

Duress occurs when one person, by the exercise of wrongful pressure, induces another to become fearful and to do something she otherwise would not do. The wrongful pressure may consist of physical violence, but usually it consists of threats. A threat to start a civil action usually is not considered to be wrongful. The threat to have someone prosecuted for a crime, though not wrongful in itself, is considered to be wrongful when made to induce someone to enter a contract. Normally, duress merely renders a contract voidable and so is not a good defense against one having the rights of a holder in due course. In its very extreme form, however, as where one party points a loaded gun at another or physically compels her to manifest her assent to contract, this duress renders the transaction void. Such duress would be a good defense even against one having the rights of a holder in due course. 3-305(a)(1)(ii). Actually, duress of this kind is very rare.

3. Lack Of Legal Capacity (Incapacity)

Incapacity may be recognized if at the time the transaction occurred the defendant was insane, intoxicated or a corporation acting outside the powers given by its charter, and in a few other special circumstances. Unlike infancy, which enables a defendant to avoid liability against a holder in due course even though her liability is merely voidable, parties limited by other types of incapacity are shielded from such liability only if the governing state law declares that such incapacity nullifies transactions -- makes them void. 3-305(a)(1)(ii). Since incapacity other than adjudicated incompetency normally renders transactions voidable and not void, incapacity other than infancy and adjudicated incompetency usually does not constitute a valid defense against holders in due course.

4. Illegality

In general, a transaction is illegal if it is contrary to public policy as provided by statute or as declared by the courts. Illegality is a real defense only if the transaction is rendered void. 3-305(a)(1)(ii). A negotiable instrument may be issued or negotiated in a transaction which is illegal because it involves gambling, usury, bribery, concealing a crime, promoting immorality, restraining trade; because it occurs on Sunday; or for many other reasons. Generally, however, the defense of illegality renders the transaction voidable only, not void. Thus, the defense is not good against a holder in due course even though the instrument in question was issued or negotiated in direct violation of a statute or was given for a consideration held to be against public policy. Before the illegality can affect a holder in due course, the courts of a state must hold, either on the basis of statutory construction or otherwise, that the particular illegality makes the transaction null and void. Then, a party who issues, accepts, or negotiates an instrument as part of the transaction can effectively defend on the ground of illegality even against a holder in due course.

See *Sandler v. Eighth Judicial District Court*, 96 Nev. 622, 614 P.2d 10 (1980) (check issued for purpose of gambling void, illegality a defense against HDC).

5. Fraud

a. Fraud In Inducement Is A Personal Defense Only

A person might be induced to sign a negotiable instrument by either of two quite different kinds of fraud. The first kind, sometimes called *fraud in the inducement* or *fraud in the procurement*, occurs when the defrauded person is fully aware of the character and essential terms of the instrument she signs but is induced to sign by deception with respect to some other matter. For example, a person might be induced to sign and deliver her check for $1,000 in payment for a stone which the seller payee has fraudulently represented to be a diamond. Fraud of the first kind is not a defense against a holder in due course.

> *Example:* B convinces M to invest in a business venture controlled by B. In doing so B misrepresents the risks involved and also misrepresents the financial state of the venture. M's investment is a note she executes payable to B, which B sells to a third party who is a holder in due course. M was a victim of fraud in the inducement, but this kind of fraud is never a real defense that can be raised against a holder in due course.

b. The Real Defense Is Fraud In Factum

The second kind of fraud, sometimes called *fraud in the factum* or *fraud in the essence*, occurs when the defrauded person is induced to sign an instrument by deception with respect to the character or terms of the instrument itself. For example, she might be induced to sign a note for $10,000 relying on a false representation that it is only a receipt or that the amount is only $1,000. The second kind of fraud might or might not be a good defense, depending on whether or not the defrauded party can prove that she lacked a reasonable opportunity to learn the true character or terms of the instrument. With this proof, fraud regarding the character or terms of the instrument is a good defense even against a holder in due course, 3-305(a)(1)(iii); otherwise not. In truth, the odds of making the defense are greatly against everyone in every case. The defense has been successful in only a tiny few reported instances.

> *Example:* B explains to her employee, M, that B has applied for a loan and needs M to sign the loan application as a character witness for B. M, who cannot read, signs what she believes is a loan application. In fact, the paper is a note. M is a victim of real fraud which is a defense against a holder in due course *if* the determination is made

that M had no reasonable opportunity before signing the note to learn its true character.

6. Discharge In Insolvency Proceedings
a. Mainly Bankruptcy
"'*Insolvency proceedings*' includes any assignment for the benefit of creditors or other proceedings intended to liquidate or rehabilitate the estate of the person involved." 1-201(22). Mainly, it means *bankruptcy* which *discharges* unsecured claims against the debtor, including the debtor's obligations on negotiable instruments. This discharge does not extinguish debts; rather, it mainly enjoins any act to collect the affected debts. 11 U.S.C.A. 524(a)(2). Therefore, the holder of a negotiable instrument cannot enforce the instrument against a debtor whose obligation on the instrument has been discharged in bankruptcy, not even if the holder is a holder in due course. Article 3 confirms this result by making insolvency discharge a real defense. 3-305(a)(1)(iv).

b. Bankruptcy Does Not Discharge The Entire Instrument
The bankruptcy injunction and the Article 3 defense work only against the debtor's obligation. They do not affect the instrument itself or the liability of any other party, not even the liability of an indorser or other party who had a right of recourse against the discharged debtor. The holder can enforce the instrument against the indorser or other party even though this person will not be able to enforce it against the debtor or otherwise recoup from her.

Example: A and B together purchase on credit from S a machine they intend to use in a business venture. They jointly sign a note payable to S. A files for bankruptcy and is, by federal law, discharged from most of her debts, including her obligation on the note to S. S sells the note to T, a holder in due course. When the note matures T sues A and B. A's bankruptcy discharge is a good defense for her. A's discharge is not, however, a defense for B, who is jointly and severally liable on the instrument and must pay the whole amount of the note to T. A's bankruptcy discharge also protects her from contribution liability to B.

7. Other Defenses Good Against Everybody
It is true that 3-305(a)(1) collects all of the defenses that are traditionally labeled as "real defenses." It is not true that they are the only reasons for not paying an instrument that are good against a holder in due course. There are other reasons for not paying that may be asserted against any person entitled to enforce an instrument, including a holder in due course. Here are the most important.

a. Forgery

A person is not liable on an instrument unless she signed it or an authorized representative signed for her. 3-401(a). This freedom from liability is effective against the world, including a holder in due course.

b. Alteration

No one can enforce an altered instrument beyond its original terms. 3-407(b-c). To the extent of the alteration, the obligor is immune to liability even when the person entitled to enforce the instrument is a holder in due course.

c. Discharge of Which There is Notice

An Article 3 discharge of a party's liability on an instrument is a personal defense, 3-601(b); but even a holder in due course takes subject to a party's discharge of which the holder has notice when she takes the instrument. The notice does not have the greater effect of preventing due-course status, and the holder who takes in due course can enforce the instrument against other parties free of their personal defenses.

> *Example:* M issues a note to P. P specially indorses the note to Q, who indorses it to R. R discharges P and Q from liability on the instrument by way of a contract supported by consideration. R also cancels Q's indorsement by striking through Q's signature on the instrument. R thereafter sells the note to T. T knows from the face of the instrument itself that Q has been discharged. This knowledge does not prevent T from being a holder in due course. Yet, because T knew of Q's discharge, Q has a good defense against T. T takes free, however, of P's discharge of which T had no notice.

d. Subsequent Claims and Defenses

A holder in due course takes free of *prior* claims and defenses only, not any arising *when or after* she becomes a holder in due course. In terms of former law, "[A] holder in due course * * * [is] subject to any claims or defenses which arise *against him* after he has taken the instrument." 3-305 comment 1 (1989 Official Text) (emphasis added). The need for good faith and other requirements for becoming a holder in due course minimize the likelihood of a defense arising from the transaction of negotiation to a holder in due course. Occasionally, however, a defense arises at that time. For example, as part of the transaction of transfer, the holder in due course may agree to cancel his transferor's obligation by striking out his signature; or unknown to the holder in due course, a transaction may be voidable on the ground of illegality; or the parties may be acting on the basis of a mutual material mistake. Also, defenses may arise after he acquires an instrument. For example, an obligor might pay the holder in due course; the latter might renounce her rights in a separate writing without giving up the instrument; the transferor or a prior party might obtain a discharge in bankruptcy; or a secondary party might be discharged by the holder's failure to make a proper presentment or to give due notice of dishonor. Another possibility is the holder impairing collateral for the instrument and thereby creating a defense for an obligor. Regardless of the nature of the defense arising when she receives the instrument or later, a holder in due course is subject to the defense just as if she were not a holder in due course.

Example: M issued a note to P who specially indorsed it to Q. Q indorsed the note to R, who became a holder in due course. M did not pay the note upon maturity, and R eventually presented it for payment so as to charge the indorsers. M dishonored. Without excuse, R delayed giving notice of dishonor to P and Q beyond the time when such notice was due. The effect of this delay was to discharge P and Q. Their discharges are good defenses against R.

Example: M issued a note to P in the amount of $5000. P, a holder, fraudulently raised the amount to $15,000, and sold the note to Q, who became a holder in due course. Q then sold the note to R, also a holder in due course. Upon maturity of the note, R could collect only $5000 from M. R can recover her loss from Q in a breach of warranty action. Q's status as a holder in due course is no defense to the action.

e. **Claims and Defenses Chargeable to the Holder**
A holder in due course is not immune to liability or other accountability for her own conduct that creates a defense or claim for relief. She is liable for her own contracts, accountable for her own actions under Article 3 that create defenses or claims, and is liable for the breach of any duty imposed on her by other law that gives the obligor an offsetting defense or counterclaim in a suit on the instrument. It makes no difference when this liability arose, either before or after the holder became a holder in due course; and it makes no difference that the liability would be a personal claim or defense not enforceable against her if a prior party were responsible for it. Taking an instrument in due course will not permit a holder to escape responsibility for her own conduct, or for the conduct of others, when the law charges the holder directly and not merely derivatively through the transfer of the instrument.

B. ORDINARY OR PERSONAL DEFENSES

Ordinary or *personal defenses* are reasons of the law for reducing or eliminating an obligor's liability on an instrument except as against a holder in due course.   The rule is:

> Except as stated in subsection (b) * * *, the right to enforce the obligation of a party to pay an instrument is subject to * * * a defense of the obligor stated in another section of this Article or a defense of the obligor that would be available if the person entitled to enforce the instrument were enforcing a right to payment under a simple contract * * *.

3-305(a)(2). Except for a holder in due course, these defenses are good against every person entitled to enforce the instrument, including the original payee and any transferee. A holder in due course takes free of the personal defenses that are attributable to prior parties, which means that the defenses cannot be asserted against a holder in due course or someone claiming through her. 3-305(b). The personal defenses are found in Article 3 itself and also in the contract law that surrounds and governs the underlying transaction that produced the instrument.

1. Article 3 Defenses

The ordinary defenses created by Article 3 itself are spread throughout the statute, but they are conveniently listed in a comment to 3-305:

- nonissuance of the instrument, conditional issuance, and issuance for a special purpose (Section 3-105(b));
- failure to countersign a traveler's check (Section 3-106(c));
- modification of the obligation by a separate agreement (Section 3-117);
- payment that violates a restrictive indorsement (Section 3-206(f));
- instruments issued without consideration or for which promised performance has not been given (Section 3- 303(b)), and
- breach of warranty when a draft is accepted (Section 3-417(b)).

3-305 comment 2. Most of these defenses are tiny and tied to a very specific situation or context discussed elsewhere. The most important defense on this list concerns the "consideration" for the instrument. Really, this defense is rooted in the contract law of the underlying transaction. Article 3 recognizes and regulates the defense but does not create it. A more appropriate place to discuss the consideration defense is later, under the heading of defenses based on contract law.

2. Discharge -- The Not-A-Defense Defense

The most important Article 3 defense is not on the list of defenses in Article 3. It is "discharge," which means that an obligor is released from liability on the instrument for reasons of Article 3 or contract law. Discharge is not thought of, technically, as a defense and therefore is not included in the ordinary defenses of 3-305(a)(2). See 3-302 comment 3. In this book, discharge is discussed under the heading of contract liability on instruments. See Chapter III supra. Nevertheless, "[d]ischarge is effective against anybody except a person having rights of a holder in due course who took the instrument without notice of the discharge." Id.; see also 3-601(b). It is, functionally, a defense and therefore warrants a cross-reference here.

3. Defenses Of Contract Law

In addition to the Article 3 defenses specifically stated in Article 3, the personal defenses to an instrument also include defenses "of the obligor that would be available if the person entitled to enforce the instrument were enforcing a right to payment under a simple contract." 3-305(a)(2). These defenses derive from the underlying obligation and are based on the contract law that governs it. *This law includes the common law and any applicable statutory law*, such as U.C.C. Article 2 when a sale of goods is involved.

a. Range of Defenses, Especially Including Problems of Consideration

The contract defenses cover a wide range. At one end are broad common-law defenses concerned with fairness in the very beginning of the contract when it was formed, such as fraud, misrepresentation, and mistake. At the other end is breach of contract which turns on precise, very narrow issues of contract interpretation and on events that often occurred at the end of the contractual relationship. There is everything in between that would be available to the obligor if contract law governed the enforceability of her promise to pay, including the age-old defense of no consideration. It is an Article 3 defense that the instrument was issued or taken without consideration, 3-303(b); but, for the most part, it is contract law that defines consideration and it is the underlying transaction that is the source of any consideration. Really, therefore, lack of consideration is a contract defense.

1) Where Consideration Fits

Consideration is not an element of the plaintiff's prima facie case in a suit on an instrument, as it is when a person sues for breach of common-law contract. Nevertheless, "[t]he drawer or maker of an instrument has a defense if the instrument is issued without consideration." 3-303(b). Moreover, the issuer has a defense to the extent that she was promised performance that has not been duly performed. Id.

2) Different Issue is Value for Holder in Due Course

It is a different issue whether or not the holder of an instrument gave "value" to qualify as holder in due course. See 3-302(a)(2), 3-303(a). The lack of value for that purpose is not itself a defense to payment of an instrument. The issue, in terms of defense to payment, is whether or not the drawer or maker got "consideration" in exchange for issuing the instrument. If not, she has a defense.

3) Terms Defined Differently

Not only are the issues different, the key terms are defined differently. "Consideration" basically keeps its common-law meaning, 3-303(b), but Article 3 gives a meaning to "value" that is both broader and more narrow that common-law consideration. See 3-303(a). Value is broader because it includes a preexisting debt, 3-303(a)(3), and more narrow because a bare executory promise is not "value." Significantly, Article 3 enlarges the definition of "consideration" to include anything that is "value." 3-303(b). Therefore, by statute, consideration -- like value -- includes preexisting debt. Because of the common-law meaning, consideration -- unlike value -- also includes an executory promise.

Nevertheless, if an obligor issues an instrument in exchange for consideration that is an executory promise, she gets a pro tanto defense to the extent that the promise is due and unperformed. 3-303(b). Correspondingly, for purposes of holder in due course, "value" includes an executory promise to the extent the promise has been performed, 3-303(a)(1), but this point is relevant here solely to complete the comparison between value and consideration.

Example: To illustrate, suppose that R gave P a $500 check as a birthday gift. The drawee dishonored the check because R stopped payment. P will not recover on the check because R has the defense of lack of consideration. 3-303(b). It is possible, however, that P can prove a local substitute for consideration that supports recovery under the common law if not on the instrument.

Example: Suppose R gave P the check as prepayment for goods that P promised, by contract, to deliver later. R stops payment. P sues. The defense of lack of consideration is not available to R. P's executory promise itself was consideration. On the other hand, R has a defense to the extent that P's promise is due and unperformed. R has no defense if the time for P's performance has not yet arrived, and R loses the defense altogether if a holder in due course takes the instrument.

b. Caveat: Defense Must be Chargeable to Plaintiff

The contract defenses that the obligor can raise are the defenses that applicable law gives to her, not the defenses of someone else. 3-305(a)(2) ("of the obligor"). Another limitation is that the defenses must be chargeable to the plaintiff against whom they are asserted. In other words, the plaintiff must be subject to the defenses by law or agreement.

Example: Suppose, for example, that A and B signed a note to Bank that evidenced a loan. Unbeknownst to Bank, A was induced to sign the note only because of B's fraud that amounted to a personal defense. A got nothing from the loan. If B paid the instrument and sued A for contribution, A would have a good defense against B. On the other hand, if Bank sued A on the note, B's fraud would not be a good defense against Bank. *Standard Finance Co. v. Ellis*, 657 P.2d 1056 (Hawaii 1983). Whether Bank is a holder in due course is irrelevant. A's obligation runs directly to Bank.   The Bank's rights against A because of this obligation are not subject to the tacky conduct of someone else that is not attributable to Bank.

Example: The result is different if B's fraud resulted in A issuing a note payable to B that B transferred to Bank. In this case, if Bank sued A on the note, B's fraud would be a good defense for A, unless Bank was a holder in due course. The difference is that, in this case, Bank's rights derive from B and are therefore subject to any defenses good against B. As a holder in due course, however, Bank's rights would be greater and Bank would take free of fraud that amounted to only a personal defense.

Example: Even if Bank is a holder in due course, the result is different in both cases if B's fraud or other tacky conduct amounts to a real defense.   Real defenses are good against the world. It would make no difference that Bank took the instrument directly from A because to the extent that a real defense exists, the law effectively deems that the obligor never became liable to anyone on the instrument.

c. Lack of Consideration No Defense for Acceptor or Indorser

Significantly, 3-303(b) does not extend the defense of no consideration to an acceptor or indorser. A probable reason is the reality that acceptors and indorsers rarely act gratuitously. Even an anomalous indorser or other surety, known as an "accommodation party," 3-419(a), typically gets consideration in the value that is given to the principal debtor. It is so common that by express provision, consideration is unnecessary to bind an accommodation party. 3-419(b). Practically, it is always there, so having to prove it is wasted effort.

C. RECOUPMENT (DEFENSIVE COUNTERCLAIMS)

1. Recoupment Distinguished From Counterclaim

Strictly speaking, *recoupment* is not a defense but accomplishes as much. A defense is a reason why *liability* is reduced, eliminated or never arises because of the plaintiff's conduct in the transaction that gives rise to her cause of action. A *claim in recoupment* is similarly related to the plaintiff's cause but reduces or eliminates *damages* by way of offset. Basically, recoupment is a related cause of action that is asserted only so far as is possible and necessary to reduce the amount of liability, only to wipe out or cut down the plaintiff's demand. In this respect recoupment differs from a counterclaim which, when it exceeds the amount of liability, is asserted both to offset damages for liability and also to produce a net recovery against the plaintiff. In sum, recoupment is essentially a counterclaim that is asserted defensively only.

Example: Because of a seller's breach of warranty, the buyer of goods may reject them and cancel the sales contract. If she is sued for the contract price, her cancellation of the contract is a defense. If the buyer accepted the goods, she is liable for the price but can assert the breach of contract as a claim in recoupment or a counterclaim. Defenses and counterclaims often go together. The buyer who defends liability because of cancellation can also counterclaim for damages because of the seller's breach of warranty.

2. Recoupment Effective As A Personal Defense Against Transferee, Not Counterclaim

When a person lacks the rights of a holder in due course, her right to enforce the instrument is subject to "a claim in recoupment of the obligor against the original payee of the instrument if the claim arose from the transaction that gave rise to the instrument * * *." 3-305(a)(3). The claim, however, can be asserted against a transferee only for purposes of recoupment, "only to reduce the amount owing on the instrument at the time the action is brought." Id. In short, it cannot be asserted as a counterclaim. If the person enforcing the instrument is the original payee, this limitation does not apply. The claim can be asserted fully, as a counterclaim, to permit an affirmative, net recovery for the obligor.

3. Holder In Due Course Answerable For Claims Against Her Personally

A holder in due course takes free of all rights of action against prior parties, whether asserted as claims in recoupment or as counterclaims, except such claims that are against the holder personally.

Example: Suppose that the seller took the buyer's note for the price. A payee can be a holder in due course by meeting the usual requirements. Yet, even if the seller is such a holder, which is possible but highly unlikely, the buyer can assert any claim for breach of warranty, and she can assert it fully as a counterclaim and not only to reduce the amount of her liability. If the seller negotiates the note, the buyer can assert her claim against the third-party holder only in recoupment, to reduce the amount owed on the note; and the buyer cannot assert the claim to any extent if the holder is a holder in due course. The third party's knowledge of the claim when she took the instrument would prevent her from becoming a holder in due course. 3-302(a)(2)(vi).

It is explicitly stated that being a holder in due course does not protect the original payee from the obligor's claims:

[t]he right of a holder in due course to enforce the obligation of a party to pay the instrument * * * is *not* subject to * * * claims in recoupment * * * against a person *other than the holder*."

3-305(b) (emphasis added).

4. Setoff Distinguished

Different from recoupment is *setoff*. It concerns *un*related debts and claims. The rule on setoff as applied to instruments is that a transferee, whether or not a holder in due course, is not subject to the obligor's setoffs against a *prior party*. Yet, in line with local procedure, the obligor should be allowed to assert any setoff she has against the transferee personally, just as it should be appropriate for her to setoff against the original payee if this person sued to enforce the instrument. The reason for protecting a transferee from a prior-party setoff is that "it is not reasonable to require the transferee to bear the risk that wholly unrelated claims may also be asserted [as well as claims arising from the transaction that produced the instrument]." 3-305 comment 3. This reason does not apply to setoff against the plaintiff herself, whether she is the original payee or a transferee and whether or not she is a holder in due course.

D. CLAIMS (PROPERTY INTERESTS)

1. General Rule

a. Claims of Ownership Survive

Holdership is different from ownership. A person can own a property interest in an instrument even though somebody else holds the instrument and is the person entitled to enforce it. On the other hand, everybody except a holder in due course takes an instrument "subject to a claim of a property or possessory right in the instrument or its proceeds, including a claim to rescind a negotiation and to recover the instrument or its proceeds * * * ." 3-306.

b. Meaning of "Claim"

Here, the term "*claim*" is broad. It includes:

not only claims to ownership but also any other claim of a property or possessory right. It includes the claim to a lien or the claim of a person in rightful possession of an instrument who was wrongfully deprived of possession. Also included is a claim * * * for rescission of a negotiation of the instrument by the claimant.

3-306 comment. It does not include a claim in recoupment which is a counterclaim used as a defense to payment rather than a property right or interest.

2. Obligor's Options When Third Party Asserts Ownership Claim

a. May Pay

An obligor safely can pay the holder of an instrument and be discharged from liability even though the obligor knows of a third person's claim to the instrument and even though the claim is valid. 3-602(a). The claimant's remedy is to sue to recover the instrument and prevent payment.

b. Must Pay Unless Owner Defends

In the meantime, the obligor is not required to pay the holder who can be forced to sue to enforce the instrument. The issue then is whether or not the obligor can defend against liability on the basis of the third-party claim. (This is sometimes referred to as the defense of *jus tertii*, meaning right of a third party.) The answer is no unless the third person "is joined in the action and personally asserts the claim against the person entitled to enforce the instrument." 3-305(c). The only exception is when the plaintiff lacks the rights of a holder in due course "and the obligor proves that the instrument is a lost or stolen instrument." Id.

c. **Defense Useless Against Holder in Due Course**
   In no event can the obligor avoid payment of an instrument, or can anyone else enforce a prior claim to it, if the instrument was taken by a holder in due course and is not held by her or someone claiming through this person. "A person having rights of a holder in due course takes free of the claim to the instrument." 3-306.

REVIEW QUESTIONS

1. T stole a note payable to P's order which P had indorsed in blank. T then sold the note to S who gave value for the instrument and took it in good faith and without notice of any claim or defense. Claiming an equitable lien on the note, P sued S to recover the instrument. In the alternative, P asked for damages for conversion. Who wins and why?

2. P loaned D $10,000 for one year. The parties agreed that the interest rate would be 25%. To evidence D's obligation for principal and interest, D made a note to P in the lump-sum amount of $12,500. The note did not disclose the interest rate. P sold the note to Q, who took as a holder in due course. D refused to pay the note at maturity. Her defense was that the interest rate on the loan exceeded the maximum rate allowed by applicable law. Is this defense good against Q?

3. M made a note to P who negotiated it by indorsement to Q. Q took as a holder in due course. Q discharged M on the note by canceling M's signature. P thereafter refused to pay the instrument, arguing that discharging M discharged her. Q's response is that discharge is a personal defense that cannot be asserted against a holder in due course. Grade Q's response.

4. B bought goods from S and paid the price with a cashier's check drawn and issued by Bank payable to S. When S presented the cashier's check to Bank for payment, Bank refused to pay it because B, who procured the cashier's check, never paid for it. S sues Bank as drawer of the cashier's check. Bank's defense is B's failure to pay for the instrument. Inasmuch as Bank and S are both parties to the check, has S dealt with Bank so that, even if S is a holder in due course, she is subject to Bank's personal defenses? Is it even possible for S to be a holder in due course inasmuch as she is the payee of the check?

5. B bought goods from S and paid the price with a personal check drawn on B's account at Bank. Bank dishonored the check at B's request. S sued B on the check. B's defense is fraudulent inducement. Is this defense good against S?

6.   M forced N, at gun point, to sign a note payable to the order of Bank. Bank was unaware of the duress. Is the duress a good defense for N if the Bank sues to enforce the note against N?

ACCOMMODATION PARTIES

Analysis

The term *surety* is probably familiar to you. Generally speaking, a surety is someone who promises to pay another person's debt. More completely defined, "[s]uretyship is the relation which exists where one person has undertaken an obligation and another person is also under an obligation or other duty to the obligee, who is entitled to but one performance, and as between the two who are bound, one rather than the other should perform." Restatement of Security § 82 (1941). The person who should perform, ultimately, is commonly called the *principal debtor.* The other person is the surety. Article 3 has a special name for a surety who joins the principal debtor in signing an instrument. The name is *accommodation party,* which generally means anyone who signs an instrument with another person for the purpose of benefiting the other person and without being a direct beneficiary of the value given for the instrument. 3-419(a) & comment 1. The other person -- the principal debtor -- is known as the *accommodated party* on the instrument.

Like any other person who signs an instrument, an accommodation party is liable on the instrument she signs. Moreover, the nature of her liability on the instrument is not determined by her role as a surety. Rather, the nature of her liability is determined, as in the case of any other signer, by the capacity in which she signed it: maker, indorser, drawer, or acceptor. In other words, with respect to whether an accommodation party is prima facie liable on an instrument, and also with respect to the existence and kind of conditions to her liability thereon, an accommodation party is treated the same as any other party to an instrument. For these purposes, her status as an accommodation party is generally irrelevant.

The relevance of accommodation status, and the different treatment that results from it, is principally in the accommodation party's rights (on and dehors the instrument) against the principal debtor, and in the accommodation party's defenses to payment of the instrument against the payee and other holders and transferees. In these regards an accommodation party is better protected, more privileged than signers of instruments who do not enjoy accommodation status.

A. DECIDING WHO IS AN ACCOMMODATION PARTY

1. Defining *Accommodation Party* And *Accommodated Party*
Article 3 indirectly defines "accommodation" and "accommodated" parties by explaining their roles when an instrument is signed "for accommodation":

> If an instrument is issued for value given for the benefit of a party to the instrument ("accommodated party") and another party to the instrument ("accommodation party") signs the instrument for the purpose of incurring liability on the instrument without being a direct beneficiary of the value given for

the instrument, the instrument is signed by the accommodation party "for accommodation."

3-419(a). In short, "[a]n accommodation party is a person who signs an instrument to benefit the accommodated party either by signing at the time value is obtained by the accommodated party or later, and who is not a direct beneficiary of the value obtained." 3-419 comment 1. This definition says much about what is required, and what is not required, to be an accommodation party.

a. What Is Required
The requirements that a person must satisfy to be an accommodation party are these:

- **The person must sign an instrument.** (See Chapter II supra.)
- **Her purpose in signing the instrument must be to benefit another party without getting any direct benefit from the value given for the instrument.** (See discussion later in this chapter about proving accommodation status.)
- **The other party, that is, the principal debtor/ accommodated party, must have signed the very same instrument, too.**

Be careful! A person who is a surety is not necessarily an accommodation party simply because she signed an instrument. She and the principal debtor must be on the instrument together.

Example: A had defaulted in repaying a loan from Lender. To forestall foreclosure against A, B agreed to repay the loan herself in 90 days if A could not come up with the money within that time. Lender agreed to this arrangement, which was essentially an extension of time for A to pay, but required B to sign a 90-day note in the amount of A's obligation. B is a surety but she is not an accommodation party. In this case, the other party, A, who is the principal debtor, was not a party to the instrument B signed.

Example: Bank was unwilling to make a loan to A. A asked her rich friend, B, to help out by promising the Bank that she, B, would repay any loan that Bank made to A. Instead of making the loan to A and having both A and B sign a note, the Bank structured the deal so that the loan was made to B and only B signed a note. B then gave the proceeds to A. If A is obligated to repay the loan, then B is a surety but is not an accommodation party. If A is not herself liable to the Bank for the loan, A is not even a surety.

b. What Is Not Required
1) Particular Capacity

Accommodation status does not depend on the person signing the instrument in a particular capacity either absolutely or in relation to the principal debtor or anyone else. "An accommodation party may sign the instrument as maker, drawer, acceptor, or indorser * * *," 3-419(b), in *any* capacity. The capacity in which she signed is never determinative of accommodation status. For instance, a maker of a note can be an accommodation party even though the principal debtor signed as indorser.

2) Indication of Accommodation

Also, in signing the instrument, the accommodation party need not indicate, through her signature or otherwise, her role as such. A person who signs with a blank signature can be an accommodation party. Yet, the capacity in which a person signs an instrument, or words added to her signature, may help her prove that she signed as an accommodation party.

2. Proving Accommodation Status
a. Proof That Establishes Accommodation Status
1) No Direct Benefit

A person is an accommodation party if she signed the instrument to benefit another party to the instrument, i.e., "for the purpose of incurring liability on the instrument without being a direct beneficiary of the value given for the instrument." 3-419(a). Ordinarily, a person proves that she signed for this purpose by presenting evidence that she received no *direct* benefit from the proceeds of the instrument. Indirect benefit does not matter.

Example: Son wished to buy a car. Bank would not loan him the money because he had no credit history. Son's Mother, who was creditworthy, promised Bank that she would repay the loan if Son defaulted. Mother and Son then executed a note to Bank. They signed as comakers. Mother is an accommodation party.

Example: Same facts, except that Mother signed the note as maker and Son signed as indorser. Mother is still an accommodation party. The capacity in which she signed does not determine accommodation status. Her purpose in signing the instrument determines accommodation status.

Example: "[I]f X cosigns a note of Corporation that is given for a loan to Corporation, X is an accommodation party if no part of the loan was paid to X or for X's direct benefit. This is true even though

X may receive indirect benefit from the loan because X is employed by Corporation or is a stockholder of Corporation, or even if X is the sole stockholder so long as Corporation and X are recognized as separate entities." 3-419 comment 1.

2) Presumption Of Accommodation

A person signing an instrument is presumed to be an accommodation party and there is notice that the instrument is signed for accommodation if:

- the signature is an anomalous indorsement, or
- is accompanied by words indicating that the signer is acting as a surety or guarantor with respect to the obligation of another party to the instrument.

3-419(c). "'*Anomalous indorsement*' means an indorsement made by a person who is not the holder of the instrument." 3-205(d). Common practice also refers to it as an *irregular indorsement*. In traditional terms, it refers to a person having signed as an indorser out of the chain of title, which usually means signing an instrument in the capacity of an indorser (in the margin or on the back other than as a primary party) prior to delivery to the payee. An irregular indorser is not a holder or otherwise an owner of the instrument, which helps explain why her indorsement is "out of the chain of title." Moreover, she does not herself transfer the instrument. Thus, although she is liable on the instrument as an indorser, she avoids warranty liability that only a transferor incurs.

Yet, neither irregularly indorsing an instrument nor adding words of guaranty to a signature establishes, conclusively, accommodation status. It establishes a rebuttable presumption only. "A party challenging accommodation party status would have to [and could possibly] rebut this presumption by producing evidence that the signer was in fact a direct beneficiary of the value given for the instrument." 3-419 comment 3. Conversely, irregularly indorsing or adding words of suretyship to a signature is not necessary to establish accommodation status.

b. Receiving Compensation for Serving as an Accommodation Party

A person who signs an instrument to benefit another person without directly benefiting from the value given for the instrument is an accommodation party even though she is paid or receives other compensation for serving as a surety, cf. 3-419(b), and even though the payment is made from the proceeds of the instrument she signs as an accommodation party. A compensated surety is nonetheless a surety.

B. LIABILITY ON THE INSTRUMENT

1. Generally: Accommodation Party Liable In The Capacity In Which She Signed

The rule is that an accommodation party's obligation on the instrument is determined by the capacity in which she signed it. 3-419(b). Capacity means maker, drawer, indorser or acceptor. If she signed as maker of a note, she is obligated thereon, i.e., has the same contract liability, that 3-412 imposes on makers generally. Similarly, if she signed as an indorser, her liability is determined by reference to the provision that describes the liability of any indorser, which is 3-415(a). Thus, "[a]n accommodation maker or acceptor is bound on the instrument without any resort to his principal, while an accommodation indorser may be liable only after presentment, notice of dishonor, and protest." 3-415 comment 1 (1989 Official Text). The very important lesson to learn here is that accommodation status, in itself, does not alter the person's liability on an instrument as defined by the usual rules governing the liability of people who sign instruments. For these rules, see Chapter III, supra.

Example: D and S sign a note as comakers, but S is an accommodation party. The note matures and is not paid. The holder sues S whose defense is that she is an accommodation party and thus cannot be liable on the instrument until the holder pursues D, the principal debtor. This defense is a loser. S's liability on the instrument is as a maker, 3-412, who as a cosigner is jointly *and severally* liable. 3-116(a). A maker engages to pay the instrument when it is due. 3-412. Her liability is primary and unconditional. Nothing in Article 3 requires a holder to first pursue someone else before she can recover from a maker. It makes no difference that S is an accommodation party. It makes no difference that the holder knows S is an accommodation party.

2. Irrelevant That Creditor Knows Of Accommodation

Generally, "the obligation of an accommodation party to pay the instrument is not affected by the fact that the person enforcing the obligation had notice when the instrument was taken by that person that the accommodation party signed the instrument for accommodation." 3-419(c). This person's notice of the accommodation can be important, however, with respect to the accommodation party's defenses, which are outlined later.

3. Exception: No Liability To Person Accommodated

Notwithstanding the general rule that an accommodation party is liable in the capacity in which she signed the instrument, she is never liable to the party accommodated either on the instrument or for contribution, 3-419(e), irrespective of the parties' capacities on the instrument.

> *Example:* D and S signed a note. S signed as accommodation maker. D indorsed. The note matured, and the holder presented it to S for payment. S dishonored the instrument. D paid it. D sued S on the instrument. A maker is ordinarily liable to an indorser, but not in this case. Because S is an accommodation party beyond being a maker, she is not liable to D who is the party accommodated on the instrument.

4. Situations In Which Accommodation Party Is Liable Only After Payment Is Sought From Someone Else

a. Where Accommodation Party Is Secondarily Liable Due to Capacity in Which She Signed

When an accommodation party signs the instrument as drawer or indorser, her liability is secondary and conditioned on dishonor. These conditions result from her role as drawer or indorser, not from her accommodation status. See Chapter III supra. Thus, the accommodation party is not liable until payment or acceptance is first demanded from, and refused by, the drawee or other payor.

> *Example:* D and S sign a note. D is the maker. S is an accommodation indorser. The note matures and D does not pay it. The holder sues S. S moves for summary disposition in her favor because the holder admittedly has not presented the note for payment to D. The motion should be granted. S's liability as indorser is conditioned on timely presentment to D, dishonor, and timely notice of dishonor to S. The holder could not necessarily salvage her action against S by presenting the instrument to D and, upon dishonor, giving S notice of same. Presentment and notice must be timely, and unexcused tardiness in either regard has the effect of discharging an indorser.

An accommodation party who is secondarily liable as an indorser or drawer can waive the conditions to her liability as early as when she signs the instrument. Such a waiver results, for example, when the accommodation party indorses a note that contains an explicit waiver of presentment. As a result, the liability of an accommodation party, even though she signed as indorser, becomes indistinguishable from that of a co-maker whose liability is not conditioned on presentment, dishonor or notice.

b. Accommodation Party Signs as Guarantor of Collectibility

When an accommodation party adds to her signature such words as "COLLECTION GUARANTEED", known as a *guaranty of collection,* she becomes a *guarantor of collectibility* and guarantees collection rather than payment of the obligation of the accommodated party. The result is that the signer is obliged to pay the amount due on the instrument to a person entitled to enforce the instrument only if:

- execution of judgment against the accommodated party has been returned unsatisfied,
- the accommodated party is insolvent or is in an insolvency proceeding,
- the accommodated party cannot be served with process, or
- it is otherwise apparent that payment cannot be obtained from the accommodated party.

3-419(d). This is the result of a guaranty of collection without regard to the capacity in which the accommodation party signed, and thus such a guaranty benefits accommodation makers and acceptors as well as accommodation indorsers and drawers.

> *Example:* D and S signed a note as comakers. S was an accommodation party and added to her signature the words, "COLLECTION GUARANTEED." The note matured, but D, the principal debtor, did not pay it. The holder sued S without pursuing D. S is not liable. Neither S's role as maker nor her status as an accommodation party requires the holder first to pursue D. Pursuing D first is required due to the guaranty of collection which S added to her signature. This addition changes her contract liability so that she promises to pay only after the holder first proceeds against the maker by suit and execution, or shows that so proceeding would be useless.

c. **Extra-Code Law**
1) Statutes
Some states have statutes, that are not part of the Code, requiring a creditor to first pursue a principal debtor before seeking payment from a surety. These laws may apply to Article 3 accommodation parties depending on the express terms of the laws and how they are interpreted by the courts.

2) Common Law
The common law of a few states includes the decisional rule of *Pain v. Packard*, 13 Johns 174 (N.Y.Sup. 1816), which limits a creditor's right to proceed against a surety upon default of the principal debtor by requiring a "due diligence" effort by the creditor to collect first from the principal debtor. The better view is that Article 3 displaces this doctrine which, therefore, cannot be relied on by accommodation parties. In any event, the protection of the *Pain v. Packard* doctrine, and similar statutory rules, can be

waived by sureties, and boilerplate language in notes and other contracts signed by sureties often accomplishes such a waiver.

5. Where There Is Collateral For The Debt

Very often, even though the principal debtor's obligation is backed by the personal liability of an accommodation party, the instrument is also backed by collateral, either personal or real property or both. Ordinarily, the collateral has been supplied by the principal debtor and is property belonging to her. If the instrument is not paid, the holder can satisfy it by foreclosing on the collateral. Accommodation parties often argue that their liability is conditioned on the holder first exhausting the collateral. This argument is unsound. It is a general principle of suretyship law, which the courts routinely apply to accommodation parties, that "the mere fact that the creditor has security from the principal affords no equitable ground for relieving the surety of his duty of immediate performance. One of the reasons why a creditor requires a surety is to avoid delay in obtaining satisfaction." Restatement of Security § 131 comment a (1941). The rule is different, and collateral that is property of the principal must first be exhausted, if the surety only guaranteed collectibility. The same is true under Article 3 when an accommodation party adds a guaranty of collection to her signature. See 3-419(d).

Example: Bank makes a loan to ABC Corp. The company president signs the note for the company. She also signs personally and individually, as an accommodation comaker. The note is secured by the equipment, inventory and receivables of the principal debtor, ABC Corp. The company president is immediately liable to the Bank when the note matures. Her liability is not conditioned on Bank first realizing on the collateral.

Example: Same facts, except that the company president adds the words "COLLECTION GUARANTEED" to her signature when she signs for herself as accommodation comaker. In this case the company president is liable only after Bank has foreclosed on the collateral and exhausted other assets of the principal debtor.

C. RIGHTS AGAINST PRINCIPAL DEBTOR

Much of the significance of accommodation status is in the rights an accommodation party enjoys against the principal debtor.

1. Exoneration

Ordinarily, a holder is not required to pursue the principal debtor before demanding payment of an accommodation party. Yet, the accommodation party enjoys the right, by suit in equity, to compel the principal debtor to pay if the principal debtor is capable of satisfying the obligation. This right is known as *exoneration.* Although an equitable right, exoneration has been confirmed by statute in some states. For example, Minnesota law provides:

> An action may be brought against two or more persons for the purpose of compelling one to satisfy a debt due to the other, for which the plaintiff is bound as surety.

Minn. Stat. Ann. 540.11 This statute has been explained as the *quid pro quo* for denying a surety relief against the creditor for failing to demand payment from the principal debtor. *MacKenzie v. Summit Nat'l Bank of St. Paul*, 363 N.W.2d 116, 120 (Minn. Ct. App. 1985).

Remember: "The surety's remedy of exoneration is solely against the principal debtor; it can in no way hinder or prejudice the rights of the creditor. Thus, the creditor may, despite the equitable suit of the surety, proceed at law to judgment and execution against the surety." L. Simpson, HANDBOOK ON THE LAW OF SURETYSHIP § 46 at 199-200 (1950).

2. Reimbursement And Recourse

Under the common law, a surety who pays the debt enjoys the right to recoup the payment from the principal debtor. This right is known as the *right of reimbursement.* An accommodation party enjoys this common-law right. She also enjoys a right of recovery on the instrument itself. By the terms of Article 3, "[a]n accommodation party who pays the instrument is entitled to reimbursement from the accommodated party and is entitled to enforce the instrument against the accommodated party." 3-419(e). An accommodation party can avail herself of these rights, including the right of recourse on the instrument, without regard to the capacity in which she signed and even though the principal debtor would not be liable to her on the instrument in the absence of the suretyship relation between them.

Example: D and S signed a note. S was the maker, who signed as an accommodation to D. D herself indorsed the instrument. When the note matured, S paid the holder. Had S not been an accommodation party, her payment to the holder would have extinguished the note and discharged D as indorser. Moreover, an indorser is not ordinarily liable to a maker. Yet, because S is an accommodation party, the note is not extinguished by her payment of it and she has a cause of action against D on the note to recover the amount S paid. The theory is that S is subrogated to the holder's rights against D on the instrument.

Correlatively, an accommodation party is never liable on the instrument to the person accommodated, 3-419(e), even though the former signs in a capacity that, in the absence of the suretyship relation, would obligate her to the latter. Thus, for example, an accommodation maker is not liable to an indorser who is the principal debtor.

3. Subrogation
a. With Respect to Creditor's Right to Payment
An accommodation party who pays the instrument is subrogated to the holder's rights on the instrument against the accommodated party, i.e., the principal debtor. This explains the accommodation party's right of recourse on the instrument as provided in 3-419(e).

b. With Respect to Creditor's Rights in Collateral
By common law, a surety (including an accommodation party) who satisfies the obligation to the creditor is subrogated to the creditor's rights in collateral that secures the debt. So, when an accommodation party pays the holder, she can enforce her rights of reimbursement and recourse out of any collateral that secures the instrument.

Example: Bank makes a loan to ABC Corp. The company president signs the note for the company. She also signs personally and individually, as an accommodation comaker. The note is secured by the equipment, inventory and receivables of the principal debtor, ABC Corp. The company president is immediately liable to the Bank when the note matures. Her liability is not conditioned on Bank first realizing on the collateral. Upon paying Bank, however, the company president is subrogated to Bank's rights in the collateral. She can dispose of the property pursuant to Part 5 of Article 9, and repay herself from the proceeds of the disposition. Any surplus proceeds belong to ABC Corp.

The creditor's rights to collateral, which pass to the accommodation party, include the priority of the creditor's security interest or other lien over the claims of third parties to the collateral.

Example: Same facts as above, except that ABC Corp. also used the collateral to secure a loan from another lender. For reasons of other law that determines priority of conflicting claims without regard to the involvement of sureties, Bank's security interest in the collateral outranks the other lender's security interest in the property. When the accommodation party is subrogated to the Bank's rights in the collateral, her claim as subrogee will also outrank the other lender's security interest.

4. Excursus: Rights Of Accommodation Parties Among Themselves

Not uncommonly, an instrument carries the signatures of two or more accommodation parties, especially when a large loan is made to an uncreditworthy company. Typically, all of these accommodation parties sign in the same capacity as part of the same transaction, and each of them is jointly and severally liable. See 3-116(a). Thus, any of them can be called upon to pay the whole amount of the instrument. In this event, however, the accommodation party who pays is entitled, under the common law, to *contribution* from the others. As among themselves, sureties are generally liable to one another, through contribution, for a proportionate share of the debt.

D. DEFENSES TO PAYMENT

1. Defenses Based On The Instrument

First and foremost, an accommodation party is a signer of an instrument. For this reason she is liable thereon in the capacity in which she signed the instrument. Correspondingly, notwithstanding her accommodation status, she is freed from liability whenever, under the rules of Article 3 generally, a person who signed in her capacity would be discharged on the instrument. Her accommodation status does not deprive her of rights, including defenses, she would otherwise have as a signer of an instrument.

Example: D and S made a note to P. D signed as maker. S, an accommodation party, signed as indorser. The note matured. D did not pay it. Weeks passed before P presented the note to D for payment. D then dishonored. P thereafter demanded payment from S. S is discharged, however. An indorser's liability is conditioned on presentment. Presentment in this case was untimely. Therefore, an indorser on the instrument is discharged. S is an indorser. She is thus discharged. Her accommodation status is irrelevant.

Example: D and S made a note to P. They signed as comakers, but S accommodated D on the instrument. P fraudulently and materially altered the instrument. D and S are both discharged.

2. Failure Of Consideration Between Creditor And Principal Debtor And Other Derivative Defenses

a. Generally

A surety's obligation is based upon the existence of a duty of the principal debtor to the creditor. Thus, the creditor cannot recover from the surety when the creditor's conduct gives the principal debtor a complete defense, i.e., excuses the principal's duty to the creditor. Thus, *failure of consideration* between principal and creditor is a defense available to the surety, Restatement of Security § 126 (1941), including an accommodation party. Further, the reasoning that allows a surety to assert such failure of consideration applies equally as well to any defense of the principal debtor against the creditor, whether the defense is want of consideration, impossibility, illegality, fraud, duress or the like. Article 3 agrees:

> In an action to enforce the obligation of an accommodation party to pay an instrument, the accommodation party may assert against the person entitled to enforce the instrument any defense or claim in recoupment * * * that the accommodated party could assert against the person entitled to enforce the instrument * * *."

3-305(d).

b. Exception for Personal Defenses

A few defenses of the principal debtor are characterized as personal to her and for this reason are unavailable to the surety. The most important examples are the principal's lack of capacity, such as infancy, and the discharge of the principal in bankruptcy. 3-305(d). When the principal debtor asserts such a "personal" defense and the surety is forced to pay the debt, the surety is not entitled to reimbursement. The characteristics of a *"personal" defense* are not entirely clear. There are no peculiar attributes common to all personal defenses which set them apart from defenses that are not personal. The real reason for denying the surety the benefit of the principal's defense of lack of capacity or discharge in bankruptcy is that "the very purpose of the suretyship was to shift the risk of the asserted defense from the creditor to the surety." Peters, *Suretyship Under Article 3 of the Uniform Commercial Code,* 77 Yale L. J. 833, 862 (1968).

c. Claims and Setoffs

Related to the question of a surety's derivative defenses is the issue whether a surety can assert, if only to the extent of reducing her own liability, the claims and setoffs that the principal debtor has against the creditor. Traditional suretyship doctrine holds that, generally, "[i]f the creditor sues the surety alone,

* * * the surety cannot use defensively a claim of the principal debtor against the creditor." L. Simpson, HANDBOOK ON THE LAW OF SURETYSHIP § 70 at 319 (1950). Accord, J. Elder, THE LAW OF SURETYSHIP § 7.4 (5th ed. 1951). Article 3 allows the accommodation party to assert related counterclaims, i.e., claims in recoupment, only to reduce the amount owing on the instrument at the time the action is brought. 3-305(a)(3) & (d). The surety cannot use for any purpose the principal debtor's unrelated setoffs.

3. Lack Of Consideration

a. Between Principal Debtor and Creditor

If no consideration supports the principal debtor's obligation to the creditor so that the former, for this reason, would have a defense against the latter, this lack of consideration is also a derivative defense for the surety that is effective against the creditor.

b. For the Surety's Undertaking

The general law of suretyship ordinarily requires consideration supporting the surety's obligation. The surety has a defense in the absence of it. In the typical case, however, the surety agrees to become a surety in order to induce the creditor to make a loan or otherwise extend credit to the principal debtor. In this event, the loan or other credit given the principal debtor is also consideration for the surety's undertaking. If the surety signs on later, after the principal and creditor have made their deal, there is no consideration for the surety's undertaking in the absence of some concession to the principal (e.g., extension of time to pay; forbearance to collect; additional credit; reduction in interest rate) or consideration paid directly to the surety. You may remember from first-year Contracts that a promise to pay a preexisting debt is, standing alone, usually unenforceable because past consideration is not itself consideration.

Here, however, there is an important difference between general suretyship law and the law of Article 3 as applied to accommodation parties. Article 3 provides:

> The obligation of an accommodation party may be enforced notwithstanding any statute of frauds and whether or not the accommodation party receives consideration for the accommodation.

3-419(b).

4. Suretyship Defenses -- U.C.C. 3-605

An accommodation party's most important defenses are a collection of reasons for discharging her from liability that are based on her status as a surety, thus the name *suretyship defenses.* Speaking very generally, these defenses, or reasons for discharge, are tied to conduct of the creditor that alters the principal's obligation or impairs collateral for the obligation. Article 3's collection of suretyship defenses is in 3-605.

Significantly, **the 3-605 suretyship defenses are also extended to** *ordinary indorsers* -- anybody who indorses an instrument whether or not for accommodation. It also includes a drawer of a draft that is accepted by a nonbank because the law treats her, upon the acceptance, as an indorser. 3-414(d), 3-605(a). The reason 3-605 covers indorsers is that, functionally, every indorser to some extent is a surety, a guarantor of payment. 3-605 comment 1. This is not to say that every indorser is, by law, an accommodation party within the meaning of 3-419. An indorser is an accommodation party only if she meets the definitional test for such status. An indorser who fails this test is treated like a surety for purposes of 3-605 only, and not for purposes of 3-419.

a. Altering the Principal Debtor's Obligation
1) The Conduct That Is Covered
a) Extending Due Date
"If a person entitled to enforce an instrument agrees, with or without consideration, to an extension of the due date of the obligation of a party to pay the instrument, the extension discharges an indorser or accommodation party having a right of recourse against the party whose obligation is extended to the extent the indorser or accommodation party proves that the extension caused loss to the indorser or accommodation party with respect to the right of recourse." 3-605(c).

b) Otherwise Materially Modifying Obligation
"If a person entitled to enforce an instrument agrees, with or without consideration, to a material modification of the obligation of a party other than an extension of the due date, the modification discharges the obligation of an indorser or accommodation party having a right of recourse against the person whose obligation is modified to the extent the modification causes loss to the indorser or accommodation party with respect to the right of recourse. The loss suffered by the indorser or accommodation party as a result of the modification is equal to the amount of the right of recourse unless the person enforcing the instrument proves that no loss was caused by the modification or that the loss caused by the modification was an amount less than the amount of the right of recourse." 3-605(d).

2) **The Main Difference Is In Burden of Proving Loss**
Extending the due date of an obligation is a material modification, but the former is dealt with in a separate rule rather than included in the latter. Why are they separate? The main reason is to treat differently the burden of proving loss because of the modification. In one way or another, the discharge is pro tanto, to the extent the conduct harms the surety. In the case of extending the due date, the surety must prove the actual loss that the extension caused her. 3-605(c). Putting the burden of proof on her seems fair and efficient because extensions of time are common and ordinarily benefit a surety. In line with this practical experience, the law effectively presumes that an extension is harmless unless the surety proves loss. Other modifications are not so common and are more likely to cause harm. Therefore, the presumption is reversed -- harm is presumed unless the holder proves otherwise. The surety's loss is deemed the amount of her right of recourse less any amount the holder proves was not lost. 3-605(d). The surety's right of recourse is measured by the amount she is entitled to recoup from the obligor if the surety pays the instrument. Usually, this amount is the full amount of the instrument so that, in the typical case of a change in the obligation other than an extension of time, the surety is completely discharged unless the holder proves that the surety's actual loss was less than the amount of the instrument.

3) **Canceling Obligation Not A Material Modification**
Surprisingly, it is not a material modification to cancel or renounce the obligation of a party against whom the surety has a right of recourse, even though the effect is fully to discharge the party. 3-604, 3-605(b). The explanation is that such a release never happens gratuitously and usually is part of a settlement with a financially troubled debtor who makes partial payment. It benefits the surety because the debt is reduced and therefore does not discharge her from liability to pay the balance. See 3-605 comment 3.

4) **Discharge Not Avoided By Reservation of Rights**
A discharge because of extension or other modification of the obligation cannot be prevented by the holder unilaterally reserving rights against the surety. Former law sanctioned this self-serving ritual that allowed the creditor to change the principal debtor's contract without releasing the surety from liability. The 1990 Article 3 abolishes the reservation of rights doctrine with respect to rights on instruments. 3-605 comment 3. A bilateral reservation remains possible, that is, no discharge results to any extent from any modification of the obligation to the extent the surety consents to the change.

b. Impairing Collateral for the Obligation

1) The Law and Its Rationale

Generally speaking, a surety who satisfies the obligation is, by law, subrogated to the creditor's rights in collateral (whether real estate, personal property, or both) that secures the obligation. The surety can then recoup what she has paid, for the principal debtor's benefit, by realizing on this collateral. Accordingly, the creditor is, as she should be, accountable to the surety for conduct that diminishes collateral or the value of it. For accommodation parties, Article 3 states the accountability this way:

> If the obligation of a party to pay an instrument is secured by an interest in collateral and a person entitled to enforce the instrument impairs the value of the interest in collateral, the obligation of an indorser or accommodation party having a right of recourse against the obligor is discharged to the extent of the impairment. The value of an interest in collateral is impaired to the extent (i) the value of the interest is reduced to an amount less than the amount of the right of recourse of the party asserting discharge, or (ii) the reduction in value of the interest causes an increase in the amount by which the amount of the right of recourse exceeds the value of the interest. The burden of proving impairment is on the party asserting discharge.

3-605(e). Notice that this discharge, like the discharges under 3-605(c-d), is proportionate or pro tanto. The holder's impairment of collateral discharges the accommodation party only in an amount of the obligation equivalent to the harm caused.

2) Unimportant Who Supplied the Collateral or When

It was true under former law, and presumably remains true, that an accommodation party can take advantage of this discharge no matter who supplied the collateral and even though she was unaware, upon undertaking the obligation, that the instrument was secured. Moreover, the discharge applies to the impairment of collateral whenever given, even to collateral that is supplied after the accommodation party signs the instrument. The explanation is that a surety's right of subrogation to the creditor's rights in collateral applies without regard to when the collateral is given and whether or not the surety is aware of its existence.

3) Conduct That Is Impairment

Impairment of collateral includes, but is not limited to, the following:

- failure to obtain or maintain perfection or recordation of the interest in collateral,
- release of collateral without substitution of collateral of equal value,
- failure to perform a duty to preserve the value of collateral owed, under Article 9 or other law, to a debtor or surety or other person secondarily liable, or
- failure to comply with applicable law in disposing of collateral.

3-605(g).

4) Excursus: Unlawful Disposition of Collateral

When the collateral for an instrument is personal property or fixtures, the disposition of the property by the holder, qua Article 9 secured party, in satisfaction of the obligation is regulated by Part 5 of Article 9. The statute requires a commercially reasonable disposition after notice to the debtor. In the event either of these requirements is not satisfied, the secured party is accountable to the debtor. This accountability is typically imposed when the secured party sues the debtor for a deficiency, meaning the balance of the secured debt that remains after the proceeds of the disposition are credited against the debt. In about half the states, this accountability results in the debtor getting a credit, against the secured debt, measured by the full market value of the collateral instead of the amount of proceeds actually produced by the secured party's disposition. In other states, accountability results in denying the secured party the right to recover any deficiency.

An accommodation party on an instrument secured by personal property is a "debtor" for purposes of Part 5 of Article 9. Thus, the accommodation party is entitled to notice of the disposition of the collateral, and can complain against the secured party if the disposition was not commercially reasonable. If the disposition is unreasonable, or if the accommodation party is not notified, the secured party is accountable to her. As a result, the liability of the accommodation party can be reduced or altogether eliminated.

This reduction or elimination of liability is not generally regarded as based on 3-605, which discharges an accommodation party when the holder impairs collateral. Rather, it is based on violation of Part 5 of Article 9. This distinction is important because the defense of impairment of collateral can be waived by an accommodation party, in advance, through language in the instrument she signs. According to express language of Article 9, however, a secured party's duty to notify a debtor cannot be waived in advance of default on the obligation, 9-504(3); and the duty to conduct a commercially reasonable disposition can never be waived by a debtor, see

9-501(3), although she is free to forego complaining about it. So, language in a note whereby an accommodation party abandons her rights in collateral, or agrees that the holder shall not be liable for her dealings or misdealings with collateral, should not deprive an accommodation party of her right, as an Article 9 "debtor," to hold a holder qua secured party liable for failing to notify the accommodation party of a disposition of the collateral, or for conducting an unreasonable disposition of the property. Be aware, however, that a minority of cases are to the contrary and allow an accommodation party or other surety to waive, in advance when she undertakes the obligation, her rights to notice and a commercially reasonable disposition of collateral under Part 5 of Article 9.

5) Loss

Impairment alone is no basis for discharge. The surety must also prove the extent to which the impairment caused her loss. She suffers loss to the extent

- the value of the interest in the collateral is reduced to an amount less than the amount of the right of recourse of the party asserting discharge, or
- the reduction in value of the interest causes an increase in the amount by which the amount of the right of recourse exceeds the value of the interest.

3-605(e). Put more generally, the surety is harmed to the extent that the impairment increased the amount by which her right of recourse is unsecured.

Example: Suppose, for example, that A accommodated B on a note for $50,000 payable to P. The note was secured by an Article 9 security interest in B's personal property worth more than $50,000. So long as the value of the collateral stays above the debt, A's right to recoup from B for paying the debt is fully secured. Unfortunately, P failed to perfect the security interest. B filed bankruptcy. Because P's security interest was unperfected, the bankruptcy trustee successfully avoided it -- wiped it out. If A pays the note, she will succeed to P's claim against B's bankruptcy estate, but the claim will be unsecured and so, too, A's right of reimbursement against B. If the collateral's value equaled or exceeded the amount of the debt, A's loss is the entire amount of the debt less any sum that will be paid on her unsecured claim in B's bankruptcy. The discharge of A's liability on the instrument is complete or almost so. If the property was worth less than the debt, A's loss and her discharge are equal to the property's value, less the distribution on her bankruptcy claim.

6) Broader Applications of Impairment Defense -- Mainly, Joint Obligor

Actually, impairment harms any party to an instrument who somehow, and to any extent, would succeed to the collateral upon paying the instrument. A party who fits this description, and who is neither an indorser nor accommodation party, is a party who is jointly and severally liable with respect to the secured obligation. Article 3 makes her liable for the whole amount of the instrument to any person entitled to enforce it, but the common law entitles her to *contribution* from the joint obligors for any amount she paid beyond her share. (The law rebuttably presumes that, among themselves, co-obligors share equally in the debt.) To secure this right of contribution, she is subrogated to the creditor's rights in the collateral. Therefore, the party who is jointly obligated is discharged to the extent that the creditor's impairment of the collateral causes the party "to pay more than that party would have been obliged to pay, taking into account rights of contribution * * *." 3-605(f). This rule also applies to an accommodation party who is not discharged under subsection (e) because the creditor was not alerted to the accommodation. In this event, the accommodation party is deemed to have a right of contribution rather than reimbursement, 3-605(f); and her loss and discharge are measured by the amount she must pay beyond her contributive share because of the impairment. The rule does not likewise benefit the accommodated party if she pays the instrument because, in this event, (f) does not even apply.

c. Holder Must Be Aware of the Accommodation

Except in the case of an indorser, the suretyship defenses of 3-605(c-e) further require that the holder knows of the accommodation, or has notice that the instrument was signed for accommodation, when she takes the action that is the basis for the defense. 3-605(h). Without being alerted to a party's accommodation status, the holder cannot know that she is affecting the obligation of someone against whom the party has a right of recourse, or that the party may succeed to her rights in collateral. Thus, the holder is not expected to account to the accommodation party for impairment. There is notice of an accommodation whenever a signature on the instrument "is an anomalous indorsement or is accompanied by words indicating that the signer is acting as surety or guarantor with respect to the obligation of another party to the instrument." 3-419(c). This further requirement is not applicable to an indorser, whether or not she is an accommodation party, because her very capacity signals her right of recourse against prior parties on the instrument and her claim to its collateral security -- by transfer, subrogation or otherwise -- if she pays the instrument.

5. Asserting Defenses Against Transferees

Typically, when an accommodation party raises defenses to payment, the plaintiff is the payee of the instrument who dealt directly with the accommodation party and the principal debtor. Sometimes, however, the instrument will have been transferred and the issue arises whether the accommodation party's defenses, which would have been valid against the transferor, are good against the transferee. In general, the answer is what you might expect: The accommodation party's defenses survive the transfer unless the transferee is a holder in due course. See 3-305(a-b). A holder in due course will take free of the accommodation party's defenses (except real defenses), including suretyship defenses. Suretyship defenses too are personal, not real defenses. Remember, however, that even a holder in due course is accountable for claims and defenses, including personal defenses, which arise against her after she has taken the instrument. Thus, conduct of a holder in due course that violates 3-605 will discharge the accommodation party.

6. Waiving Defenses

The truth is that the "suretyship defenses" of 3-605 rarely apply because they can be waived, 3-605(i), and usually are waived in the instrument or a separate writing. The whole truth is that sureties more often sign separate agreements of suretyship, commonly known as *side guaranties*, instead of or in addition to signing the instrument with the principal debtor. They commonly are called *hell-or-high-water guaranties* because, especially in business and commercial transactions, **these agreements waive virtually all defenses** -- the kinds of defenses that 3-605 covers, any derivative defenses that might arise, and every other defense possibly available to the surety. The effect is that the surety agrees to pay "come hell or high water" and usually the courts fully enforce these agreements according to their terms.

E. FTC RULE ON NOTICE TO CONSUMER SURETIES

People who sign instruments as accommodation parties, or who otherwise become sureties, are often unaware of the nature and extent of their liability. This is especially true of sureties in consumer credit transactions. A relative or friend who agrees to "*cosign*" for a debtor never expects she will be called on to pay the debt, certainly not before the creditor has looked to the principal debtor for payment. As you should know by now, an accommodation party or other surety is, in many cases, as fully liable as the principal debtor for the obligation, and in many states the creditor can rightfully demand payment from the surety without first pursuing the principal debtor. So, consumers' expectations are not reflective of reality. Moreover, suretyship agreements in consumer transactions are not much softer than side guaranties in business deals, and they are not highly regulated by government. For these reasons, the Federal Trade Commission promulgated a trade regulation rule designed to educate sureties in consumer credit transactions by requiring creditors to give any surety in such a transaction the following notice before she becomes obligated:

Notice to Cosigner

You are being asked to guarantee this debt. Think carefully before you do. If the borrower doesn't pay the debt, you will have to. Be sure you can afford to pay if you have to, and that you want to accept this responsibility.

You may have to pay up to the full amount of the debt if the borrower does not pay. You may also have to pay late fees or collection costs, which increase this amount.

The creditor can collect this debt from you without first trying to collect from the borrower. The creditor can use the same collection methods against you that can be used against the borrower, such as suing you, garnishing your wages, etc. If this debt is ever in default, that fact may become a part of *your* credit record.

This notice is not the contract that makes you liable for the debt.

16 CFR 444.3 (FTC Consumer Credit Practices Rules). A creditor who obligates a surety in connection with the extension of consumer credit in or affecting commerce without giving the surety this notice is guilty of a deceptive act or practice within the meaning of the Federal Trade Commission Act. Banks are generally beyond the FTC's jurisdiction; but the Federal Reserve Board and the Federal Home Loan Bank Board, which between themselves regulate most of the nation's banks and savings institutions, have adopted substantially similar rules requiring the same kind of notice to sureties. 12 CFR 227.14 & 535.3. Some states, by their local law, require the same or a similar warning to consumer sureties. See Uniform Consumer Credit Code (UCCC) 3.208.

REVIEW QUESTIONS

1.   What is the meaning of "accommodation party?"

2.   What is the difference between an accommodation party and a surety?

3.   Generally speaking, how does the liability of an accommodation party differ from the liability she would have on the instrument had she signed in the same capacity (maker, drawer, indorser or acceptor) but not as a surety?

4.   Inasmuch as an accommodation party is liable on an instrument in the capacity in which she signed it, just as she would have been in the absence of the suretyship relation, what is the significance in her accommodation status?

5.   D got a loan from Bank and signed a note, as maker, payable to Bank. The note was secured by personal property belonging to D. Also, S, an accommodation party, signed the note as co-maker. The note matured. D did not pay it. Bank demanded that S pay the note.

    a.   Is S's accommodation status, in itself, a defense to her liability on the note?

    b.   Must Bank exhaust the collateral before looking to either D or S for payment?

    c.   Does Article 3 require Bank to sue D before pursuing S?

    d.   Does Article 3 require Bank to demand payment of D before looking to S for payment?

    e.   Is it a defense to S's liability that she herself received nothing from Bank or D for cosigning the note?

    f.   Can Bank sue S alone, or must Bank also sue D?

    g.   If Bank sued S, can she file a third-party action against D to compel D to pay Bank?

    h.   What rights does S acquire upon paying Bank?

6.   In a situation such as Question 5, what could a person in S's position do, simply in signing the instrument, to insure that Bank first demanded payment from D before pursuing her?

7.   In a situation such as Question 5, what could a person in S's position do, simply in signing the instrument, to insure that Bank first sued D and exhausted D's estate, including property D pledged as collateral, before looking to S for payment?

8.   Same facts as Question 5 with this change: When the note matures, Bank agrees with D to extend the time for payment. Despite this concession, D is still unable to pay the note when the period of extension expires. Bank thus demands payment from S. Does this change in the facts provide S a defense?

9.   Same facts as Question 5 with this change: When the note matured and D defaulted, Bank demanded payment of the instrument, in the amount of $52,374, from S. S consulted a lawyer. The lawyer explained that S, upon paying the note, would have rights of reimbursement and recourse against D. Yet, D was in bankruptcy, and any obligation D owed S would be discharged. In other words, S could not recover anything from D personally. The lawyer also explained that, upon paying Bank, S would be subrogated to Bank's rights in the collateral that secured the note. Sadly, the property was part of the bankruptcy estate, and the trustee claimed that Bank, and thus S, had no right to it because Bank had never perfected its security interest in the property. So S would not be able to reach the collateral, valued at $40,000. S then asked the lawyer if, on these facts, she had a defense against Bank. What is your answer?

10.   Same facts as Question 5 with this change: When the note matured and was not paid, Bank repossessed the personal property collateral and disposed of it without notifying S. The proceeds, however, were not sufficient to satisfy fully the note. Bank thus sued S for the deficiency. Do these new facts suggest a defense for S?

11.   T or F   The FTC Rule that requires creditors to warn consumer sureties of the risks of suretyship provides a defense to liability for a consumer surety who is not properly notified.

Analysis

A holder in due course is Article 3's most favored person. It gives her advantages with respect to an instrument that no one else enjoys. These advantages are scattered throughout Article 3 and are discussed throughout this book. Most important, a holder in due course is immune to the personal defenses of prior parties, and takes free of all property claims to the instrument. See Chapter VI, supra. In this respect, holder in due course is an exception to the general rule of derivative title which provides that a transferee of property gets no greater rights than her transferor.

What explains this affection for the holder in due course of a negotiable instrument? Part of the answer may be historical. At common law, the bona fide purchaser of tangible personal property took free of equities and defenses while the purchaser of a chose in action did not. Once it was decided that the underlying contract right merged with the instrument upon issue, it was but a short step to the conclusion that the good faith purchasers of this form of tangible personal property also "took free." A more complete answer, however, must take into account perceived commercial needs for a protected market in which drafts and notes can be freely and safely traded. The chief hallmarks of Article 3 -- economic advantages of free and easy transferability, requirements of form on the face of the writing and in the process of negotiation, and protection of purchasers "in due course" who rely on this form as new value was given in the various credit markets -- all reflect a body of law intended to facilitate trade in instruments.

To earn the special protections of a holder in due course, the holder of an instrument must meet certain requirements. First and second, she must be the *holder* of an *instrument*. These basic requirements are discussed elsewhere. This chapter focus on the additional, peculiar requirements, commonly known as the *due-course requirements*. They require the holder to take the instrument

- **for value;**
- **without notice --**
    - ✓ **that the instrument is overdue or has been dishonored or that there is an uncured default with respect to payment of another instrument issued as part of the same series,**
    - ✓ **that the instrument contains an unauthorized signature or has been altered,**
    - ✓ **of any claim to the instrument, and**
    - ✓ **that any party has a defense or claim in recoupment described in subsection (a) of Section 3-305 of this title;**
- **without reason to question the authenticity of the instrument;**
- **in good faith; and**
- **apart from certain unusual circumstances.**

3-302(a).

A. REQUIREMENTS OF DUE-COURSE STATUS

1. For Value

a. Article 3 Definition Controls

A holder can become a holder in due course only if and to the extent that she gives value for the instrument. The Code contains two overlapping but clearly different definitions of "value." A general definition in Article 1 defines value broadly as including, among other things, "any consideration sufficient to support a simple contract." 1-201(44)(d). Article 3 defines value much more narrowly in 3-303(a) which controls the meaning of value for purposes of Article 3. This definition provides that an instrument is issued or transferred for value if:

- the instrument is issued or transferred for a promise of performance, to the extent the promise has been performed;
- the transferee acquires a security interest or other lien in the instrument other than a lien obtained by judicial proceeding;
- the instrument is issued or transferred as payment of, or as security for, an antecedent claim against any person, whether or not the claim is due;
- the instrument is issued or transferred in exchange for a negotiable instrument; or
- the instrument is issued or transferred in exchange for the incurring of an irrevocable obligation to a third party by the person taking the instrument.

3-303(a). So defined, **value is both broader and more narrow than consideration: broader because it includes preexisting debt and more narrow because it excludes an executory promise.**

b. Executory Promise Normally Not Value
1) Usual Rule
a) Promise Must Have Been Performed

Consideration can consist of a bare promise to perform even though the promise remains executory, which means unperformed. Normally, an executory promise is not value. A promise is value only to the extent the promise has been performed. 3-303(a)(1).

> *Example:* Suppose that an instrument is transferred to pay for a promise of goods or services. The promise itself is consideration, but no value is given until the promised goods or services are supplied and even then the value is proportional only.

b) Partial Performance
In the event of partial performance, "the holder may assert rights as a holder in due course of the instrument only to the fraction of the amount payable under the instrument equal to the value of the partial performance divided by the value of the promised performance." 3-302(d).

Example: If the amount of the instrument was $1,000 and only $500 worth of the agreed consideration of $900 was performed, the holder would enjoy the special protections of a holder in due course to the extent of $555.55 only ($500 / $900 = .555 X $1,000 = $555.55). She could enforce the balance of the note but only as a mere holder who is subject to personal defenses and property claims.

c) Full Performance That Is Worth Less Than The Instrument
There is no proportionality if the entire consideration is performed. In this event, the holder is a holder in due course to the full amount of the instrument even though the amount or value of the consideration is less than the amount or value of the instrument.

Example: Suppose that the payee negotiates a $1,000 instrument to a buyer who promises to pay $900 for it and does so. The buyer is a holder in due course to the extent of $1,000 because the agreed consideration, $900, was fully performed. It is irrelevant that the consideration ($900) was less than the amount of the instrument ($1,000).

d) Performance Completed After Notice
Another possibility is full performance that is accomplished only after the holder learns of a claim or defense to the instrument. In this event, the holder is a holder in due course to the proportional extent that the consideration was performed before she learned the bad news. See 3-302 comment 6 (Case # 5).

Example: M issues a note to S's order. S negotiates the note to T in exchange for T's promise to sell S widgets. At this point T has not given value. Before the widgets are delivered, T learns that M has a personal defense to payment of the note. T nevertheless delivers the widgets she promised to sell to S. By delivering the widgets, which amounts to performing the agreed consideration, T gave value, but not in ignorance of M's defense. Thus, T is not a holder in due course.

Example: M makes a $10,000 note to P. P sells it to Q in exchange for Q's promise to pay $8000 for it. Q's promise is not value. Q subsequently pays P the promised $8000. Q's payment is value. Moreover, if Q acted in good faith and without notice when the $8000 was paid, she is a holder in due course to the full amount of the note. In other words, Q can collect the face amount of the note, $10,000, free of M's personal defenses even though Q paid only $8000 for the instrument. If, however, Q performs in two installments of $4000 each and learns of a claim or defense before making the second installment, she enjoys due-course rights only to the extent of the first installment payment, that is, only to the extent that the agreed consideration has been performed before her innocence is lost. Is the extent of Q's due-course rights to be determined by the amount of the actual payment, $4000, or by such percentage of the note's face value as equals the proportion of the consideration actually paid ([4000/8000 = .50] x 10,000 = 5,000)? The answer is $5,000.

2) Exceptions

a) Irrevocable Commitment

Value is given if a holder acquires an instrument in return for an executory promise that constitutes an irrevocable commitment by the holder to a third party. 3-303(a)(5).

Example: Suppose that a bank issues an irrevocable letter of credit after receiving a third party's check intended to satisfy an unrelated debt of the customer for whose account the credit was issued. In this case the bank is obligated to pay the beneficiary of the credit regardless of any problem in the underlying transaction or any defenses to the check paid the bank. 5-114(1). Therefore, the bank is held to have given value for the instrument even though it does not pay the credit until after it has learned of a defense on the check.

b) Swapping Instruments

Value is given if a holder issues her own negotiable instrument in return for the instrument on which she seeks payment, that is, there is an exchange of negotiable instruments. 3-303(a)(4).

Example: Suppose that A buys a note and pays for it with a check. After A learns of a defense on the note, the check is paid to a transferee who is a holder in due course of the check. In this case justice obviously requires that A should not be denied the status of holder in due course merely because she learned of a defense before making a payment she was bound to make. The Code goes further, however, and provides that a person becomes a holder for value of an instrument for which she issues her own negotiable instrument even though she is never called upon to pay a holder in due course. It is reasoned that the possibility of the instrument falling into the hands of a holder in due course furnishes a sufficient basis for giving her this protection. 3-303 comment 5 ("carries the *possibility* of negotiation to a holder in due course").

Example: P is the payee of a personal check for $5000 drawn by D. P indorses the check in blank and exchanges it for a cashier's check in the same amount issued by Bank. The cashier's check is basically Bank's unperformed promise to pay. Yet, because the Bank's promise is in the form of an instrument (i.e., the cashier's check), Bank has given value for the personal check drawn by D. This means that if D's check is dishonored, the Bank, which is a holder, can enforce it as a holder in due course, assuming that the Bank took the instrument in good faith and without notice of any claim or defense.

c. Taking Instrument as Payment or Security for Debt (Including Antecedent Debt)

1) Acquiring Security Interest or Lien (Except Judicial Lien)

A security interest or other *lien* is a charge against a debtor's property that secures an obligation she owes the creditor. A lien that results from agreement between the debtor and creditor is a *security interest*. All other liens arise by force of law without the debtor's consent. Some of these liens depend on judicial proceedings; other nonconsensual liens arise apart from such proceedings. Like any property that the debtor owns, an instrument the debtor holds can be subjected to any creditor's lien that can reach personal property; and, to the extent that a creditor actually acquires a security interest or other lien in the instrument, the creditor has given value. 3-303(a)(2). The only exception is a lien obtained by judicial proceedings. In this event, the lien is perfectly valid but acquiring the lien is not value within 3-303(a)(2).

Example: The typical case is a debtor using a note payable to her as collateral for a bank loan. Article 9 governs creation of the security interest in the note, and the bank usually takes possession of it with the debtor's indorsement. The transaction is called a *pledge* of the note. If the debtor fails to repay when the loan is due, the bank can enforce the note against the maker when the note is due. If the maker has a defense to payment, the bank will take free of the defense to the extent of its rights as a holder in due course. The bank has given value by acquiring the security interest in the note.

Example: M makes a note payable to P's order. P borrows money from Bank and secures the loan by giving the Bank an Article 9 security interest in the note executed by M, which P indorses and delivers to Bank. The size of this security interest depends on the amount of value Bank gives P. 9-203(1)(b). (Interestingly, value for purposes of 9-203(1)(b) is defined by 1-201(44).) The size of the security interest determines the amount of value the Bank has given for purposes of 3-303. The Bank can be a holder in due course only to the extent of the 3-303 value it gave. To the extent that the Bank (which clearly is a holder) is a holder in due course, it can enforce the instrument free of defenses M might have against P in the event P defaults and Bank must realize on its collateral.

Example: Bank made an unsecured loan to P totaling $30,000. After getting a judgment against P, the Bank engaged the process of execution to enforce its judgment. As part of this process, the sheriff levied on, i.e., seized, certain nonexempt property belonging to P, including a $10,000 note issued by M. Bank thereby acquires a lien of execution on the note. The attachment of this lien does not constitute value for 3-303(a) purposes because the lien was acquired by legal process, not by consent as in the preceding example.

2) Value Is Pro Tanto
Although a creditor gives value by acquiring a lien or security interest in the instrument, the amount of value -- and thus the extent of due-course rights -- is limited to the size of the security interest, which is determined by the size of the secured debt. Here is the rule:

If (i) the person entitled to enforce an instrument has only a security interest in the instrument and (ii) the person obliged to pay the instrument has a defense, claim in recoupment, or claim to the instrument *that may be asserted against the person who granted the security interest,* the person entitled to enforce the instrument may assert rights as a holder in due course only to an amount payable under the instrument which, at the time of enforcement of the instrument, does not exceed the amount of the unpaid obligation secured.

3-302(e) (emphasis added).

Example: "Payee negotiates a note of Maker for $1,000 to Holder as security for payment of Payee's debt to Holder of $600. Maker has a defense which is good against Payee but of which Holder has no notice. Subsection (e) applies. Holder may assert rights as a holder in due course only to the extent of $600. Payee does not get the benefit of the holder-in-due-course status of Holder. With respect to $400 of the note, Maker may assert any rights that Maker has against Payee. A different result follows if the payee of a note negotiated it to a person who took it as a holder in due course and that person pledged the note as security for a debt. Because the defense cannot be asserted against the pledgor, the pledgee can assert rights as a holder in due course for the full amount of the note for the benefit of both the pledgor and the pledgee." 3-302 comment 6 (Case #6).

3) Securing or Paying *Preexisting Debt* Is Value Too

In the foregoing case the bank's lien secured new value. The lien was given as part of the exchange for the loan. There was value, and there was also consideration. Very often, however, a creditor's lien will attach to property, including instruments payable to the debtor, to secure a preexisting or antecedent debt. Whether or not this case is covered by 3-303(a)(2), it is covered by (a)(3) which states that an instrument is taken for value when "the instrument is issued or transferred as *payment* of, or as *security* for, an *antecedent* claim against any person, whether or not the claim is due." 3-303(a)(3) (emphasis added).

Example: Bank made a $10,000 unsecured loan to D. Later, when D's financial condition worsened, Bank got worried and demanded that D make a payment or provide collateral. D indorsed and delivered to Bank a $10,000 note drawn by M payable to P. Whether the parties intended the transfer as satisfying the loan or as securing it, the Bank in either event has given value to the extent of the preexisting $10,000 claim against D.

d. Bank Credit As Value -- 4-210 & 4-211
1) Context and Problem
U.C.C. 4-210 and 4-211 deal with the specific, very important question of when a collecting bank has given value for purposes of becoming a holder in due course with respect to checks and other items deposited with the bank for collection that are not paid. Suppose, for example, that S sells goods to B. B gives S a $1000 check for the price. B's check is drawn on First Bank. S deposits the check in her account at Second Bank, and Second Bank credits S's account with the amount of the check, $1000. Second Bank will act as S's agent in collecting the check from First Bank, the drawee-payor bank. When Second Bank presents the item for payment, First Bank dishonors it and returns the check to Second Bank. Remember that Second Bank has given S a credit for the check, expecting to recoup the credit upon payment of the check by First Bank. The check has failed, however, and Second Bank has not yet been reimbursed for the credit given S. Second Bank has several remedial options. One option is provided by 4-214(a), which empowers Second Bank to charge the check back against S's account or, if necessary, obtain a refund from S. This action against S is not an Article 3 action on the instrument itself. The action rather is pursuant to statutory rights given by Article 4. Yet, Second Bank is a transferee of the check and, most likely, a holder of it because the instrument was probably negotiated to Second Bank by delivery with any necessary indorsement. If S did not personally indorse the check, the law nevertheless makes Second Bank a holder if S was a holder. See 4-205. So Second Bank can sue, on the instrument, everybody who signed it, including B, the drawer. Suppose however, that B has a contract defense arising from her transaction with S. Second Bank will take subject to this defense unless it took the instrument as a holder in due course. Second Bank surely took in good faith and without notice of the defense. The hard question is whether Second Bank gave value for the check. Enter 4-210 and 4-211.

2) Article 4 Definition of Value
Begin with 4-211. It provides: "For purposes of determining its status as a holder in due course, a bank has given value to the extent it has a security interest in an item * * *." This rule is perfectly consistent with 3-303(a), which provides that a holder takes for value to the extent she acquires a security interest in the item. Now add 4-210(a), which describes, nonexclusively, situations in which a collecting bank, such as Second Bank,

acquires a security interest in items it takes for collection. It provides that a collecting bank has a security interest in an item:

- in case of an item deposited in an account, to the extent to which credit given for the item has been withdrawn or applied;
- in case of an item for which it has given credit available for withdrawal as of right, to the extent of the credit given, whether or not the credit is drawn upon or there is a right of charge-back; or
- if it makes an advance on or against the item.

4-210(a)(1-3).

3) **How It Works**
Applying all this to the problem at hand:
  a) **Had The Item Been Cashed**
     Second Bank clearly would have given value, and thus would have been a holder in due course of B's check, had Second Bank cashed it for S. 4-210(a)(3) (makes an advance on or against the item). The check was not cashed, however. S deposited the check in her account.

  b) **Credit for Deposit Typically Is Not Value**
     Assuming this account was typical, S has no right to withdraw uncollected funds; so 4-210(a)(2) is inapplicable. The result is that Second Bank gave value for the check only if the credit in S's account that was attributable to the check was actually withdrawn or applied. See 4-210(a)(1). In an exceptional case, the depositor may have a right to draw against the check that imposes on the bank a corresponding duty to allow withdrawals before the drawee has paid the check. Whether this right and the corresponding duty arise from an express contract between the parties or from federal or state law governing the collection process, the bank is considered as having given value immediately when the right arises and before any withdrawal against the item has been made. 4-210(a)(2). If the depositor's contract with the bank entitles her to withdraw immediately any credit given for a check that she deposits, the bank has given value in the amount of the check as soon as the check is deposited, "whether or not the credit is drawn upon or there is a right of charge-back." 4-201(a)(2).

  c) **Withdrawing Credit**
     Suppose that S's account was empty when the check was deposited. After the deposit, the balance was $1000, which was the amount of the check. There has since been no further activity in the account. So,

when the check is bounced back to Second Bank, the $1000 credit given for the item is still there. It has not been withdrawn or applied. In this event, Second Bank has no security interest in the item under 4-210(a)(1) and has not given value for it. Second Bank is therefore not a holder in due course. The effect is to force Second Bank to charge back the check against the account on the authority of 4-214(a). The result is different if S has withdrawn the $1000 credit. In this event, Second Bank has a security interest in the check under 4-210(a)(1) and is a holder in due course. It can enforce the check against B free of B's personal defenses.

d) Account Activity
    The hardest variation is presented if S's account has been active. Suppose that when S deposited the check in her account the balance was $1000. The credit given for B's check increased the balance to $2000. Upon the check's dishonor, only $1000 remains in the account. Is the $1000 that S withdrew in the interim the $1000 credit given for B's check, or the $1000 that was in S's account when B's check was deposited? If the former, Second Bank has given value for B's check pursuant to 4-210(a)(1) and 4-211. If the latter, no value has been given. The answer is that the $1000 S withdrew is attributable to the beginning balance, not to B's check because, for purposes of 4-210, "credits first given are first withdrawn." 4-210(b) (last sentence).

e) Where The Credit Is Withdrawn But Account Is Refilled
    Consider one last variation: The deposit of B's check increased S's balance to $2000. Shortly thereafter S withdrew the entire $2000, and almost immediately thereafter deposited $10,000. So, when B's check was returned to Second Bank, S's account stood at $10,000. Second Bank could (and probably would in real life) charge the dishonored check against S's account pursuant to 4-214(a). (This right of charge-back is not limited to grabbing credit specifically given for a dishonored item. Such an item can be charged against any funds in the account.) Yet, because the specific credit given for B's check was withdrawn by S under the first-in-first-out rule, Second Bank has given value for the check and thus is holder in due course of it. Second Bank can enforce the check against B free from B's defenses, even though $10,000 sits in S's account and is an easily available pot from which Second Bank could recoup the credit given S for the item.

f)   Noncash Items for Collection
Sometimes, a bank takes an instrument for collection that is not a check of its customer. For example, the customer may transfer an ordinary draft to the bank that is drawn on a buyer of goods who bought them from the seller and owes the price. The draft orders the buyer to pay the seller a sum that equals the price. The bank will forward the draft through banking channels for the purpose of having it presented to the buyer-drawee for payment or acceptance. The draft is not deposited, and there are no withdrawals against it in the usual sense. Yet, the bank may buy the draft from the customer, loan against the draft, or otherwise make advances on or against it. To this extent, the bank gives value. 4-210(a)(3).

e.   **The Setoff Problem**
A number of recent cases raise the issue whether a bank gives value for a check, that a customer deposits, by offsetting the item against a preexisting debt the customer owes the bank. This issue involves both 3-303 and 4-210. Here is the situation: As in the problem above, S sells goods to B who pays for them with a $1000 check B drew on First Bank. S deposited the check in her account at Second Bank. Second Bank immediately set off this account, including the $1000 credit for B's check, against an overdue loan that Second Bank had made to S. (The setoff is an equitable right every bank enjoys as a matter of decisional law. The right does not require the depositor's consent, and can be exercised unilaterally without notice to the customer.) The check bounces. Second Bank sues B on the check. B has a personal defense. The issue is whether Second Bank is a holder in due course and thus is immune to the defense. The answer depends on whether Second Bank gave value for the item by setting it off against S's debt to Second Bank.

Second Bank can argue that it gave value under 3-303(a)(3) (taking the instrument in payment of an antecedent claim) or 4-210(a)(1) (applying credit given for an item). Most courts seem to agree. On these facts, however, the New York Court of Appeals has held that value is not given, at least not if the credit for the check that was applied against the loan can be and is reversed at the bank's will, upon dishonor of the check, and added back to the loan balance. *Marine Midland Bank v. Graybar Electric Co.*, 41 N.Y.2d 703, 395 N.Y.S.2d 403, 363 N.E.2d 1139 (1977). Every court would agree, however, that value is given if the bank applies the check against the overdue loan with the consent of the depositor-debtor and the parties agree that the offset forever extinguishes the loan, or if the bank acquires a consensual lien on the check pursuant to a previously executed security agreement with the depositor-debtor. *Bowling Green, Inc. v. State Street Bank & Trust Co.*, 425 F.2d 81 (1st Cir. 1970).

2. Without Notice

A further requirement of holder in due course is taking the instrument "without notice" --

* that the instrument is overdue or has been dishonored or that there is an uncured default with respect to payment of another instrument issued as part of the same series,
* that the instrument contains an unauthorized signature or has been altered,
* of any claim to the instrument, or
* that any party has a defense or claim in recoupment described in 3-305.

3-302(a)(2). Notice of any of these facts should serve as a danger signal to a person who is contemplating taking an instrument for value. It should warn her that she may be buying a lawsuit and that she should not expect to occupy the favored position of holder in due course. **If a holder takes with notice of any of these circumstances, she is not a holder in due course for any purpose as against any person and is subject to all claims to the instrument, and also to the defenses of every party to the instrument, even though there is no connection between the information she knew, or is charged with, and the claims and defenses that are asserted against her.**

a. Meaning of "Notice" Beyond Actual Knowledge -- The Test Is Part Subjective and Part Objective

Of course, a person should be barred from being a holder in due course by *actual* knowledge of any of these facts. If she sees the danger signal but chooses to disregard it, she must take the consequences. But actual knowledge is not essential to "notice" of a fact. Notice is broader than knowledge which is established by any of three alternative tests:

* he has *actual knowledge* of it; *or*
* he has *received* a notice or notification of it; *or*
* from all the facts or circumstances known to him at the time in question he *has reason to know* that it exists.

1-201(25) (a-c) (emphasis added).

1) Receiving Notice of a Fact Is Notice Even Though Not Actually Known -- Read Your Mail

Receiving notice of a fact, which itself amounts to notice, does not require actually seeing or even getting in hand a writing that describes the fact: "a person receives a notice or notification when (a) it comes to his attention; *or* (b) *it is duly delivered * * * at any * * * place held out by him as the place* *for receipt of such communications.*" 1-201(26) (emphasis added). Therefore, if a person gets a letter or other communication describing a fact but does not read the communication, she is deemed to have notice of the fact described in the communication even though she does not actually know the fact. 1-201(25)(b) & 1-201(26) (when a person receives a notice or notification).

2) **Reason To Know Is As Good As Knowing -- Put "2 and 2" Together**
    "*Reason to know*" of a fact also establishes notice even though the person herself, actually, is completely unaware of the fact and has never received a notification of it. Notice by this test is sometimes referred to as *inferable knowledge.* A person is charged with knowledge of information that a reasonable person would infer from the facts and circumstances actually known to her. This test does not require a person to investigate, not even if a reasonable person would do so; but the test does require a person to open her eyes to everything she already knows. She is charged with notice of facts that others would see or discern from her own knowledge, even if she herself was subjectively blind to these facts.

3) **Constructive Notice Is Not Sufficient**
    Constructive notice does not count. For example, a public filing or recording of a property interest often works, alone, to protect the interest against subsequent lienors or purchasers of the property. Such a recording, however, "does not of itself constitute notice of a defense, claim in recoupment, or claim to the instrument" that would bar a person from becoming a holder in due course of it. 3-302(b).

4) Timing of Notice
    a) Notice in Relation to Value
        The critical time for a purchaser of an instrument to be without notice is before she takes the instrument for value. Being ignorant at the time the instrument is delivered gives no protection if the purchaser is charged with prohibited notice before having given value. In the case where notice intervenes before all of the value has been given, the holder is a holder in due course only to the extent of the value given before notice.

    b) Reasonable Opportunity to Act
        Notice is not necessarily effective as of the instant the purchaser receives it. To bar a purchaser from becoming a holder in due course, any kind of notice must be received at such time and in such manner as to give a reasonable opportunity to act on it. 3-302(f). If notice is given to an organization, it is effective when it is brought to the attention of the

person conducting the transaction or when it would have been brought to her attention with the exercise of due diligence, whichever is sooner. 1-201(27). For example, a notice received by a bank president a minute before a teller cashes a check is not likely to be effective to bar it from being a holder in due course. But if the president acts swiftly and succeeds in bringing the notice to the teller's attention before she cashes the check, the bank is charged with notice and cannot be a holder in due course of the check.

c) Forgotten Notice

Notice once given and effective does not necessarily last forever, not in the mind of the person notified and not in its legal force. In the case *Graham v. White-Phillips Co., Inc.*, 296 U.S. 27, 56 S.Ct. 21, 80 L.Ed. 20 (1935), the Court stated the doctrine of "notice forgotten in good faith:"

> [I]f the *bona fides* of the defendants must be judged of from their acts, purposes and knowledge as they existed upon the day of the purchase, then the notice served is only *prima facie* or presumptive evidence * * *, and may be rebutted by proof that the notice was lost, or its existence and contents forgotten.

Id. at 32. Because the U.C.C. does not purport to decide the "time and circumstances under which a notice or notification may cease to be effective," 1-201(25), the doctrine of forgotten notice applies under Article 3 in determining whether a holder of an instrument enjoys due-course status. *McCook Cty. Nat'l Bank v. Compton*, 558 F.2d 871, 874-75 (8th Cir. 1977) (purchaser not charged with facts that appeared in Register of Deeds reporting service published nine to seventeen months before instruments were taken). It is possible, therefore, for notice to have been received so long ago that the fact is forgotten by the time the instrument is purchased and the purchaser can be a holder in due course despite the long-ago notice.

b. Overdue, Dishonored, or Uncured Default

Holder in due course requires taking the instrument without notice that the instrument is overdue or has been dishonored or that there is an uncured default with respect to payment of another instrument issued as part of the same series. 3-302(a)(2)(iii). None of these facts is sufficient, of itself, to bar a person from being a holder in due course. It is notice of the fact that counts; but, of course, the fact must have occurred before it can be noticed.

1) Overdue
Article 3 devotes an entire section, 3-304, to explaining when an instrument is overdue. It treats demand and time instruments separately, as follows:

a) Overdue Demand Instrument
An instrument is a *demand instrument*, i.e., payable upon demand, "if it (i) states that it is payable on demand or at sight, or otherwise indicates that it is payable at the will of the holder, or (ii) does not state any time of payment." 3-108(a). Also, if an instrument is payable both at a fixed date or upon demand, it is a demand instrument until the fixed date. 3-108(c). A demand instrument becomes overdue *at the earliest* of the following times:

- on the day after the day demand for payment is duly made; or
- if the instrument is a check, 90 days after its date; or
- if the instrument is not a check, when the instrument has been outstanding for a period of time after its date which is unreasonably long under the circumstances of the particular case in light of the nature of the instrument and usage of the trade.

3-304(a). To prevent holder in due course, one of these times must have occurred **to the notice of the holder** when she took the instrument.

b) Overdue Time Instruments
A *time instrument* is an instrument that is payable at a definite time, which means "payable on elapse of a definite period of time after sight or acceptance or at a fixed date or dates or at a time or times readily ascertainable at the time the * * * [instrument] is issued, subject to the rights of (i) prepayment, (ii) acceleration, (iii) extension * * * *." 3-108(b).

- The easiest case is an instrument with principal payable in a lump sum on a fixed date. It "becomes overdue on the *day after* the due date." 3-304(b)(2) (emphasis added).
- In the case of an instrument payable in installments, it "becomes overdue upon default under the instrument for nonpayment of *an installment*, and the instrument remains overdue until the default is cured." 3-304(b)(1) (emphasis added).
- In either case, whether the principal is payable at one time or in installments, the rule is different if the due date with respect to principal is accelerated. In this event, "the instrument becomes overdue on the day after the accelerated due date." 3-304(b)(3). In

neither case does default in interest mean that the instrument is overdue. The general rule is that "[u]nless the due date of principal has been accelerated, an instrument does not become overdue if there is default in payment of interest but no default in payment of principal." 3-304(c). The rule is different after acceleration of principal which itself determines when the instrument is overdue.

2) **Default With Respect to Another Instrument**

Notice of default in payment of any other instrument is insufficient to prevent a purchaser from taking in due course, except an uncured default in another instrument of the same series. Instruments issued together as a series are collectively akin to a single instrument payable in installments. A series may be preferable for a variety of reasons, including the relative ease of selling pieces of the total obligation. When instruments issued in a series are payable at different times, a purchaser who has notice of an uncured default in one or more of the instruments cannot become a holder in due course of any of them even though none of the instruments contains an acceleration clause and the instrument she purchases has not yet matured according to its terms.

3) **Without Notice That the Instrument Has Been Dishonored**

In most cases, a dishonor occurs when a demand for payment or acceptance is properly made upon the party expected to pay, and payment or acceptance is refused or cannot be obtained within the time allowed. See 3-502, which is discussed in Chapter III supra. Very often, particularly when presentment for payment is through ordinary banking channels, a dishonored instrument bears a stamp or other notation such as "not sufficient funds," "no account," or "payment stopped." Regardless of actual knowledge, anyone purchasing such an instrument is charged with knowing that the instrument has been dishonored. Sometimes a dishonored instrument bears no evidence of dishonor, and the person selling such an instrument does not always reveal the dishonor. In these cases, whether or not a holder is charged with notice of the dishonor so as to be barred from being a holder in due course depends on whether or not the trier of fact concludes from other evidence that she had actual knowledge, had received notice, or had reason to know of the dishonor. 1-201(25).

c. **Unauthorized Signature or Alteration**

Due-course status is denied if the holder takes with notice that the instrument contains an unauthorized signature or has been altered. 3-302(a)(2)(iv). Indeed, if the forgery or alteration is apparent on the face of the instrument, this condition alone will bar due-course status, even if the holder herself --

subjectively -- is without notice of the wrongdoing. 3-302(a)(1). On the other hand, even a holder in due course usually cannot enforce an instrument against a person whose name is signed without authority, 3-403(a); and a holder in due course ordinarily cannot enforce an altered instrument beyond its original terms. 3-407(b-c). The holder gets no greater rights simply because she was unaware of the alteration or lack of authority. Nevertheless, being a holder in due course can be important in these cases because in some situations, a person who is sued on an instrument is precluded from asserting alteration or lack of authority against a holder in due course or other person who, in good faith, took the instrument for value. See, e.g., 3-406(a) (negligence contributing to forged signature or alteration). Also, it could be important to be a holder in due course against people who are fully liable on the instrument despite the forgery of somebody else's signature or an alteration that does not affect their liability.

d. Claim to the Instrument
1) Generally
A "*claim*" to an instrument means any claim of a property or possessory right in the instrument or its proceeds, see 3-306, including:

* ownership,
* a consensual or nonconsensual lien, or
* any other legal or equitable interest.

A claim might be asserted by anyone who contends that she has an adverse property interest in an instrument. Thus a claim might be asserted by one who contends that she is the legal or equitable owner of an instrument or that she has a lien against it. Perhaps the most obvious kind of claim is that which is asserted against a thief or other converter. But the most common kind of claim is that which is asserted by one who is induced to issue or transfer an instrument in a transaction that is voidable in whole or in part because it was induced by fraud, duress, mistake or similar means, or because of incapacity or illegality or for any other reason. Sometimes a claim arises from circumstances that render attempts to transfer void as when they are made by adjudicated incompetents or when they are induced by fraud in the factum that occurs despite the exercise of due care.

2) Special Case of the Dishonest Fiduciary
Claim to an instrument includes the rights of a person who is represented by a fiduciary in dealing with the instrument. A "*fiduciary*" is "an agent, trustee, partner, corporate officer or director, or other representative owing a fiduciary duty with respect to an instrument." 3-307(a)(1). A person is not charged with notice of a defense or claim merely because she has notice that

a person negotiating an instrument is or was a fiduciary; but "[n]otice of breach of fiduciary duty by the fiduciary is notice of the claim of the represented person." 3-307(b)(1). This same section, 3-307, explains in some detail certain circumstances that radiate notice of such a breach and other circumstances that are benign.

Example: Suppose, for example, that a check is drawn payable to X, as agent for Y. X cashes and negotiates the check at a depositary bank and applies the value to her own purposes rather than as directed by Y. Almost immediately, Y learns of this breach of fiduciary duty and causes the drawer to stop payment of the check. The check is dishonored and bounced back to the depositary bank which sues the drawer on the instrument. The drawer joins Y as a defendant so that Y can assert Y's claim of ownership of the instrument and its proceeds. 3-305(c). The bank loses unless it is a holder in due course. The bank is not such a holder if, in cashing the check, the bank had notice that X was breaching its fiduciary duty to Y or was planning to do so.

Example: In another common case, the fiduciary draws a check on the account of the represented person, as she is empowered to do; but the fiduciary draws the check payable to herself and uses the proceeds for own purposes. In this case, a "taker does not have notice of the breach of fiduciary duty unless the taker *knows* of the breach of fiduciary duty." 3-307(b)(3) (emphasis added).

In general, the taker must know that the instrument is taken in payment or as security for a personal debt of the fiduciary or for the personal benefit of the fiduciary. "For example, if the instrument is being used to buy goods or services, the [taker] * * * must know that the goods or services are for the personal benefit of the fiduciary. 3-307 comment 2. In other words, *notice* of the breach requires *knowledge* of the fiduciary's tacky conduct. Knowledge means actually knowing." 1-201(25). Suspicion or reason to know is not enough and investigation is not required. Moreover, in every instance, notice of the breach requires *knowledge* of the fiduciary status of the fiduciary. 3-307(b). Unless a taker actually knows of this status, the taker is unaffected by any breach of duty by a fiduciary even though the taker actually knows of the fiduciary's conduct.   On the other hand, knowledge of the fiduciary status, in itself, is benign. It must be coupled with knowledge of the fiduciary's tackiness. The commentary explains that:

[t]he requirement that the taker have knowledge rather than notice is meant to *limit Section 3-307 to relatively uncommon cases* in which the person who deals with the fiduciary knows all the relevant facts: the fiduciary status and that the proceeds of the instrument are being used for the personal debt or benefit of the fiduciary or are being paid to an account that is not an account of the represented person or of the fiduciary, as such.

3-307 comment 2 (emphasis added).

e. Defense or Claim in Recoupment

Due-course status requires taking the instrument "without notice that any party has a defense or claim in recoupment described in Section 3-305(a)." 3-302(a)(2)(vi). Section 3-305(a) describes the *personal defenses* that are good against a mere holder and also the *real defenses* that are effective even against a holder in due course. For discussion of them, see Chapter VI supra. Section 3-305(a) also explains that a person who lacks the rights of a holder in due course is subject to an obligor's *claim in recoupment* "against the original payee of the instrument if the claim arose from the transaction that gave rise to the instrument * * *." 3-305(a)(3). For discussion of recoupment, see Chapter VI supra. Even though a holder in due course takes free of the personal defenses and recoupment claims of 3-305(a), a person cannot become a holder in due course in the first place if she has prior notice that any real or personal defense or claim in recoupment is available to *any* party on the instrument. This is true even though the defense or claim of which she has notice does not affect and is not related to the defense or claim ultimately asserted against her.

1) Different Issue of Setoff

Technically, and for purposes of the due-course requirements, *setoff* is not a defense, which means that notice of setoff does not preclude due-course status. *Setoff* essentially is a counterclaim that is unrelated to the plaintiff's claim. A setoff can be effective against any plaintiff, whether holder in due course or not, but only if it is between the immediate parties and only then if applicable procedure allows or requires asserting it. A prior-party setoff is never effective, not even against a person who lacks the rights of a holder in due course. 3-305 comment 3.

2) Different Issue of Article 3 Discharge

Technically, and for purposes of the due-course requirements, *Article 3 discharge* is not a defense, which means that notice of same does not preclude due-course status. *Article 3 discharge* is a party's freedom from liability on an instrument for reasons provided by the statute itself. An important qualification that, while taking an instrument with notice of a party's discharge does not deny due-course status, the discharge is nevertheless effective against the holder. 3-302(b). A holder can take in due course even when she knows that everybody's liability on an instrument has been discharged, but in this case nobody is liable to her. The status of holder in due course is rather empty.

> *Example:* D issues a note to P who indorses in blank to Q. Q cancels the signature of P. P is discharged, but not D. Q sells the instrument to R. R can become a holder in due course, but P's discharge is effective against R.

3) Bankruptcy Discharge

Discharge in bankruptcy is altogether something else. Notice of this discharge is notice of a defense that prevents due-course status; but even a person who enjoys the rights of a holder in due course is subject to this defense of a party. Such a holder, however, is immune to the personal defenses and recoupment claims of every other party who is liable on the instrument.

4) Knowledge That Instrument Was Given for Executory Promise

A purchaser of an instrument has notice of a claim or defense if she has notice that the obligation of any party is voidable in whole or in part. On the other hand, a purchaser does not have notice of a claim or defense simply because she knows that the instrument was given in return for an executory promise, except when *the purchaser also has notice that a breach of the promise has produced a defense or claim in recoupment.*

- There is no harm in knowing that the instrument was given for an executory contractual promise and knowing, in addition, that the promisee can avoid her obligation in whole or in part *if* the promise is not performed. Also, there is no consequence in knowing that a party's liability on an instrument to another person could theoretically be reduced or eliminated, in a suit between them, by way of a counterclaim or setoff unrelated to the instrument or the obligation underlying it.
- The harm comes in having notice that an executory promise for which the instrument was given has already been breached giving the promisee an actual claim or defense arising from the terms of the underlying obligation.
- Due-course status is also precluded if the purchaser of an instrument has notice that the obligation of any party is presently voidable (whether or not any obligation has actually been voided). Voidable implies that the

party has the power to put an end to the contract. Restatement (Second) of Contracts § 7 comment b (1981). This power may result from the terms of the contract itself (e.g., a term giving the party the right to rescind), the party's lack of capacity (e.g., infancy), or serious culpability attributable to the other party (e.g., fraud, duress, material breach).

* Due-course status also is prevented by notice that an executory promise underlying the instrument has been breached, though not materially, so that a party to the instrument has a claim in recoupment, though not a basis for voiding her obligation.

Example: M issues a note payable to P's order in exchange for P's promise to install aluminum siding on P's house. P sells the note to T who knows that P has not yet performed her promise to M. This knowledge alone does not prevent T from becoming a holder in due course.

Example: Same facts, except T also knows that P is obligated to M for a loan unrelated to the siding contract, which loan M could offset in any action by P against M on the siding contract. This knowledge is irrelevant.

Example: Same facts, except that T has notice that P breached the siding contract with M. T cannot be a holder in due course even if the breach is minor so that M cannot cancel the contract and is limited to recovering damages for the breach from P.

Example: M issues a note payable to P's order in exchange for P's promise to install aluminum siding on M's house. The parties' agreement gives M the right at any time before P's performance to rescind the contract. P sells the note to T who has notice of M's right to rescind. T is not a holder in due course because she has notice that M's obligation is voidable. Whether M has actually rescinded is irrelevant. In other words, T is not a holder in due course even though, when she takes the instrument, M has not rescinded and is planning to have P install the siding pursuant to the parties' contract.

3. Authenticity Of The Instrument

Former law provided that a person has notice of a defense or claim if "the instrument is so incomplete, bears such visible evidence of forgery or alteration, or is otherwise so irregular as to call into question its validity, terms or ownership or to create an ambiguity as to the party to pay." 3-304(1)(a) (1989 Official Text). *The 1990 Article*

3 makes the condition of the instrument a wholly separate requirement of holder in due course, requiring that "the instrument when issued or negotiated to the holder does not bear such apparent evidence of forgery or alteration or is not otherwise so irregular or incomplete as to call into question its authenticity." 3-302(a)(1). The word "'authenticity' is used to make clear that the irregularity or incompleteness must indicate that the instrument may not be what it purports to be." 3-302 comment 1. It makes no difference, at least not under the new law, that the obligor's claim or defense is unrelated to the irregularity or incompleteness of the instrument. It also makes no difference, technically, that the taker is without notice of the irregularity or incompleteness; but the problem must be "apparent" and in this event the taker ordinarily would have reason to know of the problem and thus would have notice of it.

4. Good Faith
a. Distinctive Requirement

Even though a holder acquires an apparently perfect instrument for value and without prohibited notice, she does not qualify as a holder in due course unless she also takes the instrument in "*good faith*." Because the requirement of good faith is so often confused with the requirement of taking without notice, perhaps it should be emphasized that these are two separate requirements. No degree of good faith makes it possible for one who fails to meet the notice requirement to qualify as a holder in due course, and good faith is not established by showing that a person received an instrument without notice. Of course, these two requirements are closely related so that the conclusion that a holder has failed to satisfy one of these requirements is often bolstered by evidence that she failed to meet the other; but doing so is overkill. Failing either requirement is sufficient by itself to deny due-course status.

b. Test of Good Faith
1) Both Subjective and Objective

The test of good faith is both subjective and objective. It means "honesty in fact *and the observance of reasonable commercial standards of fair dealing*," 3-103(a)(4) (emphasis added), which is "concerned with the fairness of conduct rather than the care with which an act is performed." 3-103 comment 4. History explains that when this objective test is added to the subjective, "a business man engaging in a commercial transaction is not entitled to claim the peculiar advantages which the law accords to the * * * holder in due course * * * on a bar showing of 'honesty in fact' when his actions fail to meet the generally accepted standards current in his business, trade, or profession. 3-302 comment 1 (1952 Official Text).

2) Any Duty to Investigate Is Small

The most important issue of the objective test is whether or not it imposes an obligation to investigate the circumstances of an instrument before purchasing it. A purely subjective test requires no investigation, unless the failure to inquire indicates a deliberate desire to evade knowledge because of a belief that further investigation would disclose an actual claim or defense. Arguably, however, an objective test can sometimes impose a duty to investigate and can charge the holder with notice of the facts that would have been disclosed, as when persons situated as the holder would have investigated before buying the paper. Nevertheless, because accepted business practice will seldom require investigation and because the law strongly favors the free flow of negotiable instruments, it is likely that only the most compelling circumstances would trigger any duty to inquire that might be part of the objective test of good faith.

c. **Lack of Good Faith Because of Close Connection**

The courts, as a matter of decisional law, have described one situation in which a purchaser lacks good faith as a matter of law without regard to her actual intentions and motives. The situation involves a purchaser who is closely connected to the transferor which, nevertheless, is legally separate -- the latter is tied to the former in terms of a business or financial arrangement that is transactional rather than organizational or structural. Solely because of this close connection, the purchaser is deemed by law not to take in good faith when she buys instruments from the transferor. Thus, the purchaser, who therefore lacks due-course status, is always subject to claims and defenses that are available against the transferor. This "close-connection doctrine" is discussed more fully later in this chapter.

5. Apart From Certain Unusual Circumstances

Even though she satisfies the usual requirements previously described, a person does not acquire the rights of a holder in due course of an instrument taken:

- by legal process or by purchase in an execution, bankruptcy, or creditor's sale or similar proceeding,
- by purchase as part of a bulk transaction not in the ordinary course of business of the transferor, or
- as the successor in interest to an estate or other organization.

3-302(c). In these situations the transferee merely is acquiring the rights of the prior holder and there is no substantial interest in facilitating commercial transactions, which is the underlying reason for giving holders in due course their special advantages. Thus, there is no holder in due course when:

- an instrument is purchased in an execution sale or sale in bankruptcy or is acquired by other legal process;
- a representative, such as an executor, administrator, receiver or assignee for the benefit of creditors takes the instrument as part of an estate;
- a bank purchases a substantial part of the paper held by another bank which is threatened with insolvency and seeks to liquidate its assets;
- a new partnership takes over for value all of the assets of an old one after a new member has entered the firm,
- a reorganized or consolidated corporation takes over the assets of a predecessor, or
- a state bank commissioner sells the assets of an insolvent bank.

3-302 comment 5.

B. PAYEE AS HOLDER IN DUE COURSE

1. Possible But Unhelpful Between Immediate Parties

The payee of an instrument, like any other holder, can be a holder in due course so long as she meets the usual requirements, "but use of the holder-in-due-course doctrine by the payee of an instrument is not the normal situation." 3-302 comment 4. The doctrine assumes that in the typical case, the holder in due course is not the payee but is an immediate or remote transferee of the payee. When the issuer and the payee are the only parties, "the holder-in-due-course doctrine is irrelevant in determining rights between Obligor and Obligee with respect to the instrument." Id. For example:

> If Buyer issues an instrument to Seller and Buyer has a defense against Seller, that defense can obviously be asserted. Buyer and Seller are the only people involved. The holder-in-due-course doctrine has no relevance. The doctrine applies only to cases in which more than two parties are involved.

3-305 comment 2. Similarly, the Buyer can assert a breach of warranty claim or other counterclaim against the Seller. "It is not relevant whether Seller is or is not a holder in due course * * * or whether Seller knew or had notice that Buyer had the * * * claim. It is obvious that holder-in-due-course doctrine cannot be used to allow Seller to cut off a * * * claim that Buyer has against Seller." 3-305 comment 3; see also 3-305(b) ("other than the holder").

2. Exceptional Cases In Which Payee Does Not Directly Deal With Drawer Or Maker

About the only case in which it makes any difference that a payee is a holder in due course is that in which she does not deal directly with the maker or drawer but instead obtains the instrument from a remitter who obtained it from the maker or drawer. In this case, if the payee qualifies as a holder in due course, she takes the instrument free of any defense or claim based on the remitter's wrongdoing; otherwise not. See 3-302 comment 4. The examples provided by Article 3 itself are virtually exhaustive:

Example: "Buyer pays for goods bought from Seller by giving to Seller a cashier's check bought from Bank. Bank has a defense to its obligation to pay the check because Buyer bought the check from Bank with a check known to be drawn on an account with insufficient funds to cover the check. If Bank issued the check to Buyer as payee and Buyer indorsed it over to Seller, it is clear that Seller can be a holder in due course taking free of the defense if Seller had no notice of the defense." 3-302 comment 4.

Example: "X fraudulently induces Y to join X in a spurious venture to purchase a business. The purchase is to be financed by a bank loan for part of the price. Bank lends money to X and Y by deposit in a joint account of X and Y who sign a note payable to Bank for the amount of the loan. X then withdraws the money from the joint account and absconds. Bank acted in good faith and without notice of the fraud of X against Y. Bank is payee of the note executed by Y, but its right to enforce the note against Y should not be affected by the fact that Y was induced to execute the note by the fraud of X. Bank can be a holder in due course that takes free of the defense of Y." Id.

Example: "Corporation draws a check payable to Bank. The check is given to an officer of Corporation who is instructed to deliver it to Bank in payment of a debt owed by Corporation to Bank. Instead, the officer, intending to defraud Corporation, delivers the check to Bank in payment of the officer's personal debt, or the check is delivered to Bank for deposit to the officer's personal account. If Bank obtains payment of the check, Bank has received funds of Corporation which have been used for the personal benefit of the officer. Corporation in this case will assert a claim to the proceeds of the check against Bank. If Bank was a holder in due course of the check it took the check free of Corporation's claim. Section 3-306. The issue in this case is whether Bank had notice of the claim when it took the check." Id.

Example: "Employer, who owed money to X, signed a blank check and delivered it to Secretary with instructions to complete the check by typing in X's name and the amount owed to X. Secretary fraudulently completed the check by typing in the name of Y, a creditor to whom Secretary owed money. Secretary then delivered the check to Y in payment of Secretary's debt. Y obtained payment of the check. This case is similar to Case #3. Since Secretary was authorized to complete the check, Employer is bound by Secretary's act in making the check payable to Y. The drawee bank properly paid the check. Y received funds of Employer which were used for the personal benefit of Secretary. Employer asserts a claim to these funds against Y. If Y is a holder in due course, Y takes free of the claim. Whether Y is a holder in due course depends upon whether Y had notice of Employer's claim." Id.

C. EQUIVALENT RIGHTS TO HOLDER IN DUE COURSE

1. Taking Through A Holder In Due Course -- The Shelter Principle

a. Shelter Principle Gives Due-Course Rights Without Due-Course Status

A transferee of an instrument may have the rights of a holder in due course without necessarily having the status of a holder in due course. It is possible because of the *shelter principle* of 3-203(b), the "[t]ransfer of an instrument, whether or not the transfer is a negotiation, vests in the transferee any right of the transferor to enforce the instrument, including any right as a holder in due course * * *." By virtue of this broad principle (which applies to most other forms of property as well), even though a person in her own right does not satisfy the requirements for being a holder in due course, she is entitled to enjoy the benefits of that status that were enjoyed by any holder in due course prior to her in the chain of transfer of the instrument. The primary significance of the shelter principle, and the basis for its name, is the fact that it enables one who is not a holder in due course to share the shelter from claims and defenses to the extent enjoyed by a holder in due course through or from whom she acquired the instrument.

Example: A induces M by fraud to make a note payable to A. A negotiates the note to B who takes as a holder in due course. In enforcing a judgment against B, the sheriff levies on the note and sells it to C. C is not a holder in due course. C nevertheless succeeds to B's rights as a holder in due course and is not subject to the defense of fraud.

Example: A induces M by fraud to make an instrument payable to A. A negotiates it to B, who takes as a holder in due course. After the instrument is overdue, B sells it to C, who has notice of the fraud. C succeeds to B's rights as a holder in due course, cutting off the defense.

Example: Same facts, except that B gives the note to C as a gift. The result is the same. Operation of the shelter principle is not conditioned on the transferee giving value for the rights she acquired.

b. Limitations on Due-Course Rights Through the Shelter Principle

The shelter principle is not intended and should not be used to permit any holder who has herself been a party to any fraud or illegality affecting the instrument, or who has received notice of any defense or claim against, "to wash the instrument clean by passing it into the hands of a holder in due course and then repurchasing it." 3-203 comment 2. For this reason, Article 3 provides that a "transferee cannot acquire rights of a holder in due course by a transfer, directly or indirectly, from a holder in due course if the transferee engaged in fraud or illegality affecting the instrument." 3-203(b).

Example: "A induces M by fraud to make an instrument payable to A, A negotiates it to B, who takes as a holder in due course. A then repurchases the instrument from B. A does not succeed to B's rights as a holder in due course, and remains subject to the defense of fraud." 3-201 comment 3(b) (1989 Official Text).

Example: "A induces M by fraud to make an instrument payable to A, A negotiates it to B, who takes with notice of the fraud. B negotiates it to C, a holder in due course, and then repurchases the instrument from C. B does not succeed to C's rights as a holder in due course, and remains subject to the defense of fraud." 3-201 comment 3(c) (1989 Official Text).

Example: "The same facts as * * * [the immediately preceding example], except that B had no notice of the fraud when he first acquired the instrument, but learned of it while he was a holder and with such knowledge negotiated to C. B does not succeed to C's rights as a holder in due course, and his position is not improved by the negotiation and repurchase." 3-201 comment 3(d) (1989 Official Text).

2. Estoppel

Although a transferee of an instrument is not a holder in due course and does not claim through such a holder, and even though the obligation assigned to her is not in the form of a negotiable instrument, an obligor of a promise might be precluded from asserting a defense against the transferee because of equitable estoppel. Cf. 3-104 comment 2.

Example: X wrote an I.O.U. to Y. Y sold the I.O.U. to Z after X assured Z that the obligation was real and that X had no defense to it. In fact, X had a defense to the obligation and knew of the facts constituting the defense when she assured Z that none existed. X is equitably estopped to assert the defense against Z. Cf. *First State Bank v. Clark*, 570 P.2d 1144 (N.M. 1977) (pledgee of nonnegotiable note relied on maker's verbal assurances that the note was valid); compare *In re Boardwalk Marketplace Securities Litigation*, 668 F. Supp. 115 (D. Conn. 1987) (With respect to estoppel, merely executing note of questionable negotiability, even with hope that it would be negotiated, and then making payments on the note, does not estop maker from challenging negotiability.)

3. Contractual Waiver Of Claims And Defenses
a. Description and Effect

An assignee of a contract that is not a negotiable instrument cannot enjoy the rights of a holder in due course under Article 3 because she is not holding an instrument. Ordinarily, therefore, an assignee of a simple contract, such as an installment sales contract, takes subject to the claims and defenses that the buyer or other obligor could assert against the assignor. An assignee of even a simple contract can take free of these claims and defenses, however, and thereby enjoy rights equivalent to those of a holder in due course, if the contract contains a waiver-of-defenses clause. Such a clause is a provision in the contract through which the obligor agrees not to assert against any assignee any claim or defense she may have against her seller, the assignor. This clause is enforceable by the assignee as a matter of contract law, and is explicitly validated by the U.C.C. in Article 9:

> *Subject to any statute or decision which establishes a different rule for buyers or lessees of consumer goods,* an agreement by a buyer or lessee that he will not assert against an assignee any claim or defense which he may have against the seller or lessor is enforceable by an assignee who takes his assignment for value, in good faith and without notice of a claim or defense, except as to defenses of a type which may be asserted against a holder in due course of a negotiable instrument * * *. 9-206(1) (emphasis added).

Example: Farmer buys a combine on credit from Seller. The parties execute a sales contract (which is not an Article 3 instrument) that obligates Seller to deliver the combine within two weeks and obligates Farmer to pay the price in installment payments over a four-year term. The contract contains this clause: "The buyer hereby waives against any assignee any claim or defense which she may have against the seller." Seller immediately sells the contract to Finance Company. Farmer defaults under the contract, and Finance Company sues her. Farmer's defense is that the combine was never delivered. Because of the waiver-of-defense clause in the contract, this defense cannot be asserted against Finance Company.

b.   Limitations

There are three limitations on the enforceability of waiver-of-defenses clauses in contracts:

1) **"Due Course" Requirements**

    An assignee cannot enforce a waiver of defenses clause unless she purchased the contract for value, in good faith, and without notice of a claim or defense. 9-206(1). These requirements are almost identical to the requisites of due-course status under Article 3. 3-302(a). Of course, to enforce a waiver-of-defenses clause an assignee of a simple contract need not be a "holder" of an "instrument." Also, the definition of "value" for 9-206 purposes is wider than the meaning of the term under 3-302(a). For Article 3 "due course" status, value is defined in 3-303. In deciding whether an assignee has given value for purposes of 9-206, the governing definition of value is 1-201(44), which is more generous than 3-303. For example, an executory promise is value within 1-201(44), but is not value under 3-303.

2) **"Real Defenses"**

    A waiver-of-defenses clause never stops an obligor from asserting the same real defenses that are good against a holder in due course of an instrument under Article 3, that is, the defenses listed in 3-305(a). 9-206(1).

3) **Special Protection of Consumers**

    The use of waiver-of-defenses clauses in consumer transactions has been restricted by federal regulation and other law, which is discussed later in this chapter.

4.   Direct Financing

A lender who finances a person's acquisition of property or services by loaning her the purchase money directly, rather than by funneling it through the seller as happens when a lender buys the seller's instruments or sales contracts, is generally not subject to the person's claims and defenses against the seller. This immunity is not based on anything in Article 3 or Article 9. It shields the lender even when the debtor has not signed an instrument and has not agreed to waive against the lender her claims and defenses against the seller. The lender is immune from these claims and defenses simply because the debtor's promise to repay the lender the loan is, in contemplation of the law, totally independent of the seller's obligations to the debtor. The lender's rights against the debtor are not derived from the seller's rights against her. The loan and the sale are two legally separate transactions, and the lender in the loan transaction is not accountable for the sins of the seller in the sale transaction.

Example: Farmer buys a combine from Seller, and pays for it using the proceeds of a purchase-money loan from Bank. The loan is evidenced by a note Farmer issued payable to Bank. The combine is never delivered, and Farmer refuses to pay the note. The Seller's breach of the sales contract is not a good defense against payment of the note. The reason is not that Bank is a holder in due course, and it makes no difference that Bank dealt with Farmer. Bank is immune from the defense under ordinary principles of contract and sales law because Farmer's obligation to repay the loan was legally separate from Seller's obligation to deliver the combine. Bank's dealings with Farmer, and the obligations arising therefrom, are independent of the transaction between Farmer and Seller.

5. Federal Immunity

Federal law can give immunity from adverse claims and defenses to holders of contracts that are not instruments; and it can give the same immunity to transferees of instruments who are not holders in due course. The most important example is the *D'Oench* doctrine. In the controversial case, *D'Oench, Duhme & Co. v. FDIC*, 315 U.S. 447, 62 S.Ct. 676, 86 L.Ed.2d 956 (1942), the Supreme Court held that one who has dealt with a failed financial institution that is insured by the Federal Deposit Insurance Corporation may not assert a claim or defense against the FDIC that depends on some understanding that is not reflected in the insolvent bank's records. A federal statute, 12 USCA 1823(e), codifies *D'Oench, Duhme* and its progeny, and specifically directs that agreements with failed banks are unenforceable against federal insurers, including the FDIC and Resolution Trust Corporation (RTC), unless the agreements meet four formal non-secrecy requirements. This statute provides:

No agreement which tends to diminish or defeat the interest of the Corporation in any asset acquired by it under this section or section 1821 of this title, either as security for a loan or by purchase or as receiver of any insured depository institution, shall be valid against the Corporation unless such agreement-- (1) is in writing, (2) was executed by the depository institution and any person claiming an adverse interest thereunder, including the obligor, contemporaneously with the acquisition of the asset by the depository institution, (3) was approved by the board of directors of the depository institution or its loan committee, which approval shall be reflected in the minutes of said board or committee, and (4) has been, continuously, from the time of its execution, an official record of the depository institution.

12 USCA 1823(e). The statutory and common-law *D'Oench, Duhme* doctrines bar essentially the same claims and defenses. They are virtually interchangeable. Together, the doctrines protect the FDIC in its several capacities, including receiver, and also protects bridge banks and successors of any protected entity.

Example: In *Oliver v. Resolution Trust Corp.*, 955 F.2d 583 (8th Cir. 1992), the Olivers entered into two financial agreements with Sooner Federal Savings and Loan Association (Sooner) and Sooner's wholly-owned subsidiary, Tandem. In the first agreement, the Olivers gave Sooner a mortgage on their home to secure the refinancing of loans Sooner had made to several limited partnerships in which Luther Oliver was a general partner. In the second agreement, the Olivers guaranteed loans Tandem made to two corporations Luther Oliver owned as sole shareholder. Based on these agreements, Sooner threatened to foreclose on the Olivers' home and Tandem sought repayment of the funds Tandem had advanced. The Olivers brought this action against Sooner and Tandem contending both financial agreements were accompanied by separate side agreements protecting the Olivers from personal liability and guaranteeing Sooner would not foreclose on the Olivers' home. After Sooner fell into financial difficulties, the RTC was appointed receiver for Sooner and was substituted as a party in this action. On the RTC and Tandem's motion, the action was dismissed because *D'Oench, Duhme* and its statutory counterpart, 12 USCA 1823(e), precluded oral side agreements from serving as the basis for the Olivers' claims.

Significantly, the courts broadly define the "agreements" that are affected by *D'Oench*. In the landmark case of *Langley v. FDIC*, 484 U.S. 86, 108 S.Ct. 396, 98 L.Ed.2d 340 (1987), the Supreme Court read the term "agreement" expansively to include fraudulent misrepresentations since such statements are, in effect, fraudulent warranties. Later cases have further expanded the *Langley* broad definition of "agreement" to include the nondisclosure of material information.

Example: For example, in *McCullough v. FDIC*, 788 F. Supp. 626 (D. Mass. 1992), the plaintiffs sued the FDIC in its capacity as receiver of the failed Bank of New England ("BNE"). The plaintiffs alleged that BNE was the financier and co-developer of an industrial condominium project in which the plaintiffs bought four units. The plaintiffs funded this purchase with a promissory note from the BNE in the amount of $350,000 secured by a mortgage on the units. Plaintiffs alleged that at the time of this sale BNE was aware that the property was subject to a Notice of Responsibility, issued by the Massachusetts Department of Environmental Quality Engineering ("DEQE"), requiring the removal of hazardous waste located on the property and that BNE failed to inform plaintiffs of this fact. Based in part upon BNE's failure to disclose this material information, the plaintiffs sued for misrepresentation and violation of other state law. The action was dismissed because the claims made by the plaintiffs were grounded in undocumented agreements and were thus barred under the *D'Oench, Duhme* doctrine.

D. RESTRICTIONS ON DUE-COURSE STATUS AND EQUIVALENT RIGHTS

1. Federal Law

a. Federal Trade Commission Rule Concerning Preservation of Consumers' Claims and Defenses

When the holder-in-due-course doctrine, a contractual waiver of defenses, or direct financing is used in financing sales of property or services, the effect is to separate the buyer's duty to pay from the seller's obligations under the parties' contract. The holder in due course, the assignee of a contract containing a waiver-of-defenses clause, or the lender who loaned the buyer the purchase price can recover the price of the property or services even though the buyer has claims or defenses against the seller for breach of the sales transaction. More than a decade ago the Federal Trade Commission promulgated a trade regulation rule designed to prevent this separation of duties in consumer credit transactions. The rule is entitled the Federal Trade Commission Trade Regulation Rule on the Preservation of Consumers' Claims and Defenses, which provides:

> [I]t is an unfair or deceptive act or practice * * * for a seller, directly or indirectly, to:
>
> (a) Take or receive a consumer credit contract which fails to contain the following provision in at least ten point, bold face, type:
>
> **NOTICE**
>
> **ANY HOLDER OF THIS CONSUMER CREDIT CONTRACT IS SUBJECT TO ALL CLAIMS AND DEFENSES WHICH THE DEBTOR COULD ASSERT AGAINST THE SELLER OF GOODS OR SERVICES**

OBTAINED PURSUANT HERETO OR WITH THE PROCEEDS HEREOF. RECOVERY HEREUNDER BY THE DEBTOR SHALL NOT EXCEED AMOUNTS PAID BY THE DEBTOR HEREUNDER.

or, (b) Accept, as full or partial payment for such sale or lease, the proceeds of any purchase money loan (as purchase money loan is defined herein), unless any consumer credit contract made in connection with such purchase money loan contains the following provision in at least ten point, bold face, type:

NOTICE

ANY HOLDER OF THIS CONSUMER CREDIT CONTRACT IS SUBJECT TO ALL CLAIMS AND DEFENSES WHICH THE DEBTOR COULD ASSERT AGAINST THE SELLER OF GOODS OR SERVICES OBTAINED WITH THE PROCEEDS HEREOF. RECOVERY HEREUNDER BY THE DEBTOR SHALL NOT EXCEED AMOUNTS PAID BY THE DEBTOR HEREUNDER.

16 CFR 433.2.

1) When the Rule Applies

   In general terms, the FTC Rule applies in connection with any sale or lease of goods or services to consumers on credit when the seller is a person in the business of selling goods or services to consumers. For purposes of the Rule, "consumer" means "[a] natural person who seeks or acquires goods or services for personal, family, or household use." 16 CFR 433.1(b).

2) How the Rule Should Work When the Seller Extends Credit

   When the seller extends credit in a sale or lease of goods governed by the Rule, she includes the Notice (described in 433.2(a)) in any contract between her and the consumer-buyer. If only a nonnegotiable sales contract is executed, the effect of including the Notice is to negate the force and effect of any contrary waiver-of-defenses clause. So the normal rule of derivative title applies in transferring the contract, that is, any assignee of the contract steps into the shoes of the assignor-seller and is subject to the consumer-buyer's claims and defenses against the seller.

   If a negotiable instrument is executed, the Notice must be included in it and the effect is either to destroy the negotiability of the writing or to make the Notice part of the terms of the instrument. In either event, U.C.C 3-305 and 3-306 are neutered so that no transferee can take free of the consumer's claims and defenses against the seller.

3) How the Rule Should Work When a Lender Provides Direct Financing

Banks are responsible for most direct financing, but the FTC lacks jurisdiction over banks. So this FTC Rule on preserving consumers' claims and defenses could not be aimed directly at them. Instead, the FTC aimed indirectly at banks and other direct financers by prohibiting sellers, over whom the FTC does have jurisdiction, from taking the proceeds of a purchase money loan in payment for goods and services sold or leased to a consumer unless the loan contract the consumer signs contains the FTC Notice (described in 16 CFR 433.2(b)).

The seller is effectively forced to police the loan transaction to which she is not a party. If the consumer has borrowed the money to pay for the goods or services, the seller cannot lawfully take the loan proceeds unless the consumer's contract with the bank or other lender provides that the lender is subject to the consumer's claims and defenses against the seller. Although the lender is not a party to the sale or lease transaction between the seller and consumer-buyer, the lender nonetheless becomes accountable for the seller's sins by force of the Notice in the loan contract: The Notice becomes part of the loan contract and thus, by agreement, the lender assumes such accountability, even if the loan contract in which the Notice appears is a note or other Article 3 instrument.

a) Only Purchase Money Loans as Defined by the Rule Are Covered

The FTC Rule has two limitations as applied to direct financing of consumer sales and leases. The first limitation is that *only purchase money loans as defined by the rule are covered.* The FTC Rule does not apply every time a consumer borrows the purchase price of goods or services from a lender, only when the loan is a *purchase money loan* as defined by the Rule itself. This definition limits the meaning of purchase money loans, and thus the Rule's applicability to direct financing, to cash advances used to "purchase * * * goods or services from a seller who (1) refers consumers to the creditor [i.e., the lender] or (2) is affiliated with the creditor by common control, contract, or business arrangement." 16 CFR 433.1(d).

So direct financing is covered by the Rule, and a seller need worry about policing loans her customers get to pay the price of the goods and services she sells, only when a customer borrows the purchase price from a bank or other lender with whom the seller is connected by referral or affiliation. The Rule's applicability to direct financing is so limited because the FTC intended to subject a lender to a consumer's claims and defenses against a seller only where a relationship exists between lender and seller such that the lender is in a position to assess the likelihood of seller misconduct and shift the risk back to the seller.

The key concepts are "referral" and "affiliation," which are not defined by the FTC Rule itself. The definitions appear rather in staff commentary and the like.

- *Referral:* "The word "refers' is intended to reach those situations where a seller, in the ordinary course of business, is sending his buyers to a particular loan outlet, or to particular outlets, for credit which is to be used in the seller's establishment. In such circumstances the seller is effectively arranging credit for his customers. No specific number of referrals is specified in the Rule. The key distinction is between those instances where a seller is merely passing along information about places where his buyers may obtain credit and those where a seller is acting as a conduit for financing and channeling buyer-borrowers to a particular lender or limited group of lenders. * * * A seller 'refers consumers to the creditor' when his conduct indicates that he is doing more than passively engaging in an information process." Guidelines on Trade Regulation Rule Concerning Preservation of Consumers' Claims and Defenses, 41 (no. 95) Fed. Reg. 20022, 20025 (May 14, 1976).

- *Affiliation:* Affiliation is an alternative to referral for establishing the lender-seller relationship necessary for the Rule to apply to a purchase money loan. There are three types of affiliation, any one of which is sufficient in itself to trigger the Rule's applicability to a purchase money loan. The first type of affiliation is *common control,* which means that the creditor, i.e., the lender, and the seller are "functionally part of the same business entity * * * [as when] the two companies are owned by a holding company or by substantially the same individuals, * * * one is a subsidiary of the other, or * * * they are under common control in any other way." Id. at 20026. The second type of affiliation is *contract,* meaning "[a]ny oral or written agreement, formal or informal, between a creditor and a seller, which contemplates or provides for cooperative or concerted activity in connection with the sale of goods or services to consumers or the financing thereof." Id. The third and final type of affiliation is *business arrangement,* which means "[a]ny understanding, procedure, course of dealing, or arrangement, formal or informal, between a creditor and a seller, in connection with the sale of goods or services to consumers or the financing thereof." Id.; see also 16 CFR 433.1(g). These definitions of contract and business arrangement are intended to "encompass all situations where a creditor and a seller are party to any agreement, arrangement, understanding, or mutually understood procedure which is specifically related to retail sales or retail sales financing [and that is] * * * ongoing * * *. Cooperative activity on a continuing basis is what is specified by the Rule." Guidelines on Trade Regulation Rule Concerning Preservation of Consumers' Claims and Defenses, 41 (no. 95) Fed. Reg. 20022, 20026 (May 14, 1976).

b) **Only When The Seller Has Reason To Known That A Purchase Money Loan Is Involved Does The Rule Apply**

The second limitation on the FTC Rule's applicability to purchase money loans is that *only when the seller has reason to know that a purchase money loan is involved does the rule apply.* A seller cannot accept the proceeds of a purchase money loan unless the credit contract between the lender and the consumer contains the Notice. The prohibition is not strictly applied, however, without regard to whether the seller was aware of the source of the funds the consumer uses to pay the price of the goods or services. "The Rule was not intended to subject a seller to liability when he has no reason to believe he is receiving the proceeds of a 'purchase money loan.' Nor does the Rule require that the seller interrogate the buyer to determine the source of the proceeds. The objective circumstances surrounding the transaction provide the seller with information concerning the source of the proceeds. When these circumstances do not indicate the source * * * or do not provide reason to believe that the proceeds may be from a 'purchase money loan,' there is no obligation to further investigate the source * * *." Statement of Enforcement Policy Regarding Preservation of Consumers' Claims and Defenses, 41 (no. 159) Fed. Reg. 34594, 34596-7 (August 16, 1976).

4) **Consequence of Rule Violations**

The consequence of a seller violating the FTC Rule is that she has committed an unfair and deceptive trade practice and is therefore subject to civil penalties, in the nature of fines, sought by the FTC. In rare cases the FTC can seek damages on behalf of injured consumers. Consumers themselves, however, have no direct actions under the FTC Rule. Moreover, a missing Notice will not be read into a contract in which the Notice should have appeared. The result is that the FTC Rule has absolutely no effect on the enforcement of such a contract, and state law alone decides whether the holder of the contract is subject to the consumer's claims and defenses against the seller. In many states, however, local law guarantees the preservation of consumers' claims and defenses by purely local limitations on the holder-in-due-course doctrine, contractual waivers of claims and defenses, and direct financing where the seller and lender are connected.

b. Bank Credit Cards

The use of a bank card or other general credit card, such as a VISA or MasterCard, to pay for property or services not sold by the card issuer is a form of direct financing by a lender. Under the common law, the card issuer is immune from the card holder's claims and defenses against the seller of goods and services that were purchased using the credit card. So, if Jane Doe uses her First Bank VISA card to purchase a snow blower that is defective, Ms. Doe must nevertheless pay, as a matter of common law, the charge to her credit card account that represents the price of the snow blower even though the seller of the machine breached the sale contract with Ms. Doe.

Federal statutory law carves a very big hole in this common-law immunity of credit card issuers. The law provides that a credit card issuer *is* subject to all claims (other than tort claims) and defenses arising out of any transaction in which the credit card is used as a method of payment or extension of credit, subject to these limitations:

- The amount of claims or defenses asserted by the cardholder may not exceed the amount of credit outstanding with respect to such transaction at the time the cardholder first notifies the card issuer or the person honoring the credit card of such claim or defense.
- The obligor, i.e., the cardholder, must make a good faith attempt to resolve the disagreement or problem that is the source of the claim or defense.
- The amount of the transaction must exceed $50.
- The transaction must have occurred in the same state as the cardholder's mailing address or within 100 miles of that address.

15 USCA 1666i(a). The last two limitations, which deal with the amount and place of the transaction, do not apply if there are certain connections between the card issuer and the merchant who honored the card (i.e., the person with whom the cardholder disagrees concerning the underlying transaction), that is, if the merchant:

- is the same person as the card issuer;
- is controlled by the card issuer;
- is under direct or indirect common control with the card issuer;
- is a franchised dealer in the card issuer's products or services; or

♦ obtained the order for such transaction through a mail solicitation made by or participated in by the card issuer in which the cardholder is solicited to enter into such transaction by using the card issued by the card issuer.

Id.

2. State Statutory Law

a. Restricting Contractual Waivers of Claims and Defenses

Statutes in a large number of states outlaw contractual waivers of claims and defenses in consumer credit contracts involving sales of goods and services. Not only are such waivers prohibited, the statutes also declare unenforceable a waiver that is included in a consumer contract in violation of the statutory prohibition.

A typical statute outlawing waivers of claims of defenses is the following Minnesota law:

> "No contract or obligation relating to a consumer credit sale shall contain any provision by which * * * [t]he consumer agrees not to assert against an assignee any claim or defense arising out of the transaction * * *. Any assignee of the contract or obligation relating to the consumer credit sale shall be subject to all claims and defenses of the consumer against the seller arising from the sale, notwithstanding any agreement to the contrary."

Minn. Stat. Ann. 325G.16(2)(a) & (3).

b. Due-Course Status

Some states have attempted to neuter the Article 3 holder-in-due-course doctrine in consumer credit sales. The usual approach is to prohibit sellers of goods or services from taking a negotiable instrument (except a check for the purchase price) from buyers who are consumers. The theory is that a transferee of a consumer credit contract can acquire the rights of a holder in due course under Article 3, and thereby take free of claims and defenses under U.C.C. 3-305 and 3-306, only if the consumer has signed a negotiable instrument. Thus, by banning the use of negotiable instruments in consumer credit deals, consumers cannot be denied their claims and defenses under Article 3. This ban and other laws outlawing contractual waivers of claims and defenses have the combined effect of always preserving a consumer's claims and defenses against a transferee of her contract with the seller. State law banning the use of negotiable instruments in consumer credit sales does not always clearly provide that a consumer's claims and defenses are preserved when the ban is violated and a negotiable instrument is obtained from a consumer and negotiated by the seller to a person who is a holder in due course under Article 3. But see Uniform Consumer Credit Code 3.404 (1974 Official Text) (an assignee of the rights of the seller or lessor in a consumer credit sale or lease is subject to all claims and defenses of the consumer notwithstanding that the assignee is a holder in due course of a negotiable instrument issued in violation of the provisions of this Act prohibiting the use of certain negotiable instruments).

c. Direct Financing (Purchase Money Loans)

The Uniform Consumer Credit Code provides that a consumer who borrows money to purchase or lease goods or services can assert against the lender claims and defenses the consumer has against the seller in certain circumstances, which are:

- the lender knows that the seller or lessor arranged for the extension of credit by the lender for a commission, brokerage, or referral fee;
- the lender is a person related to the seller or lessor, unless the relationship is remote or is not a factor in the transaction;
- the seller or lessor guarantees the loan or otherwise assumes the risk of loss by the lender upon the loan;
- the lender directly supplies the seller or lessor with the contract document used by the consumer to evidence the loan, and the seller or lessor has knowledge of the credit terms and participates in preparation of the document;
- the loan is conditioned upon the consumer's purchase or lease of the property or services from the particular seller or lessor, but the lender's payment of proceeds of the loan to the seller or lessor does not in itself establish that the loan was so conditioned; or
- the lender, before he makes the consumer loan, has knowledge or, from his course of dealing with the particular seller or lessor or his records, notice of substantial complaints by other buyers or lessees of the particular seller's or lessor's failure or refusal to perform his contracts with them and of the particular seller's or lessor's failure to remedy his defaults within a reasonable time after notice to him of the complaints.

UCCC 3.405(1). Even in these circumstances, however, the consumer can assert her claims and defenses against the lender only if she has made a good faith attempt to obtain satisfaction from the seller or lessor.

This UCCC rule, 3.405, is similar to the federal FTC Rule Preserving Consumers' Claims and Defenses (discussed supra) as it applies to purchase money loans in direct financing arrangements. There are two important differences, however. The two rules differ in defining the circumstances under which a lender is subject to a consumer's claims and defenses against a seller or lessor. Also, and more importantly, the two rules differ with respect to operation and enforcement. The FTC Rule works only if, by the seller's policing efforts, the FTC Notice is actually included in the loan documents the consumer signs; and the consumer has no redress on her own if the Rule is violated. The UCCC rule is not dependent on including any kind of language in loan documents. Rather, the UCCC rule preserves a consumer's claims and defenses against a lender, as a matter of law, in any of the circumstances described by the law. If any of the circumstances described in UCCC 3.405(1) are present, the consumer can assert her claims and defenses against the lender simply and solely because 3.405 gives her the right to do so. The UCCC rule is aimed directly at lenders and is a matter of substantive state law.

The UCCC rule is thus a potent protection for consumers in direct financing of sales and leases of goods and services, but the UCCC has been enacted in only 11 states. Moreover, the vast majority of the other states have nothing whatsoever like 3.405. Thus, in most states, local enacted law does not subject a lender to the borrower's claims and defenses arising from the sale or service transaction in which the borrower invested the loan proceeds.

Another unique provision of the UCCC, which preserves a consumers' claims and defenses in a special form of direct financing, is 3.403, which subjects a credit card issuer (including banks issuing general purpose credit cards) to claims and defenses against a seller or lessor of goods arising from sales or leases made pursuant to the credit card. Most states have enacted nothing akin to 3.403, but the absence of this kind of provision in state law is not terribly consequential because there is a substantially similar federal statute that subjects a credit card issuer to the claims and defenses of cardholders arising from transactions in which credit cards are used. See 15 USCA 1666i, which is discussed earlier in this chapter.

3. Decisional Law
a. Close-Connection Doctrine
Legislatures and administrative agencies have not been the only sources of restrictions on due-course status and equivalent rights. The courts have developed their own restrictions that exist as a matter of decisional law, the most important of which is the *close-connection doctrine*. This doctrine is recognized almost everywhere, but its content is not uniform among the states. Moreover, no state clearly defines the doctrine. Basically, however, the close-connection doctrine holds that an assignee of a right to money cannot take free of the obligor's claims and defenses against the assignor if the assignee was so closely connected (functionally or otherwise) to the assignor (generally or with respect

to the particular transaction) that the assignee should be accountable for assignor's misdealings with the obligor.

The key to the doctrine, of course, is the degree of association, or the number and quality of ties, between the assignee and assignor that is necessary to establish the critical "close connection." The thinnest relationship to which the doctrine has been applied was the association between a car dealer and a finance company in the case, *Commercial Credit Co. v. Childs*, 199 Ark. 1073, 137 S.W.2d 260 (1940). In this case, Childs purchased a used car from Arkansas Motors, Inc. He signed a contract and note which were standard forms prepared by Commercial Credit for use by Arkansas Motors in the latter's business. On the back of the contract was a preprinted assignment of the paper to Commercial Credit. Indeed, on the very day Childs signed the forms, the paper was discounted to Commercial Credit.

Childs defaulted, and Commercial Credit sued him. Childs' defenses were misrepresentation and breach of warranty by Arkansas Motors. Commercial Credit argued that it was a holder in due course and thus took free of these defenses. The Arkansas Supreme Court disagreed:

> We think appellant [Commercial Credit] was so closely connected with the entire transaction or with the deal that it can not be heard to say that it, in good faith, was an innocent purchaser of the instrument for value before maturity. It financed the deal, prepared the instrument, and on the day it was executed took an assignment of it from the Arkansas Motors, Inc. Even before it was executed it prepared the written assignment thereon to itself. Rather than being a purchaser of the instrument after its execution it was to all intents and purposes a party to the agreement and instrument from the beginning.

Id. at 1077, 137 S.W.2d at 262.

The *Childs* case is pre-Code, but the close-connection doctrine has been applied in a great many U.C.C. cases. Indeed, the doctrine has not been limited to denying due-course status under Article 3. It has also been applied to prevent an assignee of a simple contract from enforcing a contractual waiver-of-defenses clause in the contract. Moreover, the close-connection doctrine has not been limited to consumer transactions. It has also been applied in commercial settings both to deny due-course status and prevent the enforcement of waivers of claims and defenses.

You surely have noticed that the close-connection doctrine looks very much like the FTC and UCCC rules that apply to direct financing and subject purchase-money lenders to the claims and defenses that borrowers have against the sellers of property and services purchased with the loan proceeds. The connections between lenders and sellers that trigger the application of those rules are very suggestive of connections that might invoke the close-connection doctrine. *Yet, the close-connection doctrine itself has not been applied to direct financing.* Thus far, the doctrine has been limited to tearing down barriers (e.g., due-course doctrine; waivers of claims and defenses) to an assignee's usual vulnerability, *a la* the rule of derivative title, to an obligor's claims and defenses against the assignor. The doctrine has not yet been used as a fresh, independent basis for imposing liability on a lender in a direct financing arrangement who loans purchase money and is not a party to the transaction where the money is spent.

b. Public Policy

A few courts have held that in consumer transactions, contractual waivers of claims and defenses are unconscionable, violative of public policy, or for similar reasons are not enforceable as a matter of decisional law. See, e.g., *Unico v. Owen*, 50 N.J. 101, 232 A.2d 405 (1967). No court has reached the same conclusion about Article 3's holder in due course doctrine, nor about a lender's traditional immunity in a direct financing arrangement, from the claims and defenses its borrower has against her seller.

REVIEW QUESTIONS

1.   List the holder-in-due-course requirements.

2.   Is it possible for a holder to be a holder in due course by taking the instrument in exchange for an executory promise?

3.   Suppose that a $1000 instrument is taken for a promise of goods worth $900. Only $500 of the goods is actually supplied. To what extent, if any, can the holder be a holder in due course?

4.   M issues a note to S's order. S negotiates the note to T in exchange for T's promise to sell widgets to S. Before the widgets are delivered, T learns that M has a personal defense to payment of the note. T nevertheless delivers the widgets she promised to sell to S. By delivering the widgets, which amounts to performing the agreed consideration, T gave value. Is it possible, therefore, that T is a holder in due course?

5.   Does a lender give value to the extent it acquires an Article 9 security interest in an instrument as security for a loan?

6.   Does a lender give value to the extent it acquires a judgment for a defaulted loan and obtains a execution on an instrument payable to the debtor?

7.   Bank made a $10,000 unsecured loan to D. Later, when D's financial condition worsened, Bank got worried and demanded that D make a payment or provide collateral. D indorsed and delivered to Bank a $10,000 note drawn by M payable to P. Is Bank a holder in due course if it acted in good faith and in complete innocence?

8.   Notice that will preclude due-course status can be based on inferable knolwedge. Does this mean knowledge that a person would have learned by investigating the relevant circumstances?

9.   Suppose that a check is drawn payable to X, as agent for Y. X cashes and negotiates the check at a depositary bank and applies the value to her own purposes rather than as directed by Y. Almost immediately, Y learns of this breach of fiduciary duty and causes the drawer to stop payment of the check. The check is dishonored and bounced back to the depositary bank which sues the drawer on the instrument. The drawer joins Y as a defendant so that Y can assert Y's claim of ownership of the instrument and its proceeds. 3-305(c). The bank loses unless it is a holder in due course. Is the bank a holder in due course?

10.   Is "good faith" determined by a subjective or objective test?

11.   Debtor owes Creditor $10,000 on an unsecured debt. Creditor informs Debtor that she will be forced to demand payment of the debt unless Debtor supplies collateral for it. Debtor indorses and delivers to Creditor, as security, a negotiable certificate of deposit payable to Debtor's order. If Creditor takes the instrument in good faith and without notice, is Creditor a holder in due course of the certificate of deposit?

12.   S takes B's check in payment of the price of goods and deposits the check in her account at State Bank, which credits S's account with the amount of the check. Has State Bank thereby given value for the check?

13.   A person can have notice of a fact of which she has no knowledge, but she cannot have knowledge of a fact of which she has no notice. Explain.

14.   M issued to P's order a note payable on February 14, 1992. P negotiated the note to T on February 15, 1992. T took the instrument for value, in good faith and without notice of a claim or defense to the instrument. M refused to pay the note because of a defense arising from the underlying transaction between her and P. Is T subject to this defense of which she had no notice?

15.   M issued to P's order a demand note for $10,000. P indorsed the note and sold it to T for $4000. T was completely unaware of any claim or defense to the note. M has a $7000 claim against P arising out of the underlying transaction between the two of them. Does T take subject to this claim completely, partly or not at all?

16.   B, Inc. bought a used truck on credit from Ace Used Cars, and issued to Ace a note for the price. Ace immediately discounted the note to Noreast Bank, which regularly bought paper generated by Ace's credit sales. In fact, Ace will not sell a car on credit unless Noreast indicates that the customer is creditworthy and agrees in advance to buy the customer's note from Noreast. Noreast also supplies the form notes that Ace uses, and tells Ace the rate of interest to insert in each note. Is Noreast a holder in due course of B's note so Noreast takes free of B's claims and defenses against Ace?

17.   Same facts as the preceding question, except B, Inc. signed an installment sales contract, prepared by Noreast, that contains a waiver-of-claims-and-defenses clause. Is Noreast a holder in due course who takes free of B's claims and defenses against Ace? Does Noreast take free on another basis?

18.   Reconsider Questions 16 and 17. Suppose that B is an individual who purchases the truck for personal, family and household purposes. Should Ace include the FTC Notice in the note or other credit contract B signs? What is the effect in terms of preserving, against any transferee of the note or contract, B's claims and defenses against Ace?

19.   Continue with Question 18, but change it just a bit. Suppose that B finances the purchase of the truck by getting a loan from State Bank, to which Ace Regularly refers customers whose contracts Noreast is unwilling to buy. B signs a note to State Bank evidencing the loan. Does the FTC Rule on the Preservation of Consumers' Claims and Defenses apply to this purchase money loan? Can State Bank enforce the note free from B's claims and defenses against Ace if for any reason the FTC Notice is not included in B's note?

PART TWO

BANK DEPOSITS AND COLLECTIONS

Chapters

IX

CHECK COLLECTION PROCESS

Analysis

A. *Describing (Very Generally) The Process And Its Article 3 Effects*
1. *Personal Presentment By Owners Of Checks*
2. *Direct Presentment Between Banks*
3. *Collection Through Clearinghouses*
4. *Long-Distance Collection Through Federal Reserve Banks*
B. *Forward collection process*
1. *Depositary Bank Giving Customer Credit*
2. *Collecting Banks' Indorsements*
3. *Responsibilities Of Collecting Banks*
4. *Settlements*
5. *Presentment*
C. *Main Duties Of The Payor Bank In The Return Process*
1. *Article 4 Return -- Mainly, The Midnight Deadline Rule(s)*
2. *Large-Dollar Notice*
3. *Expeditious Return*
D. *Returning Banks In The Return Process*
1. *What Is A Returning Bank*
2. *Duty Of Expeditious Return*
3. *Mechanics Of Return*
4. *Liability For Breaching Duties With Respect To Returns*
E. *Depositary Banks' RightS and duties upon return of checks*
1. *Paying For Returns*
2. *Main Rights Against Customer And Others When Returned Check Has Been Dishonored*

U.C.C. "Article 4 defines rights between parties with respect to bank deposits and collections." 4-101 comment 3. Bank collections refer, principally, to the ways and means of collecting checks -- getting them paid by the banks on which they are drawn. Article 4 is "a uniform statement of the principal rules of the bank [check] collection process * * *." 4-101 comment 1. Bank deposits refer, principally, to checking accounts. Article 4 governs the relationship between banks and their customers with respect to these accounts. It addresses such issues as when the bank must pay checks drawn on the accounts, when the bank can or must dishonor such instruments, and the bank's accountability for wrongfully dishonoring or paying checks. Article 4 also provides rules for distributing risks and losses associated with check fraud.

These matters also are affected by federal law. A principal reason is that the Federal Reserve System, an institution of the United States government, is a regular player in the check collection system. Indeed, the twelve Federal Reserve Banks and their several branches and service centers, which are spread throughout the country, form the principal structure for interbank check collection. Half or more of the checks drawn in this country are collected through the Federal Reserve, even when the collecting and payor banks are located in the same city; and, when a Federal Reserve entity is involved in the collection of a check, the application of Regulation J (12 CFR part 210) is triggered. Also, Congress has empowered the Federal Reserve "to impose on or allocate among depository institutions the risks of loss and liability in connection with any aspect of the payment system, including the receipt, payment, collection, or clearing of checks, and any related function of the payment system with respect to checks." 12 USCA 4010(f). This statute is a general delegation of power for the Federal Reserve to regulate any aspect of bank deposits and collections. It even empowers complete and comprehensive regulation of deposits and collections, totally preempting state law. The first product of this wide regulatory power is Regulation CC (12 CFR part 229) which mainly deals with funds availability in depositors' accounts and also with the return process for checks that are dishonored. For the most part, however, Regulations CC and J and other federal laws on bank deposits and check collection are supplemental rather than preemptive. They respect and treat Article 4 as the general law and add to it with respect to issues on which state law is thin or altogether lacking . So, in this Black Letter and probably in your classroom, bank deposits and check collection are discussed mainly in terms of Article 4. Federal law is discussed at the places where it embellishes -- or overrides -- the structure and rules of state law.

A. DESCRIBING (VERY GENERALLY) THE PROCESS AND ITS ARTICLE 3 EFFECTS

There are many ways in which checks are collected. Four very basic models are described here: personal presentment; direct presentment between banks; collection through clearinghouses; and long-distance collection through intermediary Federal Reserve Banks. The first model is very simple transactionally and serves mainly to introduce recurring and important legal terms and concepts. Each of the other three models builds on the one before it by adding new transactional and legal components. All of the models are followed in real life, even during the same day in the life of a single bank; but each model is always refined, modernized, and customized according to local or regional banking needs and practices and available technology. The main purposes here, however, are to acquaint you with the fundamental legal principles of check collection, and to connect them to the major rules of Article 3 regarding liability on checks. For these purposes, stripped down models of check collection work best.

1. Personal Presentment By Owners Of Checks

Suppose that Buyer purchases goods from Seller and pays for them by check. The check is drawn on PB Bank, where Buyer maintains her checking account. PB Bank is known as the *drawee* under Article 3. For purposes of Article 4, however, PB Bank is referred to as the *payor bank,* which "means a bank that is the drawee of a draft." 4-105(3). Article 4 also refers to the check as something else -- an "*item*." This term is broader than "check." Item means "an instrument or a promise or order to pay money handled by a bank for collection or payment," 4-104(a)(9), and covers any paper that typically moves through the check collection system. Seller can collect the check herself by personally presenting it for payment at PB Bank. This option exists whether or not Seller maintains an account with the Bank. If she has no account there, Seller will collect the check by getting PB to give her cash for it. If Seller has an account with PB, she can collect the check either by getting cash for the item or by getting credit to her account after depositing it. Whether Seller asks for cash or deposits the item, she is thereby presenting the check to the drawee for payment within the meaning of Article 3. See 3-501. Presentment is an essential condition to the drawer's liability on the instrument. See 3-414(b) & 3-502(b); see also Chapter III supra. Payment of the check occurs differently, however, depending on how presentment is made.

a. Presentment for Cash

Suppose that Seller takes the check to PB Bank, enters the lobby, and approaches a teller. After an exchange of pleasantries, Seller pushes Buyer's check across the counter and explains to the teller that she wants cash for the check. This is *presentment for immediate payment over the counter.* The check is dishonored if it is not paid on the day of presentment. 3-502(b)(2). Virtually always, however, the decision to pay or dishonor will be immediate, probably after the teller electronically examines the Buyer's account. PB's giving the Seller money for the item over the counter is "*payment*" of the instrument in several important senses of the word. First, because PB is the payor bank, the check is "finally paid" by PB having "paid the item in cash." 4-215(a)(1). ***Final*** *payment* **is the single most significant concept in Article 4.** It is important for a number of reasons, but principally for this reason: **After an item has been finally paid, the payor bank ordinarily cannot recover the money or monetary credit given for the item.** Payment in cash is only one way of finally paying an item. Other ways are discussed later. No matter how it happens, however, only a payor bank makes final payment. No other bank can do it.

PB's payment to Seller is also important because it triggers Buyer's discharge. When an instrument is paid by or on behalf of a party obliged to pay the instrument, and paid to a person entitled to enforce the instrument, "to the extent of the payment, the obligation of the party obliged to pay the instrument is discharged * * *." 3-602(a). Thus, when PB paid Seller in cash, the effect was to discharge Buyer on the check due to 3-602(a) and, concomitantly, to discharge her on the underlying obligation (i.e., Buyer's contractual duty to pay Seller the price of the goods). 3-310(b)(1). This obligation was only suspended when Seller took the check in payment of the goods. 3-310(b).

Upon paying any of Buyer's checks, PB Bank naturally expects to recoup the payment by charging the amount against Buyer's checking account on which the item was drawn. There may a problem. For example, the funds in the account may not be sufficient to cover the item; or the check may not be *properly payable*, which means that the item is not legally chargeable to the Buyer's account even though there are sufficient funds to cover it. A check is not properly payable, for example, if the drawer has ordered the bank to stop payment. Ordinarily, however, if the check has already been "finally paid" as defined in 4-215, the payment rightfully cannot be recovered from Seller. So, if the item cannot be charged to the account, PB will be stuck with the loss. This finality explains why PB probably will not give Seller the cash without first reviewing the size and status of Buyer's account.

The teller will therefore examine the check for irregularities, and will consult bank records (by phone or computer) to determine if Buyer's account contains sufficient funds to cover the check and will ask bank officials if there are extrinsic reasons for not paying the check. If cause not to pay the check is discovered, the teller will refuse payment and return the check to Seller. This conduct -- actually, the payor bank not paying the check on the day of presentment -- is dishonor of the instrument within the meaning of Article 3. See 3-502(b)(2). The teller may also stamp the check with the words "PAYMENT REFUSED" and write on the check the reason for refusing payment (or rather instruct the owner to "REFER TO MAKER"). This inscription is proof of dishonor, 3-505(a)(2), which Seller may use in establishing that the conditions to Buyer's secondary liability on the check as drawer of the check -- presentment and dishonor -- have been satisfied. Because of the dishonor, the Seller thereupon has an immediate right of recourse on the instrument against the Buyer. Also, the Buyer's liability on the underlying obligation is no longer suspended. The Seller, at her option, can sue Buyer on the instrument for its amount or on the underlying obligation for the price of the goods.

b. Presentment Through Deposit

Suppose that Seller also maintains her personal and business checking accounts with PB Bank. Instead of presenting Buyer's check over the counter for immediate payment, Seller includes Buyer's check in her daily deposit of money, checks and other cash items received through her business. As before, PB Bank is the *payor bank*. See 4-105(3). PB is also the *depositary bank* because it is "the first bank to take an item even though it is also the payor bank, unless the item is presented for immediate payment over the counter." 4-105(2). In banking practice, the check is called an "*on us*" item. Upon depositing the check, Seller simply expects PB to add the amount of the item to her account; but in legal effect, because PB is the drawee-payor bank, Seller's deposit of the check with PB amounts to presenting the check for payment. See 3-501.

The bank is not required to take any action with respect to the check until its *midnight deadline*, which is "midnight on its next banking day following the banking day on which it [the bank] receives the * * * item * * *." 4-104(a)(10). By then, the bank must return the check or pay for it. Failing to do so makes the bank accountable for the item -- liable for it (4-302) -- and also amounts to dishonor, 3-502(b)(1), that triggers the Buyer's liability on the check and the underlying obligation.

Probably, however, PB will credit Seller's account for the amount of the item on the day PB receives the check from Seller. It may do so quickly -- even immediately -- without first determining if Buyer's account contains sufficient funds to cover the item or if there is some other reason for not paying it. The credit, however, is revocable. Giving this credit to Seller's account is not final payment under Article 4 and is not payment that discharges Buyer-drawer on the check. Rather, the credit to Seller's account is a soft or *provisional settlement*. For a time, the Bank willy-nilly can take back the credit without liability to Seller. 4-214(c), 4-301(b) & 4-301(a). Taking back the credit from a depositor's account is also described as charging back the item against the account. This right of charge back continues until the Bank's *midnight deadline* with respect to the item. 4-301(a).

After provisionally crediting Seller's account in the amount of the check, the next major stage of the collection process involves charging or posting the check to Buyer's account. (This somewhat bass-ackward procedure of a payor bank giving someone a credit for a check and thereafter charging the item to the drawer's account is referred to as *deferred posting*. Actually, the credit and debit may occur simultaneously if the bank's electronic processing equipment is on line with its computer records of customers' accounts.) At this point the Bank may find a reason not to pay the item. Typical reasons for not paying a check are insufficient funds in the drawer's account or a direction from the drawer not to pay the item, which is known as a stop-payment order or a stop order. (A drawer's right to order her bank to stop payment of a check is discussed in the next chapter, Chapter X, infra.)

If PB finds a reason not to pay Buyer's check, PB can charge back the item to Seller's account and thereby erase the soft, provisional credit that was added to Seller's account when Seller deposited the check. 4-214(c), 4-301(b) & 4-301(a). The right of charge back would be exercised by the Bank making the appropriate accounting entry in its books; marking the check to indicate that it was not paid, which usually involves stating a reason for the nonpayment; and returning, i.e., sending, the check to Seller. 4-301(a) & (d). In Article 3 terms, these actions amount to *dishonor* of the check, see 3-502(b)(1). Thereupon, the conditions on the drawer's Article 3 liability on the check (presentment and dishonor) would be satisfied. Moreover, dishonor of the instrument would have the effect of resurrecting the underlying obligation, which was suspended when Seller took Buyer's check in payment of the price of the goods. PB Bank, however, is not liable to Seller so long as the check is returned by the bank's midnight deadline with respect to the check.

The midnight deadline is pivotal. **To dishonor the check and charge back the item to Seller's account, PB Bank must act -- must return the item to Seller -- by the Bank's *midnight deadline with respect to the item*.** The right to charge back the check expires then. 4-214(c) & 4-301(a-b). Moreover, a payor bank's failure to return a provisionally-credited item by its midnight deadline results automatically, by law, in final payment of the item. 4-215(a)(3). This provision, 4-215(a)(3), provides that an item is finally paid when the payor bank has "made a provisional settlement for the item and failed to revoke the settlement in the time and manner permitted by statute, clearinghouse rule or agreement." In initially giving Seller a credit to her account upon depositing Buyer's check, PB settled for the item, 4-104(a)(11), and this settlement was provisional. 4-201(a), 4-214(c) & 4-301(a-b). The time and manner permitted for revoking this provisional settlement are specified in 4-301(a) which requires returning the check by the midnight deadline. Thus, when PB's right of charge back expired by the rules of 4-301(a-b), the Bank failed to revoke a provisional settlement as provided by statute, and final payment thereby occurred under 4-215(a)(3). Also, somewhat circuitously, final payment cuts off a payor bank's right of return, 4-301(a-b), and thus its right of charge back. The credit for the check to Seller's account thereby becomes hard or firm and is available for withdrawal as of right at the opening of the bank's next banking day, which is the bank's second banking day following receipt of the item. 4-215(e)(2).

Final payment thus means PB cannot *rightfully* return and charge back the check and erase the credit given Seller. Of course, even when the right to return a check is lost because of final payment, the payor bank nevertheless retains the raw power to bounce the item. If this power were exercised in the present case -- if the bank wrongfully charged back the check to Seller's account -- Buyer would nevertheless not be liable to Seller or anyone else on the check. Remember that Buyer's liability on the check, as drawer, is conditioned on dishonor of the instrument. 3-414(b). "If the drawee bank does not return the check * * * within the midnight deadline, the settlement becomes final payment * * *. Thus, no dishonor occurs regardless of whether the check is retained or is returned after the midnight deadline." 3-502 comment 4. Moreover, when the 4-301(a) midnight deadline is missed and the item thereby is finally paid, 4-215(a)(3), the provisional credit to Seller's account becomes hard funds available for withdrawal as of right. 4-215(e)(2). Payment is not defined by 3-602(a) but naturally must include making hard funds available to the payee. If so, the final payment under Article 4 results in payment under Article 3 that discharges Buyer-drawer on the check, 3-602(a), and, concomitantly, on the underlying obligation. 3-310(b)(1).

Seller is not whipsawed. She can complain against PB on several bases. First, the charge back was wrongful and unlawful in violation of Article 4 and for this reason alone should be reversed. Additionally, PB's charge back amounted to conversion of Seller's funds. It might also be argued that because PB did not return the item by the midnight deadline, the bank itself is personally *accountable* for the item, 4-302(a)(1), which means that PB "is liable to pay it." 4-302 comment 3. The flaw in this argument is that PB already paid the check -- already accounted for it -- when the provisional settlement to Seller's account became final. The complaint is that PB unlawfully took back this final payment. Liability for accountability under 4-302 probably applies only when a payor bank fails to make a timely return of a check for which it had *not* provisionally settled. Correspondingly, dishonor of a check because of a payor bank's accountability (3-502(b)(1)) probably is limited to the same situation.

If PB's reason for wanting to dishonor the check was insufficient funds in Buyer's account, PB's recourse when it is too late to return the item is to charge it against the account and create an overdraft. Buyer is liable to PB for this overdraft, which is the equivalent of a loan. This liability is based on the deposit agreement between PB and Buyer, implied contract, and also on 4-401(a), which allows charging overdrafts against a customer's account. Overdrafts are properly payable items.

Usually, there is no reason not to pay a check. So, if Buyer's check to Seller is typical, PB will complete the process of posting the item to Buyer's account. Completing this process can occur on the very day the item was received by PB or sometime later. The check, which by this time will have been stamped "PAID" or the like, will eventually be returned to Buyer together with other checks drawn and paid against her account during the preceding month. Under former law, completing the process of posting the check resulted itself in final payment of Buyer's check, even if the process was completed before the midnight deadline with respect to the item. PB could not thereafter change its mind and take back the credit to Seller's account -- not even if it acted before the midnight deadline. Completing the posting process was final payment which terminated the Bank's right of charge back and made the bank accountable for the item. *Completing the process of posting is no longer a means of final payment.* The right of PB to return the check and charge it back to Seller's account is unaffected by the posting process. As long as the midnight deadline has not expired, PB can return a check and avoid liability to Seller even though the bank has completed the process of posting the item to the Buyer-drawer's account.

2. Direct Presentment Between Banks

Suppose that Buyer and Seller do not share the same bank and that Seller does not personally present Buyer's check to PB Bank. Rather, Seller either deposits the check in her account at a different bank, DB Bank, or cashes it there. In this variation of the hypothetical case, PB is still the payor bank but is NOT the depositary bank. DB is now the depositary bank. 4-105(2). If Seller deposits the check, DB will credit the amount of the check to Seller's account. Doing so amounts to settling for the item. If Seller cashes the check at DB, the cash advance is also a form of settlement. Either kind of settlement by DB Bank -- credit to Seller's account or cash in her hand -- is provisional, meaning it can be reclaimed by DB if the check is properly dishonored by PB Bank. 4-201 & 4-212(a). Be careful to distinguish the earlier example in which PB Bank gave Seller cash for the check. Seller getting cash was final payment there, but not here. DB Bank's cash advance is not final payment within the meaning of 4-215(a)(1) because DB is not the payor bank. PB Bank is the payor bank. Only a

payor bank finally pays an item. A payor bank that cashes a check finally pays it.
Any other bank that cashes a check provisionally settles for it.

After making a settlement with Seller, DB will then act as Seller's agent in collecting
the check, see 4-201(a), i.e., getting payment from PB. Because DB will act in this
role for Seller, DB is also known as a *collecting bank,* which "means a bank handling
an item for collection except the payor bank." 4-105(5). A payor bank, such as PB
Bank in the present example, is not a collecting bank even though it is, of course,
very much involved in the collection process and, indeed, is the target of collection
activities.

Because both DB and PB are in the same city, collection of the check will probably --
in real life -- be accomplished through a third bank there or, more likely, through a
clearinghouse or other clearing arrangement to which DB, PB and other local banks
belong. Collection through clearinghouses is discussed later. For now, assume that
DB decided to collect the check by presenting it directly to PB for payment. This
method of collecting a check is always an option for depositary-collecting banks such
as DB Bank when a bank is a payor. See 4-204(b)(1).

After receiving the check from Seller, DB Bank must forward the item to PB within a
reasonable time, presumably before midnight of DB's next banking day following its
receipt of the item. 4-202(a)(1) & (b). Remember: Because the item is being sent
directly to PB Bank, which is the drawee-payor, DB technically is presenting the
check for payment on behalf of Seller. DB thus gets an additional label -- the
presenting bank, which "means a bank presenting an item except a payor bank."
4-105(6).

Upon receiving the check from DB Bank, PB must either return the check or settle
for it *by midnight of the banking day of receipt.* 4-302(a)(1). (Sooner action is
required if the item is received directly or indirectly from a Reserve Bank . PB must
act by close of its banking day. 12 CFR 210.9.) Otherwise, PB becomes accountable
-- liable for the item. In normal practice, PB will give DB credit for the item as soon
as the item is presented and received.   This credit is referred to as a settlement
between the banks. Under state law, this settlement is provisional. Prior to final
payment, PB can revoke the settlement credit if some reason exists for not paying the
check (e.g., Buyer's account is empty or the check is not properly payable). 4-301(a).
Under preemptive federal law, however, this settlement between banks is final when
made. 12 CFR 229.36(d). Nevertheless, also by federal law, PB retains a
substantively similar right to return the check to DB and recoup for the item if PB
decides not to pay the item and acts seasonably under Article 4 in returning it.

Actually effecting the settlement between PB and DB can occur in a variety of ways. See 4-213(a). For example, PB may credit an account that DB maintains with PB for settlement purposes. This settlement may be effected through the Federal Reserve Bank (Fed Bank) in the Federal Reserve District where the banks are located or a branch of a Federal Reserve Bank. (Federal Reserve Banks are banks for banks. They do not directly serve the general public.) Both PB and DB will probably have their own accounts at the Fed Bank, or can use another bank's account at the Fed Bank through a *correspondent relationship.* These Fed accounts are maintained for various purposes, including as a means of making settlements with and between other banks in the check collection process. The Fed Bank will debit PB's account in the amount of Buyer's check to Seller and will credit the same amount to DB's Fed account.

Of course, DB will not present only Seller's check to PB. Rather, DB will present all the checks drawn against PB that DB received during the same period as Seller's check. PB will settle for all of these items as soon as they are presented, probably by a debit to an account on the Reserve Bank's books; but DB will not necessarily get a credit to its Fed account equaling the total sum of the checks that it presents. The reason is that, when DB presents checks to PB, PB may simultaneously present checks it received that were drawn against DB. PB will thus be entitled to a settlement from DB, and this settlement will be set off against the credit that PB owes DB. The result of the offset is known as *net settlement.* If the settlement due PB is greater than the settlement due DB, the former bank gets an appropriate credit to its Fed account, and a corresponding debit is charged to DB's account.

Now return to the trail of Buyer's check to Seller. Having settled for this item, PB bank will follow the same routine for posting the item to Buyer's account as was followed in the earlier example where Buyer and Seller both banked with PB. As before, PB has until its midnight deadline to decide whether or not to pay the check. Until then, PB can return the item to DB Bank. The reason is 4-301(a). It provides that "[i]f a payor bank settles for a demand item * * * before midnight of the banking day of receipt, the payor bank may revoke the settlement and recover the settlement if, before it has made final payment and before its midnight deadline, it * * * returns the item * * *." So, by returning the item by the midnight deadline, PB can recover the settlement. It does so under state law by revoking the very settlement that PB gave DB. By state law, this settlement was provisional only. Federal law changes this detail of the scheme because, by federal law, the settlement was final when made. Yet, the same federal law provides that if PB returns the check to DB by PB's Article 4 midnight deadline, DB must pay PB for the return. "A depositary bank shall pay the returning or paying bank returning the check to it for the amount of the check prior to the close of business on the banking day on which it received the check * * *." 12 CFR 229.32(b). The substantive, net effect is the same.

The procedures for return are largely governed by federal law, Regulation CC. Its big rule is that a dishonored check must be *expeditiously returned*. There are tests to determine whether or not this requirement has been met, and there is liability for not meeting it. Yet, Regulation CC honors Article 4's rules on final payment, especially including the 4-301(a) midnight deadline with respect to returns. With a couple of tiny exceptions, nothing in Regulation CC overrides or contradicts final payment and accountability defined in terms of Article 4. Complying with CC does not change the consequences of not complying with Article 4. On the other hand, the consequences of failing to comply with CC are not defined in terms Article 4. The consequences are not final payment or accountability. Regulation CC defines the consequences differently in its own terms. Basically, the penalty for not expeditiously returning a check is negligence liability and damages proximately caused, not exceeding the amount of the item. 12 CFR 229.38.

If PB timely returns the item pursuant to 4-301(a), which amounts to dishonor of the check for Article 3 purposes (see 3-502(b)(1)), DB Bank can charge it back against Seller's account, 4-212(b), because the credit DB gave Seller, on the basis of Buyer's check, was provisional. 4-201(a). Federal law does not deny that this credit is provisional and confirms the depositary bank's right of charge back against its customer. 12 CFR 229.32(b) Commentary. DB will effect this charge back by debiting Seller's account, notifying Seller of the dishonor, and, usually, by returning the check itself to Seller. Seller then can sue Buyer on the check, or on the underlying obligation Buyer owes Seller.

If PB retains the check beyond the midnight deadline of 4-301(a), PB cannot rightfully return the check to DB. The check is finally paid, 4-215(a)(3), and the settlement that DB received upon presentment becomes final. 4-215(c). For this reason, the credit DB gave Seller also becomes final and DB is itself accountable to its customer for the amount of the item. 4-215(d). Finally, because of PB's final payment, DB loses the right to charge back the item against Seller's account in the event that PB, notwithstanding final payment and acting without right, bounces the check to DB. 4-214(a) (last sentence). If PB takes this unlawful action and DB charges back the check against Seller's account, Seller can recover from either DB or PB. DB can recover over from PB for breach of a warranty that PB made in returning the item that the return was timely and proper under the UCC. 12 CFR 229.34(a).

Seller cannot recover from Buyer. PB's final payment means that Buyer is discharged on the check under 3-602(a). Pause just a minute, and see how 3-602 works here. It conditions a person's discharge on her -- or someone acting for her -- paying a person entitled to enforce the instrument, such as a holder. In this case, PB acts for Buyer. Payment by PB Bank was equivalent to payment by Buyer herself.

The person who was paid, DB Bank, was a holder derivatively and in its own right. First, DB Bank was acting for Seller who, as the payee, was a holder of the check. Second, DB Bank was a holder itself. DB was in possession of the instrument, and the instrument was almost certainly indorsed to it. Seller probably indorsed the check when she transferred it to DB Bank. Even if Seller failed to indorse personally, DB Bank became a holder at the time it received the item for collection if the customer at the time of delivery was a holder of the item, whether or not the customer indorses the item. 4-205(1).

If this case is typical, the check will be finally paid by the passage of the midnight deadline without any return, rightful or wrongful. By the same rules, Buyer is discharged on the check. In any event, payment of the check also discharges Buyer on the underlying obligation for the price of the goods. 3-310(b)(1).

3. Collection Through Clearinghouses

Suppose that DB and PB are not the only banks in town. Bilateral, direct presentment between each set of banks would be possible but very cumbersome and inefficient. Commonly, therefore, banks grouped in a city or larger region will agree among themselves to a multilateral collection process, known as a *clearinghouse,* for the principal purpose of collecting checks they receive that are drawn on one another. Article 4 splits the word in two, *clearing house,* and defines it sparingly as "an association of banks or other payors regularly clearing items." 4-104(a)(4). (The word "*clear*" or "*clearing*" is a non-technical, bankers' term referring essentially to the process of getting final payment of a check by a payor bank.) A somewhat fuller definition is "any arrangement by which three or more participants exchange checks on a local basis, including an entire metropolitan area. * * * [It] may include arrangements using the premises of a Federal Reserve Bank, but it does not include the handling of checks for forward collection or return by a Federal Reserve Bank." 12 CFR 229.2(l).

In simple terms, a clearinghouse operates in this manner: "[B]anks present checks to a central point -- a separate facility or a back office room of one of the banks in the arrangement. There, checks are physically exchanged among participants, and collection is made by crediting the amounts presented by each bank against one another. Today, settlement for the transactions of the nation's major clearinghouses is made against accounts that participating banks maintain at the Federal Reserve banks." D. Friedman, DEPOSIT OPERATIONS 73 (1982). (Sometimes the "central point" where checks are exchanged among members of the clearinghouse is the local Fed Bank or a branch of it.)

Assuming DB and PB are members of a clearinghouse, DB Bank (the depositary-collecting bank which took the check for collection from Seller) will forward the item to the clearinghouse rather than to PB Bank directly. Presentment of the check on PB occurs through the clearinghouse, and the clearinghouse rules will provide for crediting DB and debiting PB for the item when the clearinghouse receives it. This settlement for the item between the banks will occur through the clearinghouse as part of its process for computing the daily net settlements among all the banks belonging to the clearinghouse. PB will then acquire the item from the clearinghouse and put the item through PB's own internal process that decides whether or not to pay it.

PB Bank can return the item before its midnight deadline if it decides not to pay the item. The return may be through the clearinghouse or directly to DB. Again, by federal law, DB is required to pay for the return. Be aware, however, that clearinghouse rules are usually very elaborate and detailed, and often prescribe procedures and time limits different from Article 4's provisions. Such variations from Article 4, whether agreed to by banks acting bilaterally or collectively through a clearinghouse arrangement, are expressly permitted, 4-103, except that no agreement can "disclaim a bank's responsibility for its lack of good faith or failure to exercise ordinary care or limit the measure of damages for the lack or failure." 4-103(a). Not uncommonly, clearinghouse rules reduce the period during which a payor can return an item. The result is to shorten the Article 4 "midnight deadline." The consequence of a payor bank failing to meet the earlier time limit is final payment of the affected item under 4-215(a)(3).

4. Long-Distance Collection Through Federal Reserve Banks

Suppose that DB and PB are located in distant cities. DB could collect Buyer's check for Seller by sending the item directly to PB. 4-204(b)(1). Rarely, however, do banks so situated engage in direct presentment of items between themselves. The reasons that oppose direct presentment among banks grouped locally argue even more strongly against following that bilateral process on a nationwide basis. A typical bank, even in a small city, daily receives checks drawn on scores of different banks spread throughout the country. Just imagine the time and expense that would be involved in directly dealing with each payor bank every banking day. The problem of long-distance check collection is principally answered by the Federal Reserve whose twelve banks, bank branches and regional service centers spread throughout the country operate collectively as a kind of a national clearinghouse.

Assume that Seller and DB Bank are located in Atlanta, Georgia. Buyer and PB Bank are located in Minneapolis, Minnesota. Upon receiving the check from Seller for collection, DB Bank will not send the item to PB Bank. Rather, DB will transfer it to the Federal Reserve Bank in Atlanta, where DB maintains a reserve account. Upon receiving the check, the Atlanta Fed will credit DB's account for the amount of the item. In so doing the Atlanta Fed is settling for the item. The Atlanta Fed will forward the item to the Federal Reserve Bank of Minneapolis.

Of course, Buyer's check will not travel alone on the trip to Minneapolis. On the day the Atlanta Fed receives the item, the Bank also receives jillions of other checks from banks throughout the multi-state Sixth District of the Federal Reserve System, which is the area served by the Atlanta Fed. The Bank then sorts these items according to the Federal Reserve Districts in which the payor banks are located. All of the checks drawn on banks in the Ninth Federal Reserve District, which is served by the Minneapolis Fed, are physically sent there all together in very weighty bundles.

When the Minneapolis Fed receives these bundles, the Atlanta Fed will be entitled to a credit for the total amount of the items. Of course, the Atlanta Fed will similarly have received bundles from the Minneapolis Fed and an offsetting credit will be in order. Accounting for these crisscrossing credits is accomplished electronically through the *Interdistrict Settlement Fund* in Washington, D.C., which in simple terms is a funds switching mechanism for Federal Reserve Banks. The Fund makes net settlements between Reserve Banks daily.

The Minneapolis Fed will sort the bundles of items from Atlanta according to the payor banks on which the items are drawn. The total of the items for each payor bank is then debited to the bank's account at the Minneapolis Fed (or to the account of a correspondent through which the payor bank indirectly participates in the Federal Reserve collection system). This debit is a provisional settlement, which federal law requires by close of the payor bank's banking day. 12 CFR 210.9(a)(1). The checks are thereafter sent to the payor bank. (In the case of a correspondent relationship, checks may be sent to the correspondent bank which will then forward the items to the respondent-payor bank.) In this way PB Bank will eventually receive, and be charged with, Buyer's check.

At every point along the collection route the checks are proofed and sorted by machines that read the information encoded on the items in the little numbers that appear on standard form checks. These numbers are the *MICR* numbers, meaning Magnetic Ink Character Recognition. They identify:

- the federal reserve district and state in which the payor bank is located and the federal reserve office or a special collection arrangement;
- the payor bank itself;
- the account number against which the check is drawn;
- the check number; and
- the dollar amount of the check encoded by the payee or depositary bank.

In the present example, the Atlanta and Minneapolis Federal Reserve Banks are acting as *collecting banks,* as is DB Bank. Unlike DB, however, the two Reserve Banks are not depositary banks. Only DB is a depositary bank. Here, as in all the other examples, PB Bank is the payor bank. In this example, the Federal Reserve Banks are in between the depositary and payor banks and thus, in addition to being a collecting bank, each of them is known as an *intermediary bank,* which means "a bank to which an item is transferred in course of collection except the depositary or payor bank." 4-105(4).

Upon PB receiving the check from the Minneapolis Fed, which is also the "presenting bank," the "midnight deadline" clock begins to tick with respect to the item. As usual, PB can return the check before the midnight deadline if it decides not to pay the item. This right of return is recognized in 4-301(a), which repeatedly has been discussed in connection with the other collection models. The right is confirmed in this case by Federal Reserve Regulation J. See 12 CFR 210.12(a). (Regulation J applies because the check was received through a Reserve Bank.)

Article 4 would require PB to return the check to PB's transferor, 4-301(d), which would be the Minneapolis Fed. On this detail, however, federal law Regulation CC overrides. It allows a payor bank to "send a returned check to the depositary bank, or to any other bank agreeing to handle the returned check expeditiously * * *." 12 CFR 229.30(a)(2). The aim is to speed up the return process by allowing the payor bank to use any expeditious route for returning a dishonored check. Whether PB returns the check directly to the depositary bank, DB, or indirectly through another bank (i.e., a "returning bank"), the bank to which PB sends the item must pay PB for it. A returning bank gets paid by the bank to which it sends the item, whether another returning bank or the depositary bank. If the check is for $2500 or more, PB is required by Regulation CC to notify DB directly that the check is being returned unpaid, whether or not PB returned the check itself directly to DB. 12 CFR 229.33.

If PB returns the item to the Minneapolis Fed, this bank will send the item back to Georgia, probably to the Atlanta Fed. The Atlanta Fed will return it to DB which will send it to Seller. In the wake of the check on its return trip is a series of debits and credits, with each bank that returns getting paid by the bank to which the item is sent. In the end, DB Bank charges back the check against Seller's account and sends the item to her. See 4-214(a). Seller, of course, is left with actions against Buyer on the check itself and on the underlying obligation. Dishonor of the check by PB Bank triggered the Buyer's secondary liability thereon as drawer of the instrument, and also resurrected the Buyer's liability for the price of the goods under Article 2. The same charge back and liabilities would result if PB returned the check directly to DB or through some other indirect route other than the Federal Reserve Banks.

If PB retains the check beyond its midnight deadline, the right of return is lost, and final payment occurs under state law, see 4-215(a)(3), with all the consequences -- already discussed -- that ordinarily flow from final payment of a check.

B. FORWARD COLLECTION PROCESS

1. Depositary Bank Giving Customer Credit

A person who wants to "collect" a check will take it to her bank and ask for cash or credit to her account. The depositary bank is not legally obliged to give cash for the item immediately; and, if the bank credits the customer's account for the item, the bank is not legally required to allow withdrawal of the credit (i.e., make the funds available) immediately. The check may be dishonored. Moreover, a credit to the account is provisional only and can be revoked in case of dishonor. Unless the bank is also the payor bank, even a cash settlement for the check is provisional. The customer must repay the cash settlement if the check is dishonored, and the bank can charge the amount of the settlement against the customer account as a means of self-help recoupment. If the depositary bank is also the payor bank, a cash settlement is final payment that ordinarily cannot be recovered.

Federal law dictates how soon funds must be made available for a check that a customer deposits for credit with her bank. It largely depends on the nature of the check and whether the check is local or nonlocal. This law is discussed in Chapter X infra. In any event, the federal funds availability law does not affect the depositary bank's right to revoke provisional settlements; but the law does affect the bank's ability to enforce this right. If funds must be made available for a check before it is returned or the depositary bank otherwise learns of dishonor, the account may be emptied before the bank is even aware of the need to charge back the check and thereby revoke the settlement given the customer. The customer will remain personally liable to the depositary bank for the amount of the settlement, but collecting the debt as an ordinary unsecured creditor is much more difficult than doing so by setting off against the account, which would have been possible had the funds not been paid out of the account. Thus, it is important to depositary banks that checks move quickly during forward collection and also during their return to the depositary bank in the event of dishonor by payor banks.

2. Collecting Banks' Indorsements

Every bank (other than the paying bank) that handles a check during forward collection must add a standardized, legible indorsement, including the depositary bank and intermediary banks. 12 CFR 229.35(a) Appendix D.1. & 2. The purpose is the protection of depositary banks. A full and clear indorsement reduces the time necessary to return a check that has been dishonored by the payor bank. The faster a check is returned, the smaller is the risk that the depositary bank will make funds available for the check in ignorance of the dishonor. Among other information, each indorsement must include the bank's nine-digit routing number and the indorsement date. The depositary bank's indorsement must be placed on the back of the check so that the routing number is wholly contained in the area 3.0 inches from the leading edge of the check to 1.5 inches from the trailing edge of the check. Id. Appendix D.1. The leading edge is defined as the right side of the check looking at it from the front. The trailing edge is defined as the left side of the check looking at it from the front. An intermediary bank must indorse in the area on the back of the check from 0 inches to 3.0 inches from the leading edge of the check. 12 CFR part 229 Appendix D.2. Properly indorsing is most significant for the depositary bank. Failure to follow the indorsement standard may increase the risk of unrecoverable loss to the depositary bank. Paying and returning banks may be relieved of the duty of expeditious return, and thus of liability for delay in return, if the delay is due to a nonstandard indorsement. 12 CFR 229.30(b); 12 CFR 229.38(c) Commentary.

3.   Responsibilities Of Collecting Banks
a.   The Role Of Collecting Banks

Any bank handling a check or other item for collection, except the payor bank, is a *collecting bank*. 4-105(5). This term includes the *depositary bank* (4-105(2)) and any *intermediary bank* (4-105(4)), but not the payor bank. The collecting bank that actually presents the check to the payor bank for payment is also known as the *presenting bank* (4-105(6)). None of these collecting banks pays a check that it takes for collection. Only a payor bank, the drawee, which is not a collecting bank, pays a check. The role of a collecting bank is rather to assist the owner of the check in getting payment from the payor bank by forwarding the item for presentment for payment and, if the item is dishonored, to assist in returning it to the owner if the item is returned through the collecting bank.

b.   The Agency Status Of Collecting Banks
1)   Under Article 4

In their role of helping the owner of a check get payment from the payor bank, collecting banks ordinarily serve as agents of the owner. Actually, the depositary bank is the agent, and intermediary banks are sub-agents. 4-201(a); 12 CFR 229.36(d) Commentary. Article 4 reasons that this agency status continues until final payment is made by the payor bank. At this point, each collecting bank becomes a debtor of its transferor and a creditor of its transferee. The explanation is that the settlements each bank gave its transferor in the collection process are initially provisional and become final -- they "firm up" -- when the payor bank finally pays the items. 4-215(c-d). "Thus the collection is completed, all agency aspects are terminated and the identity of the item has become completely merged in bank accounts, that of

the customer with the depositary bank and that of one bank with another."
4-201 comment 4.

2   Effect of Regulation CC

Regulation CC affects the form of this analysis by declaring, as a matter of
preemptive federal law, that settlements between collecting banks for the
forward collection of checks are final when made, not provisional. 12 CFR
229.36(d). This declaration, however, does not necessarily abolish the
agency status of collecting banks in the forward-collection process; and in
any event does not immunize collecting banks from liability for negligently
handling forward-collection items. Regulation CC expressly provides that "a
collecting bank handling a check for forward collection may be liable to a
prior collecting bank, including the depositary bank, and the depositary
bank's customer," and thereby "preserves the liability of a collecting bank
* * * for negligence during the forward collection of a check under the
U.C.C., even though * * * settlement between banks during forward
collection is 'final' rather than 'provisional.'" Id. Commentary.

c. Duties and Standard of Care

Because collecting banks are agents or subagents of the owner of the item, the
banks are responsible to her for their collection conduct. In general, they owe
the owner a duty of good faith, 1-203, and they must also act reasonably,
according to a standard of ordinary care, in carrying out tasks with respect to
both forward-collection and return of items. 4-202(a). For example, a collecting
bank must exercise ordinary care in

- presenting an item or sending it for presentment;
- sending notice of dishonor or nonpayment or returning an item after learning
  that the item has not been paid;
- settling for an item when the bank receives final settlement; and
- notifying its transferor of any loss or delay in transit within a reasonable time
  after discovery thereof.

Id. Specifically, with respect to sending items, "[a] collecting bank shall send
items by reasonably prompt method taking into consideration any relevant
instructions, the nature of the item, the number of those items on hand, the cost
of collection involved and the method generally used by it or others to present
those items." 4-204(a). With respect to the timing of its actions, the general rule
is that a collecting bank acts seasonably if it takes proper action before its
midnight deadline following receipt of an item, notice, or settlement. 4-202(b).

d. Measure of Damages

A collecting bank that acts unreasonably in its collection tasks is NOT strictly accountable for the amount of an item as is a payor bank upon failure to settle or return it by the midnight deadline. Rather, a collecting bank's liability for negligence in mishandling an item for collection is measured by "the amount of the item *reduced by* an amount that could not have been realized by the exercise of ordinary care * * *." 4-103(e) (emphasis added). Consequential damages are recoverable only where there is bad faith. Id.

Example: B paid by check for goods purchased from S. The check was drawn on PB Bank where B maintained her checking account. S deposited the check in her account with DB Bank. For unexplained reasons, DB Bank sat on the check for a week before finally sending it for presentment. Because DB and PB were located far apart, the normal collection process called for the check to pass through two intermediary banks on its way to PB Bank. The check was eventually received by PB Bank eight banking days after S deposited it with DB Bank. PB Bank dishonored the check because B's account contained insufficient funds to cover it. DB is liable, prima facie, to S for mishandling the item. Ordinary care required DB to act before its midnight deadline in sending the check on its way to PB Bank. Yet, DB Bank can avoid having to pay damages, i.e., the amount of the item, if it can show that the check would not have been paid even if DB Bank had exercised ordinary care. So, for example, DB will avoid damages by proving that B's account was empty at the time when the check would have been presented for payment had DB acted seasonably in sending the item for payment.

e. No Vicarious Liability

Each intermediary bank involved in the collection process owes a duty of reasonable care to the owner just as does the initial collecting bank, i.e., the depositary bank. Thus, the owner can recover the amount of the item directly from an intermediary bank that negligently mishandles it, subject to usual offset for the amount which would have been in any event uncollectible. 4-103(e). The owner cannot, however, recover from the depositary bank, or another collecting bank prior to the negligent party in the collection chain, on the theory that the prior bank is vicariously liable for the sins of all later collecting banks. Each collecting bank is liable only for its own negligence and not for the default of any other bank. 4-202(c). A collecting bank remains responsible, however, "for using ordinary care in selecting properly qualified intermediary banks and agents and in giving proper instructions to them." 4-202 comment 4.

Example: B paid by check for goods purchased from S. The check was drawn on PB Bank where B maintained her checking account. S deposited the check in her account with DB Bank. The same day DB forwarded the check to IB Bank, an intermediary bank, in route to PB Bank. IB Bank unreasonably held the check for more than a week and finally presented it to PB for payment. PB dishonored the item. If IB had acted seasonably in making presentment, the check would have been paid. IB Bank is liable to S. DB is not liable to S for IB's negligence even though DB selected IB as an intermediary, unless DB's selection of IB was, in itself, unreasonable.

f. No More Special Treatment of Reserve Banks

Federal Regulation J applies when an item is collected through a Federal Reserve Bank. 12 CFR 210. This regulation formerly provided that a Reserve Bank is an agent only of the sender of an item. The meaning of the term "sender" was limited to banks and clearing agencies, which meant that federal law immunized a Reserve Bank from liability to the owner of an item if the Bank acted negligently in handling the item. This rule has changed. Regulation J now provides in language like Article 4 that "[a] Reserve Bank shall act * * * as agent or subagent of the owner with respect to an item," 12 CFR 210.6(a)(1), and that "[a] Reserve Bank may be liable to the owner, to the sender, to a prior collecting bank, or to the depositary bank's customer with respect to a check * * * for the Reserve Bank's own lack of good faith or failure to exercise ordinary care * * *." Id.

Example: Same facts as in the immediately preceding example, except that IB Bank is the Minneapolis Federal Reserve Bank. Under former law, the Minneapolis Fed would not have been liable to S. Moreover, DB Bank is not vicariously liable for the negligence of the Minneapolis Fed, 4-202(c), and presumably was not itself negligent in selecting the Minneapolis Fed as an intermediary bank. Thus, S would be stuck with the loss. Now, however, the Minneapolis Fed is accountable for its negligence to S.

4. Settlements

a. Under Article 4

As a check is deposited and moves from bank to bank in the collection process, everybody usually gets an almost immediate credit or settlement for the item. Article 4 provides that these settlements in the forward collection process generally are provisional -- between the depositor and depositary bank and also between banks involved in the collection process. 4-201(a), 4-214(a)&(c) & 4-301. They become final upon final payment by the payor bank. If the payor bank dishonors the item instead of paying it, the item is returned by the same path that took it to the payor bank. Each transferee in the return process takes back (revokes) the provisional credit the transferee gave for the item. It is by this revocation of settlements that a bank returning a check gets paid for the return.

b. By Federal Law

Overriding federal law declares that settlements between banks for the forward collection of a check are final when made. 12 CFR 229.36(d). Yet, "[s]ettlement by a paying bank is not considered to be final payment for the purposes of [Article 4], because a paying bank has the right to recover settlement from a returning or depositary bank to which it returns a check under this subpart [C of Regulation CC]." Id. Commentary. Correspondingly, a returning bank can recover from the bank to which it returns the item, and the depositary bank can recover from the depositor. More is said later on this right of recovery. The immediate point is that making recovery independent and unrelated to forward-collection settlements eliminates any reason for these settlements to be provisional.

5. Presentment
a. Place Of Presentment

Regulation CC lists the locations at which a paying bank must accept presentment of checks:

- At a location to which delivery is requested by the paying bank;
- At an address of the bank associated with the routing number on the check, whether in magnetic ink or in fractional form;
- At a branch, head office, or other location consistent with the name and address of the bank on the check if the bank is identified on the check by name and address; or
- At any branch or head office if the bank is identified on the check by name without address.

12 CFR 229.36(b) & Commentary.

b. Truncation

A major cost in check collection, both in time and money, is the cost of forwarding the paper between banks and between the payor and its customer. Check truncation, which is sometimes called check safekeeping, reduces this cost, which explains why the trend in check collection is truncation. Generally, the payee, the depositary bank, or another bank -- known as the "keeper" -- retains the checks themselves and electronically forwards only the information or images of the checks. The payor is presented with electronic notices instead of paper items. The drawers receive reports of items charged to their account but do not receive the items themselves unless a special request is made. Even then the customer may receive only a copy of image of the check. For many years a similar system has worked well for credit cards.

1) Tpes of Truncation

There are three major forms of truncation:

- *Payor Bank Truncation*. The impetus for having truncation occur at the payor bank is basically savings in postage arising from not including the items in the envelope with the periodic statement. Many business entities reconcile with check numbers and corresponding amounts, calling for actual checks only if discrepancies are found. Individuals can do the same quite readily where the payor bank's computerized system places the serial number of the paid check and its amount on the periodic statement in serial number order, signaling gaps in serial numbers in some appropriate way.

- *Intercept Truncation*. Here the paper item is held by an intermediary bank and the entire MICR line is then forwarded directly or through others to the ultimate payor. A typical example is found in the handling of credit union share drafts by the payable through bank designated thereon. The bank's reader-sorters take off the entire MICR line and forward to the paying credit union the drawer's account number, the serial number of the item and the dollar amounts. The intermediary bank retains the item and provides necessary retrieval of original items, or after their destruction of the microfilm copies. Here also retrieval must be accomplished if the payor institution wires nonpayment as to a particular item, as a paper return item channel will be followed.

- *First Bank Truncation*. Here the paper stops at the first bank in the chain of collection having truncating capabilities, hopefully a depositary bank. Naturally, the forwarding process must include an audit trail designation so that subsequent banks can effect a return for credit of the unpaid items. Storage and retrieval will be as in the case of the intermediary banks.

Leary, *Adapting the Substantive Law to Check Safe-Keeping (Truncation) in Paper and Electronic Payments Litigation* 321-22 (ALI-ABA 1983). It is even possible that a business that receives lots of checks could serve as the keeper of checks. It would electronically capture the information from the checks and "deposit" or present them by forwarding the electronic data through its bank or directly to the payor banks.

2) Truncation and the Law
  a) Agreements Allowed
      Truncation is governed less by law than by contract, principally
      including agreements governing retention and other aspects of electronic
      presentment. U.C.C. Article 4 sanctions such agreements, 4-103, and
      defines an "agreement for electronic presentment" to mean "an
      agreement, clearing-house rule, or Federal Reserve regulation or
      operating circular, providing that presentment of an item may be made
      by transmission of an image of an item or information describing the
      item ('presentment notice') rather than delivery of the item itself."
      4-110(a). Regulation CC warns that "[a] truncation agreement may not
      extend return times or otherwise vary the requirements of [Regulation
      CC] with respect to parties interested in the check that are not party to
      the agreement." 12 CFR 229.36(c).

  b) Article 3 Sanctions Electronic Presentment
      Article 3 accommodates truncation by allowing presentment by
      "electronic communication" where it is commercially reasonable.
      3-501(b)(1). Regulation CC adds that "[a] bank may present a check to
      a paying bank by transmission of information describing the check in
      accordance with an agreement with the paying bank." 12 CFR
      229.36(c). "Presentment of an item pursuant to an agreement for
      presentment is made when the presentment notice is received."
      4-110(b). "If presentment is made by presentment notice, a reference to
      'item' or 'check' in this Article means the presentment notice unless the
      context otherwise indicates." 4-110(c).

  c) Retention and Encoding Warranties
      Two warranties apply when truncation occurs.

      ◆ First, the keeper warrants to subsequent collecting banks and payors
        that its retention and presentment of the checks comply with the
        keeper's truncation agreements. 4-209(b).
      ◆ Second, any person who encodes information with respect to the
        checks "warrants to any subsequent collecting bank and to the payor
        bank or other payor that the information is correctly encoded."

      4-209(a). The encoding warranty applies, too, even in the absence of
      truncation. In the traditional collection process which moves the checks
      themselves, the depositary bank usually will encode on every check the
      amount of the item. This encoding enables electronic processing.
      Sometimes, encoding and retention, too, are done by customers who are

payees of a large volume of checks. Whoever encodes information on a check, whether the depositary bank or its customer, warrants the accuracy of the encoding. Id.

3) Regulation CC Endorses Truncation
Regulation CC endorses truncation by agreement in providing that a bank may present a check to a paying bank by transmission of information describing the check in accordance with an agreement with the paying bank. 12 CFR 229.36(c). The check is presented when the transmission is received by the paying bank. Id. Commentary. A truncation agreement may not, however, extend return times or otherwise vary the requirements of Regulation CC as they affect parties interested in the check who are not party to the agreement. 12 CFR 229.36(c).

C. MAIN DUTIES OF THE PAYOR BANK IN THE RETURN PROCESS

Article 4 deals thoroughly with the forward-collection process -- getting the check from the depositary bank to the payor bank and presenting it for payment. The statute says less about the return process -- getting a dishonored check from the payor to the depositary bank and, ultimately, to the depositor. Together, Articles 3 and 4 define dishonor of a check in terms of the payor bank seasonably returning a dishonored check in order to avoid accountability for the item or finally paying it. These state statutes are very sketchy, however, on the details and duties of this return process, especially after the item leaves the payor banks. Federal law fills the gaps, principally with Regulation CC which requires and explains "expeditious return" of dishonored checks. Regulation CC also requires special, quick notice when a large-dollar item is dishonored.

This combination of Articles 3 and 4 and Regulation CC produces three main responsibilities of payor banks with respect to the return of checks for nonpayment: pay or dishonor by returning by the Article 4 midnight deadline; return expeditiously; and quickly notify the depositary bank when a large-dollar item is dishonored. The main rights and duties of returning and depositary banks with respect to returned checks are separately discussed later in this chapter.

1. **Article 4 Return -- Mainly, The *Midnight Deadline* Rule(s)**
    a. **The Requirement That The Payor Bank Return A Check To Avoid Having To Account For The Item -- Avoiding Accountability Under 4-302**
        A payor bank cannot indefinitely retain a check that has been presented for payment. The check usually belongs to the depositor who expects payment, and federal law will require the depositary bank to make funds available for the

check in fairly short order unless the check is sooner dishonored. 12 USCA 4001-4010. By rule of Article 4 -- 4-302 -- the payor bank becomes accountable for the item -- liable for it -- unless it returns the check by the **midnight deadline** with respect to the item -- **midnight of the next banking day following the banking day on which the item is received**, 4-301(a)(1); and a payor bank that is not the depositary bank can retain the item this long only if the bank settles for the item -- gives credit for it -- by midnight of the banking day of receipt. Id. If the item is presented through a Federal Reserve Bank, accountability results at the end of the banking day unless the payor bank settles by then. 12 CFR 210.9(a). In practice, a payor bank almost always settles for an item on the day the item is received and often immediately, even when the payor bank is also the depositary bank. Accountability under 4-302 is thus avoided. Settlement is an accounting. Until the midnight deadline, however, this settlement can be recovered by a return that is timely under 4-301 and in compliance with other provisions of state law and federal Regulation CC. Failure to make such a timely return results in the settlement becoming final -- final payment occurs. The settlement cannot be recovered lawfully. Unlawfully recovering the settlement result in liability for converting the funds.

b. Overview And Importance Of Return Under 4-301 To Recover Settlement

   1) **Payor Bank Is Also The Depositary Bank -- "On Us" Items**
   When a payor bank receives an item that is presented for payment, quick action is necessary to dishonor the item. If the payor bank is also the depositary bank, it must return the item (which is called an "on us" item) or send notice of dishonor before its midnight deadline, which is midnight of the next banking day following the banking day of receipt. Delaying beyond this deadline makes the bank accountable for the item whether or not the item actually is returned. 4-302(a)(1). In practice, a payor bank almost always "accounts" for an "on us" item at the time the bank receives it, usually by giving the customer a credit to her account. This accounting is a settlement. A payor bank that settles for an "on us" item by such a credit on its books can recover the settlement by returning the item by the bank's midnight deadline. See 4-301(a)&(b). Failing to comply with 4-301 means that the settlement becomes final -- final payment occurs -- and cannot be recovered. If the payor bank accounts for the item by paying in cash rather than by crediting the customer's account, the settlement is final when made -- final payment occurred -- and usually cannot be recovered.

   2) **Payor Bank Is NOT The Depositary Bank**
   If the payor bank is not the depositary bank, even quicker action is necessary. The bank becomes accountable for the item at midnight of the

banking day of receipt unless the bank by this time either returns the item or settles for it. 4-302(a)(1). In the case of an item a payor bank receives directly or indirectly from a Federal Reserve Bank, the payor bank becomes accountable for the check at the close of the banking day on which it received the item unless the bank settles for the item by then. 12 CFR 210.9(a). Practically always, the payor bank settles for an item that is presented for payment as soon as the bank receives the item, usually by crediting an account of the presenting bank. The bank thereby avoids 4-302 accountability. Despite this settlement, the bank can dishonor the item and recover the amount of settlement by returning the check before the bank's midnight deadline in compliance with 4-301. The same is true with respect to items presented through a Federal Reserve Bank. 12 CFR 210.12(a). Complying with 4-301 is the only way to dishonor the item and is the essential trigger to any lawful recovery of the bank's settlement. Failing to comply with 4-301 means that the settlement is final -- final payment has occurred. This payment usually cannot be recovered.

c. When To Return

1) General Rule -- "Midnight Deadline" But Not Beyond Final Payment

To comply with 4-301 and thereby win the right to recover a settlement given for an item, the payor bank must return the item before the bank has made final payment and before its *midnight deadline*. 4-301(a). The outside time limit is the *midnight deadline*, meaning midnight of the bank's next banking day following the banking day on which the bank received the item. The right to return and recover for the return can be sooner lost, however, by final payment before this deadline. Final payment by the payor cuts off the right to return a check and to recover for it even though the midnight deadline has not expired. Failing to return by the midnight deadline is itself a means of final payment and is the usual means a check is finally paid, but final payment can otherwise and sooner occur. Final payment is defined by 4-215(a) and is separately discussed later in this chapter.

2) Exceptions

a) Extension for Expedited Delivery

The 4-301 midnight deadline "is extended if a paying bank, in an effort to expedite delivery of a returned check to a bank, uses a means of delivery that would ordinarily result in the returned check being received by the bank to which it is sent on or before the receiving bank's next banking day following the otherwise applicable deadline. The deadline is extended further if a paying bank uses a highly expeditious means of transportation, even if this means of transportation would ordinarily result in delivery after the receiving bank's next banking day * * *." 12 CFR 229.30(c).

> *Example:* "A paying bank may have a courier that leaves after midnight to deliver its forward collection checks. This paragraph removes the constraint of the midnight deadline for returned checks if the returned check reaches either the depositary bank or the returning bank to which it is sent on that bank's banking day following the expiration of the midnight deadline or other applicable time for return. The extension also applies if the check reaches the bank to which it is sent later than the close of that bank's banking day, if highly expeditious means of transportation are used. For example, a West Coast paying bank may use this further extension to ship a returned check by air courier directly to an East Coast depositary bank even if the check arrives after the close of the depositary bank's banking day." Id. Commentary.

b) **Excuse for Delay**
Failing to meet the 4-301 midnight deadline is sometimes excused by law, and in such a case there is no final payment under 4-215(a)(3). Such an excuse is provided by Article 4, which provides:

> Delay by a * * * payor bank beyond time limits prescribed or permitted by this Act or by instructions is excused if (i) the delay is caused by interruption of communication or computer facilities, suspension of payments by another bank, war, emergency conditions, failure of equipment, or other circumstances beyond the control of the bank , and (ii) the bank exercises such diligence as the circumstances require.

4-109(b). This excuse is not limited to situations where the payor bank's right to revoke a settlement is governed by 4-301(a). Rather, 4-109(b) "operates not only with respect to time limits imposed by the Article itself but also time limits imposed by special instructions, by agreement or by Federal Reserve regulations or operating circulars, clearing-house rules or the like. The latter time limits are 'permitted' by the Code." 4-109 comment 3.

c) **Agreement That Shortens Deadline**
The 4-301 right to return can be varied by agreement (e.g., a clearinghouse arrangement) or preempted by federal law. In this event,

the limits of the payor bank's right to revoke, including the time and manner of exercising the right, are set by the agreement or law that overrides 4-301. If the time limit for return is sooner than the midnight deadline, failing to meet this earlier limit is final payment, 4-215(a)(3), and cuts off the 4-301 right of return even if the midnight deadline has not expired.

Example: "It is very common for clearing house rules to provide that items exchanged and settled for in a clearing, (e.g., before 10:00 a.m. on Monday) may be returned and the settlements revoked up to but not later than 2:00 p.m. on the same day (Monday) or under deferred posting at some hour on the next business day (e.g., 2:00 p.m. Tuesday). Under this type of rule the Monday morning settlement [can be recovered but only in line with law and the clearing house rules] * * *." 4-215 comment 4. "[I]f the time limit for the return of items received in the Monday morning clearing is 2:00 p.m. on Tuesday and the provisional settlement has not been revoked at that time in a manner permitted by the clearing house rules, the * * * settlement made on Monday morning becomes final at 2:00 p.m. on Tuesday." Id. comment 7. The item cannot be returned or the settlement recovered. This is true even though, under 4-301(a), the right to return extended until midnight on Tuesday because the clearinghouse rules, as a form of agreement among the parties, override 4-301(a).

Example: Buyer pays by check for goods purchased from Seller, a local merchant. The check is drawn on PB Bank, which is Buyer's bank where she maintains her checking account. Seller deposits the check in her account at DB, another local bank, or she cashes the item there. PB and DB are members of the Metropolitan Clearinghouse Association (MCA), along with most of the other local banks. The same banking day, DB transferred the check to the MCA, which provisionally credited DB with the amount of the check. PB picked up the check and decided, the next banking day, to dishonor it because Buyer's account is empty. The time is 9:00 p.m. MCA rules prohibit returns by payor banks after 2:00 p.m. on the banking day following the banking day on which items are received. Under Article 4, however, returns are permitted until midnight of the day after receipt.

4-301(a). PB *cannot* properly return the item. The MCA
rule overrides Article 4 in this case. Moreover, the
consequence of PB retaining the item beyond the MCA time
limit for returns is final payment of Buyer's check,
4-215(a)(3), with all of the consequences of final payment
already mentioned. For example, the provisional credit to
DB becomes firm or final, and the provisional settlement
between DB and seller also becomes final.

3) **When a Payor Bank Receives an Item So as to Start Running the
Midnight Deadline or Other Time Limit on the Right to Revoke**
Whether the time limit on the right to trigger the midnight deadline of
4-301(a) or some other time set by an overriding agreement or other law,
there is always the issue as to when the payor bank received an item so as to
start the applicable time period running

a) **Cutoff Hour**
For accounting purposes, banks commonly establish a "cutoff" hour so
that final figures can be computed, during normal working hours, to
establish the bank's position for the day. Items received after this time
are deemed received on the next banking day. Article 4 approves a
cutoff hour of this type provided it is not earlier than 2:00 p.m.,
4-108(a), and provides that "[a]n item or deposit of money received on
any day after a cutoff hour so fixed or after the close of the banking day
may be treated as being received at the opening of the next banking
day." 4-108(b). It is not clear that this treatment applies in determining
when a payor bank receives an item for purposes of 4-301(a) or any
other right to revoke settlements. The express terms of 4-108(a) approve
a cutoff only "[f]or the purpose of allowing time to process items, prove
balances, and make the necessary entries on its books to determine its
position for the day * * *." Probably, however, the language "time to
process items" is sufficiently broad, in spirit if not in letter, so that it
should include marking the time for settlement revocation rights among
the purposes for which a cutoff hour is properly used. Cf. 12 CFR
210.9(a) n.2 (A paying bank is deemed to receive a cash item on its next
banking day if the bank receives the item after a cutoff hour established
by it in accordance with state law.).

b) **Data Processing Facilities**
Commonly, checks are presented to and received by payor banks at data
processing centers that are separate facilitates from the banks. In this
case, does the time limit for returns begin to run when the center

receives the item or when the item is actually transferred to the payor bank itself? There is conflicting authority, but the majority of courts facing this question have held that the item is received, for purposes the midnight deadline, when the data processing center receives the item. This holding applies whether the center is part of the payor bank or is an independent organization that contracts with the bank to provide check clearing services.

c) Branch Banks

The same question can arise when a check drawn on a branch of a bank is received first by another branch, the main banking house, or other physically separate offices of the bank. In this event the issue turns on whether the payor branch functions as a separate bank for purposes of paying items. See 4-107 & comment 2.

5) Re-presented Items

A number of courts have considered whether a re-presented item is deemed finally paid, under 4-215(a)(3), if the item is not timely returned pursuant to 4-301(a) upon re-presentment. A re-presented item is an item that has earlier been presented and properly returned by the payor bank. In other words, the check bounced and the owner has again sent it through the collection process, hoping the check will be paid the second time. The majority of courts hold that 4-215(a)(3) & 4-301(a) apply to re-presented items so that the items are deemed finally paid if the payor bank fails to return them in the proper manner by its midnight deadline.

d. **What To Return**

1) General Rule

Section 4-301 requires returning the item itself -- the check. Giving notice of dishonor is generally *not* an acceptable substitute. 4-301(a)(1-2); see also 12 CFR 229.30(a) ("If a paying bank determines not to pay a check, it shall *return the check* * * *.") (emphasis added).

Example: Buyer gave Seller a check drawn on PB Bank. Seller deposited the check with DB Bank. DB directly presented the check to PB Bank on Monday, and on the same day PB settled with DB for the item by crediting an account of DB for the amount of the item. PB can return the item and recover for it by sending the item back to DB before midnight on Tuesday. Sending includes mailing. 1-201(38). If PB delays beyond this time in returning the item to DB, final payment has occurred. Thus, final payment will occur if PB takes no action before Tuesday midnight, or if PB's only action before Tuesday midnight is sending DB notice of dishonor. A return by the midnight deadline requires returning the item itself, except when the item is unavailable for return.

At least for purposes of Regulation CC's different requirement of expeditious return, which is discussed later, the returned check must bear (i) a clear indication on its face that it is a returned check and (ii) the reason for the return. 12 CFR 229.30(d). "A check is identified as a returned check by a reason for return stamp, even though the stamp does not specifically state that the check is a returned check. A reason such as 'Refer to Maker' is permissible in appropriate cases." 12 CFR 229.30(d) Commentary.

2) Exception -- When Item Unavailable

If the check itself is unavailable for return, as when it has been lost or destroyed, a copy of the check or written notice of dishonor is a permissible substitute. This copy or notice is called a *notice in lieu* of return. 4-301(a)(2); 12 CFR 229.30(f). "If a check is unavailable for return, the paying bank may send in its place a copy of the front and back of the returned check, or, if no such copy is available, a written notice of nonpayment containing [the same descriptive information that is necessary when giving large-dollar notice] * * *. The copy or notice shall clearly state that it constitutes a notice in lieu of return." 12 CFR 229.30(f). Electronic notice is not sufficient. Id. A legible facsimile or similar image of both sides of the check is acceptable, however, even if electronically conveyed. Id. A notice in lieu of return is considered a returned check subject to the requirements of federal and state law that would apply if the check itself were returned. Id.

This specificity with regard to the form and information of a notice in lieu is not required by Article 4. It simply provides for sending "written notice of dishonor * * * if the item is unavailable for return." 4-301(a)(2). Nevertheless, the detailed requirements of federal law Regulation CC supersede, even for purposes of Article 4. 12 CFR 229(f) Commentary.

e. Where To Return (And How Returns Are Paid For)

1) In Terms of Article 4

Under Article 4, how an item is returned depends on how the payor bank received the item. If the item was presented through a clearinghouse, the item is returned "when it is delivered to the presenting or last collecting bank or to the clearing house or is sent or delivered in accordance with clearing-house rules." 4-301(d)(1). In all other cases an item is returned "when it is *sent* or delivered to the bank's customer or transferor or pursuant to instructions." 4-301(d)(2) (emphasis added). In short, the item returns by the same route it reached the payor bank. Incidentally, to "send" includes "to deposit in the mail or deliver for transmission by any other usual means of communication with postage or cost of transmission provided for and properly addressed and in the case of an instrument to an address specified thereon or otherwise agreed, or if there be none to any address reasonable under the circumstances." 1-201(38).

2) Overriding Federal Law

a) The Rule

With the aim of expediting returns, Regulation CC preempts 4-301(d) by allowing a payor bank to "send a returned check [directly] to the depositary bank, or to any other bank agreeing to handle the returned check expeditiously * * *," 12 CFR 229.30(a)(2), regardless of whether or not the returning bank handled the check for forward collection. Id. Commentary. All Federal Reserve Banks agree to handle returned checks expeditiously. 12 CFR 229.30(a)(2).

- ◆ In every case, a paying bank may return a returned check based on any routing number designating the depositary bank appearing on the returned check in the depositary bank's indorsement. 12 CFR 229.30(g).
- ◆ In a case where the paying bank is unable to identify the depositary bank despite use of ordinary care and good faith, the paying bank is authorized to return the check to any bank that handled the item for forward collection even if that bank does not agree to handle the check for expeditious return to the depositary bank. In such a case the paying bank is excused from the requirement of an expeditious return, except when the paying bank is itself responsible for the inability to identify the depositary bank. There is no excuse, however, for violating the midnight deadline rule because of inability to identify the depositary bank. 12 CFR 229.30(b).

b) The Explanation

It is important to understand how and why federal law overrides state law in this matter. Article 4 essentially requires returning the check along the same route it followed in getting to the payor bank, which means that the payor bank must return the item to its transferor. The payor and each returning bank is paid for the returned item by revoking the settlement the bank gave its transferor in the forward-collection process. This scheme explains why Article 4 deems that forward-collection settlements are provisional only.

Federal law rejects this approach by allowing the payor bank to use any route for returning the check, subject to the federal rule of expeditious return which is discussed later. The payor bank can return directly to the depositary bank, even though the depositary bank did not make direct presentment of the item to the payor bank. Alternatively, the payor bank can send the item indirectly to the depositary bank through any intermediary bank agreeing to handle the returned check expeditiously, whether or not the intermediary bank was involved in forward collection. The intermediary bank in the return process is called a *returning bank*.

♦ In case the paying bank returns to a returning bank, that bank "shall settle with * * * [the paying bank] by the same means that it settles or would settle with the sending bank for a check received for forward collection drawn on the depositary bank. This settlement is final when made." 12 CFR 229.31(c). In case the return is directly to the depositary bank, that bank "shall pay * * * the paying bank * * * prior to the close of business on the banking day on which * * * [the depositary bank] received the check." 12 CFR 229.32(b). Such a payment is final when made. Id.

♦ A returning bank can return directly to the depositary bank or indirectly through another returning bank. Every returning bank, like the paying bank, is entitled by federal law to be paid for the returned check by the bank to which the item is returned.

Because of this direct right to payment for a returned check from any bank to which the check is returned and because the return path of an item may be different from its path on forward collection, Regulation CC provides that forward-collection settlements between banks are final when made. The reason that Article 4 deems them provisional -- as part of Article 4's traditional scheme for recouping for dishonored checks -- no longer applies in light of Regulation CC's modern scheme that directly obligates any bank that takes a returned check to pay the transferor for the item. It is an independent obligation unconnected to the forward collection of the item.

2. Large-Dollar Notice
a. The Notice Requirement

Even when a payor bank makes a timely and otherwise proper return under 4-301, the bank is also bound to give quick, special notice if the item is for $2,500 or more. This special notice is required by a rule of Regulation CC commonly called the large-dollar notice requirement:

If a paying bank determines not to pay a check in the amount of $2,500 or more, it shall provide notice of nonpayment such that the notice is received by the depositary bank by 4:00 p.m. (local time) on the second business day following the banking day on which the check was presented to the paying bank.

12 CFR 229.33(a). The notice carries no value, and is no substitute for returning the check in compliance with Regulation CC (the expeditious return rule) and U.C.C. Article 4-301 (the midnight deadline rule). To reiterate, this large-dollar notice requirement is in addition to the rule of Article 4 requiring a timely, proper 4-301 return in order to recover a settlement. Satisfying the large-dollar notice requirement does not satisfy 4-301. On the other hand, the large-dollar notice requirement is not part of 4-301, so that failing to meet the requirement does not bar a payor bank from recovering a settlement if 4-301 is met. The consequence of violating the large-dollar notice requirement is liability for damages under Regulation CC.

b. Who Gives The Notice

Any "paying bank" as Regulation CC defines the term must give the large-dollar notice. Significantly, the definition of "paying bank" is broad and includes:

- The bank by which a check is payable, unless the check is payable at another bank and is sent to the other bank for payment or collection;
- The bank at which a check is payable and to which it is sent for collection; or
- The bank whose routing number appears on a check in magnetic ink or in fractional or magnetic form and to which the check is sent for payment or collection.

12 CFR 229.2(z). The effect is to require large-dollar notification in a wider range of circumstances. Part of the purpose for doing so is surely to combat MICR fraud. This crime cannot as easily succeed as in the past because a bank named magnetically as payor must now give large-dollar notification even when the indicated account is somehow bogus and thus, in real terms, the dishonored check is not payable by the bank.

Example: "On November 7, 1979, a customer of plaintiff [Northpark National Bank] -- a Dallas Bank -- deposited with it a $62,500 check and thereby set in motion a clever fraud which would result in his bilking plaintiff out of some $60,000 * * *. Two features of the modern check collection process are central to the understanding of this fraud. The first is that, notwithstanding the colloquial suggestion to the contrary, checks deposited for collection do not generally clear. That is, provisional credits -- on the customer's account at the depositary bank and on the accounts of intermediary banks involved in the collection process -- become final by the mere passage of time, rather than by an advice of actual payment. * * * It being statistically unlikely that a particular check will not be paid, * * * the practicalities of the process call for giving actual notice (down the chain of collection) only in the event a check is not paid. Accordingly, the temporary hold which a depositary bank customarily places on the withdrawal of proceeds from a check deposited for collection is intended to give the collection chain an opportunity to notify the depositary bank, if it be necessary, that the check has not been paid. Thus, the hallmark of the normal completion of collection -- i.e., the check having been paid -- is the receipt of no notice by the depositary institution.

"The second important feature is that the collection process has been, of course, automated by the use of check-sorting computers. * * * The vast amount of items processed allows no practical alternative. * * * Along the bottom of a check's face there are so-called MICR numbers [Magnetic Ink Character Recognition] which identify the drawer's bank, branch, and account number. A computer reads these numbers and automatically routes the check to the appropriate destination for collection. The initial destination depends, therefore, entirely on the MICR routing number printed on the check.

"With the foregoing in mind it is clear how a fraud of this type is accomplished. Its object is to cause a worthless check deposited for collection to take a sufficiently long detour in its progress to the drawee bank, to insure that the notice of nonpayment will not arrive at the depositary bank until after the expiration of the hold which it placed on the availability of the proceeds from transit items. Having received no such notice before the expiration of the hold, the depositary bank supposes the items to have been paid and allows its proceeds to be withdrawn. By the time notice arrives the malefactor has, of course, absconded with the spoils. The crucial detour is caused by imprinting the fraudulent check with the wrong MICR routing number -- i.e., one that does not correspond to the bank designated on the face of the check as the drawee bank, but to a different bank, preferably one that is distant from the institution designated as the drawee bank on the face of the check. The

fraudulent check in our case bore the MICR routing number of
Bankers Trust Co. in New York and identified the Bank of Detroit
-- a fictitious institution -- as the drawee bank.

"A brief chronology is now in order. The malefactor deposited the
fake check in his account with plaintiff on November 7, 1979.
Plaintiff put a 14- day hold -- through November 20 -- on the
availability of the check's proceeds. On the next day, November 8,
the check was presented to the Republic National Bank of Dallas --
plaintiff's correspondent bank for out-of-state collections -- which,
in turn, presented the check on November 9 directly to the FRBNY
[Federal Reserve Bank of New York] for collection, without routing
the item through the local Federal Reserve Bank of Dallas.   The
* * * check bears a stamp showing that it had been presented to
Bankers Trust Co. for collection on November 13. The precise
timing of events during the next few days has not yet been
established. It is clear, however, that at some time after November
13, Bankers Trust determined that the check was not drawn on it
and returned the item to the FRBNY. The FRBNY, having now
extracted the check from the computer-directed addressing system,
then forwarded the check to the FRBC on the strength of the
designation Bank of Detroit which the check bore on its face.   The
complaint states that the check is stamped as having been in the
hands of the FRBC [Federal Reserve Bank of Chicago] on
November 20. Meanwhile, back in Dallas, the malefactor withdrew
$9,000 from his account on November 21 and an additional $40,250
on Saturday, November 24. The precise schedule of the check's
vicissitudes after November 20 is yet undetermined. It must,
however, have been sent to the Detroit branch of the FRBC, which
branch, in turn, established that the Bank of Detroit did not exist.
The check must then have followed the self-same route back to the
FRBC and then to the FRBNY. * * * [T]he FRBNY again received
the check on November 29, well after the malefactor had eloped
with the plundered funds, leaving -- we suppose -- a barren account.
What happened to the check thereafter is immaterial. Suffice it to
say that the Federal Reserve Bank of Dallas advised plaintiff some
time in December that the check would be returned unpaid, and
upon the check's return debited plaintiff's account at the Dallas Fed
for the amount of the phony check." *Northpark Nat'l Bank v.
Banker's Trust Co.*, 572 F.Supp. 524, 525-27 (S.D. N.Y. 1983).
Under the current large-dollar notice rule, Banker's Trust would be a

paying bank and would be liable to the depositary bank for having failed to provide the large-dollar notice.

c. How The Notice is Given

"Notice may be provided by any reasonable means, including the returned check, a writing (including a copy of the check), telephone, Fedwire, telex, or other form of telegraph." 12 CFR 229.33(a). As for the contents of the notice, it must include the:

* name and routing number of the paying bank;
* name of the payee(s);
* amount;
* date of the indorsement of the depositary bank;
* account number of the customer(s) of the depositary bank;
* branch name or number of the depositary bank from its indorsement;
* trace number associated with the indorsement of the depositary bank; and
* reason for nonpayment.

The message must be clear and unequivocal:

> Regardless of the means used to effect notification, we perceive that [the] Regulation * * * contemplates an unqualified notice from the paying bank that it will not pay the item. The primary purpose of requiring timely notification of nonpayment is to alert the depositary bank so that it may protect itself from potential loss. To this end, the notification must identify the instrument and state in sufficiently specific terms that it will not be honored. * * * To qualify, the notice of dishonoring must be specific, precise, unequivocal, and certain, and it must be delivered to a responsible person at the depositary bank.

Federal Deposit Ins. Corp. v. Lake Country Nat'l Bank, 873 F.2d 79, 81-82 (5th Cir. 1989).

d. Damages

A bank must exercise ordinary care and act in good faith in complying with the notice requirement. This duty extends to the depositary bank, the depositary bank's customer, the owner of the check, or another party to the check. Damages for negligence are measured by the amount of the loss incurred, up to the amount of the check, reduced by the amount of the loss that would have been incurred even if the bank had exercised ordinary care. A bank that bank fails to act in good faith may be liable for other damages, if any, suffered as a proximate consequence. 12 CFR 229.38(a).

e. **Warranties**
Warranties accompany the notice in order to give the depositary bank more confidence in relying on notices of nonpayment. In giving the notice the paying bank warrants that

* the check was or will be returned within the midnight deadline;
* the bank is authorized to send the notice; and
* the check has not been materially altered.

12 CFR 229.34(b). Damages for breach of a warranty that accompanies a large-dollar notification "shall not exceed the consideration received by the paying * * * bank, plus finance charges and expenses related to the returned check, if any." 12 CFR 229.34(c).

3. **Expeditious Return**
Banks returning checks must also abide by Regulation CC's requirement of *expeditious return*. This requirement is imposed not only on the payor bank that returns an item, but also on intermediary banks involved in the return process (known as returning banks). As applied to payor banks, the expeditious return rule is separate from and in addition to the large-dollar notice requirement and is also in addition to the midnight deadline rules of Article 4. A check must be timely returned under Article 4 and must also be expeditiously returned under Regulation CC. The midnight deadline and expeditious return rules are closely related but different. It is possible to meet one rule and not the other, and the consequences of violating the rules are different. A way to view the relationship between the two requirements is that a return must begin by the midnight deadline of state law and must be accomplished expeditiously under federal law.

a. **Requirement Of Expeditious Return**
Upon dishonoring a check, the paying bank must return it in an "expeditious manner." 12 CFR 229.30(a). There are two alternative tests for expeditious return:

1) **Two-Day/Four-Day Test**
A check is considered expeditiously returned if the check is returned such that it would normally be received by the depositary bank by 4:00 p.m. (local time of the depositary bank) two business days after the banking day of presentment in the case of a local check, or by 4:00 p.m. four business days after presentment in the case of a nonlocal check. 12 CFR 229.30(a)(1).

2) Forward Collection Test

A check is nonetheless considered returned expeditiously if the paying bank uses transportation methods and routes for return comparable to those used for forward collection checks, even if the check is not received by the depositary bank within the two-day or four-day period. 12 CFR 229.30(a)(2). Essentially, to satisfy the forward collection test, the bank must use means of routing and transporting a returned check that are as efficient as the means a similarly situated bank uses for forward collection of a similar item deposited with the bank by noon on the banking day following the bank day of presentment of the returned check. **In effect, the paying bank should treat a returned check as if the check were drawn on the depositary bank and deposited with the paying bank by noon on the banking day following the bank day of presentment of the returned check.**

The reference to a "similarly situated bank" indicates a general community standard. In the case of a paying bank, a similarly situated bank is a bank of similar asset size, in the same community, and with similar check handling activity as the paying bank. A paying bank has similar check handling activity to other banks that handle similar volumes of checks for collection. 12 CFR 229.30(a) Commentary.

b. Payable-At or -Through Banks

Regulation CC includes a payable-at or payable-through bank within its definition of "paying bank," so that those banks are subject to the both the expeditious return and notice of nonpayment requirements, see 12 CFR 229.2(z); 12 CFR 229.36(a), although such a bank is not subject to Article 4's midnight deadline. 12 CFR 229.30(a) Commentary. In applying the expeditious return rule to a payable-at or payable-through bank, the "requirement begins when the * * * bank receives the check during forward collection, not when the payor returns the check to the * * * bank." Id. The requirement of expeditious return does not apply, however, to checks deposited in a depositary bank that does not maintain transaction accounts. 12 CFR 229.30(e).

c. Relation To Article 4's Midnight-Deadline Rule

Nothing in or about the expeditious return rule relieves the payor bank from the state-law midnight deadline rule. Regulation CC is explicit on this issue, providing that the rule of expeditious return "does not affect a paying bank's responsibility to return a check within the deadlines required by the U.C.C. * * *." 12 CFR 229.30(a)(2); see also 12 CFR 229.30(b) Commentary ("A paying bank's return under [Regulation CC's rules of expeditious return] is also subject to its midnight deadline under U.C.C. § 4-301 * * *."). Thus, satisfying the rule of expeditious return does not prevent a payor bank's liability for accountability or final payment of a check that it unseasonably bounces in violation of Article 4. On the other hand, the consequences of violating the expeditious return rule are described by Regulation CC, not by Article 4. The violation can result in damages but not accountability or final payment. In the event the payor bank violates both the midnight deadline rule of Article 4 and the Regulation CC rule of expeditious return, the bank is liable under the former law or the latter, *but not both*. 12 CFR 229.38(b).

d. Extension Of Time

The deadline for expeditious return, like the state-law midnight deadline of 4-301, is extended in the event of expeditied delivery. 12 CFR 229.30(c).

e. Qualifying Returned Checks

In order to facilitate electronic processing of returned checks, paying banks are allowed (but not required) to convert returned items to *qualified returned checks* (QRCs), 12 CFR 229.30(a), which means an item that is prepared for handling by automated check processing equipment for return to the depositary bank by encoding the check with the routing number of that bank, the amount of the check, and a return identifier ("2") in position 44 of the MICR line. 12 CFR 229.2(bb) & 229.30(a)(2). Paying banks, however, are not allowed extra time for qualifying returns. Their incentive is that qualified returns will be handled at a lower cost by returning banks.

f. Liability For Breach Of Expeditious Return Rule And Other Requirements Of Regulation CC

1) Basis Of Liability -- Negligence And Lack of Good Faith

Apparently, a bank is not liable for simple failure to comply with the rule of expeditious return or other requirements of Subpart C of Regulation CC ("Collection of Checks). Rather, in literal terms, liability is triggered only if the bank fails to exercise ordinary care and good faith in complying with the requirements. 12 CFR 229.38(a). This implies that a bank that breaches Regulation CC can avoid liability by establishing that, notwithstanding the breach, it acted reasonably and in good faith.

2) Liability To Whom

Liability runs to the depositary bank, the depositary bank's customer, the owner of a check, or another party to the check.

3) Damages

Compensatory damages for negligence are measured by the amount of the loss incurred, up to the amount of the check, reduced by the amount of the loss that would have been incurred even if the bank had exercised ordinary care. 12 CFR 229.38(a). Consequential damages are recoverable only if the bank failed to act in good faith. Id.

4) Comparative Fault

Liability under Subpart C is comparative. If the plaintiff failed to exercise ordinary care or to act in good faith, the damages recoverable must be reduced in proportion to the amount of negligence or bad faith attributable to the plaintiff. 12 CFR 229.38(c).

a) Where Delay Is Due to Difficulty In Identifying Depositary Bank

"This comparative negligence rule may have particular application where a paying or returning bank delays in returning a check because of difficulty in identifying the depositary bank. Some examples will illustrate liability in such cases. In each example, it is assumed that the returned check is received by the depositary bank after it has made funds available to its customer, that it may no longer recover the funds from its customer, and that the inability to recover the funds from the customer is due to a delay in returning the check contrary to the standards established by 229.30(a) or 229.31(a)." 12 CFR 229.38(c) Commentary.

Example: "If a depositary bank fails to use the indorsement required by this regulation, and this failure is caused by a failure to exercise ordinary care, and if a paying or returning bank is delayed in returning the check because additional time is required to identify the depositary bank or find its routing number, the paying or returning bank's liability to the depositary bank would be reduced or eliminated.

Example: "If the depositary bank uses the standard indorsement, but that indorsement is obscured by a subsequent collecting bank's indorsement, and a paying or returning bank is delayed in returning the check because additional time was required to identify the depositary bank or find its routing number, the paying or returning bank may not be liable to the depositary bank because the delay was not due to its negligence. Nonetheless, the collecting bank may be liable to the depositary bank to the extent that its negligence in indorsing the check caused the paying or returning bank's delay.

Example: "If a depositary bank accepts a check that has printing, a carbon band, or other material on the back of the check that existed at the time the check was issued, and the depositary bank's indorsement is obscured by the printing, carbon band, or other material, and a paying or returning bank is delayed in returning the check because additional time was required to identify the depositary bank, the returning bank may not be liable to the depositary bank because the delay was not due to its negligence. Nonetheless, the paying bank may be liable to the depositary bank to the extent that the printing, carbon band, or other material caused the delay." 12 CFR 229.38(c) Commentary.

b) Responsibility for Back of Check
"The indorsement standard in 229.35 [that applies to collecting banks] is most effective if the back of the check remains clear of other matter that may obscure bank indorsements. Because bank indorsements are usually applied by automated equipment, it is not possible to avoid preexisting matter on the back of the check. For example, bank indorsements are not required to avoid a carbon band or printed, stamped, or written terms or notations on the back of the check. Accordingly, this provision places responsibility on the paying bank or depositary bank, as appropriate, for keeping the back of the check clear for bank indorsements during forward collection and return." 12 CFR 229.38(d) Commentary.

Example: "The paying bank * * * is responsible for the condition of the check when it is issued by it or its customer. (It would not be responsible for a check issued by a person other than such a bank or customer.) Thus, the paying bank would be responsible for the adverse effect (if any) of a carbon band or other material placed on the back of a check before issuance. The paying bank may contract with its customers with respect to such responsibility.

Example: "The depositary bank is responsible for the condition of the check arising after it is issued and before it is accepted by the depositary bank, as well as any condition of the check arising during its handling of the check. The depositary bank would be responsible for the adverse effect (if any) of a stamp placed on the check by its customer or a prior indorser. The depository bank may refuse to accept a check whose back is unreasonably obscured or contract with its customers with respect to such responsibility.

"Responsibility under [this paragraph] is treated as negligence for comparative negligence purposes, and the contribution to damages under [this paragraph] is treated in the same way as the degree of negligence under paragraph (c) of this section." 12 CFR 229.38(d) Commentary.

5) Defenses
  a) Extraordinary Circumstances
     If a bank is delayed in acting beyond the time limits set forth in Subpart C because of interruption of communication or computer facilities, suspension of payments by a bank, war, emergency conditions, failure of equipment, or other circumstances beyond its control, its time for acting is extended for the time necessary to complete the action, if it exercises such diligence as the circumstances require. 12 CFR 229.38(e).

  b) Statute Of Limitations
     Any action under Subpart C must be brought within one year after the violation occurred. 12 CFR 229.38(g).

  c) Reliance On Board Rulings
     No provision if Subpart C imposing any liability applies to any act done or omitted in good faith in conformity with any rule, regulation, or interpretation thereof by the Board, regardless of whether the rule, regulation or interpretation is amended, rescinded, or determined by judicial or other authority to be invalid for any reason after the act or omission had occurred. 12 CFR 229.38(h).

D. RETURNING BANKS IN THE RETURN PROCESS

1. What Is A Returning Bank
A returning bank is a bank (other than a paying or depositary bank) handling a returned check or notice in lieu of return. 12 CFR 229.2(cc). A paying bank is authorized to return a dishonored check through a returning bank rather than directly to the depositary bank, so long as doing so is expeditious and the returning bank has itself agreed to handle the returned check expeditiously. A bank so agrees if it:

- Publishes or distributes availability schedules for the return of returned checks and accepts the returned check for return;
- Handles a returned check for return that it did not handle for forward collection; or,
- Otherwise agrees to handle a returned check for expeditious return.

12 CFR 229.31(a) Commentary. In effect, all Federal Reserve Banks agree to handle returned checks expeditiously. 12 CFR 210.12. A return may be made to a returning bank whether or not the bank handled the check for forward collection.

2. Duty Of Expeditious Return

A returning bank is required to return a returned check expeditiously, that is, according to standards that are similar to the tests of expeditious return established for paying banks. 12 CFR 229.31(a) & Commentary.

a. Tests of Expeditious Return

1) Two-Day/Four-Day Test

A returning bank returns a check in an expeditious manner if it sends the returned check in a manner such that the check would normally be received by the depositary bank not later than 4:00 p.m. (local time of the depositary bank) of

- The second business day on which the check was presented to the paying bank if the paying bank is a local paying bank, i.e., is in the same check processing region as the depositary bank; or
- The fourth business day following the banking day on which the check was presented to the paying bank if the paying bank is a nonlocal paying bank, i.e., is located in a different check-processing region than the depositary bank.

12 CFR 229.31(a)(1). If the last business day on which the returning bank may deliver a returned check to the depositary bank is not a banking day for the depositary bank, the returning bank meets this requirement if the returned check is received by the depositary bank on or before the depositary bank's next banking day. Id.

"While a returning bank will not have first-hand knowledge of the day on which a check was presented to the paying bank, returning banks may, by agreement, allocate with paying banks liability for late return based on the delays caused by each. In effect, the two-day/four-day test protects all paying and returning banks that return checks from claims that they failed to return a check expeditiously, where the check is returned within the specified time following presentment to the paying bank, or a later time as would result from unforeseen delays."   12 CFR 229.31(a) Commentary.

2) **Forward Collection Test**
A returning bank also returns a check in an expeditious manner if it sends the returned check in a manner that a similarly situated collecting bank would normally handle a check

- Of similar amount as the returned check;
- Drawn on the depositary bank; and
- Received for forward collection by the similarly situated bank at the time the returning bank received the returned check.

12 CFR 229.31(a)(2). Under this test a returning bank must accept returned checks, including both qualified and raw returns, at approximately the same times and process them according to the same general schedules as checks handled for forward collection. Thus, a returning bank generally must process even raw returns on an overnight basis, unless its time limit is extended by one day to convert a raw return to a qualified return check. 12 CFR 229.31(a) Commentary.

A returning bank may, however, establish earlier cutoff hours for receipt of returned checks than for receipt of forward collection checks, but the cutoff hour for returned checks may not be earlier than 2:00 p.m. Thus, a returning bank may allow itself more processing time for returns than for forward collection checks. Nevertheless, all returned checks received by a cutoff hour for returned checks must be processed and dispatched by the time the returning bank would dispatch forward collection checks received at a corresponding forward collection cutoff hour that provides for the same or faster availability for checks destined for the same depositary banks. Id.

b. **Extension Of Time For Qualifying Returns**
Except when a returning bank is returning a check directly to the depositary bank, the returning bank may extend by one business day the time for return in order to convert a returned check to a qualified returned check. 12 CFR 229.31(a). This extension applies, however, only to the forward-collection test for expeditious return, not to the alternative two-four/four-day test.

3. **Mechanics Of Return**
   a. **Where Returning Bank Sends Return**
   A returning bank can send the return check to:

+ the depositary bank; or
+ any returning bank agreeing to handle the returned check expeditiously, regardless of whether or not the returning bank handled the check for forward collection.

12 CFR 229.31(a)(2). A returning bank may return a returned check based on any routing number designating the depositary bank appearing on the returned check in the depositary bank's indorsement or in magnetic ink on a qualified returned check. 12 CFR 229.31(g) . A returning bank that is unable to identify the depositary bank may send the returned check to

+ any collecting bank that handled the check for forward collection if the returning bank was not a collecting bank with respect to the returned check; or
+ a prior collecting bank if the returning bank was a collecting bank with respect to the check,

even if that collecting bank does not agree to handle the returned check expeditiously. 12 CFR 229.31(b).

b. Indorsement Of Returns

Every bank (other than a paying bank) that handles a returned check must indorse the check, 12 CFR 229.35(a), and in such a manner that protects the identification and legibility of the depositary bank indorsement by

+ Using an ink color other than purple; and
+ Staying clear of the area on the back of the check from 3.0 inches from the leading edge of the check to the trailing edge of the check. 12 CFR part 229 Appendix D.3.

c. Settling For Returns

1) Returning Bank Must Settle For Returns

A returning bank shall settle with a bank sending a returned check to it for return by the same means that it settles or would settle with the sending bank for a check received for forward collection from the sending bank. 12 CFR 229.31(c). This is true even if the returning bank handled the check during forward collection. Id. Commentary. The settlement becomes final when made. 12 CFR 229.31(c).

2) Recouping Settlement In The Event Returning Bank Is Not Paid

Any bank that handles a check for forward collection or return is liable to any bank that subsequently handles the check to the extent that the subsequent bank does not receive payment for the check because of suspension of payments by another bank or otherwise, whether or not the prior bank so handling the check has indorsed it. 12 CFR 229.35(b). For example, if a returning bank returned a check to an insolvent depositary bank, and did not receive the full amount of the check from the failed bank, the returning bank could obtain the unrecovered amount of the check from any bank prior to it in the collection and return chain, including the payor bank. Because each bank in the collection and return chain could recover from a prior bank, any loss would fall on the first collecting bank that received the check from the depositary bank. To avoid circuity of actions, the returning bank could recover directly from the first collecting bank. 12 CFR 229.35(b) Commentary. Under the U.C.C., the first collecting bank might ultimately recover from the depositary bank's customer or from the other parties on the check. (A bank has the rights of a holder with respect to each check it handles. 12 CFR 229.35(b) (last sentence).) Alternatively, the returning bank has a preferred claim against the failed depositary bank. 12 CFR 229.39(b). If the returning bank elects to recover from a prior bank, then this prior bank is subrogated to the returning bank's preferred claim against the insolvent depositary bank. 12 CFR. 229.39(b) Commentary.

4. Liability For Breaching Duties With Respect To Returns

a. Regulation CC

Regulation CC imposes the duties of a returning bank that are described here. Thus, the bank's liability for breaching them is prescribed by CC, and is the same liability that a payor bank suffers for violating CC. Basically, it is liability for negligence in failing to comply with CC that causes damages measured by the actual loss suffered, up to the amount of the check and reduced by the amount of the loss that would have been incurred even if the bank had exercised ordinary care. Consequential damages are recoverable only if the bank fails to act in good faith. 12 CFR 229.38(a).

b. Article 4

Article 4 echoes CC by separately requiring a collecting bank to act reasonably in returning a check. 4-202(a)(2). Damages under this rule are "the amount of the item reduced by an amount that could not have been realized by the exercise of ordinary care. If there is also bad faith it includes any other damages the party suffered as a proximate consequence." 4-103(e).

E. DEPOSITARY BANKS' RIGHTS AND DUTIES UPON RETURN OF CHECKS

1. Paying For Returns

"A depositary bank shall pay the returning or paying bank returning the check to it for the amount of the check prior to the close of business on the banking day on which it received the check ('payment date') by

- debit to an account of the depositary bank on the books of the returning or paying bank;
- cash;
- wire transfer; or
- any other form of payment acceptable to the returning or paying bank.

These payments are final when made." 12 CFR 229.32(b).

2. Main Rights Against Customer And Others When Returned Check Has Been Dishonored

a. Charging Back Against Customer's Account

1) The Right of Charge Back And How It Works

Probably the longest sentence in the UCC, perhaps in the whole of recorded law, is this rambling first sentence of 4-214(a):

> If a collecting bank has made provisional settlement with its customer for an item and [the bank] fails by reason of dishonor, suspension of payments by a bank or otherwise to receive a settlement for the item which is or becomes final, the bank may revoke the settlement given by it, charge back the amount of any credit given for the item to its customer's account or obtain refund from its customer, whether or not it is able to return the item, if by its midnight deadline or within a longer reasonable time after it learns the facts it returns the item or sends notification of the facts.

This sentence allows a depositary bank, that is not the payor bank, to recover the amount of credit it gave its customer for a check if the check is dishonored or for some other reason the depositary bank is not paid for the check. It is self-help recovery. The bank simply debits the customer's account for the amount of the check even though the specific credit attributable to the check has been withdrawn or applied. If the account is insufficient to cover the charge back, the bank can sue to "obtain refund from its customer." 4-214(a). The customer is personally liable for the refund.

Example: Here is the easiest case for applying 4-214(a). Buyer gives Seller a check drawn on PB Bank. Seller deposits the check at DB Bank and gets a credit to her account in the amount of the item. In giving Seller this credit, DB Bank is thereby settling for the item, see 4-104(a)(11), and the settlement is presumably provisional. 4-201(a). DB Bank presents the check directly to PB Bank which itself immediately settles for the item by giving DB Bank a credit through accounts maintained between them. Later the same day, PB Bank discovers that Buyer's account is empty, and thus the item is returned to DB before PB's midnight deadline. DB can charge back the item to Seller's account under 4-214(a) if the conditions for applying the section are satisfied. The conditions are satisfied because:

- DB, a collecting bank, provisionally settled with Seller, its customer, for Buyer's check, an item; and,

- DB did not get not paid for the item, i.e., failed to get a final settlement. PB's timely return of the item to DB, pursuant to 4-301(a), amounted to dishonor as defined by 3-502(b)(1).

- Thus, DB may revoke the settlement it gave Seller. This means that DB can debit Seller's account for the amount of Buyer's check even if the funds in the account are not attributable to that particular item. If Seller's account is insufficient to cover the debit, the Seller is personally liable for the deficiency and DB can sue Seller to recover it, i.e., "obtain refund from its customer." 4-214(a).

Example: The same result would follow if Buyer's check had gone through an intermediary, returning bank (RB), on its way to PB Bank. PB would have returned the check to RB, and RB would have paid PB for the return. RB, in turn, would have returned to and recovered from DB.

Example: The same result would also follow if DB Bank had cashed Buyer's check for Seller. Giving cash for the item was a settlement because "settle" is defined to include payment in cash. 4-104(a)(11). (The term "pay," when used in this definition, is probably not limited to payment by a payor bank but also includes cash advances by other banks. The drafters intended a very broad definition of settle, encompassing any form of credit given by banks and other persons. See 4-104 comment 10.) A settlement can be either provisional or final, and any settlement given by a collecting bank is presumably provisional. 4-201(a). Thus, DB's cashing the check for Seller would be a provisional settlement that could be revoked pursuant to 4-214(a) if DB failed to get a final settlement for the check.

2) **Bank's Duty To Customer When Charging Back (Article 4 and Regulation CC) -- Giving Seasonable Notice**

By the literal terms of 4-214(a), charge back or refund is conditioned on the bank returning the item or sending notice of the facts by the bank's midnight deadline or within a longer reasonable time after it learns the facts. 4-214(a) (first sentence). "A collecting bank returns an item when it is sent or delivered to the bank's customer * * * or pursuant to its instructions." 4-214(b). There is authority that written notice is not required. Oral notice is sufficient. In any event, the time limit is the collecting bank's midnight deadline *or* a longer reasonable time. Thus, the collecting bank acting by its midnight deadline is not a hard-and-fast requirement.

3) **Affect On Right of Charge-Back of Failing To Give Seasonable Notice**

Giving seasonable notice is not a condition in the sense that failing to give the notice bars the charge back or refund. "If the return or notice is delayed beyond the bank's midnight deadline or a longer reasonable time after it learns the facts, the bank may revoke the settlement, charge back the credit, or obtain refund from its customer, but it is liable for any loss resulting from the delay." 4-214(a).

4) **Affect of Regulation CC**

"This regulation does not affect a depositary bank's right to accept or reject a check for deposit, to charge back the customer's account based on a returned check or notice of nonpayment, or to claim a refund for any credit provided to the customer." 12 CFR 229.19(c) Commentary; see also Commentary id. 229.32(b) ("This paragraph and this subpart do not affect the depositary bank's right to recover a provisional settlement with its nonbank customer for a check that is returned."). Regulation CC simply echoes the Article 4 requirement of notifying the customer:

> If the depositary bank receives a returned check or notice of nonpayment, it shall send notice to its customer of the facts by midnight of the banking day on which it received the returned check or notice, or within a longer reasonable time.

12 CFR 229.33(d). The consequence of violating this version of the notice requirement is the same as violating Article 4's requirement -- liability for damages the customer incurs as a result of the bank's failing to give timely notice. Id. Commentary.

5) Depositary Bank That Is Also The Payor Bank

A depositary bank that is also the payor bank enjoys rights of charge back and refund against its customer, 4-214(c), but for this bank the rights are governed by 4-301(a). See 4-301(b). In effect, when the depositary bank is the payor bank, charging back equates with returning and dishonoring the item, so that the limits of the 4-301 midnight deadline rule and sooner final payment apply. Most significantly, if the bank credits the depositor's accounts and fails to return the check by its midnight deadline, final payment has occurred and the rights of charge back and refund are lost. Also, if the bank cashes the item, the effect is final payment of the item then and there. There is no right to return, charge back or seek refund even if the bank bounces the check, notifies the customer, or takes other action prior to the midnight deadline.

b. Suing On The Check

1) Bank As Holder And Holder in Due Course

The payor bank's dishonor of the check triggers the secondary liability of the drawer and any indorser. Thus, the depositary bank can sue them on the check. With respect to the bank's status:

* The depositary bank will be a holder even if the customer-depositor neglected to indorse the check so long as the customer herself was a holder. In this case the bank's holder status results not from the shelter principle but by declaration of law. 4-205(1).
* The depositary bank typically will also satisfy the other requirements for holder in due course. This status most commonly is important in suing the drawer of the check. It allows the bank to take free of the drawer's defenses against the payee, who typically is the bank's customer. Usually, the only issue that presents any difficulty is whether or not the bank gave value. See 4-211 & 4-210.

2) Timeliness of Notice to Indorsers

An indorser's liability is conditioned on timely notice of dishonor, 3-503(a). Untimely notice will discharge the indorser's liability. 3-415(c). Unless notice or delay in giving notice is excused, "with respect to an instrument taken for collection by a collecting bank, notice of dishonor must be given * * * by the bank before midnight of the next banking day following the banking day on which the bank receives notice of dishonor of the instrument * * *." 3-503(c). Delay that discharges the indorser on the instrument is inconsequential if the indorser is the bank's customer. The bank retains the right of refund against her and charges back against her account. 4-214(a). The delay in notice does not affect these rights but only subjects the bank to liability for any loss that the delay caused the customer, and usually there is none.

3. Rights When Returned Check Was Not Dishonored And Was Unlawfully Returned In Violation Of Midnight Deadline

a. No Right of Charge Back or Refund -- Payor Bank's Final Payment Terminates Depositary Bank's Right of Charge Back

The third sentence of 4-214(a) provides: "These rights to revoke, chargeback and obtain refund terminate if and when a settlement for the item received by the [depositary or other collecting] bank is or becomes final." In terms of Article 4, a settlement given or received by a depositary bank becomes final when the payor bank finally pays the item. See 4-215(a) & (c). So, when the payor bank finally pays an item, as described in 4-215(a)(3) and 4-301(a), a depositary bank loses the 4-214(a) rights of charge back and refund and thus cannot recover the credit the bank gave its customer for the item.

b. No Actions On The Check

The liability of the drawer or any indorser of the check is conditioned on dishonor of the instrument. Thus, if the payor bank violates 4-301 and thereby finally pays an item, the depositary bank cannot sue anybody on the check. There was payment rather than the dishonor that is necessary to charge the drawer or an indorser. Moreover, the payment discharged liability on the instrument.

c. Warranties

In the end, therefore, the depositary bank is left with a returned check for which it paid and for which it cannot lawfully recover. The answer is to look for recovery in the other direction -- back up the collection stream toward the payor bank which wrongfully returned the item despite final payment. The best theory is federal warranty law:

> Each paying bank or returning bank that transfers a returned check and receives a settlement or other consideration for it warrants to the transferee returning bank, to any subsequent returning bank, to the depositary bank, and to the owner of the check, that
>
> - *The paying bank timely returned the check within its deadline under the UCC*, Regulation J and Regulation CC (regarding expeditious return);
> - It is authorized to return the check;
> - The returned check has not been materially altered; and
> - In the case of a notice in lieu of return, the original check has not and will not be returned.

12 CFR 229.34(a) (emphasis added). "Damages for breach of these warranties shall not exceed the consideration received by the paying or returning bank, plus finance charges and expenses related to the returned check, if any." Id. 229.34(c). In truth, however, the depositary bank is very likely to charge the item back against the customer's account even though the bank lacks the right to do so.

d. How "Return" Is Even Possible After Final Payment

Some people might think that a payor bank that has finally paid an item cannot return it (see 4-301(a)), and thus they will wonder why a collecting bank would have reason to sue on the check or charge the item back against its customer. While it is true that final payment takes away the payor bank's right of return, the bank nevertheless retains the rare power to return an item that it has finally paid; and, when this power is exercised, a ripple of wrongful recoveries for the returned item is the result: between the payor bank and the returning bank; between returning banks; between a returning bank and the depositary bank; and, finally, between the depositary bank and its customer. The bank to which the payor bank returns the item could prevent the ripple effect by contesting the payor bank's return, arguing that payor bank lost any right of return because of final payment bank. This argument is sound. Yet, banks seldom try to stop a wrongful return because they often are unaware that it has been returned wrongfully. They rotely send it back through usual banking channels for returns and it is charged back to the depositor's account as though proper dishonor had occurred.

e. Customer's Predicament And Rights When She Is Charged With Wrongful Return

Consider the position of the depositary bank's customer in the event of a wrongful return in violation of 4-301. The customer's account will be debited for the amount of the item, yet there is no one to whom she can pass the loss. Because the payor bank finally paid the item, the drawer of the check is discharged, and there is no dishonor that is necessary to charge the drawer or indorsers. The customer's rights are against the banks:

- The customer can force the depositary bank to recredit her account for the item because the bank's charge back to her account was wrongful. Moreover, upon final payment by the payor bank, the settlement between the customer and the depositary bank became final. 4-215(d).
- The depositary bank could then shift the loss back to any returning bank or directly to the payor bank because the bank breached the federal warranty that the check was timely returned under the UCC, Reg J and Regulation CC. 12 CFR 229.34(a).

- ◆ The customer could sue directly any returning bank or the payor bank because the federal warranty runs to the customer herself. Id.

The analysis is slightly different if the payor bank never settled for the item but became accountable for it under 4-302(a) as a result of not returning the item by the deadlines of that section. In this case of late return:

- ◆ The customer has no claim against the depositary bank. Dishonor occurred, 3-502(b)(1), so that the depositary bank's 4-214(a) charge back was rightful.
- ◆ On the other hand, the dishonor triggered the liability of the drawer and prior indorsers. The customer can sue them on the check.
- ◆ Also, even though the item was not finally paid, the payor bank is accountable -- liable for the item -- to the customer.

F. FINAL PAYMENT

1. Why Final Payment Is Important

This chapter repeatedly illustrates the importance of final payment and how it is the key concept of Article 4. Final payment is the point beyond which payor banks cannot dishonor checks that have been presented for payment and cannot lawfully return the checks and take payment for them from the depositary bank or a returning bank. In short, a payor bank that finally pays a check is usually stuck with it as against persons upstream in the collection process, even if the drawer's account is empty or the check cannot properly be charged against the account. Usually, the payor bank's only lawful remedy is to charge the drawer's account, and this remedy is possible only if the item is properly payable. If there are not sufficient funds in the drawer's account to cover the check, the customer is liable for the amount of the overdraft because of common-law contract. (The bank's payment discharged the drawer on the check itself.) If the customer is insolvent, the bank takes the loss.

Final payment under Article 4 also has consequences under Article 3 because it gives meaning to the term "payment" as used in important provisions 3-602 (discharge through payment to a holder) and 3-418 (payment is final in favor of certain classes).

All of these matters have already been stressed throughout this chapter. The effects of final payments are fully demonstrated in various contexts. You must understand these effects in order to appreciate fully the meaning and significance of final payment. So reread carefully the earlier parts of this chapter. The main purposes here are to emphasize a few fundamental aspects of final payment and to describe some details about the mechanics of final payment. The assumption is that, by this point, the effects of final payment already are known.

2. Who Makes Final Payment

Only a payor bank, i.e., the drawee of a check, makes final payment! The Code is clear: "An item is finally paid by a *payor bank * * *.*" 4-215(a) (emphasis added). Collecting banks settle for items by crediting accounts or, in the case of depositary banks, by cashing the items, i.e., giving money "over the counter" for them. Collecting banks, however, do not pay checks or other items, not finally or otherwise. True, a credit (whether cash or other form of settlement) given by a collecting bank does become final upon final payment so that the bank cannot revoke the credit from the customer. Yet, the reason is not because the collecting bank finally paid the item. *Only a payor bank makes final payment!* The reason is that final payment by a payor bank has the derivative effect of finalizing settlements by collecting banks. See 4-215(c) & (d); 4-214(a) (third sentence).

Example: Buyer gave Seller a check drawn on PB Bank. Seller cashed the check at her bank, DB Bank, which then presented the check for payment to PB. PB dishonored the item by a timely return pursuant to 4-301(a). Acting pursuant to 4-214(a), DB immediately charged the item against Seller's account, i.e., debited Seller's account for the amount of the item. Seller argues that a collecting bank's right of charge back terminates upon final payment; that final payment occurs when an item is paid in cash, 4-215(a)(1); and thus that DB could not charge back the item because the item was finally paid when DB cashed it. The flaw in this argument is equating DB's cashing of the check with final payment of the item. *Only a payor bank finally pays an item!* See 4-215(a).

3. How Final Payment Is Made

Article 4 describes three different, alternative means of finally paying an item. 4-215(a). Each of them is discussed below in an order that varies from the statutory listing of them. Remember that each method of final payment is an alternative to the others, and that final payment occurs as soon as the payor bank has first done any of them.

a. Paid In Cash

A check is finally paid when the payor bank pays the item in cash. 4-215(a)(1). Cash payment usually occurs only when the check is presented "over the counter" for immediate payment, which might be done by the payee or other owner of a check but is rarely done by collecting banks acting for a customer. Payor banks rarely settle in cash with collecting banks. The typical case of final payment by payment in cash involves the owner of an item personally presenting a check to the payor bank and asking for payment in money. Upon the teller complying with this request, the payor bank thereby makes final payment. This is the consequence whether the owner of the item maintains her own account at the payor bank or is a stranger who banks elsewhere. Though straightforward and easily understood and applied in the great bulk of cases, final payment by payment in cash raises a couple of important issues.

1) **What Is Cash?**

Cash is money. The term also includes instruments issued by the payor bank that are generally regarded as money equivalents, such as a cashier's check, which is a draft drawn by the bank on itself.

> *Example:*   Buyer pays Seller for goods with a $1000 check drawn on PB Bank. Seller herself presents the check over the counter for payment in cash. The teller gives Seller ten $100 bills. PB then discovers that Buyer's account is empty. Too bad. PB cannot recover the money under Article 4. The payment was final because PB paid in cash.

> *Example:*   Same facts, except that Seller asks for a cashier's check payable to herself instead of money. PB complies with the request. When Seller needs the money, she returns to PB and asks the Bank to pay the cashier's check. Can PB rightfully refuse to pay the check inasmuch as Buyer's account was empty? No. In essence, the refusal would be an attempt to reclaim the payment/credit/settlement given for Buyer's check. This payment, however, was final because it amounted to payment in cash.

2) **Can a Payor Bank Avoid Final Payment When It Pays in Cash by Declaring That the Cash Payment Is Provisional Only and Not Final?**

This question may sound like double-talk, but it's double-talk you may have agreed to when opening your own checking account. Suppose that Seller, from the preceding examples, takes Buyer's check to PB Bank, where Seller also maintains an account. Rather than depositing the check, Seller asks for cash over the counter. She gets it. The same day PB discovers that Buyer's account is empty and immediately debits Seller's account for the amount of the item. On these facts, PB acted wrongfully. The payment by PB was final because the Bank paid in cash, and there is no recourse against Seller. Add this fact: The deposit agreement between PB and Seller declares that "every settlement made between Bank and account holder is provisional, whether settlement is made in cash, for deposit credit or otherwise, and Bank can recover from account holder on every item settled between them that fails for whatever reason." This new fact changes the analysis if PB and Seller were free to negate, by contract, the effect of 4-215(a)(1), and if their contract withstands attack under various policing doctrines apart from Article 4 that guard against substantive and procedural unfairness. On the first point, see 4-103(a) (effect of Article 4 provisions may be varied by agreement).

b. Settled Without Right to Revoke

A check is finally paid if the payor bank settles for it without having a right to revoke the settlement under statute, clearinghouse rule, or agreement. 4-215(a)(2). In terms of state law, final payment by this means almost never occurs because, by state law and usual practice, settlements are almost always provisional. Regulation CC provides the overriding rule that settlements between banks in the forward-collection process are final when made. Putting this rule together with 4-215(a)(2) would seem to mean that anytime a collecting bank presents a check for payment, the payor bank's usually immediate settlement would be final rather than provisional, final payment would therefore occur, and the payor bank therefore would not have the not have a right to return under 4-301 because final payment had occurred. This analysis cannot be true for practical reasons even if it is technically, literally correct, and the comments to Regulation CC obligingly reject it.

> [Even though 12 CFR 229.36(d)] makes settlement between banks during forward collection final when made * * *[s]ettlement by a paying bank is not considered to be final payment for the purposes of U.C.C. [4-215(a)(2) or (3)], because a paying bank has the right to recover settlement from a returning or depositary bank to which it returns a check under [Regulation CC].

12 CFR 229.36(d) Commentary. Regulation CC elsewhere provides that a payor bank that returns a check by the 4-301 midnight deadline has a federal right to recover the amount of the check from the bank to which the check is returned -- whether this bank is the depositary or an intermediary returning bank. This right of recovery is discussed below, under the heading of where returns are sent and how they are paid for. In the end, therefore, what was said in the beginning still applies -- final payment by means of 4-215(a)(2) will almost never happen and only in extraordinary cases.

c. Failed Properly To Recover Provisional Settlement

A payor bank finally pays a check by making a provisional settlement for the item and failing to revoke the settlement in the time and manner permitted by statute, clearing-house rule, or agreement. 4-215(a)(3). Of course, 4-301 is such a statute, so that failing to make a return by the midnight deadline is final payment and is the way in which final payment usually occurs. There is more, however, to 4-215(a)(3). The 4-301 right to return can be varied by agreement (e.g., a clearinghouse arrangement) or preempted by federal law. In this event, the limits of the payor bank's right to revoke, including the time and manner of exercising the right, are set by the agreement or law that overrides 4-301. If the time limit for return is sooner than the midnight deadline, failing to meet this earlier limit is final payment and cuts off the 4-301 right of return even if the midnight deadline has not expired.

Example: "It is very common for clearing house rules to provide that items exchanged and settled for in a clearing, (e.g., before 10:00 a.m. on Monday) may be returned and the settlements revoked up to but not later than 2:00 p.m. on the same day (Monday) or under deferred posting at some hour on the next business day (e.g., 2:00 p.m. Tuesday). Under this type of rule the Monday morning settlement [can be recovered but only in line with law and the clearing house rules] * * *." 4-215 comment 4. "[I]f the time limit for the return of items received in the Monday morning clearing is 2:00 p.m. on Tuesday and the provisional settlement has not been revoked at that time in a manner permitted by the clearing house rules, the * * * settlement made on Monday morning becomes final at 2:00 p.m. on Tuesday." Id. comment 7. The item cannot be returned or the settlement recovered. This is true even though, under 4-301(a), the right to return extended until midnight on Tuesday because the clearinghouse rules, as a form of agreement among the parties, override 4-301(a).

When a payor bank receives an item directly or indirectly from a Federal Reserve Bank, Regulation J governs the bank's right to return the item. In this respect, Regulation J defers to Article 4. The federal right is as follows:

A paying bank that receives a cash item directly or indirectly from a Reserve Bank, other than for immediate payment over the counter, *and that pays for the item as provided in § 210.9(a) of this subpart,* may, before it has finally paid the item, return the item in accordance with Subpart C of Part 229 [Regulation CC], the Uniform Commercial Code, and its Reserve Bank's operating circular. The rules or practices of a clearinghouse through which the item was presented, or a special collection agreement under which the item was presented, may not extend these return times, but may provide for a shorter return time.

12 CFR 210.12 (emphasis added). The emphasized language is important because the effect of incorporating 210.9(a) is to limit the federal right to return to items for which the payor bank has settled by *close of the banking day* on which the items were received. In contrast, the 4-301(a) right is available with respect to settlements made by *midnight* of the day of receipt.

4. Liabilities That Are Excepted From Final Payment (And 4-302 Accountability)

A payor bank can sometimes, in effect, avoid (by end run) the finality of final payment. Even though a settlement has become final under the rules of Article 4, the bank can recover damages on collateral theories and thereby effectively recoup the payment made, even when the payment was made in cash. With respect to an item that has been finally paid, the principal bases of recoupment are: breach of warranty of presentment, restitution for mistaken payment, and subrogation to rights of the drawer.

a. Breach of Warranty

A payor bank that pays an item is the beneficiary of certain warranties made upon presentment, see 4-208 and 4-209, and can recover damages upon breach of any of these warranties. A payor's damages are usually measured by the amount of the item plus any finance charges and expenses related to it. Warranty liability is discussed in general terms earlier in this chapter, and is also discussed in Chapter X as a means of shifting loss in check fraud cases. The only reason for mentioning warranty liability here is to make the very important point that final payment is no bar to a payor bank recovering for breach of any warranty of which the payor is a beneficiary. Indeed, final payment stops no one from recovering for breach of any warranty with respect to an instrument.

Example: Buyer gives Seller a check drawn on PB Bank. Seller's employee steals the check, forges Seller's indorsement, and cashes the item at DB Bank. DB presents the check for payment, and PB finally pays the item. Notwithstanding final payment of the check, DB Bank is liable to PB for breach of the warranty that DB was a person entitled to enforce the item. 4-208(a)(1). This warranty was breached because, as a result of the forged indorsement, DB was not such a person. PB will have reason to press this claim because a check with a forged indorsement is not properly payable. This means that Buyer can force PB to recredit her account for the amount of the item. Buyer will be prompted to take this action because she remains liable to Seller both on the instrument and on the underlying obligation for which it was taken.

Also, in case the payor bank made no settlement but became accountable for the item under 4-302 as a result of having failed to settle or return in a timely fashion, the bank's liability for the item "is subject to defenses based on breach of a presentment warranty or proof that the person seeking enforcement of the liability presented or transferred the item for the purpose of defrauding the payor bank." 4-302(b).

b. Restitution for Mistaken Payment

The common law of restitution permits, in limited circumstances, the recovery of money or other credit mistakenly paid. See Restatement of Restitution §§ 23, 29, 33 & 34 (1937). Article 3 defers to common-law restitution, 3-418(b), and even codifies restitutionary recovery in certain cases. 3-418(a) (paying despite a stop order or a forged drawer's signature). On this basis, payor banks commonly seek to recover final settlements for items (even cash payments), arguing that final payment was a mistake because the bank was unaware, at the time of the payment, that the drawer's account was empty or that, for some other reason, the item was not properly payable. Common-law restitution, 3-418, and the limits and defenses to such a restitution action are discussed earlier in Chapter V supra. It is sufficient here to emphasize the two large hurdles that stand in the way of the bank's recovery. First, local law may not support the claim. Second, 3-418(c) provides a wide defense to any restitutionary claim.

1) **Content of Local Common Law**

The common law of restitution permits the recovery of money paid by mistake only in limited cases, and only when the mistake is of a kind that the law excuses. These restrictions on restitutionary recovery vary some among the states, some being more generous than others with respect to the range of circumstances in which recovery is allowed. So, a payor bank cannot revoke or otherwise reclaim a final payment simply because, in the bank's view, a mistake in payment was made. The facts of the particular case must fit within the range of circumstances under which the local law of restitution authorizes recovery. Possibly, however, 3-418 goes beyond the common law and liberalizes recovery for certain mistakes. The statute affirmatively declares that a drawee can recover the amount of a draft paid "on the mistaken belief that (i) payment of the draft has not been stopped * * * or (ii) the signature of the drawer of the draft was authorized * * *." 3-418(a).

2) **The Defense of 3-418(c)**

a) **The Reach Of The Defense**

Without question, the defense of 3-418(c) is the highest hurdle a payor bank must jump to succeed in winning restitution of final payment. The defense applies whether the action is based on common-law or statutory restitution of 3-418(a), and provides that restitutionary remedies "may not be asserted against a person who took the instrument in good faith and for value or who in good faith changed position in reliance on the payment or acceptance." 3-418(c). The defense is intended specifically to stop a drawee, in the ordinary case, from recovering payment of an overdraft or a draft that was not signed by the drawer. The rationale for the defense is that "the drawee is responsible for knowing the state of the account before he accepts or pays." 3-418 comment 2 (1989 Official Text).

> **Example:** Buyer gives Seller a check drawn on PB Bank. Seller deposits the check with DB Bank which provisionally credits Seller's account. DB presents the check for payment to PB Bank. PB immediately settles with DB, and does not return the check before PB's midnight deadline. Thus, the check is deemed finally paid, 4-215(a)(3), and the credit to Seller's account is final. 4-215(c). PB thereafter discovers that Buyer's account is empty. Because PB cannot now revoke the payment under Article 4, PB sues DB to recover in restitution for payment mistakenly made. Even if local common law would allow restitution on these facts, 3-418(c) is a defense for DB if it was a holder in due course of the check (see 3-302(a)) or changed its position in reliance on PB's payment. DB probably was a holder in due course. Value was given in that, upon final payment by PB, the credit to Seller's account was available for withdrawal as of right. See 4-210(a) & 4-211. PB might alternatively sue Seller to recover the payment, but Seller too is protected by 3-418(c).

b) The Limits of the Defense
   There are three main limitations on the 3-418(c) defense:

   ◆ First, 3-418(c) protects only two classes of people -- persons who took the instrument in good faith and for value (obviously including holders in due course) and persons who in good faith changed their position in reliance on payment. A defendant who is not among these classes cannot rely on 3-418(c) as a defense to a payor bank's suit in restitution to recover a payment mistakenly made.
   ◆ Second, the defense is not a bar to a payor bank's right of return under Article 4 (4-301) and Regulation CC. As against persons seeking to collect a check, the payor bank has a free right to return under 4-301

by taking appropriate action before its midnight deadline and before final payment otherwise occurs.

+ Finally, 3-418(c) is not a defense to a breach of warranty action by a payor bank. 3-418(c) (second sentence).

c. Subrogation to Drawer's Rights

Sometimes, a drawee bank finally pays a check that cannot be charged to the drawer's account because the check is not properly payable, which basically means that the customer who owns the account has a good reason for objecting to her payment of the check. It happens, for example, when a payor bank ignores an effective stop payment order. In this event, the bank is subrogated to the rights of the drawer against the payee or any other holder of the item with respect to the transaction out of which the item arose. 4-407(3). The bank can assert these rights despite having made final payment of the check; and 3-418(c), which is a defense to a payor's restitution action, does not apply.

Example: "If, for example, the payee was a fraudulent salesman inducing the drawer to issue a check for defective securities, and the bank pays the check over a stop-payment order but reimburses the drawer for such payment, the bank should have a basis for getting the money back from the fraudulent salesman." 4-407 comment 3.

REVIEW QUESTIONS

1. Buyer gives Seller a check drawn on PB Bank located in Minneapolis. Seller deposits the check in her account at DB Bank located in northern Minnesota. Upon making this deposit DB Bank credits Seller's account for the amount of the item. DB Bank immediately sends the check for payment, but forwards the item through the Minneapolis Federal Reserve Bank which presents the check to PB Bank. Identify the banks using the appropriate Article 4 labels.

2. Continue with the same facts. PB and DB maintain accounts with the Minneapolis Fed. Upon receiving the check, the Minneapolis Fed promptly debited PB Bank's account for the amount of the item and gave DB Bank a corresponding credit. PB Bank receives the check on Monday morning and decides, on Monday afternoon, to dishonor it. Can PB revoke the settlement effected through the Minneapolis Fed and thereby recoup the debit to PB's account at the Fed?

3. Suppose that PB Bank properly returns the item and the Minneapolis Fed reverses the credit to DB Bank's account. Can DB Bank, in turn, debit Seller's account?

4.   Suppose that the dishonored check is returned to DB Bank on Tuesday, but the Bank waits until Thursday to pass the check along to Seller. Does this delay beyond DB Bank's midnight deadline preclude DB Bank from charging the item back against Seller's account?

5.   Explain Seller's recourse upon the return of the dishonored check to her following DB Bank's charge back of the item against her account.

6.   Reconsider Question 2. Suppose that PB Bank had already decided to pay the check and had completed the process of posting it to Buyer's account. Does this affect PB Bank's right to return the item?

7.   Reconsider Question 2. Suppose that PB Bank decides on Wednesday to to return the check. Is it too late to make a proper return?

8.   Continue with Question 7. Despite having finally paid the item, PB Bank bounced the check back to DB Bank which charged it back against Seller's account. Can Seller sue Buyer on the check or the underlying obligation?

9.   Follow up on Question 8. In the event Buyer is freed from liability, is Seller altogether without recourse?

10.   Suppose that PB Bank finally paid Buyer's check because of a mistake in computing the balance of Buyer's account. Can PB recover the payment notwithstanding that it has lost the right to revoke the payment under Article 4?

11.   Is PB stuck with the loss if payment cannot be recovered under Article 4 or otherwise?

X

THE RELATIONSHIP BETWEEN A PAYOR BANK AND ITS CHECKING ACCOUNT CUSTOMERS

Analysis

A. *Wrongful Dishonor*
   1. What Is "Wrongful Dishonor"
   2. What Damages Are Recoverable
   3. Who Can Complain Of Wrongful Dishonor
   4. Which Funds Are Counted In Determining The Sufficiency Of The Account
      -- The Problem And Law Of Funds Availability
   5. Other Problems In Determining If Dishonor Is Rightful Or Wrongful

B. *Overdraft Liability*
   1. Overdrafts Chargeable To The Drawer's Account
   2. Overdraft Liability Of Joint Account Holders
   3. Contrary Agreements Regarding Overdrafts

C. *Stopping Payment*
   1. The Right To Stop Payment (Or Close An Account)
   2. Payor Bank's Liability For Payment Over A Valid Stop-Payment Order
   3. Requisites Of An Effective Stop-Payment Order
   4. Stopping Payment Against A Holder In Due Course
   5. Cashiers' Checks

D. *Untimely Checks*
   1. Stale Checks
   2. Postdated Checks
   3. Mitigating Liability For Paying Untimely Checks

E. *Effect Of A Customer's Incompetence Or Death*

F. *Check Fraud*
   1. Basis Of Payor Bank's Liability To Its Checking-Account Customer
   2. Payor Bank's Defenses

The fundamental relationship in the check collection process is between the drawee-payor bank and the drawer of the check who, generally and technically, is a *customer* of the payor bank because she has an account there. See 4-104(a)(5). The account upon which the drawer writes a check is the source of funds to which the payor bank looks for reimbursement upon paying the check. Actually, the account is a balance sheet reflecting the amount of money the bank owes the customer (or vice versa if the account is overdrawn). Money deposited in an account is not really held *in species* by the bank for the customer's benefit. The money becomes the bank's funds, but the customer becomes a general creditor of the bank for the total of her deposits. Checks that can rightfully be charged against the account are debits that reduce the bank's indebtedness to the customer.

The debtor-creditor relationship that a checking account creates is basically founded upon a contract between the payor bank and the customer. The contract is typically expressed in a written deposit agreement which often takes the simple form of a signature card. In exchange for having the use of the customer's money deposited in a checking account and, perhaps, for a further fee, the bank agrees to pay checks drawn on the account over the signature of the person or persons named in the deposit agreement.

Certain aspects of the relationship are also governed by U.C.C. Article 4. Most importantly, Article 4 explains that, "[a] bank may charge against the account of a customer an item that is properly payable from the account even though the charge creates an overdraft. An item is properly payable if it is authorized by the customer and is in accordance with any agreement between the customer and bank." 4-401(a). On its face, this provision appears only to create a right in the bank's favor. As applied, however, 4-401(a) imposes a duty on a payor bank: *The bank must pay properly payable items.* Failing to do so makes the payor bank liable to its customers for *wrongful dishonor,* 4-402, which includes any unauthorized or unjustified refusal to pay a check.

The negative implication of 4-401(a) imposes another duty on a payor bank: *The bank cannot charge its customer's account for an item that is not properly payable, and the bank should therefore dishonor the item.* Otherwise, the bank is guilty of *wrongful payment.* A variety of circumstances render an item not properly payable. A good example is a check that the drawer has ordered the bank not to pay by issuing a stop-payment order. See 4-403. Another good example is a check that bears a forged or otherwise ineffective signature of the drawer or an indorser. If a bank pays a check that is not properly payable, the item cannot rightfully be charged against the customer's account. If the account is nevertheless charged for the item, the bank thereby breaches 4-401(a) and on this basis the customer can ordinarily sue to force the bank to recredit her account.

These twin duties that a payor bank owes its checking account customer, i.e., to pay properly payable items and to dishonor items that are not properly payable, account for most of the instances in which a bank is liable to such a customer. Yet, a payor bank's liability for breaching either of these duties is not absolute. Article 4 and supplemental law establish a host of defenses and conditions to the bank's liability, some of which take the form of duties that are imposed on the customer.

This chapter briefly outlines wrongful dishonor in general terms, and then separately discusses various sets of circumstances that most often raise the question of wrongful payment.

A. WRONGFUL DISHONOR

"A payor bank is liable to its customer for damages proximately caused by the wrongful dishonor of an item." 4-402(b).

1. What Is "Wrongful Dishonor"

Simply put, *wrongful dishonor* is dishonoring a check that is properly payable and thus should have been paid. 4-402(a). (For the meaning of dishonor, see 3-502(b).) "An item is properly payable if it is authorized by the customer and is in accordance with any agreement between the customer and bank." 4-401(a). Put more fully, wrongful dishonor is any dishonor of a check by the drawee/payor bank that is not permitted or justified by law or the terms of the deposit contract between the payor bank and its customer. Thus, there is no wrongful dishonor where the drawer has no credit extended by the drawee, or where the draft lacks a necessary indorsement or is not properly presented. In contrast, a bank wrongfully dishonors by refusing to pay a check that is properly presented and properly drawn on an account having sufficient funds to cover the item.

Example: B drew a $500 check to S in payment for goods. The check bounced (i.e., was dishonored) because the payor bank's computer system malfunctioned and erroneously determined that B's account contained only $25. In fact, B's account contained $2500. The payor bank is guilty of wrongful dishonor.

Example: Same facts, except that B's account actually contained only $25 and was not covered by an agreement requiring the bank to pay overdrafts. In this case, there is no wrongful dishonor because the check was not properly payable.

2. What Damages Are Recoverable

a. Kinds of Damages

The express terms of 4-402 describe the customer's recovery for wrongful dishonor as "damages proximately caused." 4-402(b). This includes consequential damages of all sorts, including damages for an arrest or prosecution of the customer (as when the customer is charged with writing bad or hot checks), for loss of credit, and for other mental suffering. Though punitive damages are not authorized by the statute, there is caselaw permitting recovery of such damages in appropriate circumstances, as when the payor bank acted intentionally or with malice. See also 4-402 comment 1 ("Whether a bank is liable for noncompensatory damages, such as punitive damages, must be decided by Section 1-103 and Section 1-106 ('by other rule of law').")

b. Proof of Damages and the "Trader Rule"

A statutory action for wrongful dishonor did not exist under pre-Code law. The wrong was addressed through a common-law action for breach of contract or an action in tort, such as defamation. In a defamation case, the customer could recover substantial damages without proving that damage actually occurred if she was a merchant, trader or fiduciary. Damages were presumed because defaming a person in her business, trade or profession was a defamation "per se." Presuming damages in such a case was known as the *Trader Rule*. Section 4-402 does not "retain" this Rule. 4-402 comment 1. By the terms of the statute, liability is limited to actual damages proved. 4-402(b). It could be argued that the common-law Trader Rule supplements 4-402; but it is likely that by not retaining the rule, 4-402 also displaces it.

3. Who Can Complain Of Wrongful Dishonor

a. "Its Customer"

A payor bank is liable to "its customer" for wrongful dishonor. 4-402(b). Defined most restrictively, this means the person who has the account on which the dishonored item was drawn. See 4-104(a)(5).

b. Recovery by Individuals When the Customer Is a Business Entity

Following the restrictive definition of customer, most courts have held that an individual who signed a check on behalf of a partnership or corporation cannot herself recover for wrongful dishonor of the item even though the individual maintains a separate personal account with the payor bank. A few courts have concluded, however, that upon the wrongful dishonor of a check of a business entity such as a partnership or a corporation, an individual member or officer of the entity is a customer for purposes of 4-402, and is entitled to recover damages thereunder in her own right, where -- in fact and as perceived by the payor bank -- the business entity had no viability as a separate and distinct legal creature;

its affairs and the individual's were closely intertwined; and the individual was treated, for practical purposes, as the real customer. It is also possible that supplemental common law gives the individual a separate cause of action if the dishonor of the other entity's check actually impugns her own reputation. The statute does not displace such a common-law action. 4-402 comment 5.

c. Payees

A payee or other holder of a check that is wrongfully dishonored cannot recover from the payor bank under 4-402. See 4-402 comment 5. (The statute "confers no cause of action on the holder of a dishonored item.") Yet, if the payor bank finally pays a check or becomes accountable for it under other rules of Article 4, the bank is liable to the holder. It is not clear whether the holder could recover from the bank upon the dishonor of a check that, while not finally paid, was entitled to priority under 4-303. In this case the basis of recovery would have to be 4-303(a) itself. This provision contains no language expressly imposing accountability. On the other hand, the payor bank is culpable, in general terms, when it dishonors an item that is entitled to priority under 4-303(a), inasmuch as the bank thereby interferes with and frustrates the superior rights of the owner of the item.

4. Which Funds Are Counted In Determining The Sufficiency Of The Account -- The Problem And Law Of *Funds Availability*

The most common reason for dishonoring a check is insufficient funds in the drawer's account. Dishonor for this reason is wrongful, however, if the payor bank errs in deciding that the account is insufficient to cover the check. Whether or not an account is sufficient depends partly on how soon the bank must account for funds that the customer deposits in the account. This timing issue concerns the law of *funds availability*, which determines when the customer has the right to withdraw or apply credit to her account that results from deposits of cash, checks or other items. This law is mainly federal. If a check is dishonored because funds are not counted that should have been available to the customer, the dishonor is wrongful under any applicable federal law that is violated and is also wrongful under state law 4-402.

a. Article 4

Article 4 says very little about funds availability and, in any event, is subject to preemptive federal law.

1) Cash

"[A] deposit of money becomes available for withdrawal as of right at the opening of the bank's next banking day after receipt of the deposit." 4-215(f).

2) "On Us" Items

When the customer deposits a check in a bank that is also the payor bank and the check is finally paid, credit given for the item in the customer's account becomes available for withdrawal as of right "at the opening of the bank's second banking day following receipt of the item." 4-215(e)(2).

Example: "[I]f A and B are both customers of a depositary-payor bank and A deposits B's check on Monday, time must be allowed to permit the check under the deferred posting rules of Section 4-301 to reach the bookkeeper for B's account at some time on Tuesday, and, if there are insufficient funds in B's account, to reverse or charge back the provisional credit in A's account. Consequently this provisional credit in A's account does not become available for withdrawal as of right until the opening of business on Wednesday. If it is determined on Tuesday that there are insufficient funds in B's account to pay the check, the credit to A's account can be reversed on Tuesday. On the other hand if the item is in fact paid on Tuesday, the rule of subsection (e)(2) is desirable to avoid uncertainty and possible disputes between the bank and its customer as to exactly what hour within the day the credit is available." 4-215 comment 12.

3) Other Checks

When the customer deposits and gets credit for a check that is drawn on another bank, the credit becomes available for withdrawal as of right if and when

- the settlement to the depositary bank "becomes final" and also
- "the bank has had a reasonable time to receive return of the item and the item has not been received within that time." 4-215(e)(1).

In this context "reasonable" depends "on the distance the item has to travel and the number of banks through which it must pass (having in mind not only travel time by regular lines of transmission but also the successive midnight deadlines of the several banks) and other pertinent facts." 4-215 comment 11.

b. Federal Law -- Expedited Funds Availability Act and Regulation CC

The federal Expedited Funds Availability Act, 12 USCA 4001 - 4010, specifies the maximum length of time that a depositary bank can delay before making a customer's deposits "available for withdrawal." The Act does not require any delay and would approve immediate availability of all deposits. It sets an outside limit -- an *availability schedule* -- that shortens any longer state law and that varies the time of availability with the nature of the deposit. This law is greatly amplified -- in huge detail -- by Subpart B of Regulation CC. 12 CFR 229.10 - 229.21.

1) The Meaning Of Availability

At such time as the law requires making funds "available for withdrawal," the bank must make them "available for *all* uses generally permitted to the customer for actually and finally collected funds under the bank's account agreement or policies, such as for *payment of checks drawn on the account*, certification of checks drawn on the account, electronic payments, withdrawals by cash, and transfers between accounts." 12 CFR 229.2(d) (emphasis added).

2) When Funds Must Be Available -- Availability Schedule

The availability of funds is determined by a complicated schedule that turns on the nature of the deposit. Deposits that carry a low risk of fraud must be made available sooner than ordinary checks; and availability varies for ordinary checks depending on whether they are local or nonlocal. The schedule assumes that the time a depositary bank can hold credit for ordinary checks should roughly correspond to the time ordinarily required to collect the items. The time is longer for nonlocal checks because collection takes longer, and thus the time for availability of nonlocal checks is longer. Availability that is earlier than the time usually needed for collection increases the risk of fraud because of the greater chance that the funds will become available and will be withdrawn before notice of dishonor.

Outlined here is a shortened, summary version of the availability schedule that shows only its biggest, most general points. Be aware that the schedule distinguishes between business and banking days. *"Business day"* means a calendar day other than a Saturday, Sunday, or certain stated dates that are holidays observed by the Federal Reserve. 12 CFR 229.2(g). *"Banking day"* means the part of any business day on which an office of a bank is open to the public for carrying on substantially all of its banking functions. 12 CFR 229.2(f).

a) Low-Risk Deposits -- Next-Day Availability

The following kinds of deposits must be available for withdrawal at the start of business on the next business day following the banking day of receipt:

- **Cash**
  Cash deposits get next-day availability but only when the deposits are made in person to an employee of the depositary bank. Other cash deposits must be available on the second business day after the banking day on which the deposits are made. 12 CFR 229.10(a).

- **Electronic Payments** including
  - Wire transfers
  - Automated Clearing House (ACH) credit transfers

  An electronic payment is not received until the bank receives both (1) payment in actually and finally collected funds, and (2) payment instructions identifying the account to be credited and the amount. 12 CFR 229.10(b)(2).

- **Government Checks** such as
  - United States treasury checks
  - Postal Service money orders
  - Checks drawn on a Federal Reserve Bank or Federal Home Loan Bank
  - Checks issued by the state where the depositary bank is located
  - Checks drawn by a unit of general local government within the state

- **Bank Checks**
  - Cashier's checks
  - Certified checks
  - Teller's checks

- **"On Us" Items**
  These items include any check deposited in a branch of the depositary bank and drawn on the same or another branch of the same bank if both branches are located in the same state or in the same check processing region. 12 CFR 229.10(c)(vi). The item is "on us" if the two branches are located in the same state but not in the same check processing region. 12 CFR 229.10 Commentary. Deposits at facilities that are not located on the premises of a brick-and-mortar branch of the bank, such as off-premise ATMs and remote depositaries, are not considered deposits made at branches of the depositary bank. Id. "On us" items do not include payable through drafts deposited in the payable through bank even though this bank is the "paying bank" within the definition of that term.

Overview of Regulation CC (12 CFR Part 229), 53 Fed. Reg. 19396 (May 27, 1988).

- ♦ **$100 Of All Other Checks Deposited On The Same Banking Day**
  Up to $100 of the aggregate deposit by check or checks that are not subject to next-day availability, which includes ordinary local and nonlocal checks, must be made available on the next business day. The $100 that must be made available under this rule is in addition to the amounts of other low-risk deposits that are entitled to next-day availability. A depositary bank may aggregate all local and nonlocal check deposits made by a customer on a given banking day for the purposes of the $100 next-day availability rule. Thus, if a customer has two accounts at the depositary bank, and on a particular banking day makes deposits to each account, $100 of the total deposited to the two accounts is all that this rule subjects to next-day availability.

b) Local Checks -- Second-Day Availability
Availability. **Local checks** must be available for withdrawal at the start of business on the **second business day** following the banking day when the funds were deposited. 12 CFR 229.12(b). For example, a local check deposited on Monday must be available for withdrawal on Thursday.

Definition. A local check is a check that is not entitled to next-day availability and is drawn on, payable through, or payable at a local paying bank. A local paying bank is a paying bank to which a check is sent for forward collection located in the same check processing region (of which there are 48) as the depositary bank. 12 CFR 229.2(r)&(s). The term also includes certain exceptional government and bank checks that do not qualify for next-day availability. 12 CFR 229.12(b) & Commentary.

c) Nonlocal checks -- Fifth-Day Availability
Nonlocal checks are checks that are not entitled to next-day availability that are drawn on banks in different check processing regions than the depositary bank. These checks must be available for withdrawal on the **fifth business day** following the banking day on which funds are deposited.

3) **Adjustment For Cash Withdrawals With Respect to Local and Nonlocal Checks**

There is an adjustment to the availability rules for cash and similar withdrawals against local and nonlocal checks. Funds from these checks need not be available for cash withdrawal until 5:00 p.m. on the day specified in the schedule instead of the start of business on that day. Even then, at 5:00 p.m., only $400 of the deposit must be made available for such withdrawal. This $400 is in addition to the first $100 of a day's deposit which always is entitled to next-day availability. The remainder of the funds must be available for cash or similar withdrawal at the start of business on the next business day following the business day specified in the schedule. If the proceeds of local and nonlocal checks become available for withdrawal on the same business day, the $400 withdrawal limitation applies to the aggregate of the funds that became available for withdrawal on that day. 12 CFR 229.12(d).

Means of withdrawal similar to cash withdrawal include electronic payment, issuance of a cashier's or teller's check, certification of a check, or other irrevocable commitment to pay, but do not include the granting of credit to a bank, Federal Reserve Bank, or Federal Home Loan Bank that presents a check to the depositary bank for payment. 12 CFR 229.11(b)(2).

4) **Exceptions For High-Risk Deposits**

The statute and its regulations create six "safe guard" exceptions that allow depositary banks to extend the availability times in certain narrow situations involving high risks of fraud.

a) **New Accounts**

If a customer establishes an account with a depositary bank with which it has no other current or recent account relationship, that customer is considered a new depositor and may be subject to the new account exception for the first 30 calendar after the account is opened. During the new account period, the schedules for local and nonlocal checks do not apply, but deposits received by cash and electronic payment must be given their usual next-day or second-day availability. The first $5000 of funds deposited to a new account on any one banking day by Treasury checks, checks drawn on Federal Reserve Banks or Federal Home Loan Banks, U.S. Postal money orders, state and local government checks, and bank checks must be made available at the start of business on the following business day if the deposit is made in person at a staffed location, or on the second business if not made over-the-counter. Funds in excess of the first $5000 must be available for withdrawal not later than at the start of business on the ninth business day following the banking day of deposit. For the purposes of new accounts only, traveler's checks are treated as bank checks. The usual availability requirements with respect to "on us" items and the first $100 of a day's deposit do not apply during the new-account period.

b) Large Deposits

A depositary bank may extend the hold placed on deposits of local and nonlocal checks (but not low-risk deposits) to the extent that the amount of the aggregate deposit on any banking day exceeds $5000. The first $5000 is subject to the availability schedules.

Where a customer has multiple accounts with a depositary bank, the bank may apply the large-dollar deposit exception to the aggregate of deposits to all of the customer's accounts even if the customer is not the sole holder of the accounts and not all of the holders of the customer's accounts are the same. Thus, a bank may aggregate the deposits made to two separate accounts at that bank held by the same individual, and also aggregate the deposits of an individual and a joint account for the purposes of this exception.

c) Redeposited Checks

The schedules with respect to local and nonlocal checks do not apply to a check that has been returned unpaid and is redeposited by the customer or the depositary bank, except that this exception does not apply to:

- a check that has been returned due to a missing indorsement;
- a check that has been returned because it was postdated if it is no longer postdated when redeposited.

In the cases of both checks with missing indorsements and postdated checks, the time for making the funds available begins to run again as of the date of redeposit.

d) Repeated Overdrafts

The local and nonlocal check availability schedules are suspended for six months as to any account or combination of accounts of a customer that has been repeatedly overdrawn. There are two tests to determine when accounts are repeatedly overdrawn.

- First, a customer's accounts are repeatedly overdrawn if on six banking days within the preceding six months the balance of the accounts is negative or would have been negative if checks or other charges to the accounts had been paid. This test can be met based on separate occurrences, or based on one occurrence, except that if the bank dishonors a check that otherwise would have created a negative balance the incident is considered an overdraft only on that day.

♦ Under the second test, a customer incurs repeated overdrafts if, on two banking days within the preceding six months, the available balance in any account held by the customer is negative in an amount of $5,000 or more, or would have become negative in such amount if checks or other charges to the account had been paid.

The exception applies not only to overdrafts caused by checks drawn on the account, but also overdrafts caused by other debit charges, including account fees. The exception does not apply to accounts with overdraft lines of credit, unless the credit line has been exceeded or would have been exceeded if the checks or other charges to the account had been paid.

e) Reasonable Cause To Doubt Collectibility
With respect to local and nonlocal checks, a check drawn on a Federal Reserve Bank or a Federal Home Loan Bank, or bank checks, a depositary bank may place or extend a hold if the bank has reasonable cause to believe the check is uncollectible. For example:

♦ If the bank received a notice of return from payor bank;
♦ Check is stale (more than six months old);
♦ Check is postdated;
♦ Reasonable belief that depositor is engaging in check kiting;
♦ Reasonable belief that the drawer is insolvent.

The determination that a check is uncollectible cannot be based, however, on a class of checks or persons.

f) Emergency Conditions
The holds placed on deposits of local and nonlocal checks may be extended due to delay in the collection or return of checks, or delay in the processing and updating of customers' accounts, caused by:

♦ An interruption of communications or computer or other equipment facilities;
♦ A suspension of payments by another bank;
♦ A war; or

◆ An emergency condition (including weather condition) beyond the control of the depositary bank.

The bank, however, must exercise such diligence as the circumstances require.

5) Availability Of Deposits Subject To High-Risk Exceptions

Holds placed on deposits subject to any of the high-risk exceptions, other than the new account exception, shall not exceed a reasonable period of time, which is presumed to be four business days beyond what the schedule provides. In the case of emergency conditions, however, the hold may be extended for a reasonable period after the emergency ends. There are no limits on holding funds deposited in new accounts.

6) Notice Of Reliance On High-Risk Exception

a) Content Of Notice

If any of these exceptions are invoked, other than the new account exception, the bank must provide a notice to the customer stating the customer's account number, the date and amount of the deposit, the amount of the deposit that is being delayed, the reason the exception was invoked, and the day funds will be available for withdrawal. 12 CFR 229.13(g)(1).

b) Timing Of Notice

Person-To-Person Deposits. For deposits made in person to an employee of the depositary bank, the notice generally must be given to the depositor at the time of deposit, even though the depositor is not the customer holding the account. 12 CFR 229.13(g)(2).

Other Deposits. For other deposits, such as deposits received at an ATM, lobby deposit box, night depository, or through the mail, notice must be mailed to the customer not later than the close of the business day following the banking day on which the deposit was made. Id.

Exception. Notice to the customer may be provided at a later time if the facts upon which the determination to invoke the exception do not become known to the depositary bank until after notice would otherwise have to be given. In these cases, the bank must mail the notice to the depositor as soon as practicable, but not later than the business day following the day the facts become known. Id.

7) General Disclosure Requirements

A bank must disclose to customers, in writing and in various forms, the specifics of the bank's availability policy, and must notify customers of changes in the policy. 12 CFR 229.15. Appendix C to Regulation CC contains model forms, clauses, and notices. Although their use is not required, banks using them properly to make required disclosures are deemed to be in compliance.

8) Consequences Of Violating Law

a) Federal Liability for Damages

The Act and Regulation CC themselves provide for damages for violating the funds availability rules of federal law. A bank that fails to comply with any of these rules is liable to the injured person for:

- Any actual damages sustained by that person as a result of the failure;
- Such additional amount as the court may allow, except that in the case of an individual action this liability shall not be less than $100 nor greater than $1000; and
- In the case of a successful action to enforce the foregoing liability, the costs of the action, together with a reasonable attorney's fee as determined by the court.

12 CFR 229.21(a)(1-3). Any action under this section may be brought either in federal or state court within one year after the date of the occurrence of the violation involved. Id. 229.21(d).

b) State Liability for Wrongful Dishonor

The Expedited Funds Availability Act preempts state law only narrowly, as where the state law allows longer holds than the federal law or contradicts the federal disclosure requirements. See 12 CFR 229.20. It does not preempt alternative, more generous recovery under state law when the wrongful refusal to make funds available results in wrongful dishonor of the customer's check.

5. Other Problems In Determining If Dishonor Is Rightful Or Wrongful

a. Unaccounted New Credits

"Banks commonly determine whether there are sufficient funds in an account to pay an item after the close of banking hours on the day of presentment when they post debit and credit items to the account. The determination is made on the basis of credits available for withdrawal as of right or made available for withdrawal by the bank as an accommodation to its customer. When it is determined that payment of the item would overdraw the account, the item may be returned * * *." Before the item is returned new credits that are withdrawable as of right may have been added to the account. 4-402 comment 4. Should these new credits be counted in deciding whether or not the account is sufficient? Article 4 answers this uncertainty, for its own purposes, in favor of the bank. The bank's failure to make a second determination before the item is returned is not a wrongful dishonor if new credits are added that would have covered the check. 4-402(c) & comment 4.

Two limitations on this general rule should be noted. First, even under Article 4, if the bank elects to make a "subsequent balance determination * * * for the purpose of reevaluating the bank's decision to dishonor the item, the account balance at that time is determinative of whether a dishonor for insufficiency of available funds is wrongful." 4-402(c). Second, while 4-402(c) protects against Article 4 liability for wrongful dishonor, it cannot protect against liability under federal funds availability law if this federal law is violated by the bank's failure to make a subsequent balance determination.

b. The Problem of Priority Between Checks

The sufficiency of an account with respect to a particular item can depend on when the item is considered in relation to other checks drawn against the account. This will be true, for example, in a case where several checks are presented at roughly the same time, and there are sufficient funds to cover one or more of the items but not all of them. Whether the item or items that are not paid were dishonored rightfully or wrongfully will depend on whether the bank dealt with the checks in the proper order. The proper order, however, is "any order." 4-303(b). "This is justified because of the impossibility of stating a rule that would be fair in all cases, having in mind the almost infinite number of combinations of large and small checks in relation to the available balance on hand in the drawer's account; the possible methods of receipt; and other difficulties. Further, where the drawer has drawn all the checks, the drawer should have funds available to meet all of them and has no basis for urging one should be paid before another * * *." 4-303 comment 7.

Example: At a time when B's account contained $500, she drew two checks totaling $600. One check in the amount of $100 was payable to her aunt; the other check in the amount of $500 was payable to her stockbroker. Both checks were presented for payment on the same day. The bank paid the check to the aunt, and dishonored the check to the broker. There is no wrongful dishonor.

c. Another Priority Problem: When Legal Events Against The Account Trump Checks Drawn On The Account

1) The Problem

There are a variety of legal events that can eliminate or freeze a drawer's account. For example, an account is effectively frozen upon being garnished by a creditor of the account holder. Also, an account can be reduced or entirely wiped out by the payor bank itself exercising its equitable, self-help right of setoff to satisfy a matured debt the account holder owes the bank. Any such event can thereby compete with a check drawn on the affected account in the sense that if the event is recognized before the check is considered for payment, there may not be sufficient available funds to pay the check. Whether the resulting dishonor is rightful or wrongful in such a case depends on whether the legal event or the check was entitled to priority.

2) The Rule

To solve this and similar conflicts, 4-303(a) determines priority between certain events that affect an account and checks drawn against the account.

The provision rather awkwardly provides:

> **Any knowledge, notice or stop-payment order received by, legal process served upon or setoff exercised by a payor bank comes too late to terminate, suspend or modify the bank's right or duty to pay an item or to charge its customer's account for the item if the knowledge, notice, stop-payment order or legal process is received or served and a reasonable time for the bank to act thereon expires or the setoff is exercised after the earliest of the following:**
>> **(1) the bank accepts or certifies the item;**
>> **(2) the banks pays the item in cash;**
>> **(3) the bank settles for the item having reserving a right to revoke the settlement under statute, clearing-house rule or agreement;**
>> **(4) the bank becomes accountable for the amount of the item under Section 4-302 dealing with the payor bank's responsibility for late return of items; or**
>> **(5) with respect to checks, a cutoff hour no earlier than one hour after the opening of the next banking day after the banking day on which the bank received the check and no later than the close of that next banking day or, if no cutoff hour is fixed, the close of the next banking day after the banking day on which the bank received the check.**

4-303(a). In essence, the rule is that if any one of the circumstances listed in subsections (1) through (5) occurs before notice of the legal event is received or served and a reasonable time for the bank to act thereon expires or, in the case of setoff, before the setoff is exercised, the check has priority over the event. Dishonoring the check due to or after to the event would thus be wrongful as against the account customer. Violating 4-303 would not be wrongful, in itself, against the payee or other holder.

Example: B drew a $10,000 check to S. On the banking day the check was presented for payment, which was Monday, the balance in B's account was $11,000. The next banking day, which was Tuesday, the bank took some action indicating an intention to pay the check, but then the bank changed its mind. Later on Tuesday all of B's account was set off in satisfaction of a $25,000 loan the bank has made to B. Whether the setoff came too late depends on whether the setoff was exercised before or after the bank's Tuesday cutoff hour. If the setoff occurred after the cutoff hour, the $10,000 check was entitled to priority under 4-303(a), and dishonor of the check was wrongful as between the bank and its customer.

a) The "Reasonable Time to Act" Factor
When the competing legal event is anything other than setoff by the payor bank, "the effective time for determining whether they [i.e., the legal events] were received too late * * * is receipt [of the knowledge, notice, stop-order or legal process] *plus* a reasonable time for the bank to act on any of these communications." 4-303 comment 6 (emphasis added). In the case of a setoff exercised by the payor bank, the effective time is not similarly extended because the setoff is itself action by the bank.

b) Priority Versus Final Payment
Be careful! It is easy to confuse 4-303(a) with 4-215(a) which describes the circumstances constituting final payment of an item. Certain of the tests determining the priority status of the item for purposes of 4-303(a) are the same as for final payment under Section 4-215(a), *but other tests apply in the context of 4-303(a).* The tests for priority that are not tests for final payment are:

- acceptance or certification of the item; and,
- passing of the bank-fixed cut-off hour on the day after the check is received.

This means that an item can attain priority for purposes of 4-303(a) even before the item has been finally paid within the meaning of 4-215(a).

B. OVERDRAFT LIABILITY

1. Overdrafts Chargeable To The Drawer's Account

An *overdraft* is a check drawn on an account that contains insufficient funds to cover the item. Ordinarily, of course, the payor bank can and will dishonor an overdraft. The bank usually is not obligated to pay a check that is not fully backed by collected funds (e.g., cash and finally paid checks) in the drawer's account. An exception is the unusual case in which the bank has agreed to pay overdrafts in the deposit agreement or otherwise. The bank's right to dishonor an overdraft does not, however, create a duty to do so. A bank can pay an overdraft and charge the amount to the customer's account even in the absence of an agreement with the customer authorizing the payment of overdrafts. See 4-401(a) (as against its customer a payor bank may charge her account with an overdraft). In other words, paying an overdraft is *not* an instance of wrongful payment. The customer is personally liable to the bank for the amount of the negative balance created by an overdraft because the overdraft "itself authorizes the payment for the drawer's account and carries an implied promise to reimburse the drawee." 4-401 comment 1 (1989 Official Text & Comments).

2. Overdraft Liability Of Joint Account Holders

In the past the courts disagreed whether or not a joint owner of an account is liable for an overdraft that she did not sign or otherwise authorize and from which she received no benefit. Former law seemed to authorize such an overdraft "as against its customer." It defined "customer" broadly to include any person having an account with the bank, and "account" was broad enough to include a joint account. "There is [thus] some judicial authority for the proposition that A can be held personally liable for an overdraft in a joint account where the overdraft is created by B. Given the broad definition of 'customer' in Article 4, this decision seems correct." B. Clark, THE LAW OF BANK DEPOSITS, COLLECTIONS AND CREDIT CARDS ¶ 2.08[4] (1990).

On the other hand, the basis for imposing overdraft liability is the implied promise to reimburse the drawee which the instrument itself carries. Presumably, this implied promise is made only by the person who actually drew the instrument, not by other owners of the account against which the instrument is drawn. So there is contrary judicial authority holding that a joint account holder is not liable for overdrafts simply because she is joint owner of the account. She must have signed the check, authorized its issuance, benefited from its payment, or have agreed in the deposit contract or otherwise to be responsible for overdrafts created by another owner of the account.

The 1990 version of Article 4 settles this disagreement. It "adopts the view of case authority holding that if there is more than one customer who can draw on an account, the non-signing customer is not liable for an overdraft unless that person benefits from the proceeds of the item" 4-401 comment 2. The rule is: "A customer is not liable for the amount of an overdraft if the customer neither signed the item nor benefited from the proceeds of the item." 4-401(b). Expect the courts to define "benefit" fairly generously for this purpose.

3. Contrary Agreements Regarding Overdrafts

a. Bank Agreeing To Pay Overdrafts

A bank is obligated to pay an overdraft if it has made an enforceable agreement to do so. An overdraft that is within the terms of such an agreement is, in effect, properly payable, and the bank commits wrongful dishonor by not paying the item.

Customers often argue that an agreement to pay overdrafts resulted from the bank's habit and practice of gratuitously paying the customer's overdrafts in the past. It is true that as a matter of contract law, such a contract need not be expressed and can be inferred from circumstances such as a pattern of conduct between the parties. On the other hand, the pattern itself must be so well established as to imply a promise by the bank to pay future overdrafts; and there must be consideration, reliance, or some other legal basis for enforcing this promise. The deposit contract that the customer signed might very well argue against both promise and enforceability. In *Thiele v. Security State Bank*, 396 N.W.2d 295 (N.D. 1986), the deposit contract provided that "'[w]e [the bank] do not in any way obligate ourselves to pay any item which would overdraw this account regardless of the frequency with which we may do so hereafter as a matter of practice.'" Id. at 298. The court decided that this "language explains any course of dealing which may have occurred before the execution of the account agreement and negates any informal modification of express terms subsequent to the written agreement." Id. at 302. Moreover, an agreement to pay overdrafts is really a promise to loan money, and many states recently have enacted statutes of frauds that condition the enforcement of such a promise (often called a "credit agreement") on a writing signed by the bank.

b. Joint Account Customer Assuming Liability For Another Customer's Overdrafts

A customer on an account who neither signed an overdraft nor benefited from it is nevertheless liable for the overdraft, despite 4-401(b), if she agreed (before or after) to pay overdrafts drawn by another customer on the account, ratified the overdraft, or is estopped to deny liability for it.

C. STOPPING PAYMENT

Stopping payment refers to the drawer of a check or other authorized person ordering the payor bank, usually after the check has already been issued, to dishonor the item upon presentment for payment even though the item is otherwise properly payable. The intent of an order to close an account is the same with respect to outstanding items.

1. The Right To Stop Payment (Or Close An Account)
a. The Basis of the Right

"A customer or any person authorized to draw on the account if there is more than one person may stop payment of any item drawn on the customer's account or close the account by an order to the bank describing the item or account with reasonably certainty * * *." 4-403(a). "[S]topping payment or closing an account is a service which depositors expect and are entitled to receive from banks notwithstanding its difficulty, inconvenience and expense." 4-403 comment 1. The right is absolute, and is fettered only by certain procedural requirements that must be satisfied for the stop-order to be valid and effective. In other words, a customer can order payment stopped on any check she has written for whatever reason, or for no reason, without having to explain her motives to the payor bank.

b. The Policy Behind It

According to Professor Hal Scott: "One of the fundamental policies underlying the right to stop payment is to improve the bargaining position of the drawer (buyer) with its payee (seller) in a dispute on the underlying transaction. Stop payment allows the drawer to retain *funds and goods* pending resolution of any dispute, subject, of course, to the seller's right to reclaim the goods by peaceful repossession, *see* 2-507. Without stop payment the drawer would usually only have the goods -- it may not even have this if payment is required in advance -- and would have to go after the seller for damages or a rescission remedy." Permanent Editorial Board for the Uniform Commercial Code, Uniform New Payments Code § 425 comment 1 (Draft No. 3 June 2, 1983) (emphasis in original).

c. Persons Entitled to Exercise the Right

The right to stop payment belongs to any customer on the account against which the item is drawn. This means:

♦ "[I]f there is more than one person authorized to draw on a customer's account any one of them can stop payment of any check drawn on the account or can order the account closed," 4-403 comment 5, even if the person did not sign the check on which she orders payment stopped.

♦ "[I]f there is a customer, such as a corporation, that requires its checks to bear the signatures of more than one person, any of these persons may stop payment on a check." Id.

Also, upon a customer's death, payment of her checks can be stopped by any person claiming an interest in the account, including a surviving relative or a creditor of the customer. See 4-405 comment 3. Otherwise, "a payee or indorsee has no right to stop payment." 4-403 comment 2.

d. Items and Drawees Subject To The Right

The right to stop payment ordinarily is exercised against checks, but the right is not limited to checks and applies to any "item" drawn against a customer's account. Therefore, the right "extends to any item payable by any bank. If the maker of a note payable at a bank is in a position analogous to that of a drawer (Section 4-106) the maker may stop payment of the note. By analogy the rule extends to drawees other than banks." 4-403 comment 3.

2. Payor Bank's Liability For Payment Over A Valid Stop-Payment Order

a. Basis of Liability

A valid stop order renders the affected check not properly payable. Therefore, a "payment in violation of an *effective* direction to stop payment is an improper payment, even though it is made by mistake or inadvertence." 4-403 comment 7 (emphasis added).

b. Disclaimer of Liability

Banks would like to disclaim this liability and often will try to do so in the deposit agreement or otherwise, but any such agreement "is invalid * * * if in paying the item over the stop-payment order the bank has failed to exercise ordinary care." 4-403 comment 7; see also 1-102(3) & 4-103(a). Moreover, an agreement disclaiming or limiting a bank's liability "which is imposed upon a customer as part of a standard form contract would have to be evaluated in the light of the general obligation of good faith." 4-403 comment 7; see also 1-203 & 4-104(c).

c. Damages

Because a check covered by a valid stop order is not properly payable, it can be argued that a charge to the drawer's account is improper and must be reversed. By this argument the measure of the payor bank's liability is the amount of the item. It may be, however, that the bank's wrongful payment over the stop order actually caused the drawer no loss, as where the drawer has no reason for refusing to pay the payee or other holder. In such a case, holding the bank strictly liable for the amount of the item would give the drawer a windfall. So a payor bank is liable for paying over a stop order only if the drawer suffered actual loss. The question is whether the drawer's recovery should be conditioned on her proving the loss, or the absence of loss should be a defense proved by the payor bank.

The statute itself expressly provides:

> The burden of establishing the fact and amount of loss resulting from the payment of an item contrary to a[n] [effective] stop-payment order or order to close an account is on the customer.

4-403(c). Arguably, however, this provision is contradicted by 4-407, which gives subrogation rights of various parties to a payor bank that has paid over a stop order. The purpose is to prevent unjust enrichment. These rights include the rights of the payee (or any other holder of the check) against the drawer, either on the instrument or the underlying transaction. 4-407(2). The purpose of this specific subsection is to prevent unjust enrichment of the drawer by allowing the payor bank to recover from the drawer whatever is legitimately owed the payee or other person to whom the drawer would be liable in connection with the instrument. Naturally, when relying on 4-407, the payor bank would have the complete burden of proving the rights to which it is subrogated. It would seem, therefore, that the drafters intended that concerns about a windfall to the drawer should be addressed through 4-407, which puts the burden squarely on the payor bank to prove, in effect, the absence of loss from its failure to honor the drawer's stop order.

Several courts have resolved this apparent conflict between 4-403 and 4-407 by dividing the burden of proof. Under their compromise approach, the payor bank must plead the absence of loss as a defense and bear the burden of going forward with some evidence to substantiate the defense. Thereafter, the drawer bears the burden of persuading the trier of fact as to the fact and amount of loss.

d. Compounding Damages By Wrongful Dishonor

An item covered by an effective stop-order must be ignored in determining the sufficiency of an account to cover other items. An account balance will be artificially and inaccurately low if the bank violates a stop-order, pays the check, and debits the account. If the bank then bounces checks due to this inaccurate insufficiency in the account, the bank is guilty of wrongful dishonor with respect to these items. The statute is explicit that the customer's loss for violating a stop payment order "may include damages for [wrongful] dishonor of subsequent items under Section 4-402." 4-403(c).

e. Subrogation

As just mentioned, 4-407 gives to a payor bank, that has paid over a stop order, subrogation rights of various parties. The payor bank is subrogated to the rights

- of any holder in due course on the item against the drawer or maker; and
- of the payee or any other holder of the item against the drawer or maker either on the item or under the transaction out of which the item arose; and
- of the drawer or maker against the payee or any other holder of the item with respect to the transaction out of which the item arose.

4-407(1-3). The purpose is to prevent unjust enrichment. This purpose is achieved because, by exercising the subrogation rights appropriate for the case, the payor bank can shift responsibility for the instrument or the underlying transaction to the party who properly should bear it.

Example: D, a law student, had just learned in her commercial paper class that a payor bank is liable to its customer for violating a stop-payment order. So D had an idea. She purchased a new, pinstriped suit from Brooks Bros. to wear to job interviews. She paid by check and immediately ordered the drawee to stop payment of the item, hoping that the bank would screw up and violate the order. Sure enough the bank paid the check and charged it to D's account. D then demanded that the bank recredit her account because the check was paid over her valid stop-payment order. Bank refuses. D sues. D loses. First, D suffered no loss because she would have been liable on the check, and on the underlying obligation to Brooks Bros., if the bank had complied with the stop-payment order and dishonored the check. Second, the bank is subrogated to the rights on the check and the underlying obligation that the payee, Brooks Bros., would have enjoyed against D had the check been dishonored. 4-407(2).

Example: B drew a check to S in payment for goods. Upon inspecting the goods, B discovered they were defective and rightfully rejected them. At the same time she ordered the drawee not to pay the check to S. Even though B's stop-payment order was valid, the bank paid the check and charged it to B's account. B sues bank, demanding that the bank recredit her account for the amount of the item. Bank files a third-party action against S. B should win against bank, and bank should have recovery against S. B suffered a loss because she would not have been liable to S on the check or the underlying obligation had the check been dishonored, inasmuch as her rightful rejection entitled B to cancel the sales contract. See 2-711(1).

Bank, however, is subrogated to B's rights against S with respect to the sales transaction. Because B could recover from S the price paid, id., bank can recover the same from S. 4-407(3).

f. Common-Law Defenses

Apart from and beyond subrogation, the payor bank retains common-law defenses against its customer who complains about the bank paying over an effective stop order. For example, the defense of ratification is available to the bank, e.g., "that by conduct in recognizing the payment the customer has ratified the bank's action in paying over a stop-payment order." 4-403 comment 7.

g. Restitution

In addition, people whom the bank pays are potentially accountable to the bank for restitution -- unjust enrichment resulting from payment by mistake. Id. This accountability is subject, however, to the beneficiary's bona fide-purchaser defense of 3-418, which usually is a good and complete defense to restitution.

3. Requisites Of An Effective Stop-Payment Order

Payment in violation of a stop order is improper only if the stop order was effective with respect to the item. To be effective a stop order "must be received at a *time* and in a *manner* that affords the bank a reasonable opportunity to act on it before any action by the bank with respect to the item described in Section 4-303." 4-403(a).

a. Manner
1) Form

A stop order can be oral or written, but a written order is effective for a longer time. A written order is effective for six months. An oral stop order lasts only 14 calendar days unless confirmed in writing within the 14-day period. 4-403(b). "If there is written confirmation within the 14-day period, the six-month period dates from the giving of the oral order." 4-403 comment 6.

- "A stop-payment order may be renewed any number of times by written notice given during a six-month period while a stop order is in effect.
- "A new stop-payment order may be given after a six-month period expires, but such a notice takes effect from the date given.
- "When a stop-payment order expires it is as though the order had never been given, and the payor bank may pay the item in good faith * * * even though a stop-payment order had once been given." Id.

2) Content

A stop order is effective only if it contains sufficient information to allow the bank to act. The order must describe the item with "reasonable certainty." 4-403(a). This "reasonableness standard * * * does not rise to the level of [complete or absolute] certainty," and it tolerates "certain discrepancies in the description of an otherwise adequate order" so that a stop order may be effective even though there are mistakes in the customer's description of the item. *Best v. Dreyfus Liquid Assets, Inc.*, 215 N.J.Super. 76, 81, 521 A.2d 352, 355 (1987). The reasonableness of an inaccurate description is ordinarily, of course, a factual question.

In the *Best* case, the customer erroneously stated the date of the check and the check number. The court nevertheless held that the customer's stop order was not unreasonable as a matter of law. Similarly, in the case *Kunkel v. First Nat'l Bank of Devils Lake*, 393 N.W.2d 265 (N.D. 1986), the court determined that a stop order was not necessarily unreasonable simply because the customer listed the amount of the check as $7400 when, in fact, the amount was $7,048.27. In contrast, the stop order was unreasonable in *Marine Midland Bank v. Berry*, 123 A.D.2d 254, 506 N.Y.S.2d 60 (1986), because the order misstated the check number, incorrectly named the payee, and misstated the amount of the check.

b. Time of Receipt

To be effective, a stop order must be received a reasonable time before any of these circumstances has occurred:

- the bank accepts or certifies the item;
- the bank pays the item in cash;
- the bank settles for the item without having a right to revoke the settlement under statute, clearing-house rule or agreement;
- the bank becomes accountable for the amount of the item under Section 4-302 dealing with the payor bank's responsibility for late return of items; or
- with respect to checks, a cutoff hour no earlier than one hour after the opening of the next banking day after the banking day on which the bank received the check and no later than the close of that next banking day or, if no cutoff hour is fixed, the close of the next banking day after the banking day on which the bank received the check.

4-303(a)(1-5). This section, which is discussed earlier in this chapter, determines priority between the right of a customer to stop payment and the right and duty of the payor bank to promptly process checks presented for payment. If any one of the circumstances in 4-303(a) has occurred with respect to a check before the bank has had a reasonable chance to act on a stop order covering the item, the stop order comes too late, which means that the order is ineffective and paying the item is not wrongful.

4. Stopping Payment Against A Holder In Due Course

Technically speaking, payment can be stopped against a holder in due course. On the other hand, "the drawer remains liable on the instrument * * * and the drawee, if it pays, becomes subrogated to the rights of the holder in due course against the drawer." 4-403 comment 7. The practical result is that the drawer cannot complain against the bank for violating the drawer's stop order if the drawer had no defense that was good against the holder in due course. At a minimum, the bank's recovery as subrogee is offset against its liability for wrongful dishonor.

5. Cashiers' Checks

In a very large number of recent cases the courts have considered if payment can be stopped on a cashier's check, which is a draft drawn by a bank on itself. 3-104(g). This broad concern involves two entirely separate issues. The easier issue is whether the bank that issues the cashier's check becomes liable to the person who procured it, i.e., the remitter, by refusing to dishonor the instrument upon the remitter's request. The second and harder issue is whether an issuing bank that refuses payment of its cashier's check, either on its own or at the request of the remitter, can escape liability to the payee or other holder of the instrument.

a. Remitter's Right to Stop Payment

Suppose that B buys goods from S who demands payment in the form of a cashier's check. B purchases a cashier's check from Bank and delivers the instrument to S. B quickly learns that the goods are defective and asks Bank not to pay the cashier's check and to return to B the money she paid Bank for the check. Must Bank honor B's request?

The answer is no, unless Bank and B have an enforceable agreement giving B the right to stop payment of the check. B does not have the right apart from such an agreement. 4-403 does not apply for two reasons: First, 4-403 is limited to checks drawn on the customer's account. A cashier's check is drawn by the issuing bank against the bank's own account. Second, a stop order comes too late, i.e., is ineffective, if received after the item it covers has been accepted. See 4-303(a)(1). A draft drawn by the drawer on itself is accepted upon issuance. Therefore, there can never be a timely stop order of a cashier's check.

b. Issuer's Liability When Payment Denied

A bank that issues a cashier's check may wish to dishonor the item either as a courtesy to the remitter who requests that payment be stopped, or for the bank's own reasons. The problem in doing so is that the bank, as issuer of the check, is liable on the instrument to the payee or a subsequent holder. 3-412. In a conflict between the bank and a holder of the cashier's check, is the bank always and inevitably liable, or can the bank raise defenses to its liability on the instrument? The courts disagree on this issue.

1) Overgeneralized View

Some courts have suggested, in applying a variety of technical justifications, that the bank that issues a cashier's check is strictly, absolutely liable thereon to any holder of the instrument. The rationale for this view is that a cashier's check is regarded in the commercial world as the equivalent of cash, and to allow the issuing bank to assert defenses to payment would undermine the useful purposes of cashier's checks as substitutes for money.

2) Better View

A far preferable view is that an issuing bank can raise defenses to the payment of a cashier's check according to the usual rules governing an obligor's liability on a negotiable instrument. Unless the holder is a holder in due course, the bank can raise the full range of its defenses permitted under 3-305 and 3-306, including the defenses of want or failure of consideration and all other defenses of the bank which would be available in an action on a simple contract. If the holder enjoys "due course" status, the bank can raise only its real defenses. Yet, even if the holder lacks due-course status, the bank can assert only its own defenses. It cannot raise defenses that are personal to the remitter, such as breach of contract between the remitter and the payee of the cashier's check. Such matters are properly left for decision in an action between those parties.

Example: B satisfied an obligation to S by giving S a cashier's check B procured from Bank. In exchange for the cashier's check, B had given Bank her personal check drawn on another financial institution. B's personal check bounced. For this reason Bank dishonored the cashier's check when S presented it for payment. S sued Bank on the cashier's check. Bank can raise its defense of lack or failure of consideration unless S is a holder in due course who did not deal with the Bank. S may be a holder in due course even though she is the payee of the cashier's check.

Example: S sold goods to B who paid for them using a cashier's check issued by Bank. The goods were defective, and B asked Bank to stop payment of the check. Because B was a valued customer, Bank dishonored the cashier's check when S presented it for payment. S sued Bank on the instrument. Bank should not be allowed to assert B's breach of contract claim as a defense.

c. Damages When Issuer Wrongfully Refuses to Pay Cashier's Checks or Similar Bank Items

When a bank refuses payment of a cashier's, certified, or teller's check on which it is liable and for which it has no good defense, the damages against the bank naturally include the amount of the item; but the damages are not limited to this amount. The damages also can include "compensation for expenses and loss of interest resulting from the nonpayment and may [include] * * * consequential damages if the obligated bank refuses to pay after receiving notice of particular circumstances giving rise to the damages." 3-411(b). Expenses and consequential damages are not recoverable, however, even though the bank is liable on the instrument, if payment was refused because:

- the bank suspends payments;
- the obligated bank asserts a claim or defense of the bank that it has reasonable grounds to believe is available against the person entitled to enforce the instrument;
- the obligated bank has a reasonable doubt whether the person demanding payment is the person entitled to enforce the instrument; or
- payment is prohibited by law.

3-411(c).

d. Rights of a Claimant Who Lost a Cashier's Check

Because of the large damages that can flow from the wrongful dishonor of a cashier's check, the issuing bank naturally will be reluctant to honor the rights of a person who claims to have lost a cashier's check. To honor these rights requires the bank to risk (minimally) the truth of the person's claim, which can unduly burden honest people in some cases. Many states therefore have enacted a statute that attempts to accommodate the interests of the bank and original claimant in such a case. The statute usually is included in Article 3 as section 3-312 and provides in full:

(a) In this section:
    (1) "Check" means a cashier's check, teller's check, or certified check;
    (2) "Claimant" means a person who claims the right to receive the amount of a cashier's check, teller's check, or certified check that was lost, destroyed, or stolen;
    (3) "Declaration of loss" means a written statement, made under penalty of perjury, to the effect that
        (i) the declarer lost possession of a check,

(ii) the declarer is the drawer or payee of the check, in the case of a certified check, or the remitter or payee of the check, in the case of a cashier's or teller's check,

(iii) the loss of possession was not the result of a transfer by the declarer or a lawful seizure, and

(iv) the declarer cannot reasonably obtain possession of the check because the check was destroyed, its whereabouts cannot be determined, or it is in the wrongful possession of an unknown person or a person that cannot be found or is not amenable to service of process; and

(4) "Obligated bank" means the issuer of a cashier's check or a teller's check or the acceptor of a certified check.

(b) A claimant may assert a claim to the amount of a check by a communication to the obligated bank describing the check with reasonable certainty and requesting payment of the amount of the check, if

(i) the claimant is the drawer or payee of a certified check or the remitter or payee of a cashier's check or teller's check,

(ii) the communication contains or is accompanied by a declaration of loss of the claimant with respect to the check,

(iii) the communication is received at a time and in a manner affording the bank reasonable time to act on it before the check is paid, and (iv) the claimant provides reasonable identification if requested by the obligated bank.

Delivery of a declaration of loss is a warranty of the truth of the statements made in the declaration. If a claim is asserted in compliance with this subsection, the following rules apply:

(1) The claim becomes enforceable at the later of (i) the time the claim is asserted, or (ii) the ninetieth (90th) day following the date of the check, in the case of a cashier'scheck or teller's check, or the ninetieth (90th) day following the date of the acceptance, in the case of a certified check;

(2) Until the claim becomes enforceable, it has no legal effect and the obligated bank may pay the check or, in the case of a teller's check, may permit the drawee to pay the check. Payment to a person entitled to enforce the check discharges all liability of the obligated bank with respect to the check;

(3) If the claim becomes enforceable before the check is presented for payment, the obligated bank is not obliged to pay the check; and (4) When the claim becomes enforceable, the obligated bank becomes obliged to pay the amount of the check to the claimant if payment of the check has not been made to a person entitled to enforce the check. Subject to paragraph (1) of subsection (a), payment to the claimant discharges all liability of the obligated bank with respect to the check.

(c) If the obligated bank pays the amount of a check to a claimant under paragraph (4) of subsection (b) of this section and the check is presented for payment by a person having rights of a holder in due course, the claimant is obliged to

(i) refund the payment to the obligated bank if the check is paid, or (ii) pay the amount of the check to the person having rights of a holder in due course if the check is dishonored.

(d) If a claimant has the right to assert a claim under subsection (b) of this section and is also a person entitled to enforce a cashier's check, teller's check, or certified check

which is lost, destroyed, or stolen, the claimant may assert rights with respect to the check either under this section or Section 60 of this act.

Essentially, 3-312 allows the claimant to make a claim for payment by providing the bank with a declaration of loss. The claim is enforceable at the later of the time the claim is made or the 90th day following the date or certification of the check. If the claim becomes enforceable before the check is presented for payment, the bank is obliged to pay the claim and is discharged of all liability with respect to the check. The claim is legally ineffective prior to the time the claim become enforceable, and the bank must pay the check if the check is presented prior to the time of the claim's enforceability. The reasoning seems to be that if 90 days pass without presentment of the check, the claim of loss is probably legitimate and the possibility is small that someone will appear as a holder in due course of the instrument. In the unlikely event that such a person appears after the bank has honored an enforceable claim, the claimant is accountable for the check.

D. UNTIMELY CHECKS

1. Stale Checks
a. Defined
A *stale check* is an uncertified check of a customer which is presented more than six months after the check's date.

b. Two Basic Rules
There are two rules with respect to stale checks.

1) Bank Is Not Obligated To Pay
First, the payor bank is not obligated to pay them. 4-404. Thus, dishonor of a stale check is not wrongful dishonor.

2) Bank May Pay In Good Faith
Second, although not bound to pay a stale check, the payor bank has the right to do so *in good faith*. Id. Thus, paying a stale check in good faith is not wrongful payment and the item rightfully can be charged to the customer's account. A bank pays a stale check in good faith if, for example, the bank knows that the drawer wants payment made. "Certified checks are excluded [from these rules on stale checks] * * * because they are the primary obligation of the certifying bank * * * [which] runs directly to the holder of the check." 4-404 comment.

2. Postdated Checks

a. Defined

A postdated check is a check issued before the stated date of the instrument.

b. Notice of Postdating Renders Check Not Properly Payable

It could be argued that premature payment of a postdated check is wrongful because the drawer ordered payment at a later date. Payor banks, however, cannot easily discover postdates. Finding them would be very costly in time and money. Therefore, in order to enforce a postdate against a payor bank, the customer "must notify the payor bank of its postdating in time to allow the bank to act on the customer's notice before the bank has to commit itself to pay the check." 4-401 comment 3. Here is the rule:

> A bank may charge against the account of a customer a check that is otherwise properly payable from the account, even though payment was made before the date of the check, unless the customer has given notice to the bank of the postdating describing the check with reasonable certainty.

4-401(c).

c. When And How Long Notice Is Effective (Like Stop Order)

In effect, a notice of postdating is akin to a stop order that orders the bank to delay payment rather than to stop payment. Therefore, some of the procedural rules are the same:

- The period of effectiveness of a notice of postdating is the same as that for a stop order. See 4-401(c) & 4-403(b) (14 days oral and six months written).
- Like a stop order, a notice of postdating must be received at such time and in such manner as to afford the bank a reasonable opportunity to act on it before the bank takes any action with respect to the check described in Section 4-303, that is,
  - √ the bank accepts or certifies the item;
  - √ the banks pays the item in cash;
  - √ the bank settles for the item having reserving a right to revoke the settlement under statute, clearing-house rule or agreement;
  - √ the bank becomes accountable for the amount of the item under Section 4-302 dealing with the payor bank's responsibility for late return of items; or
  - √ with respect to checks, a cutoff hour no earlier than one hour after the opening of the next banking day after the banking day on which the bank received the check and no later than the close of that next banking day or, if no cutoff hour is fixed, the close of the next banking day after the

banking day on which the bank received the check. 4-303(a)(1-5) &
4-401(c).

d. Damages
If a bank violates an effective notice of postdating by charging the check against
the customer's account before the date stated in the notice, the bank is liable for
damages for any resulting loss, including loss resulting from dishonor of
subsequent items. 4-401(c).

3. Mitigating Liability For Paying Untimely Checks
As in the case where a stop order is violated, a payor bank that wrongfully pays a
stale or postdated check should not be liable if the drawer suffered no actual loss as a
result of the wrongful payment. Moreover, 4-407 subrogates the bank to the rights of
various parties to the instrument.

E. EFFECT OF A CUSTOMER'S INCOMPETENCE OR DEATH

A check drawn by a customer who was then incompetent, or who later dies or becomes
incompetent, is properly payable so long as the bank is unaware of the death or an
adjudication of incompetency. The check becomes not properly payable, however, a
reasonable time after the bank knows of the death or adjudication. That is, when a
customer has been adjudged incompetent, or has died, the payor bank loses the authority
to pay the customer's checks as of the time "the bank knows of the fact of death or of an
adjudication of incompetence *and* has reasonable opportunity to act on it." 4-405(a)
(emphasis added). There is an exception in the case of a customer's death: "Even with
knowledge a bank may for 10 days after the date of death pay or certify checks drawn on
or before that date unless ordered to stop payment by a person claiming an interest in the
account." 4-405(b).

Arguably, paying the checks of an incompetent or dead customer without authority, i.e.,
in violation of 4-405, is -- by analogy or otherwise -- a case in which the payor bank has
paid an item "under circumstances giving a basis for objection by the drawer or maker
* * *." 4-407. In this event, as when there is wrongful payment over a stop order or
payment of an untimely check, the payor bank is subrogated to the rights of various
parties under 4-407 for the purpose of preventing unjust enrichment of the customer's
estate.

F. CHECK FRAUD

Check fraud mainly refers to wrongfully altering checks or making signatures on them that are unauthorized or otherwise ineffective. Who bears the loss in case of check fraud as between the payor bank and the customer whose account is charged with the tainted item? The usual answer is that the loss falls on the payor bank, unless the bank can establish a defense provided by Article 3 or 4 or extra-Code law. This chapter explains the basis of the payor bank's liability to its customer for the major kinds of check fraud, and also outlines the bank's major defenses against its customer in each case. The next chapter moves beyond the bilateral relationship between the payor bank and its customer to consider if and how, in check fraud cases, the loss should properly be shifted to a third person. The assumption here and in the next chapter is that collecting the loss from the wrongdoer, who in every case is ultimately responsible, is practically impossible because she is financially or otherwise unavailable.

1. Basis Of Payor Bank's Liability To Its Checking-Account Customer

In every instance of check fraud the fundamental basis of a payor bank's accountability to its customer, where the item has been charged to the customer's account, is the rule that only properly payable items can be charged against a customer's account. See 4-401(a). Checks that have been materially altered, or that carry an ineffective signature, are not properly payable.

a. Ineffective Drawer's Signature

The deposit contract between a payor bank and its customer determines who can draw against the customer's account by specifying whose signature is necessary on checks that are chargeable against the customer's account. Therefore, a check drawn against the account of an individual customer that is signed by someone other than the customer, and without authority from her, is not properly payable and is not chargeable to the customer's account, inasmuch as any "unauthorized signature [on an instrument] is ineffective" as the signature of the person whose name is signed. 3-403(a). Similarly, a check is not properly payable that is drawn on the account of a corporate customer by someone other than the person or persons authorized to draw against the account. Also, in the case where a deposit contract requires multiple signatures on checks drawn against the account, a check not signed by all of the required signatories is unauthorized, 3-403(b), and is not properly payable.

Example: T steals D's checkbook and, using D's name or her own name, draws a check against D's account. The drawee-payor bank pays the check and charges it to D's account. D can force the bank to recredit her account for the amount of the item.

Example: The deposit contract between D Corp. and Bank provides that Bank can and will pay checks drawn on the account by the president *or* the comptroller of D Corp. Without authority, an employee of D Corp. draws a check on the account using the president's name. The check is not properly payable and cannot rightfully be charged against the account of D Corp.

Example: The deposit contract between D Corp. and Bank provides that Bank can and will pay checks drawn on the account by the president *and* comptroller of D Corp. Both officers must sign the checks. Bank pays a check drawn against the account of D Corp. that is signed only by the comptroller. The check is not properly payable and cannot rightfully be charged against the account of D Corp.

Example: Same facts (both officers must sign), except that the comptroller, without authority, also signs the president's name. The check is not properly payable. The unauthorized signature of the president is not operative as the president's signature. So the check lacks a necessary signature.

b.   Ineffective Indorsement

1)   What Is The Wrong To The Drawer?

A check that bears a forged or otherwise unauthorized or ineffective indorsement cannot rightfully be charged against the drawer-customer's account because the check was not paid consistently with the drawer's (or subsequent holder's) order and was not properly presented to the payor bank. (Presentment is a demand for payment made by or on behalf of the person entitled to enforce the instrument, usually a holder. 3-501(a). A transferee of a check with an ineffective indorsement cannot be a holder. See Chapter IV supra.) In short, a check with any forged indorsement, or an indorsement that is otherwise ineffective, is not properly payable because it was not properly presented and paid. Because the check is not properly payable, it cannot rightfully be charged against the customer's account.

Example: B drew a check to S in payment for goods. An employee of S indorsed the check and cashed it at the payor bank. This employee had no responsibilities with respect to D's checks, acted without any authority from S to indorse for S, and used her own name. The bank then charged the amount of the check against B's account. B can force bank to recredit her account. The result is the same if the employee used S's name or indorsed in both her name and S's.

Example: B drew a check to H and W jointly. H indorsed the check and
also forged W's indorsement. The payor bank paid the check
and charged B's account for the amount of the item. W never
got a dime of the payment. Payor bank must recredit B's
account, at least to the extent of W's interest in the check.
(Remember: "If an instrument is payable to two or more persons
not alternatively, it is payable [only] to all of them and may be
negotiated, discharged or enforced only by all of them."
3-110(d).)

2) Where Is The Loss To The Drawer?

An important side issue here is why, in either example, *B* would complain
against the payor bank for charging the item to her account. A loss to S is
obvious. Where is the loss to *B*? In the first of the two examples, payment
was improper because it was not made to a holder. In the second example
payment was improper because payment was not made to all of the joint
payees. As a result, B was not discharged on the instrument, see 3-602(a)
(discharge requires payment to holder); so she was not discharged on the
underlying obligation. 3-310(b). B thus remains liable to the payee. If this
liability to the payee is enforced, B effectively will "pay" twice, inasmuch
as her account has already been debited for the amount of the check. There
is the loss to B. (The fuller truth, however, is that S usually enjoys
additional actions against other people and often shifts the loss to them
instead of B. These other actions are considered in the next chapter.)

c. Alteration

A check is properly payable only on the terms ordered by the drawer. So an
altered check, i.e., a check on which the terms have been wrongfully changed by
the payee or someone else, is not properly payable. In the usual case of
alteration, the wrongdoer raises the amount of the check. In this case, the check
is not properly payable to the extent of the alteration. The payor bank can
charge the customer's account according to the original tenor of the item (i.e., in
the amount ordered by the customer), 4-401(d)(1), but the difference between
the original and raised amounts of the check cannot be charged against the
account.

Example: B drew a $50 check to S who cleverly and fraudulently raised the
amount to $500, and cashed it, for $500, at payor bank. The bank
then charged B's account for $500. B can force the bank to recredit
her account for $450.

d. Wrongfully Completed Checks

For some purposes, a check that is completed other than as authorized is treated as an altered instrument. See 3-115 & 3-407. This is not true in deciding who, as between a payor bank and its customer, bears the loss from a wrongfully completed check. The rule is: A bank which in good faith makes payment to a holder may charge the indicated account of its customer according to the tenor of the check as actually completed, not just in the amount or as otherwise authorized by the customer. 4-401(d)(2). It makes no difference that the bank knows that the item was completed by someone other than the customer so long as the bank was unaware that the *completion* itself was improper. Id.

> *Example:*   B drew a check to S, leaving the amount blank. S was authorized to complete the check in an amount not exceeding $50. S filled in the amount of $500 and cashed the item at payor bank. The bank can charge B's account to the full extent of $500.

> *Example:*   B drew a $500 check, leaving blank the name of the payee. B then gave the check to T and directed T to use the check to purchase certain goods for B, filling in the name of the seller. T filled in her own name and cashed the check at payor bank. The bank can charge the check to B's account.

2. Payor Bank's Defenses

The U.C.C. and other law provide an array of defenses for a payor bank or another defendant in a check fraud case as against a customer or other person who complains of a loss. The most important of these defenses are considered below as they might be applied when determining, as between the payor bank and its customer, who bears the loss for check fraud. Most of these defenses are applicable whether the complaint involves an allegedly ineffective signature or an alteration, but the emphasis here is on problem signatures because, in real life, the usual complaint in the vast majority of check fraud cases is lack of authority, forgery or an otherwise ineffective signature rather than alteration.

a. Authority
1) The Effect Of The Defense -- It Undercuts Wrong

When a customer demands the recrediting of her account for the amount of an item that carried an allegedly ineffective signature, or that has been altered, the payor bank's most basic defense is that the alteration or signature was authorized by a proper person. Authority denies the wrong that is the foundation of the complaint.

2) Rules About Agents Authorized To Sign for Their Principals

The rules on signatures by agents are very important in establishing the defense of authority with respect to signatures. In practice, problem signatures usually are not made by strangers. Problem signatures commonly are made by wrongdoers who were associated with the person whose signature was necessary. They could have been authorized to sign for her. Here are the rules:

* A person's signature on an instrument may be made by an agent or other representative.
* The signature is deemed to be the signature of the represented person, and she is fully bound on the instrument as if she personally had signed it, if the represented person would be bound if the signature were on a simple contract. 3-402(a).
* Whether or not the represented person is so bound is determined by extra-Code agency law. "If under the law of agency the represented person would be bound by the act of the representative [or purported representative] in signing either the name of the represented person or that of the representative, the signature is the authorized signature of the represented person." 3-402 comment 1
* By reference to this extra-Code law, the defense that a signature on an instrument was authorized can be based on express authority, may be implied in law or in fact, or may rest merely on apparent authority.
* Article 3 does not bar parol evidence to prove or deny the authority.
* Article 3 requires no particular form of appointment or form of signature to establish the authority.
* In particular, if the represented person would be bound on a simple contract under extra-Code law, she is bound on the instrument whether or not she is identified in the instrument.

Example: B has a checking account with Payor Bank. The deposit contract specifies that B is the sole signatory on checks payable against the account. C drew a check on B's account, using C's own name or B's name. Payor Bank paid the check and charged B's account for the amount of the item. C fled with the proceeds of the check. B sued Bank to force the recrediting of her account. Bank proves at trial that B had expressly or implicitly authorized C to draw checks against the account. Bank wins.

Example: The deposit contract between D Corp. and Bank provides that Bank can and will pay checks drawn on the account by the president or comptroller of D Corp. The contract also authorizes the bank to pay checks drawn over the facsimile signature of either of these people, as through the use of a rubber stamp. Without authority, an employee of D Corp. draws a check on the account using a rubber stamp bearing the president's name. The courts are split on whether the check in such a case is properly payable. Some authority says that the check is properly payable and chargeable to the corporation's account due to the terms of the deposit agreement. Other authority argues that the deposit agreement protects the bank only when the facsimile signature is used with appropriate authority. Perhaps the case is better resolved in the bank's favor on the basis of estoppel or the like rather than authority.

Example: B drew a check to H and W jointly. H indorsed the check by signing his name and also W's name. Payor Bank paid the check and charged B's account for the amount of the item. W never got a dime of the payment. W complained to B who satisfied the amount she owed W. B then sued Payor Bank who established at trial that W had approved H indorsing the check on her behalf. Bank is not accountable to B. (In fact, B was not accountable to W. Inasmuch as H acted rightfully in dealing with the check, B was discharged on the instrument and the underlying obligation to both H and W.)

Example: B gave P a check in settlement of a tort action. The check was payable to P and her attorney in the action, L. Unbeknownst to P, L indorsed the check, which was paid, and used the proceeds for her own purposes. P got nothing. Believing she remained obligated on the settlement, B paid P and attempted to shift the loss to Payor Bank. Whether or not the bank is accountable -- i.e., whether or not the item was properly payable -- depends on whether or not L, as P's attorney in the action, was authorized to sign the settlement check for P. Also, if L had this authority, payment of the check to L discharged B's liability on the instrument and on the underlying settlement.

b. Ratification

1) Signature Becomes Effective As That Of Represented Person
A customer cannot recover against a payor bank on the basis that her signature or an indorsement was forged if the person whose name was signed ratifies the signature. "An unauthorized signature may be ratified for all purposes of this Article." 3-403(a). The effect is that "[t]he unauthorized

signature becomes valid so far as its effect as a signature is concerned." 3-403 comment 3. Ratification is retroactive and may be found in conduct as well as in express statements.

Example: The deposit contract between D Corp. and Bank provides that Bank can and will pay checks drawn on the account by the president or comptroller of D Corp. Without authority, an employee of D Corp. draws a check on the account using the president's name. The check is used to purchase widgets. The Bank pays the check and debits the account of D Corp. Upon discovering the fraud, D Corp. fires the employee and confiscates the widgets for the use of D Corp. By retaining the benefits received in the transaction with knowledge of the unauthorized signature, D Corp. thereby ratifies the employee's signature. The signature is thus effective even though the employee was not an authorized agent of D. Corp. So the check is deemed to have been properly payable and D Corp. cannot complain that the check was charged to the corporate account.

2) Effect On Signer's Liability

When a person makes an unauthorized signature of somebody else, the signer herself can be liable even though the represented person is not liable because of the lack of authority. See 3-403(a). If the represented person ratifies the signature, she thereby adopts it as her own and the actual signer may thereby be relieved of liability. Nevertheless:

- The ratification does not relieve the signer of liability to the person represented.
- It does not in any way affect the signer's criminal liability.

3-403 comment 3.

c. **Preclusion By Estoppel**

Former law expressly provided that an unauthorized signature could operate as the signature of the represented person when, because of the peculiar circumstances, the person was "precluded from denying it." 3-404(1) (1989 Official Text). It recognized "the possibility of an estoppel against the person whose name is signed, as where he expressly or tacitly represents to an innocent purchaser that the signature is genuine * * *." 3-404 comment 4 (1989 Official Text). Even in the absence of this express provision in the new law, preclusion by estoppel remains possible because of 1-103, which allows principles of common law and equity to supplement the Code.

d. 3-406 -- Negligence

The defense of 3-406 covers preclusion because of certain negligence:

> A person whose failure to exercise ordinary care *substantially contributes* to an alteration of an instrument or to the making of a forged signature on an instrument is precluded from asserting the alteration or the forgery against a person who, in good faith pays the instrument or takes it for value or for collection.

3-406(a) (emphasis added).

Example: Using a No. 2 soft-lead pencil, D draws a $100 check to P's order. With no trouble at all, P erases the amount of the check and raises it to $1000. The check is properly chargeable to D's account in the amount of $1000.

Example: The deposit contract covering the checking account of D Corp. authorized the payor bank to pay checks drawn over the actual signature of the president of D Corp., or over her facsimile signature imprinted with a rubber stamp whenever the stamp was used by her personally or by someone else authorized to sign for her. Because the company was negligent in looking after the rubber stamp, it was used by an unauthorized person to draw several checks on the corporate account. These checks were paid and charged to the account. D Corp. cannot complain against the payor bank. The company is precluded by 3-406 from asserting the employee's lack of authority.

Example: During a two-year period a secretary in the law partnership of Olson & Olsen embezzled more than $100,000 from the firm. He drew checks on the firm's trust account, forging the name of the managing partner who was the only authorized signatory on the account. The secretary was not authorized to draw against the account and had no responsibilities with respect to the firm's checks. The firm was aware that someone was stealing from the account as soon as two months after the secretary's embezzlement began, but took no action to prevent further forgeries. The firm is precluded from complaining about forgeries that occurred after it learned of the problem and had a reasonable time to take preventive action.

> ***Example:*** Jane Smith filed an insurance claim with her carrier, Assured
> Equity. Upon approval of the claim, the insurer drew a check to
> Jane Smith but negligently mailed it to the wrong person whose
> name was the same as the insured. The check was paid, upon the
> unauthorized signature of the intended Jane Smith, and charged to
> Assured Equity's account. The payor bank is not accountable to the
> insurer which is precluded, on the basis of 3-406, from asserting the
> unintended Jane Smith's lack of authority.

1) The "Substantially Contributes" Requirement

Not just any negligence effects preclusion under 3-406. The negligence
must actually "contribute" to the forgery or alteration. That is, it must afford
an opportunity of which advantage is in fact taken. Moreover, the
contribution must be *substantial*. The test is less stringent than direct and
proximate cause. It is an easier test requiring only that the negligence was a
substantial contributing factor in bringing about the alteration or forgery.
3-406 comment 2. "The Code has thus abandoned the language of the older
cases (negligence which 'directly and proximately affects the conduct of the
bank in passing the forgery') and shortened the chain of causation which the
defendant bank must establish. * * * In the instant case, the trial court
could readily have concluded that plaintiff's business affairs were conducted
in so negligent a fashion as to have 'substantially contributed' to the * * *
forgeries, within the meaning of 3-406." *Thompson Maple Products, Inc.
v. Citizens Nat. Bank of Corry*, 234 A.2d 32, 34-35 (Pa.Super. 1967).

2) The Effect of the Payor's Culpability

The defense of 3-406 does not entirely fail if the payor bank or other person
asserting the preclusion also acted unreasonably in dealing with the
instrument. A concept of comparative negligence applies.

> [I]f the person asserting the preclusion fails to exercise ordinary care
> in paying or taking the instrument and that failure substantially
> contributes to loss, the loss is allocated between the person
> precluded and the person asserting the preclusion according to the
> extent to which the failure of each to exercise ordinary care
> contributed to the loss.

3-406(b). "'Ordinary care' in the case of a person engaged in business means
observance of reasonable commercial standards, prevailing in the area in
which the person is located, with respect to the business in which the person
is engaged." 3-103(a)(7). Significantly, "[i]n the case of a bank that takes
an instrument for collection or payment by automated means, reasonable

commercial standards do not require the bank to examine the instrument if the failure to examine the instrument does not violate the bank's prescribed procedures and the bank's procedures do not vary unreasonably from general banking usage not disapproved by this Article or Article 4." Id.

> *Example:*   Janitor steals Employer's blank check form that was negligently left on a desk in Employer's office. Janitor draws a check to herself, signing the name of Employer's president who is the only person authorized to draw on the account.   The check is paid and charged to Employer's account. Employer may be precluded from complaining about the forgery because of Employer's negligence. It happens, however, that the payor bank did not attempt to verify the authenticity of the drawer's signature. This failure may be comparative negligence that dilutes the preclusion defense. It can be comparative negligence if the bank's own procedures were violated or, if they were met, if general banking practice was violated by not requiring verification. Banks commonly verify signatures only on items that exceed a certain dollar amount. The likelihood that verification is required increases with the amount of the check.

e.   4-406(c-d) (Breach of Conditional Duty to Discover and Report Check Fraud)

Typically, a bank sends its checking-account customer a statement of account that shows payment of items from the customer's account. In so doing the bank returns or makes available to the customer either the items themselves or information sufficient to allow the customer reasonably to identify the items. Article 4 does not directly require this accounting; but if the bank provides such a statement, Article 4 imposes a duty on the customer to examine the items or information with "reasonable promptness * * * *to determine* whether any payment was not authorized because of an alteration of an item or because a purported signature by or on behalf of the customer was not authorized. If, based on the statement or items provided, the customer should reasonably have discovered the unauthorized payment, the customer must promptly *notify* the bank of the relevant facts." 4-406(c) (emphasis added).

1)   When Duty On Customer Is Triggered

The duty on the customer is not imposed unless the bank either (1) returns or makes available the checks paid or (2) provides information sufficient to allow the customer to identify them. Which course the bank follows is a matter of bank-customer agreement; but if their agreement requires the bank only to provide identifying information, the duty on the customer requires adequate information -- "sufficient to allow the customer reasonably to identify the items paid." 4-406 comment 1. Images of the items will do but are not required. It is sufficient that the bank describes the checks by item numbers, amount, and dates of payment. Id. It is not necessary for the bank to identify the payee of each item and the item's date. The customer should be able to determine these two pieces of information from her own records based on the number of the check, its amount and date of payment supplied by the bank.

2) Effect of Customer's Breach of the Duty

The effect of a customer's breach of the 4-406(c) duty is described by 4-406(d):

- If the bank proves that it suffered a loss because the customer failed to discover or report an unauthorized payment, the customer is precluded from asserting the alteration or the customer's unauthorized signature against the bank. 4-406(d)(1).

- Whether or not the bank can prove a loss, the customer is precluded from asserting her unauthorized signature or an alteration by the same wrongdoer on any item paid in good faith by the bank "if the payment was made before the bank received notice from the customer of the unauthorized signature or alteration and after the customer had been afforded a reasonable period of time, not exceeding 30 days, in which to examine the item or statement of account and notify the bank." 4-406(d)(2). This language covers the case of a string of forgeries or alterations by the same wrongdoer. The bank need not establish that it suffered a loss because, in this kind of case, the law presumes loss.

3) Coverage of Forged Indorsements.

The 4-406(d) preclusion is limited to alterations and forgeries and unauthorized signatures of the customer -- the person who has the account and whose name should have been signed as drawer. The preclusion of (d) therefore never applies to forged indorsements. Typically, the checking account customer has no way of verifying indorsements.

4) Missing Drawer's Signature

Under former law the courts were divided on whether or not the duty and preclusion of 4-406 applies in the case where multiple signatures on a check are required by the deposit contract, but the bank pays checks missing one or more of the required signatures. The decisive question is whether or not, in such a case, there is an "unauthorized signature." Article 3 now clearly ends this dispute because the statute expressly provides that "[i]f the signature of more than one person is required to constitute the authorized signature of an organization, the signature of the organization is unauthorized if one of the required signatures is lacking." 3-403(b). This rule will apply even when two natural persons jointly hold an account in their individual capacities because "organization" is a broad term. It includes "a corporation, government or governmental subdivision or agency, business trust, estate, trust, partnership or association, *two or more persons having a joint or common interest*, or any other legal or commercial entity." 1-201(28) (emphasis added).

5) **Bank's Comparative Negligence Dilutes the 4-406(d) Defense**
Even if the customer was negligent so that the preclusion of 4-406(d) applies against her, the bank nevertheless shares the loss if the customer proves that the bank failed to exercise ordinary care in paying the item and that the failure substantially contributed to the loss. 4-406(e). In this event loss is allocated between the customer and the bank according to the extent to which the customer's negligence in not finding or reporting the wrong and the bank's negligence in paying the item contributed to the loss.

6) **Bank's Lack of Good Faith Denies the Defense**
If the customer proves that the bank did not pay the item in good faith, the bank completely forfeits the 4-406(d) preclusion defense despite negligence by the customer. 4-406(e).

f. **4-406(f) (One-Year Outside Limit on Customer's Complaints About Customer's Unauthorized Signature or Alteration)**
Application of the 4-406(d) preclusion rule, which is discussed immediately above, depends upon determinations as to ordinary care of the customer and the bank. In contrast, 4-406(f) places an *absolute* limit on the right of a customer to make a claim for payment of altered or unauthorized checks *without regard to care or lack of care of either the customer or the bank.* In any event, "a customer who does not within one year after the statement or items are made available to the customer * * * discover and report the customer's unauthorized signature on or any alteration on the item is precluded from asserting against the [payor] bank the unauthorized signature or alteration." 4-406(f). On the other hand, subsection (f) is like 4-406(d) in that neither preclusion defense applies to indorsements. "Section 4-406 imposes no duties on the drawer to look for unauthorized indorsements." 4-406 comment 5. Customers' complaints about ineffective indorsements are covered, however, by the general three-year statute of limitations that applies to any action to enforce any obligation, duty, or right arising under Article 4. See 4-111.

g. Special Rules for Unauthorized Indorsements in Certain Circumstances

Section 3-404 and 3-405 provide three different rules whereby indorsements of payees are deemed effective in law even though, in fact, they are unauthorized. These rules cover circumstances where, for overriding policy reasons, the loss is generally better left with the drawer-customer -- she cannot shift her loss to the payor bank -- because, in the covered cases, the customer is in the best position to protect against it. Generally, the rules operate in the same way. When an indorsement involves fraud that a rule covers, an indorsement by *any person* in the name of the identified payee is deemed effective as the payee's indorsement in favor of the person who pays or people who take the instrument for value or collection. Section 3-404 applies in certain cases involving impostors and nominal or fictitious payees, and section 3-405 involves fraudulent indorsements by employees on instruments for which their employment gives them some responsibility. Although the main purpose of the statutes is to insulate payor banks from customers' complaints of losses in certain instances of unauthorized indorsements, neither 3-404 nor 3-405 is limited to this purpose, this situation, or to checks. Each statute is generally applicable to any instrument and in any situation that meets its peculiar requirements.

1) 3-404 -- When Payees are Impersonated or Imagined

a) Impostor Rule -- 3-404(a)

i) The Fraud

In the *impostor case*, a drawer is induced to issue an instrument because a thief impersonates someone else whom the drawer intends and names as payee. The thief indorses in the name of the payee and induces a third person to take or pay the instrument. Finally, the thief departs with her loot, and the law must determine which of the two innocent and defrauded parties must bear the cost of the wrong. The drawer often complains against her bank for paying the item, arguing that the indorsement was ineffective because the check was payable to the person whom the drawer intended rather than to the thief. Therefore, the item was not properly payable and not chargeable against the customer's account.

ii) Pre-Code Law

Before the Code, the outcome of these cases usually depended on what the court found to be the dominant intent of the defrauded party. If she dealt face to face with the impostor, her dominant intent was usually found to be to deliver the instrument to the impostor. Consequently, the impostor was treated as holder, and the party who gave the instrument to the impostor bore the loss rather than the person who purchased the instrument or paid the impostor.

If the parties dealt by mail or telegram, it usually was reasoned that the defrauded party intended to deliver the instrument to the person the impostor pretended to be. Consequently, the impostor did not become the holder and so the loss was borne by the person who purchased the instrument or paid the impostor.

iii) **The Code Rule When Payee Impersonated**
The dominant intent test was criticized as a fiction because in the eyes of the deceived drawer or maker, the payee named and the defrauder are the same person so that there is only one intention, or if there are two, they are so intertwined as to be inseparable. The Code therefore rejects the test of dominant intent and refuses expressly to distinguish between imposture face to face and by correspondence. It states this wider *impostor rule* of 3-404(a):

> If an impostor, by use of the mails or otherwise, induces the issuer of an instrument to issue the instrument to the impostor, or to a person acting in concert with the impostor, by impersonating the payee of the instrument or a person authorized to act for the payee, an indorsement of the instrument by any person in the name of the payee is effective as the indorsement of the payee in favor of a person who, in good faith, pays the instrument or takes it for value or for collection.

Under the Code, regardless of how the imposture is carried out, when the impostor or her confederate or anyone else indorses the instrument, it is as if the real payee of an ordinary order instrument indorsed it. If the indorsement is in blank, the instrument immediately becomes payable to bearer so that the impostor or anyone else in possession of it becomes the holder and the proper person to negotiate it or to receive payment. If the instrument is indorsed specially, by anyone, and delivered to the special indorsee, the latter becomes the holder; and if she otherwise qualifies, she becomes a holder in due course who is entitled to enforce the instrument -- free from defenses -- against the defrauded maker or drawer. If a drawee pays the holder, whether she be the impostor or anyone else, the drawee is entitled to charge the drawer's account because a payment to the holder is in accordance with the drawer's order. The net result is that the ultimate loss is normally borne by the defrauded maker or drawer rather than by the transferee from the defrauder or by the drawee who pays the impostor or a transferee.

Example: Upon answering a knock at her door, D, a religious fundamentalist, found a man who said his name was Pastor Oral Roberts and asked for a contribution to his cause of returning God to the classroom. The man represented himself as THE Oral Roberts who is a famous evangelist and faith healer. D thus gave the man a check for $500 payable to the order of Oral Roberts. In fact, the man was a crook who used the proceeds of the check for his own purposes. Upon discovering that she had been swindled, D demanded that the drawee-payor bank recredit her account. D argued that the indorsement on the check was not the signature of the intended payee, the real Oral Roberts, and that consequently the check was not properly payable. D loses. The crook's signature was effective under 3-404(a).

Example: Same facts, except that the impostor had obtained the check as a result of a solicitation letter sent through the mail to D. The result is the same.

iv) Impersonation of An Agent of the Named Payee
In a variant case, the defrauder, instead of misrepresenting herself to be another, misrepresents herself to be the agent of another, and thereby induces a maker or drawer to issue the negotiable instrument made payable to her alleged principal. The impostor rule of former law did not apply in this case, and effective negotiation of the instrument was not possible unless the alleged principal, herself, indorsed the instrument. The impostor rule of 3-404(a) changes this result. It is wider and expressly applies when an impostor impersonates "the payee of the instrument *or a person authorized to act for the payee*." 3-404(a). An indorsement in the payee's name by the supposed "agent" or anyone else is effective. The defrauded maker or drawer again bears the loss.

Example: Suppose that the man at D's door falsely represented that he was an assistant minister to the real Oral Roberts and was authorized to act for Pastor Roberts. D gave the man a check payable to Oral Roberts. D indorsed the check using the name of Oral Roberts and cashed it. The check was paid and charged to D's account. 3-404(a) does protects the drawee against D's demand that her account be recredited with the amount of the check.

b) Rule of the Nominal or Fictitious Payee -- 3-404(b)
   i) The Fraud
      The *nominal or fictitious payee* is an entirely different kind of fraud but is handled similarly by 3-404. Suppose that X gives Y general authority to issue checks drawn on B Bank to pay X's creditors and employees. Intending to cheat X, and enrich herself, Y draws a check for $3,000 on B Bank payable to the order of F, and signs X's name as drawer. F is neither a creditor nor an employee, and Y intends F to have no interest in the check. Y indorses the check in the name of F naming herself as special indorsee. Y promptly cashes the check at B Bank and retains the proceeds. B Bank charges X's account for the $3,000. When X learns of Y's duplicity, X demands that the bank recredit her account for $3,000. When B Bank refuses, X sues B Bank. Both X and B Bank agree that X was liable on the check and that B Bank had a right to charge X's account if, but only if, the check was properly payable, which requires that Y was a holder. See 4-401(a). X contends that Y was not a holder because the check was payable to the order of F, who was therefore the only appropriate party to indorse. Because the instrument was never indorsed by F, Y could not become holder. Logically, there is much to be said for X's position.

   ii) The Code's Rule Favors the Bank
      As a matter of policy, the Code favors B Bank. It does so by this rule:

      If (i) a person whose intent determines to whom an instrument is payable * * * does not intend the person identified as payee to have any interest in the instrument, or (ii) the person identified as payee of an instrument is a fictitious person, the following rules apply until the instrument is negotiated by special indorsement:
      (1) Any person in possession of the instrument is its holder.
      (2) An indorsement by any person in the name of the payee stated in the instrument is effective as the indorsement of the

payee in favor of a person who, in good faith, pays the instrument or takes it for value or for collection.

3-404(b). In terms of this rule, Y's intent determined to whom the check was payable because Y was the person who signed the check, even though Y was signing on behalf of X. 3-110(a). At the time of issuing the check, Y did not intend F to have any interest in the check. Therefore, because of 3-404(b)(1), Y was a holder before the special indorsement. Also, the indorsement of Y (or her confederate or anyone else), in the name of F, the named payee, had the same effect as if F, the named payee, had indorsed. Consequently, after the special indorsement to herself, Y was a holder because she was still in possession of an instrument that ran to her. When a person draws a negotiable draft or check she orders the drawee to pay the holder. Therefore, when the bank in good faith paid Y who was a holder, the bank was obeying X's order and so was entitled to charge X's account.

The result is the same even with these variations in the problem:

- F was an actual creditor of X . The key is that Y did not intend F to have an interest in the check.
- F was nonexistent, made-up, fictitious. Ditto.
- Checks of X must be signed by two persons, Y and Z. They both sign the check to F. As far as Z knows, the check is intended to pay a legitimate debt owed F. Y intends to keep the check for himself.

iii) **Where Stealing Instrument Is Afterthought**
Section 3-404(b) would not apply if F, the payee, were a real person and Y did not decide to steal the check until after issuing it. If the payee is fictitious, it is irrelevant when Y makes the decision to steal the instrument.

iv) **Where Actual Drawer Is Not Involved**
The rule of 3-404(b) also would not apply if Y had not actually signed the check as, or for, the maker or drawer of the instrument. Suppose that, instead of actually drawing the check, Y merely prepared it for X's signature and that X signed it thinking that F was a creditor. Or suppose that instead of preparing the check, Y merely prepared a list or report on which F's name falsely appeared as creditor. In these situations, 3-404(b) does not apply because Y is

not the person whose intent determined to whom the check is payable. It was X. The person to whom an instrument is payable is determined by the intent of the "person, whether or not authorized, signing as, or in the name or behalf of, the issuer of the instrument." 3-110(a). In effect, when the payee is a real person, 3-404(b) only applies if the actual "drawer or maker does not intend the payee to have any interest in the instrument." 3-404 comment 2.

It is a different case, however, if the payee is fictitious. In this event, 3-404(b) applies regardless of the intent of the actual drawer or maker.

It is also a different case, even if the payee is a real person, if X's signature is made by a check-writing machine or other automated means that Y uses to issue the check payable to F. In this event, the payee is determined by the intent of the person supplying the name of the payee. 3-110(b). On these facts, this person is Y. It would seem, therefore, that 3-404(b) applies. 3-404 comment 2 (Case # 4). Section 3-405 may also apply if Y is an employee.

v)   Where Drawer's Signature Is Unauthorized
Take note that 3-404 works only on indorsements. Unauthorized drawer's signatures are not deemed effective by either 3-404(a) or (b). If in any of these examples the signature of X, the drawer, is ineffective, X is not liable to anyone on the check (but Y may be liable). The check, therefore, is not properly payable with respect to X's account and cannot be charged against this account by the drawee-bank whether or not 3-404 applies. Suppose, for example, that Y has no authority to act for X in any regard. Y drew a check on X's account using X's name. To hide the fraud, Y drew it payable to F, a person with whom X regularly does business. Y did not intend F to have an interest in the instrument. The drawee paid it. The check, however, is not properly payable because X did not draw it. Section 3-404 does not solve this problem. The bank cannot charge X's account.

c)   Common Requirements of the Two Rules of 3-404
Although 3-404(a) and (b) are different rules that address different kinds of fraud, they share certain elements and are alike in certain respects.

i)   Signature Of Someone As Payee Is Required
The rules of 3-404(a) and (b) share an uncertainty. It is not clear whether an instrument that is payable to a fictitious payee or to an

impersonated payee is payable to order or to bearer. Arguments can be made for either and neither. Perhaps it is best to recognize that such an instrument is anomalous and that although it is governed by some well established principles in the law of commercial paper, it is treated in a way that cannot be reconciled with some other equally well recognized principles. The Code starts with a desire to help the good faith purchaser or drawee who pays. It might have done this simply by declaring such paper to be payable to bearer so as not to require any indorsement, as is essentially done by 4-205 with respect to instruments deposited for collection. But had the Code done so, it would have abandoned the appearance of a regular chain of indorsements and it did not wish to go this far. So it required that someone at least appear to sign on behalf of the person named as payee before anyone could become a holder of it.

ii) Signature Must Be "In the Name of the Payee"
A similarity between 3-404(a) and (b) is that the only bogus indorsement that either rule makes effective is an indorsement "in the name of the payee." Under former law, some cases required the indorsement to be in exactly the same name as the named payee. These cases are rejected. Under 3-404(a) or (b), an indorsement is effective if in a name "substantially similar" to the name of the payee. 3-404(c). Moreover, an indorsement that is wildly different, or no indorsement at all, is effective if the instrument is deposited in a depositary bank to an account in a name substantially similar to that of the payee. Id. This allowance is based on the rule that checks may be deposited for collection without indorsement. See 4-205(1).

d) Whom The Rules Protect
Another similarity between 3-404(a) and (b) is that they both protect not only a person who pays an instrument in circumstances to which the rules apply. Both rules also protect a person who takes an instrument for value or for collection. For example, using the 3-404(b) problem to illustrate, suppose that instead of Y herself presenting the check and getting payment from the drawee bank, she promptly indorsed in F's name and cashed or deposited the check at C Bank. This bank presented the item for payment but B Bank, the drawee, dishonored. C Bank is a holder because of 3-404(b). It can sue Y as indorser and, more important, X as drawer. Moreover, if C Bank is a holder in due course, it can take free of X's defenses and claims, including any defense based on Y's tackiness.

e) Effect Of Comparative Fault

Subsections 3-404(a) and (b) are also alike in that both rules equally take into account the negligence of the person who pays or takes the instrument for value or collection. They do so by this qualification to both rules:

> With respect to an instrument to which subsection (a) or (b) applies, if a person paying the instrument or taking it for value or for collection fails to exercise ordinary care in paying or taking the instrument and that failure substantially contributes to loss resulting from payment of the instrument, the person bearing the loss may recover from the person failing to exercise ordinary care to the extent the failure to exercise ordinary care contributed to the loss.

3-404(d). Such negligence can be even more potent. Suppose that in the example immediately above, C Bank was negligent in not detecting the wrongdoing when Y deposited or cashed the check there. In this event, even if C Bank was a holder in due course, X could discount its liability by the value of D Bank's negligence. Yet, becoming a holder in due course requires taking the instrument in good faith, which "means honesty in fact *and the observance of reasonable commercial standards of fair dealing*." 3-103(a)(4) (emphasis added). Arguably, then, C Bank's negligence prevents it from being a holder in due course so that X would have a complete defense to liability. The result is probably the same either way.

On the other hand, establishing that C Bank was negligent is not a slam dunk. Look at this definition of "*ordinary care*," which certainly applies to 3-404 and maybe also applies to the meaning of good faith:

> "Ordinary care" in the case of a person engaged in business means observance of reasonable commercial standards, prevailing in the area in which the person is located, with respect to the business in which the person is engaged. In the case of a bank that takes an instrument for processing[,] for collection or payment by automated means, *reasonable commercial standards do not require the bank to examine the instrument if* the failure to examine does not violate the bank's prescribed procedures and the bank's procedures do not vary unreasonably from general banking usage not disapproved by this Article or Article 4.

3-103(a)(7) (emphasis added). The outcome in C Bank's case may depend on whether it dealt with Y through an individual who normally would be required to examine the instrument and check identification, or by some other means less likely to trigger such a duty.

f) Same Basic Policy Behind The Rules
Finally, 3-404(a) and (b) are most fundamentally alike because the same basic policy supports both of them. It puts the risk of these kinds of fraud on the drawer or maker because (1) she is in a better position to avoid the risks and (2) the costs of protecting against them is more appropriately borne by her rather than by the completely innocent payor or purchaser of the instrument. Adjustments are made in particular cases where negligence of the payor or purchaser dilutes her innocence, where she had the last chance to prevent the loss and bungled the job. In the end, it is a kind of comparative fault.

h. **3-405 -- When Employees Steal Checks for Which They Are Responsible**
Section 3-405 focuses on employee fraud. It was added in 1990 and is among the two or three most important innovations of the 1990 changes in Article 3. Formerly, employers often could shift and avoid losses caused by employee fraud if the fraud did not fit the relatively narrow rules of 3-404 covering impostors, nominal or fictitious payees and did not involve employer negligence that would trigger 3-406. The drafters of the 1990 Article 3 reconsidered how fairly to distribute losses caused by employee fraud. The balance they reached is different from former law, and less favorable to employers. It is expressed in the policy and language of 3-405 that employers should be originally responsible for a wider range of employee fraud when, and solely because, the fraud is committed by an employee who was entrusted with responsibilities with respect to instruments. The basic reason is that employee fraud is really an employment matter and is better dealt with as such.

Although 3-405 applies to any kind of instrument, the normal case for applying 3-405 will involve checks, and will usually be between the employer, as drawer or payee, and a collecting bank that cashed the checks or a drawee bank that paid them. The issue is always who bears the loss between the employer and the bank. The loser always has a right to recover over from the wrongdoer; but, almost always, the wrongdoer is financially unavailable.

Section 3-404, which is discussed earlier, overlaps with 3-405. Some cases fit both sections. As to these cases, 3-405 may eclipse 3-404 because the elements of the former may be easier to prove. The eclipse is not total, however, because 3-404 is not limited to employee fraud. On the other hand, the kinds of fraud that 3-404 covers are usually committed by employees, so that 3-404 will not work nearly as hard as its statutory predecessors or be as important in Article 3's scheme for distributing fraud losses. Section 3-405 will be worked to death because, although it is limited to employee fraud, it alone covers a wider range of fraudulent conduct than all of the former rules of check fraud combined, and also because most check fraud is committed by employees.

1) How 3-405 Works

The section is big but the core rule of 3-405 is small and easy to understand. It is the first sentence of subsection (b):

> [I]f an employer entrusted an employee with responsibility with respect to the instrument and the employee or a person acting in concert with the employee makes a fraudulent indorsement of the instrument, the indorsement is effective as the indorsement of the person to whom the instrument is payable if it is made in the name of that person.

3-405(b). In some respects this rule is similar to the rules of 3-404. For both 3-404 and 3-405(b):

* The same standard determines if the indorsement is in the same name as the payee, "substantially similar."
* The indorsement is effective only in favor of a person who, in good faith, pays an instrument or takes it for value or for collection.
* Finally, the effectiveness is discounted by such a person's negligence in paying or taking the instrument.

These matters, however, are details. In the main, 3-405 is very different and much broader than 3-404, covering cases of employee fraud that would fit 3-404 and more. Most significantly, 3-405 covers the simple case in which an employee with certain responsibility does nothing more than steal checks that are issued *by* her employer for accounts payable, or checks that are issued *to* her employer for accounts receivable.

Example: Suppose that X gives Y, an employee, the job of verifying, electronically recording, and sending checks that X draws to pay accounts she owes other people. Y plays no role in deciding to whom these checks are payable. In fact, she plays no other role whatsoever with respect to the checks. One day, Y stole several checks and forged the payees' indorsement. The instruments were paid. Ordinarily, because of the missing indorsements of the payees, the checks are not properly payable; and the drawee bank cannot charge them to X's account. Because of 3-405, however, the indorsements are effective since X entrusted Y with responsibilities with respect to the checks. Because the indorsements are effective, the checks are properly payable and thus chargeable to X's account. The loss stays with X. She cannot shift it to anyone other than Y, who is financially unavailable. Of course, the result is the same if Y's duties include deciding to whom the checks are payable, as by determining and reporting accounts payable.

Example: Suppose that the stolen checks were received by X rather than issued by X. Instead of drawer, X was payee. Y could easily take the checks because her job also involved processing payments on accounts receivable. Y forged X's indorsement and the checks were cashed by D Bank, a depositary bank, and paid by the drawee. Ordinarily, X could shift the loss to either bank by way of a conversion action based on her forged indorsements. Because of 3-405, however, the indorsements by Y are effective. There is no basis for conversion against anyone. The loss once again stays with X.

Both of these examples are beyond 3-404. In the absence of 3-405, the employer very likely could shift the losses to the banks, which frequently happened under former law. The loss now stays with the employer.

2) Key Terms
The real keys to 3-405, which largely determine its reach, are four terms:

+ "employee,"
+ "responsibility with respect to instruments,"
+ the employee having been "entrusted" with the responsibility, and
+ "fraudulent indorsement."

a) "Employee"
There is no special definition of "*employee.*" Its ordinary meaning controls, except that the term includes an independent contractor and employee of an independent contractor. 3-405(a)(1). Officers, executives, and other white-collar workers are included equally with other employees.

b) "Entrusted"
"*Entrusted*" likewise lacks any special meaning. It probably includes any conduct whereby the responsibility is expressly given or assigned to

the employee by the employer, and also the employer's acquiescence in the employee keeping responsibilities that she otherwise assumed. Cf. 2-403(3).

c) **"Responsibility With Respect to Instruments"**
The most critical term is *"responsibility with respect to instruments."* It is a new term of art with a special (and very long) definition which generally means having authority to act as to instruments in a responsible capacity. 3-405(a)(3)(vi). It includes authority:

- to sign or indorse instruments on behalf of the employer;
- to process instruments received by the employer for bookkeeping purposes, for deposit to an account, or for other disposition;
- to prepare or process instruments for issue in the name of the employer;
- to supply information determining the names or addresses of payees of instruments to be issued in the name of the employer; and
- to control the disposition of instruments issued in the name of the employer.

3-405(a)(3)(i-v). The term "does not include authority that merely allows an employee to have access to instruments or blank or incomplete instrument forms that are being stored or transported or are part of incoming or outgoing mail, or similar access." 3-405(a)(3). This access does not empower the employee to act in a sufficiently *responsible capacity* with respect to instruments. Thus, a janitor or mail room clerk does not have "responsibility with respect to instruments" even though the job gives her constant access to checks going from and coming to the employer.

Example: Suppose that a janitor steals a batch of checks from the desk of the accounts payable clerk. They are properly drawn by the employer and payable to various of the employer's suppliers. The janitor's unauthorized indorsements in the suppliers' names are not made effective under 3-405. It is inapplicable because the janitor is not an employee entrusted with responsibility with respect to instruments. Section 3-404 is also inapplicable. Likewise, neither section applies if the mail room clerk steals and indorses incoming checks payable to the employer.

d) "Fraudulent Indorsement"

The last term, *"fraudulent indorsement,"* also limits the kinds of fraud that 3-405 covers. It means:

- in the case of an instrument payable to the employer, a forged indorsement purporting to be that of the employer, or
- in the case of an instrument with respect to which the employer is the issuer, a forged indorsement purporting to be that of the person identified as payee.

3-405(a)(2). An indorsement is not fraudulent that a person is authorized to make. Therefore, 3-405 will not apply when the wrongdoer causes the employer to issue the checks payable to the wrongdoer herself that she then indorses. It is also inapplicable when the employee steals checks that, as part of her job, she stamped with the employer's unrestrictive, blank indorsement. In both cases the indorsements are authorized, not forged. In both cases there is fraud, but not in the indorsements themselves.

It is more obvious, but very significant, that 3-405 is also inapplicable to any forged or unauthorized signature of the employer as drawer, maker, or acceptor. Thus, whenever an employee without authority issues checks in the name of the employer, 3-405 does not make the signatures effective against the employer even if the employee was entrusted with responsibility with respect to instruments. The rule of 3-405 applies only to indorsements, not signatures in any other capacity. Because of the ineffective drawer's signature, the drawee bank cannot charge the checks to the employer's account unless some other rule prevents the employer from shifting the loss to the bank.

3) Comparative Fault

Like 3-404 and 3-406, 3-405 also accounts for comparative fault. "If the person paying the instrument or taking it for value or for collection fails to exercise ordinary care * * * and that failure substantially contributes to loss resulting from the fraud, the person bearing the loss may recover from the person failing to exercise ordinary care to the extent the failure to exercise ordinary care contributed to the loss." 3-405(b) (second sentence).

Example: A computer that controls Employer's check-writing machine was programmed to cause a very large check to be issued to a well-known national corporation, such as General Motors, Inc. (GM), to which Employer owed money. Employee fraudulently changed the address of GM in the computer data bank to Employee's post office box. Employee was an accounts payable clerk whose duties included entering information into the computer. The check was subsequently produced by the check-writing machine and mailed to the Employee's box. She got the check, indorsed it in the name of GM, and deposited the check to an account in Depositary Bank which Employee had opened in GM's name. The Bank had opened the account without requiring Employee to produce any resolution of the corporation's board or other evidence of authorization of Employee to act for GM. In due course, the check is presented for payment; Depositary Bank receives payment; and Employee is allowed to withdraw the credit by wire transfer to a foreign bank. Employer remains obligated to General Motors, and cannot recover from the drawee bank because the indorsement was effective and thus the item was properly payable. Employer can recover from Depositary Bank, however, to the extent the finder of fact concludes (as it should) that Depositary Bank was negligent and that its negligence contributed to Employer's loss.

REVIEW QUESTIONS

1.   Identify the principal, twin duties that a payor bank owes its checking account customer and that are the foundation of the relationship between them.

2.   Section 4-402 subjects a payor bank to liability for "wrongful dishonor of an item." Explain "wrongful dishonor" and give an example of it.

3.   Bank wrongfully dishonored checks of ABC, Inc. Of the following people, who can recover damages from the bank under 4-402 (which subjects a bank to liability to its customer for wrongful dishonor)?
    •   ABC, Inc.
    •   the president of ABC, Inc.
    •   the payees of the checks.

4.   In the action by ABC, Inc. against the bank, can the company recover substantial damages without proving that damages actually occurred as a result of the wrongful dishonor?

5.   T or F   A payor bank can pay an overdraft and charge the item to the customer's account, but is not obligated to pay it.

6. Why is a payor bank liable for paying over a valid stop-payment order?

7. T or F   A bank is not liable for violating a valid stop-payment order if the customer suffered no actual loss as a result.

8. B issued a valid stop-payment order covering a check issued to S in payment for goods. The goods were defective, and B properly rejected all of them. The payor bank violated B's order and paid the check. The bank cannot properly charge the check to B's account. Yet, the loss will not necessarily rest finally with the bank. Explain.

9. T or F   Payment of a cashier's check cannot be stopped.

10. T or F   A stale check is not properly payable.

11. A week after the death of a customer, the payor bank was presented with a check she drew on the day of her death. The bank knows of the customer's death. Can the bank safely pay the check?

12. Generally speaking, as between a customer and the payor bank, which of them bears the loss resulting from check fraud, including forged signatures and alterations on items drawn against the customer's account? Explain.

13. Identify in summary fashion a payor bank's major defenses to liability when the bank pays a check over the signature of a person not authorized by the deposit agreement to write checks on the customer's account.

14. The foregoing list should not include U.C.C. 3-404 or 3-405, which contain defenses that apply when the wrongdoer is an impostor or an employee entrusted with responsibility with respect to checks. Why not?

Chapter X ends by explaining who usually bears the losses from check fraud (alteration or unauthorized signature) as between a payor bank and its checking account customer. The losses often fall on the bank. This chapter begins by considering whether or not losses borne by the payor bank can be shifted to someone else involved in the collection of the tainted items. The remainder of this chapter considers other combinations of plaintiffs and defendants in check fraud suits (especially those involving forged indorsements) that permit the more direct and efficient shifting of losses to the persons who ultimately should bear them.

A. PAYOR BANK VERSUS PEOPLE UPSTREAM IN THE COLLECTION CHAIN -- PRIMARILY, PRESENTMENT WARRANTIES

A check that has been altered, or that carries an unauthorized signature of the drawer or an indorser, is not properly payable and cannot rightfully be charged to the account against which it was drawn. Thus, if the payor bank pays the check, the payment cannot be recouped from the account. So, as against its checking account customer, the bank must bear the check fraud loss. Usually, the only way the payor bank can shift the loss to someone else is by a claim for breach of warranty based on 4-208. It establishes implied warranties that benefit payor banks which pay or accept items:

> **If an unaccepted draft is presented to the drawee for payment or acceptance and the drawee pays or accepts the draft, (i) the person obtaining payment or acceptance, at the time of presentment, and (ii) a previous transferor of the draft, at the time of transfer, warrant to the drawee that pays or accepts the draft in good faith that:**
>
> > **(1) the warrantor is, or was, at the time the warrantor transferred the draft, a person entitled to enforce the draft or authorized to obtain payment or acceptance of the draft on behalf of a person entitled to enforce the draft;**
> > **(2) the draft has not been altered; and**
> > **(3) the warrantor has no knowledge that the signature of the purported drawer of the draft is unauthorized.**

4-208(a). As is apparent, these presentment warranties do not cover every kind of check fraud. Thus, the payor bank cannot unload every kind of check fraud loss.

1. Who Makes Presentment Warranties To The Payor Bank Under 4-208

The warranties that run in favor of a payor bank are made by the person who obtains payment and also by every previous transferor.

♦ The warranties arise automatically, that is, the warranties are implied by law and are not conditioned on the warrantor expressly making them or even being aware that warranties are made as part of the collection process.

♦ The warranties arise -- they are triggered -- whenever a check is presented and paid, but the person obtaining payment is not the only warrantor. Also making the presentment warranties to the bank is every previous transferor of the check. This means that a payor bank is not limited, in a breach of warranty action on a check, to suing the person who presented the item and obtained payment. The payor bank can recover from any collecting bank or other person in the collection chain or from any prior transferor if a 4-208 warranty was breached at the time of this person's transfer. A previous transferor would not be responsible for breach of the warranty against alteration if the check was altered after she transferred it.

2. Scope Of Presentment Warranty Protection Under 4-208

With respect to checks paid by payor banks, 4-208(a) implies three presentment warranties:

a. Alteration

Section 4-208(a)(2) very clearly provides a warranty that "the draft has not been altered." Article 4 does not define "altered." Presumably, the definition in Article 3 applies. If so, for purposes of this warranty an alteration is "(i) an unauthorized change in an instrument that purports to modify in any respect the obligation of a party, or (ii) an unauthorized addition of words or numbers or other change to an incomplete instrument relating to the obligation of a party." 3-407(a).

b. Unauthorized Indorsement

In so many words 4-208(a) creates a warranty against unauthorized indorsements. The words are a warranty that "the warrantor is * * * a person entitled to enforce the draft" or is authorized by such a person. 4-208(a)(1). To be such a person ordinarily implies that the check or other item contains all necessary indorsements, and that the indorsements are genuine or otherwise effective. So, if the indorsement of a payee or special indorsee is missing or is signed without her authority, the 4-208(a)(1) warranty is breached, *even though the warrantor is completely unaware of any problem with the indorsement.* The warrantor's knowledge or lack of knowledge is totally irrelevant.

Example: B drew a check on her account at PB Bank, and gave it to S in payment for goods. T stole the check from S and cashed it at DB Bank, after forging S's indorsement. DB Bank forwarded the item for collection through an intermediary bank, IB Bank. IB presented the check for payment to PB Bank which paid the item and charged it to B's account. Upon learning of the theft, S demanded the price of the goods sold to B. B paid S in cash and then demanded that PB Bank recredit her account for the amount of the check because the check was not properly payable. PB Bank did so. Now PB Bank can sue, for breach of warranty of presentment, any of the following: IB Bank, DB Bank, or T.

c. Unauthorized Drawer's Signature

There is only a limited warranty with regard to the drawer's signature. It is that the warrantor "has *no knowledge* that the signature of the purported drawer of the draft is unauthorized." 4-208(a)(3) (emphasis added).

Example: Forging B's name, T drew a check against B's checking account at PB Bank. T used this check to pay for goods purchased from S. S deposited the check in her account at DB Bank and forwarded the item for collection through IB Bank, which presented the check to PB Bank for payment. PB Bank paid the check and charged it to B's account. When the forgery was discovered, PB Bank recredited B's account because the check was not properly payable. PB Bank is probably stuck with the loss, however, because T, the wrongdoer, was the only person who breached the limited presentment warranty regarding an unauthorized drawer's signature.

3. Damages
a. Kinds

The damages for breach of a presentment warranty include:

* Compensatory damages equaling the amount paid by the drawee less the amount the drawee received or is entitled to receive from the drawer because of payment.
* Incidental damages for expenses and loss of interest resulting from the breach.

4-208(b).

b. Disclaimer

The presentment warranties or, presumably, damages for breaching them can be limited or entirely disclaimed except with respect to checks. 4-208(e).

4. Major Defenses In Warranty Action

a. Payor Bank's Lack of Good Faith

No one is liable to a payor bank for breach of warranty with respect to a check the bank paid if, in paying the item, the payor bank acted without good faith. The presentment warranties of 4-208 are made only to a payor which *in good faith* pays or accepts the item. On the other hand, the drawee's negligence -- failure to exercise ordinary care in making payment -- is irrelevant. 4-208(b).

b. Laches

In asserting breach of warranty, a payor bank must notify the warrantor within 30 days after acquiring "reason to know of the breach and the identity of the warrantor." 4-208(e). Otherwise, "the warrantor is discharged to the extent of any loss caused by the delay in giving notice of the claim." Id.

c. Failure to Assert Defenses Against Customer

Remember that Articles 3 and 4 provide a payor bank with various defenses in check fraud cases. (See Chapter X, supra.) In certain situations, ineffective indorsements are deemed valid; and for various reasons a drawer is precluded from complaining about an unauthorized indorsement or alteration. See 3-404, 3-405, 3-406 & 4-406. A payor bank should not be allowed to ignore these defenses, accept the check fraud loss from its customer, and then pass the loss to someone upstream in the collection process by way of a warranty or other action. To allow such shifting of the loss would undermine the purposes and policies behind the Code defenses or upset the balancing of liabilities that the whole scheme of defenses is designed to achieve. For this reason, Article 4 encourages a payor bank to assert its defenses against a customer by giving warrantors this derivative protection:

> If a drawee asserts a claim for breach of warranty under subsection (a) [4-208(a)] based on an unauthorized indorsement of the draft or an alteration of the draft, the warrantor may defend by proving that the indorsement is effective under Section 3-404 or 3-405 or the drawer is precluded under Section 3-406 or 4-406 from asserting against the drawee the unauthorized indorsement or alteration.

4-208(c).

Example: B drew a check to S who fraudulently raised the amount of the item. S cashed the item at DB Bank which presented the item for payment to the drawee, PB Bank. The check, as altered, was paid and charged to B's account. B did not discover the alteration until 14 months after receiving from PB the canceled item and a statement of account covering it. B demanded that PB recredit her account, arguing that the check was not properly payable beyond the original tenor of the item. Although B's claim against PB was barred by 4-406(f), PB recredited B's account for the amount of the alteration and, in the process, waived the 4-406 defense against B's claim. PB then sued DB Bank for breach of the 4-208(a) payment warranty against alteration. DB wins. Because PB waived its 4-406 defense to B's claim, 4-208 and 4-406 preclude PB from asserting any claim against DB based on the alteration.

Example: B drew a check to S and negligently mailed it to another person named S. This person cashed the check at DB Bank, after indorsing the item in her name. PB Bank, the drawee, paid the check and charged it to B's account. After satisfying her debt to S, B sued PB Bank for charging her account with an item that was not properly payable, and PB Bank filed a third party claim against DB Bank for breach of the 4-208(a)(1) presentment warranty. PB Bank decided to recredit B's account, ignoring the advice of DB Bank that B's claim was precluded by 3-406 (negligence substantially contributing to unauthorized signature). In the third-party action, DB Bank can defend against PB's warranty action by proving that B was precluded by 3-406 from asserting the unauthorized indorsement against PB. It is uncertain whether or not this defense is pro tanto. Suppose that B's negligence would have reduced her recovery against PB but would not have provided a complete defense. Is DB's derivative reliance on 3-406 similarly reduced?

d. Forged Signature Not Unauthorized

When a payor bank's breach of warranty claim is based on an unauthorized signature, it is a good defense that the signature was actually authorized (expressly or impliedly) by the person whose name was signed, or was otherwise effective under agency law or other extra-Code law. This defense is asserted by the warrantor in its own right and directly against the payor bank, and is not premised on the payor bank having failed to raise the defense against the bank's customer. The defense, if proved, undermines completely the very foundation of the payor bank's claim.

Example: B drew a check to S on an account at PB Bank. Signing S's name, T indorsed the check and cashed it at DB Bank. PB Bank paid the check and charged it to B's account. When B complained that the check was not properly payable because it lacked S's indorsement, PB Bank recredited B's account and sued DB Bank for breach of the 4-208(a)(1) warranty. DB Bank wins if it can establish that T had authority to indorse the check on S's behalf, just as DB would win (because of 4-208(c)) if the case were covered by 3-404 or 3-405 so that any person's indorsement in S's name was deemed effective.

5. Recovery Over (Passing The Buck) Through 4-207 Transfer Warranties

A person who is liable to a payor bank for breaching a 4-208 presentment warranty can often pass the loss to someone else further upstream in the collection process on the basis of the transfer warranties implied by 4-207, which provides:

A customer or collecting bank that transfers an item and receives a settlement or other consideration warrants to the transferee and to any subsequent collecting bank that:
> **(1) the warrantor is a person entitled to enforce the item;**
> **(2) all signatures on the item are authentic and authorized;**
> **(3) the item has not been altered;**
> **(4) the item is not subject to a defense or claim in recoupment (Section 3-305(a)) of any party that can be asserted against the warrantor; and**
> **(5) the warrantor has no knowledge of any insolvency proceeding commenced with respect to the maker or acceptor or, in the case of an unaccepted draft, the drawer.**

4-207(a). In addition, each customer and collecting bank that transfers an item and receives a settlement or other consideration is obligated to pay the item if the item is dishonored. 4-207(b).

As you can see, the 4-207 transfer warranties cover the same kinds of fraud and more that are covered by the presentment warranties of 4-208. So, in any case where a presentment warranty is breached, there is a corresponding transfer warranty. The transfer warranties thus ordinarily insure that any check fraud loss unloaded by a payor bank can be passed upstream to the very beginning of the collection chain, thereby protecting every collecting bank through which the check passed. This is possible because the transfer warranties are made, in seriatim order, by *each* customer and collecting bank who transfers an item and receives a settlement or other consideration for it, and they run in favor of the customer's or collecting bank's "transferee and to *any subsequent collecting bank.*" 4-207(a). A transferee not protected by 4-207 may find protection among the similar warranties of 3-416 which covers transfers of instruments outside of the check collection process. See Chapter V supra.

Example: B drew a check on her account at PB Bank, and gave it to S in payment for goods. T stole the check from S and cashed it at DB Bank, after forging S's indorsement. DB Bank forwarded the item for collection through an intermediary bank, IB Bank. IB presented the check for payment to PB Bank which paid the item and charged it to B's account. Upon learning of the theft, S demanded the price of the goods sold to B. B paid S in cash, and then demanded that PB Bank recredit her account for the amount of the check because the check was not properly payable. PB Bank did so. Now PB Bank can sue, for breach of the presentment warranty of 4-208(a)(1), any of the following: IB Bank, DB Bank, or T. Suppose that PB Bank sues IB Bank. IB Bank, in turn, can sue DB Bank or T for breach of the corresponding transfer warranty. See 4-207(a)(1). If IB Bank sues DB Bank, the latter bank can rely on the same transfer warranty to recover from T.

Upon scanning the 4-207 transfer warranties, you will notice that the list includes a warranty that "all signatures on the item are authentic and authorized," 4-207(a)(2), which is not limited by a requirement that the warrantor know of the problem. You might conclude that this warranty would permit a payor bank to shift a loss resulting from a forged drawer's signature where prior parties were unaware of the forgery. You are wrong! Remember: The 4-207 transfer warranties do not run in favor of payors. The only warranties to payors are the payment warranties of 4-208, which are less inclusive than the transfer warranties.

6. Payor Bank's Restitution Action To Shift Losses Not Covered By Payment Warranties

a. The Claims for Restitution

You surely will notice that certain check fraud and other kinds of losses that a payor bank can suffer are not covered by the 4-208 payment warranties. Most noticeable are losses resulting from checks bearing unauthorized drawers' signatures when the lack of authority is unknown to prior parties, payments over valid stop orders, and losses resulting from overdrafts (a/k/a NSF checks) that cannot be collected from customers because the customers are insolvent or otherwise unable or unavailable to satisfy the overdrafts.

Payor banks sometimes argue mistake and rely on restitution law or some other common-law theory to recoup these losses from persons who obtained payment of such items or who otherwise received the proceeds of them. Section 3-418 sanctions the common-law restitution claim in 3-418(b) and, to some extent, codifies restitutionary liability in 3-418(a) which covers the two most common cases of mistaken payment: payment of forged checks and checks on which the drawer has stopped payment. If the case does not fit within (a), however, the bank is then free under (b) to resort to the common law which, rather than 3-418, will determine liability:

> **(a) Except as provided in subsection (c), if the drawee of a draft pays or accepts the draft and the drawee acted on the mistaken belief that (i) payment of the draft had not been stopped pursuant to Section 4-403 or (ii) the signature of the drawer of the draft was authorized, the drawee may recover the amount of the draft from the person to whom or for whose benefit payment was made or, in the case of acceptance, may revoke the acceptance. Rights of the drawee under this subsection are not affected by failure of the drawee to exercise ordinary care in paying or accepting the draft.**

> **(b) Except as provided in subsection (c), if an instrument has been paid or accepted by mistake and the case is not covered by subsection (a), the person paying or accepting may, to the extent permitted by the law governing mistake and restitution, (i) recover the payment from the person to whom or for whose benefit payment was made or (ii) in the case of acceptance, may revoke the acceptance.**

3-418(a-b).

b. The Defense to Restitution

At the same time, 3-418 creates a huge defense to both common law and statutory restitution:

> **The remedies provided by subsection (a) or (b) may not be asserted against a person who took the instrument in good faith and for value or who in good faith changed position in reliance on the payment or acceptance. * * ***

3-418(c). It is a defense to any action by any payor to recover payment or escape acceptance made on any instrument without regard to the nature of the error the payor made as to the state of the drawer's account. So the defense is available whether the loss to the payor was caused by a forged drawer's signature; an overdraft; payment over a stop order; or any other circumstance giving reason for the payor bank's complaint. Behind 3-418(c) is the argument for finality of payment, and this argument applies whatever the payor's reason for avoiding payment or acceptance. Also behind 3-418(c) is the additional reason that the drawee is responsible for knowing the state of the account before acceptance or payment.

There are two limitations on the 3-418(c) defense:

* First, the defense is only available to a holder in due course (or other good faith purchaser) or a person who in good faith changed her position in reliance on the payment. As against anyone else, the equities favor allowing the payor to recover payments mistakenly made. (Practically speaking, however, in most cases any solvent party who benefited from payment will have taken the check in good faith and for value so that the defense is available to her.)
* Second, 3-418(c) is no defense for anyone to a payor's recovery for breach of a presentment warranty or to recovery of a bank settlement under 4-301. In these cases other concerns override the policies behind 3-418(c).

7. Policy Underpinnings

Together, the 4-208 presentment warranties and the 3-418(c) defense to restitution allocate check losses on the basis of whether the payor bank or someone else was in a better position to protect against the loss. In the case of a forged drawer's signature or an overdraft, for example, the payor bank occupies the superior position because the bank should know the balance of the customer's account, and (in theory) can check the authenticity of a drawer's signature on a check by comparing it to the customer's signature on the deposit contract on file with the bank. For this reason, a loss caused by the payor bank paying an overdraft or a check bearing a forged drawer's signature is not covered by a warranty (except when the forgery is known to the prior party), and shifting the loss by way of a common-law action is barred by 3-418(c).

On the other hand, detecting forged indorsements is practically impossible (even in theory) for a payor bank. The person best able to uncover such an unauthorized signature is the person who deals with the forger. So, a payor bank can shift a loss resulting from paying a check with a forged indorsement because this problem is covered by a payment warranty. Moreover, recovery on this basis, i.e., warranty, is not barred by 3-418(c). The transfer warranties of 4-207 allow passing the loss to the start of the check collection process. If the loss is not thereby placed on the person who dealt with the forger, the loss can ultimately reach this person by way of the transfer warranties of 3-416, which are similar to 4-207 but apply to transfers beyond the check collection chain. For discussion of the warranty provisions of 3-416, see Chapter V supra.

B. PAYEE VERSUS DEPOSITARY-COLLECTING BANK

1. Setting Up And Justifying The Direct Action In The Typical Check Fraud Case

The most common kind of check fraud involves forged indorsements. In the typical case, a thief steals checks payable to someone else, forges the payee's indorsements, and deposits the checks at a bank where the thief maintains an account. The thief may have opened the account in the name of the payee, posing as a representative of the payee who is authorized to deal with the account; or the thief may have opened the account in some other name, even her own name. The stolen checks are eventually paid by the payor bank. The thief's account thus swells, and the drawers' accounts correspondingly shrink.

Obviously, the payee is the person who initially suffers loss from this fraudulent scheme. We know, however, that the payee can shift the loss to the drawers of the stolen checks. Because the checks carried forged indorsements, the checks were not paid to a holder. Therefore, the drawers of the checks were not discharged on the instruments or on their underlying obligations to the payee. The drawers thus remain liable to the payee.

Upon satisfying their obligations to the payee, the drawers thereby assume the check fraud loss, inasmuch as their checking accounts have already been reduced by the amounts of the stolen checks. The drawers have, in effect, paid twice. The drawers, however, can pass the loss to the payor banks. The stolen checks paid by the banks were not properly payable and could not rightfully be charged to the drawers' accounts. Therefore, their accounts must be recredited.

The check fraud loss passes to the payor banks when they recredit the drawers' accounts. Of course, the payor banks can shift the loss back up the collection chain by relying on the presentment warranty that the warrantor was entitled to enforce the checks. 4-208(a)(1). The collecting banks that obtained payment of the checks, and each prior customer and collecting bank, made this warranty to the payor banks. They effectively warranted that the checks carried all necessary indorsements, and that the indorsements were authorized. Sooner or later, the loss will come to rest on the first collecting bank, i.e., the depositary bank, which is the bank where the thief deposited or cashed the stolen checks. In theory, this bank can recoup from the thief who herself breached the 4-207(a)(1) transfer warranty of right to enforce. By this time, however, the thief is long gone, physically or financially.

So the loss rests ultimately with the depositary-collecting bank in line with the policy of putting the loss on the person in the best position to protect against it. Yet, implementing this policy involves a very long, circuitous route of claims and recoveries over: payee v. drawers; drawers v. payor banks; payor banks v. depositary bank or intermediary banks; intermediary banks v. depositary bank. It would be much more efficient if the payee sued the depositary bank directly. After all, in this case the payee is the real victim of the check fraud, and the depositary bank is the entity who, in the end, is ultimately responsible.

2.   Theory Of The Direct Action -- Conversion

The holder of a check is the owner of it and the only rightful recipient of its proceeds unless she, or someone acting by her authority, directs otherwise. Therefore, when a check is stolen from a payee, her indorsement forged and the proceeds of the instrument are misappropriated, the thief is guilty of converting the payee's property and is liable to the payee for common-law conversion; and so is every transferee involved in the misappropriation even though the transferee acted innocently and without knowledge of the payee's superior rights. As a result, the bank at which the thief cashes the stolen check, or deposits it, is liable for conversion to the payee. Article 3 recognizes and codifies this conversion liability by providing:

> An instrument is * * * converted if it is taken by transfer, other than a negotiation, from a person not entitled to enforce the instrument or a bank makes or obtains payment with respect to the instrument for a person not entitled to enforce the instrument or receive payment.

3-420(a). "This covers cases in which a depositary or payor bank takes an instrument bearing a forged indorsement." 3-420 comment 1.

3.   Damages For Conversion

"[T]he measure of liability is presumed to be the amount payable on the instrument, but recovery may not exceed the amount of the plaintiff's interest in the instrument." 3-420(b).

Example: T steals a check from Payee, forges Payee's indorsement, and cashes the check at DB Bank. The check is presented for payment and charged to the drawer's account at PB Bank. Payee sues DB Bank. In the absence of a defense, DB Bank is liable for the amount of the check. In case an instrument that pays interest is converted, the damages are presumed to include the loss of interest.

Example: Same facts except that the check is payable jointly to two payees who are a building contractor and a supplier of building material. The check is delivered to the contractor who forges the supplier's indorsement. "The supplier should not, without qualification, be able to recover the entire amount of the check from the bank that converted the check. Depending upon the contract between the contractor and the supplier, the amount of the check may be due entirely to the contractor, in which case there should be no recovery, entirely to the supplier, in which case recovery should be for the entire amount, or part may be due to one and the rest to the other, in which case recovery should be limited to the amount due to the supplier." 3-420 comment 2.

4. No Defense Of Good Faith To The Direct Action

a. Former Law

Under former law the depositary-collecting bank's principal defense was 3-419(3), which provided:

> [A] representative, *including a depositary or collecting bank*, who has in good faith and in accordance with the reasonable commercial standards applicable to the business of such representative dealt with an instrument or its proceeds on behalf of one who was not the true owner is not liable in conversion or otherwise to the true owner beyond the amount of any proceeds remaining in his hands.

3-419(3) (1989 Official Text) (emphasis added). According to the usual interpretation of 3-419(3), a depositary-collecting bank acted as a *representative* when it took checks for deposit and collection from a thief who had stolen them and forged the payee's indorsement, even though the person represented was not the owner of the items. So, when the payee sued the bank for conversion, the section operated as a defense, except to the extent of proceeds remaining in the bank's hands. As usually interpreted, however, "remaining proceeds" meant funds attributable to the forged checks that remained available in the wrongdoer's account. The bank thus was not liable for amounts attributable to the checks that had been withdrawn from the account. Ordinarily, most of the funds had been withdrawn, and 3-419(3) thus operated as a complete, or almost complete, defense for the bank. There were contrary interpretations of 3-419(3) that very narrowly defined the term "representative," or the "remaining proceeds" language, so that 3-419(3) did not apply to any extent as a defense for the depositary-collecting bank. Most cases, however, rejected these interpretations, with the ultimate effect that the payee's direct action against the depositary-collecting bank was usually fruitless -- except where the wrongdoer had left tainted funds in her account, or where the peculiar circumstances of the particular case made the 3-419(3) defense unavailable by its own terms.

b. Change in Law Denies Defense to Depositary Bank

In 1990, 3-419(3) became 3-420(c) and more than the number was changed. The section was rewritten to provide:

A representative, *other than a depositary bank*, who has in good faith dealt with an instrument or its proceeds on behalf of one who was not the person entitled to enforce the instrument is not liable in conversion to that person beyond the amount of any proceeds that it has not paid out.

3-419(c) (emphasis added). This change in substance denies to depositary banks the defense of having acted reasonably and in good faith in dealing with converted items. The reason for the change is clear and sound, inasmuch as former law allowed the payee to shift the loss directly or indirectly to the payor bank which could shift it ultimately to the depositary bank:

> The depositary bank is ultimately liable in the case of a forged indorsement check because of its warranty to the payor bank under Section 4-208(a)(1) and it is usually the most convenient defendant in cases involving multiple checks drawn on different banks. There is no basis for requiring the owner of the check to bring multiple actions against the various payor banks and to require those banks to assert warranty rights against the depositary bank.

3-420 comment 3.

C. OTHER DIRECT ACTION SUITS

1. Payee Versus Payor Bank
a. Basis of the Action
In the typical check fraud case involving a payee's unauthorized indorsement, there is no doubt that the payee can recover directly from the payor bank for conversion if the check is paid. Paying a check over a forged indorsement amounts to conversion. 3-420(a). Because the payee is the owner of the check and is entitled to its proceeds, she is a proper party to complain of the wrong by the payor bank. Section 3-420 covers any case in which a check is paid over an unauthorized or missing indorsement.

b. Inapplicability of the 3-420(c) Defense
The defense of 3-420(c), which bars or limits a conversion action against a "representative" who deals with converted checks in good faith, is not available to the payor bank. The payor bank is not a "representative" within the meaning of the section, which has no applicability here whatsoever.

c. **Jurisdiction Is a Problem**

When the payee and payor bank are located in different states, the payee may be unable to sue the bank locally for jurisdictional reasons. Even if the local long-arm statute supports jurisdiction, constitutional due process will not permit exercising that jurisdiction if the bank's only connection with the payee's state is that checks drawn against the bank have circulated there. In this event, the payor bank has not purposefully acted in the payee's state or deliberately directed its activities at residents of the state. Therefore, traditional notions of justice and fair play, which define jurisdictional due process, would be offended by forcing the bank to answer for the conversion there. The payee would be required to sue where the payor bank is located.

Example: B draws a check to S whose employee, T, takes the check, forges S's indorsement and deposits the item in her account at DB Bank. The check is paid by the drawee, PB Bank. T cleans out her account and leaves town. S could recover from DB Bank but decides not to pursue this local bank. S can nevertheless recover from PB Bank. If, however, PB Bank is located in a different state and has insufficient local connections for jurisdictional purposes, S cannot pursue her conversion action against the bank locally. In case PB can be sued locally and "suit is brought against both the payor bank and the depositary bank, the owner, of course, is entitled to but one recovery." 3-420 comment 3.

2. Drawer Versus Depositary-Collecting Bank
a. Traditional View and Conversion Liability

The traditional view is that in the typical unauthorized indorsement case, the drawer of the check cannot directly recover from the depositary-collecting bank for conversion, money had and received, or otherwise. Article 3 expressly adopts this view, at least with respect to conversion. It provides that "[a]n action for conversion of an instrument may not be brought by * * * the issuer or acceptor of the instrument * * *." 3-420(a). The explanation is that the drawer of the check is not the holder or owner of the item, and has no right to the proceeds of it. Moreover, even though the check was paid and the drawer's account charged with the item, this charge was not authorized or effective against the drawer because the check was not properly payable, inasmuch as it carried an unauthorized indorsement. Therefore, any wrong committed by the depositary-collecting bank in dealing with the check violated no valuable property or other rights of the drawer. The drawer's recourse is to recover from the payor bank for paying an item that was not properly payable.

b. Other Theories of Liability -- *Sun 'N Sand*

Under former law, a few cases would allow the drawer of an altered check or a check with a forged indorsement to sue -- on other theories -- a depositary bank that took the check. The best example is *Sun 'N Sand, Inc. v. United California Bank*, 21 Cal.3d 671, 148 Cal. Rptr. 329, 582 P.2d 920 (1978), in which the California Supreme Court recognized that a drawer of a check might possibly recover directly from the depositary-collecting bank in a check fraud case on the basis of breach of warranty or negligence.

1) Breach of Warranty

Sun "N Sand held that the presentment warranties of former law ran in favor of the drawer of a check, as well as the payor bank. The technical analysis is that the drawer of a check pays the item, or is a payor of it, within the meaning of those warranty provisions. Because the payment warranties are made by any collecting bank in the collection chain of a check, the drawer could hold the depositary-collecting bank accountable in a forged indorsement case because the warranty against forged indorsements would have been violated directly as to the drawer. This theory will no longer hold. The 1990 Articles 3 and 4 make clear that no presentment warranties are made to the drawer of a check upon presentment to the drawee-payor bank. 3-417 & 4-208. With respect to the breach of warranty theory, *Sun 'N Sand* is flatly rejected.

2) Negligence

Sun 'N Sand also holds, though much more narrowly, that a depositary-collecting bank owes a limited duty of reasonable care to the drawer of a check, and that the drawer can recover from the bank on a negligence theory if the bank acts unreasonably in dealing with the item. By the terms of the court's opinion, however, the duty is narrowly circumscribed and is activated only when checks drawn payable to a bank are presented to the same bank by a third person who seeks to negotiate them for her own benefit. This aspect of *Sun `N Sand* is not so clearly rejected by the 1990 changes in Articles 3 and 4 and probably stands. Moreover, the duty of care has already been widened by the California Court of Appeals, holding that a drawer stated a cause of action in negligence against a depositary-collecting bank where an employee of the drawer stole checks payable to various persons, forged the payees' indorsements, and deposited the checks in the employee's personal account. *E.F. Hutton & Co., Inc. v. City Nat'l Bank*, 149 Cal. App.3d 60, 196 Cal. Rptr. 614 (1983). In *Hutton,* the key fact triggering the bank's duty of care to the drawer was that the bank knew, or should have known, that the employee worked for the drawer.

REVIEW QUESTIONS

B drew a check to S for the price of goods. T wrongfully took the check, forged S's indorsement, and deposited the check in her account at DB Bank. The check was paid by the drawee, PB Bank, and charged to B's account.

1. Can S require B to pay the price of the goods even though B's check, taken by S for the underlying obligation, has been charged to B's checking account?

2. Can B recover from PB Bank?

3. Can B recover instead from DB Bank?

4. Rather than pursuing B, can S recover from DB Bank?

5. Can S recover instead from PB Bank?

PART THREE

ORDINARY DRAFTS USED WITH OTHER COMMERCIAL PAPER

Chapters

XII

ORDINARY DRAFTS AND DOCUMENTS OF TITLE IN SALES FINANCING

Analysis

A check is not an entirely reliable means of paying for property or services. A seller who takes the buyer's check in exchange for property or services is not certain to get payment from the drawee-bank. The check can be dishonored for a variety of reasons (insufficient funds, stop order, etc.) that leave the seller-payee with nothing more than a cause of action against the buyer-drawer. The result is that, although the seller intended a cash deal, she ends up having sold on credit. To make matters worse, this unintended credit is probably unsecured.

A seller of goods can insure that she is actually paid by not delivering the property until she gets cash, or its equivalent, in hand. Of course, the typical buyer will not wish to pay for the goods in advance of delivery. The answer is a simultaneous exchange of goods for cash. When the seller and buyer are located far apart, this kind of exchange is made possible through the use of a documentary draft and a payment scheme known as "payment against documents."

In this scheme, the seller ships the goods by carrier to the buyer's city. The carrier gives the seller a receipt for the goods which is known as a bill of lading. A bill of lading is a kind of document of title and, as such, it represents the goods and controls their disposition. The seller attaches this document to a draft drawn by her against the buyer. The set of two writings is called a *documentary draft,* which is handled for collection by banks. The seller's bank will take the documentary draft and, as agent for the seller, send it to a bank in the buyer's city. The latter bank, upon receiving the documentary draft, will present it to the buyer for payment. Upon paying it, the buyer gets the document of title and thereby gets control of the goods. The payment is then sent by the presenting bank to the seller's bank and deposited in the seller's account.

Payment against documents is fully discussed below, immediately following a short lesson on the law of documents of title. Considered also in this chapter are other schemes in which documents and drafts other than checks are used as vehicles of payment or credit to finance sales of goods.

A. DOCUMENTS OF TITLE

Negotiable instruments embody rights to the payment of money. Documents of title represent title to goods.

The principal source of state law on documents of title is U.C.C. Article 7, which is the basis of what is said here about documents. Be aware, however, that preemptive federal law often applies. See, e.g., United States Warehouse Act, 7 USCA 241-272 (governing the licensing of warehouses, the grading of agricultural commodities, and the contents of warehouse receipts, among other things); Pomerene Act, 49 USCA App. 81-124 (interstate shipment of goods); Carriage of Goods by Sea Act, 49 USCA 1300-1315 (shipments of goods from and to U.S. ports in foreign trade). These federal laws and Article 7 share many basic principles.

Under Article 7, a *document of title* (or its short-form synonym, *document,* 7-102(1)(e)) is a writing "which in the regular course of business or financing is treated as adequately evidencing that the person in possession of it is entitled to receive, hold and dispose of the document and the goods it covers." 1-201(15). Examples are: "bill of lading, dock warrant, dock receipt, warehouse receipt or order for the delivery of goods." Id. Among these examples, the most common and familiar are the bill of lading and the warehouse receipt, which explains why the balance of this discussion focuses exclusively on them.

A *bill of lading* is a "document evidencing the receipt of goods for shipment issued by a person engaged in the business of transporting or forwarding goods * * *." 1-201(6). Railroads and trucking lines, for example, issue bills of lading, as do other kinds of businesses who carry, i.e., transport, goods from one location to another. A *warehouse receipt* is "a receipt issued by a person engaged in the business of storing goods for hire." 1-201(45). A farmer who stores grain in an elevator gets a warehouse receipt covering her crop. A law student who wins a mansion full of furniture on Wheel of Fortune gets a warehouse receipt upon storing the goods in a terminal near her law school. (There is no space for the booty in her studio apartment.) Notice that both kinds of documents originate with professional bailees, that is, people whose business -- at least in part -- is shipping or storing other people's goods.

In more general terms, a bill of lading or a warehouse receipt is, basically, evidence of a *bailment* that sets out the major terms of the contract between the bailor and bailee, including when and to whom the bailee should release the goods. A bill or receipt is also indicia of title to the bailed goods so that third parties can acquire ownership of, or other interests in, the goods by addressing the document rather than the goods themselves. In these roles, bills of lading and warehouse receipts serve two principal, closely related functions: controlling access to the goods and controlling ownership of them.

How a document serves these functions, and its effectiveness in doing so, are largely determined by whether the document is negotiable or non-negotiable.

1. Distinguishing Negotiable Documents
a. The Test for Negotiability

Recall (fondly?) the difficulties in determining whether a right to the payment of money is negotiable under Article 3. U.C.C. 3-104(a) lists the requisites of Article 3 negotiability, but another dozen or so provisions in Part I of Article 3 amplify the listing. All of Chapter II, supra, is devoted to explaining those provisions.

Deciding if a document is negotiable under Article 7 is much easier. Except in overseas trade, the test is whether "by its [the document's] terms the goods are to be delivered to bearer or to the order of a named person." 7-104(1). That's it! "Any other document is non-negotiable." 7-104(2). Restated in language you learned in studying Article 3, an Article 7 document is negotiable if it contains "words of negotiability." If these words are missing, the document is non-negotiable.

b. Article 7's Coverage of Non-negotiable Documents
If a right to the payment of money is not negotiable under the provisions of Article 3, the consequences are that the writing is not an instrument and Article 3 is altogether inapplicable. Article 7 is different in this regard. It generally applies to both negotiable and non-negotiable documents. Making the distinction is important only in applying particular rules within Article 7, not in deciding whether the statute, as a whole, is the general source of governing law.

2. How Documents Control Access To The Goods
The bailee of goods who has issued a document of title, whether a bill of lading or a warehouse receipt, is generally obligated to "deliver the goods to a *person entitled under the document* * * *." 7-403(1) (emphasis added). The meaning of "person entitled under the document," which is the key to deciding who is entitled to the goods, depends on whether the document is negotiable or not.

a. When the Document Is Non-negotiable
The person entitled to the goods under a non-negotiable document is "the person to whom delivery is to be made by the terms of or pursuant to written instructions * * *." 7-403(4). Such written instructions, directed to a bailee who has issued either a warehouse receipt or a bill of lading, are referred to as a *delivery order,* 7-102(1)(d), which is itself a document of title. 1-201(15).

> *Example:*   O stores goods with W who issues a non-negotiable warehouse receipt providing that the goods are "Received for the account of O." (There are no words of negotiability.) X steals the receipt and presents it to W. W would act wrongfully as against O by releasing the goods to X. W must deliver the goods to O or pursuant to O's instructions, and O has not instructed delivery to X.

> *Example:*   Same facts except that O gives X a delivery order instructing W to deliver the goods to X. X presents this order to W. W is justified in releasing the goods to X.

A delivery order can be seen as Article 7's version of a check. A bank holds monetary credit that belongs to a customer. By her check the customer orders the bank to pay the credit to someone else. A warehouser or carrier, who is the bailee, holds goods that belong to the bailor. By a delivery order the bailor orders the bailee to deliver the goods to a third person.

The person named in a delivery order may not wish to take possession of the goods. Of course, the bailee is not bound to hold the goods for such person's account. If, however, the bailee agrees to hold the goods for the account of the person named in the delivery order, this agreement can be established by the bailee accepting the order, much as a drawee of a draft becomes liable thereon by accepting the instrument. "When a delivery order has been accepted by the bailee it is for practical purposes indistinguishable from a warehouse receipt." 7-102 comment 3. Thereafter, the bailee is obligated to deliver to the person entitled under the accepted delivery order.

Example: O stores goods with W who issues a non-negotiable receipt. O writes a delivery order instructing W to deliver the goods to X. W accepts the order, which is itself non-negotiable. W is now obligated to deliver the goods to X or pursuant to the instructions of X.

b. When the Document Is Negotiable

The person to whom the bailee is obligated to deliver goods covered by a negotiable document is the *holder* of the document. 7-403(1) & (4). The term "holder" has the same basic meaning here that it has for purposes of Article 3, except that documents are held instead of instruments: "'Holder' with respect to a document of title means the person in possession [of the document of title] if the goods are deliverable to bearer or to the order of the person in possession." 1-201(20). Deciding if a person is a holder depends, as under Article 3, on whether the paper is order or bearer paper.

1) Upon Issuance

If the bailee issues a negotiable document running to the order of a named person, only this person can be a holder upon issuance, and she acquires the status upon getting possession of the document which names her. If the document runs to bearer, any person in possession of it is a holder.

2) Subsequent Holders

A person can become the holder of a document issued to the order of someone else only if the person named in the document indorses it. If the indorsement is a blank indorsement, which means that the named person signs her name without specifying a person to whom delivery should be made, the document becomes bearer paper, and anybody in possession of it is a holder. If the indorsement is a special indorsement, meaning that the named person identifies someone to whom delivery should be made, no one can thereafter become a holder without the indorsement of the special indorsee. If the special indorsee indorses in blank, the document becomes bearer paper, and anyone in possession of it is a holder.

Of course, as is true with respect to instruments, a bearer document can be converted into order paper by a special indorsement. This is true whether the document was issued as bearer paper, or became bearer paper through a blank indorsement. In either event, after the special indorsement, no later taker could become a holder without the special indorsee's signature on the document.

Observe that these rules are essentially the same as the rules on the negotiation of instruments. Compare 3-201 and 3-205 with 7-501(1)-(3).

Example: O stores goods with W, a warehouser, who issues a negotiable document covering the goods. The document runs to O's order. T steals the document, presents it to W and demands the goods. W should not deliver the goods to T because T is not a holder and, thus, is not entitled under the negotiable document.

Example: Same facts except that O indorses the document in blank before it is stolen by T. W delivers the goods to T. W is not accountable to O for delivering the goods to T because T was a holder.

Example: O stores goods with W, a warehouser, who issues a negotiable document covering the goods. The document runs to O's order. O gives to T a delivery order instructing W to deliver the goods to T. Thereafter, O indorses to P the document issued by W. T and P both demand the goods from W. W is obligated to deliver to P. She is the person entitled under the document.

c. **Bailee's Accountability for Non- or Misdelivery**
A bailee is obligated to surrender goods to a person entitled to their delivery under a document covering the goods. A bailee who refuses to deliver the goods to such a person or is unable to do so because the goods have been lost or destroyed (nondelivery), or who cannot deliver them because she has given the

goods to someone else (misdelivery), is liable, usually for conversion, to the person entitled to delivery.

d. Excuses for Non- or Misdelivery

Article 7 provides a list of seven excuses for nondelivery and misdelivery. See 7-403(1)-(3). Only the most important excuses are discussed here.

1) Major Excuses for Nondelivery

a) Goods Lost or Destroyed

A bailee is excused for nondelivery when the reason is "damage to or delay, loss or destruction of the goods for which the bailee is not liable." 7-403(1)(b). Warehousers and carriers are obligated to exercise reasonable care in keeping goods bailed with them. See 7-204(1) & 7-309(1). If the goods are lost or destroyed despite the bailee's due care, the bailee is not liable for their nondelivery. In some states the bailee is burdened with proving due care. In other states, the person entitled under the document must prove negligence by the bailee to establish the bailee's liability for failing to deliver lost or destroyed goods.

b) Bailee's Lien Unsatisfied

A bailee, whether a warehouser or a carrier, acquires a lien, by law, on goods in her possession that are covered by a document to secure charges for storage and transportation. 7-209 (lien of warehouser) & 7-307 (lien of carrier). "A person claiming goods covered by a document of title *must* satisfy the bailee's lien where the bailee so requests * * *." 7-403(2) (emphasis added). A bailee who makes such a request is justified in not delivering the goods until the lien is satisfied, 7-403 comment 4, even if the person entitled to delivery of the goods is not the person who stored or shipped them. If the lien is not paid, the bailee is entitled to sell the goods herself, at a public or private sale, and apply the proceeds in satisfaction of the charges owed her. 7-210(1) & 7-308(1). A purchaser in good faith of goods sold to enforce a bailee's lien takes the goods free of any rights of persons against whom the lien was valid, even though the bailee's sale of the property failed to comply with the requirements of the law governing such a sale. 7-210(5) & 7-308(4).

c) Negotiable Document Not Surrendered

A person claiming under a negotiable document of title must surrender the document for cancellation upon taking possession of the goods. 7-403(3). Otherwise, the bailee is not obligated to deliver the goods even though the person's claim is, in fact, rightful. This requirement of surrender of the document "is limited to cases of delivery to a claimant; it has no application, for example, where goods * * * are lawfully sold to enforce the bailee's lien." 7-403 comment 5.

2) Major Excuse for Misdelivery: Claimant With a Better Right
A bailee is not liable for having delivered the goods to someone other than the person entitled under the document if the bailee made "delivery of the goods to a person whose receipt was rightful as against the claimant." 7-403(1)(a). According to the commentary, the principal case covered by this excuse "is delivery to a person whose title is paramount to the rights represented by the document." 7-403 comment 2.

Example: O stores goods with W, a warehouser, who issues a negotiable receipt covering the goods. The receipt runs to O's order. After O indorses the document in blank, T steals it. Both T and O appear at W's warehouse to claim the goods. W is justified in delivering to O even though T is a holder and is entitled under the document.

Example: O gives Bank a security interest in widgets to secure a loan. O then stores the goods with W who issues a document covering the goods. Upon O's failure to repay the loan, Bank traces the goods to W and demands delivery of them. W is justified in delivering to Bank.

a) Minor Difficulty With 7-403(1)(a) in Practice
The practical difficulty for the bailee in these situations is knowing for sure who has the better claim to the goods. If her determination is wrong, the bailee is liable for misdelivery. For this reason, Article 7 provides: "If more than one person claims title or possession of the goods, the bailee is excused from delivery until he has had a reasonable time to ascertain the validity of the adverse claims or to bring an action to compel all claimants to interplead and may compel such interpleader, either in defending an action for nondelivery of the goods, or by original action, whichever is appropriate." 7-603.

b) Major Implication of 7-403(1)(a) in Theory
There is an extremely important theoretical implication in this rule that excuses a bailee from misdelivery when the goods were surrendered to a person having a better claim to them than the person entitled under the document. It is this: *A person who is, as against the bailee, entitled to delivery of goods under a document may not be entitled to them as*

against third parties. As the following discussion reveals, documents facilitate transferring interests in the goods, but title to goods is not in all instances controlled by documents covering them.

3. How (And The Extent To Which) Documents Control Title To The Goods

In a sale of goods transaction, title ordinarily passes when the seller completes her performance with reference to the physical delivery of the goods. 2-401(2). Delivery and passage of title can be accomplished, however, without the buyer herself actually taking possession of the goods. When the goods are covered by a document, "title [to the goods] passes at the time when and the place where [the seller] delivers such documents." 2-401(3)(a). The reason is that title to goods covered by a document is reified, that is, embodied, in the document because, by law, a transferee of a document, whether negotiable or non-negotiable, acquires the transferor's title to the goods that the document covers. 7-504(1).

a. The Security of Documented Title (Protection Against Subsequent Claims)

When a buyer of goods actually takes and keeps possession of the property itself, her title is safe. No one else can defeat her title by thereafter dealing with the seller. The seller's rights passed to the buyer upon delivery, 2-401(2), and the seller is left with nothing to sell. Thus, if the seller purported to resell the goods to a third person, the third person would acquire only her transferor's rights, 2-403(1), and her transferor -- the seller -- had no rights in the goods to convey. All her rights had already passed to the first buyer.

A buyer's possession of a document covering the goods never provides as much security of title as possession of the goods themselves, not even when the document is negotiable. Yet, as between negotiable and non-negotiable documents, the former provide more security than the latter.

1) Resale by Transferor

In the case of a sale of goods covered by a non-negotiable document, title to the goods, i.e., the seller's rights, passes to the buyer when she gets the document. 7-504(1). Yet, her title can be defeated by certain creditors of, and buyers from, her transferor until such time as the bailee receives notification of the sale to the buyer. See 7-504(2)(a) & (b), which applies only in the case of a non-negotiable document. Most threatening to the buyer is the rule of 7-504(2)(b) that if the seller resells the goods in the ordinary course of business to a third person, this person will defeat the original buyer's rights if the bailee has delivered the goods to the third person, or received notice of the third person's rights, before learning of the original buyer's claim to the goods. 7-504(2)(b). Cf. 2-403(2).

Example: O owns goods stored with W, who issued to O a non-negotiable document covering the goods. O sells the goods to B1 who takes the document but neglects to notify the bailee of the sale to her. (O had written on the document an instruction to W that she deliver the goods to B1.) O thereafter resells the goods to B2 in the ordinary course of business, and sends W a delivery order directing surrender of the goods to B2. Upon receipt of the delivery order, W surrenders the goods to B2 without knowledge of the transfer to B1. B1 sues B2 and W.

As against B2, B1 argues that she acquired title to the goods, 7-504(1); that O was therefore left with no interest in the goods; and thus that B2 acquired nothing. This line of argument would prevail in the absence of 7-504(2)(b), which applies in favor of B2 and entitles her to judgment over B1.

As against W, B1 will argue that W was obligated to deliver the goods to a person entitled under the document, 7-403(1); that she, B1, was entitled under the document inasmuch as the document was non-negotiable and she was the person to whom delivery was to be made by the terms of instructions that O had written on the document itself, 7-403(4); and, therefore, that W is liable to her for nondelivery. This argument fails. B2 was also entitled under the document. Moreover, a bailee is not liable for misdelivery if she surrendered the goods "to a person whose receipt was rightful as against the claimant." 7-403(1)(a). B2's receipt was rightful as against B1 under the rule of 7-504(2)(b), which is the reason why B1 would not recover from B2.

B1's only recourse is to sue O for breach of contract.

Example: Same facts except that W learned of the sale to B1 before learning of the transfer to B2. Both B2 and W are liable to B1.

Example: Same facts as the original example, except that the document was negotiable and B1 became a holder of it. Both B2 and W are liable to B1. With respect to B1 v. B2, 7-504(2) does not apply in the case of a negotiable document. With respect to B1

v. W, B1 was the only person entitled under the document. 7-403(1) & (4).

2) Sale By Bailee

A buyer's title to goods covered by a document might be threatened by the bailee's sale of the property. As a general rule, however, a transferee of the bailee cannot defeat the buyer's title whether the title is represented by a negotiable or non-negotiable document. The transferee acquires only the rights of her transferor, 2-403(1), and in this case the transferor, i.e., the bailee, had nothing but a limited right of possession.

Example: O owns equipment she stores with W whose only business is storing goods. W issues a non-negotiable warehouse receipt covering the goods. O sells the equipment to B who acquires the document and written instructions directing W to deliver to B. W thereafter sells and delivers the goods to T, who purchases innocently, in good faith and for value. B sues T to replevy the goods or to recover damages in conversion. B wins. The result would be the same if the document were negotiable.

There is an important exception, however: "A buyer in the ordinary course of business of fungible goods sold and delivered by a warehouseman who is also in the business of buying and selling such goods takes free of any claim under a warehouse receipt even though it has been duly negotiated." 7-205. Cf. 2-403(1) & 9-307(1).

Example: O stores grain with W, an elevator, which buys and sells grain in addition to storing such goods for farmers. W issues to O's order a negotiable document covering the grain. O sells the grain to B and indorses the documents to B. W thereafter sells and delivers the grain to T in the ordinary course of business. B sues T for conversion. T wins. The result would be the same if the document were non-negotiable.

b. The Credibility of Documented Title (Protection Against Prior Claims)

1) Post-Documentation Claims

a) General Rule

A transferee of goods generally acquires only the rights of her transferor. 2-403(1). Thus, the transferee takes the property subject to legal and equitable claims against the goods existing at the time of the transfer to her. The same is true, as a general rule, when goods are covered by a document, whether negotiable or non-negotiable. 7-504(1).

Example: O stored goods with W who issued a non-negotiable document covering the property. O sold the goods to B1 and gave B1 a delivery order instructing W to deliver the goods to B1. W followed the instructions and delivered to B1. O thereafter resold the goods to B2, and transferred the original document to her. Upon discovering the prior sale and delivery to B1, B2 sued B1 and W.

Example: B2 loses her action against B1. B2 acquired the title and rights which O had authority to convey. 2-403(1) & 7-504(1). O had no rights to convey to B2 because O had already sold her rights to B1.

Example: B2 loses her action against W. B1 was a person entitled under the document. 7-403(1) & (4).

b)   Exception: "Due Negotiation"
In some cases, property is negotiable, meaning that a transferee of it can potentially acquire rights greater than the rights of her transferor. An example you know well is the Article 3 instrument. See 3-305. Also negotiable in this sense is a negotiable document of title. Just as a holder in due course of an instrument takes free of all claims to the instrument, 3-306, "a holder to whom a negotiable document of title has been duly negotiated acquires thereby * * * title to the document [and] title to the goods," 7-502(1)(a) & (b), which essentially means that a holder of a document by due negotiation takes free of all claims to the document and the goods.

There are three keys to this freedom from claims under Article 7. Two of the keys have already been discussed: The transferee must be a *holder,* and she must be holding a *negotiable document.* The third key is *due negotiation,* which has several requirements. The holder must purchase the document

♦ in good faith,
♦ without notice of any defense against or claim to it on the part of any person,
♦ for value other than receiving the document in settlement or payment of a money obligation, and

♦ in the regular course of business or finance.

7-501(4). Be careful! These requirements are very similar to the requisites for the status of holder in due course of an instrument under Article 3, but there are two important differences.

Meaning of Value. First, the meaning of value for due negotiation under Article 7 is different. For purposes of due negotiation, value is defined by 1-201(44), as modified by 7-501(4). The modification excludes from the meaning of value taking a document in satisfaction of a preexisting money debt. Value for purposes of Article 3 due-course status is defined in 3-303. This definition includes taking an instrument in satisfaction of an antecedent claim.

The definition of value for Article 3 due-course purposes excludes an executory promise. See 3-303(a) (agreed consideration must have been performed). For Article 7 due-negotiation purposes, value includes any consideration sufficient to support a simple contract, 1-201(44)(d), which includes an executory promise.

Regular Course of Business or Finance. Another difference is the requirement under Article 7, for due negotiation of a document, that the purchase occur in the regular course of business or finance, which requirement applies both to the person making the transfer and also to the transaction itself. 7-501 comment 1. There is no such regular-course requirement for Article 3 due-course status.

Example: O, a farmer, stores grain with W who issues to O's order a negotiable warehouse receipt. O sells the grain to B1 and the parties agree that title immediately passes to B1, but O does not transfer the document to her. O thereafter sells the grain to B2, a cereal manufacturer, and negotiates the document to B2. B2 takes possession of the grain from W. B1 sues B2 and W. B1 loses.

As against B2, B1 will argue that O had already transferred her rights to B1, and thus B2 acquired nothing in B2's deal with O. This argument would prevail but for 7-502(1), which provides that a holder of a negotiable document through due negotiation acquires title to the document and to the goods. B2 is a holder of a negotiable document who acquired it through due negotiation, as defined in 7-501(4).

As against W, B1 will lose because B2 was a person entitled under the document inasmuch as the document was negotiable and B2 was a holder. See 7-403(1) & (4).

Example: Same facts except that B2 is a law professor. B1 will prevail as against B2 because, in this case, the document would not have been duly negotiated to B2. The reason is that the negotiation to B2 was not in the regular course of business or financing inasmuch as B2, a law professor, is certainly not a person in the trade. See 7-501 comment 1. B1 will still lose as against W. Although B2 did not take through due negotiation, she was a holder and thus was the person entitled under the document.

Example: O, a farmer, stores grain with W who issues to O's order a negotiable warehouse receipt. O indorses the document in blank. T steals the document and sells it to B, a cereal manufacturer, who innocently pays substantial value for it. B then takes possession of the grain from W. O sues B. B was a holder of a negotiable document, but she prevails only if she took the document through due negotiation. This depends on whether the negotiation was in the regular course of business, which turns on whether T was a person in the trade.

Example: Same facts except that T was a person in the trade, but the price B paid for the document was well below market value. O's action against B will succeed. B did not take through due negotiation because the purchase was not in the regular course of trade. "[A] price suspiciously below the market * * * is * * * clearly outside the range of regular course." 7-501 comment 1.

2) Pre-Documentation Claims
Even a holder of a negotiable document who acquires it through due negotiation is generally not protected from claims to the goods that existed before the document was issued. For example, suppose that T steals goods from O and stores them with W. W issues a negotiable warehouse receipt to T's order. T duly negotiates the document to B, and B takes possession of the goods from W. O finds the goods in B's possession and sues B for conversion. B will rely on 7-502(1) and argue that because she took the document through due negotiation, she acquires title to the document and the

goods. This argument is flawed: 7-502(1) is subject to the rule of 7-503. This section, 7-503, provides that, as a general rule, "[a] document of title confers no right in goods against a person who before issuance of the document had a legal interest or a perfected security interest in them," not even if the document is negotiable. O will prevail over B.

Note, however, that O would not prevail in an action against W. The reason is this rule:

> A bailee who in good faith including observance of reasonable commercial standards has received goods and delivered or otherwise disposed of them according to the terms of the document of title or pursuant to this Article is not liable therefor. This rule applies even though the person from whom he received the goods had no authority to procure the document or to dispose of the goods and even though the person to whom he delivered the goods had no authority to receive them.

7-404.

There are exceptions to the rule of 7-503. This rule, which preserves pre-documentation claims, does not apply if the true owner:

- delivered or entrusted them or any document of title covering them to the bailor or his nominee with actual or apparent authority to ship, store or sell or with power to obtain delivery under this Article (7-403) or with power of disposition under this Act (2-403 & 9-307) or other statute or rule of law; or,
- acquiesced in the procurement by the bailor or his nominee of any document of title.

7-503(a) & (b). These exceptions are summarized as follows:

> In general it may be said that the title of a purchaser *by due negotiation* prevails over almost any interest in the goods which existed prior to the procurement of the document of title *if* the possession of the goods by the person obtaining the document derived from any action by the prior claimant which introduced the goods into the stream of commerce or carried them along that stream.

7-503 comment 1 (emphasis added).

Example: First Bank has a perfected security interest in O's crops. First Bank agrees that the crops should be stored. O stores them, gets a negotiable document that runs to bearer, and pledges the document to Second Bank to secure a loan. Second Bank's claim prevails over First Bank's, notwithstanding that First Bank perfected first. (Section 9-312(5)(a) is inapplicable here. Article 9 defers to the due-negotiation principle of Article 7. 9-309.)

Example: Same facts except that First Bank in no way authorized the storage. First Bank prevails over Second Bank, which in this case is not protected by 7-503(a) or (b).

Example: O owns goods and authorizes T to store them on behalf of O. T takes the goods and stores them with W. Because T represents that she is the owner of the goods, W issues a negotiable document to T's order. T then duly negotiates the document to B. B gets title to the goods and thereby defeats O's rights in them.

Example: Same facts except that for some reason, the document is not duly negotiated to B. In this event, O prevails against B. "A transferee of a document, whether negotiable or non-negotiable, to whom the document has been delivered but not duly negotiated, acquires the title and rights which his transferor had or had *actual authority to convey.*" 7-504(1) (emphasis added). T had no rights of her own; and, although she may have had actual authority to store and apparent authority of some other kind, she had no actual authority to convey O's rights. The exceptions to the rule of 7-503 do not apply. In effect, they work only in favor of a holder through due negotiation. B is not such a holder.

B. PAYMENT AGAINST DOCUMENTS

Now that you understand the basic principles of documents of title law, you can better appreciate and more critically evaluate the payment scheme known as *"payment against documents."* This scheme permits a simultaneous exchange of goods for cash or other payment, even when the buyer and seller are located far apart, by addressing payment to documents covering the goods rather than to the goods themselves.

1. How The Payment Scheme Works

a. Step One: Creating the Documentary Draft

Upon shipping the goods to the buyer, the seller has the carrier issue a negotiable bill of lading to the seller's order. The bill of lading is, of course, a document of title, as discussed above. The bill will probably direct the carrier to notify the buyer when the goods arrive in the buyer's vicinity. Yet, because the bill is a negotiable document, the carrier cannot properly deliver the goods to anyone except a holder of the document. 7-403(1) & (4). So, even though the carrier is asked to notify the buyer of the arrival of the goods, the carrier cannot surrender the goods to the buyer unless the buyer holds the bill of lading.

At the time of shipment, the holder of the bill is the seller. 1-201(20). It was issued to her order, and she is in possession of it. So, even though the seller has shipped the goods, she remains in control of them because she holds the negotiable document covering the goods and thereby holds the key to getting possession of them from the carrier. Moreover, by shipping the goods under a negotiable document to her own order, the seller effectively retains, by law, a security interest in the goods, 2-505(1)(a). This interest is important to the seller because, if the contract is a shipment contract, title to the goods will pass to the buyer when they are shipped despite the seller having procured a negotiable document covering the goods. See 2-401(2)(a).

The seller will attach the bill of lading to an Article 3 draft, in the amount of the price of the goods, drawn against the buyer. The seller is both the drawer and payee of the draft, which is payable at sight or on demand. The draft with the accompanying bill of lading is referred to as a *documentary draft.* 4-104(a)(6). The seller will not send the documentary draft directly to the buyer. Rather, she will ask her bank to send the draft through banking channels for the purpose of collecting it from the buyer.

b. Step Two: Sending the Documentary Draft for Collection

The collection activities of banks, and the scope of 4, are not limited to checks. Banks collect, and Article 4 regulates, other kinds of items. "'*Item*' means an instrument or a promise or order to pay money." 4-104(a)(9). A documentary draft is an item, and a seller who seeks payment against documents can have her bank collect the documentary draft she has drawn against the buyer. Part 5 of Article 4 deals with the collection of documentary drafts.

The seller will indorse both the draft and document that comprise her documentary draft and transfer them to her bank. The bank's treatment of the draft, however, is very different from its treatment of a check. A check is treated as cash, and the depositor's account is credited with the amount of the item immediately upon deposit because the bank assumes that the item will be paid. Banks thus commonly refer to checks as *cash items.* There is no assumption that a documentary draft will be paid. So, when the bank takes a documentary draft for collection, the seller's account is usually not credited with the item. Thus, instead of referring to the draft as a cash item, it is labeled a *collection item,* which means that credit will be given to the seller's account only if and when the draft is actually collected, that is, when payment by the buyer is made and remitted to the depositary bank.

Upon taking a documentary draft for collection, the seller's bank, which in Article 4 terms is the depositary-collecting bank, "shall present or send the draft and accompanying documents for presentment * * *." 4-501. The bank, however, does not send the documentary draft to the buyer. Rather, it is sent, through banking channels, to a bank where the buyer is located for the purpose of having the latter bank present the item to the buyer for payment. In this regard Article 4 requires the seller's bank, which is a collecting bank, to "exercise ordinary care in * * * sending [the item] for presentment," 4-202(a)(1), which requires the bank to "send [the item] by reasonably prompt method," 4-204(a), and to send the item before the bank's midnight deadline. 4-202(b).

The documentary draft will end up in the hands of a bank where the buyer is located. This bank is known as the *presenting bank,* see 4-105(6), which is not a payor bank. The presenting bank is not the drawee of the draft. The buyer is the drawee. The presenting bank is acting solely as the agent, or sub-agent, of the owner of the item, i.e., the seller, for the purpose of collecting the item from the buyer. So, like the seller bank, the presenting bank is a collecting bank whose duties are very different from a payor bank.

c. **Step Three: Presenting the Documentary Draft for Payment**
The presenting bank is obligated to present the documentary draft to the buyer-drawee for payment. The bank can, and probably will, make presentment by sending the buyer, who is the drawee, a written notice that the bank holds the item for payment. See 4-212(a). In this event, the draft is deemed presented when the notice is received by the buyer-drawee. 3-501(b)(1). Upon receiving payment of the draft, the presenting bank is obligated to deliver the documents to the drawee. 4-503(1).

Here is the exact point at which the simultaneous exchange of goods for cash takes place. The buyer tenders actual payment, which is cash or a cash equivalent in the form of a bank obligation and not just the buyer's own commitment. This payment is sent back down the collection chain to the seller's bank which will credit it to the seller's account. In return, the buyer gets the bill of lading covering the goods. Remember that the bill was indorsed in blank by the seller to whose order the bill was issued. Thus, the buyer, by taking possession of the bill, becomes the holder of the document, and thus the holder of the key to the goods, because the carrier-bailee's obligation to deliver the goods now runs to the buyer qua holder of the negotiable bill of lading. 7-403(1) & (4).

2. Buyer's Protections

The buyer who pays against documents actually gets, at the time of payment, a piece of paper which, in itself, is worthless. The credibility of the document, and the value in it, are based on rights which accompany the transfer of the document to her and provide some protection, i.e., some insurance, that the buyer will get the goods she bargained for.

a. Exclusive Access to the Goods

By taking possession of the negotiable bill of lading which the seller has indorsed in blank, the buyer becomes the holder of the document, 1-201(20) & 7-501(1), and is the only person to whom the carrier can rightfully deliver the goods. 7-403(1) & (4). The carrier would therefore become liable to the buyer for misdelivery should the carrier deliver the goods to the seller or otherwise follow the seller's orders after the buyer has taken up the document. The carrier is also liable to the buyer for loss or damage to the goods caused by the carrier's negligence.

b. Title to the Goods

If title to the goods has not already passed to the buyer by the time she gets the document of title, see 2-401, transfer of the document to her will pass the seller's title, that is, the buyer will thereby acquire the title and rights the seller had or had actual authority to convey. 7-504(1).

c. Rights Acquired Through Due Negotiation

The document is not merely transferred to the buyer. It is negotiated to her, 7-501(1), and in the typical case she will undoubtedly acquire the document in good faith, for value, without notice, and in the regular course of business. Thus, the buyer will be a holder through "due negotiation." 7-501(4). As a result, she will take title to the document and also title to the goods free of claims to them that arose after the document was issued. 7-502.

d. Warranties

1) Upon Issuance of the Document

Ordinarily, when the sales contract provides for payment against documents, the buyer is not entitled to inspect the goods before paying for them.

2-512(1) & 2-513(3). So, when the seller's draft is presented to the buyer for payment, the buyer will inspect the document of title to insure that the bill describes goods of the kind and quantity she ordered. The credibility of this description is backed by what is, in effect, a warranty by the issuer of the document that the issuer has the goods described and that the goods are as described in the document. This warranty is stated in terms of the carrier's liability for nonreceipt or misdescription:

> A consignee of a non-negotiable bill who has given value in good faith or a holder to whom a negotiable bill has been duly negotiated relying in either case upon the description therein of the goods, or upon the date therein shown, may recover from the issuer damages caused by the misdating of the bill or the nonreceipt or misdescription of the goods, except to the extent that the document indicates that the issuer does not know whether any part or all of the goods in fact were received or conform to the description, as where the description is in terms of marks or labels or kind, quantity, or condition or the receipt or description is qualified by "contents or condition of contents of packages unknown," "said to contain," "shipper's weight, load and count" or the like, if such indication be true.

7-301(1) (applicable to bills of lading). For similar liability with respect to warehouse receipts, see 7-203.

In turn, the shipper (i.e., the seller) warrants to the carrier "the accuracy at the time of shipment of the description, marks, labels, number, kind, quantity, condition and weight as furnished by him * * *." 7-301(5).

2) **Upon Negotiation of the Document**
In negotiating the bill of lading to the buyer, the seller warrants, in addition to any warranty made in selling the goods, that

- the document is genuine; and
- he has no knowledge of any fact which would impair its validity or worth; and
- his negotiation or transfer is rightful and fully effective with respect to the title to the document and the goods it represents.

7-507. This warranty is not made by the seller's bank, the presenting bank or any other intermediary in the collection chain. Such a party warrants "only its own good faith and authority." 7-508.

3) Upon Sale of the Goods

The seller also makes warranties with respect to the goods themselves. 2-313 (express warranties), 2-314 (merchantability) & 2-315 (fitness for a particular purpose).

e. Contract Remedies

In the event the goods, or the seller's performance, fail to conform to the sales contract, the buyer may pursue against the seller the remedies that Article 2 provides for breach of contract, including breach of warranty. See 2-711 & 2-714.

3. Seller's Protections Upon Breakdowns In The Scheme

a. Buyer Dishonors

1) Procedure Upon Dishonor

- The buyer dishonors the documentary draft by refusing to pay it, or by not paying it within the prescribed time. 3-502(c). If the presenting bank has made presentment by sending the buyer-drawee notice, 3-501(b)(1), the draft is deemed dishonored if the buyer does not respond by the close of business on the third banking day after notice was sent. 3-502(c) & 4-212(b).
- In the event of dishonor, the presenting bank "must use diligence and good faith to ascertain the reason for dishonor, must notify its transferor of the dishonor and of the results of its effort to ascertain the reasons therefor and must request instructions." 4-503(2).
- "[U]pon learning that the draft has not been paid or accepted in due course," the bank which took the documentary draft for collection, i.e., the seller's bank, "shall seasonably notify its customer [the seller] of the fact * * *." 4-501.

2) Seller's Reaction

The buyer's dishonor is a breach of contract which trigger's the seller's Article 2 remedies. See 2-703. In most instances the seller will react by reselling the goods and suing the buyer for the difference between the contract price and the resale price. See 2-706.

There is no problem, of course, in the seller getting access to the goods for the purpose of reselling them. The goods are still in the seller's control because, through the collecting and presenting banks, she retains possession of the document of title and is the holder of it. The carrier is thus obligated to deliver the goods to her. 7-403(1) & (4). The seller may have the goods returned to her, or she may sell them where they sit. The resale may occur, without the goods themselves being moved, by the seller delivering to the new buyer the document of title covering the goods.

The presenting bank, however, is not obligated to act, on its own, with respect to the goods. The bank's only duties are to request instructions and to follow any reasonable instructions seasonably received. 4-503. In the absence of such instructions, the presenting bank may, but need not, "store, sell, or otherwise deal with the goods in any reasonable manner." 4-504(a). If the bank takes action with respect to the goods pursuant to instructions from the seller, the bank has a right to reimbursement for its expenses. Indeed, the bank can require prepayment or indemnity for such expenses. 4-503. If the bank takes action in the absence of instructions, it acquires, by law, "a lien upon the goods or their proceeds." 4-504(b).

b. Bailee Misdelivers Goods
Payment against documents reduces the seller's risks because she controls the goods until the buyer pays for them by honoring the documentary draft. The seller's control, however, depends on the carrier fulfilling its obligation to deliver only to a person entitled under the document, which is the seller in the case of a negotiable document still in possession of the seller or her agent. If the carrier violates this obligation, as by delivering the goods to the buyer before the buyer gets the document, the seller's insurance for payment is altogether lost. In this event, the carrier is liable to the seller for misdelivery.

c. Presenting Bank Misdelivers Documents
The seller's control of the goods until the buyer pays is also undermined if the presenting bank surrenders the document prior to the buyer honoring the draft. With the document in hand, the buyer is a holder of it, and the carrier can rightfully surrender the goods to her. The presenting bank, however, is liable to the seller for violating 4-503, under which the bank can deliver the document to the buyer only upon payment of the draft. This violation amounts, at the very least, to a breach of the presenting bank's duty of ordinary care which the bank, as a collecting bank, owes to the seller as the owner of the documentary draft. See 4-202 & 4-103(e).

d. Depositary Bank Is Negligent
The seller's bank, which is the depositary bank, owes the seller a duty of ordinary care in handling the documentary draft for collection. If the bank violates this duty, as by delaying in sending the draft for collection or by acting unreasonably in giving the seller notice of dishonor or in forwarding instructions to the presenting bank, the depositary bank is liable for damages. In the absence of bad faith, however, the seller's maximum recovery is the amount of the draft

less "an amount that could not have been realized by the exercise of ordinary care." 4-103(e). Bad faith by the bank exposes it to liability for consequential damages. Id.

4. Variations In The Scheme

a. Discounting Documentary Drafts

Typically, when a depositary bank takes a documentary draft for collection, the amount of the draft is not credited against the seller-customer's account until the draft is actually paid by the buyer-drawee and payment is remitted through banking channels to the depositary bank. The seller, however, may convince her bank to purchase the draft from her rather than simply take it for collection. This arrangement is referred to as *discounting the draft.*

Obviously, by discounting a documentary draft, the depositary bank assumes the risk of the buyer's dishonor. This risk is well insured, however. In effect, the goods become collateral for the bank's advance, inasmuch as the bank acquires a security interest in the document, 4-210(a); and the bank enjoys the control and rights of a holder of the document who acquired it through due negotiation. Also, upon the buyer's dishonor and notice to the seller-drawer, the latter party becomes liable on the draft to the bank. Arguably, though not certainly, the bank has the 4-214(a) right to charge back the amount of the item to the seller's account, see 4-201(a) (last sentence). In any event, because the seller will be liable to the bank as drawer of the draft should the buyer dishonor it, the bank can debit the seller's account through its common-law right of setoff, whether or not the 4-214(a) right of charge back is available to the bank.

b. Shipping Under a Non-negotiable Document

So far, the discussion of payment against documents has assumed that the goods are covered by a negotiable document. Payment against documents can be structured, however, so that the goods are shipped under a non-negotiable bill of lading. In this event, the seller retains control of the goods by consigning them to herself or her agent so that the carrier is obligated to deliver the goods according to the seller's instructions. 7-403(1) & (4). The seller or her agent will instruct the carrier to surrender the goods to the buyer upon the buyer's payment of the draft.

This variation is less acceptable to the buyer for two basic reasons: First, paying the draft does not give the buyer exclusive control of the goods, as is true when she pays and gets a negotiable document covering them. Even after a buyer pays a draft against a non-negotiable document, the carrier can rightfully deliver the goods to whomever the seller instructs (at least if the carrier has not received notice of the buyer's claim). This is true even if the buyer receives, upon paying the draft, a delivery order in her favor. Second, a buyer who pays against a non-negotiable document cannot have the rights of a holder who takes through due negotiation. These rights are possible only when a negotiable document is negotiated. Thus, the buyer would have no protection against preexisting claims to the document or the goods themselves.

C. CREDIT AGAINST DOCUMENTS: TRADE ACCEPTANCES

1. Description Of The Scheme

Payment against documents requires the buyer to pay the documentary draft upon presentment to her. The seller may agree, however, that the buyer can acquire the documents accompanying the draft by accepting the instrument upon presentment instead of paying it. "Acceptance means the drawee's signed agreement to pay a draft as presented," and is accomplished by the drawee signing the draft. 3-409(a). The buyer qua acceptor "is obliged to pay the draft according to its terms at the time it was accepted * * *." 3-413(a). A draft accepted by a buyer in a sale of goods arrangement such as that described here is referred to as a *trade acceptance*. The arrangement as a whole could be labeled, quite accurately, credit against documents because the effect is an extension of credit to the buyer for a period of time specified by the terms of the draft. For example, if the draft provides for payment "60 days after sight," the drawee turned acceptor must pay the draft, to the payee or her transferee, 60 days after accepting it.

The procedure for getting the buyer's acceptance is basically the same as that involved in getting payment from the buyer when she is to pay against documents. There are only two basic differences, both of which are obvious: First, in credit against documents, the seller draws a time draft, rather than a demand draft, ordering the buyer to pay the instrument following a specified period after acceptance. Second, although the documentary draft is routed to the buyer through banking channels (just as in the case of a draft requiring payment), the presenting bank presents the draft for acceptance rather than for payment. See 4-503(1).

2. Advantages To Seller Compared To Sale On Account

The obvious question is why the seller would insist on a trade acceptance instead of simply sending the goods to the buyer on unsecured credit and relying on the buyer's Article 2 obligation to pay the price. In either case the seller depends on the buyer's promise to pay. The difference is that a trade acceptance captures the buyer's promise to pay in a negotiable form, which is easier to enforce (even for the seller-payee) than a mere contractual promise, see 3-308, and for which there may be a wider market should the seller-payee decide to discount her rights against the buyer.

In the event the seller discounts the draft, the purchaser will acquire the buyer's obligation thereon as acceptor, 3-413(a), and also the obligations of the seller as both drawer and indorser. 3-414(b) & 3-415(a). Moreover, the typical purchaser would satisfy the requirements for holder-in-due-course status, see 3-302(a), so that she would acquire the draft free from claims and defenses. 3-305(b) & 3-306. Thus, the purchaser of the draft could enforce it against the buyer-acceptor notwithstanding that the seller breached the underlying sales contract between her and the buyer.

3. **Advantage To Buyer Compared To Signing Instrument Up Front**
From the buyer's perspective, credit against documents is preferable to signing a note at the time the sales contract is made because, in accepting a documentary draft, her engagement on an instrument is concurrent with acquiring control of the goods. In signing an instrument beforehand, as when the contract is made, the buyer risks having to pay a holder in due course for goods she never received.

D. BANKER'S ACCEPTANCES

Another means for financing the buyer's purchase of goods is the *bankers' acceptance*. By this means the buyer usually can get funds more easily and more cheaply because the buyer's draft is accepted by a bank and thereby is backed by the credit of the acceptor-bank as well as the buyer's own credit. The very best explanation of bankers' acceptances is by a top expert, Reade H. Ryan, Jr. He explains:

Take a very simple example -- that of a bank customer which is an importer or buyer of oil. The importer wants to finance its importation of oil for 120 days, the time it takes the importer to import, re-sell and get paid for the oil purchased from the exporter. To extend the acceptance financing, the bank first has the importer execute an appropriate acceptance credit agreement under which the importer agrees that, in consideration for the bank's accepting one or more drafts drawn by the importer on the bank, the importer will pay the bank the amount of each draft the bank may accept and will pay that amount on or before the last business day before its maturity (or at maturity in same day funds), together with an appropriate acceptance commission for the bank's taking the credit risk of its customer. Technically, the acceptor bank does not need the acceptance credit agreement in order to have the drawer's reimbursement obligation. Such obligation is imposed by law. See UCC, § 4-401. The draft sometimes makes this obligation clear by expressly authorizing the drawee to 'charge' the draft 'to account of' the drawer. However, the acceptance credit agreement is important to make clear the terms of payment, of the acceptance commission and other amounts payable by the customer, and of the other agreements, representations, and provisions which protect the credit position of the bank.

Having executed the acceptance credit agreement, the importer will draw a 120-day time draft on the bank payable to the order of the importer (though the draft could be payable to the order of the bank or to the order of bearer). Then the bank accepts that draft by stamping 'Accepted', and dating and signing, across the face of the draft. Once accepted, the draft, now a negotiable instrument known as a banker's acceptance, may be transferred by the importer by its endorsement and delivery. The importer will get the money to pay for the imported oil either by selling or having the acceptor bank (as the importer's agent) sell, at a discount, the banker's acceptance in the acceptance market or, typically, by having the acceptance discounted by the acceptor bank, which may then or later rediscount the acceptance in the acceptance market.

The market for bankers' acceptances is an over-the-counter market made by about 30 dealers and a dozen brokers, with investors ranging from foreign central banks and foreign governments to domestic and foreign private investors of all kinds. Dealers quote bid and asked prices for round lots of $5 million. If the transaction to be financed is large, several drafts of $5 million each will be drawn. For smaller transactions, a number of drafts of similar maturities drawn on the same bank will be packaged to trade as a round lot. Typical maturities are one, three and six months, with the average reportedly around three months.

The acceptor bank which discounts its acceptance may hold the acceptance until maturity, but commonly the bank will, on the same day it discounts the acceptance, rediscount the acceptance in the market to put itself back in funds. The rediscount rate will normally be lower than the discount rate. In theory that is because the rediscounted paper carries with it the obligation of at least two parties, the acceptor and the drawer, and possibly a third, an endorser; in practice, the discounting bank sets its discount rate by applying a margin over the rediscount rate. Thus, in ordinary course, a bank will make a small profit on rediscount at the same time that it converts its paper into cash.

Ultimately the accepted draft will mature -- in our example, after 120 days -- but by then (hopefully) the importer will have sold its oil acquired with the proceeds of the acceptance and will, pursuant to the acceptance credit agreement, have paid the acceptor bank an amount equal to the face amount of the accepted draft.

Upon its payment of its acceptance, the acceptor bank can look back on a transaction in which the bank never had to use its own funds, only its credit, and received an acceptance commission and made profit on the discount and rediscount of the acceptance. (Of course, if the acceptor bank holds its acceptance for a day or more without rediscounting the acceptance, the bank will use its own funds.) The bank's customer, the importer, can look back on a transaction in which it financed the importation of oil using the bank's credit and paid an acceptance commission and the discount.

An exporter can also use acceptance financing. Assume the customer is an oil exporter which has a sales contract with a foreign buyer for its oil and expects to export, sell and get paid for its oil in 120 days. At the outset the bank will require the customer to execute an acceptance credit agreement under which the customer agrees to furnish the bank the funds with which to pay the acceptance at maturity. Having executed this agreement, the exporter will draw a 120-day draft on the bank, will have the draft accepted by the bank, and will realize the proceeds of the oil sale by having the accepted draft discounted. Upon maturity of the acceptance, the exporter repays the bank out of the oil proceeds from the foreign buyer.

    * * *

A banker's acceptance is often connected to a letter of credit issued by the accepting bank to finance the sale of goods. For example, the importer-buyer could instruct its bank to issue to the exporter-seller a commercial documentary letter of credit under which the bank issuer is not to pay cash against a sight draft, but rather to accept time drafts drawn by the exporter- seller on the bank against stipulated documents and in accordance with specified terms. When the exporter presents the stipulated documents, together with its time drafts drawn on the issuing bank, the bank would accept the drafts, and the exporter would receive its cash payment from the sale of the bankers' acceptances.

Letters of credit and bankers' acceptances may be used separately or in conjunction.

R. Ryan, *Bankers' Acceptances* in PLI COMMERCIAL LAW AND PRACTICE COURSE HANDBOOK ON LETTERS OF CREDIT AND BANKERS' ACCEPTANCES (1988); see also *United States v. Dougherty*, 763 F.2d 970, 972 (8th Cir. 1985) (discussing exporter's use of bankers' acceptances to finance foreign sales).

Bankers' acceptances ordinarily are used only to finance international sales of goods. The reason is that certain advantages attach to acceptances that are "eligible" for discount or purchase by the Federal Reserve, and federal law limits eligible acceptances to those

having not more than six months' sight to run, exclusive of days of grace-- (i) *which grow out of transactions involving the importation or exportation of goods*; (ii) which grow out of transactions involving the domestic shipment of goods; or (iii) which are secured at the time of acceptance by a warehouse receipt or other such document conveying or securing title covering readily marketable staples.

12 USCA 372(a) (emphasis added). Import or export transactions mean sales between the United States and another country or between foreign countries. Domestic acceptances are eligible to finance shipment alone and not to provide working capital, i.e., finance purchases of goods.

Ineligible acceptances are not necessarily illegal and are sometimes done, but they do not qualify for Federal Reserve discount. In truth, the Federal Reserve no longer rediscounts acceptances to any significant extent, but the eligibility of acceptances for discount remains important to banks for reasons of reserve requirements and lending limits. See generally W. Todd, *A Regulator's View of Bankers' Acceptances* in PLI COMMERCIAL LAW AND PRACTICE COURSE HANDBOOK ON LETTERS OF CREDIT AND BANKERS' ACCEPTANCES (1988).

REVIEW QUESTIONS

1.   O hires C, a law student, to transport goods from Pittsburgh to Philadelphia. C gives O a receipt for the goods. Is this receipt a warehouse receipt or a bill of lading within the meaning of U.C.C. Article 7?

2.   Same facts as Question 1 except that C is in the business of transporting other people's goods. When the goods arrive in Philadelphia, X appears at C's office there with a writing, signed by O and addressed to C, that directs C to deliver the goods to X. What is the technically proper name for this writing, and is it a document of title?

3.   Continue with Question 2. Waving the writing in the face of C's employee, X demands possession of the goods. Is C obligated to deliver to X?

4.   O hires C, a professional carrier, to transport goods from Pittsburgh to Philadelphia. C gives O a bill of lading covering the goods that runs to O's order. When the goods arrive in Philadelphia, X appears at C's office there with a writing, signed by O and addressed to C, that directs C to deliver the goods to X. O had sold the goods to X. Waving the writing in the face of C's employee, X demands possession of the goods. C surrenders the goods to X. The next day, Ms. BFP enters C's office in Philadelphia. In her hand is the bill of lading that C issued to O. The bill has been indorsed by O to BFP upon the two of them agreeing to a sale of the goods by the former to the latter. This sale occurred before O dealt with X. Is C liable to Ms. BFP for misdelivery?

5.   Same facts as Question 4, except that O sold the goods to X first.

6.   T runs a legitimate heavy equipment dealership during the day. At night, however, T is an equipment thief, stealing equipment from construction sites. While waiting for the "hot" equipment to cool, T stores it at W, a warehouser, who issues to T negotiable documents covering the property. After a cooling off period, T sells the equipment to out-of-state buyers by negotiating the documents to them. These buyers are contractors who purchase the goods, and take the documents, for value, in good faith and innocently. Eventually, the buyers take delivery of the equipment from W, who knows nothing and has acted reasonably in all respects.

    a.   Are these buyers holders through due negotiation?

    b.   Can the people from whom the equipment was stolen replevy it from the buyers?

    c.   Is W liable to (i) the people from whom the equipment was stolen or (ii) the buyers?

7.   Seller ships goods to Buyer, who has agreed to pay against documents. Upon presentment of the draft to Buyer, she pays it and the presenting bank gives her a negotiable document that describes the kind and quantity of goods she contracted to buy from seller. Buyer then contacted the carrier about taking delivery of the goods. The carrier explained that the seller had telephoned and given instructions to deliver the goods to BFP, to whom Seller had sold the goods. Is the carrier or BFP accountable to Buyer?

8.   Same facts as Question 7, except that Seller had not double-dealt. In other words there was no resale to BFP. The carrier had the goods and gladly surrendered them to Buyer. Yet, there was a small problem: The bill of lading described the shipment as ten cartons of widgets, which is the amount buyer had ordered from seller. The carrier, however, delivered to buyer only nine cartons. Further investigation revealed that seller only shipped nine cartons. Who among the seller, the presenting bank and the carrier is liable to Buyer?

9.   Seller ships goods to Buyer, who has agreed *to pay* against documents. Upon presentment of the *demand draft* to buyer, she accepts it instead of paying the instrument. The presenting bank then surrenders to Buyer the negotiable document, in bearer form, which had accompanied the draft. The bank returns the accepted draft through banking channels to Seller. Buyer gets possession of the goods from the carrier.

    a.   Is the carrier liable to Seller?

    b.   Is the presenting bank liable to Seller?

    c.   In the trade, what is the name of a draft drawn by a seller of goods on the buyer and accepted by the buyer?

10.   Why would a seller of goods prefer a banker's acceptance over a trade acceptance?

<table>
<tr><td style="border: 1px solid black; text-align: center; padding: 40px;">

XIII

LETTERS OF CREDIT

</td></tr>
</table>

Analysis

Seller and Buyer are negotiating a contract for the sale of goods. Seller is unwilling or unable to commit herself without payment in advance. Buyer does not wish to pay for the goods until she gets them. This impasse can be broken by the buyer having her bank issue the seller an Article 5 *letter of credit,* which is "an engagement by a bank or other person made at the request of a customer * * * that the issuer will honor drafts or other demands for payment upon compliance with the conditions specified in the credit." 5-103(1)(a).

This engagement, which is an enforceable promise, runs directly to the person named as beneficiary in the letter of credit, which would be the seller in the hypothetical case described here. The engagement is an independent obligation of the issuer to the beneficiary. The obligation is separate from the sales contract between the buyer and seller and separate from the bank's relationship with its customer who requested the credit. The seller thereby acquires, up front, a bank's promise to pay her upon the seller satisfying conditions described in the letter of credit. These conditions are decided by the buyer and seller, although nothing requires the buyer's bank to issue a credit on conditions that are objectionable to it. Typically, the principal condition is the presentation of documents of title covering goods the customer has ordered from the seller. Satisfaction of the conditions of the credit trigger the issuer's obligation to pay without the seller first looking to the buyer for payment. In this sense, the issuer's obligation to the seller is primary rather than secondary, which distinguishes a letter of credit from a guaranty.

Under the letter of credit arrangement the seller does not get payment in advance, but she gets the next best thing: A virtually undeniable promise by a person likely to remain solvent that the seller will be paid once control of the goods passes to the buyer by the transfer of appropriate documents.

The buyer is required to reimburse the issuer for paying the letter of credit. In effect, therefore, the buyer is paying for the goods when the bank honors the seller's demand for payment under the letter of credit. Thus, the buyer must pay for the goods before actually getting them. The buyer, however, gets the next best thing. She gets control of the goods upon payment because the bank will not pay the seller unless the seller transfers documents covering the goods.

If the goods are nonconforming, the buyer can sue the seller for breach of contract. Herein, however, is the ultimate effect of using a letter of credit. Ordinarily, a buyer is not required to pay for goods until after she has inspected them following delivery. The seller thus bears the risk of the buyer's dissatisfaction and the burden of having to sue to recover the price or other damages if the buyer breaches by rejecting conforming goods. When a letter of credit is used, the seller is paid regardless of the buyer's dissatisfaction with the goods. The buyer must sue to recoup her damages if the seller has breached the contract, as by shipping nonconforming goods. In effect, therefore, using a letter of credit shifts, from the buyer to the seller, the advantage of holding the price of the goods pending the resolution of contractual disputes between the parties. Significantly, the risk of insolvency also shifts. The buyer, rather than the seller, gambles that the other party will have available assets from which to satisfy her damages in the event she is the victim of a breach of contract.

The foregoing overview illustrates the traditional use of a letter of credit, which is facilitating sales of goods (especially in international transactions) by insuring payment of the price to the seller-beneficiary upon her performance in accord with the terms of the letter of credit. A letter of credit so used is referred to as a *commercial credit*. The remainder of this chapter is primarily concerned with filling in the most important details about commercial credits. Some attention is paid, however, to *standby credits*. A standby credit is a letter of credit that insures payment to the beneficiary not for her performance in a sale or other transaction with the customer, but for the customer's default in the transaction.

The principal source of law for the discussion here is U.C.C. Article 5. In practice, an equally important source of law is the Uniform Customs and Practice for Commercial Documentary Credits (UCP), promulgated by the International Chamber of Commerce. The UCP often governs rights and duties under letters of credit, and the interpretation of their terms, either because the credit itself declares that it is issued subject to the UCP, or because the courts rely on the UCP as evidence of trade usage and common understanding with respect to letters of credit. In most important respects, Article 5 and the UCP are entirely consistent.

A. DEFINING BASIC TERMS AND RELATIONSHIPS

1. Commercial Credits

a. The Main Players

In the commercial letter of credit, the *issuer,* 5-103(1)(c), usually a commercial bank, issues the *credit,* which is shorthand for *letter of credit,* 5-103(1)(a), in favor of the seller of goods. The bank acts in response to a request or application of the buyer, who is known as the *customer.* 5-103(1)(g). The seller is known as the *beneficiary* of the credit. 5-103(1)(d). The *credit* is a writing in which the issuer engages that it will pay or accept drafts or other demands for payment that comply with the terms of the credit. See 5-102(1), 5-103(1)(a) & 5-104. Typically, the terms require the seller to present documents, which usually consist of the seller's invoice; a shipping document (e.g., bill of lading, airway bill); an insurance certificate; various additional certificates (e.g., of inspection or origin); and consular documents, if necessary. The terms of credit also typically require presenting the documents together with a draft, or other form of a demand, ordering the issuer to pay or accept.

The nature of the draft gives rise to an important distinction in credit law: The distinction between *payment credits* and *time, usance,* or *acceptance credits.* With a payment credit, the beneficiary presents a sight or demand draft calling for payment, and the issuer honors the credit by paying the draft. With a time, usance, or acceptance credit, the beneficiary draws a draft payable at a specified future date after presentation, and the issuer honors the draft by accepting it, thereby creating a *banker's acceptance. (Banker's* acceptances are discussed in Chapter XII, supra.) In either case, the seller-beneficiary gets her money sooner or later, but the delay in payment under an acceptance credit is a cost to the seller which she may shift to the buyer in negotiating the price of the goods. This cost is incurred whether the seller holds the accepted draft until maturity or sooner discounts the draft to a third party.

The terms of a letter of credit, including the required documents and whether drafts are presented for payment or acceptance, are really decided by the seller and buyer. They decide how little, or how much, is required of the seller in order to get payment or acceptance of drafts drawn under a credit. The buyer then asks her bank, through an *application agreement,* to issue a letter of credit containing the terms agreed to by the seller. In this role the buyer is known, technically, as the *customer.* 5-103(1)(g). In practice the buyer is also referred to as the *applicant,* because of the application agreement she makes with the issuer-bank, or the *account party,* because it is on the buyer's account that the issuer-bank issues the credit.

If the buyer's bank is unwilling to establish a credit on the terms agreed to by the buyer and seller, they must find another bank willing to accept their terms or change the terms to suit the bank.

b. The Relationship Between Issuer and Beneficiary: Duty to Honor
A letter of credit is *established* as regards the beneficiary, meaning that the issuer becomes liable thereon to the beneficiary, when the beneficiary receives the credit itself from the issuer, or when she receives written advice, i.e., notice, from another bank acting for the issuer that the credit has been issued. 5-106(1)(b). A credit that has been established cannot be modified or revoked unilaterally by the issuer unless the credit is a *revocable credit.* See 5-106(3). Practically speaking, however, a revocable credit is not really a letter of credit because it has no legal significance. See 5-106 comment 2. So nothing more will be said here about revocable credits. The entire discussion before and after this paragraph refers to *irrevocable credits,* which cannot be modified or

revoked as regards the customer or the beneficiary without her consent. See 5-106(2).

Once a credit is established, the issuer is burdened with a statutory *duty to honor* owed directly to the beneficiary. This duty is stated in 5-114(1), which is the heart and soul of Article 5 and the statute's most important provision: "An issuer must honor a draft or demand for payment which complies with the terms of the relevant credit *regardless* of whether the goods or documents conform to the underlying contract for sale or other contract between the customer and the beneficiary."

The clause in 5-114(1) that begins with the word "regardless" is terribly important because it states the *independence principle,* which is that:

> The letter of credit is * * * independent of the underlying contract between the customer [buyer] and the beneficiary [seller]. * * * [T]he issuer is under a duty to honor the drafts or demands for payment which in fact comply with the terms of the credit without reference to their compliance with the terms of the underlying contract. * * * The duty of the issuer to honor where there is factual compliance with the terms of the credit is also independent of any instructions from its customer once the credit has been issued and received by the beneficiary.

5-114 comment 1.

An issuer that violates the duty to honor is guilty of *wrongful dishonor* and is liable to the beneficiary for "the face amount of the draft or demand * * * less any amount realized by resale or other use or disposition of the subject matter of the transaction [i.e., the goods]." 5-115(1). Moreover, "the customer is entitled to compensation for the issuer's failure to perform the customer/issuer contract [i.e., the application agreement], and thus to recover as if for nondelivery under a contract for the sale of goods." H. Harfield, LETTERS OF CREDIT 62 (1979).

c. **The Relationship Between Issuer and Customer: The Right of Reimbursement**

Upon duly honoring a draft or demand for payment under a credit, the issuer acquires a *right of reimbursement* against the customer. 5-114(3). This right entitles the issuer to recoup "any payment made under the credit and to be put in effectively available funds not later than the day before maturity of any acceptance made under the credit." Id. Usually, the issuer's right of reimbursement is also confirmed in the application agreement or another writing that is part of the contract between it and the customer. Their contract will also provide for a commission to be paid to the issuer for issuing the credit, and the means for securing the right of reimbursement and the commission. Significantly, the right of reimbursement depends on the issuer having "duly honored" a demand under a credit. The issuer cannot recoup payment from its customer in the event of *improper payment* or *wrongful* or *improper honor,* meaning payment or acceptance against documents that did not factually comply with the terms of the credit. In this event, the issuer is left with pursuing the beneficiary, who may be liable for restitution or for breach of warranty. See, e.g., 5-111(1) (warranty that the necessary conditions of the credit have been complied with); 7-507 (warranties upon transfer of documents, including genuineness of documents and lack of knowledge of facts which would impair validity or worth of documents). The issuer also is secured by the documents and the goods they represent either through a common-law banker's lien or otherwise, such as by the issuer's rights to the documents and the goods by virtue of its status as a holder through due negotiation. 7-502(1).

2. Standby Credits

The main players, and the basic rights and duties of the issuer, are the same in both commercial and standby letters of credit. Yet, a standby credit differs fundamentally from a commercial credit. While the traditional commercial credit directs a bank to pay the beneficiary upon the shipment of goods or other performance by her in favor of the customer, the standby credit "directs the bank to pay the beneficiary not for his own performance but upon the customer's default, thereby serving as a guarantee device." Note, *"Fraud in the Transaction": Enjoining Letters of Credit During the Iranian Revolution,* 93 HARV. L. REV. 992, 993 (1980). For this reason, standby credits are often referred to as *guaranty letters of credit.* A standby credit differs from a common-law guaranty, however, in "'that the former is a direct obligation to pay upon "specified documents showing default" while the latter is a secondary obligation requiring proof of the fact of default.'" *American Nat'l Bank & Trust Co. v. Hamilton Industries Internat'l, Inc.,* 583 F.Supp. 164, 169 (N.D. Ill. 1984).

Example: O hires C to construct a building. Pursuant to their agreement, C, the customer, gets her bank, the issuer, to establish a letter of credit in favor of O, the beneficiary. The credit provides that the issuer will honor drafts presented by O together with O's certified statement that C has breached the terms of the construction contract.

Often, however, the beneficiary of a standby credit is a bank or other financer that gives credit to a third party.

Example: C borrows money from State Bank to begin construction of a building for O. As collateral for the loan, C assigns to State Bank her right to payment from O. State Bank worries that O might be unwilling or unable to pay sums owed C under the construction contract. So C convinces O to get National Bank to issue a letter of credit in favor of State Bank. The credit provides that National Bank will pay drafts accompanied by certificates to the effect that C has performed and is entitled to payment from O.

Example: "Defense Contractor (Contractor) negotiates the sale of high technology optical equipment with Foreign Government (Buyer). * * * Contractor insists on a twenty percent downpayment, progress payments of an additional sixty percent during the course of performance, and the balance upon installation and satisfactory operation of the equipment. Buyer balks at these terms. It is concerned that Contractor may not perform at all or may perform unsatisfactorily. In these events Contractor will have Buyer's money, and Buyer will have a cause of action that it will have to pursue in a distant jurisdiction, Buyer being situated in one country, Contractor in another. Buyer is also concerned that its cause of action may become worthless in the face of Contractor's insolvency. * * *

"[T]he parties agree that a strong financial institution, usually a foreign bank or the foreign subsidiary of a United States bank, will issue two guaranties in favor of Buyer, one to cover return of the downpayment, the other to cover return of the progress payments. Under those guaranties * * * the guaranty issuer will pay Buyer promptly and without inquiry upon Buyer's demand, provided that the demand is made in the time and manner specified in the guaranty. [These guaranties are not letters of credit. Rather, they are more like bonds or other suretyship contracts governed by the common law.]

"The guaranty issuer insists that it have security for its guaranty, so the parties agree further that Contractor will cause a financially strong party (usually a commercial bank) to issue two standby credits in favor of the guaranty issuer. The first credit engages to pay the guaranty issuer a sum equal to the downpayment upon the guaranty issuer's order. The second engages to pay a sum equal to or less than the progress payments, as the guaranty issuer orders. If Buyer draws on a guaranty, the guaranty issuer will draw on the corresponding standby.

"Contractor is concerned that there may be a draw on the credits when Contractor is not in default and asks that the credits contain conditions that protect against unauthorized drafts. Buyer refuses. It argues that any attempt to condition payment of the credit on the question of performance may force Buyer to litigate performance questions before payment and may force Buyer to litigate them in Contractor's forum. It is against these risks that Buyer is attempting to guard, and Buyer insists that the credits contain only paper conditions and that they are to be simple. The bank issues, then, two credits under which it engages to pay * * * drafts provided that they: (1) are presented prior to the respective credit's expiry; (2) bear a legend identifying the credit; and (3) are accompanied by a certificate reciting, in the downpayment credit, that the guaranty issuer paid on the downpayment guaranty, and in the performance credit, that the guaranty issuer paid on the progress-payments guaranty. Ultimately, Contractor will bear the cost of draws under the guaranties, for when Buyer draws on a guaranty, the guaranty issuer will draw on the standby; and in the event of draw under the standby, the bank issuer [of the letters of credit] will seek reimbursement from Contractor." Dolan, *Standby Letters of Credit and Fraud (Is the Standby Only Another Invention of the Goldsmiths in Lombard Street?)*, 7 CARDOZO L. REV. 1, 3-5 (1985).

B. DETERMINING COMPLIANCE WITH THE CREDIT

An issuer's fundamental and principal duty under Article 5 is to "honor a draft or demand for payment which complies with the terms of the relevant credit * * *." 5-114(1). Then, upon having duly honored the draft or demand for payment, the issuer is entitled to the primary right Article 5 gives it: reimbursement from the customer. Due honor means, basically, having paid or accepted only in compliance with the terms of the credit. Obviously, the procedure and substance of compliance are central to credit law both with regard to the relationship between the issuer and the beneficiary and the relationship between the issuer and the customer.

1. What Determines Compliance

The most important point to remember about credit law is that the issuer deals only in documents (and other papers), not in performance. The issuer's duty to honor turns on whether the "draft or demand for payment * * * complies with the terms of the relevant credit * * *." 5-114(1). This means that the issuer's duty to honor depends exclusively on whether the beneficiary has presented the kinds of documents and other papers called for in the credit, not on whether the beneficiary has otherwise satisfied the underlying contract with the customer. Thus, when a demand is made under a credit, the issuer simply compares what the beneficiary actually presents with what she is required to present by the terms of the credit. A match here triggers the issuer's duty to honor "regardless of whether the goods or documents conform to the

underlying contract for sale or other contract between the customer and beneficiary."
Id.

When there is such a match and the issuer fulfills its duty to honor, the right of reimbursement arises despite the beneficiary's breach of its contract with the customer because the "issuer's obligation to its customer * * * does not include liability or responsibility * * * for performance of the underlying contract for sale or other transaction between the customer and the beneficiary." 5-109(1)(a). The right of reimbursement also arises even though the documents presented to the issuer, and against which the issuer paid or accepted, were not what they purported to be. In deciding if the papers presented by the beneficiary satisfy the credit, the issuer is obligated only to "examine documents with care so as to ascertain that *on their face* they appear to comply with the terms of the credit * * *." 5-109(2) (emphasis added). "The fact that the documents may be false or fraudulent or lacking in legal effect is not one for which the issuer is bound to examine. His duty is limited to apparent regularity on the face of the documents." 5-109 comment 2.

> *Example:* At Buyer's request, Issuer established a credit in favor of Seller. The credit required the issuer to pay Seller's drafts accompanied by bills of lading covering "widgets shipped to Buyer." Seller presented a draft with such a bill at a time when a dispute raged between Seller and Buyer regarding the quality of the widgets Seller was supplying. Issuer must pay despite the contract dispute, and, upon paying, is entitled to reimbursement from Buyer even if, in fact, Seller breached her contract with Buyer.

> *Example:* Credit required Beneficiary to present a warehouse receipt, issued by a warehouse in Customer's vicinity, covering a certain quantity of widgets that Customer had agreed to buy from Beneficiary. Upon making a demand for payment under the credit, Beneficiary tendered a writing that appeared, on its face, to be a document like that required by the credit. Issuer honored the credit and paid Beneficiary. Customer resisted reimbursing Issuer because the document was a fake. It was purportedly issued by Ace Terminal Warehouse, and no such business existed anywhere. Issuer is nevertheless entitled to reimbursement.

2. Degree Of Compliance
a. General Rule Applicable in Deciding Whether There Has Been Wrongful Dishonor

The issuer's right of reimbursement from its customer depends on the issuer having "duly honored" the beneficiary's draft or demand for payment, 5-114(3), meaning that the beneficiary presented documents and other papers that complied with the terms of the credit. Mainly to safeguard the issuer's right of reimbursement, and also to limit the issuer's obligation to the terms it agreed to, the courts generally follow the rule that a beneficiary is not entitled to acceptance or payment unless the documents she presents *comply literally, precisely and strictly* with the terms of the credit. A dishonor in the face of less than strict compliance with the terms of the credit is not wrongful. Only in a few cases have the courts embraced a less stringent test of "reasonable" or "substantial" compliance. Yet, even the courts that adhere to the stricter standard recognize that a little looseness is necessary to preserve the commercial utility of credits.

Example: Commercial letter of credit required beneficiary to present bill of lading that required carrier to notify "Mohammed Soran" upon the arrival of the goods. In making a demand for payment under the credit, the beneficiary presented a bill that listed, as the person entitled to notice, "Mohammed Sofan." The issuer dishonored because of the misspelling. The beneficiary sued for wrongful dishonor. Issuer wins.

Example: Standby credit required the beneficiary to "certify in writing" that the customer owed the beneficiary the amount of the draft presented to the issuer for payment under the credit. The beneficiary's demand letter stated that "the amount is due." Because the demand letter did not use the word "certify," the issuer dishonored. The issuer would be liable for wrongful dishonor if the substantial compliance test is applied. Liability is less certain under the test of strict compliance, but is possible if no one could have been misled by the different wording and the credit did not explicitly prescribe use of the word "certify."

b. Caveats to the General Rule

1) Distinguish the Issue of Interpretation

In interpreting the language of a credit for the purpose of deciding the meaning of the terms with which a beneficiary must strictly comply, the courts almost always resolve ambiguities and doubts against the issuer and in favor of the beneficiary. The familiar theory is that a contract or other writing will be construed against the person who drafted it.

2) Different Standard in Deciding the Issue of Reimbursement

When an issuer has honored a credit and the customer resists the issuer's right of reimbursement, the decision whether the payment was rightful or wrongful is not made according to the standard of strict compliance that applies in determining if a dishonor was wrongful as against the beneficiary. Rather, on the issue of reimbursement, the standard is substantial compliance.

3. Timing Of Compliance

A typical credit specifies an expiration date, also known as *expiry date*, upon which the issuer's duty to honor terminates. This date is part of the terms of the credit, and any draft or demand for payment that violates the date is not in compliance with the credit even though the documents are in perfect form and otherwise satisfy the terms of the credit.

4. Procedural Concerns

a. Presentment

Typically, the terms of a credit require presentment of a draft, drawn against the issuer, together with certain accompanying documents. The batch, as a whole, is a documentary draft, the presentment of which is therefore generally controlled by Article 3, especially the many technical rules in Part 5 of Article 3, except to the extent these rules on presentment are modified by Article 5 and by the credit itself.

b. Examination

1) General Obligation

"An issuer must examine documents with care so as to ascertain that on their face they appear to comply with the terms of the credit * * *." 5-109(2).

2) Time Allowed for Honor or Rejection

Notwithstanding provisions such as 4-301(a) on the time allowed for the acceptance or payment of ordinary drafts and checks, an issuer is allowed three banking days to determine whether to honor or reject a documentary draft or demand for payment that is presented under a credit. 5-112(1)(a). Failure to honor the draft within this time constitutes dishonor of it and the credit. 5-112(1).

c. Dishonor

1) Returning the Documentary Draft

Ordinarily, a payor bank that dishonors a documentary draft must physically return the instrument to accomplish dishonor. See 4-302(a)(2). In the case of such an instrument presented under a credit, the issuer can, consistent with dishonor, retain the draft and accompanying documents as bailee for the presenter if it advises the presenter of its retention for that purpose. See 5-112(2) & comment 2.

2) Providing Reasons for Dishonor

Article 5 does not require the issuer to give reasons for the dishonor or rejection of a draft or other demand for payment. The courts reason, however, that unexplained dishonor breeds litigation, and that persons claiming under a credit should, in fairness, be given a chance to remedy defects in documents, or correct other problems leading to dishonor, by re-presenting in compliance with the credit. Thus, there is judicial authority that an issuer who fails to give any reasons for dishonor may thereby waive all objections to the beneficiary's presentation. Moreover, when an issuer formally places its refusal to pay upon specified grounds, the issuer is held to have waived all other defects that the beneficiary could have cured had she known of them. Neither of these rules applies, however, to incurable defects in the beneficiary's presentment, that is, defects that could not have been avoided by making a timely re-presentation to the issuer. Moreover, a beneficiary cannot take advantage of the waiver rules if she knowingly tenders nonconforming documents.

Example: Bank issued a credit in favor of S providing for payment of S's draft accompanied by certain documents and papers, including "invoice # 11046" and a negotiable bill of lading covering the goods. In making a demand under the credit, S mistakenly presented invoice # 11064, which was connected to a separate deal between S and the customer. Bank dishonored, without explanation. A week later, after having discovered her mistake, S presented the proper papers, including invoice # 11046. The Bank again dishonored but on the ground that the credit had expired the preceding day. S sues Bank for wrongfully dishonoring the first time S presented. Bank may be deemed to have waived all objections to S's presentation, including the problem with the invoice, and will therefore have no defense to the action. Thus, Bank will be liable.

Example: Same facts, except that S's first presentation occurred on the day before the credit expired. The Bank dishonored without explaining its action. The result will probably be different. On these facts the defect was incurable inasmuch as a re-presentment would have been untimely.

C. RIGHTFUL DISHONOR DESPITE FACIAL COMPLIANCE

1. Overview

An issuer must honor a draft or demand for payment that complies with the terms of the relevant credit. 5-114(1). Compliance means that the draft or demand, and the documents presented with it, appear on their face to satisfy the terms of the credit. Thus, as a general rule, an issuer is guilty of wrongful dishonor, and is accordingly liable to the beneficiary, by refusing to pay a demand that facially complies with the credit. There are, however, a few exceptions, themselves qualified, which justify an issuer dishonoring a letter of credit despite facial compliance with the credit's terms.

The exceptions are that dishonor is rightful, despite facial compliance, when:

- a required document does not in fact conform to the warranties made on negotiation or transfer of a document of title (Section 7-507) or a certificated security (Section 8-306);
- a required document is forged or fraudulent; or,
- there is fraud in the transaction.

5-114(2).

Remember! For purposes of the immediate discussion, the assumption is that the demand for payment and accompanying documents appear on their face to comply with the terms of the credit. The reasons for dishonor under 5-114(2) involve latent or hidden problems that the issuer is not obligated to search for when a demand is made. See 5-109. How then will the issuer know of these problems so that, on the basis of them, it can dishonor? The informant is usually the customer who asks the issuer to dishonor a credit because, the customer alleges, there is a hidden defect or problem that justifies dishonor under 5-114(2).

All's well if the customer is right. If the customer is wrong, however, the issuer will have wrongfully dishonored and thus will be liable to the beneficiary. The credibility and overall utility of credits would be seriously undermined if the issuer were allowed to dishonor solely on the basis of the customer's allegations, or if the issuer were required, or even allowed, to suspend a credit while it investigated the customer's allegations "since these matters frequently involve situations in which the determination of the fact of the non-conformance may be difficult or time-consuming * * *." 5-114 comment 2.

Article 5 resolves this problem, in the first instance, against the customer by providing: "[In all] cases as against its customer, an issuer acting in good faith may honor the draft or demand for payment despite notification from the customer of

fraud, forgery or other defect not apparent on the face of the documents * * *."
5-114(2)(b). This means that when an issuer honors a credit despite the customer's
warning of a hidden defect, the issuer nevertheless has a right of reimbursement
against the customer even though, in fact, the customer was right. The only
requirement is that the issuer must have acted in good faith, which is judged by a
subjective standard. See 1-201(19).

The customer is not completely without recourse in this situation. Upon the issuer
deciding to ignore the customer's warning and honor the credit, "a court of
appropriate jurisdiction may enjoin such honor." 5-114(2)(b). To win an injunction,
however, the customer must establish a hidden defect that justifies dishonor under
Article 5 and must also satisfy the usual prerequisites for an injunction under the
local, extra-Code law of remedies.

Notwithstanding the foregoing, a hidden defect never justifies an issuer's dishonor,
and never supports an injunction against honor, when the person demanding honor is
"a negotiating bank or other holder of the draft or demand which has taken the draft
or demand under the credit and under circumstances which would make it a holder in
due course and in an appropriate case would make it a person to whom a document of
title has been duly negotiated or a bona fide purchaser of a certificated security."
5-114(2)(a). The person will have purchased drafts that the beneficiary has drawn
under the credit, as is explained below in a discussion of the alienability of credits.
In essence, the person is a good faith purchaser for value who has innocently relied
on the issuer's engagement to honor the credit. Thus, the issuer must honor the credit
despite hidden defects, and the customer must then reimburse the issuer. In effect,
therefore, "[t]he risk of the original bad-faith action of the beneficiary is thus thrown
upon the customer who selected him rather than upon innocent third parties or the
issuer. So, too, is the risk of fraud in the transaction placed upon the customer."
5-114 comment 2.

Now the details.

2. Hidden Defects That Justify Dishonor
a. Breach of Warranty

An issuer rightfully dishonors a draft or other demand made under a credit, even
though the demand and accompanying documents facially comply with the terms
of the credit, if *a required document does not in fact conform to the warranties
made on negotiation or transfer of a document of title or of a certificated
security.* 5-114(2). Securities are very rarely involved in a letter of credit
transaction. Documents are almost always involved. The warranties with
respect to documents, that are referred to in 5-114(2), are as follows:

Where a person negotiates or transfers a document of title for value * * * he warrants to his immediate purchaser

- that the document is genuine; and
- that he has no knowledge of any fact which would impair its validity or worth; and
- that his negotiation or transfer is rightful and fully effective with respect to the title to the document and the goods it represents.

7-507(a-c).

b. Document Forged or Fraudulent

That a document is forged or fraudulent is a good reason for dishonor by the issuer even though the document appears, on its face, to be regular and in full compliance with the terms of the credit. This hidden defect is also largely, if not fully, covered by the 7-507(a) warranty "that the document is genuine," the breach of which is a basis in itself for not honoring a credit. Both reasons for dishonor address the authenticity of the document itself.

c. Fraud in the Transaction

The most troubling issue under Article 5 is the meaning of the phrase in 5-114(2), "fraud in the transaction," which justifies dishonoring a credit even though the documents appear on their face to comply with the terms of a credit. The source of the phrase is well known. It codifies the holding of *Sztejn v. J. Henry Schroder Bank Corp.*, 177 Misc. 719, 31 N.Y.S.2d 631 (Sup. Ct. 1941). In the *Sztejn* case, Schroder had issued, for the account of Sztejn, an irrevocable credit in favor of Transea Trading. The credit required the beneficiary to present, among other things, a bill of lading covering a quantity of bristles. The issue in the case was whether the issuer was required to honor the credit if the beneficiary presented a document in perfect order, that is, a genuine bill of lading describing the goods as bristles, when, in fact, the seller-beneficiary had shipped cowhairs and other worthless materials. The court decided that, on these facts, payment of the credit should be enjoined.

Neither the *Sztejn* case nor the phrase "fraud in the transaction" justifies dishonor simply because of a breach of warranty or other breach of contract in the underlying transaction between the customer and the beneficiary. What is required is *intentional, active fraud on the part of the seller.* Moreover, the fraud must be serious, that is, *of such an egregious nature as to vitiate the entire transaction.*

Look at it this way: The very purpose of the letter of credit is to insure that the money is in the seller's hands during any period of dispute between the buyer and seller as to performance of their underlying contract. The risk of recovering for nonperformance is therefore on the buyer. She agrees to assume this risk by agreeing to the letter of credit arrangement. So, breach of contract is not "fraud in the transaction" justifying dishonor of a credit. The buyer does not accept, however, the risk of recovering the price in circumstances where the seller hoodwinked her. Putting the money in the seller's care in such a case is thus beyond the purpose of the letter of credit, and therefore dishonoring the credit in such a case does not undermine its legitimate commercial utility.

3. Issuer's Dilemma And Privilege Upon Notification Of Hidden Defects

There is a huge problem for an issuer in dishonoring a credit because of these hidden defects, i.e., breach of warranty, forged or fraudulent documents, and fraud in the transaction. The defects are not apparent. Whether they really exist is a fact-bound inquiry that will take time to determine and that, even with all the facts in hand, usually involves making a legal judgment call. Whether the issuer decides to honor or dishonor the credit, there is a large risk of accountability if the decision is wrong. If the credit is dishonored and the defect is not established, the issuer is liable to the beneficiary for wrongful dishonor. If the credit is honored and the defect is proved real, the issuer might lose the right to reimbursement from its customer. In any event, the issuer's credibility will suffer.

Therefore, an issuer is given this privilege: "[In all] cases as against its customer, an issuer *acting in good faith* may honor the draft or demand for payment despite notification from the customer of fraud, forgery or other defect not apparent on the face of the documents [including fraud in the transaction] * * *." 5-114(2)(b) (emphasis added). This means that even if there was, in fact, a hidden defect justifying the issuer in not honoring the credit, the issuer nevertheless enjoys the right of reimbursement against the customer so long as the issuer acted in good faith in honoring the credit.

The privilege carries an important limitation, however: "a court of appropriate jurisdiction may enjoin such honor." Id.

4. Enjoining Payment Because Of Hidden Defects

Letters of credit are misused when they are honored despite fraud or other hidden defects as described above. Giving the issuer a privilege to honor a credit in good faith despite allegations of such a defect does not facilitate misuse. The privilege is intended only to allow the issuer to avoid having to make a judgment on whether misuse has occurred. The privilege does not prevent the customer from otherwise stopping honor. Even when an issuer has decided to ignore the customer's allegations of hidden defects, such as fraud in the transaction, "a court of appropriate jurisdiction may enjoin such honor." 5-114(2)(b).

There are two principal requirements for an injunction in such a case:

* First, there must in fact be a hidden defect. That is, the customer must prove that the documents do not conform to pertinent warranties, that the documents are forged or fraudulent, or that there is fraud in the transaction.
* Second, the usual, traditional prerequisites for an injunction must be satisfied, as in any other case where the extraordinary, equitable remedy of injunction is sought. In general, the customer must show that without the injunction, she will suffer irreparable harm that legal remedies are inadequate to address. This means that honor of a letter of credit should not be enjoined, even in the face of forgery or fraud in the transaction, if the customer's loss is fairly and likely compensable through money damages, which is often the case.

5. Absolute Duty To Pay Certain Innocent Third Parties

In no event can an issuer dishonor a credit, or a court enjoin such honor, even if there is in fact a hidden defect such as forgery or fraud in the transaction,

> if honor is demanded by a negotiating bank or other holder of the draft or demand which has taken the draft or demand under the credit and under circumstances which would make it a holder in due course and in an appropriate case would make it a person to whom a document of title has been duly negotiated or a bona fide purchaser of a certificated security.

5-114(2)(a). In this case, "[t]he risk of the original bad-faith action of the beneficiary [including engaging in fraud in the transaction and other egregious hoodwinking] is * * * thrown upon the customer who selected him rather than upon innocent third parties or the issuer." 5-114 comment 2.

Example: B ordered bristles from S. Payment was to be made through a negotiation credit, which B got Bank to issue in favor of S. The terms of the credit provided for payment upon presentation of a draft and a bill of lading covering 50 cases of bristles. S delivered 50 cases of material to carrier and represented that the cases contained bristles. The carrier therefore issued a bill of lading describing 50 cases of bristles. In fact, the cases contained worthless cowhairs. S then drew a draft on Bank payable to herself, and negotiated the instrument and document of title, for value, to X. X was totally unaware of S's fraud, and acted in good faith. When X presents the documentary draft and demands payment under the credit, X must pay notwithstanding the fraud in the transaction. Moreover, a court cannot enjoin such honor, notwithstanding proof of the fraud.

An important point about the foregoing example is the reason the Bank is obligated to pay despite the fraud, which ordinarily would be grounds for dishonoring the credit. The reason is not that the Bank is liable on the instrument to X and that X is a holder in due course of the instrument who thereby takes free of claims and defenses under 3-305. On these facts, X is a holder in due course; but the Bank is not liable *on the instrument* to anyone, even in the absence of a reason for dishonoring the credit. A drawee, which is the Bank's role, is not liable on the instrument unless and until it accepts the instrument. 3-408. The Bank is liable to X because of Article 5, and the issuer's commitment, in a negotiation credit, to pay not only the beneficiary but also holders of drafts drawn under the credit. The Bank is denied its usual right to dishonor when there is fraud in the transaction because of the express language of 5-114(2)(a) which borrows the due-course doctrine of Article 3. Because X, as the transferee of a draft drawn under the credit, is a holder in due course of the instrument, the issuer is obligated *by Article 5* to honor the credit notwithstanding the misconduct of S which would give the issuer the right, as against S, to dishonor the credit.

One other point: For no reason whatsoever, the issuer could rightfully dishonor the credit upon B's demand for payment if the letter of credit had been a straight credit rather than a negotiation credit. See the following discussion on the alienability of letters of credit. In short, except where a credit is a negotiation credit, the issuer is obligated only to the beneficiary and no one else.

D. ALIENABILITY OF CREDITS

Whether a letter of credit is alienable depends upon what aspect of alienability is involved. Credits may be alienable in three, wholly different senses which concern the beneficiary transferring the right to draw under the credit; negotiating drafts drawn by the beneficiary under the terms of the credit; and assigning the right to proceeds paid under the credit. Only in the last sense is there an absolute right of alienation.

1. Transferring The Right To Draw

A letter of credit identifies, by name or otherwise, who is to draw drafts or perform other acts that will trigger the bank's 5-114(1) obligation to honor a draft or demand for payment. This person(s), who is the beneficiary, cannot transfer her right to draw, i.e., she cannot delegate performance of the conditions under the credit, unless "the credit is expressly designated as transferable or assignable." 5-116(1). More precisely, only when a credit declares its transferability is the issuer obligated to honor the demand of a person to whom the beneficiary has delegated the right to draw. A credit that is alienable in this sense is a *transferable credit.* Otherwise, the credit is a *nontransferable credit.*

The purpose is to protect the customer who procured the letter of credit. In initiating the credit the customer may have "put his faith in performance or supervision of performance by a beneficiary of established reputation * * *." 5-116 comment 1. If the beneficiary were allowed freely to transfer the right to perform the conditions of the credit, the customer could thereby "be deprived of real and intended security." Id. Of course, a customer assumes this risk by allowing the issuance of a transferable credit, which does require the customer's consent.

Example: B orders goods from S. Upon B's application, Bank issues a credit in favor of S. The terms provide for payment upon S drawing and presenting a draft against the Bank, together with other documents evidencing the shipment of goods to B. S sells to T the sales contract between S and B. In other words, S delegates to T her duty to perform the contract with B, and also her right to receive payment under the contract. Also, S "assigns" the letter of credit to T, including the right to draw under the credit. T manufactured the goods B ordered and shipped them to B. T then drew a draft against Bank and presented it to Bank, together with documents required by the credit. Bank is obligated to honor the draft only if the credit, as issued or amended by the Bank, expressly provides that the credit is transferable. If there is no such provision, the Bank is not liable to T for dishonoring the draft.

2. Negotiating Drafts

Negotiating drafts drawn under a letter of credit is very different from transferring the right to draw. The former refers to the beneficiary assigning, to a third party, a draft that the beneficiary has herself drawn. The beneficiary is not thereby delegating performance of a condition of the credit if, as is usual, the credit requires the presentation of drafts drawn by the beneficiary. The draft the beneficiary assigns was, in fact, drawn by her.

Yet, by established custom and practice, as well as by the terms of the UCP, the issuer is not obligated to honor the beneficiary's drafts negotiated or assigned to third parties unless the credit itself includes a commitment to such persons, or the issuer otherwise effectively authorizes negotiation of drafts under the credit. A credit that contains no commitment of this type is known as a *straight credit.* Where the commitment is provided for, the credit is known as a *negotiation credit,* because the third parties who purchase drafts drawn under a letter of credit are usually banks which, in this role, are known as *negotiating banks.* The typical negotiation clause in

Nickles Comm. Paper 2nd—18

a credit provides that the credit runs in favor of "drawers, endorsers and bona fide holders of drafts drawn under and in compliance with the terms of this credit."

A negotiation credit is not necessarily a transferable credit.

Example: Upon ordering goods from S, B gets State Bank to issue a letter of credit in favor of S, requiring in part the presentation of draft(s) drawn on State Bank by S. Upon shipping the goods to B, S draws a draft against State Bank and sells the draft to National Bank, which also acquires from S whatever documents and other writings are required by the terms of the credit. This transaction between S and National Bank may have occurred for no other reason than that dealing with National Bank is quicker and more convenient for S than traveling to an outpost of State Bank. National Bank then presents the documentary draft to State Bank, expecting State Bank to honor the draft. State Bank is obligated to do so only if the credit is a negotiation credit and National Bank is within the class of third parties to whom the credit commits the issuer.

3. Assigning Right To Proceeds

Even though a credit is straight and nontransferable, the beneficiary may assign her right to proceeds of the credit, and she may do so even before performance of the conditions of the credit. 5-116(2). In assigning proceeds, the beneficiary is transferring her Article 5 right to the money that the issuer is obligated to pay upon compliance with the terms of the letter of credit.

This right to assign proceeds is not conditioned on the credit allowing such an assignment. Indeed, the right is not abridged by a provision in the credit purporting to prohibit assignment of proceeds. See 5-116 comment 3 & 9-318(4).

Assigning the right to proceeds of a credit is treated, with a few exceptions, as "an assignment of an account [9-106] under Article 9 on Secured Transactions and is governed by that Article * * *." 5-116(2). Essentially, therefore, the assignment is treated as the creation of a security interest, and the assignee is regarded as a secured party with a security interest in the letter of credit or, at least, in the fruits of it. This is appropriate inasmuch as in the vast majority of cases in which rights to proceeds of credits are assigned, the purpose is to collateralize a loan or credit.

a. How Is the Assignment Effected?

An assignee is concerned that the assignment be effective between her and the beneficiary-assignor. Otherwise, the assignee's right to proceeds is not established as against anyone. Because the assignment is generally governed by Article 9, the assignee should first consult 9-203(1), which explains how a security interest is created. The formalities are simple: The parties sign a written security agreement, or the creditor takes possession of the property in which the security interest is to be created, i.e., the collateral. The latter option is unavailable where the collateral is purely intangible so that possession is impossible, as when the collateral is accounts. Because the assignment of proceeds of a letter of credit is treated as an assignment of an account, 9-203(1) would require a written security agreement.

At this point, however, Article 5 intervenes, either to add a requirement or to preempt 9-203(1), by this language: "[T]he assignment is ineffective until the letter of credit is delivered to the assignee." 5-116(2)(a). Whether this requirement is in addition to a written security agreement, or in place of it (as is more likely), is not entirely clear. It is clear, however, that the assignment is not effective as against anyone, even if there is a written security agreement, unless and until the credit itself is in the hands of the assignee or her agent.

b. **What Is Necessary to Make the Issuer Accountable to the Assignee?** The assignee of the proceeds of a letter of credit is also concerned about binding the issuer to account to her. That is, the assignee wants to insure that the issuer will be liable to her for proceeds paid to the beneficiary or someone else in derogation of the assignment. Such an obligation to account does not arise as soon as, and simply because, the assignment is effective between the beneficiary-assignor and the assignee. In order to bind the issuer so that the issuer must respect the assignment, the issuer must receive "a notification of the assignment signed by the beneficiary which reasonably identifies the credit involved in the assignment and contains a request to pay the assignee." 5-116(2)(b). Until the issuer receives such a notification, the issuer may honor drafts or demands for payment drawn under the credit without any accountability to the assignee, id., notwithstanding that the assignment was fully effective between the assignee and beneficiary.

Even when this notice has been received, the issuer may rightly withhold the proceeds from an assignee "until the letter of credit * * * is exhibited to the issuer." 5-116(2)(c). The assignee, of course, will have the letter and can exhibit it because delivery of the letter to her, and presumably her continued possession, are necessary to the effectiveness of the assignment. See 5-116(2)(a).

IMPORTANT! Although a beneficiary may assign her right to proceeds even before performance of the conditions of the credit, 5-116(2), neither she nor her assignee, or anyone else, is entitled to honor of the credit, i.e., actually to get the proceeds ($$$$), from the issuer until such time as there is compliance with the terms of the credit. This is true even though the issuer has been fully notified of an assignment of the proceeds that is fully effective. There are no proceeds to claim from the issuer until compliance with the credit.

c. How Does the Assignee Protect Her Right to Proceeds Against Subsequent Transferees

A beneficiary's right to proceeds of a letter of credit is property that remains alienable despite an effective assignment, and despite a provision in the assignment prohibiting any further transfer or making the transfer constitute a default. See 9-311. The beneficiary can subsequently transfer the right to proceeds, voluntarily or involuntarily, by way of another assignment, an attachment, levy, garnishment, or other judicial process.

An assignee's rights, as against other claimants of the proceeds, is determined by the priority principles of Article 9. Believe me! This is not the place to review those principles in detail. A fairly reliable general rule is that a security interest enjoys priority over claims that arise after the interest is perfected. See, e.g., 9-301(1) & 9-312(5). So, to protect her rights against subsequent claimants, the assignee should perfect. Ordinarily, perfection requires filing an Article 9 filing statement in a public office, usually with the Secretary of State. See 9-302(1); 9-401(1); 9-402(1). Here again, however, Article 5 intervenes and, in this instance, clearly overrides Article 9 by providing that an assignment of a right to proceeds of a letter of credit is perfected by delivery of the credit to the assignee. 5-116(2)(a). Of course, in the absence of such delivery, there is no effective assignment in the first place.

4. Back-To-Back Credits

Back-to-back credits describes a financing and security arrangement in which a bank issues a letter of credit on the strength of an assignment of the right to proceeds of a separate credit. On back-to-back credits, and the alienation of credits generally, see J. Dolan, THE LAW OF LETTERS OF CREDIT ch. 10 (1991).

Example: "Distributor is the beneficiary of a letter of credit issued by Retailer's bank. Under the terms of the letter, Distributor is to ship widgets to Retailer under documentary drafts. The letter requires that the drafts be accompanied by proper bills of lading, invoices, and insurance certificates. If the documents are in order, the issuing bank is obligated to pay the drafts to Distributor * * * In order to help finance Distributor's operation, Distributor's bank extends to Distributor a line of credit secured by an assignment of Distributor's rights to proceeds of drafts drawn under the letter [issued by Retailer's bank]. * * * Distributor's bank could use the security interest in proceeds under the * * * letter as collateral to support either a direct line of credit to Distributor or the issuance of a *second* letter with Distributor as customer and Distributor's supplier as beneficiary. In this way, Distributor's bank could finance the purchase of inventory one link up the chain of distribution. Under such an arrangement, Distributor's bank would be required to honor drafts drawn by Supplier that conform to the second letter, but in turn could be assured of the proceeds from drafts drawn by Distributor upon Retailer that conform to the first letter." B. Clark, THE LAW OF BANK DEPOSITS, COLLECTIONS AND CREDIT CARDS ¶¶ 10.12[2] & [3] (1990) (emphasis in original).

E. INVOLVEMENT OF OTHER BANKS

1. Advising Bank

An *advising bank* is "a bank which gives notification of the issuance of a credit by another bank." 5-103(1)(e). An advising bank is almost always a bank convenient to the beneficiary. An advising bank is most often used to relay notice that the credit has been issued when this communication between the issuer and beneficiary would be more easily and reliably accomplished by going through a local bank. Banks everywhere chat easily among themselves by way of fax, telex and other electronic communication devices.

Upon receiving a request of an issuer to advise a letter of credit, the advising bank will typically issue a written advice of credit, and give notice of the credit, by sending the advice of credit to the beneficiary. In important ways, this advice of credit stands as a substitute for the issuer's credit. Sending the advice to the beneficiary establishes the credit against the customer, and the beneficiary's receipt of the advice establishes the credit as regards her. Also, an assignment of the right to proceeds of a credit is effective upon delivery of the advice of credit to the assignee. 5-116(2)(a). Clearly, however, an advising bank is only a messenger, and assumes no obligation to honor drafts drawn or demands for payment made under the credit, 5-107(1), not even when the advising bank has issued a written advice of credit. Its principal duty is simply to transmit accurately information about the credit that has been issued by another bank. See 5-107(1).

2. Confirming Bank

A *confirming bank* is "a bank which engages either that it will itself honor a credit already issued by another bank or that such a credit will be honored by the issuer or a third bank." 5-103(1)(f). Unlike a bank that only advises a credit, a confirming bank is itself "directly obligated on the credit to the extent of its confirmation as though it were its issuer." 5-107(2). Therefore, to the extent of the confirmation, Article 5

saddles a confirming bank with the same fundamental duty of the issuer under
5-114(1): to honor a draft or demand for payment which complies with the terms of
the relevant credit. In so honoring, the confirming bank acquires a right of
reimbursement from the issuer which procured the confirmation. See 5-114(3) (In
applying 5-114(3), remember: A confirming bank is treated "as though it were" the
issuer and enjoys the rights of an issuer, 5-107(2), and the definition of "customer"
includes a bank which procures confirmation of a credit on its customer's behalf.
5-103(1)(g).)

3. Negotiating Bank

A *negotiating bank* is a bank that purchases drafts drawn by the beneficiary of a letter
of credit. Neither the issuer nor a confirming bank is obligated to honor these drafts
unless the credit is a negotiation credit, or the issuer otherwise authorizes negotiation
of drafts under the credit. (See earlier discussion about the difference between
negotiation and straight credits.)

REVIEW QUESTIONS

1.   From the seller's perspective, what is the advantage of payment through a letter of
credit compared to the buyer paying against documents?

2.   Upon establishment of a letter of credit, what is the issuer's principal responsibility
to the beneficiary?

3.   What right does the issuer enjoy against the customer-account party upon duly
honoring a draft or demand for payment presented under a letter of credit?

4.   Explain the issuer's accountability to the beneficiary for wrongful dishonor, i.e.,
violating the issuer's duty to honor.

5.   Explain the consequence of improper payment, i.e., the issuer honoring a draft or
demand that failed to comply with the terms of the credit.

6.   When can an issuer rightfully dishonor a draft or demand for payment under a
letter of credit?

7.   T or F   An issuer loses the right of reimbursement from its customer by
honoring a draft or demand for payment after receiving notice from
the customer that the beneficiary is guilty of fraud in the transaction.

8.   T or F   A customer cannot stop payment under a letter of credit when the
                   beneficiary is guilty of fraud in the transaction.

9.   What is the meaning of "fraud in the transaction?"

10.   Is a letter of credit alienable?

```
┌─────────────────────────────────────────────────────────┐
│                                                         │
│                    APPENDIX A                           │
│                                                         │
│  ─────────────────────────────────────────────          │
│                                                         │
│                                                         │
│            ANSWERS TO REVIEW QUESTIONS                   │
│                                                         │
│                                                         │
│                                                         │
└─────────────────────────────────────────────────────────┘
```

I. INTRODUCTION TO INSTRUMENTS AND NEGOTIABILITY

1. U.C.C. Article 3 governs **negotiable instruments.**

2. The most recent significant amendments to the uniform version of Article 3 were made in **1990**.

3. The two basic kinds of instruments are the note and the draft.

4. *True.* A certificate of deposit is a type of note.

5. *True.* A check is a type of draft.

6. All Article 3 instruments share the same essential characteristics of form that are called the **requisites of negotiability**, which are outlined in U.C.C. 3-104(a) and discussed in Chapter 2 of this book.

7. This question is the same but is asked differently. The point is important. All Article 3 instruments are alike in form in that they share the same essential requisites of negotiability.

8.   The different kinds of instruments are distinguishable in terms of form in that a **note carries an explicit promise** by the maker to pay the instrument, and a **draft carries the drawer's order** to pay the instrument.

9.   The principal significance of embodying a right to the payment of money in an instrument is **negotiability**, which means that a transferee of an instrument can acquire rights therein (but does not always do so) that are greater or better than the rights of the transferor.

10.   Negotiability is an exception to derivative title.

11.   *False.*   Generally, a transferee of property acquires only the transferor's rights therein, and takes subject to claims to the property that were good against the transferor. This principle of derivative title, as applied to the right to the payment of money, is often expressed in these familiar terms: An assignee steps into the shoes of the assignor, and in enforcing the right assigned to her is subject to whatever defenses the obligor could have raised against enforcement by the assignor. A transferee of property takes free of these claims and defenses only in limited and narrow circumstances specifically defined, and closely circumscribed, by law.

12.   *False.*   Lord Mansfield decided *Miller v. Race* in the late 18th Century. It was later that Judge Posner joined the United States Court of Appeals for the Seventh Circuit.

II. THE MEANING OF INSTRUMENT: ARTICLE 3's REQUISITES OF NEGOTIABILITY

1.   An "instrument" within the meaning of U.C.C. Article 3 is a writing that satisfies the requisites of negotiability described in 3-104(a).

2.   Article 3's requisites of negotiability are a writing that contains an unconditional promise or order to pay a fixed amount of money, with or without interest or other charges described in the promise or order, so long as the it:

> (1) is payable to bearer or to order at the time it is issued or first comes into possession of a holder;
> (2) is payable on demand or at a definite time; and
> (3) does not state any other undertaking or instruction by the person promising or ordering payment to do any act in addition to the payment of

money, but the promise or order may contain (i) an undertaking or power to give, maintain, or protect collateral to secure payment, (ii) an authorization or power to the holder to confess judgment or realize on or dispose of collateral, or (iii) a waiver of the benefit of any law intended for the advantage or protection of an obligor.

3-104(a).

3. The two basic kinds of instruments are the note and the draft. The note is an instrument that promises payment, and the draft is an instrument that orders payment.

4. The writing is not negotiable for two reasons: First, the time for payment is indefinite because it is tied to the date of the writing which is undated. Second, the writing lacks words of negotiability, that is, it is not payable to order or to bearer.

5. Yes. It would be a 3-104(c) check that is negotiable despite the missing words of negotiability.

6. Because the Note is not negotiable, nothing in Article 3 governs the Bank's right to payment. Most significantly, there can be no Article 3 holder in due course of the right to payment. Ms. Jones is nevertheless accountable for the loan, and the Bank can assign its rights against her. Any such assignment, however, would not be governed by Article 3.

7. *Yes*.

8. a. *Yes*. It would be an instrument.

    b. *No*. It would not be an instrument.

    c. *No*.

    d. *Yes*.

    e. *Yes*.

    f. *Yes*.

    g. *Yes*.

h.   *Yes*.

9.   The promise is **not** an instrument because there is an express condition to payment.

10.   *No*.

11.   *No*.

12.   *Yes*.

13.   *Yes*.

14.   *Yes*.   Although the recital of the executory promise of Doe to convey Blackacre might be read as an implied condition that the promise be performed, the condition is not an express promise as required by Section 3-106(a)(i).

15.   *No*.

III. CONTRACT LIABILITY ON INSTRUMENTS

1.   The **most basic rule governing liability on negotiable instruments** is that "a person is not liable on an instrument unless (i) the person signed the instrument, or (ii) the person is represented by an agent or representative who signed the instrument and the signature is binding on the represented person under Section 3-402." 3-401(a).

2.   **You are not liable** on a check on which a thief has forged your name. The unauthorized signature is not effective as your signature. Thus, your signature does not appear on the instrument. 3-401(a) & 3-403(a). The thief is liable on the check to any person who in good faith pays the instrument or takes it for value because, as against these people, your unauthorized signature by the thief operates as the thief's own signature. 3-403(a).

3.   An agent should **identify the represented person** and **indicate that the signature is made on behalf of the represented person**. By following this form the agent most surely **avoids personal liability** on the instrument.

4.   The liability of a person who is **primarily liable** on an instrument is not conditioned on someone else refusing to pay it. A party who is **secondarily liable** engages to pay only upon presentment to, and dishonor by, someone else. The liability of a maker or acceptor is ordinarily primary. A drawer or indorser is secondarily liable.

5.   *False.*   Notice of dishonor is not a condition to a drawer's liability.

6.   The indorser's liability is **discharged**.

7.   Ordinarily, in the case of bank collections, a check is dishonored by the drawee-payor bank **seasonably returning the item** by the drawee-payor bank's midnight deadline.

8.   The drawee of a draft is not liable in this role because the drawee has **not signed** the instrument. Also, Article 3 explicitly declares that a drawee is not liable unless and until she accepts the item. A drawee qua drawee has **not accepted**.

9.   Although a drawee bank on a check is not liable on the instrument as drawee, the bank will become liable thereon by **certifying** the check. Certification is acceptance. The drawee thereby becomes, and has the liability of, an acceptor. Certification is rare, however. A drawee bank is more likely to become liable with respect to the instrument on theories of **express assignment** (although the check itself does not itself constitute an assignment), **de facto acceptance** (liability under contract as by orally promising to pay a check), and **Article 4 accountability** (e.g., retaining an item beyond the bank's midnight deadline).

10.   *False.*   Only payment to a *person entitled to enforce the instrument* discharges a person's liability on an instrument.

11.   *False.*   A discharge results only if the alteration is fraudulent. In the event of an alteration that is not fraudulent, the instrument remains enforceable to the extent of its original, unaltered terms.

12.   Ordinarily, taking of an instrument for an underlying obligation affects the obligation by **suspending** it.

13.   Taking an instrument discharges the underlying obligation if (a) the **parties agree** to such an effect, or (b) the instrument is a certified check, cashier's check, teller's check, or any other **instrument on which a bank is liable as maker or acceptor**.

14.   A discharge results only if:

    *   the check was tendered in good faith to the claimant as full satisfaction of the claim,

- the instrument or an accompanying written communication contained a conspicuous statement warning that the instrument was tendered in full satisfaction,
- the amount of the claim was unliquidated or subject to a bona fide dispute, and
- the claimant obtained payment of the check.

15. Discharge is avoided only if the claimant was **unaware** that the check was tendered in full payment of the debt.

IV. INSTRUMENTS AS PROPERTY: ENFORCEMENT, TRANSFER, AND NEGOTIATION

1. *False.*   Principles of property law beyond Article 3 determine who owns an instrument. Article 3 determines who can use and enjoy an instrument, that is, who can enforce and exercise its other rights.

2. Transfer is the conveyance of a person's rights in an instrument to a transferee with the result that the transferee acquires the transferor's rights and nothing more. Negotiation is a special form of transfer that enables the transferee to acquire rights with respect to the instrument that are greater or better than the rights of the transferor. Through negotiation a transferee becomes a holder, and a holder who holds in due course takes the instrument free from all claims and most defenses even though the claims and defenses could have been asserted against the transferor.

3. *True and False.*   The transferor must indorse the instrument if the instrument is order paper, that is, issued or indorsed to her order. The transferor's indorsement is not necessary if the instrument is payable to bearer either because it was issued to her in that form or has been indorsed in blank.

4. *True and False.*   There can never be a holder of an instrument following transfer by a thief if the thief forged a necessary indorsement. On the other hand, a person in possession of bearer paper is a holder even though she claims through a thief.

5. An indorsement is (a) qualified or unqualified; *and* (b) blank or special; *and* (c) restrictive or unrestrictive.

6. *False.*   In specifying a person, A, to whom the instrument is payable, the indorser has specially indorsed, and the instrument is payable to A's

order even though the words of negotiability are actually missing from the indorsement. The absence of express words of negotiability in the indorsement has no affect on the negotiability of the instrument.

7. The indorsement "P, Pay to A" is an unqualified, special, restrictive indorsement, implying that the instrument can be transferred to no one else and is properly handled only by paying A. This restriction is ineffective, however, to prevent further transfer or negotiation by A, and is treated in law as an unrestrictive indorsement to her. The special indorsee, A, can negotiate the instrument to anyone by indorsement and delivery.

8. The response is improved by adding that the indorsement is restrictive because of the language, "For Deposit Only," and that T could have become a holder in due course of the instrument only by applying the value she gave consistently with the indorsement. Because T did not so apply the value she gave, she did not acquire due-course status even though she was a holder. Moreover, because T violated the restrictive indorsement, she is liable to P for conversion of the instrument.

V. WARRANTY AND RESTITUTION: INSURING ENFORCEABILITY

1. T, U and V breached the presentment warranty that they are people entitled to enforce the instrument. T breached the transfer warranty to the same effect that T made to U and V. U breached the same transfer warranty to V if U transferred for consideration. Having a breach of warranty claim is important to M because she remains liable on the instrument, and also on the underlying obligation, to P. If M is forced to pay P, M can most easily and certainly recoup the payment made to V through a breach of warranty claim.

2. Yes. R has a breach of warranty claim against Q, whether or not Q signed the note, even though Q was a holder in due course of the note and was ignorant of the alteration.

3. Q's actions against P are for breach of the transfer warranty that all signatures are authentic and authorized, and maybe also on P's indorsement. M cannot recoup if she mistakenly pays. A payor receives no presentment warranty covering the genuineness of the maker's signature. Moreover, a restitution action would probably be barred by the *Price v. Neal* doctrine and 3-418.

4.   In the case of transfer warranties, the basic measure of damages is the amount of the loss suffered as a result of the breach not to exceed the amount of the instrument. 3-416(b). For presentment warranties in the case of a payor, the measure is the amount she paid, which naturally is her loss. 3-417(b) & (d).

5.   The drawee-payor bank must recredit ABC's account for $45,000 because the item was properly payable only to the extent of $5,000. The loss can be shifted back to Computer because of the warranty of correct encoding that the law implied and imposed on Computer. 4-209(a).

VI. CLAIMS AND DEFENSES TO INSTRUMENTS

1.   S wins because she is a holder in due course of the instrument and thus takes free of all claims to it on the part of any person. This freedom from claims immunizes S from both the equitable lien and the conversion action.

2.   The defense is good against Q only if, because of other local law, violation of the usury limit "nullifies the obligation of the obligor" -- makes the obligation entirely null and void. 3-305(a)(1).

3.   Unless Q is a graduating senior, her response should be graded "F." A holder in due course takes free of defenses not attributable to her that exist when she takes the instrument. A holder in due course is fully accountable for defenses that arise against her personally after she takes the instrument.

4.   A payee can be a holder in due course, and S probably is such a holder and probably is not subject to Bank's defense.

5.   The defense is good against S even if she is a holder in due course. Even a holder in due course takes subject to personal defenses attributable to the holder herself, even if the defenses are based on facts occurring before the instrument was issued.

6.   Yes. This form of duress is a real defense that is good against everyone, including any holder in due course.

VII. ACCOMMODATION PARTIES

1.   An accommodation party is one who signs the instrument in any capacity for the purpose of incurring liability on the instrument without being a direct beneficiary of the value given for the instrument, which value is given for the benefit of another party to the instrument. 3-419(a).

2.   An accommodation party is a kind of surety. A surety is anyone who agrees to pay the debt of another person. An accommodation party is a surety who makes the agreement by signing an instrument that the principal debtor, i.e., accommodated party, has also signed. In other words, an accommodation party is a surety whose liability is on an instrument, and she is the surety for another party to the same instrument.

3.   Generally speaking, there is no difference. An accommodation party is liable on an instrument in the capacity in which she signed even though the taker knows of the accommodation. 3-419(b-c).

4.   The significance in accommodation status is threefold. First, an accommodation party is never liable on an instrument to the person accommodated. 3-419(e). Thus, for example, although a maker or drawer is liable to an indorser, an accommodation maker or drawer is not liable to an indorser who is the accommodated party. Second, an accommodation party has certain rights against the principal debtor on the instrument and de hors it: exoneration; reimbursement and recourse; and subrogation. Finally, an accommodation party enjoys certain defenses to liability on the instrument, as against the holder, that are dependent on her accommodation status, meaning she can assert the defenses only because she is a surety.

5.   a.   *No.*   Any person who signs an instrument is liable thereon in the capacity in which she signed it, including an accommodation party. Accommodation status, in itself, is no defense to liability and, indeed, is not a distinguishing factor even in determining the nature of the accommodation party's liability to a holder of the instrument.

    b.   *No.*

    c.   *No.*

    d.   *No.*

    e.   *No.*

    f.   Bank can sue S alone. S is liable as a maker, just as is D; and co-makers, who sign as part of the same transaction, are jointly and *severally* liable.

g.   ***Yes.***   The action would be based on S's equitable right of exoneration.

h.   S's rights against D, upon paying the obligation, are these:
- Common-law right of reimbursement from the principal debtor, D;
- Right of recourse on the instrument itself, which is wholly dependent on S's accommodation status inasmuch as co-makers ordinarily are not liable to each other on the instrument; and,
- Right of subrogation to the Bank's rights in the collateral that secures the note, which permits S to recoup her payment from the proceeds of a disposition of the property.

6.   She could sign as an indorser because her contract liability in this capacity would depend on presentment, dishonor and notice of dishonor.

7.   She could add words such as "collection guaranteed" to her signature. See 3-419(d).

8.   An extension of time results in discharge only to the extent the surety proves that the extension caused loss. 3-605(c).

9.   D's bankruptcy, in itself, is no defense for S. Although the bankruptcy will discharge any personal obligation of D to Bank, this discharge, while a defense for D, cannot be asserted derivatively by S. The bankruptcy defense is personal to D. (Of course, if S herself filed bankruptcy and obtained a discharge therein, her suretyship obligation to Bank would be wiped out.) On the other hand, by failing to perfect the security interest in the collateral so that the property was lost to the bankruptcy estate, Bank impaired the collateral and thereby discharged S to the extent of the value of the property. S is thus liable for $52,374 less $40,000, or $12,374. 3-605(e) & comment 6.

10.   When a creditor disposes of personal property collateral, Part 5 of Article 9 requires her to give prior notice to the debtor. U.C.C. 9-504(3). Failing to give this notice makes her accountable to the debtor for damages, and in some states results in the creditor losing the right to recover any deficiency from the debtor. An accommodation party on a secured note, or other surety on a debt secured by personal property, is a debtor for purposes of Part 5 of Article 9 who is entitled to notice of a planned disposition of the collateral. Therefore, in this problem, the Bank is accountable to S for failing to notify her. The precise nature of this accountability depends not on Article 3, but on how local courts have defined the consequences of a creditor violating the requirements of Part 5 of Article 9.

11.   *False.*   A creditor who violates the FTC Rule is accountable under the federal law, but the violation is not a defense for the surety.

VIII. HOLDER IN DUE COURSE

1.   Holder in due course means and requires:
-       a holder
-       of an instrument
-       the instrument when issued or negotiated to the holder does not bear such apparent evidence of forgery or alteration or is not otherwise so irregular or incomplete as to call into question its authenticity;
-       the holder took the instrument
    --   for value
    --   in good faith
    --   without notice
        ---   that the instrument is overdue or has been dishonored or that there is an uncured default with respect to payment of another instrument as part of the same series
        ---   that the instrument contains an unauthorized signature or has been altered
        ---   of any claim to the instrument
        ---   that any party has a defense or claim in recoupment.
        3-302(a).

2.   *No.*   The promise itself is consideration, but no value is given until the promised goods or services are supplied and even then the value is proportional only.

3.   If the amount of the instrument was $1,000 and only $500 worth of the agreed consideration of $900 was performed, the holder would enjoy the special protections of a holder in due course to the extent of $555.55 only ($500 / $900 = .555 X $1,000 = $555.55). She could enforce the balance of the note but only as a mere holder who is subject to personal defenses and property claims.

4.   *No.*   By delivering the widgets, which amounts to performing the agreed consideration, T gave value, but not in ignorance of M's defense. Thus, T is not a holder in due course.

5.   *Yes.*

6.   *No.*

7.   *Yes.*   Whether the parties intended the transfer as satisfying the loan or as securing it, the Bank in either event has given value to the extent of the preexisting $10,000 claim against D.

8.   *No.*   "*Reason to know*" of a fact establishes notice even though the person herself, actually, is completely unaware of the fact and has never received a notification of it. Notice by this test is sometimes referred to as *inferable knowledge*. A person is charged with knowledge of information that a reasonable person would infer from the facts and circumstances actually known to her. This test does not require a person to investigate, not even if a reasonable person would do so; but the test does require a person to open her eyes to everything she already knows. She is charged with notice of facts that others would see or discern from her own knowledge, even if she herself was subjectively blind to these facts.

9.   The bank is not such a holder if, in cashing the check, the bank had notice that X was breaching its fiduciary duty to Y or was planning to do so.

10.   The test of good faith is both subjective and objective. It means "honesty in fact *and the observance of reasonable commercial standards of fair dealing*," 3-103(a)(4) (emphasis added), which is "concerned with the fairness of conduct rather than the care with which an act is performed." 3-103 comment 4. History explains that when this objective test is added to the subjective, "a business man engaging in a commercial transaction is not entitled to claim the peculiar advantages which the law accords to the * * * holder in due course * * * on a bar showing of 'honesty in fact' when his actions fail to meet the generally accepted standards current in his business, trade, or profession. 3-302 comment 1 (1952 Official Text).

11.   The Creditor is a holder in due course. The certificate was indorsed and delivered to her, and thus she is a holder. She gave value because she took the instrument as security for an antecedent claim against Debtor.

12.   State Bank has given value for the check by crediting it against S's account only if S has the right to withdraw the credit immediately. Depositors rarely have this right, which ordinarily is based on an agreement with the bank. In the absence of this right of immediate withdrawal, State Bank will give value for the check only if credit given for the item is actually withdrawn or applied, or if State Bank makes an advance on or against the item.

13. The definition of notice, which contains an objective element, encompasses, and goes beyond, the meaning of knowledge, which is subjective only.

14. T is subject to the defense. She had notice that the note was overdue and thus is not a holder in due course. Therefore, she is subject to all of M's defenses. It makes no difference that the reason T lacks due-course status is unrelated to the defense M asserts.

15. T has given value by paying $4000 for the note. If T took in good faith and without notice, this payment gives her due-course status and protection as to the full amount of the note. So T is completely free from personal defenses, and can collect the full $10,000. Yet, the substantial discount, that is, paying $6000 less than the face value of the note, is perhaps evidence (though not conclusive in itself) of lack of good faith. The fact that the instrument was payable on demand is, in itself, irrelevant. The holder must have notice that demand for payment has been made or that the note has been outstanding for an unreasonable period of time.

16. Noreast might be denied the immunity of a holder in due course on the basis of the close-connection doctrine. There is doubt because B is not a consumer. Technically, the doctrine is not limited to consumer transactions, but the courts have applied the doctrine less freely in commercial cases.

17. Noreast is not a holder in due course because an installment sales contract is not an instrument. Noreast nevertheless can take free of B's claims and defenses against Ace through enforcement of the waiver-of-defenses clause in the contract, which is enforceable if Noreast took the contract for value, in good faith and without notice of any claim or defense. 9-206(1). The enforceability of the waiver depends, more than anything else, on whether the close-connection doctrine is applied.

18. The FTC Notice should be included on these facts if Ace is in the business of selling or leasing goods or services to consumers. Inserting the Notice in B's note either destroys the negotiability of the note so that there can not be a holder in due course of it, or includes as a term of the note, which is enforceable against any transferee or holder, B's right to assert claims and defenses against Ace. The same right becomes a controlling term in any installment sales contract in which the Notice is included.

19.   The loan to B is a purchase money loan within the meaning of the FTC Rule because of the pattern of referrals that Ace makes to State Bank. Thus, Ace should not take the proceeds of the loan unless any note or other credit contract between State Bank and B contains the FTC Notice. If the Notice is not included, State Bank can collect the loan free from B's claims and defenses against Ace, although State Bank might be answerable to B on some theory if State Bank failed to act on knowledge that the Notice properly should have been included.

IX. CHECK COLLECTION PROCESS

1.   PB Bank is the payor bank. CB Bank is the depositary bank, 4-105(2), and is also a collecting bank. The Minneapolis Fed is a collecting bank, too, and is also an intermediary bank. In addition, the Minneapolis Fed is the presenting bank.

2.   *Yes.*   PB Bank can recover the settlement if it acts by its midnight deadline, which is Tuesday midnight, and before it has finally paid the item. 4-301(a). To revoke the settlement PB Bank must return the check before its midnight deadline or, if the item is unavailable for return, send written notice of dishonor.

3.   *Yes.*   See 4-214(a).

4.   *No.*   The delay renders the bank liable to its customer for negligence, and the customer can recover damages proximately caused by the delay.

5.   Seller's recourse is to notify Buyer of the dishonor of the check and sue on the instrument. The Buyer's liability thereon, as drawer, is triggered because the check was presented and dishonored, and she has received notice of the dishonor. In the alternative, Seller can sue Buyer on the underlying obligation between them inasmuch as dishonor of the check revives this obligation.

6.   *No.*   Final payment terminates the 4-301(a) right of return, even though PB Bank's midnight deadline has not yet expired; but completing the process of posting is not final payment. PB Bank thus can return the item.

7.   *Yes.*

8.   *No.*   Because PB Bank finally paid the check, Buyer was discharged on the check, and on the underlying obligation.

9.   Seller is not without recourse. She can recover from CB for wrongful charge back.
      Final payment by PB Bank terminated CB Bank's right to charge back the check
      against Seller's account. CB can then recover over against PB Bank. 4-213(5)(c).
      Alternatively, Seller can recover from PB Bank directly on the theory that PB
      Bank become accountable to her upon final payment.

10.   Section 3-418 and the local common law of restitution might provide for recovery
      of the payment, but CB and Seller will probably have a defense in 3-418.

11.   In theory, no. PB Bank can charge the item to Buyer's account even though the
      account contains insufficient funds to cover the check, and Buyer is personally
      liable to PB Bank for the overdraft.

X. THE RELATIONSHIP BETWEEN A PAYOR BANK AND ITS CHECKING ACCOUNT CUSTOMERS

1.   The twin duties are: First, the bank must pay items drawn against the account that
      are properly payable. Second, the bank should not pay items that are not properly
      payable.

2.   Simply put, *wrongful dishonor* is dishonoring a check that is properly payable and
      thus should have been paid. 4-402(a). (For the meaning of dishonor, see
      3-502(b).) "An item is properly payable if it is authorized by the customer and is
      in accordance with any agreement between the customer and bank." 4-401(a). Put
      more fully, wrongful dishonor is any dishonor of a check by the drawee/payor
      bank that is not permitted or justified by law or the terms of the deposit contract
      between the payor bank and its customer. Thus, there is no wrongful dishonor
      where the drawer has no credit extended by the drawee, or where the draft lacks a
      necessary indorsement or is not properly presented. In contrast, a bank wrongfully
      dishonors by refusing to pay a check that is properly presented and properly drawn
      on an account having sufficient funds to cover the item.

3.   ABC, Inc. can recover; in some states, the president may be allowed to recover;
      the payees cannot recover.

4.   A statutory action for wrongful dishonor did not exist under pre-Code law. The
      wrong was addressed through a common-law action for breach of contract or an
      action in tort, such as defamation. In a common-law defamation case, the
      customer could recover substantial damages without proving that damage actually
      occurred if she was a merchant, trader or fiduciary. Damages were presumed
      because defaming a person in her business, trade or profession was a defamation

"per se." Presuming damages in such a case was known as the *Trader Rule.* Section 4-402 does not "retain" this Rule. 4-402 comment 1. By the terms of the statute, liability is limited to actual damages proved. 4-402(b). It could be argued that the common-law Trader Rule supplements 4-402; but it is likely that by not retaining the rule, 4-402 also displaces it.

5.   ***True*** (unless the deposit contract requires payment of overdrafts).

6.   A check covered by a valid stop-payment order is not properly payable even though it was properly payable upon issuance.

7.   ***True.***

8.   The bank is subrogated to the rights of B against S with respect to the transaction out of which the check arose. Thus, inasmuch as B could have recovered the price of the goods paid to S, 2-711, the bank can recover same.

9.   ***False.***   The remitter has no right to force the issuing bank to stop payment, but the issuing bank enjoys the power to dishonor payment for its own reasons or as a courtesy to the remitter. The issues are whether, upon dishonor of a cashier's check, the issuing bank can assert defenses when sued on the instrument by the payee or subsequent holder; and, if so, the nature and range of defenses that the issuing bank can properly raise against the plaintiff.

10.   ***False.***   A payor bank is authorized to make payment of a stale check in good faith.

11.   So far as Article 4 is concerned, the bank can safely pay the check: "Even with knowledge a bank may for 10 days after the date of death pay or certify checks drawn on or before that date unless ordered to stop payment by a person claiming an interest in the account." 4-405(b).

12.   The payor bank generally bears the loss, in the absence of an effective defense, because an item that has been altered, or that carries a forged or otherwise ineffective signature of a drawer or indorser, is not properly payable. An altered check, however, is not properly payable only to the extent of the alteration. The bank is authorized to charge the customer's account to the extent of the original tenor of the altered item.

13. The potentially available major defenses are these:

- The customer authorized the person to draw the check.
- The customer ratified the signature.
- The customer's negligence substantially contributed to the making of the unauthorized signature. See 3-406.
- The customer violated her duty of ordinary care that requires her promptly to discover the unauthorized signature and report it to the bank. See 4-406(c-d).
- Without regard to ordinary care, or lack thereof, on anyone's part, and whether or not there is a resulting loss to bank, the customer failed to discover and report the unauthorized signature within one year from the time the item, along with the bank statement covering it, were made available to her. See 4-406(f).

14. U.C.C. 3-404 and 3-405 provides defenses in certain cases involving forged *indorsements* of payees. Under the circumstances covered by any of these defenses, an unauthorized indorsement is deemed effective in law so that, for instance, the drawer cannot complain against the payor bank for paying the check carrying the indorsement.

XI. SHIFTING CHECK FRAUD LOSSES

1. *Yes.* Due to the forged indorsement, the check was not paid to a holder. Therefore, the payment did not discharge B on the instrument, and she also remained liable on the underlying transaction.

2. *Yes.* A payor bank can only charge to a customer's checking account items that are properly payable. A check with an unauthorized indorsement is not properly payable.

3. *No.*

4. *Yes.* S has a conversion claim against DB Bank.

5. *Yes.* PB Bank's payment of the check was a conversion of property belonging to S.

XII. ORDINARY DRAFTS AND DOCUMENTS
OF TITLE IN SALES FINANCING

1. *Trick question.* The receipt is neither a warehouse receipt nor a bill of lading because it was not issued by a professional bailee. See 1-201(6) (definition of "bill of lading") & 1-201(45) (definition of "warehouse receipt"). The receipt is not a document of title of any kind unless (1) in the regular course of business or financing the receipt would be treated as adequately evidencing that the person in possession of it is entitled to receive, hold and dispose of the document and the goods it covers, and (2) the law student is a "bailee". 1-201(15) (definition of "document of title"). Although Article 7 purports to cover, in broad terms, documents of title, most of its provisions deal specifically with warehouse receipts and bills of lading.

2. The writing is a "delivery order," 7-102(1)(d), which is a document of title. See 1-201(15).

3. The answer depends on whether the document that C issued to O is negotiable or non-negotiable. If the document is non-negotiable, C's obligation is to deliver pursuant to O's written instructions, 7-403(1) & (4), which means C should deliver the goods to X. If the document C issued is negotiable, her obligation is to deliver to the "holder" of the document. Id. The facts are insufficient to determine whether X is a holder. 1-201(20). Moreover, even if X is a holder of a negotiable document issued by C to O, C is not obligated to deliver to X until X surrenders the document. 7-403(3).

4. The bill that C issued to O was negotiable because, by its terms, the goods were to be delivered to the order of a named person, O. 7-104(1)(a). Thus, C's obligation was to deliver to the holder of the document. 7-403(1) & (4). BFP was the holder because she was in possession of a document indorsed to her. 1-201(20). A bailee is excused from misdelivery, however, if she delivered the goods to a person whose receipt was rightful as against the claimant. 7-403(1)(a). So C is not accountable to BFP if, as between BFP and X, X has the better claim. BFP has the better claim, however, not X. Upon the sale to BFP and transfer of the document to her, title to the goods (i.e., O's rights) passed to BFP. 2-401(3) & 7-504(1). In the deal between O and X, the latter got the former's rights. By this time, however, O had no rights. C is liable to BFP.

5. Now C can argue that X acquired O's rights, leaving nothing for O to transfer to BFP so that, as between X and BFP, X has the better claim. Consequently, C is

excused for having delivered the goods to X even though X was not entitled under the document. There is possibly a flaw in this argument, however. If BFP was a holder to whom the document had been duly negotiated, see 7-501(4), she acquired title to the document and the goods free from X's claim to them. 7-502(1). In this event, BFP has the better claim to the goods, and C is liable to BFP for misdelivery.

6. a. The buyers are holders through due negotiation. 7-501(4). Article 7 provides that such a holder acquires "title to the document", "title to the goods," 7-502(1)(a) & (b), and is, in sum, "owner" of both. 7-502 comment 1.

    b. The people from whom the equipment was stolen can replevy the property from the buyers. Although the buyers acquired their rights through due negotiation, the good title they acquired through 7-502(1) is subject to a big exception in 7-503. This exception is that "[a] document of title confers no rights in goods against a person who before issuance of the document had a legal interest * * * in them," 7-503(1), assuming such person did not introduce the goods into the stream of commerce.

    c. (i) Under the common law, W would be liable for conversion to the people from whom the equipment was stolen, but Article 7 immunizes W from liability: "A bailee who in good faith including observance of reasonable commercial standards has received goods and delivered or otherwise disposed of them according to the terms of the document of title or pursuant to this Article is not liable therefor. *This rule applies even though the person from whom he received the goods had no authority to procure the document or to dispose of the goods and even though the person to whom he delivered the goods had no authority to receive them.*" 7-404 (emphasis added).

    (ii) W is not liable to the buyers. A warehouseperson makes no warranty with respect to the rights of the bailor in the goods covered by the document. This is not a case of non-receipt or misdescription of the goods for which a bailee is liable. See 7-203.

7. See the answers to Questions 4 and 5.

8. The seller and carrier are both liable. The seller is liable for breach of contract under Article 2. The carrier is liable for misdescribing the goods in the document of title. 7-203. The presenting bank is not liable for the misdescription, having

warranted only its own good faith and authority in acting to collect the documentary draft. See 7-508.

9.   a.   The carrier is not liable. The carrier was justified in delivering to the buyer because she was the holder of the negotiable document and thus was entitled to the goods thereunder. 7-403(1) & (4).

     b.   The presenting bank is liable to seller. The bank's obligation was to present the draft for *payment* and to withhold the document until payment was made. 4-503(1).

     c.   Trade acceptance.

10.   The buyer is the acceptor on a trade acceptance. A bank is the acceptor on a banker's acceptance. The main reasons a seller would prefer the latter to the former are (1) the risk of the obligor's insolvency is less when the obligor is a bank, and (2) a banker's acceptance bank is more marketable because the risk of insolvency is smaller, there is an established secondary market for banker's acceptances, and banks can rediscount them to Federal Reserve Banks.

XIII. LETTERS OF CREDIT

1.   When the buyer agrees to pay against documents, the seller gambles that the buyer will be willing and able to pay at the time of the exchange. When payment is through a letter of credit, the seller enjoys the independent commitment of a bank to pay her the price, as described in the credit, when the documents are presented. This commitment is made well before the seller is obligated to perform.

2.   The responsibility is a duty to honor: The issuer must honor the seller's "draft or demand for payment which complies with the terms of the relevant credit regardless of whether the goods or documents conform to the underlying contract for sale or other contract" between the seller and buyer. 5-114(1).

3.   "[A]n issuer which has duly honored a draft or demand for payment is entitled to immediate *reimbursement* of any payment made under the credit * * *." 5-114(3) (emphasis added).

4.   An issuer that violates the duty to honor is liable to the beneficiary for "the face amount of the draft or demand * * * less any amount realized by resale or other use or disposition of the subject matter of the transaction [i.e., the goods]." 5-115(1).

5. The issuer loses the right of reimbursement from the customer.

6. An issuer can rightfully dishonor when:
- A draft or demand for payment fails to comply with the terms of the credit;
- A required document does not conform to applicable warranties, or is forged or fraudulent; or,
- There is fraud in the transaction.

7. *False.* "[A]s against its customer, an issuer *acting in good faith* may honor the draft or demand for payment despite notification from the customer of fraud, forgery or other defect not apparent on the face of the documents * * *." 5-114(2)(b) (emphasis added).

8. *True and False.* The statement is true in the sense that the issuer is not obligated to obey a customer's order to dishonor because the issuer owes an independent obligation to the beneficiary, and also because the issuer is privileged by Article 5 to honor a credit, notwithstanding notice of fraud in the transaction, so long as the issuer acts in good faith. The statement is false in the sense that, in any event, the customer can petition a court to enjoin honor. 5-114(2)(b).

9. "Fraud in the transaction" is intentional, active fraud by the beneficiary that is so egregious as to vitiate the entire transaction between the beneficiary and customer.

10. The right to draw under a credit is alienable under a *transferable credit*. Drafts drawn by the beneficiary can be negotiated to purchasers, and collected by them from the issuer, under a *negotiation credit*. The beneficiary's right to proceeds, upon compliance with the credit, is always assignable.

Most of these 15 questions were selected from *bar examinations* of several states, but any of them would be appropriate for a final examination in a commercial paper, U.C.C. or commercial transactions course. A commercial paper final exam would likely include five or six of these questions to be answered in three to four hours. Law professors typically allow students to refer to a copy of the Uniform Commercial Code in taking any examination covering the U.C.C. Bar examiners are seldom so indulgent.

QUESTION I
(Suggested Time: 15 Minutes)

On March 1, for value, Morris signed and delivered to Tom two promissory notes. Both notes recited that they were payable to Tom or bearer on May 1, at Farmers' State Bank.

(a) On May 1, during banking hours, a person other than Tom and unknown to Farmers' State Bank, presented one of the notes to the Bank and demanded payment. The note bore no indorsement. At that time there were sufficient funds in Morris' checking account with the Bank to pay the note. The Bank Vice President telephoned Morris' office to inquire whether payment should be made, but Morris' secretary stated that Morris was in Europe and could not be reached. The Bank then calls you requesting advice as to whether it should pay the note and charge Morris' account. Advise the Bank.

(b) On May 3, Tom indorsed the other note in blank and delivered it to Cecil for value. When Cecil presented the note to Farmers' State Bank for payment during banking hours on July 15, the Bank refused to pay it because by then Morris had returned and told the Bank not to pay. When Cecil sues Morris and Tom on the note, can either of them defend solely on the ground of late presentment? Give your reasons.

QUESTION II
(Suggested Time: 15 Minutes)

Rich Nephew, as Independent Executor of Poor Uncle's Estate, opened an Estate checking account with Bank to which he deposited a $2500 check from a purchaser to whom he had sold all of the meager assets of the Estate. The next day he wrote two checks on the Estate account, one for $2,000 payable to the order of Resten-Pease Funeral Home in payment of Poor Uncle's funeral expenses, and the other for $500 payable to the order of Needy Niece as a distribution to her under Poor Uncle's will. Both checks were negotiable and were signed "Rich Nephew, Independent Executor," but did not bear the name of the Estate. He sent the $2,000 check to the Funeral Home with a transmittal letter stating "enclosed is check of Poor Uncle's Estate in payment of your statement." He delivered to Needy Niece the $500 check, which she promptly indorsed in blank and delivered to her landlord in payment of back rent. The landlord then indorsed the check in blank and gave it to his son, Tom, as a present for graduation from law school. When Funeral Home and Tom timely presented the checks to the Bank for payment, both checks were dishonored because the $2,500 check previously deposited had been returned unpaid, leaving nothing in the Estate account. Funeral Home and Tom then made timely demand upon Rich Nephew individually for payment of their respective checks. When he refused, each sued him individually. What result in each case, and why?

QUESTION III
(Suggested Time: 20 Minutes)

Murray signed and delivered to his son, Paul, a negotiable check drawn on First Bank payable to the order of Paul in the amount of $100.00 as a gift. Paul skillfully and fraudulently altered the check by changing the amount to $8,100.00. He then indorsed the check and delivered it to Acme Motor Company in payment for a new automobile. When Acme presented the check to First Bank for payment, Murray's account balance was less than $8,100.00 and the Bank called Murray for a deposit. Upon doing so the Bank learned that the check had been altered and, at Murray's request, timely refused payment. Assuming timely and proper notice of dishonor what rights, if any, does Acme have against Murray? What difference, if any, would it make if in a suit by Acme against Murray it was determined that Murray's negligence substantially contributed to the alteration?

QUESTION IV
(Suggested Time: 30 Minutes)

D drew and delivered to P a $100 check on X-Bank to P's order. P, despite the fact the check was not drawn negligently, skillfully altered the check to raise its amount to $1,000. P then negotiated the $1,000 check to R, R taking it for value and wholly innocent of any knowledge of the artful alteration. R then took the check to X-Bank and procured its certification, X-Bank certifying the check with a stamp reciting, in part, "CERTIFIED PAYABLE ONLY AS ORIGINALLY DRAWN AND WHEN PROPERLY INDORSED. /s/ X-BANK." R then specially indorsed the check to S who took it in good faith in payment for merchandise purchased from S and delivered to R. S then presented the check to X-Bank and received payment in the certified amount. When D discovered X-Bank had charged $1,000 to his account, D protested. X-Bank removed the overcharge to D's account and brought suit against both R and S asking for the return of the $900 on the grounds both of alleged breach of UCC warranties and the bank's contractual limitation of liability under its conditional certification that it should not be liable beyond the check's original tenor, viz., $100. Both R and S demurred to X-Bank's complaint. Should the demurrers be sustained? Explain.

QUESTION V
(Suggested Time: 20 Minutes)

Alice Able owed Barbara Brown $100.00. To pay the debt Alice Able signed and delivered to Barbara Brown a check payable to Barbara Brown in the amount of $100.00. Barbara Brown indorsed the check as follows: "Pay to the order of Cathy Columbus (signed) Barbara Brown." Barbara Brown then gave the check to Cathy Columbus who, intending promptly to deposit it, indorsed it simply "Cathy Columbus" and placed it in her desk drawer. Cathy Columbus forgot about having indorsed the check and several days later it was stolen by Tom Trickey. Tom Trickey forged the indorsement of Frank Fictitious on the check and representing himself as Frank Fictitious used it to buy a ten speed bicycle from Harry Holder. Harry Holder took the check in good faith and without notice. May Harry Holder recover from Alice Able?

QUESTION VI
(Suggested Time: 30 Minutes)

Mary owns a retail store. She executed and delivered to Peter her negotiable promissory note dated August 1, 1986 payable to the order of Peter in the principal sum of $1,000, without interest, on or before February 1, 1987. The note was given in payment for goods shipped by Peter to Mary on August 1, 1986, as inventory for her store. On August 10, 1986, Peter indorsed the note in blank and delivered it to Henry, who paid $900 in cash. On August 15, 1986, Mary returned the goods to Peter, the goods being defective, and demanded return of the note. Peter told Mary he had sold the note to Henry. On September 1, 1986, Mary told Henry that the goods were defective and that she would not pay the note. Henry, on September 15, 1986, indorsed the note in blank and delivered it to John, who was aware of Mary's contention but who paid Henry $700 in cash. On February 15, 1987, John indorsed the note in blank and delivered it to Kenneth, who paid John $1,000 in cash and knew nothing about Mary's contention. On February 20, 1987, when Kenneth presented the note to Mary, she refused to pay.

    (a)   Kenneth sues Mary on the note. What result and why?

    (b)   If Kenneth elects not to sue Mary, can he recover from any other party? Explain why as to each of them. You may assume any required notice has been given.

QUESTION VII
(Suggested Time: 30 Minutes)

Tom Dupe entered into an oral agreement to purchase several large air conditioning units from Bobby Slick and tendered as a down payment a $2,000.00 check drawn on Dupe's local bank, the Friendly Bank of Ozark. On the same afternoon, Dupe discovered that Slick was in fact a con man and that he never intended to deliver the air conditioning units. Dupe contacted the Friendly Bank when the doors opened the next morning and requested a stop order on his check.

In the meantime, Slick had deposited the $2,000.00 check for collection in his personal account at the Citizens Bank of Mulberry. Slick was frequently overdrawn and on the day of this deposit he had a negative balance of $50.00. Both Dupe and the Friendly Bank knew that Slick banked at Citizens, but made no effort to notify that Bank of the stop order. After the stop order had been requested, but before the check had cleared, Slick withdrew the new balance of $1,950.00 from his account at Citizens Bank and disappeared. Since Dupe's check had been dishonored when presented for collection, Citizens Bank was left with a $1,950.00 overdrawn account.

Does Citizens Bank have any recourse against Dupe or Friendly Bank? Please discuss fully.

QUESTION VIII
(Suggested Time: 30 Minutes)

Axel applied to a bank for a loan of $50,000. The bank would not make the loan to Axel unless he procured someone approved by the bank "to sign the Note with him." Axel's two uncles, Wilford and Parnell, each agreed to sign a Note for half of Axel's loan.

One instrument for $25,000.00 was signed by Axel as maker and by his Uncle Wilford as co-maker. A second instrument for $25,000.00 was signed by Axel as maker, and Uncle Parnell as indorser-guarantor. Neither instrument referred to presentment or notice of dishonor or protest. The bank took a mortgage on Axel's restaurant property, including land, building and contents. Axel was required to carry insurance on the properties. Axel failed to pay the Notes when due. Nine months passed without payment or activity on the Notes. The bank neither presented the Notes for payment nor gave notice of dishonor or protest. One night the restaurant was totally destroyed by fire. It had been uninsured for several months.

Upon learning that the restaurant building and its contents had burned, the bank demanded payment of Wilford and Parnell. They refused to pay, whereupon the bank sued each. Decide and discuss the rights of the parties.

QUESTION IX
(Suggested Time: 45 Minutes)

Buyer drew a check to Seller in payment for goods. Seller deposited the check in her account at State Bank, which credited Seller's account with the amount of the item. State Bank presented the item to the payor, Bay National Bank, for payment. Bay National refused to pay the check and returned the item to State Bank within a day or two after presentment. Buyer had issued a stop order covering the check because of a dispute with Seller over the quality of the goods purchased by Buyer. Two banking days after the check was returned to State Bank, having taken no action of any kind against anyone, State Bank asks you to explain the full range of its remedial options. What is your explanation?

QUESTION X
(Suggested Time: 45 Minutes)

When D's checking account balance was $300, she drew two checks totaling $1100. One of the checks was drawn for $800 payable to D's mortgage company. The other check was drawn payable to a finance company affiliated with the payor bank, and represented a $300 payment on an installment car loan. The $800 check was deposited in the mortgage company's account at the payor bank on Tuesday, and on the same day the payor bank determined to pay the item. On Wednesday, the $300 check was presented. Also on Wednesday, the bank reversed its decision to pay the check to the mortgage company, stamped this check "INSUFFICIENT FUNDS," and returned it to the mortgage company. The $300 check was paid. The mortgage company accelerated D's mortgage and initiated foreclosure proceedings. Who is liable to whom for what?

QUESTION XI
(Suggested Time: 15 Minutes)

Paul obtained a series of Marty's personal checks and forged Marty's signature to a number of these checks payable to "cash." Paul then indorsed and negotiated the checks to George who deposited them into his own bank account. Marty's bank, the Citizens Bank, paid the checks. Marty failed to notice the forged checks when they were returned to him with his monthly bank statements over a two-year period. Marty finally discovered the forgeries at the end of the two-year period when he was going over his checks for an IRS audit. What are Marty's rights against George, Citizens Bank and George's Bank?

QUESTION XII
(Suggested Time: 30 Minutes)

Sly heard Dobbs was interested in purchasing Smith's five acres of cantaloupes for $2500. Seizing the opportunity, Sly executed a bill of sale for the melons in Smith's name as seller, went to a bar and approached a stranger, Jones, introduced himself as being Smith, and offered Jones $100 to take the bill of sale to Dobb's office and bring back Dobb's $2500 check. Jones eagerly accepted, delivered the bill of sale and was handed Dobb's $2500 check to Smith's order, plus a second $1000 check to Smith's order to "give to Smith also because I owe him this on another deal." Jones, realizing only one check was expected to be brought back, delivered only the $2500 check. Sly indorsed it in the name of its payee and then in his own name and got it paid by its drawee, X-Bank. Jones indorsed the $1000 check in the name of its payee and then in his own name and got it paid by its drawee, X-Bank. Meanwhile, when Dobbs took a truck to the melon field, Smith had him ejected and arrested for trespassing. Dobbs now sues Smith, X-Bank and Jones. Dobbs prays against Smith for possession of the melons and also a paid-in-full receipt for the $1000 debt. Alternatively, against X-Bank, Dobbs prays that $3500 be recredited to his checking account. Alternatively, Dobbs prays against Jones $3500 damages for alleged fraud and deceit. Dobbs agrees he is entitled to only $3500 overall recovery. Does Dobbs have, as against any of those parties, the rights prayed for? Explain. Limit discussion to civil aspects only.

QUESTION XIII
(Suggested Time: 45 Minutes)

Mild-mannered T, who worked in the mailroom at P Corporation, stole a $10,000 check that P's customer, D, had sent in payment for goods sold to her by P. T also stole a rubber stamp bearing P's name and logo. Using this device, T stamped the back of the stolen check and deposited it in an account with First Bank. T had opened the account under the name P Company and listed herself, on the signature card, as president of the fictional organization. D's check was paid by the drawee, Second Bank, the following week and charged against D's account. Shortly thereafter, T withdrew everything from the account at First Bank and left town. Who is liable to whom for what? Why?

QUESTION XIV
(Suggested Time: 45 Minutes)

Buyer (B) ordered 10,000 fondue pots from Seller (S). Pursuant to the parties' agreement, B got Bank to issue a letter of credit in favor of S. By the terms of this letter, Bank undertook to pay S's draft drawn against the Bank that is accompanied by a negotiable document covering "10,000 fondue pots manufactured by S." S filled B's order and shipped the pots in compliance with the delivery terms of the sales contract. The carrier issued a negotiable bill of lading, to S's order, which covered "10,000 fondue pots supplied by S." S drew a draft on Bank payable to S's own order. S then indorsed, in blank, both the draft and the negotiable document, and discounted the documentary instrument to X, an innocent purchaser for value. Upon presentment by X, Bank dishonored the draft. Disappointed, but not defeated, X visited the carrier to check on the fondue pots. Surprise! Upon instructions from S, the carrier had released the goods to B. Against whom does X have actions?

QUESTION XV
(Suggested Time: 30 Minutes)

On February 1, 1987, Bank, at the request and for the account of its customer, Carl, issued its irrevocable letter of credit in favor of Bryon as beneficiary. By the terms of the credit, the Bank engaged that it would honor at any time before February 1, 1988, any written demand for payment not to exceed $10,000 signed by Bryon and stating that Carl had not paid for goods sold to him by Bryon. The credit further provided that it was nontransferable. On April 1, 1987, Bryon, to secure his indebtedness to Thrifty Finance Company, executed and delivered to Thrifty a security agreement and financing statement describing the collateral as "all inventory and accounts receivable now owned or hereafter acquired by Bryon." Thrifty filed the financing statement in the office of the Secretary of State the next day and delivered to Bank a copy of the security agreement with a transmittal letter stating that the accounts receivable included proceeds that might become payable under the letter of credit. On May 1, 1987, for value Bryon executed and delivered to Alec a written assignment of Bryon's right to all proceeds under the letter of credit, properly identifying it. At the same time, Bryon delivered to Alec the letter of credit and delivered to Bank a written notification signed by Bryon identifying the letter of credit and requesting Bank to pay Alec any proceeds that might thereafter be due under the letter of credit. On July 1, 1987, Bryon presented to Bank a written demand for payment in the amount of $9,000 referring specifically to the letter of credit and stating that Carl had not paid for goods sold to him by Bryon.

(a)   If Bryon insists that the Bank pay him rather than Thrifty or Alec on the ground that the letter of credit was nontransferable, is Bryon legally correct?

(b)   If Bryon concedes that the Bank may pay Thrifty or Alec, which of them is entitled to payment?

(c)   If Carl timely instructs the Bank not to honor the letter of credit at all on the ground, which is true, that the goods he purchased from Bryon do not conform to the contract between them, may Bank properly refuse payment?

APPENDIX C

TEXT CORRELATION CHART

Black Letter Commercial Paper	Farnsworth: Commercial Paper (3d ed.)	Jordan & Warren: Negotiable Instruments and Letters of Credit	Nickles, Matheson & Dolan: Credit & Payment Systems	Rubin & Cooter: The Payment Stystem	Speidel, Summers & White: Commercial Paper	Whaley: Payment Law
Chapter I Introduction To Instruments And Negotiability	15-60	1-19	96-122	—	21-30 81-84	1-4
Chapter II The Meaning Of Instruments: Requisites Of Negotiability	71-76	20-27	123-74	—	85-96	4-19
Chapter III Contract Liability On Instruments	84-86 119-40 276-83	93-107 118-31	175-235	—	30-51 71-80	97-109 146-79
Chapter IV Instruments As Property: Enforcement, Transfer And Negotiation	182-87 204-11	4-13 27 299-301	236-61	—	96-98	21-29
Chapter V Warranty And Restitution: Insuring Enforceability	137 147-48 267-70	97-98 230-40	262-75	—	138-41 170-72 245-51 272-77	180-86
Chapter VI Claims And Defenses To Instruments	61-83 214-15	16-19	278-90 253-375	—	117-37	67-95
Chapter VII Accommodation Parties	445-83	107-18	438-76	—	51-70	109-46
Chapter VIII Holder In Due Course	54-60 188-204 212-13	28-92	276-78 290-352	—	81-117	31-67

Chapter IX Check Collection Process	87-104 140-81 231-40	132-69	478-557	159-76 209-51 293-403 439-45	228-318 327-46	258-99
Chapter X The Relationship Between A Payor Bank And Its Checing Account Customers	111-19 215-31 240-64 299-314 320-29 334-39	302-44 216-29	558-614	176-209 251-78 419-38 445-99 522-50	198-227 347-407	213-58 301-16 327-58
Chapter XI Shifting Check Fraud Losses	265-99 329-34	240-76 283-99	615-78	499-522 550-82	138-97	186-211 316-27
Chapter XII Ordinary Drafts And Documents Of Title In Sales Financing	340-83	345-84	680-733	—	318-27	—
Chapter XIII Letters Of Credit	384-444	385-431	736-97	—	468-574	—

APPENDIX D

INDEX OF KEY TERMS

APPENDIX E

TABLE OF UNIFORM COMMERCIAL CODE CITATIONS

<table>
<tr><td>

APPENDIX F

TABLE OF FEDERAL STATUTES AND REGULATIONS

</td></tr>
</table>